# The Collected Essays of Leslie Fiedler

BY LESLIE A. FIEDLER

Nonfiction

*An End to Innocence*
*No! in Thunder*
*Love and Death in the American Novel*
*Waiting for the End*
*The Return of the Vanishing American*
*Being Busted*

Fiction

*The Second Stone*
*Back to China*
*The Last Jew in America*
*Nude Croquet*

# The Collected Essays of Leslie Fiedler

## VOLUME II

STEIN AND DAY/*Publishers*/New York

First published in 1971
Copyright © 1971 by Leslie A. Fiedler
Library of Congress Catalog Card No. 76-122420
All rights reserved
Published simultaneously in Canada by Saunders of Toronto Ltd
Printed in the United States of America
Stein and Day/*Publishers*/7 East 48 Street, New York, N.Y. 10017
SBN 8128-1352-9

71-11585

# Contents

v

*Unfinished Business*

*Cross the Border—Close the Gap*

# Acknowledgments

THE AUTHOR wishes to thank the editors and publishers of the following firms and periodicals under whose imprints parts of this book originally appeared:

AMERICAN JUDAISM for "Marx and Momma," Winter, 1965–66; "Some Jewish Pop Art Heroes," Passover, 1966; "This Year We Are Slaves— Next Year We Shall Be Free," Summer, 1966; "Myths of the Jews on Stage and Screen," December, 1966; "Crimes and Punishments," Spring, 1967.

COMMENTARY for "Prophet Out of Israel," January, 1951; "Henry Roth's Neglected Masterpiece," August, 1960; "John Peale Bishop and the Other Thirties," April, 1967.

EDIZIONE DI STORIA E LETTERATURA for "Caliban or Hamlet: A Study in Literary Anthropology," from *Friendship's Garland*, ed. V. Gabrieli, Rome, 1966.

ENCOUNTER for "Negro and Jew," Summer, 1956; "The Middle Against Both Ends," August 1955.

FOREIGN SERVICE for "Antic Mailer—Portrait of a Middle-Aged Artist," January 2, 1960; "John Barth: An Eccentric Genius," January 7, 1961.

FREE PRESS for "Voting and Voting Studies" from *American Voting Behavior*, Glencoe, Illinois, 1959.

HERZL PRESS for *The Jew in the American Novel*, New York, 1959.

JOURNAL OF THE CONFERENCE ON COLLEGE COMPOSITION AND COMMUNICATION for "On Remembering Freshman Comp," February, 1962.

THE LISTENER for "The Shape of Moby Dick," 1967.

MIDSTREAM for "The Image of Newark and the Indignities of Love: Notes on Philip Roth," Summer, 1959.

MONTANA OPINION for "Montana: P.S.," June, 1956.

NEW AMERICAN REVIEW for "Toward a Centennial: Notes on Innocents Abroad," 1966.

NEW LEADER for "On Living with Simone Weil," June 10, 1957; "The Pleasures of John Hawkes," December 12, 1960.

NEW YORK HERALD TRIBUNE MAGAZINE for "The Death of Avant-Garde Literature," May 17, 1964.

ODYSSEY PRESS for "In Quest of George Lippard," first published as an Introduction to *Quaker City*, 1970.

PARTISAN REVIEW for "Master of Dreams: The Jew in a Gentile World," Summer, 1967; "Our Country and Our Culture," May-June, 1952; "An Almost Imaginary Interview: Hemingway in Ketchum," Summer, 1962; "The New Mutants," Fall, 1965.

PERSPECTIVES, U.S.A. for *"Partisan Review:* Phoenix or Dodo?" Spring, 1956.

PLAYBOY for "Academic Irresponsibility," December, 1968; "Cross the Border—Close the Gap," December, 1969.

PRAIRIE SCHOONER for "Saul Bellow," Summer, 1957.

RAMPARTS for "The Antiwar Novel and the Good Soldier Schweik," January, 1963.

RUNNING MAN for "Some Notes on the Jewish Novel in English or Looking Backward from Exile," July-August, 1969.

SHOW for "A Night with Mr. Teas," October, 1961.

SOUTHERN ILLINOIS UNIVERSITY PRESS for "The Two Memories: Reflections on Writers and Writing in the Thirties," from *Proletarian Writers of the Thirties*, 1968.

# Introduction to the Collected Essays

THE FOLLOWING essays were written over a period of slightly more than two decades extending from my thirtieth year to just beyond my fiftieth. They record impressions and responses, therefore, to a period bounded by two Cold Wars: the first between the two great powers on either pole of Europe, who came inevitably into conflict once their initial revolutionary impetus had turned into imperialist expansionism; the second between the old and the young, parents and children in the whole region between those two poles. Some of these essays deal directly with the politics created by the first of the two Cold Wars, and some with the cultural changes created by the second. Others are concerned primarily with literature, but these, too, are necessarily influenced by the series of cultural revolutions and political counterrevolutions through which we have all been living over the past twenty years.

Almost all of these essays were occasional to begin with, which is to say, were prompted by public events or the appearance of certain books, as well as by the demands of editors or the organizers of forums and symposia. They seem to me, however, to have survived their occasions, which is why I have chosen them out of the several hundred similar articles which I wrote and published between 1948 and 1970. Even when I have changed my mind radically about matters treated in one or another essay, I have not revised or altered anything. The reader patient enough or moved enough to read through to the end of these two volumes will discover not only where I am now in my feelings and ideas, but also where I have been all along the way. It is tempting to falsify one's past in the light of the present, but really impossible

for a writer like me who has always insisted in rushing into print
before he has had time enough for second thoughts.

This collection is intended to record not only one man's sentimental and political education, but an experience shared by the
overlapping generations who have come of age within the two
decades it spans, generations which now find it mutually useful to
pretend that a cultural "gap" separates them. What separates them
in fact, however, is precisely what they have in common: the living
memory recorded here of a loss of innocence which has kept the
twice-born fathers of my own generation disconcertingly young, so
that their sons have had, in order to seem even younger, to retreat
from adolescence to childhood—from the show of sophistication
to the profession of naïveté. If I were as close to twenty-five or
thirty-five at the moment as I am to fifty-five (and if in addition I
were blessedly Black), I would be writing just such an anatomy of
the New Innocence as I once wrote of the Old; but trapped in time,
I must content myself with the republication of old criticisms, hoping for new readers capable of perceiving in these volumes analogies
to their own situation which it would be mischievous or irrelevant
or downright boring for me to make clear.

# Introduction to Volume II

THIS VOLUME represents the first collection of my own essays that I have put together since 1960, but the material it contains is not confined to articles written in the decade between then and now. Some of the material, as a matter of fact, is as old as anything in Volume I. What I have attempted to do is to rescue from the dusty files of periodical rooms and library stacks whatever uncollected writing of mine in essay form that seems to me at this point worth preserving. I have organized that material into three thematic sections for the benefit of readers who love a semblance of order, and also for my own sake, which is to say, in order to demonstrate to myself that, after all, everything I have written comes finally to focus about a few general themes, and can be made to show in perspective a kind of development.

The first section of this volume is called "To the Gentiles" and includes essays on Jewish writers, chiefly but not exclusively Americans, as well as reflections on the plight of such writers when they abandon the traditional tongues of their people, holy or secular, to address the Gentile world in the language of the Gentiles. In a way, this section must be understood as valedictory, my farewell to a subject which has concerned me for a long time, but which seems to me at the moment exhausted, both in terms of my own interests and that of the young audiences who no longer find in Jewish experience viable images of their own character and fate.

The second section, on the contrary, is precisely what its title indicates, "Unfinished Business"—perhaps unfinishable business. I have included essays dealing with Montana, for instance, which I may have left physically, but with which I shall obviously never be done in my fantasies and dreams. Other essays deal with writers like Shakespeare, Melville, and Mark Twain about whom no one ever feels he has said the last word; and with such newer writers as John Hawkes and John Barth about whom I have the sense of just having begun to talk. The remainder of the section consists of pieces dealing with the thirties and with the university, which is to say, with the period of time which seems to have made my mind once and for all, and with the institution in which I have been trying to remake it ever since.

The final section of the volume is intended to gather together examples of my most recent thinking about the literary and cultural changes through which we are all uncomfortably living. Almost half of the articles I have included, however, were written before the Cultural Revolution had become apparent to everyone—some as long as ten years ago—and represent my first fumblings toward the critical position best expressed in the essay which gives this section its title, "Cross the Border—Close the Gap."

As I continue to write critical essays in the decades to come (if, indeed, I do not abandon them utterly for fiction or fantasy or, best of all, movies), it is from this place that I will be starting: from the very heart, that is, of what until only yesterday I considered still to be "The Future," and beyond which, therefore, I can scarcely imagine anything else.

# TO THE GENTILES

# Introduction

GATHERED TOGETHER in this section the reader will find all of my essays on Jewish subjects not included in the two earlier collections which make up Volume I. I have a strong sense of having said my say on the subject. Doubtless I will be tempted into further comments from time to time on Jewish writers and the world out of which they come, if indeed that world remains distinguishable from the larger community around it. But I think that in no case will I try to preserve such later essays, since in "Master of Dreams" I have come as near as I suspect I ever shall to a final mythical definition of the situation which defines me as well as many of the writers whom I most love. It would be a shame to turn from the central myth to peripheral detail, and I shall try to resist the temptation.

Believing the record of my dealings with the books of fellow Jews necessarily bears witness to the special kinds of difficulties one falls into when speaking *en famille,* I have begun this section with an essay on Simone Weil (the earliest of the pieces reprinted here) and an account of the troubles that essay caused me. It should be noted further that, though there is no record of it in the text, "Straddling the Wall" was an equal source of *tsooris.* It is, in fact, the only book review I ever wrote in my life which was refused publication, apparently at the behest of the American Jewish Committee whose deepest pieties it offended. Similarly, my essay on the *Partisan Review* brought down on my head actual excommunication, in the form of an indignant letter from the editors of that journal barring me forever from its pages. That "forever" actually lasted, I believe, three years, which seems good enough for a Jewish "forever," and perhaps explains why, despite considerable doubts, I

3

have included an analysis of that periodical and my relationships with it in this particular section.

The long critical study called "The Jew in the American Novel" has lived a fairly respectable life as a paperback publication issued by the Herzl Foundation; and, in addition, I have cannibalized it from time to time, using pieces of it in certain of my longer works. Nonetheless, I have chosen to include it, since it represents the closest thing I have produced to a continuous exposition of my view of the Jewish American writer. I no longer quite believe everything in it, but I leave it unrevised because I have recorded later changes of heart and shifts of emphasis in the essays which immediately follow it, including those which I did every two months for nearly two years in the pages of *American Judaism.*

The next to the last essay included here moves into the tenderest and most difficult area in which American Jewish literature and American Jewish culture are presently involved; that of relationships between the Jews and Blacks in the United States. The reader will find here a continuation of certain speculations begun in a time which now seems relatively peaceful and innocent, speculations recorded in the essay in Volume I called "Negro and Jew: Encounter in America." Taken together these two essays constitute, as I have already warned the reader, a last word on these matters. I see on rereading them, however, that they represent by no means a conclusive one. But to have been anything more or less than inconclusive on this subject would have been not only misleading, but finally not even quite Jewish.

# Prophet Out of Israel

SINCE HER DEATH, Simone Weil has come to seem more and more a special exemplar of sanctity for our time—the Outsider as Saint in an age of alienation, our kind of saint. In eight scant years, this young Frenchwoman, whom scarcely anyone had heard of before her sacrificial death in exile at the age of 34, has come to possess the imagination of many in the Western world. Catholic and Protestant, Christian and Jew, agnostic and devout, we have all turned to her with the profound conviction that the meaning of her experience is our meaning, that she is really *ours*. Few of us, to be sure, would find nothing to dissent from in her religious thought; fewer still would be capable of emulating the terrible purity of her life; none could measure himself, without shame, against the absolute ethos toward which she aspired. And yet she does not seem strange to us, as other mystics and witnesses of God have seemed strange; for though on one side her life touches the remote mysteries of the Divine Encounter, on the other it is rooted in a world with which we are familiar.

She speaks of the problems of belief in the vocabulary of the unbeliever, of the doctrines of the Church in the words of the unchurched. The *askesis,* the "dark night of the soul," through which she passed to certitude, is the modern intellectual's familiar pattern of attraction toward and disillusionment with Marxism, the discipline of contemporary politics. The day-to-day struggles of trade unionism, unemployment, the Civil War in Spain, the role of the Soviet Union, anarchism, and pacifism—these are the determinants of her ideas, the unforeseen roads that led her to sanctity. Though she passed finally beyond politics, her thought bears to the end the mark of her early interests, as the teaching of St. Paul is influenced by his Rabbinical schooling, or that of St. Augustine by his training in rhetoric.

Before her death, scarcely any of Simone Weil's religious writings had been published. To those in France who thought of her still, in terms of her early political essays, as a somewhat unorthodox Marxist moving toward anarchism, the posthumous Christian books must have come as a shock. Surely, no "friend of God" in all history had moved more unwillingly toward the mystic encounter. There is in her earlier work no sense of a groping toward the divine, no promise of holiness, no pursuit of a purity beyond this world—only a conventionally left-wing concern with the problems of industrialization, rendered in a tone at once extraordinarily inflexible and wonderfully sensitive.

The particular note of conviction in Simone Weil's testimony arises from the feeling that her role as a mystic was so *unintended,* one for which she had not in any sense prepared. An undertone of incredulity persists beneath her astonishing honesty: quite suddenly God had taken her, radical, agnostic, contemptuous of religious life and practice as she had observed it! She clung always to her sense of being an Outsider among the religious, to a feeling that her improbable approach had given her a special vocation, as an "apostle to the Gentiles," planted at "the intersection of Christianity and everything that is not Christianity." She refused to become, in the typical compensatory excess of the convert, more of the Church than those born into it; she would not even be baptized, and it is her unique position, at once in and out of institutionalized Catholicism, that determines her special role and meaning.

To those who consider themselves on the safe side of belief, she teaches the uncomfortable truth that the unbelief of many atheists is closer to a true love of God and a true sense of his nature, than the kind of easy faith which, never having *experienced* God, hangs a label bearing his name on some childish fantasy or projection of the ego. Like Kierkegaard, she preached the paradox of its being easier for a non-Christian to become a Christian, than for a "Christian" to become one. To those who believe in a single Revelation, and enjoy the warm sensation of being saved in a cozy circle of friends, she expounded the doctrine of a gospel spread in many "languages," of a divine Word shared among rival myths, in each of which certain important truths, implicit elsewhere, are made explicit. For those to whom religion means comfort and peace of mind, she brings the terrible reminder that Christ promised not peace but the sword, and that his own last words were a cry of absolute despair, the *"Eli, Eli, lama sabachthani!"* which is the true glory of Christianity.

But she always considered that her chief mission was to those still "submerged in materialism," that is, to most of us in a chaotic and disenchanted world. To the unbeliever who has rather smugly despised the churchgoer for seeking an easy consolation, she reveals the secret of his own cowardice, suggesting that his agnosticism may itself be only an opiate, a dodge to avoid facing the terror of God's reality and the awful burden of his love.

She refused to cut herself off from anyone by refusing to identify herself completely with anyone or any cause. She rejected the temptation to withdraw into a congenial group, once associated with which she could be disowned by all outside of it. She rather took upon herself the task of sustaining all possible beliefs in their infinite contradictions and on their endless levels of relevance; the smugness of the false elect, the materialism of the shallowly rebellious, self-deceit and hypocrisy, parochialism and atheism—from each she extracted its partial truth and endured the larger portion of error. She chose to submit to a kind of perpetual invisible crucifixion; her final relationship to all those she would not disown became that of the crucified to the cross.

The French editors of Simone Weil's works, Gustave Thibon, a lay theologian who was also her friend, and Father Perrin, the nearest thing to a confessor she ever had, have both spoken of Simone Weil's refusal to be baptized as a mere stage in her development, a nonessential flaw in her thinking, which, had she only lived longer, would probably have been remedied. M. Thibon and Father Perrin are, of course, Catholics, and speak as they must out of their great love for Mlle Weil and their understandable conviction that such holiness could not permanently have stayed outside of the Church; but from Simone Weil's own point of view, her outsideness was the very *essence* of her position. This is made especially clear in the present volume.

"I feel," she wrote once, "that it is necessary to me, prescribed for me, to be alone, an outsider and alienated from every human context whatsoever." And on another occasion, she jotted in her journal the self-reminder, "Preserve your solitude!" What motivated her was no selfish desire to withdraw from the ordinary concourse of men, but precisely the opposite impulse. She knew that one remains alienated from a particular allegiance, not by vainly attempting to deny all beliefs, but precisely by sharing them all. To have become rooted in the context of a particular religion, Simone Weil felt, would on the one hand have exposed her to what she calls "the patriotism of the Church," with a consequent blindness to the faults of her own group and the virtues of others, and would, on the other hand, have separated her from the common condition here below, which finds us all "outsiders, uprooted, in exile." The most terrible of crimes is to collaborate in the uprooting of others in an already alienated world; but the greatest of virtues is to uproot oneself for the sake of one's neighbors and of God. "It is necessary to uproot oneself. Cut down the tree and make a cross and carry it forever after."

Especially at the moment when the majority of mankind is "submerged in materialism," Simone Weil felt she could not detach herself from them by undergoing baptism. To be able to love them as they were, in all their blindness, she would have to know them as they were; and to know them, she would have to go among them disguised in the garments of their own disbelief. Insofar as Christianity had become an exclusive sect, it would have to be remade into a "total Incarnation of faith," have to become truly "catholic," catholic enough to include the myths of the dark-skinned peoples from a world untouched by the churches of the West, as well as the insights of post-Enlightenment liberals, who could see in organized religion only oppression and bitterness and pride.

". . . in our present situation," she wrote, "universality . . . has to be fully explicit." And that explicit universality, she felt, must find a mouthpiece in a new kind of saint, for "today it is not nearly enough merely to be a saint, but we must have the saintliness demanded by the present moment, a new saintliness, itself also without precedent." The new kind of saint must possess a special "genius," capable of blending Christianity and Stoicism, the love of God and "filial piety for the city of the world"; a passive sort of "genius" that would enable him to act as a "neutral medium," like water, "indifferent to all ideas without exception, even atheism and materialism. . . ."

Simone Weil felt that she could be only the forerunner and foreteller of such a saint; for her, humility forbade her thinking of herself as one capable of a "new revelation of the universe and human destiny . . . the unveiling of a large portion of truth and beauty hitherto hidden. . . ." Yet she is precisely the saint she prophesied!

Despite her modesty, she spoke sometimes as if she were aware that there was manifest in the circumstances of her birth (she had been born into an agnostic family of Jewish descent) a special providence, a clue to a special mission. While it was true, she argued in her letters to Catholic friends, that the earlier saints had all loved the Church and had been baptized into it, on the other hand, they had all been born and brought up in the Church, as she had *not*. "I should betray the truth," she protested, "that is to say, the aspect of the truth that I see, if I left the point, where I have been since my birth, at the intersection of Christianity and everything that is not Christianity."

It must not be thought that she was even troubled by the question of formally becoming a Christian; it vexed her devout Catholic friends and for *their* sakes she returned again and again to the problem; but as for herself, she was at peace. Toward the end of her life, the mystic vision came to her almost daily, and she did not have to wonder (in such matters, she liked to say, one does not believe or disbelieve; one *knows* or does not know) if there were salvation outside an organized sect; she was a living witness that the visible Church and the invisible congregation of the saints are never one. "I have never for a second had the feeling that God wanted me in the Church. . . . I never doubted. . . . I believe that now it can be concluded that God does not want me in the Church."

It is because she was capable of remaining on the threshold of organized religion, "without moving, quite still . . . indefinitely . . . " that Simone Weil speaks to all of us with special authority, an Outsider to outsiders, our kind of saint, whom we have needed (whether we have known it or not) "as a plague-stricken town needs doctors."

To what then does she bear witness? To the uses of exile and suffering, to the glory of annihilation and absurdity, to the unforeseen miracle of love. Her life and work form a single document, a document which we can still not read clearly, though clearly enough, perhaps, for our needs. On the one hand, the story of Simone Weil's life is still guarded by reticence; and on the other hand, her thought comes to us in fragmentary form. She completed no large-scale work; she published in her lifetime no intimate testimony to the secret religious life that made of her last few years a series of experiences perhaps unequaled since St. Theresa and St. John of the Cross. If she has left any detailed account of those experiences we have not yet seen it.

Since her death, four volumes of her work have been published in France. *La Pesanteur et la Grâce (Gravity and Grace),* is a selection from her diaries, chosen and topically rearranged by Gustave Thibon; the effect is that of a modern *Pensées*—no whole vision, but a related, loosely linked body of aphorisms, always illuminating and direct, sometimes extraordinarily acute. We do not know, of course, what M. Thibon has chosen to omit; and he has not even told us how large a proportion of the notebooks he has included in his selection.

*L'Enracinement (The Need for Roots)* is the longest single piece left by Simone Weil. Begun at the request of the Free French Government in exile, it takes off from a consideration of the religious and social principles upon which a truly Christian French nation might be built and touches upon such subjects as the humanizing of factory work, the need for freedom of purely speculative thought, and the necessity for expunging from our books a false notion of the heroic which makes us all guilty of the rise of Hitler. It is a fascinating though uneven book, in parts ridiculous, in parts profound, but motivated throughout by the pity and love Simone Weil felt in contemplating a society that had made of the apparatus of government an oppressive machine by separating the secular and religious.

The third book, of which the present volume is a translation, is in many ways the most representative and appealing of the three. It

is not, of course, a whole, but a chance collection, entrusted to
Father Perrin during the time just before Simone Weil's departure
for America. It includes some material originally written as early as
1937, though recast in the final years of her life; but in the main it
represents the typical concerns of the end of Simone Weil's life,
after she had reached a haven of certainty. Among the documents
(which survived a confiscation by the Gestapo) are six letters, all
but one written to Father Perrin, of which letter IV, the "Spiritual
Autobiography," is of special importance. Among the essays, the
meditation on the *Pater Noster* possesses great interest, for this was
the single prayer by which Simone Weil attained almost daily the
Divine Vision of God; and the second section of the study called
"Forms of the Implicit Love of God," I find the most moving and
beautiful piece of writing Simone Weil ever did.

Another volume of her collected essays and meditations, under
the title *La Connaissance Surnaturelle* (Supernatural Knowledge)
has recently appeared in France, and several other volumes made
up of extracts from her notebooks are to be published soon. Simone
Weil apparently left behind her a large body of fragments, drafts,
and unrevised sketches, which a world that finds in her most casual
words insights and illuminations will not be content to leave in
manuscript.

Several of her poems and prose pieces not included in any of
these volumes, have been published in various French magazines
(notably in *Cahiers de Sud),* and three or four of her political essays have appeared in this country in *Politics.* But the only really
consequential study, aside from those in the three books, is her
splendid, though absurdly and deliberately partial, interpretation of
the *Iliad,* which has been excellently translated into English by
Mary McCarthy and published in pamphlet form under the title of
*The Iliad: or, the Poem of Force.*

These are the chief sources of her thought; and the introduc-
tions to the volumes edited by M. Thibon and Father Perrin provide, along with briefer personal tributes printed at the time of her
death, the basic information we have about her life. In a profound
sense, her life is her chief work, and without some notion of her biography it is impossible to know her total meaning. On the other
hand, her books are extensions of her life; they are not *literature,*

not even in the sense that the writings of a theologically oriented author like Kierkegaard are literature. They are confessions and testimonies—sometimes agonized cries or dazzled exclamations—motivated by the desire to say just how it was with her, regardless of all questions of form or beauty of style. They have, however, a charm of directness, an appealing purity of tone that makes it possible to read them (Simone Weil would have hated to acknowledge it!) for the sheer pleasure of watching a subtle mind capture in words the most elusive of paradoxes, or of contemplating an absolute love striving to communicate itself in spite of the clumsiness of language.

## Her Life

We do not know, as yet, a great deal about the actual facts of Simone Weil's life. Any attempt at biographical reconstruction runs up against the reticence and reserve of her parents, who are still living, and even more critically, it encounters her own desire to be anonymous—to deny precisely those elements in her experience, which to the biographer are most interesting. She was born in 1909, into a family apparently socially secure (her father was a doctor) and "completely agnostic." Though her ancestors had been Jewish, the faith had quite disappeared in her immediate family, and where it flourished still among remoter relatives, it had become something cold, oppressive, and meaninglessly legalistic to a degree that made Simone Weil all of her life incapable of judging fairly the merits of Judaism. She appeared to have no sense of alienation from the general community connected with her Jewishness (though in appearance she seems to have fitted exactly a popular stereotype of the Jewish face), but grew up with a feeling of belonging quite firmly to a world whose values were simply "French," that is to say, a combination of Greek and secularized Christian elements.

Even as a child, she seems to have troubled her parents, to whom being comfortable was an end of life and who refused to or could not understand her mission. They frustrated again and again, with the greatest of warmth and goodwill, her attempts to immolate herself for the love of God. Her father and mother came to represent, in an almost archetypal struggle with her, the whole solid bourgeois world, to whom a hair shirt is a scandal and suffering only a blight to be eliminated by science and proper familial care. Yet she loved her parents as dearly as they loved her, though she was from childhood quite incapable of overt demonstrations of affection.

At the age of five, she refused to eat sugar as long as the soldiers at the front were not able to get it. The war had brought the sense of human misery into her protected milieu for the first time, and her typical pattern of response was already set: to deny herself what the most unfortunate were unable to enjoy. There is in her reaction, of course, something of the hopeless guilt of one born into a favored position in a society with sharp class distinctions. Throughout her career, there was to be a touch of the absurd in her effort to identify herself utterly with the most exploited groups in society (whose own major desire was to rise up into the class from which she was trying to abdicate), and being continually "rescued" from the suffering she sought by parents and friends. A little later in her childhood, she declared that she would no longer wear socks while the children of workers had to go without them. This particular gesture, she was later to admit in a typically scrupulous bit of self-analysis, might have been prompted as much by an urge to tease her mother as by an unselfish desire to share the lot of the poor.

At fourteen, she passed through the darkest spiritual crisis of her life, feeling herself pushed to the very verge of suicide by an acute sense of her absolute unworthiness and by the onslaught of migraine headaches of an unbearable intensity. The headaches never left her afterward, not even in her moments of extremest joy; her very experiences of Divine Love would come to her strained through that omnipresent pain which attacked her, as she liked to say, "at the intersection of body and soul." She came later to think of that torment, intensified by the physical hardships to which she compulsively exposed herself, as a special gift; but in early adolescence, it was to her only a visible and outward sign of her inner misery at her own total lack of talent.

The root of her troubles seems to have been her relationship with her brother, a mathematical prodigy, beside whose brilliance she felt herself stumbling and stupid. Her later academic successes and the almost universal respect accorded her real intelligence seem never to have convinced her that she had any intellectual talent. The chance phrase of a visitor to her mother, overheard when she was quite young, had brought the whole problem to a head. Simone Weil never forgot the words. "One is genius itself," the woman had said, pointing to the boy; and then, indicating Simone, "the other beauty!" It is hard to say whether she was more profoundly disturbed by the imputation of a beauty she did not possess or by the implicit denial of genius.

Certainly, forever afterward, she did her best to destroy what in her was "beautiful" and superficially charming, to turn herself into the antimask of the appealing young girl. The face in her photographs is absolute in its refusal to be charming, an exaggeration, almost a caricature, of the intellectual Jewess. In a sentence or two, Father Perrin recreates her for us in her typical costume: the oversize brown beret, the shapeless cape, the large, floppy shoes, and emerging from this disguise, the clumsy, imperious gestures. We hear, too, the unmusical voice that completes the ensemble, monotonous, almost merciless in its insistence. Only in her writing is Simone Weil betrayed into charm; in her life, she made a principle of avoiding it. "A beautiful woman," she writes, "looking at her image in the mirror may very well believe the image is herself. An ugly woman knows it is not."

But though her very appearance declares her physical humility, we are likely to be misled about Simone Weil's attitude toward her own intelligence. Father Perrin tells us that he never saw her yield a point in an argument with anybody, but on the other hand, he is aware, as we should be, too, of her immense humbleness in the realm of ideas. Never was she able to believe that she truly possessed the quality she saw so spectacularly in her own brother, the kind of "genius" that was honestly to be envied insofar as it promised not merely "exterior success" but also access to the very "kingdom of truth."

She did not commit suicide, but she passed beyond the temptation without abandoning her abysmal sense of her own stupidity. Instead, she learned painfully the *uses* of stupidity. To look at a mathematical problem one has inexcusably missed, she writes, is to learn the true discipline of humility. In the contemplation of our crimes or our sins, even of our essential proneness to evil, there are temptations to pride, but in the contemplation of the failures of our intelligence, there is only degradation and the sense of shame. To know that one is mediocre is "to be on the true way."

Besides, when one has no flair for geometry (it is interesting that her examples come always from the field of her brother's special competence) the working of a problem becomes not the really irrelevant pursuit of an "answer," but a training in "attention," which is the essence of prayer. And this in turn opens to us the source of a higher kind of genius, which has nothing to do with natural talent and everything to do with Grace. "Only a kind of perversity can force the friends of God to deprive themselves of genius, because it is enough for them to demand it of their Father in the name of Christ, to have a superabundance of genius . . ." Yet even this final consideration never brought her absolute peace. She wrote toward the end of her life that she could never read the parable of the "barren fig tree" without a shudder, seeing in the figure always a possible portrait of herself, naturally impotent, and yet somehow, in the inscrutable plan of God, cursed for that impotence.

However she may have failed her own absolute standards, she always seems to have pleased her teachers. At the *Ecole Normale Supérieure,* where she studied from 1928 to 1931, finally attaining her *agregée de philosophie* at the age of 22, she was a student of the philosopher Alain, who simply would not believe the report of her early death years afterward. "She will come back surely," he kept repeating. "It isn't true!" It was, perhaps, under his instruction that the love of Plato, so important in her thought, was confirmed in her once and for all.

But at that point of her career she had been influenced by Marx as well as the Greek philosophers; and it was as an earnest and committed radical, though one who had never joined a particular political party, that she took up her first teaching job at Le Puy. It was a time for radicals—those utterly bleak years at the pit of a world-wide depression. She seems, in a way not untypical of the left-wing intellectual in a small town, to have horrified the good citizens of Le Puy by joining the workers in their sports, marching with them in their picket lines, taking part with the unemployed in their pick and shovel work, and refusing to eat more than the rations of those on relief, distributing her surplus food to the needy. The bourgeois mind seems to have found it as absurd for this awkward girl to be playing ball with workers as to be half-starving herself because of principles hard to understand. As for crying for a Revolution—!

A superintendent of instruction was called in to threaten Simone Weil with revocation of her teacher's license, at which she declared proudly that she would consider such a revocation "the crown of her career!" There is a note of false bravado in the response, betraying a desire to become a "cause," to attain a spectacular martyrdom. It is a common flaw in the revolutionary activity of the young; but fortunately for Simone Weil, this kind of dénouement, of which she would have been ashamed later, was denied her. She was only a young girl, harmless, and her license was not revoked. Irked at the implied slur, perhaps, and certainly dissatisfied in general with halfway participation in the class struggle of a teacher-sympathizer, she decided to become a worker once and for all by taking a job at the Renault auto plant.

It is hard to know how to judge the venture. Undoubtedly, there is in it something a little ridiculous: the resolve of the Vassar girl of all lands to "share the experience" of the working class; and the inevitable refusal behind that resolve to face up to the fact that the freedom to *choose* a worker's life and the consciousness of that choice, which can never be sloughed off, make the dreamed-of total identification impossible. And yet for the sake of that absurd vision, Simone Weil suffered under conditions exacerbated by her sensibility and physical weakness beyond anything the ordinary worker had to bear; the job "entered into her body," and the ennui and misery of working-class life entered into her soul, making of her a "slave," in a sense she could only understand fully later when her religious illumination had come.

She was always willing to take the step beyond the trivially silly; and the ridiculous pushed far enough, absurdity compounded, becomes something else—the Absurd as a religious category, the madness of the Holy fool beside which the wisdom of this world is revealed as folly. This point Simone Weil came to understand quite clearly. Of the implicit forms of the love of God, she said, ". . . in a sense they are absurd, they are mad," and this she knew to be their special claim. Even unhappiness, she learned, in order to be pure must be a little absurd. The very superiority of Christ over all the martyrs is that he is not anything so solemn as a martyr at all, but a "slave," a criminal among criminals, "only a little more ridiculous. For unhappiness is ridiculous."

An attack of pleurisy finally brought Simone Weil's factory experience to an end (there were always her parents waiting to rescue her), but having rested for a while, just long enough to regain some slight measure of strength, she set off for Spain to support the Loyalists, vowing all the while that she would not ever learn to use the gun they gave her. She talked about Spain with the greatest reluctance in later years, despite the fact, or perhaps because, it was undoubtedly for her, as for many in her generation, a critical experience: the efflorescence and the destruction of the revolutionary dream. From within and without, the Marxist hope was defeated in a kind of model demonstration, a paradigm for believers. Simone Weil was fond of quoting the Homeric phrase about "justice, that fugitive from the camp of the victors," but in those years it was absent from the camp of victor and vanquished alike. Not even defeat could purify the revolution!

While the struggle in Spain sputtered toward its close, Simone Weil endured a personal catastrophe even more anticlimactic; she was wounded—by accident! The fate that preserved her throughout her life for the antiheroic heroism of her actual death brought this episode, too, to a bathetic conclusion. Concerned with the possibilities of combining participation and nonviolence, pondering the eternal, she forgot the "real" world of missteps and boiling oil and ineptly burned herself, a victim of that clumsiness which seems to have been an essential aspect of her denial of the physical self. Badly hurt and poorly cared for, she was rescued from a field hospital by her parents—once more coming between her and her desired agony!

The Spanish adventure was her last purely political gesture; afterward, during the Second World War, she was to work up some utterly impractical plan for being parachuted into France to carry spiritual solace to the fighters in the underground resistance; and she was even to consider at one point going to the Soviet Union, where she could doubtless not have lived in freedom for a month. Among the Communists in France she had been known as a Trotskyite and had once been threatened with physical violence for delivering an anti-Stalinist report at a trade union convention. But at a moment when the Russians were retreating before the German attack, she felt obliged to "add a counterweight" in order to restore that equilibrium which could alone make life here below bearable. One can barely imagine her in the field with the Red Army, this quixotic, suffering "friend of God," flanked by the self-assured killers of "Fascist Beasts," and carrying in her hand the gun that would doubtless have blown off her fingers had she tried to fire it.

These later projects were, as their very "impossibility" attests, different in kind from her early practical ventures: the picketing with the unemployed, the participation in Spain. She had passed into the realm of the politics of the absurd, of metapolitics, having decided that "the revolution is the opiate of the people," and that the social considered in itself is "a trap of traps . . . an *ersatz* divinity . . . irremediably the domain of the devil." The lure of the social she believed to be her special temptation. Against the love of self she was armored by her very temperament. "No one loves himself," she wrote in her journal. "Man wants to be an egoist and cannot." But a nostalgia for collective action seemed ever on the point of overwhelming her defenses. Simply to join together with others in any group whatsoever would have been for her "delicious." "I know that if at this moment I had before me a group of twenty young Germans singing Nazi songs in chorus," she once said, "a part of my soul would instantly become Nazi. . . ." Yet the "we" can lead away from God, she knew, as dangerously as the "I." "It is wrong to be an 'I,' but it is worse to be a 'we,' " she warned herself. "The city gives us the feeling of being at home. Cultivate the feeling of being at home in exile."

Yet charity took her continually back into the world of social action. "Misery must be eliminated in so far as possible from life in society, for misery is useful only in respect to grace, and society is not a society of the elect. There will always be enough misery for the elect." If there is a certain inconsistency in her position, it is easy to forgive. Even the "wrong" politics of her revolutionary youth she would not write off as wholly mistaken; she never repented her early radicalism, understanding it as a providential discipline through which she had been unconsciously learning how to emancipate her imagination from its embroilment with the social. "Meditation on the social mechanism is a purification of the first importance in this regard. To contemplate the social is as good a means of purification as retiring from the world. That is why I was not wrong in staying with politics for so long."

It was after her Spanish experience that Simone Weil reached the critical point of conversion; but the decisive event in her spiritual education had been, she always felt, her work in the factory. She had not known what she was seeking at the machine, but she had found it nonetheless: branded with the red mark of the slave, she had become incapable of resisting "the religion of slaves." In one sense, Simone Weil insisted afterward, she had not needed to be converted; she had always been *implicitly,* in "secret" even from her lower self, a Christian; but she had never knelt, she had never prayed, she had never entered a church, she had never even posed to herself the question of God's existence. "I may say that never in my life have I 'sought for God,' " she said toward the end of her life; but she had been all the time waiting, without daring to define what she awaited.

Taken off by her parents to Portugal to recuperate from her burns and her chagrin, she made her way to Solesmes, where, listening to a Gregorian chant at the moment when her migraine was at its worst, she experienced the joy and bitterness of Christ's passion as a real event, though still so abstractly that she did not attach to it any name. And there, too, she had met a young English Catholic, who introduced her to the work of the British metaphysical poets of the seventeenth century, and so gave her a key to the beyond in the place of conventional prayer to which she had not yet been able to turn.

Like no saint before her, Simone Weil distrusted the conventional apparatus of piety and grace; and it is typical of her role that it was through forms of art acceptable to the most skeptical anti-Christian (Gregorian chant and metaphysical poetry—two of the special rediscoveries of our irreligious time) that she approached her encounter with God. "In a moment of intense physical suffering," she tells us, "when I was forcing myself to feel love, but without desiring to give a name to that love, I felt, without being in any way prepared for it (for I had never read the mystical writers) a presence more personal, more certain, more real than that of a human being, though inaccessible to the senses and the imagination. . . ." She had been repeating to herself a piece by George Herbert, when the presence came. "I used to think I was merely reciting it as a beautiful poem," she writes, "but without my knowing it the recitation had the virtue of a prayer." It is worth quoting the poem as a whole, for its imagery is vital, as we shall see later, to an understanding of Simone Weil's essential thought.

Love bade me welcome: yet my soul drew back,
  Guiltie of lust and sinne.
But quick-ey'd Love, observing me grow slack
  From my first entrance in,
Drew nearer to me, sweetly questioning,
  If I lack'd any thing.

A guest, I answer'd, worthy to be here:
  Love said, You shall be he.
I the unkinde, ungratefull? Ah my deare,
  I cannot look on thee.
Love took my hand, and smiling did reply,
  Who made the eyes but I?

Truth Lord, but I have marr'd them: let my shame
  Go where it doth deserve.
And know you not, sayes Love, who bore the blame?
  My deare, then I will serve.
You must sit down, sayes Love, and taste my meat:
  So I did sit and eat.

Even after such an experience, this astonishingly stubborn friend of God could not *for more than five years* bring herself to pray conventionally (though she tells us that in 1937 she knelt for the first time, at the shrine in Assisi), finally persuading herself to say the *Pater Noster* daily with so special a concentration that apparently at each repetition, Christ himself "descended and took her." It is her remarkable freedom from, her actual shamefastness before the normal procedures of Christian worship that lends a special authority to Simone Weil's testimony. Nothing comes to her as a convention or a platitude; it is as if she is driven to reinvent everything from the beginning. Of her first mystical experience she writes, "God had mercifully prevented me from reading the mystics, so that it would be clear to me that I had not fabricated an absolutely unexpected encounter." Surely, no mystic has ever been so scrupulously his own skeptical examiner.

Afterward, Simone Weil found in St. John of the Cross and the *Bhagavad-Gita* accounts of encounters similar to her own; and she even decided upon rereading her old master Plato in the light of her new experience that he, too, must have achieved the mystical union. Before her own encounter, she had thought that all such alleged experiences could be only a turning of the natural orientation of the sexual desire toward an imaginary object labeled God—a degrading self-indulgence, "lower than a debauch." To distinguish her own secret life from such *ersatz* mysticism became one of the main objects of her thought.

After her first mystical union, the inner existence of Simone Weil becomes much more important than anything that superficially happens to her. Even the War itself, the grossest fact of our recent history, shrinks in the new perspective. Nonetheless, Simone Weil continued to immerse herself in the misery of daily life. Driven by her constant desire not to separate herself from the misfortune of others, she refused to leave Paris until it was declared an open city, after which she moved with her parents to Marseilles. But there she was caught by the anti-Jewish laws of the Vichy Government which made it impossible for her to teach any longer; and so she went to Gustave Thibon, a lay theologian, in charge of a Catholic agricultural colony in the South of France. Under his guidance, she worked in the vineyards with the peasants (whom she astonished and bored with lectures on the Upanishads!), sleeping as they slept, and eating their meager fare until her feeble health broke down once more. M. Thibon at first immensely mistrusted her motives—a radical intellectual "returning to the soil!"—then became closely attached to her, and it was to him that she entrusted her journals and occasional jottings, which he finally decided to publish after her death despite her request to the contrary.

The chief external influence on Simone Weil during these last years of her spiritual progress was not M. Thibon, but Father Perrin, with whom she was apparently able to talk as she had never been able to before and to whom she communicated what of her secrets could be spoken at all. He was truly and deeply her friend. One has the sense of Simone Weil as a woman to whom "sexual purity" is as instinctive as breath; to whom, indeed, any kind of sentimental life is scarcely necessary. But a few lines in one of her absolutely frank and unguarded letters to Father Perrin reveal a terrible loneliness which only he was able to mitigate, to some degree, and a vulnerability which only he knew how to spare. "I believe that, except for you, all human beings to whom I have ever given, through my friendship, the power to harm easily, have sometimes amused themselves by doing so, frequently or rarely, consciously or unconsciously, but all of them at one time or another. . . ."

It is no evil in them, she hastens to add, that prompts this infliction of pain, but an instinct, almost mechanical, like that which makes the other animals in the chicken yard fall on the wounded hen. The figure of the wounded hen is one to which she returns elsewhere, and in contemplating it, one knows suddenly the immense sensitivity beneath the inflexible surface, her terrible need *not* to be laughed at or pitied for her patent absurdities. One remembers another heart-rending figure she used once to describe herself, "Indeed for other people, in a sense I do not exist. I am the color of dead leaves, like certain unnoticed insects." And the phrases from her journal recur, "never seek friendship . . . never permit oneself to dream of friendship . . . friendship is a miracle!"

It was at Father Perrin's request that Simone Weil "experientially" took communion, and it was with him that she argued out the question of her baptism: Would she lose her intellectual freedom in entering the Church? Did Catholicism have in it too much of those "great beasts" Israel and Rome? Did Christianity deny the beauty of this world? Did excommunication make of the Church an instrument of exclusion? Her friendship for the priest made her problem especially difficult: she did not want to hurt him personally by refusing baptism at his hands, nor did she certainly want to accept merely out of her love for him.

In the end, she decided to wait for an express command from God, "except perhaps at the moment of death." Searching, she believed, leads only to error; obedience is the sole way to truth. "If," she wrote in one of her most splendid paradoxes, "it were conceivable that one might be damned by obeying God and saved by disobeying him, I would nonetheless obey him." The role of the future spouse is to wait; and it is to this "waiting for God" that the title of the present collection refers. Simone Weil finally remained on the threshold of the Church, crouching there for the love of all of us who are not inside, all the heretics, the secular dreamers, the prophesiers in strange tongues; "without budging," she wrote, "immobile, εν υπομενη . . . only now my heart has been transported, forever I hope, into the Holy Sacrament revealed on the altar."

In May, 1942, she finally agreed to accompany her parents, who had been urging her for a long time, and set sail for America. Before her departure she remarked ruefully to a friend, "Don't you think the sea might serve me as a baptismal font?" But America proved intolerable to her; simply to *be* in so secure a land was, no matter how one tried to live, to enjoy what most men could not attain. She finally returned to England, where she tried desperately to work out some scheme for re-entering France and where she refused to eat any more than the rations allowed her countrymen in the occupied territory. Exhausted and weakened by her long fast, she permitted herself to be borne off into the country by well-meaning protectors, but on August 24th in 1943, she succeeded at last in dying, completing the process of "de-creation" at which she had aimed all her life.


## Her Method

Simone Weil's writing as a whole is marked by three characteristic devices: extreme statement or paradox; the equilibrium of contradictions; and exposition by myth. As the life of Simone Weil reflects a desire to insist on the absolute even at the risk of being absurd, so her writing tends always toward the extreme statement, the formulation that shocks by its willingness to push to its ultimate conclusion the kind of statement we ordinarily accept with the tacit understanding that no one will take it *too* seriously. The outrageous (from the natural point of view) ethics of Christianity, the paradoxes on which it is based, are a scandal to common sense; but we have protected ourselves against them by turning them imperceptibly into platitudes. It is Simone Weil's method to revivify them, by re-creating them in all their pristine offensiveness.

"He who gives bread to the famished sufferer for the love of God will not be thanked by Christ. He has already had his reward in his thought itself. Christ thanks those who do not know to whom they are giving food." Or "Ineluctable necessity, misery, distress, the crushing weight of poverty and of work that drains the spirit, cruelty, torture, violent death, constraint, terror, sickness—all these are God's love!" Or "Evil is the beautiful obedience of matter to the will of God."

Sometimes the primary function of her paradoxes is to remind us that we live in a world where the eternal values are reversed; it is as if Simone Weil were bent on proving to us, by our own uncontrollable drawing back from what we most eagerly should accept, that we do not truly believe those things to which we declare allegiance. ". . . every time I think of the crucifixion of Christ I commit the sin of envy." "Suffering: superiority of man over God. We needed the Incarnation to keep that superiority from becoming a scandal!"

Or sometimes it is our sentimentality that is being attacked, that *ersatz* of true charity which is in fact its worst enemy, "[Christ] did not however prescribe the abolition of penal justice. He allowed stoning to continue. Wherever it is done with justice, it is therefore he who throws the first stone." "Bread and stone are love. We must eat the bread and lay ourselves open to the stone, so that it may sink as deeply as possible into our flesh."

Or the paradox may have as its point merely the proving of the *impossibility* of God's justice, the inconsequentiality of virtue and grace. "A Gregorian chant bears testimony as effectively as the death of a martyr." ". . . a Latin prose or a geometry problem, even though they are done wrong, may be of great service one day, provided we devote the right kind of effort to them. Should the occasion arise, they can one day make us better able to give someone in affliction exactly the help required to save him, at the supreme moment of his need."

Corresponding to Simone Weil's basic conviction that no widely held belief is utterly devoid of truth is a dialectical method in which she balances against each other contrary propositions, not in order to arrive at a synthesis in terms of a "golden mean," but rather to achieve an equilibrium of truths. "One must accept all opinions," she has written, "but then arrange them in a vertical order, placing them at appropriate levels." Best of all exercises for the finding of truth is the confrontation of statements that seem absolutely to contradict each other. "Method of investigation—" Simone Weil once jotted down in a note to herself, "as soon as one has arrived at any position, try to find in what sense the contrary is true."

When she is most faithful to this method, her thought is most satisfactory; only where some overwhelming prejudice prevents her from honoring contradictions is she narrow and unilluminating—as, for instance, toward Israel, Rome, Aristotle, or Corneille. These unwitting biases must be distinguished from her deliberate strategic emphases, her desire to "throw the counterweight" on the side of a proposition against which popular judgment is almost solidly arrayed; as she does most spectacularly by insisting, in the teeth of our worship of happiness and success, that "unhappiness" is the essential road to God, and the supreme evidence of God's love.

One can see her method of equilibrium most purely in her remarks on immortality of the soul, in her consideration of the rival Protestant and Catholic theories of the Eucharist, and especially in her approach to the existence of God. "A case of contradictories, both of them true. There is a God. There is no God. Where is the problem? I am quite sure that there is a God in the sense that I am sure my love is no illusion. I am quite sure there is no God, in the sense that I am sure there is nothing which resembles what I can conceive when I say that word. . . ."

There are three main factors that converge in Simone Weil's interest in the myth (this is yet another aspect of her thought with which the contemporary reader of Jung and Joyce and Eliot and Mann feels particularly at home): first, there is the example of her master, Plato, who at all the great crises of his thought falls back on the mythic in search of a subtle and total explication; second, there is her own belief in multiple revelation, her conviction that the archetypal poetries of people everywhere restate the same truths in different metaphoric languages; and third, there is her sense of myth as the special gospel of the poor, a treasury of insights into the Beauty of the World, which Providence has bestowed on poverty alone, but which, in our uprooted world, the alienated oppressed can no longer decipher for themselves.

To redeem the truths of the myths, they must be "translated." Sometimes this is a relatively simple process of substituting for unfamiliar names, ones that belong to our own system of belief: Zeus is God the Father, Bacchus God the Son; Dionysus and Osiris "are (in a certain manner) Christ himself." In the fragment of Sophocles, Electra is the human soul, and Orestes is Christ; but in this latter example we are led, once we have identified the protagonists, to a complex religious truth: as Electra loves the absence of Orestes more than the presence of any other, so must we love God, who is by definition "absent" from the material world, more than the "real," present objects that surround us.

In a similar manner, other folk stories and traditional poems can lead toward revelations of fundamental truths: the "two winged companions" of an Upanishad, who sit on a single branch, one eating the fruit of the tree, the other looking at it, represent the two portions of the soul: the one that would contemplate the good, the other (like Eve in the Garden) that would consume it. Or the little tailor in Grimm's fairy tale who beats a giant in a throwing contest by hurling into the air a bird rather than a stone teaches us something about the nature of Grace. And finally, we discover from "all the great images of folklore and mythology" what Simone Weil considers to be the truth most necessary to our salvation, namely, "it is God who seeks man."

The fate of the world, she knew, is decided out of time; and it is in myth that mankind has recorded its sense of its true history, the eternal "immobile drama" of necessity and evil, salvation and grace.

## Her Essential Thought

It is no accident that Simone Weil has left behind no single summation of her thought; for she is not in any sense a systematic thinker. Some of her profoundest insights were flashed off as detached aphorisms; and, as we have seen, she sought, rather than avoided, inconsistency. To reduce her ideas to a unified body of dogma would be, therefore, misleading and unfair; yet there are certain central concepts to which she always returned, key images that she might extend or vary, but which she could never entirely escape. These figures which adumbrate the core of her commitment are those of eating, looking, and walking toward; of gravity *(pesanteur)* and light; of slavery, nudity, poverty, and de-creation.

The first group seems almost instinctive, rooted below the level of thought in Simone Weil's temperament itself, and provides a way into the others. The whole pattern of her life is dominated by the concepts of eating and not eating; from her childhood refusal of sugar, through her insistence at Le Puy on eating only as much as the relief allowance of the unemployed, to her death from semistarvation in England, her virtue seems naturally to have found its expression in attitudes toward food. The very myths that most attracted her: the Minotaur, Eve and the apple, the two birds of the Upanishad are based on metaphors of eating; and the final line of the poem of George Herbert, which was the occasion of her first mystical experience, reads, we remember, "So I did sit and eat."

There are two kinds of "eating" for Simone Weil, the "eating" of beauty and the beloved here below, which is a grievous error, "what one eats is destroyed, it is no longer real," and the miraculous "eating" in Heaven, where one consumes and is consumed by his God. "The great trouble in human life is that looking and eating are two different operations. Only beyond the sky, in the country  inhabited by God, are they one and the same single operation. . . . It may be that vice, depravity, and crime are nearly always, or even perhaps always, in their essence, attempts to eat beauty, to eat what we should only look at."

Here below we must be content to be eternally hungry; indeed, we must *welcome* hunger, for it is the sole proof we have of the reality of God, who is the only sustenance that can satisfy us, but one which is "absent" in the created world. "The danger is not lest the soul should doubt whether there is any bread [God], but lest, by a lie, it should persuade itself that it is not hungry. It can only persuade itself of this by lying, for the reality of its hunger is not a belief, it is a certainty."

Not to deny one's hunger and still not to eat what is forbidden, there is the miracle of salvation! It is true even on the level of human friendship, "a miracle by which a person consents to view from a certain distance, and without coming any nearer, the very being who is necessary to him as food." And how much more true on the level of the divine! "If [Eve] had been hungry at the moment when she looked at the fruit, if in spite of that she had remained looking at it indefinitely without taking one step toward it, she would have performed a miracle analogous to that of perfect friendship."

It is "looking" which saves and not "eating." "It should also be publicly and officially recognized that religion is nothing else but a looking." Looking, the mere turning of the head toward God, is equated by Simone Weil with desire and that passive effort of "waiting for God" which gives the present book its name; while eating is equated with the will, and the false muscular effort to seize that which can only be freely given. Man's "free will" consists in nothing but the ability to turn, or to refuse to turn, his eyes toward what God holds up before him. "One of the principal truths of Christianity, a truth that goes almost unrecognized today, is that looking is what saves us. The bronze serpent was lifted up so that those who lay maimed in the depths of degradation should be saved by looking upon it."

Besides the temptation to consume what should only be regarded, man is beset by the longing to march toward the unapproachable, which he should be willing merely to look at from afar; and worst of all, he ends by persuading himself that he *has* approached it. "The great error of the Marxists and of all the nineteenth century was to believe that by walking straight ahead one had mounted into the air." What we really want is above us, not ahead of us, and "We cannot take a single step toward heaven. It is not in our power to travel in a vertical direction. If however we look heavenward for a long time, God comes and takes us up." We are free only to change the direction of our glance; we cannot walk into heaven; we cannot rise without being lifted by grace.

The vertical is forbidden to us because the world is the province of gravity and dead weight *(pesanteur)*. The whole universe, as we know it through the senses and the imagination, has been turned over by God to the control of brute mechanism, to necessity and blind force, and that primary physical law by which all things eternally *fall*. The very act of creation entailed the withdrawal of the Creator from the created, so that the sum total of God and his world and all of its creatures is, of course, less than God himself. Having withdrawn from the universe so that it might exist, God is powerless within it, ineffective except as his grace penetrates on special occasions, like a ray of light, the dark mechanical realm of unlimited misery.

Yet we must *love* this world, this absence of God by virtue of which we are, for only through it, like the smile of the beloved through pain, can we sense the perfectly nonpresent Being who alone can redeem it. "In the beauty of the world, brute necessity becomes an object of love. What is more beautiful than the action of gravity on the fugitive folds of the sea waves or on the almost eternal folds of the mountains?"

This world is the only reality available to us, and if we do not love it in all its terror, we are sure to end up loving the "imaginary," our own dreams and self-deceits, the utopias of the politicians, or the futile promises of future reward and consolation which the misled blasphemously call "religion." The soul has a million dodges for protecting itself against the acceptance and love of the emptiness, that "maximum distance between God and God," which is the universe; for the price of such acceptance and love is abysmal misery. And yet it is the only way. "If still persevering in our love, we fall to the point where the soul cannot keep back the cry 'My God, my God, why hast thou forsaken me?' if we remain at this point without ceasing to love, we end by touching something that is not affliction, not joy, something that is the central essence, necessary and pure, something not of the senses, common to joy and sorrow: the very love of God."

The final crown of the life of holiness is the moment of utter despair in which one becomes totally a "slave," naked and abandoned and nailed to the cross in imitation of the absolute spiritual poverty of Christ. "Extreme affliction . . . is a nail whose point is applied at the very center of the soul, whose head is all necessity spreading throughout space and time. . . . He whose soul remains ever turned toward God though pierced with a nail finds himself nailed to the center of the universe . . . at the intersection of creation and its Creator . . . at the intersection of the arms of the Cross."

On the cross, deceit is no longer possible; we are forced to "recognize as real what we would not even have believed possible," and having yielded ourselves in love to spiritual poverty, spiritual nudity, to death itself, even to the point of provisionally renouncing the hope of immortality, we are ready for the final gesture of obedience: the surrender of the last vestiges of selfhood. In the ultimate "nuptial yes," we must de-create our egos, offer up everything we have ever meant by "I," so that the Divine Love may pass unimpeded through the space we once occupied, close again on Itself. "We are created for this consent, and for this alone."

*Missoula, Montana*
—1951

# On Living with Simone Weil

To WRITE about Simone Weil* is an act of engagement terrifying in its implications. I have never hesitated to take up living issues either from the fear of being proved wrong by developing events or out of tenderness toward the vanity and self-deceit of others. Pious footnotes on established reputations have seemed to me as unattractive as retrospective insights into yesterday's causes. But I have never dealt with a personality so painfully and inexhaustibly contemporaneous as Simone Weil; though ten years dead, she remains living in a way that Alger Hiss, for all the resurrection of his name in the press and on the radio, is not. Beside her, the Rosenbergs, McCarthy seem ghosts, less real than what one has written about them. Only she among recent figures with whom I have dealt in print has really *happened* to me, become an event in my life as well as an item in my bibliography; or, to put it more precisely, I have become an event in hers, a minor event in the pathos and comedy of a life which is not yet through.

It is for this reason that I am almost tempted to believe that, given the chance, I would not write on her again. It all seemed innocent enough in the beginning: the brief note from Irving Kristol asking me to read *La pesanteur et la grâce* and to put something down if I felt moved to, my own passionate response to that selection of aphorisms from her notebooks, my first piece on her in *Commentary,* my introduction to *Waiting for God,* and then—the deluge.

---

\* Simone Weil, *The Notebooks* (tr. by Arthur Wills), 2 vols.

31

To this day I am not sure that the day's mail will not bring me a new volume of "mystical" poems, shamelessly turgid and printed at the author's expense; or another letter from Ceylon or Cuba or the Philippines thanking me for my essay and hinting shyly that the writer, too, has had experiences like Simone Weil's. Visiting clergymen in Missoula, Montana, Episcopal or Catholic, will stop in to see me, or intellectual priests exiled in obscure towns in the West send me clippings from parochial magazines.

I have finally the sense of a fragmented, ill-assorted community of admirers of Simone Weil, nuts, lonely neurotics, ex-radicals, existentialists, discontented kids trying to find each other, to tell someone who will listen their love for her. It is more than a little embarrassing sometimes: too many confessions more intimate than one should be asked to share; too many muddled confusions that end equating Simone Weil's terrible, bleak vision with the blurred nature-mysticism of Walt Whitman; too many correspondents who have only read excerpts from my piece in *Time*. And, of course, there is *Time* itself, hot always on the trail of the Latest Thing in Religion from Kierkegaard to the Lubovitcher Rebbe, *Time* in whose pages everything sinks to the dead level of the interesting.

I will not pretend that a first appearance in *Time* (where I made my début flanked by a picture of Simone Weil, uncompromisingly ugly and intent) is easy to take for one brought up on left-wing politics, especially since the twinge of guilt is inevitably balanced by a small flush of pride. But there were favorable responses, too, from Herbert Read and Upton Sinclair—even offers of audiences with the Pope and Sholem Asch, both of which temptations I managed finally to resist; in short, distinguished recognition and some comic relief.

But this is only a part of the picture, in a sense the least fascinating; for at the same moment that a doctor in the Celebes was sitting down to write me a note of appreciation, a professor in the Hebrew University (I am told) was hurling the *Commentary* containing my article through a window. When I tried not long ago to persuade my publisher to include one of my Weil pieces (I *would* still write them, after all) in my collection of essays, I was assured from the friendliest of sources that "everybody" considers these tributes to contemporary sanctity well below my usual standards. It all de-

pends on who your "everybody" is. Certainly, Simone Weil has
stirred up—and continues to excite—a resistance whose strength I
at first underestimated. Though her flirtation with the Roman
Church has never quite satisfied the staunchest guardians of orthodoxy, it has seemed sufficiently compromising to justify hysteria to
a certain kind of middle-class mind, for which anti-Catholicism
plays the role of anti-Semitism among the lower classes. And my
willingness to abide this flirtation has led to a still circulating series
of rumors about my own conversion to Catholicism, of which my
article seemed in some quarters to be an encoded confession.

I do not want to gloss over the problems of Simone Weil's attitude toward her own Jewishness, which are complex and deserve a
treatment equally complex, at which I have made an attempt in my
*Commentary* essay. I want to remark here only how various other
attitudes are involved with and disguised by the righteous protest
against her alleged anti-Semitism. The first of these is a psychoanal-
ytically oriented distrust of such "neurotic symptoms" as the denial
of the self and the belief in a direct communion with God—as if supreme goodness were not as likely to look like mental disease as
mental health. The second and more important is the desire among
those whose former radicalism has shrunk to little besides antireli-
gion to resist the "failure of nerve" and the "return to God." Like
color distinctions to the poor whites, it is their last claim to a kind
of superiority; and I know now that one must be cautious in hack-
ing away at such a claim as if only principle and truth rather than
prestige and self-respect were involved.

In any case, the opposition is formidable, entrenched in the
most fashionable tolerance of the moment and even commercially
enough of a threat to have scared the publishers of the English
translation of *Waiting for God* into expurgating that book. What
they removed from the volume in question was a piece, included in
the French version, in which Simone Weil retold the myth of
Noah's drunkenness to prove that Shem was the evil son, Ham the
real chosen of God. I first learned of this bowdlerization when I
protested the cutting of a reference to it in my own introductory
essay and an editor from Putnam's wrote: "As you know, it has
been considerably criticized in Jewish circles. . . ." He went on to
assure me that it was being saved for "possible future publication,"

but it has not, of course, yet appeared. This strikes me, I must confess, as sheer comedy—self-censorship out of the purest commercial motives; but my next adventure was more pathetic, the motives at stake more confused.

There has been going on, since the publishing of Simone Weil's work began, a struggle between her Jewish family and her Catholic literary executors, in which each would like by selection and emphasis to make it clear that at the end of her life she was clearly moving away from or toward the Roman Church. Since I had expressed a view that she would never have become a Catholic because she found too great a "Jewish" element in that church, I had apparently succeeded in offending both, certainly in pleasing neither. At any rate, I found myself in the dead center of a fight, a vulnerable target between two strongly entrenched forces. As a result, my introductory note (which Herbert Read had suggested be published with the British edition of *Lettre à un réligieux* and perhaps translated for appearance in France) was vetoed by her parents. They seem to have been deeply hurt by my view of them as urging against their daughter's ideal of self-immolation the desirability of sustaining one's life in at least minimum security. My description of the absurd conflict between their desire as parents to see Simone happy and her desire to die they read as a reproach to them for pandering to their own comfort. Mme. Weil wrote bitterly of her thankless labors as a housewife, her husband's self-sacrifice as a doctor. To justify myself seemed impossible; but I tried at least to say something of my dismay at having cost them pain—bourgeois father myself and knowing how I could not have resisted wishing for my own child that she *not* achieve sainthood at such a cost; and I welcome the chance to repeat this in print.

No matter—except as I sit over these latest volumes of Simone Weil to appear in America and live again my relationship with her: my role in introducing her to this country (the publisher's canniness I appreciate only now in having a Jew to do the job), my implication with her family and with her mission of spreading the scandal and pain she thought to be the way to God. It is from these journals before me that the selections I first read were chosen, well chosen, for there is little new in the larger work: the same concept of the Void; the same obsessive metaphors of eating and female ugliness; the same desire to substitute for Judaism an Egyptian-Greek beginning for Christianity; the same hatred of war and the state and the self; the same realization that in our age the nonbeliever may be closer to a knowledge of God than the pious communicant. All that is added is a further sense of the hash of incomplete projects and half-completed syntheses out of which Simone Weil's aphorisms were extracted; of the sometimes nearly incoherent jumble of mathematics and comparative mythology, politics, and bodily pain against which she defined her vision. It is a true vision all the same: a vision capable still of giving offense and illumination; testimony to a life no one would dare wish for his child or pray for himself, but which he is proud to know was lived in his time by one who fought for causes that he, too, dreamed, and who was like him (whatever the word finally means) a Jew.

—1957

# THREE

# Straddling the Wall

*THE WALL,* we are told in an "Editor's Prologue," is actually the work of a certain Noach Levinson, Archivist of the Warsaw Ghetto, whose collection of documents and notes on Jewish life in the days of the destruction was dug up from its hiding place just after the war; "the Editor" has merely cut and arranged items from the collection. But a note on the back of the title page warns us that the "archive" is merely a hoax, and the book jacket assures us that we are reading a novel by John Hersey—presumably on the principle that there is no use taking chances and that more people are likely to read novels than histories. And what of the misguided reader who avoids the blurbs on book jackets? After all, there *was* a Warsaw Ghetto, and everyone knows that Hersey's book on Hiroshima was non-fiction, and therefore. . . . A further note adds to the confusion, asserting that "the substance is history" but that "the details are invented." Why so elaborate a pretense of subterfuge?

If *The Wall* gains anything from all this machinery, it does not gain enough to make a difference; for it remains on the whole a dull and unconvincing novel. Given its subject, before which the private imagination falters and the public imagination takes refuge in rhetoric, the unconvincingness is expected, perhaps inevitable; but the dullness demands a special talent. Indeed, that dullness is, in a sense, deliberate, the product of the very good sense and good taste that here and there win for Mr. Hersey some local successes. There is practically none of the overwriting one might look for in connection with such a theme; and any sentimentality that creeps in is reasonably quiet and well-behaved. There is, too, a solid core of carefully accumulated fact that is impressive, though never moving, beneath the conscientious underwriting.

Within the book's well-bred American limitations, the East European Jews it pretends to evoke are stifled; when they momentarily materialize, we catch them squirming. One has the impression of a Gentile with good intentions retelling a Yiddish story but avoiding the extreme intonations that make the point—in order to keep from giving offense. The language of the protagonists suffers especially; what there is in Yiddish of the richly vulgar, the outrageously exaggerated, has almost disappeared. It is typical that one characteristically gross idiom which slips by Mr. Hersey's guard is expurgated in translation, *"Geh, kak' oif'm yam"* becoming "Go use the ocean for a toilet seat."

In its attempt to seem merely the jottings of an archivist the book succeeds in being, in the Jamesean sense, scarcely *written* at all. Avoiding the poetic tone, the epic ambition, it is drawn toward the low-keyed prose of the report. Stylistically, it exists at the point where history, journalism, and fiction blur into that un-form which we may as well call, as the movies have taught us to, the "documentary." Overwhelmed, perhaps, by the political fact which was his occasion, Hersey does not dare to give the demands of form precedence over those of documentation; and yet he is no longer content to do the modest job of reportage that made *Hiroshima* effective. In the end, he merely flirts with fiction: sketching characters, tentatively striving for inwardness, but always retreating to the "facts" of the researcher.

The dry, matter-of-fact approach of the reporter is viable in literature only when, as in Defoe or Swift, the fable is not "true," but merely the outward form of a consistent and serious symbolism trying to get by in a literal-minded age. In Hersey's book, the opposite is the case; his book is an allegory stood on its head, with its literal story being verified history but its inner meanings essentially false. What one resents is *The Wall's* effort to bully us into accepting moral and political insights that we know are invalid by insisting on the documentary veracity of a historical event that we cannot deny. As a result, we are left feeling that the value of the book depends entirely on the truth of its statements down to their last detail; the whole structure, we suspect, would collapse if it turned out that in Warsaw during the March of 1941 there were not 1,668 but 1,669 deaths from typhus.

How different this is from what may properly be considered a novel we can see by reminding ourselves of the opening of Kafka's *Amerika,* in which the very "mistake" of placing a sword in the hand of the Statue of Liberty assures us that the book we are beginning is not less but more true than a document. When a writer compels us outward toward the world of statistics, he betrays a basic uncertainty about his ability to convey poetic conviction and inward truth, which can lead him only into further difficulty and confusion. To maintain the kind of verisimilitude he has chosen, Hersey is forced to impose unnecessary strains on our credulity. Wishing his account to seem more archive than fiction, Hersey narrates it all from the point of view of the single archivist Levinson; but to make this probable, he asks us to believe that scores of people have chosen to confess to one man their most intimate thoughts and have recollected, while doing so, the most insignificant details of their past. The author himself feels the absurdity of this from time to time and apologizes in a backhand way, putting into the mouth of Levinson the reader's objections. "Why does she remember, and why does she feel that she has to tell me, a detail like that?" "He spoke to me as an ear, not as a man."

But the most palpable piece of stage-managing required by Hersey's machinery comes in the final scene, the theatrical *finale* in which a handful of survivors crouch in a sewer just outside the wall of the burning Ghetto, and Levinson *interviews* them: a *Time* reporter on the spot or a Gallup Poll man taking notes. "Some of my friends have mentioned seeing a change in you during recent months. Have you felt such a change. . . . Could you describe this change? Why this change?" And they all, in excrement halfway to their knees, dutifully answer. It is a picture not only of the Warsaw Ghetto, but of a world we continue to inhabit, trapped between the crap and the well-intentioned inquisitors.

This, of course, Hersey does not know, being aware only that his quizzees must (even as we must) answer so that his charade can end on a note of hope. To symbolize that hope, *Hatikvah* is played offstage on the concertina of a doomed man, even as Hersey's protagonists make their affirmations like the convicted defendants in a

Soviet trial. If he had been content merely to aim at a good book, he might have avoided such embarrassments; but he is driven by the desire to write a *great* one, a work of art as great as its subject. In the interest of such greatness, he feels obliged to go beyond the mere evocation of horror and despair and defeat, feels compelled to demonstrate that the ordeal of the Ghetto was, for a chosen few at least, a school for nobility. It is possible that this was, in fact, true; but for a writer to convince us of it is another matter. In this regard, Hersey's plight is rather like that of an author who has imagined a great poet as his protagonist and finds himself forced to invent verses capable of persuading us of his protagonist's talent. So Mr. Hersey must persuade us that his ennobled survivors are, indeed, noble; and to do this, he must find for them a language appropriate to their redeemed state rather than to the editorial demands of the *New Yorker*.

Realizing the difficulty of this, he seeks refuge at first in quotation, putting in the mouth of his archivist certain phrases from the eminent Jewish writer Peretz. When the German flamethrowers have driven the last Jewish resisters underground, we are permitted to listen to Levinson addressing a gathering in an airless bunker. He speaks to his comrades of Peretz, rehearsing for them the remembered words of that dead author.

> Now I am not advocating that we shut ourselves up in a spiritual ghetto. On the contrary, we should get out of such a ghetto. But we should get out as Jews, with our own spiritual treasures. We should interchange, give and take, but not beg.
>
> Ghetto is impotence. Cultural cross-fertilization is the only possibility for human development. Humanity must be the synthesis, the sum, the quintessence of all national cultural forms and philosophies.

As rhetoric this is not disgraceful, but as relevant wisdom it is of doubtful worth. Peretz was dead before even the first of the World Wars was over; and repeated after the final outbreak of terror, his phrases seem old-fashioned, inadequate with their proffered hope of cultural assimilation and a commonwealth of enlightened men. This was the battered hope men carried still in their hearts before Warsaw and the concentration camps; but with what was it replaced? This question, too, Levinson-Hersey tries to answer, listing one by one, as in a morality play, the partial answers of the handful left in the sewers to confront their inevitable death.

First the Zionist speaks ("the Jewish ethical tradition is worth preserving—it is the basis of all Western monotheism, after all . . . and the best way of preserving it is to give it a home"), then the Socialist ("Judge me, Levinson. Have I or have I not tried to put human understanding into my politics. . ."), then Rachel Apt, heroine of the tale, and representative of a modern religiosity without religion ("I am rather unclear as to God. But so far as the rest of religion is concerned, I think there is only one thing: not to hurt anybody"). It is a crescendo of clichés which it seems impossible to augment; but Levinson has already outdone the hoariest of them, declaring: "I think we are indeed involved in the struggle of Humanity against Anti-Humanity. Here, we are outnumbered. We are a little hysterical. We may all die. But we will win." The Zionist, the Socialist, the Jewish Heroine, the subtle Scholar among them can do no better; and, indeed, the final condemnation of the book is that we are prepared to believe that out of the mouths of Hersey's characters precisely such platitudes would come: after the Terror, such pious banalities. Poor Jews!

—1950

# FOUR

# Partisan Review: Phoenix or Dodo?

I CANNOT WRITE about the *Partisan Review* objectively and coolly. In dealing with it, I have the sense of beginning my own autobiography, or, more precisely, of treating that part of my life which is typical rather than peculiar: my life as an urban American Jew, who came of age intellectually during the Depression: who discovered Europe for the imagination before America: who was influenced by Marxist ideas, Communist and Trotskyist; who wanted desperately to feel that the struggle for a revolutionary politics and the highest literary standards was a single struggle (but who had more and more trouble believing it as the years went on); whose political certainty unraveled during the second World War. . . I forget after a while whether I am writing about myself and my friends or about the magazine we used to fight for and argue over in 1937 and '38 and '39. I do not mean we *liked* it, then—far from it! Every issue seemed to us to fail some large, abstract notion of *Partisan Review*-ness, some ideal, it now seems clear to me, of ourselves. No sooner was *Partisan* a year old than this year's level seemed to us a vast falling off from the year before. The point is, of course, that what is merely typical of oneself is bound to appear comic, embarrassing, depressing and a bore; and yet—I remember K., now the author of two novels, one of whose first ambitious pieces of fiction was a parody of a *Partisan Review* story we all mailed off together as a huge joke, but who, ten years later, was publishing regularly in *PR*. I remember my own sense of being misrepresented when I, in turn, began to appear in its pages; and my special horror when, after only three contributions, I was men-

41

tioned in two separate attacks on *Partisan* as representative of its intellectual vices.

By now I have come a long way from the pattern of my past: a Professor of English Literature, improbably asked for letters of recommendation by aspiring students; a father of six children, who lives over five hundred miles from the nearest big city and is surrounded by those who, if they know *Partisan* at all, have picked it up in a university library rather than off the "literature table" of a deviationist Marxist sect. Yet I have accepted my fate with all its contradictions: I stand somehow for *PR* and *PR* for me; I do not like it, but I cannot deny it. I know that even my feeling of being misrepresented is typical, as is my lack of love for the magazine. It is not a publication one loves; only its enemies are passionate. Nor does *PR* love its own children; I am aware that at the very moment I am losing a good academic job because I have appeared too often on its pages (and am therefore obviously "negative" as well as Jewish), *PR* is preparing to blast me publicly for believing in God. This strikes me as reasonably just as well as amusing—as amusing almost as the letter I had not long ago from a writer who is perhaps the best of the younger American novelists. "As for *PR*," he writes, "you know I never took that dodo for a phoenix. . . ." We both remember, of course, that it was *Partisan* which almost alone published him in the days when he was fighting to establish his reputation; but his comment is also just and a joke and part of the history of the magazine.

The real riddle of *Partisan Review* has always seemed to me the question of how the mouthpiece of so small and special a group as I have been defining (I should be much more surprised to discover that I am a "typical American" than that I am a typical *Partisan* writer) has managed to become the best-known serious magazine in America, and certainly, of all American magazines with intellectual ambitions, the one most read in Europe. That these are facts, I think there can be no doubt; at least, they are invariably mentioned with horror in anti-*Partisan* tirades. For better or for worse, *PR* has come to symbolize highbrow literature in America, and to suffer the twin indignities of the highbrow in our world: to be despised without understanding, and to be taken up by the culturally fashionable in equal ignorance.

Two examples, picked at random out of many, may serve to make the point. In a recent article, a certain reputable professor of American Literature sought to make clear his contempt for the politics of Mark Twain by writing, "We know this type well: the liberal who is not the tough realist. . . . You will find him vending his misanthropy in the *Partisan Review*." The reputable professor feels free to assume that there will be no doubt among academic readers about the meaning of his allusion. But the symbol is effective in Hollywood as well as at Princeton or Harvard. A couple of years ago, I paid a brief visit to an acquaintance who had been translated from an editorship in a publishing house to the position of a movie producer; and I found him in the midst of the appropriate splendor: white rugs on the floor, ponies for each of his children—and in the middle of a large, free-form cocktail table—a single copy of *PR*—to show, I suppose, that he was not yet lost to intellectual respectability.

Not only the purveyors of culture, however, high and low, accept this equation of *Partisan* and highbrow; it holds water for people who have never even seen the periodical, perhaps have never known one of its readers in their lives. It is, as a matter of fact, by no means easy to meet such readers. In its nearly twenty years of history, *PR* has never claimed more than ten thousand subscribers, and probably has considerably fewer at the present moment; and yet it is referred to in such mass-circulation journals as *Life* and *Time* with perfect confidence that it will stir the proper responses in their vast audience. Most of its subscribers have, to be sure, clustered about the two great cities of New York and Chicago (44%, according to a poll taken one year by the editors); and New York, at least, has been traditionally the taste-making center of the nation.

Besides, the split among the various kinds of art in America and their appropriate audiences into low, middle, and high has surrendered the creation, consumption, and judgment of serious literature into the hands of the very few. It is against those few that *Partisan*'s five to ten thousand faithful must be measured, and not against the 160,000,000 of the latest census figures. In that relatively restricted group, the thirties were marked by a turning away from the hinterland of America to Europe in a search for literary materials and examples. In that constant turning from East to West to East which characterizes our culture, the vanes pointed East once more; and no one seemed better suited for mediating between Europe and America than the kind of second generation Jew who in America's big cities was trying to find his own identity in the pages of *transition* and Karl Marx's *Capital*. Certainly, the Jews were the only immigrant group that had brought with it a considerable Old World culture to which it clung, refusing to cast it into the melting pot with the same abandon with which southern European or Scandinavian peasants were willing to toss away their few scraps of European spiritual goods.

It was the sons of the original Jewish immigrants, disabused of the legend of a Golden America by the Great Depression and attracted toward the Communist Party, who formed the core of the John Reed Club of New York which first sponsored the *Partisan Review*. In a handful of American cities, such "cultural" organizations, controlled by the Communists and called after native American radicals like John Reed or Jack London, flourished in the late thirties—as part of a strategy aimed at capturing the prestige of the "intellectuals" for the cause of the Soviet Union. It is important to remember that *PR* was born of such a marriage of Greenwich Village and Marxism—or more properly, from the attempt to woo the disaffected, rootless American, who wandered into New York in search of cultural freedom, from Bohemianism to Radicalism.

*Partisan Review* in its present form, however, begins with a declaration of independence from the orthodox Communists who ordained its beginnings. Its emergence as an independent journal is one symptom among many of the growing uneasiness of a certain segment of American writers, whom the Depression and the Spanish Civil War had persuaded into a temporary alliance with the Communist Party. From 1937 on (the new *PR* appeared first in the fall of that year), the Communists in America lost more and more of their respectable, intellectual fellow-travelers—indeed, almost deliberately jettisoned them for movie stars, script writers, and authors of detective stories as the Popular Front reached its peak of development. Into the cultural vacuum thus created, moved the *Partisan Review*. It was for many a transition from "revolutionary art" back to old-style "aestheticism" or forward to middle-class accommodation (though of this they were not then aware): for others merely the way into a lonelier and lonelier non-conformism.

From the Communists, the new periodical inherited, first of all, a name (at one point later on, when no one was any longer clear exactly what they were "partisan" *for*—there was an unsuccessful attempt to change that name); second, two editors: Philip Rahv and William Phillips, who alone have remained with the publication through countless editorial shifts, thus giving the magazine what continuing character it has; and third, a certain kind of bad manners, traditional in the Marxist movement. There is a polemical vigor and toughness about *PR* which has survived almost all its causes; occasionally that toughness hardens into a pose, but it is always a safeguard against stuffiness and gentility. Born into a dispute (thirty days after its inception, its editors were already labeled by their old comrades "slanderers of the working class . . . turncoats . . . agents provocateurs . . . strikebreakers!" and they were returning abuse for abuse), it has continued to ignore the rules of gentlemanly debate. Often when its collaborators have no one else to attack, they gouge and kick each other like marines stirred up to fight among themselves, just to keep their hands in. Though its founding fathers tend more and more to show their old scars rather than risk getting new ones, they have remained old soap-boxers, which for me, at least, seems preferable to the young academicians or genteel undergraduate admirers of Wyndham Lewis who are found, for example, in *The Hudson Review*. Of all American magazines of discussion, only *Partisan* can be said never to talk to itself; to a few, yes, or to a crowd expected in advance to be hostile—but that is something else again.

There were two motives which impelled the editors of the new *PR* to break from the domination of the Communist Party: first, a desire for cultural autonomy, a feeling that orthodox Stalinism was hedging literature about with the "zeal of vigilantes"; and second, political disagreements of a Trotskyist hue with the official Communist line. Both led to long-term difficulties that have helped determine the nature of the magazine. From their second motive, the editors of *PR* (though most of them did not in fact ever become official Trotskyites) inherited a minor but troublesome vice: an obsessive anti-Stalinism and a myopic concern with sectarian Marxist politics, that, especially in the earlier years, hedged the magazine about with a technical jargon and the sort of parochial fervor which baffles and bores an outsider. After a while, even the insiders, who were not of the sternest, began to wilt at the prospect of yet another scholastic debate on the nature of the Soviet State.

From the first motive, *PR* inherited a whole Chinese nest of interlocking questions, which they have never solved theoretically but which their whole career has been an attempt to answer in practice. If one really believes (as *PR* declared in an early manifesto) that "the tradition of aestheticism" is dead or ought to be and that literature finds its "final justification" in the "historic process," how can one avoid setting political standards for art and eventually harrying the artist precisely as the Communists have done? This is an especially acute problem if one's approach to the "historic process" is revolutionary or even liberal; for it is a baffling fact of our time that many contemporary artists of the first rank are politically reactionary, as in the cases of Yeats, Eliot, Pound, Lawrence, etc. Does one print the work of such misguided writers for the sake of some presumed independent aesthetic value? And how can such values exist if works of art are really rooted in history?

The *de facto* answer of *PR* has been to print Allen Tate, T. S. Eliot, and other artists whose politics it abhors. For a while, indeed, it was the chief American outlet for Eliot, not only his poetry but even an occasional essay on social matters; and as time went on, certain old standbys like James T. Farrell seemed actually to be pushed aside in favor of defter though less "revolutionary" authors, especially those enjoying critical acclaim. What lay behind such a strategy? Unkind critics accused *PR* of institutionalizing schizophrenia; unkinder ones insisted that its editors were shamelessly pursuing "big names."

The truth is, I think, that *PR* has been obsessed with the notion of a two-fold *avant-garde,* political and artistic, both segments regarded as a threat by middle-class philistines. Since the magazine actually came into being at the end of a period rather than a beginning, at the moment when experimentalism in art was being consolidated and academicized all over the world, the concept that serious art is, *per se,* as revolutionary as Marxism has been difficult to maintain. It has been somewhat easier to foster that illusion in respect to painting by espousing the newer versions of abstractionism, or in music, with a spirited apology for the twelve-tone row, than to sustain it in defense of these newer writers, who (aside from such "standards" as Eliot) have been the actual official favorites of *PR:* Malraux, Silone, Koestler, Sartre, Moravia, or George Orwell, to whom *Partisan* once awarded a one thousand dollar literary prize. Ideologically, these writers may represent progressive trends; but technically, they are not very interesting, ranging from glib traditionalism to simple ineptness; and in Orwell's case actually being on record against "advanced" art. Just as *PR* comes into existence at the instant of the liquidation of revolutionary politics as a force in American intellectual life, so it presides (quite unconsciously at first) over the liquidation of experimentalism in art. This has irked various defenders of post-World War I "new literature," ranging from Parker Tyler to Paul Goodman to Harold Rosenberg, men who began as collaborators of the magazine but have one by one withdrawn from its pages. Rosenberg has written a valedictory attack on what *Partisan* has become, dubbing its present writers a "herd of independent minds" and treating them as enemies of serious art.

Despite the fact that *PR*'s notions of an *avant-garde* reach nostalgically back to the very twenties whose values it betrays, those notions have helped develop one of its most valuable features: a series of acute exposés of certain highly regarded writers who pander to the timid, cheery bourgeois mind, which, even after fifty years, persists in the belief that the aging purveyors of the "new literature" (even Eliot!) somehow subvert morality and patriotism. The second World War brought to America a peculiarly violent recrudescence of this attitude; philistine apologists like Archibald MacLeish cried out that the antiwar, antisentimental nature of our literature in the twenties and thirties had left us powerless in the forties to combat Fascism, while Van Wyck Brooks was insisting that the "secondary" literature of Joyce or Proust or Eliot had all along been an offense to the human spirit.

Dwight Macdonald in an essay called *Kulturbolschewismus* and M. D. Zabel in *The Poet on Capitol Hill* demonstrated with wit and passion how such arguments, proposed in the name of American democracy, actually represent totalitarian impulses, paralleling the attacks on the arts of Germany and Russia. In the atmosphere of controversy and self-congratulation which surrounded these two pieces, the editors were able to defend their previous principles of selection against the charges of contradictoriness by declaring, "It is coming to be something of a revolutionary act simply to print serious creative writing." When the culture-censors ten years later closed in on Ezra Pound, who had been awarded a coveted literary prize, *Partisan*'s editors, troubled by his anti-Semitism, were no longer so certain where their hearts lay; but in 1941 they were courageous and unequivocal.

Our entry into the war followed hard on these polemics, bringing a crisis in the history of *Partisan Review*. The editors found themselves not only confused but not even sharing a common confusion about the attitude to take toward our participation in the fight against Hitler. Dwight Macdonald, who had played a leading editorial role in the years just before Pearl Harbor and was still maintaining the traditional revolutionary position (the defeat of Hitler could only be forwarded by a redoubled struggle for socialism in the United States), left the board of editors; and with his going the magazine came to take political stands on specific issues less and less often. McCarthyism for a little while stirred it to specific political discussion and forced the resignation of the most right-wing of its long-time associates, James Burnham; but in general *PR* tended more and more to invest its post-Marxian zeal in considering broadly defined problems of American culture. The clash of High Brow and Low Brow has gradually usurped the place of Class War in its working mythology.

The editors have moved since variously toward skepticism, New Dealism and non-Marxian socialism; and though occasionally a cry is raised in its columns against the "Age of Conformism," most of its collaborators have been able to imagine no formulation of their plight which transcends the dilemma of adapting to current American life or sighing for the good old revolutionary days. Yet despite all changes, *PR* has remained in tone and tactics different from other American magazines of its category: the only periodical in our intellectual community for which politics in the European sense (something beyond choosing between Democrats and Republicans on set occasions) has ever existed. That old political passion survives in two forms: in the conviction that art is rooted in society, however one understands that society, and must be discussed in terms of those roots; and in a stubborn secularism which has outlived the revolutionary beliefs which once sustained it. From Edmund Wilson to Lionel Trilling, the most characteristic critical voice of *PR* has attempted to assert the sociological thesis against an evergrowing tendency toward intrinsic or "pure" textual criticism, and has sought to defend it against its profanation by the Stalinist or liberaloid theory that art must embody "progressive" ideas.

Occasionally in reading *Partisan* these days one has the sense of a weary but gallant voice crying, "Rosinante to the road again," as the editors print the replies to their latest questionnaire on the Return to Religion. When they reconsider their other long-time favorite problem: the Relation of the Intellectual to American Culture, they cannot help being aware of how far they have come since, say, Dreiser's offhand dismissal of official "Americanism" in the earliest of their symposia. But when it is a matter of "the retreat to faith," the old forces rally round and the majority opinion, naturalist and "scientific," rings out loud and clear, as if nothing had happened in twenty years—and we were all rebels still—with no income tax returns to trouble us.

In 1950, a symposium on "Religion and the Intellectuals" took up where an earlier discussion labeled "The New Failure of Nerve" had left off seven years before; but whereas in the earlier forum, part at least of *Partisan*'s fervor was directed against doctrinaire Marxism, this time the Marxist issue was left far out on the periphery. The finish of the first Symposium had found Professor Sidney Hook (who is almost the official spokesman for *PR* in these matters) closed in argument with an orthodox Socialist; the close of the second found the same Professor Hook grappling with a slippery Christian apologist, Ernest van den Haag. Hook has always struck me as a brilliant though cruel polemicist and a courageous man, but his views on religion are vitiated by the fact that he can, apparently, never really credit the fact that anyone actually believes in God. His attitude in this regard is like that of an uninitiated small boy toward sex: he has heard of it, and he pretends to give credence to its reality, but that papa and mama really *do* it is unthinkable!

It remains further to be said that its origin in the Village-Marx-
ist atmosphere of New York has influenced *PR* in two other significant ways: leaving it peculiarly "European" and resolutely anti-
"academic." Its European flavor is partly a matter of the taste of its
editors; its favorite literary ancestors are Dostoevsky and Tolstoi;
its favorite moderns, Malraux, Koestler, Silone, Kafka, Musil,
Sartre, Moravia, etc; and translations of their works will frequently
be the only imaginative literature in a given issue. Even more characteristic, perhaps, are those communications from European cultural centers, which lend much of its peculiar tone to *PR:* the Paris
letters of H. J. Kaplan and Nicola Chiaramonte, as well as the Italian letters of the latter and the London letters by Koestler and Orwell (attempts to institute similar regular communications from
American centers away from New York have always stuttered out
to nothing) have kept *Partisan*'s readers in touch not only with the
literary and political news but with the very gossip of Europe—a
narrow and sometimes *chic* Europe, to be sure, but a real one. The
*PR* reader has, by virtue of these letters, always felt a good deal
closer to Paris than to, say, Missoula, Montana; and though there is
something a little absurd about this, there is also something valuable. *PR* has kept open a dialogue between our writers and certain
writers on the continent; and it alone has been able to do this because it alone among our periodicals has been interested in and articulate about those "general ideas," with which the continental
mind engages so passionately but which most Americans notoriously ignore in favor of documented facts or textual analysis. The
most famous of these general ideas is the somewhat ambiguous one
of "alienation": a concept which joins together the Marxist beginnings of *PR* with its early leanings toward depth psychology and its
later interest in existentialism.

The belief in the "alienation" of the writer and intellectual from
the community in a time of decaying values has seemed to certain
of its critics to obsess the *Partisan Review,* and to lend a characteristic note of melancholy to its fiction and poetry as well as to its
more ideological pieces. Protests have rung out from the beginning
against the mixture of self-pity and bravado implicit in this view of
the writer at odds with his world; and just lately, for instance, the
editor of a provincial little magazine has described it as an "attitude

which seems to come from reading *The Golden Bowl* on the B.M.T. subway." In one sense, such a view is indeed a peculiarity, almost a disease of the social group out of which *Partisan* comes: a development of the special sense of loneliness of the city-dweller, the Jew, the Marxist in an un-Marxist America—and especially of the left-wing Communist cut off even from the comforting sense of solidarity with the Soviet Union and "right-minded" liberalism. On the other hand, it is the traditional European view of the artist in America from Baudelaire on Poe to D. H. Lawrence on the classic American authors; and as mass culture advances throughout the Western world, it comes to describe the plight of the artist everywhere. It is true enough that "alienation" has sometimes been celebrated by *PR*, rather than explored; but on the other hand, its writers have done more than any others I know to describe the situation of a minority high culture in a mass society committed to the majoritarian principle.

In its earliest manifesto, *PR* declared its defiance of all "academicians from the University"; and it has continued its rather harried financial existence via "angels" and begging letters—but always without the sponsorship of any educational institution.[1] This has been especially difficult in America, where the intellectual and his pursuits are granted full recognition and status only when they are associated with "higher education" and the universities have stood almost alone in subsidizing serious magazines. Even the Rockefeller Foundation, which in recent years has given support of one kind or another to such ventures, has invested only in periodicals whose respectability was already insured by an institutional connection, *Kenyon Review, Sewanee Review,* etc. *Partisan* has accordingly remained quite different in tone from those magazines that have defined themselves against the tendencies of old-line literary scholarship and whose *raison d'être* has been the struggle to reform the teaching of literature in the college classroom. *PR*'s ideo-

---

[1] In 1963, Richard Poirier, Chairman of the English Department at Rutgers University, became chief editor of *Partisan Review,* and William Phillips, one of its founders, was made a professor at the same institution. Since then it has largely been supported by that institution; but to what degree this represents a change in *Partisan Review* and to what degree one in the American university is the subject for another article which I am resolved never to write.

logical center has never become (no matter how many professors it lists among its contributors) the argument between the "New Critics" and the "Old Scholars," that is, a debate about pedagogy. It arises rather from that strange mingling of malicious gossip and disinterested argument about ideas that characterizes a social evening in New York. What the café is for Europe, such parties are for America—and it is out of them that *Partisan* has drawn its reigning concerns and its tone.

There are certain obvious limitations implicit in originating in so tight and isolated a world; obviously, personalities will play too large a part in any magazine nurtured by that milieu. Marriages and divorces, the falling out with an old mistress or the acquiring of a new one may end by influencing a political manifesto or the review of a new novel. Even the fiction of *PR* tends inevitably toward the *roman à clef,* its contributors feeding on each other like a mutual benefit association of cannibals. And the final absurdity (which I am not inventing but reporting) is the *PR* writer who produces a novel pillorying another *PR* writer (thinly disguised) for having in a previous book portrayed too bitterly still another *PR* contributor.

Moreover, the editors, to whom the literary cocktail party has been not only a source of images and ideas but also a university, end up without the protection of a traditionally acquired education —and are helplessly jostled by fad and fashion in a frantic drive to keep up with the latest thing. A critic of *PR* writing in 1949 could quite justly observe that up until that time, the magazine had never printed any full-scale article on a literary figure who flourished earlier than the latter half of the nineteenth century. This is, I think, an inevitable consequence of the scrappy, disordered, and largely contemporary culture out of which *PR* is improvised; it is a big price to pay for avoiding the curse of "academicism."

Yet certain qualifications must be made to these more general charges. On the one hand, *Partisan* has always included among its key contributors such generally cultured men as Edmund Wilson; and on the other hand, the American universities have undergone a revolutionary change since 1937 so that the sort of writer who once would have free-lanced out of some big city Bohemia ends up at Iowa State or North Carolina College for Women; and consequently, there has been an inevitable rapprochement between *PR* and what it likes to call "the academy." Not only have professors become its contributors, but its contributors have become professors. The last few years have seen an odd sort of united front between *PR* and *Kenyon Review*,[2] the best of the academic-New Critical quarterlies, whose editor, John Crowe Ransom, not only writes for *Partisan* but has enlisted two of its editors, Rahv himself and Delmore Schwartz, to serve with him in the "School of Letters," a Rockefeller sponsored set-up which grants an M.A. in literature.

Besides, there has always been a loose, hard-to-define but nonetheless real connection between *PR* and Columbia University, which, trapped in the midst of New York City and fed by the subways, manages to be in certain important respects the least academic of academies. Since the death of the old Village and the institutionalization of the American writer, Columbia has come more and more to serve as a kind of intellectual center for the city and consequently for the New York-oriented throughout the nation. *Partisan Review* represents, in the light of this, one more colonizing attempt on the part of a university which has also made its influence felt decisively in such ventures as Readers' Subscription (the highbrow book club of the United States), and Anchor Books, whose distribution of serious, large format books in paper binding has revolutionized American publishing. Among the editors of *Partisan Review,* there have always been professors from Columbia like F. W. Dupee and Lionel Trilling; and in the list of *PR's* regular contributors still others play a large part, including Meyer Shapiro, whose shadowy but enormous reputation among New York intellectuals as a polymath and whose formative influence on many of those intellectuals cannot be assessed in terms of his relatively limited publication. Lionel Trilling is, of course, the most interesting and influential of the group; much of his criticism has appeared in *PR*, as well as the two short stories which made him a reputation as a fictionist; yet he manages to preserve a remarkable aura of respectability not granted any of his colleagues. Those who condemn all else about the magazine, specifically exempt him from the gen-

---

[2] Just a year or two ago *Kenyon Review* was officially buried, after having dragged out a kind of posthumous half-life for a long time; and its last fiction editor is now filling the same post on *Playboy.*

eral blame; yet he is in most ways not untypical: Jewish, a New York who refuses to leave that city, an exploiter of the themes of anguish and alienation, a naturalist searching for tragedy. But in him the ordinarily annoying pose is mitigated by a soft-spoken style which is modesty itself—and combined with the stance of a nineteenth-century English gentleman-dissenter to produce a version of the *PR* writer as a belated Matthew Arnold.

Whereas Trilling embodies and modifies, in a secondary way, the *PR* spirit, another Columbia figure has presided over the very definition of that spirit: the figure of the eminent philosopher John Dewey, who himself wrote occasionally for *PR,* but whose influence has made itself felt even more effectively through his disciples, Ernest Nagel and Sidney Hook. As a matter of fact, it is the Naturalism of the Columbia school that has outlasted the collapse of its Marxism and that shores up the secularist tough-mindedness of *Partisan Review. PR* was, as one might expect, attracted for a while to the French version of Existentialism. Its atheism, its attempt to find a non-Marxian basis for the revolutionary attitude, its early defiance of Stalinism—all these seemed especially sympathetic to the *Partisan Review* mind. William Barrett, a former professor of philosophy, who finally filled the editorial vacuum left by the resignation of Dwight Macdonald, led the enthusiastic acclaim of Sartre, who threatened for a while to stand permanently in the niche left empty for *PR* by the fall of Karl Marx. But there was something too hasty and *willed* about this allegiance, which has in the last couple of years been struggling vainly to survive the personal encounter of *PR*'s editor with the representatives of Sartrean philosophy. No, Existentialism was for *PR* only an adventure, an affair; their true love has waited patiently for them at home: the spirit of John Dewey. In an unexpected way this alienated, Europe-oriented periodical comes to rest with the most "American" of philosophical systems: the same Deweyan pragmatism which, on another front, has nurtured the progressive educationist. It is a final irony.

What then shall I say at last of *Partisan* and the piece of myself which it represents? After scanning nearly twenty years' worth of it all at once, I feel bound to report that I have felt it to be frequently pontifical and boring, occasionally ritualistic in its repetition of a few sacred themes, generally depressing in the sense it gives of the narrowing down and drying up of political adventurousness and aesthetic experimentalism. I have found its symposia heavy-handed and its culture spotty. I have been appalled by its genuflecting to big names, amused by its occasional compensatory indulgences in the grayest sort of Germanic scholarship, exasperated by its over-adulation of Silone; and at one point I found myself muttering that if I came across the name of Kafka or Jean-Paul Sartre once more I would burn the whole damned pile of back issues. I have been provoked by the number of its contributors, who, having no apparent love for literature, deal with it like a subject they have drawn at random out of a hat; and I have turned away in disgust from certain young operators who by learning to say "milieu" and "situation" have imposed themselves on the editors.

Yet I cannot despise a magazine which has never been afraid of ideas or paralyzed by worries about "good taste"; which has served as a bridge between Europe and America, the free lance and the university; which above all has printed, often before anyone else, such writers of fiction as Saul Bellow, Mary McCarthy, Lionel Trilling, and Delmore Schwartz, such poets as Randall Jarrell, Robert Lowell, and John Berryman, such critics as Edmund Wilson and Lionel Trilling. It is a strange enough bird, the *Partisan Review,* a scraggier, shabbier, more raucous phoenix than we might have hoped for, and one not above crying out its own name at the top of its voice; but it is our only real contender for the title. Blasted into ashes by its enemies, mourned prematurely by its friends, despaired of by its own editors—it yet somehow survives; and that is, after all, the point.

*Missoula, Montana*
—1956

# Saul Bellow

WITH THE PUBLICATION of *Seize the Day,* Saul Bellow has become not merely a writer with whom it is possible to come to terms, but one with whom it is *necessary* to come to terms—perhaps of all our novelists the one we need most to understand if we are to understand what the novel is doing at the present moment. Bellow has endured the almost ritual indignities of the beginning fictionist: his first novel a little over-admired and read by scarcely anyone; his second novel once more critically acclaimed, though without quite the thrill of discovery, and still almost ignored by the larger public; his third novel, thick, popular, reprinted in the paperbacks and somewhat resented by the first discoverers, who hate seeing what was exclusively theirs pass into the public domain; and now a fourth book: a collection of stories, most of which have appeared earlier, a play, and a new novella.

Suddenly, the novelist whom we have not ceased calling a "young writer" (it is a habit hard to break and the final indignity) is established and forty, a part of our lives and something for the really young to define themselves against. But it has become clear that he will continue to write, that he is not merely the author of a novel or two, but a *novelist;* and this in itself is a triumph, a rarity in recent American literary history and especially among the writers with whom we associate Bellow. We think of the whole line of Jewish-American novelists, so like him in origin and aspiration, of Daniel Fuchs and Henry Roth and Nathanael West, those poets and annalists of the thirties who did not survive their age, succumbing to death or Hollywood or a sheer exhaustion of spirit and subject. Or we think of Bellow's own contemporaries, the *Partisan Review* group, urban Jews growing up under the threat of failure and terror, the Depression and Spain and the hopelessly foreseen coming of war. We remember, perhaps, Isaac Rosenfeld or H. J. Kaplan or Oscar Tarcov or Delmore Schwartz or even Lionel Trilling, who had also to be twice born, committed first to Stalinism and then to disenchantment, but who were capable of using imaginatively only the disenchantment. And remembering these, we recall beginnings not quite fulfilled, achievements which somehow betrayed initial promises. Certain short stories remain in our minds (flanked by all those essays, those explanations and rejoinders and demonstrations of wit): Kaplan's "The Mohammedans," Rosenfeld's "The Pyramids," Schwartz's "In Dreams Begin Responsibilities," Trilling's "The Other Margaret"; but where except in *The Dangling Man* and *The Victim* and *Augie March* do the themes and motifs of the group find full novelistic expression?

We must begin to see Bellow, then, as the inheritor of a long tradition of false starts and abject retreats and gray inconclusions. There is a sense in which he fulfills the often frustrated attempt to possess the American imagination and to enter the American cultural scene of a line of Jewish fictionists which goes back beyond the postwar generation through Ben Hecht and Ludwig Lewisohn to Abe Cahan. A hundred, a thousand one-shot novelists, ephemeral successes and baffled eccentrics stand behind him, defining a subject: the need of the Jew in America to make clear his relationship to that country in terms of belonging or protest—and a language: a speech enriched by the dialectic and joyful intellectual play of Jewish conversation.

Bellow's own story is, then, like the archetypal Jewish dream a success story since, like the standard characters in the tales of my grandfather (Socialist though he was!), the novelist, too, has "worked himself up in America." Bellow's success must not be understood, however, as exclusively his own; for he emerges at the moment when the Jews for the first time move into the center of American culture, and he must be seen in the larger context. The background is familiar enough: the gradual breaking up of the Anglo-Saxon domination of our imagination; the relentless urbanization which makes rural myths and images no longer central to our experience; the exhaustion as vital themes of the Midwest and of the movement from the provinces to New York or Chicago or Paris; the turning again from West to East, from our own heartland back to Europe; and the discovery in the Jews of a people essentially urban, essentially Europe-oriented, a ready-made image for what the American longs to or fears he is being forced to become.

On all levels in the years since World War II, the Jewish-American writer feels imposed on him the role of being The American, of registering his experience for his compatriots and for the world as The American Experience. Not only his flirtation with Communism and his disengagement, but his very sense of exclusion, his most intimate awareness of loneliness and flight are demanded of him as public symbols. The Southerner and the Jew, the homosexual out of the miasma of Mississippi and the ex-radical out of the iron landscape of Chicago and New York—these seem the exclusive alternatives, contrasting yet somehow twinned symbols of America at mid-century. *Partisan Review* becomes for Europe and *Life* magazine the mouthpiece of intellectual America, not despite but because of its tiny readership and its specially determined contributors; and in Saul Bellow a writer emerges capable of transforming its obsessions into myths.

He must not, however, be seen only in this context. His appearance as the first Jewish-American novelist to stand at the center of American literature is flanked by a host of matching successes on other levels of culture and subculture. What Saul Bellow is for highbrow literature, Salinger is for upper middlebrow, Irwin Shaw for middle middlebrow and Herman Wouk for lower middlebrow. Even on the lowbrow levels, where there has been no such truce with anti-Semitism as prosperity has brought to the middle classes, two young Jews in contriving Superman have invented for the comic books a new version of the Hero, the first purely urban incarnation of the most ancient of mythic figures. The acceptance of Bellow as the leading novelist of his generation must be paired off with the appearance of Marjorie Morningstar on the front cover of *Time*. On all levels, the Jew is in the process of being mythicized into the representative American.

There is a temptation in all this to a kind of assimilation with the most insipid values of bourgeois life in the United States. It is to

Bellow's credit that he has at once accepted the full challenge implicit in the identification of Jew with American, and yet has not succumbed to the temptation; that he has been willing to accept the burden of success without which he might have been cut off from the central subject of his time; and that he has accomplished this without essential compromise. In *Augie March,* which is the heart of his work (though technically not as successful as *The Victim* or *Seize the Day),* he has risked the final absurdity: the footloose Jewish boy, harried by urban Machiavellians, the picaresque *schlimazl* out of Fuchs or Nathanael West, becomes Huck Finn; or, if you will, Huck is transformed into the foot-loose Jewish boy. It is hard to know which way of saying it gives a fuller sense of the absurdity and importance of the transaction. The point is, I think, that the identification saves both halves of the combination from sentimental falsification: Huck Finn, who has threatened for a long time to dissolve into the snub-nosed little rascal, barefoot and overalled, and the Jewish *schlimazl,* who becomes only too easily the liberals' insufferable victim, say, Noah Ackerman in Irwin Shaw's *The Young Lions.*

The themes of Saul Bellow are not, after all, very different from those of the middlebrow Jewish novelists in step with whom he has "worked himself up"; but in treatment they become transformed. Like Wouk or Shaw, he, too, has written a War Novel: a book about the uncertainty of intellectual and Jew face to face with a commitment to regimentation and violence. But unlike Wouk and Shaw, Bellow has not merely taken the World War I novel of protest and adulterated it with popular front pieties. His intellectual is not shown up like Wouk's Keefer; his Jew does not prove himself as brave and brutal as his anti-Semitic buddies like Shaw's Ackerman or Wouk's Greenspan, whose presumable triumphs are in fact abject surrenders. The longing to relinquish the stereotyped protest of the twenties, no longer quite believed in, is present in Bellow's *Dangling Man,* but present as a *subject:* a temptation to be confronted, not a value to be celebrated.

*Dangling Man* is not an entirely successful book; it is a little mannered, a little incoherent, obviously a first novel. But it is fresh beyond all expectation, unlike any American war book before or since; for Bellow has realized that for his generation the war itself is an anticlimax (too foreknown from a score of older novels to be really lived), that their real experience is the waiting, the dangling, the indecision before the draft. His book therefore ends, as it should, with its protagonist about to leave for camp and writing in his journal: "Hurray for regular hours! And for the supervision of the spirit! Long live regimentation!" In the purest of ironies, the slogans of accommodation are neither accepted nor rejected, but suspended.

Similarly, in *The Victim* Bellow takes up what is, perhaps, the theme *par excellence* of the liberaloid novel of the forties: anti-Semitism. In proletarian novels, though many were written by Jews, this was a subject only peripherally treated; for the Jew in the Communist movement, Judaism was the enemy, Zionism and the Jewish religion the proper butt of satire and dissent. But Hitler had made a difference, releasing a flood of pious protests against discrimination; from Arthur Miller's *Focus* to John Hersey's *The Wall*, via *Gentleman's Agreement*, *The Professor's Umbrella*, etc., Jew and Gentile alike took up the subject over and over. In a time when the Worker had been replaced by the Little Man as a focus for undiscriminating sympathy, the Little Jew took his place beside the Little Negro, the Little Chinese, the Little Paraplegic as a favorite victim. Even what passed for War Novels were often merely anti-anti-Semitic fictions in disguise, the war itself being treated only as an occasion for testing a Noble Young Jew under the pressure of ignorant hostility.

In the typical middlebrow novel, it was seldom a real Jew who was exposed to persecution; rather some innocent gentile who by putting on glasses mysteriously came to look Jewish or some high-minded reporter only pretending to be a Jew. In part what is involved is the commercial necessity for finding a gimmick to redeem an otherwise overworked subject; but in part what is at stake is surely a confusion in the liberal, middlebrow mind about what a Jew is anyhow: a sneaking suspicion that Jew-baiting is real but Jews are imaginary, just as, to the same mind, witch-hunting is real but witches only fictions.

In Bellow's book about anti-Semitism, *The Victim,* once more the confusion becomes the subject. It is Asa Leventhal, not the author, who is uncertain of what it means to be a Jew because he does not know yet what it is to be a man; and neither he nor his author will be content with the simple equation: the victim equals the Jew, the Jew the victim. In *The Victim,* Jew and anti-Semite are each other's prey as they are each other's beloved. At the moment when the Jew in general, when the author himself as well as his protagonist, have moved into situations of security, however tenuous, inflicting injury in their scramble to win that security, Bellow alone among our novelists has had the imagination and the sheer nerve to portray the Jew, the Little Jew, as victimizer as well as victim. Allbee may be mad, a pathological anti-Semite and a bum, but his charge that Leventhal's success was achieved somehow at his expense is not utter nonsense. It is the necessary antidote to the selfpity of the Jew, one part of a total ambiguous picture. In the slow, gray, low-keyed exposition of *The Victim,* Leventhal's violence and his patience, his desire to exculpate himself and his sense of guilt, his haunting by the anti-Semite he haunts, become for us truths, part of our awareness of our place as Jews in the American scene.

As *The Victim* is Bellow's most specifically Jewish book, *Augie March* (in this, as in all other respects, a reaction from the former) is his most generally American. Its milieu is Jewish-American, its speech patterns somehow molded by Yiddish, but its theme is the native theme of *Huckleberry Finn:* The rejection of power and commitment and success, the pursuit of a primal innocence. It is a strangely non-Jewish book in being concerned not with a man's rise but with his evasion of rising; and yet even in that respect it reminds us of *David Levinsky,* of the criticism of David implicit in the text and entrusted to the Socialist characters. It is as if David had been granted a son, a grandson, to try again—to seek a more genuine Americanism of noncommitment. Certainly, Bellow's character is granted a symbolic series of sexual successes to balance off the sexual failures of Cahan's protagonist. But the Socialism of Cahan does not move his descendant; it has become in the meanwhile Soviet Communism, an alternative image of material success, and has failed; so that there is left to Augie only the denial of the values of capitalism without a corresponding allegiance, a desire to flee success from scene to scene, from girl to girl, from father to father—in favor of what? The most bitter of Happy Endings as well as the most negative, the truly American Happy Ending: no reunion with the family, no ultimately happy marriage, no return to the native place—only a limitless disponibility guarded like a treasure. It is, of course, the ending of *Huckleberry Finn,* an ending which must be played out as comedy to be tolerable at all; but unlike Twain, Bellow, though he has found the proper tone for his episodes, cannot recapture it for his close. *Augie,* which begins with such rightness, such conviction, does not know how to end; shriller and shriller, wilder and wilder, it finally whirls apart in a frenzy of fake euphoria and exclamatory prose.

*Seize the Day* is a pendant and resolution to *Augie March.* Also a study of success and failure, this time it treats them in contemporary terms rather than classic ones, reworking directly a standard middlebrow theme. Call it *The Death of a Salesman* and think of Arthur Miller. It is the price of failure in a world dedicated to success that Bellow is dealing with now; or more precisely, the self-consciousness of failure in a world where it is not only shameful but rare; or most exactly of all, the bitterness of success and failure become pawns in the deadly game between father and son. Bellow is not very successful when he attempts to deal with the sentimental and erotic relations that are the staples of the great European novels; his women tend to be nympholeptic projections, fantasies based on girls one never had; and his husbands and wives seem convincing only at the moment of parting. But he comes into his own when he turns to the emotional transactions of males inside the family: brother and brother, son and father—or father-hating son and Machiavellian surrogate father. It is the muted rage of such relationships that is the emotional stuff of his best work; and in *Seize the Day,* it is the dialogues of Tommy and his old man, Tommy and the sharper Tamkin, that move us, prepare us for Tommy's bleakest encounter: with himself and the prescience of his own death.

But how, we are left asking, has Bellow made tragedy of a theme that remains in the hands of Arthur Miller sentimentality and "good theater"? It is just this magical transformation of the most travestied of middlebrow themes which is Bellow's greatest triumph. That transformation is in part the work of style, a function of language. Bellow is in no sense an experimental writer; the scraps of *avant-garde* technique which survive in *The Dangling Man* are purged away in *The Victim;* yet he has managed to resist the impulse to lifeless lucidity which elsewhere has taken over in a literature reacting to the linguistic experiments of the twenties. There is always the sense of a living voice in his prose, for his books are all dramatic; and though this sometimes means a deliberate muting of rhetoric for the sake of characterization, it just as often provides occasions for a release of full virtuosity. Muted or released, his language is never dull or merely expedient, but always moves under tension, toward or away from a kind of rich, crazy poetry, a juxtaposition of high and low style, elegance and slang, unlike anything else in English except *Moby Dick,* though at the same time not unrelated in range and variety to spoken Yiddish.

Since Bellow's style is based on a certain conversational ideal at once intellectual and informal, dialogue is for him necessarily a distillation of his strongest effects. Sometimes one feels his characters' speeches as the main events of the books in which they occur; certainly they have the impact of words exchanged among Jews, that is to say, the impact of actions, not merely overheard but *felt,* like kisses or blows. Implicit in the direction of his style is a desire to encompass a world larger, richer, more disorderly and untrammeled than that of any other writer of his generation; it is this which impels him toward the picaresque, the sprawling, episodic manner of *Augie March.* But there is a counterimpulse in him toward the tight, rigidly organized, underplayed style of *The Victim:* and at his best, I think, as in *Seize the Day,* an ability to balance the two tendencies against each other: hysteria and catalepsy, the centrifugal and the centripetal in a sort of perilous rest.

But the triumphs of Bellow are not mere triumphs of style; sometimes indeed they must survive the collapse of that style into mannerism, mechanical self-parody. Beyond an ear, Bellow possesses a fortunate negative talent: a constitutional inability to dissolve his characters into their representative types, to compromise their individuality for the sake of a point. It is not merely that his protagonists refuse to blur into the generalized Little People, the Victims of sentimental liberalism; but that they are themselves portrayed as being conscious of their struggle against such debasement. That struggle is, indeed, the essence of their self-consciousness, their self-definition. Their invariable loneliness is felt by them and by us not only as a function of urban life and the atomization of culture, but as something *willed:* the condition and result of their search to know what they are.

More, perhaps, than any other recent novelist, Bellow is aware that the collapse of the proletarian novel, which marks the starting place of his own art, has meant more than the disappearance of a convention in the history of fiction. With the disappearance of the proletarian novel as a form there has taken place the gradual dissolution of the last widely shared definition of man: man as the product of society. If man seems at the moment extraordinarily lonely, it is not only because he finds it hard to communicate with his fellows, but because he has lost touch with any overarching definition of himself.

This Bellow realizes, as he realizes that it is precisely in such loneliness, once man learns not to endure but to *become* that loneliness, that man can rediscover his identity and his fellowship with others. We recognize the Bellow character because he is openly what we are in secret, because he is us without our customary defenses. Such a protagonist lives nowhere except in the City; he camps temporarily in boardinghouses or lonely hotels, sits by himself at the corner table of some seedy restaurant or climbs backbreaking stairways in search of another whose existence no one will admit. He is the man whose wife is off visiting her mother or has just left him; the man who returns to find his house in disorder or inhabited by a squalid derelict; the man who flees his room to follow the funeral of someone he never knew.

He is essential man, man stripped of success and belongingness, even of failure; he is man disowned by his father, unrecognized by his son, man without woman, man face to face with himself, which means for Bellow face to face not with a fact but a question: "What am I?" To which the only answer is: "He who asks!" But such a man is at once the Jew in perpetual exile and Huck Finn in whom are blended with perfect irony the twin American beliefs that the answer to all questions is always over the next horizon and that there is no answer now or ever.

—1957

# SIX

# The Jew in the American Novel

## Foreword

THIS ESSAY is intended to be not exhaustive but representative. The few writers who are discussed at any length are those who seem to me (and my personal taste plays a role of which any reader enamored of objectivity should be warned) both most rewarding as artists and most typical as actors in the drama of Jewish cultural life in America. I have not deliberately, however, omitted as untypical any Jewish American fictionist of first excellence. I am aware of how many rather good novelists I have slighted (along with some rather bad ones whom I am glad to pass over in silence); but I will not try to list them here, thus risking further injustice to those whose names fail to come to mind.

What I hope emerges from my study is a general notion of the scope and shape of the Jewish American tradition in fiction—useful to Gentile and Jew, reader and writer alike, not merely as history but as a source of pleasure and self-knowledge. The bonus of satisfaction for the critic engaged on such a job is the privilege of saying once more how much joy and terror and truth he has found, not only in certain widely respected authors but also in such relatively neglected ones as Abraham Cahan, Daniel Fuchs and Henry Roth.

## 1. Zion as Eros

The novel in which the Jewish writer attempts to make meaningful fiction of his awareness of himself as a Jew in America remains for a long time of merely parochial interest. In the first fifty years of such writing, only four novelists emerge whose work seems worth remembering; yet even of these none is mentioned in the most recent standard history of the American novel. The omission does not arise from ignorance or discrimination; it is a matter of simple justice. The fiction of Sidney Luska, Abraham Cahan, Ludwig Lewisohn, and Ben Hecht appears in retrospect not merely to fall short of final excellence, but to remain somehow irrelevant to the main lines of development of fiction in the United States.

For American Jews, their achievement has, of course, a symptomatic, an historical importance since they act as surrogates for the whole Jewish-American community in its quest for an identity, a symbolic significance on the American scene. Such early novelists begin to establish an image of the Jew capable not only of satisfying the Jews themselves, but also of representing them to their Gentile neighbors. The writing of the American-Jewish novel is essentially, then, an act of assimilation: a demonstration that there is an American Jew (whose Jewishness and Americanism enrich each other) and that he feels at home!

The striving of Jews to become in the United States not merely facts of the census but also of the imagination is only half of a double process that must be seen whole to be understood at all. As the Jewish writer goes out in search of himself, he encounters the Gentile writer on a complementary quest to come to terms with the Jew, the stranger in his land. Collaborators or rivals, whether willingly or not, Jewish fictionist and Gentile engage in a common enterprise. For a long time, indeed, it is hard for the Jewish novelist to compete with the Gentile in the creation of images of Jewishness. Ludwig Lewisohn's *The Island Within* may not be recorded in the standard history, but *The Sun Also Rises* is; for it is a subtler and truer book, and Robert Cohn, middleweight boxing champion from Princeton, is a realer Jew than any of Lewisohn's. That he is the product of anti-Semitic malice rather than love is from a literary point of view irrelevant. For better or worse, it is Hemingway's image of the Jew which survives the twenties: an overgrown boy scout and hangdog lover—an outsider still, even among outsiders, and in self-imposed exile.

It is hardly surprising that as late as 1930, Gentile writers are more effective at representing American Jews than are Jews themselves; for behind them there is a longer tradition of working with the American scene, and even a longer experience in projecting images of the American Jew than we are likely to remember. The first Jewish character in American fiction is the creation of the first professional novelist in the United States, Charles Brockden Brown. In 1799, he published *Arthur Mervyn,* the protagonist of which, after two volumes of being buffeted by a stubbornly perverse destiny, finds himself with a haven in sight. Like the typical Brown hero, he is about to redeem his fortune by marriage to a woman mature and well-to-do; and like all such heroes, he addresses her more as a mother than as a bride—though this time with an overtone of terror. "As I live, my good mamma," he says gazing into the eyes of Achsa Fielding, "those eyes of yours have told me a secret. I almost think they spoke to me. . . . I might have been deceived by a fancied voice . . . but let me die if I did not think they said you were —a *Jew.*" "At this sound," the author tells us, "her features were instantly veiled with the deepest sorrow and confusion."

Arthur Mervyn has, indeed, guessed right, and for a moment the promised Happy Ending trembles in the balance; but Jewess or not, Mrs. Fielding offers too great a hope of security to be rejected, and Mervyn marries her. So sane and bourgeois a climax infuriated Shelley, who, though an admirer of Brockden Brown, could never forgive him for allowing his hero to desert an Anglo-Saxon "peasant girl" for a rich Jewish widow. Despite so prompt an appearance in American literature, however, the Jewish character does not immediately prosper, remaining an exotic or occasional figure until our own century. When present at all in classic American fiction, the image of the Jew is likely to appear, as it had in *Arthur Mervyn,* in female form—superficially just another variant of the Dark Lady, who is otherwise Mediterranean or vaguely "Oriental" (though, indeed, the term seems sometimes a mere euphemism for Jewish) or even Negro. The Ruth of Melville's long narrative poem *Clarel* or the Miriam of Hawthorne's *The Marble Faun* are, like Brockden Brown's prototype, dark projections of sexual experience or allure, foils to the pale, Anglo-Saxon maiden. Though objects of great erotic potency, they do not ordinarily survive to their book's endings, being death-ridden as well as death-bearing, but are consigned to imprisonment or an early grave.

The American writer is attracted toward the archetypal pattern of Shylock and Jessica, the sinister Jew deprived of his lovely daughter; but he cannot treat it with the comic aplomb of Shakespeare or even the Romantic blitheness of Scott. In his work, a tragic blight falls over the Gentile myth of assimilation, the dream of rescuing the desirable elements in the Judaic tradition (maternal tenderness and exotic charm: the figure of Mary) from the unsympathetic (patriarchal rigor and harsh legalism: the figure of the High Priest and Father Abraham). Indeed, except as the threatening guardians of sloe-eyed ambiguous beauties, male Jewish characters seldom make more than peripheral appearances in earlier American fiction. There are neither American Riahs nor Fagins though one of the villains in George Lippard's *The Quaker City, or the Monks of Monk Hall* is called, unsubtly enough, Gabriel von Gelt. ("Vot you scratch your fingersh on te floor? Hey?" Gabriel is reported as saying in the earliest of literary "Jewish accents.")

This novel, an astonishing blend of home-grown socialism, violence, and genteel pornography, appeared in 1844 and won rapidly an immense number of readers, who probably did not single out the lone Jew from the crew of thugs who run a Gothic whorehouse for the off-hours amusement of Philadelphia's respectable citizens. Yet it is not unimportant that in the nightmare phantasmagoria of the populist imagination run wild—among the hunchback dwarfs, deaf and dumb Negroes, corrupt clergymen, and millionaires gloating over the bared breasts of drugged virgins—the figure of the hawk-nosed, conniving Jew takes his due place. Gabriel von Gelt is the ancestor of the fictional Jewish gangster, the Wolfsheim, say, of Fitzgerald's *The Great Gatsby*.

Long before the Jewish novelist existed in America, at any rate, the Jewish character had been invented, and had frozen into the anti-Jewish stereotype. Indeed, one of the problems of the practicing Jewish-American novelist arises from his need to create his protagonists not only out of the life he knows, but *against* the literature on which he, and his readers, have been nurtured. In order to become a novelist, the American Jew must learn a language (learn it not as his teachers teach it, but as he speaks it with his own stubborn tongue) more complex than a mere lexicon of American words. He must assimilate a traditional vocabulary of images and symbols, changing even as he approaches it—must use it, against the grain as it were, to create a compelling counter-image of the Jew, still somehow authentically American.

No wonder Jews are not only businessmen and workers, trade-union officials and lawyers, psychoanalysts and theater-owners but even actors, singers, musicians, composers of popular songs and makers of movies before they are writers. First the world of work and commerce, then of the professions, next that of popular culture, and only last of all, that of serious literature opens up to the American Jew. He can make the nation's songs like Irving Berlin or define its dream of the vamp like Theda Bara; he can even provide the *ersatz* of fiction like Fannie Hurst or Edna Ferber, act out for the laughs travesties of himself on the vaudeville stage with Smith and Dale or in the *Saturday Evening Post* with Montague Glass's Potash and Perlmutter. On such a level he speaks neither as a Jew becoming an American nor as an American who was a Jew; he communicates in the nonlanguage of anticulture, becomes his own stereotype. It is for this reason that the popular arts in the United States continue to this day to speak with a stage "Jewish accent." This is, however, only one more hindrance in the way of the serious Jewish writer, who must come to terms not only with Achsa Fielding and Gabriel von Gelt, but also with Sophie Tucker and Eddie Cantor.

Yet even before the triumph of the Jews in the world of mass culture, even before the perfection of the movies which sealed that victory, the Jewish-American novel had been created, the Jewish-American writer invented. The author of this achievement was, however, a *goy*—one of the most elusive and riddling figures in all American literature. He emerges in the 1880's out of those rather high-minded, assimilationist circles in German-Jewish New York, in which Ethical Culture seemed to promise a revivifying intellectual movement, at once secular and morally committed, Jewish and American. The name on the title pages of his "Jewish" books *(As It Was Written, Mrs. Peixada, The Yoke of the Thorah,* etc.) is Sidney Luska, a pseudonym obviously intended to suggest that the writer was himself Jewish; but he had apparently been born Henry Harland, a Protestant American, as discontented with his past, as uncertain of his identity as any alienated Jew. There is a certain appropriate irony in the fact that the first Jewish-American novelist was not a Jew at all, or that, more precisely, he was the creation of his own fiction, an imaginary Jew.

It is not easy to find the truth about so elusive an existence. Henry Harland was above all else an inveterate poseur, a liar who lied for his soul's sake; and the ordinary biographical sources are likely to contain whatever fabrication suited his view of himself at the moment he was asked for information. The ordinarily quite dependable *Dictionary of National Biography,* for instance, reports that Harland was born in St. Petersburg, that he was educated in Rome and studied at the University of Paris, "acquiring a knowledge of the life of the Latin Quarter"; the groundless romance of a provincial aesthete. Actually, he seems to have been born in Connecticut, to have moved early in life to New York, to have attended the Harvard Divinity School for one year—and then to have fallen under the influence of Felix Adler, who changed his whole life.

There still exists in my own mind a vestigial doubt (unsupported by any fact I have been able to discover) that Luska-Harland may, after all, have been a Jew pretending to be a Gentile pretending to be a Jew; it would be the best joke of all! More probably, however, he was a refugee from Protestantism who passed via Ethical Culture into the German-Jewish society of late nineteenth-century New York, and who tried even growing what he liked to think of as a "Jewish beard" to pass for a Jew. His books are Jewish not only in theme and point of view, but are meticulously documented with references to Jewish-American customs and to the rituals of Judaism. In one of his novels, the pursuit of verisimilitude (or exoticism!) is carried to the point of printing the name of God only as the two letter abbreviation used in Hebrew to avoid profaning the Holy Name.

Though he is now almost forgotten, Luska was in his own day a success, hailed not only by self-conscious spokesmen for Jewish culture, but greeted by William Dean Howells himself as one of the most promising younger realists. At the peak of his first fame, however, Luska committed a kind of suicide, becoming once again Henry Harland and fleeing America in one of the earliest acts of literary expatriation. He reappeared in England as the editor of *The Yellow Book,* chief journal of the *fin de siècle,* in which his own crepuscular prose (a new collection of his work was called *Grey Roses)* appeared beside the elegantly obscene decorations of Aubrey Beardsley. Harland proved to be a first-rate editor, printing, among other representatives of the advanced literature of his time, Henry James, who responded with a grateful tribute to Harland's own fiction; but his old schizoid doubts about who he was were not allayed by his new role.

During his entire term on the magazine, he wrote letters to himself signed "The Yellow Dwarf," attacking his own editorial policy. Only he knew the identity of this constant critic and relished, as he had before, his own secret duplicity. Still restless, however, he felt impelled to move once more, this time quite out of anglosaxondom, to France, where he was converted to Catholicism and ended by writing a best-seller called *The Cardinal's Snuffbox.* This piece of pseudo-aristocratic, pious fluff, whose title reveals its appeal for the provincials Harland had left behind, earned him $75,000 in its first year and enabled him to live out his life in elegant conversation amid the elegant bricabrac of pre-World War I Europe.

In his final reincarnation, he was asked once by a reporter about Sidney Luska and answered, "I never knew a Sidney Luska . . . ," and spoke of a nightmare, dimly remembered, from which he was now awakened. There is, indeed, something sufficiently nightmarish about the whole episode, though it is from this nightmare that the Jewish novel in the United States begins. But what precisely did Henry Harland dream himself in that bad dream from which it took him so long to wake? He dreamed himself the excluded artist, poor, passionate, gifted and antibourgeois, offering to a world that rebuffed him the dowry of sensibility and insight amassed by an ancient suffering race. For Harland, such mythic Jews seemed to promise the redemption of American culture, a revitalization of American life. But where were they to be found outside of his own books?

He thought, perhaps, that he had discovered the embodiment of his ideal in Felix Adler and in his own deepest self which Adler had revealed to him; but actually Harland's Jewish heroes seem to have been derived first of all from literature. The protagonist of his first book, *As It Was Written: A Jewish Musician's Story*, seems to have been suggested by the Daniel Deronda of George Eliot, who was one of Harland's favorite writers. But that oddly sexless portrait of the female artist as a Young Jew he naturalized to the American scene endowed him with a particularly American mission. "It is the Jewish element that will leaven the whole lump . . ." he writes in his novel. "The English element alone is, so to speak, one portion of pure water; the German element one portion of *eau sucrée;* now add the Jewish—it is a dose of rich strong wine. . . . The future Americans, thanks to the Jew in them, will have passions, enthusiasms. They will paint great pictures, compose great music, write great poems, be capable of great heroism. . . ." In such praise lurks an implicit threat. What if the Jew refuses the obligation, rejects even the assimilation which is the first step demanded of him in his role of secular savior?

Harland-Luska does not at first face up to this question; but there is present in his work from the start an undertone of hostility, lurking beneath the exaggerated philo-Semitism of the surface. Though his conscious mind writes the editorials that make the avowed point of his fictions, his ambivalent unconscious is writing the plots. Ernest Neuman, the artist of *A Jewish Musician's Story*, is only one-half artist; the other half is murderer! He is a Jekyll and Hyde character not merely because the exigencies of Harland's Gothic plot demand it, but because the deeper exigencies of Harland's divided mind demanded that plot to begin with. Neuman is a schizophrenic who has murdered his wife and remains unaware of it, who is consciously horrified and baffled until an experiment in automatic writing reveals to him, and to us, his guilt. This "new man," the new Jewish-American proposed as a symbol of assimilation, of the mating of the Jewish and American psyche, ends by killing his Gentile bride and proves capable only of destruction.

In *Mrs. Peixada,* Harland does permit the mating of Gentile and Jew, though he returns to the pattern of Brockden Brown and makes his symbol of Judaism a woman. It is always easier to breach the barriers against intermarriage in the popular mind by permitting the assimilation of the forbidden group through the female rather than through the male. So in the the earliest novel, marriages of aristocrats and lower-class women were applauded, while the Lady who ran off with her groom was held up as an object of contempt; and so now in the movies, Marlon Brando is allowed a Japanese wife, but his abandoned Caucasian girl is forbidden anything more than sympathetic conversation with a Japanese male. At any rate, Mrs. Peixada represents the return of the Jessica-figure in her American form; though this time she is not only stained by sexual experience (she is a widow, of course, rather than anything less genteel), she is the murderer of her first husband. Legally, to be sure, she is innocent, having acted in self-defense against that husband, who is the monstrous projection of all the evil ever attributed by the Gentile mind to the Jew: a pawnbroker, "gaunt as a skeleton . . . a hawk's beak for a nose, a hawk's beak inverted for a chin—lips, two thin, blue, crooked lines across his face, with yellow fangs behind them. . . ."

But there is worse to come. Though Luska was able to maintain in his mind not only Shylock and Jessica, but Daniel Deronda as well—nightmare and idealization in a dreamlike truce—none of those mythic figures could survive the intrusion of real Jews. Real Jews do, however, take over in *The Yoke of the Thorah,* which is perhaps the first genuine genre study of American-Jewish life in the New World. They are no longer mere projections of Anglo-Saxon self-hatred or guilt, these German-Jewish merchants of the eighties, eating, matchmaking, talking over the market. They are coarse, vulgar, platitudinous, loud, sentimental, gregarious, not saviors at all but only human beings; and the character who represents Harland moving among them shrivels and withdraws in their presence. But he cannot help listening to them, and catches for the first time (ironically, *loses* by catching) what is to be the real material of the Jewish writer.

> "Oh my daughter," Mrs. Morgenthau returned. "She works like a horse. . . . And such a *good* girl. Only nineteen years old and earns more than a hundred dollars a month. . . . She's grand. She's an angel."
> "Tillie's all wool from head to foot," put in Mr. Koch, "and a yard wide."

"Such a brilliant musician," said Elias.
"Musician," echoed her mother. "Well, I should say so. You
ought to hear her play when she really knuckles down to it.
Why you—you'd jump, you'd get so excited. The other night
she was only drumming—for fun. I tell you what you do. You
come around and call on us some evening."

Where now is the "rich strong wine"? Even music, which represented for Harland the essence of Jewish genius, becomes in such
scenes bait in the matrimonial trap and matrimony itself merely an
adjunct of business. Such an insight into the discrepancy between
the traditional mission of the Jew and his actual accommodation to
the American scene might have provided Harland the cue for genuine comedy or tragedy; it became instead merely the occasion for
personal disillusion. It is hard to tell whether he is more distressed
because the Jews will not assimilate to his heroic, artistic ideal or
because they have already assimilated to the actual values of the
world around them. Their very vitality parodies the American
mores they accept; and face to face with that vitality as it exists not
in the imaginary artist but in the real businessman, Harland experiences only a desire to go away.

The divorce to which this desire will eventually lead him is already signalled in *The Yoke of the Thorah*. The fable is a simple
one: a young Jew, talented but weak and superstitious, is bullied
out of marrying a sensitive and beautiful Gentile girl by the chica-
nery of his uncle who is a rabbi. He marries instead the gross
daughter of a family of German-Jewish merchants; and having rejected a union with the Gentile world which would have redeemed
him, dies lonely and disenchanted. His final gesture is to commit
suicide in the middle of Central Park; but that gesture only ac-
knowledges the fact that inwardly he had died long since. The publication of such a book by their former champion and literary hope
apparently stirred the Jews of New York to bitterness. They had
taken Harland in, and he had turned on them and attacked them
—quite as their own writers would do in the years to come. That
his attack was rooted in a burgeoning anti-Semitism, Harland himself did not at first realize; but he arose to defend himself in public
forums at Jewish synagogues and temples and even wrote a couple
of other "Jewish" books, quite innocent of innuendo or offense.

He was, however, really through; he had exhausted Jewishness as a subject and as a mask and was preparing for his next removal. In England and in France, he exiles the Jews from the center of his fiction to its periphery, and his last word on the subject is a casual sneer in the book that made his fortune. The words are put into the mouth of a lovely though improbable lady with an equally improbable Italian title, his gentle heroine: "The estate fell into the hands of the Jews, as everything more or less does sooner or later; and if you can believe me—they were going to turn the castle into . . . one of those monstrous, modern hotels, for other Jews to come to." The sentence foreshadows one theme of a somewhat later and certainly much greater expatriate American, with similar yearnings for orthodoxy and "the tradition."

> And the Jew squats on the window sill, the owner,
> Spawned in some estaminet of Antwerp.

> . . . On the rialto once
> The rats are underneath the piles. The Jew is underneath the lot.

The history of Henry Harland is, finally, even more ridiculous than pathetic, a success story in the end: From Rags to Riches, from Ethical Culture on the East Side to Roman Catholicism on the Riviera. Yet before his last metamorphosis, Harland had defined what was to be the obsessive theme of the American-Jewish novel through the twenties: the theme of intermarriage, with its ambiguous blending of the hope of assimilation and the threat of miscegenation. The tradition that begins with Luska-Harland descends in one line to *The Island Within* and in another to the Cohens and the Kellys and *Abie's Irish Rose*.

It is self-evident that the Jewish-American novel in its beginnings must be a problem novel, and its essential problems must be those of identity and assimilation. The very concept of such a novel involves an attempt to blend two traditions, to contribute to the eventual grafting of whatever still lives in Judaism onto an ever-developing Americanism. One cannot, however, propose to lose himself without raising the question of what the self is which may be surrendered or kept; and the Jewish-American writer who is, of course, almost necessarily non-orthodox finds a riddle in the place where he looks for an answer. *Is* there a Jewish identity which survives the abandonment of ghetto life and ghetto beliefs, which for so long defined the Jew? Or has the Jew left in Europe, along with the pain and squalor he fled, the possibility of any definition?

What is unexpected is that these problems be posed in terms of sexual symbols, that the Jewish-American novel before 1930 be erotic fiction. The approach to and retreat from the Gentile community, the proffering of himself and the shying away out of fear of acceptance or rejection, becomes in the imagination of the Jewish writer a kind of wooing, an act of timid and virginal love. It becomes associated in his thinking with his attitude toward the new sexual freedom offered him by the breakdown of ghetto life and with the erotic subject matter that takes a central place in art once religion has been replaced as the essential subject. The Jewish-American novelist begins his attempts at a moment when the triumphs of European naturalism make it possible for fiction in the United States to break through the taboos of gentility, when the antibourgeois writer, in particular, delights in portraying himself as the exponent of the instinctual life, as the lover.

There is a real pathos in the efforts of the Jewish intellectual to see himself as Don Juan, an essential vanity in his striving to embody current theories of sexual freedom. There is nothing, either in his own deepest traditions or in the stereotypes imposed on him by Western fiction, to justify such a mythicization of himself: Shylock as Don Juan, Rashi as Don Juan, Daniel Deronda as Don Juan— they are all equally improbable. Yet it is in the role of passionate lover that the American-Jewish novelist sees himself at the moment of his entry into American literature; and the community with which he seeks to unite himself he sees as the *shikse*. Don Juan and the *shikse*—it is this legend, this improbable recasting of Samson and Delilah, which underlies American-Jewish fiction up to the end of the twenties.

The erotic theme had already been proposed by Henry Harland, and it is taken up again by Abraham Cahan in *The Rise of David Levinsky,* certainly the most distinguished novel written by an American Jew before the 1930's. It is easy to forget the sense in which Cahan's book is a love story, or even more precisely a story of the failure of love; for superficially it is another up-from-the-ghetto book, its concerns chiefly social. Indeed, it appeared in 1917, the year of the Russian Revolution, when for a little while it seemed possible that the dream of Socialism might become a fact and the Jew really assimilate to the emancipated Human Race instead of to the nation in which he happened to find himself. No wonder that even the more perspicuous critics were content to talk about *David Levinsky* as a social document: a commentary on the rise of the garment industry and its impact on American life; a study of the crisis in American-Jewish society when the first wave of German immigrants were being overwhelmed by Jews from Galicia and the Russian Pale; a case history of the expense of spirit involved in changing languages and cultures; a portrayal of New World secularism which made of City College a Third Temple and of Zionism and Marxism enlightened religions for those hungry for an orthodoxy without God.

Certainly, *David Levinsky* is all these things, as it is also the account of a Jew who dissipated the promise of his life in the pursuit of wealth; it is a rich and complex book, a retrospective and loving essay on the failures of his people by a man nearly sixty when he wrote it. An anti-Semitic book, the conservative Jewish reviewers blindly called it: "Had the book been published anonymously, we might have taken it for cruel caricature of a hated race by some anti-Semite. . . ." It is to remain the typical response of the "guardians of the Jewish Community" to any work which treats with art and candor the facts of Jewish life in the United States. Both the traditions of the European naturalist novel, on which Cahan really drew, and those of the American novel, to which he aspired, prescribe for the author a "negative" attitude toward the philistine society around him; and as a Jew he found especially abhorrent the drift of his own people, the chosen remnant, toward delusive bourgeois values. The disenchantment that became anti-Semitism in the imaginary Jew, Harland, becomes in Cahan a prophetic rage which is really love, an apparent treason which is the profoundest loyalty. In this respect, he remains the model for all serious Jewish-American novelists.

His ultimate subject is, aptly enough, loneliness: the loneliness of the emancipated Jew, who has lost the shared alienation of the ghetto to become a self-declared citizen of a world which rejects even as it rewards him. The unique loneliness of the "successful" immigrant Jew, however, suggests to Cahan the common human loneliness of those who have failed at love; and in the end it is hard to tell with which loneliness his book is primarily concerned. It is with the melancholy of David Levinsky that the novel begins; he came to America, he tells us, with four cents in his pocket and has now $2,000,000, but his life is "devoid of significance." To explain his joylessness David has certain theories. It is all due, he insists, to "a streak of sadness in the blood of my race"; to be a Jew is to be sad! But he asserts, too, that it is his wealth and the devices by which he has pursued it that have cut him off from the sources of happiness: "There are cases when success is a tragedy."

Yet Cahan makes the point with some care that David is only *incidentally* a capitalist, that he is not fundamentally different from other immigrant Jews of his generation who have become trade-unionists and socialists; what is peculiar in his development has occurred almost by accident. "Had I chanced to hear a socialist speech," he says at one point, "I might have become an ardent follower of Karl Marx." Instead he read Spencer and Darwin! What, then, is *essentially* wrong with David? Cahan does not answer unequivocally, but at times at least he suggests that he is somehow sexually or affectively incapacitated; that no boy brought up in the Talmudic tradition "that to look at the finger of a woman in desire is equivalent to seeing her whole body naked" can enter into the full heritage of modernity, which includes an ideal of sexual freedom as well as the hope of a classless society. Like Peretz, he considers the vestiges of ghetto Puritanism one of the hindrances that stand between the Jew and his full humanity.

Each failure of David Levinsky at winning a woman (and the book is in effect a tally of such failures) is given a symbolic social meaning. He does not get Matilda, his first love whom he desires while still in Europe, because he is not yet sufficiently emancipated from his Talmudic training; he cannot keep Dora, the wife of a friend with whom he carries on an inconclusive affair, because he has stepped outside of the Jewish family and cannot smuggle his way back in; he cannot win Anna Tevkin, young socialist and daughter of an eminent Hebrew poet, because he has learned to sing *The Star-Spangled Banner* with tears in his eyes, because he is a "Good American."

But for all his "Americanism," he remains still in some baffling sense a Jew and is, therefore, forbidden the possibility of marrying a Gentile. His last real chance at love seems, indeed, to be offered him by a Gentile woman "of high character," who all but proposes to him; yet at the last moment he feels between them "a chasm of race." There is always something! Though he cannot abide loneliness and prowls the streets ("I dream of marrying some day. I dread to think of dying a lonely man. Sometimes I have a spell of morbid amativeness and seem to be falling in love with woman after woman. . . ."), it is no use; some deep impotence dogs him. They are not symbols only, these failed love affairs of David Levinsky; they are real failures of the flesh and spirit, failures of a Jew in love with love and money.

In Ludwig Lewisohn and Ben Hecht, the two most admired Jewish novelists of the twenties, the erotic theme is restated in exaggerated, almost hysterical tones. There is something about their work not merely brash and provocative (this they intended), but vulgar and crude; and it becomes hard to remember that they seemed once the most promising of young novelists, before one was translated into a prophet of the new Zion and the other into a maker of successful movies. "More gross talent than net accomplishment," a disgruntled critic finally said of Hecht, and the phrase will do for Lewisohn, too. They chose to begin with such different masks, the professor and the reporter, that it is difficult to see how much they had in common, how both contrived sexual melodramas to project the plight of the Jew in the Jazz Age. A pair of titles, however, Lewisohn's *Don Juan* (1923) and Hecht's *A Jew in Love* (1931), frame the period and define its chief concern.

Unlike Cahan, who preceded them, and the Proletarian novelists, who were to follow them, Lewisohn and Hecht are hostile to Marxism; and the Marxists (most of them Jewish, of course) who appear in their books are portrayed as self-deceivers, attempting to conceal their personal anguish behind an artificial fog of socialist cant. The secular Jewish prophet honored by Hecht and Lewisohn is not Marx but Freud; and the secular religion to which they respond is what they call Freudianism, though, like many intellectuals in their time, they were not quite sure where Freud ends and D. H. Lawrence begins. Psychoanalysis seemed to them primarily one more device for mocking the middle class, one more source for arguments in defense of sexual emancipation. Beyond this, their interest remained superficial. Lewisohn's novel, *The Island Within,* contains what is probably the most unconvincing psychoanalyst in literature and manages to tuck away an utterly improbable description of an analysis, somewhere between its "epical" beginning and the little sermon on mixed marriages with which it ends.

Their common devotion to Eros and to Freud as his prophet, Lewisohn and Hecht develop in quite different ways. Lewisohn sets his in a context of belated German Romanticism, from which he derives a mystique of passion somehow synthesized with internationalism, pacifism, and a Crocean commitment to art. Hecht, on the other hand, adjusts his to a provincial version of *symbolisme,* which means for him a dedication to disorder and cynicism in art and life. Celebrated in his day as a new American Huysmans, he has become for us undistinguishable from the pressroom heroes of his *Front Page,* flip hard-guys to whom whiskey is the Muse and Chicago the Earthly Paradise. Lewisohn typically identifies himself with his protagonists, harried by women and bourgeois taboos, but pledged to fight for freedom with the sole weapon of art; Hecht presumably separates himself from the scoundrels who are the heroes of his books, though he covertly sympathizes with their amoral contempt for decency and tenderness.

The leading characters of both, though presumably intellectuals, are notable not for their ideas but for their efforts, successful or baffled, to find in themselves the demonic, impulsive sources of life. In this they are the authentic products of their age, though uneasy projections of their Jewish authors. What has a Jew to do finally with the primitivism and phallic mysticism which possessed the era? Only when he revolts not merely against philistinism but against his own most authentic traditions can he espouse such a cause. It is illuminating to remember that writers like D. H. Lawrence and Sherwood Anderson, the real high priests of the erotic religion, portrayed Jews in their fiction as natural enemies of the primitive ideal, antitypes of the passionate hero: cold, cerebral, incapable of the dark surrender of the self.

It is true enough that when Lewisohn uses *Don Juan* as a book title, he does so ironically and that he somehow feels obliged to pretend (however unconvincingly) that his protagonist is not a Jew; but he is all the while *living* the role in his own much-publicized life. In the news and gossip columns as well as in the pages of his novels, Lewisohn concentrated on justifying his love life—with time off for belaboring the poor women who failed him and the divorce laws which hampered his style. The only subject to which Lewisohn responds in his fiction with real fervor, the single spring of his creative work, is his own sex life desperately projected as typical.

*The Island Within*, his attempt at a major novel, opens with a manifesto declaring his epic ambitions and defending them against the proponents of the novel of sensibility, just then replacing the older, objective form. His declared intent is esthetically reactionary enough, but he cannot abide even by that; before the book is half over, he has abandoned the broad-canvas portrayal of three generations of Jewish life in Poland and Germany for a more intimate evocation of modern marital difficulties, for his usual blend of self-pity and editorial. No sooner has he reached America, than he heads for the bedroom, the old battle ground on which the sensitive Jew, a psychoanalyst this time, still struggles with the *shikse* (in the teeth of public opinion and benighted law) for the possession of his own soul.

Hecht, on the other hand, goes immediately to his theme—in this case not a direct exculpation of himself but the satirizing of another, a successful Jew. When the book first appeared, it was read as a *roman à clef;* and those in the know were more than willing to let the ignorant in on the secret of who Jo Bosshere, the publisher-protagonist, *really* was. At this point, when we no longer care about such revelations, it becomes clear that the book is more than a wicked jibe at an identifiable public figure; it is a work of inspired self-hatred: a portrait of the Jewish author as his own worst (Jewish) enemy. At any rate, the hero of Hecht's novel, whose original name was Abe Nussbaum, juggles a wife, a mistress, a whore whom he really loves, the wife of a good friend, in a frenzy of erotic machiavellianism, behind which there is no real desire. He braces himself for each sexual encounter with an energy so neurotically tense that it is dissipated by a knock at the door, a chance remark, the slightest shift in affective tone. What drives him is not passion but the need to force from the world unwilling avowals of love for his absurdly horrifying Jewish face. Bosshere-Nussbaum is portrayed by Hecht as the caricature of the anti-Semite come to life: not merely the Jew, but the nightmare of the Jew (as hawkbeaked and vulpine as Mr. Peixada) as Don Juan.

Of all the women he has possessed without desire, the one to whom Bosshere most desperately clings is, of course, the single *shikse* among them: the pure blonde tantalizing image of a world which all of his assaults and betrayals cannot make his own. Toward her he is impelled by something deeper than sadism and self-hatred, by what Hecht calls brutally "the niggerish delight of the Jew in the blonde." If he is defeated in the end, however, it is not because of the resistance of his *shikse* so much as because of his own inability to accept himself as the seducer and scoundrel. "To himself he was only this greedy, monogamous Jew full of biblical virtues. . . ." To himself he was only the child of his people, not a great lover but a martyr to women, who cries out finally in the unexpected scriptural allusion, "My God, my God, why hast Thou forsaken me," and does not know whether he is invoking Eros or the God of Abraham, Isaac, and Jacob.

This is implicitly at least a self-criticism of the Jewish intellectual that cuts much deeper than personal satire, but it is marred by an imprecision of language and an uncertainty of tone that ends in incoherence. Lewisohn is explicit, however pat and superficial, and in *The Island Within* (actually published three years before *A Jew in Love*) he gives to the erotic-assimilationist novel its final form. Arthur Levy, the protagonist of Lewisohn's novel, never abandons his vocation as a lover; he merely transfers his desire from the representative of an alien world to the symbol of his own people, thus reinforcing a battered Romantic faith in sexual passion with an equally Romantic commitment to Zionism. As he has earlier com-

bined the advocacy of sexual freedom with a vaguely internation-
alist humanism, so now he combines it with a revived Judaism,
adapted to the modern scientific mind.

He pretends, indeed, to find in the Jewish tradition sanctions
for his view of love. Is not Jewish divorce, he asks rhetorically, easier than Christian? Were not the Jews always skeptical about the
notion of marriage as a sacrament? Have Jewish women historically
not represented a *tertium quid:* neither servile like the slave-
women of the Anglo-Saxon world before modern times, nor hopelessly lost like the "emancipated" Gentile women of the current
era? Have they not remained at the heart of the tradition the Jewish
intellectual has temporarily abandoned, waiting to bestow on him
when he returns the warm fulfillment he has vainly sought in
strangers? We have come full circle from Cahan's view of ghetto
Judaism as a castrating force.

But Lewisohn is prepared to go even further than this, from a
defense of Zion as the true Eros, to an attack on the Gentile woman
as the false Aphrodite. It has all been the fault of the *shikse* and of
the Jewish intellectual only so far as he has become her victim. It is
no longer the Gentile world which rejects the Jew in Lewisohn's fiction (that world is, indeed, eager to draw him in and suck him
dry), but the Jew who rejects it—even as Arthur Levy rejects the
hope of assimilation and sets out at his story's end back to Europe,
back to his people's past, to investigate the plight of his fellow Jews
in Rumania.

We have reached at last the reverse of Harland-Luska's theory
in *The Yoke of the Thorah;* Jessica has yielded to Delilah. Not by
rejecting the Gentile girl for the Jewish one but by preferring her,
the sensitive Jew commits spiritual suicide. The *shikse* represents
no longer the promise of fulfillment, of a blending of cultures, but
only the threat of death, of the loss of identity. The reversal, however, like the original thesis, remains a little too pat, more suited for
sermonizing than poetry; at any rate, in neither case did the authors
make of their themes moving and memorable fictions. Yet with
Lewisohn's establishment of the antistereotype in its classic form
something has been accomplished, that is to say, the last possibility
of the erotic-assimilationist novel has been exhausted. His novel

rests like a melancholy capstone on the whole period which reaches from the eighties to the dying twenties, a monument to an unsuccessful quest by whose example later writers have profited. After *The Island Within,* the Jewish-American novelist knew at least one direction in which he could not go.

## 2. Zion as Armageddon

Though there were American Jewish novelists of real distinction in the first three decades of the twentieth century, it is not until the thirties that such writers play a critical role in the total development of American literature. From that point on, they have felt themselves and have been felt by the general public as more than pioneers and interlopers, more than exotics and eccentrics. Indeed, the patterns of Jewish speech, the experiences of Jewish childhood and adolescence, the smells and tastes of the Jewish kitchen, the sounds of the Jewish synagogue have become, since 1930, staples of the American novel.

It is, of course, Jewish urban life in particular which has provided a standard décor for the novel: the life of New York, and especially of the ghettos of the East Side, Williamsburg, etc. In a certain sense, indeed, the movement of Jewish material from the periphery to the center is merely one phase of a much larger shift within the world of the American novel: that urbanization of our fiction which accompanies the urbanization of our general culture.

Our literary twenties were dominated by provincial writers like Theodore Dreiser, Sherwood Anderson, and Sinclair Lewis, even Faulkner and Hemingway, who close that period and provide a bridge into the age that succeeds it. Whatever their talent, they remained essentially country boys who had come to the big city, who had wandered under their own power into New Orleans or New York, who had been transported by the A.E.F. to Paris. Whether they stayed or returned home again did not finally matter; even when they wrote about the city, they wrote about it as seen through the eyes of one who had come late into it and had remained a stranger.

Despite an occasional sport like Myron Brinig, who writes about Montana, or MacKinlay Kantor, whose subject matter includes hound dogs, Jewish writers do not fit into such a provincial pattern, which does not, in any case, reflect the typical, the *mythical* Jewish experience in America. Their major entry into the American novel had to await its urbanization, though that entry is not, to be sure, only a function of such urbanization. It is an extension, too, of the break-up of the long-term Anglo-Saxon domination of our literature which began in the generation just before the First World War. The signal that this double process had started was the emergence of Dreiser as the first novelist of immigrant stock to take a major position in American fiction. There is something ironic in the fact that the breach through which succeeding Jewish writers poured was opened by one not innocent of anti-Semitism; but once the way was opened for immigrants in general, it was possible for Jews to follow.

At any rate, by the end of the thirties (a recent historian of Jewish literature points out) there were some sixty American Jewish writers of fiction who could be called without shameless exaggeration "prominent." A close examination of that historian's list proves rather disheartening; for of the sixty-odd names he mentions, fewer than ten seem to me worthy of remembering; and three of these (Abe Cahan, Ludwig Lewisohn and Ben Hecht) belong, in theme and significance, to the twenties in which their major work was accomplished. The writers who remain of the original sixty are Edward Dahlberg, Leonard Ehrlich, Daniel Fuchs, Meyer Levin (recently come to life by reaching back into the Jewish Society of the twenties for an image of violence and disgust stark enough to move us) and Henry Roth. Even if one were to add to these certain others not included in the original group, say, Waldo Frank, Maurice Samuel, Isidor Schneider and Michael Gold, who are at least symptomatically important, it would make a constellation by no means inspiring; for no one of them is a figure of first importance even in the period itself.

Fuchs and Roth are writers of considerable talent, even of major talent, perhaps; but for various reasons, their achievement is limited. Roth is the author of a single novel, *Call It Sleep;* and

Fuchs, though he wrote three before his retreat to Hollywood and popular fiction for ladies' magazines (and despite a recent comeback in short fiction) wrote only one book of considerable scope: *Homage to Blenholt*. There remains, of course, Nathan Wallenstein Weinstein, who preferred to call himself Nathanael West—and whose long neglect by official writers on the period is now being overbalanced by his enthusiastic rediscoverers. For a long time, scarcely anyone but Henry Popkin* considered him worth touting; but now the republication of his whole works and his translation into a Broadway play have given West back a full-scale existence. There is no use being carried away, however, no use in concealing from ourselves the fact that what has been restored to us is only another tragically incomplete figure, whose slow approach to maturity ends in death. And there remains further the troublesome question: is West in any effective sense a Jew?

Though the thirties mark the mass entry of the Jewish writer into American fiction, they do not last long enough to see any major triumphs. There is no Jewish writer among the recognized reigning figures of the period: no Dos Passos, no Farrell, no Steinbeck; there is no Jewish writer who played a comparable role to the continuing major novelists of the twenties: no Fitzgerald, no Hemingway, no Faulkner. There is no Jewish author (with the possible exception of West) who can rank even with middle-generation fictionists like Robert Penn Warren, who seemed at the end of the thirties promising young men.

Even in the creation of images of the Jew, a job the Jewish writer in the United States has long been struggling to take out of the hands of the Gentiles, there is no Jewish writer who can compare in effectiveness to Thomas Wolfe. Just as Sherwood Anderson and Hemingway and Fitzgerald succeeded in making their hostile images of Jews imaginative currencies in the twenties, Wolfe succeeded in imposing on his period a series of portraits derived from his experiences at New York University: enameled Jewesses with melon breasts; crude young male students pushing him off the side-

---

* I have in conversation, as well as through reading his articles, so long exchanged ideas with Henry Popkin on the American Jewish novelist that I am indebted to him everywhere.

walk; hawkbeaked Jewish elders, presumably manipulating the world of wealth and power from behind the scenes.

What, then, was the modest contribution of the Jewish writer to the fiction of the thirties, and how did this prepare for later successes going beyond anything he himself achieved? Predictably enough, a large number of American Jewish writers of the period were engaged in the production of the best-advertised (though, alas, quite infertile) art-product of the period: the Proletarian Novel. Perhaps the best way to define that subform of the novel is to remind ourselves that it is the major result of applying to the creation of literature the theory that "art is a weapon"; and that therefore it was in intent anti-art, or at least, opposed to everything which "petty-bourgeois formalism" considered art to be. Perhaps because of the contradictions inherent in such a view, it had one of the shortest lives ever lived by a literary genre. One speaks of the Proletarian Novel as a form of the thirties, but in fact it was finished by 1935 or 1936, becoming at that point merely formula writing, completely at the mercy of political shifts inside the Communist movement.

In any case, the Proletarian Novel is not, as its name suggests, merely a book about proletarians; it is alternatively about poor farmers, members of the lower middle class; and most often, in *fact* if not in theory, about intellectuals, specifically about the intellectual's attempt to identify himself with the oppressed and with the Movement which claimed to represent them. The Proletarian Novel was, then, ideological fiction dedicated to glorifying the Soviet Union and the Communist Party and to proving that the Party was the consciousness of the working class in America as well as in the rest of the world. Yet the most characteristic aspect of such novels escapes ideological definition completely, for it is a product of the age as it worked on writers beneath the level of consciousness of class or anything else. This is the *tone* of the Proletarian Novel: a note of sustained and self-satisfied hysteria bred on the one hand of Depression-years despair and on the other of the sense of being selected as brands to be snatched from the fire.

The Stalinist movement in the United States has always attracted chiefly marginal and urban groups; and if one thinks of the marginal and urban in the United States, he thinks, of course, largely of Jews. Especially in its cultural activities, in the John Reed Clubs, in the *New Masses* (and those cultural activities were of major importance in the thirties when the Communists captured few factories but many publishing houses), Jews participated in a proportion completely out of accord with their role in the total population. Indeed, the Movement was by way of being the typical strategy of the ambitious young Jew in a time of Depression for entering fully into American life. Jews who would have been dismayed by older kinds of bourgeois assimilation embraced this new method which allowed them at once to identify themselves with America and protest against certain aspects of its life.

Similarly, the intellectual, whether Jewish or not, found in the Movement an escape from the sense of alienation from American society which the twenties had brought to acute consciousness. One must realize the attractiveness of the orthodox Communist "culture" sponsored by the *New Masses* for the young man who was both an intellectual and a Jew. It is scarcely surprising that so many of them turned to the Proletarian Novel as their chosen form; even those who for aesthetic reasons found the genre unpalatable apologized for their apostasy, or tried to make up for it: like Nathanael West feeding his more orthodox contemporaries at the family hotel and boasting of having walked the picket line with James T. Farrell and Leane Zugsmith.

Still, no matter how alluring the Proletarian Novel might have been to the unproletarian Jewish writer, he could not, of course, write such a novel *as a Jew*. It was during the thirties, one remembers, that the Stalinists were officially condemning Jewish chauvinism in Palestine, and attacking Ludwig Lewisohn (who had entered his Zionist phase) as the blackest of reactionaries; and in those days, "race consciousness" was thought to be inimical to class consciousness. It is not surprising, after all, that a recent survey of the literature of the period, in a book called *The Radical Novel in America,* can point out only *one* Proletarian Novel which dealt specifically with anti-Semitism. This is a problem which must wait for the Popular Front novel and the Middlebrow Liberal Novel, which is to say, for the forties.

All of which does not mean, of course, that a Jewish writer could not *begin* with his Jewishness; and, as a matter of fact, Michael Gold's *Jews Without Money,* which appeared in 1930, was the prototype of the Proletarian Novel, going through eleven printings in its first year and setting a pattern for succeeding writers. Not quite a novel, really, or quite an autobiography, it seems more than anything a collection of vignettes of Jewish life making a moral point—a conversion tract illustrating the passage of a thinking man from Judaism to Communism. The pattern is simple enough (it is picked up and reinforced later in Isidor Schneider's *From the Kingdom of Necessity):* to make of "Jewish nationalism" and the Jewish religion the chief symbols of reaction; the pious man, the pillar of the synagogue, appears as a landlord and an owner of whorehouses; the rabbi becomes an old lecher; and the rituals of the Jews instances of hypocrisy and backwardness. The *Seder* (one thinks of what Herman Wouk will be doing fifteen years later to redeem all this!) an especial horror: "Ironical, isn't it? No people has suffered as the Jews have from the effects of nationalism and no people has held to it with such terrible intensity. . . ."

Can there be, then, in the American Jewish proletarian writer any Jewishness beyond a peculiarly Jewish self-hatred, a Jewish anti-Jewishness? To be sure, there is always available to him Jewish local color: the stumbling speech, the squalor, the joy peculiar to the Lower East Side or Brownsville; but these are by the thirties already sentimentalized clichés also available to the makers of Cohen and Kelly type movies. There is, beyond this, the constant awareness of alienation which belongs to the Jew: the sense of loneliness not as an accident but as a kind of chosenness; and in a writer like Gold the ancestral cry of *"Eli, Eli . . ."* persists. "In my ears still ring the lamentations of the lonely old Jews without money: 'I cash clothes, I cash clothes, my God, why hast thou forsaken me!' "

Not only has the concept of the choosing of all Israel in an election which seems an abandonment been transferred from the whole people to a part—to the poor alone—but in the process, what began as a mystery has become hopelessly sentimentalized. It is not for nothing that Mike Gold has been called the Al Jolson of the Communist Movement; indeed, in and through him, a cloying tradition of self-pity, which is also, alas, Jewish, and which had already possessed the American stage, moves on into literature. If the Communist Jewish writer can sing *"Eli, Eli . . ."* to his own tune, he can also sing *"A Yiddishe Mamme"* in a proletarian version. Here is Mike Gold once more: "My humble funny little East Side mother. . . . She would have stolen or killed for us. . . . Mother! Momma! I am still bound to you by the cords of birth. . . . I must remain faithful to the poor because I cannot be faithless to you."

All of this is secondary, however; the special meaning of Judaism for the radical writer of the thirties is, expectedly enough, its Messianism. "I believed," Gold writes, "the Messiah was coming, too. It was the one point in the Jewish religion I could understand clearly. We had no Santa Claus, but we had a Messiah." It is understandable, after all, that Marxism should feel at home with the Messianic ideal, since Marx seems to have envisaged himself, more often than not, as a prophetic figure: the last of the prophets promising a new heaven and a new earth. With the Russian Revolution, however, and the differentiation of Bolshevism, a new tone is apparent in Socialist messianism: a note at once apocalyptic and violent.

The old-fashioned sanity that characterizes Abraham Cahan is abandoned; and especially anything that smacks of the pacifism of the twenties is rejected in favor of an ideal of "hard Bolshevism" and class war. Two quite different sorts of feelings are involved, often confused with each other but logically quite separable: on the one hand, the desire, compounded of the self-hatred of the Jew and the self-distrust of the intellectual, that the good, clean, healthy workers of the future take over and destroy all that has come before them; on the other, an impulse to identify oneself with the future, to feel oneself for once strong and brutal and capable of crushing all that has baffled and frustrated one's dreams. "Oh workers' Revolution," Gold's protagonist cries out at the book's climax. "You brought hope to me, a lonely suicidal boy. You are the true Messiah. . . ."

Jewish American fiction in the thirties, whether specifically "proletarian" or not, is characterized by this frantic religiosity without God, this sense of the holiness of violence. Wherever one turns, there is the sense of a revelation, mystic and secular and terrible, as the only possible climax: the challenge to an unbelieved-in God to redeem Williamsburg at the end of Fuchs' first novel; the prayer to Pure Mathematics as a savior in Maurice Samuel's *Beyond Woman;* the invocation of the holy rage of John Brown in Leonard Ehrlich's *John Brown's Body;* the baffled and self-destructive attempt of Nathanael West's Miss Lonelyhearts to become Christ in a Christless world.

The Jewish novel of the twenties has as its typical theme assimilation and as its typical imagery the erotic; but the novel of the thirties is in theme and imagery, as well as politics, apocalyptic. Sex does not disappear from it completely, for the conquest of erotic taboos is a continuing concern of the contemporary novel; but its meaning and importance alike have been altered as compared with, say, *The Rise of David Levinsky* or Ben Hecht's *A Jew in Love.* From the Jew in love to the Jews without money of the thirties is a long way whose direction is indicated by Maurice Samuel's title *Beyond Woman.* Where erotic material does appear, it is likely to have the function which it assumes in Gold's book, to have become one more exhibit in the Chamber of Horrors: evidence of the evils of prostitution or the prevalence of the homosexual rape of small boys under Capitalism. More generally speaking, after Mike Gold, sex tends to be treated as just another sort of violence in a violent America.

In the 1930's, the Jewish-American novelists, like most of their Gentile fellows, become subscribers to the cult of violence, though for the Jewish writer such an allegiance has a special pathos because of the long opposition to violence in the Jewish inheritance. It is one more way of denying his fathers. And what could he do in any case? In those shabby, gray years, the dream of violence possesses the American imagination like a promise of deliverance. Politics is violent and apolitics equally so; whatever else a man accepts or denies, he does not deny terror.

Obviously, the thirties did not invent terror and violence in our fiction; as far back as our books go, there are images of horror: the torn corpse stuffed up the chimney; the skull split by a tomahawk; the whale spouting blood. Even a "funny book" like *Huckleberry Finn* has more corpses than anybody can ever remember. There are, however, two transformations in the thirties of the role and handling of violence.

The first is the *urbanization of violence;* that is to say, violence is transferred from the world of nature to the world of society, from what man must endure to what man has made. There is, of course, a special horror in considering the law of fang and claw walled in but unmitigated by the brick and glass of the city planners. Even a provincial writer like Faulkner is driven in those years to move into the city streets for images of terror adequate to the times; and *Sanctuary* remains of all his books the most appalling and Popeye, his sole urban protagonist, his most monstrous creation.

But the thirties mark the climax of an even more critical change: the ennobling of violence as "the midwife of history." Under the name of the Revolution, violence becomes not something to be fled, not the failing of otherwise admirable men, not a punishment for collective guilt—but the crown of social life. What had begun just after 1789 with the Terror and been hailed in America by the theoretically bloody Jefferson received in an age of mechanized warfare and mass production its final form. The lust for pain of Nietzsche and the hypostasizing of history by Hegel culminated in the twin horrors of Nazi and Soviet brutality; but a worse indignity had already been worked on the minds of intellectuals, conditioned in advance to accept one or the other.

In light of this, it is easy to understand that questions of ideology are secondary, that it is the pure love-fear of violence which distinguishes the novel of the thirties: a kind of passion not unlike that which moved the Germans before their final defeat, a desire for some utter cataclysm to end the dull-dragging-out of impotent suffering. Not only Communist-oriented writers produced such horror literature, but southerners like John Peale Bishop (in *Act of Darkness)* or Robert Penn Warren (in *At Heaven's Gate);* Hemingway made his obeisance to the mode in *To Have and Have Not;* and even so mild an upper-middlebrow traditionalist as James Gould Cozzens produced in *Castaway* a novella of the required shrillness.

In the official Communist version, the vision of the apocalypse is translated into that of the "Final Conflict" between worker and boss, Good and Evil; but this pat formula the better Jewish-American novelists could not quite stomach. Rather typically they temper the violence they cannot reject with humor, an ironic refusal to enter the trap completely. At the close of Daniel Fuchs' *Homage to Blenholt,* the three *shlemiels* who are his protagonists have reached the end of their illusions and are looking at each other in despair. One has come to realize that he will run a delicatessen for the rest of his life; another has come to see that the greatest event in his career will be winning three hundred dollars on a long shot.

> "Well," said Coblenz, "don't take it so hard. Cheer up. Why don't you turn to Communism?"
> "Communism?" cried Mrs. Balkin. "Listen to Mr. Bungalow. Communism!"
> "What has Communism got to do with it?" Munves sincerely wanted to know.
> "It's the new happy ending. You feel lousy? Fine! Have a revelation and onward to the Revolution!"

Fuchs' protagonists remain to the end victims and antiheroes, incapable of any catastrophe more tragic than the pratfall; but this is the traditional strategy of the comic writer. In a more complex way, Nathanael West and Henry Roth manage to achieve at once the antiheroic and the almost-tragic. In West, the comic butt is raised to the level of Everybody's Victim, the skeptical and unbelieved-in Christ of a faithless world; in Roth, the *shlemiel* is moved back to childhood, portrayed as the victim of circumstances he can never understand, only transcend.

West, of course, remains a humorist still; though in him humor is expressed almost entirely in terms of the grotesque, that is to say, on the borderline between jest and horror. In his novels, violence is not only subject matter; it is also technique, a way of apprehending as well as a tone and theme. Especially in the *Dream Life of Balso Snell,* one can see what West learned from the Surrealists during his stay in France: the violent conjunctions, the discords at the sensitive places where squeamishness demands harmony; the bellylaugh that shades off into hysteria.

Yet he is a peculiarly American case, too. In one of his few published critical notes he announces: "In America violence is idiomatic, in America violence is daily." And it is possible to see him as just another of our professional tough guys, one of the "boys in the backroom" (the phrase is Edmund Wilson's—the title of a little book in which he treated West along with John O'Hara). But West is, despite his own disclaimers, in a real sense, a Jew. He is racked, that is to say, by guilt in the face of violence, shocked and tormented every day in a world where violence *is* daily. In *Miss Lonelyhearts,* he creates a kind of portrait of himself as one all nerves and no skin, the fool of pity whom the quite ordinary horror of ordinary life lacerates to the point of madness. His protagonist is given the job of answering "letters from the lovelorn" on a daily newspaper and finds in this job, a "joke" to others, a revelation of human misery too acute to bear.

But this is West's analogue for the function of the writer, whom he considers obliged to regard unremittingly a suffering he is too sensitive to abide; and in no writer is there so absolute a sense of the misery of being human. He is child enough of his age to envision an apocalypse; but his apocalypse is a defeat for everyone. The protagonist of *Miss Lonelyhearts* is shot reaching out in love toward a man he has (against his will) offended; the hero-*shlemiel* of *A Cool Million: or The Dismantling of Lemuel Pitkin* goes from one absurd anti-Horatio-Alger disaster to another, and after his death becomes the hero of an American Fascist movement. But the real horror-climax of his life and the book comes when, utterly maimed, he stands on a stage between two corny comedians who wallop him with rolled up newspapers in time to their jokes until his wig comes off (he has been at one point scalped), his glass eye falls out, and his wooden leg falls away; after which they provide him with new artificial aids and begin again.

It is in *The Day of the Locust,* however, West's last book and the only novel on Hollywood not somehow trivialized by its subject, that one gets the final version of The Apocalypse according to Nathanael West. At the end of this novel, a painter, caught in a rioting mob of fans at a Hollywood premiere, dreams, as he is crushed by the rioters, his masterpiece, "The Burning of Los Angeles":

> Across the top he had drawn the burning city, a great bonfire of architectural styles. . . . Through the center . . . spilling into the middle foreground, came the mob carrying baseball bats

and torches—all those poor devils who can only be stirred by the promise of miracles and then only to violence, a great United Front of screwballs and screwboxes to purify the land. No longer bored, they sang and danced joyously in the red light of the flames.

West does not seem to be finally a really achieved writer; his greatness lies like a promise just beyond his last novel and is frustrated by his early death; but he is the inventor for America of a peculiarly modern kind of book whose claims to credence are perfectly ambiguous. One does not know whether he is being presented with the outlines of a nightmare endowed with a sense of reality or the picture of a reality become indistinguishable from nightmare. For the record, it must be said that the exploiters of such ambiguity are typically Jews: Kafka for the continent, West for us.

But in what sense is West a Jew at all? There is a violent flight from Jewish self-consciousness in his work; indeed, in *Balso Snell,* there is a bitter portrait of the kind of Jewish artist who feels obliged to insist on his origins:

"Sirrah!" the guide cried in an enormous voice, "I am a Jew! and whenever anything Jewish is mentioned, I find it necessary to say that I am a Jew. I'm a Jew! A Jew!"

Indeed, whenever a Jew is directly identified in West, he is portrayed viciously enough to satisfy the most rabid anti-Semite; although one must hasten to add that this is balanced by portraits of anti-Semites which would gratify any Jew. Finally, however, anti-Semitism and anti-anti-Semitism do not really add up to Jewishness, much less cancel each other out. West's changed name is surely a clue; he is the first American Jewish writer to wear a name which is a disguise; the exact opposite of Henry Harland, first author of an American book with a Jewish milieu, who called himself Sidney Luska and tried to pass as a compatriot of his protagonists.

West, we are told, made a point of dressing in a Brooks Brothers suit, carrying a tightly rolled umbrella and going, conspicuously, on hunting trips—which is to say, he insisted in all ways on making himself the antitype of the conventional Jewish intellectual. Yet it seems to me inconceivable that anyone but an urban, second-generation Jew in revolt against his background could have produced the novels from *Balso Snell* to *The Day of the Locust*. Certainly, the epigram of C. M. Doughty, which he himself quotes, seems applicable to Nathanael West: "The Semites are like to a man sitting in a cloaca to the eyes, and whose brows touch heaven."

Henry Roth is quite another matter. *Call It Sleep,* which appeared in 1935, and which no one will reprint despite continuing critical acclaim, is a *specifically* Jewish book, the best single book by a Jew about Jewishness written by an American, certainly through the thirties and perhaps ever. Technically, Roth owes a great deal to James Joyce; and, indeed, it is the strategy of intense concentration on fragmented detail and the device of stream-of-consciousness (both learned from *Ulysses)* which protect his novel from the usual pitfalls of the ghetto book. He reverses the fatal trend toward long-winded chronicle, which had at once inflated and dimmed the portrayal of Jewish immigrant society from Abe Cahan's lifelong study of David Levinsky to Ludwig Lewisohn's "saga" of four generations. The events of *Call It Sleep* cover two years of ghetto life, from 1911 to 1913, and are funneled through the mind of a boy who is six at the start of the book. It is through the sensibility of this sensitive, poetic, mama-haunted, papa-hating Jewish child, full of fears and half-perceptions and misunderstandings, that the clichés of the form are redeemed to poetry.

But he serves another purpose, too, that of helping the author, apparently committed to the ends of the Movement, evade ideology completely. In the place of the Marxian class struggle, Roth sets an almost Dickensian vision of the struggle between the child and society, of the child as Pure Victim. The lonely boy and the hostile city make only the first in a series of counterpoints on which the book is based: the greenhorn and the American; a subtle and lovely Yiddish and a brutal, gray English; grossness and poetry; innocence and experience, finally Gentile and Jew. In a way, quite unexpected in the thirties, Roth plays off the values of the *Cheder* against the values of an outside world dedicated to a pagan hunger for sex and success.

The climax of the book comes when David, the young protagonist, thrusts the handle of a milk ladle down into a crack between streetcar rails and is shocked into insensibility. He has learned earlier of the power of the rails, when captured and tortured by a gang of Gentile hoods on the previous Passover, and has come somehow to identify that power with the coal of fire by which the mouth of Isaiah was cleansed. He feels the need of a similar cleansing, for young as he is, he has the sense of having played pander to his cousin Esther and a Gentile boy in order to be accepted in that boy's world. Just before he passes into complete unconsciousness, David is granted a vision—once more the apocalypse—in which all that troubles him is healed: his father's paranoiac rage and fear of cuckoldry; his mother's mute suffering and erotic fantasies; his own terrors and apostasies. Blended into his vision are the harsh cries of the street and the voice of a Socialist speaker prophesying the day on which the Red Cock will crow. For the vision, neither the eight-year-old David nor the author has a name; and as the boy falls from consciousness, he thinks: "One might as well call it sleep."

After this spectacular achievement, Roth wrote no more novels; he works now, one hears, in an insane asylum in upstate New York —and an occasional story reveals him still haunting his old material without conviction or power. It is not an untypical case in the history of American Jewish writers in the thirties. Gold and Schneider lapsed into mere pamphleteering: West and Fuchs moved off to Hollywood, where the former died; no promises were fulfilled. Looking back, one sees a series of apparent accidents and ideological cripplings, acts of cowardice and despair; and yet there is a sense that this universal failure is not merely the function of personal weakness but of a more general situation. Although all outward circumstances in the time of the Great Depression conspired to welcome the Jewish writer, the inward life of the Jewish community was not yet defined enough to sustain a major writer, or even to provide him with something substantial against which to define himself in protest.

### 3. Zion as Main Street

It is only during the past fifteen or twenty years that such a definition has been achieved. In this period, Jewish self-consciousness in

America has endured certain critical readjustments under pressure from world events: the rise and fall of Hitler; the consequent dissolution of virtually the whole European Jewish community; the establishment of the State of Israel, and the need to redefine the allegiance of American Jews as Jews and as Americans. Other less spectacular developments have exercised an influence, too: the closing off of mass immigration and the slow disappearance of Yiddish as a spoken language; the elimination of the "greenhorn" as a typical Jewish figure—all this accompanied by an increasing general prosperity for the majority of American Jews. No longer is our story that of the rise of an occasional David Levinsky, but that of almost the whole Jewish people on the march toward the suburbs; of the transformation of essential Jewish life into bourgeois life.

At the same moment, there has been a complementary entry of the Jews into the academic world. One reads with surprise and incredulity that when Ludwig Lewisohn graduated from Columbia, he was advised not to hope for a job teaching English anywhere in America. More and more these days, even in this sensitive Anglo-Saxon area, Jews have come to write and teach; and only the most unreconstructed backwoods anti-Semite is heard to murmur bitterly about men named Greenspan or Schwartzstein lecturing on Emerson or Thoreau. Jews, indeed, have come to control many of the positions of prestige in the intellectual world of America, as editors and journalists and lay critics as well as teachers and writers.*

We live at a time when there exists what can be called either a temptation or an opportunity, at any rate the possibility of Jews en-

---

* Only an occasional crackpot these days raises an unheard voice against the trend, as Mr. Jack Feltz (dealer in uranium property) protests in a recent mimeographed leaflet: "According to studies of . . . *Publishers' Weekly,* as high as one-third or more of many publishers' lists are the works of Jewish authors, while the Jewish people constitute something like one-thirtieth of our population. . . . The authorities of our literature are, chiefly, members of a minority group who . . . have their own especial bias and prejudice. Every book that goes into print . . . is either written by, edited by, advertised by, published by, or, what is common—all four—Jewish people. . . .

"Why are the works of degenerate authors declared 'Great American Writing,' when often they are in extremely poor English, and are demoralizing and dangerous to our youths? Is it not probable that literary careers are bought from these publishers, just as we would buy a box of soap at the supermarket? There is only one other possibility: these publishers are at war with the American intelligence, as well as its Christian morality."

tering fully into the suburban-exurban pattern of success, conformity, and acceptance in an America where right-minded citizens protest teaching *The Merchant of Venice,* and blatant anti-Semitism exists chiefly in the most backward elements of the working class and in the backwoods of the South. For better or for worse, the task of the Jewish-American novelist now is to give some sense of the settling down of Jews in our steam-heated, well-furnished *Galut* —or to struggle against it, if such a struggle is still possible.

For this reason, we are through with the traditional "up from the ghetto" kind of Jewish fiction as a living form. In such books as Alfred Kazin's *A Walker in the City,* Isaac Rosenfeld's *Passage from Home,* or *An End to Dying* by the very young writer Sam Astrachan, one sees attempts to redeem the old pattern; but such attempts seem finally nostalgic and vestigial—echoes of yesterday's concerns. What, then, is central and vital in the recent novel as written by American Jews? Perhaps the best way to begin to answer this is to consider the situation left by the collapse of the Proletarian Novel and the exhaustion of the messianic spirit.

Even before the end of the thirties, when the most aware began to feel that the post-World War I era was over and the pre-World War II era had already begun, proletarian fiction was officially liquidated. The Communist Party through its cultural organs began to prepare for the Popular Front Novel, for a kind of fiction *pious* rather than *apocalyptic* in its approach. No longer was intransigence the keynote, but cooperation; no longer were the "workers" the subject, but "the little people"; no longer was the *International* required mood music, but *America the Beautiful.* Sentimentality had replaced terror; and those who looked back longingly toward bloodier days were condemned as "infantile leftists."

Most crucial of all, the American Left, which had traditionally associated itself with the *avant-garde* in literature, turned away toward Hollywood and Broadway and nightclub folksingers from the Village. The concept of Art as a Weapon no longer led to old-fashioned Agitprop productions, but to slick creations provided by movie writers or Madison Avenue ad-men with bad consciences. The distinguished names, available in the thirties at least for petitions and pamphlets, Dreiser or Farrell or Dos Passos, began to be replaced by Rex Stout and Donald Ogden Stewart, Dashiell Hammett and Howard Fast.

Fast is particularly interesting as the last full-time bard of the Movement, its most faithful middlebrow servant in the arts. He has recently reached a final crisis of conscience and has made at last a public break with the Communist Party; but for some fifteen years beginning in 1942 he managed almost alone to create a kind of subliterature in tune with its changing political line. In *The Unvanquished* and *Citizen Tom Paine,* he found a way of adapting the historical novel to Stalinist uses, of making its sentimentality underwrite the pieties of "progressive politics," and thus broke out of the long silence which had followed the collapse of proletarian fiction. If he turned at last into the most dogged sort of formula writer, it was due only in part to his natural limitations. No one could have stood up long under the demand to redeem George Washington when "Americanism" becomes respectable; to refurbish Judah Maccabee when Judaism comes back into fashion; or to get Sacco and Vanzetti out of the mothballs when all else fails. That the official Popular Front hack be a Jew is in some ways ironical but not unexpected; for among the last faithful left to the Communists in America were certain Jews clinging to the ragged cliché that in the Soviet Union, at whatever price, anti-Semitism had been eliminated.

The accommodation of the Stalinist left to middlebrow pressures (and the more complicated adjustment of the anti-Stalinist left in the pages of *Partisan Review)* has left no place for the instinctively radical writer to turn. There is no more dismaying prospect than the loneliness and bewilderment of the belated apocalyptic writer, especially when he is too young for the experience of the thirties and has to make a secondhand, home-made version of class struggle fiction—out of G.I. platitudes and memories of Marxism. James Jones is, perhaps, the outstanding representative of the group; and Norman Mailer its chief Jewish proponent. In the latter's *The Naked and the Dead,* for instance, the Fascist villain out of a hundred weary Agitprop entertainments appears as General Cummings, surely one of the most improbable characters in all fiction.

Such writers, having no center, are provincials in the deepest sense of the word: that is to say, they repeat what they have never heard and invent all over again what is already worn out. Mailer is a case in point, recapitulating the whole recent history of literature before him: he rewrites the antiwar novel in *The Naked and the Dead*, the anti-Hollywood novel in *The Deer Park*, the novel of political disillusionment in *Barbary Shore*. Only the hectic sexuality, which threatens, despite his conscious intent, to replace politics completely, seems his own; the rest is unacknowledged (I suspect, unaware) quotation.

As in the writers of the thirties, in Mailer what remains of Jewishness is translated into social protest; though the chief rebels of his books are (like West's) almost pointedly *not* Jews. And yet in one sense, he is more the child of his sentimental times than he would be pleased to admit; certainly there appears for the first time in *The Naked and the Dead*, what is to become a standard character in the liberal-middlebrow war book: the Jewish Sad Sack. In Mailer's Goldstein, who finds the chief horror of war anti-Semitism in his own ranks, there is present in embryo Irwin Shaw's Noah Ackerman—and the protagonist of a score of movies to come.

Such lapses into the banal vocabulary of the middlebrows are, however, rare in Mailer. He may be clumsy and provincial, but he is above all things honest; and he refuses to endorse the clichés of enlightened liberalism. There is something healthy, I think, in preferring yesterday's platitudes to today's; for they are at least unfashionable, assurances that the writer is not merely on the make. Mailer is not, in any case, a typical figure, standing apart as he does from the two major developments which have followed the collapse of the Proletarian Novel.

Both these developments are of considerable importance for an understanding of Jewish writers in America since both are in large part products of Jewish writers, and both help to establish the background against which the later Jewish writer defines himself. The first development is a kind of literary Jacobinism: a resistance to the separation of radical politics and *avant-garde* art. Its adherents would reconstitute the alliance of antibourgeois social criticism and antibourgeois literary experiment; but this they would do outside of any party orthodoxy. The second is a species of literary liberalism which aims at rescuing Popular Front art, that is, self-righteous, middlebrow art, from the Communists in favor of an enlightened segment of the bourgeoisie. Let us consider them in reverse order.

The middlebrow liberal or liberal-colored fictionist responds to the demands of a certain novel-reading section of the middle class which would like to be Philistine in a really arty kind of way. Such readers are more concerned with social problems than with art and turn to novels merely as occasions for thinking about such "important problems." The kind of middlebrow fiction produced for their benefit has established itself everywhere from *Good Housekeeping* and the *Saturday Evening Post,* on the one hand, to the *New Yorker,* on the other.

One of its newer subvarieties, science fiction, has opened up a whole series of periodical and book-length markets. The first lower-middlebrow form of fiction to challenge the long dominance of the Western and the detective story, science fiction is in large part a Jewish product. There are a score of Jewish writers among its most widely read practitioners, as compared with practically none among those of the two older types of institutionalized fantasy. The basic myths of science fiction reflect the urban outlook, the social consciousness, the utopian concern of the modern, secularized Jew. The traditional Jewish Waiting-for-the-Messiah becomes in lay terms the *commitment to the Future,* which is the motive force of current science fiction. The notion of the Jewish cowboy is utterly ridiculous, of a Jewish detective, Scotland Yard variety or private eye, nearly as anomalous; but to think of the scientist as a Jew is almost tautological.

Much science fiction, set just before or after the Great Atomic War still to come, embodies the kind of guilty conscience peculiar to such scientist-intellectuals (typically Jewish) as Robert Oppenheimer; while the figure of Einstein presides over the whole New Heaven and New Earth such literature postulates, replacing the earlier Hebrew God who is—for most science fiction fans, certainly —dead. Even in its particulars, the universe of science fiction is born judaized; the wise old tailor, the absurd but sympathetic *yiddishe mamme* plus a dozen other Jewish stereotypes whiz unchanged across in space and time. Even secret Jewish jokes are made for the cognoscenti: the police on a corrupt, transgalactic planet called in the exotic tongue of that world *Ganavim.* And in the Superman comic books (lowbrow equivalent of science fiction) the same aspirations and anxiety are projected in the improbable disguise of the Secret Savior, bespectacled Clark Kent, who may look like a *goy* but who is invented by Jews. The biceps are the biceps of Esau, but the dialogue is the dialogue of Jacob.

The more "serious" middlebrow novel in form combines a clear narrative line (no confusing flashbacks or troublesome experiments in style) with a pious celebration of social protest in favor of Negroes, Jews, children of adulterous mothers, paraplegics, Hungarians—whatever is thoroughly unexceptionable and, of course, *up to date;* for such books must compete with the daily newspaper. In these works, a new, urban, professional, liberalized, and, I think, largely Jewish elite comes to terms with its own vague feelings of guilt at being so prosperous in a troubled world. The kind of people who learn all about their children from reading Gesell, who go to the Museum of Modern Art, who subscribe to *The Reporter,* who vote for Adlai Stevenson, also buy the novels of Budd Schulberg and Irwin Shaw to get the latest word on the "little people," with whom they sentimentally identify themselves.

Naturally enough, considering the strength of Jewishness in this group and the impact of Hitler on the whole newspaper-reading world, the first "little people" to be celebrated in the liberal novel were the "little Jews." Not only Jewish writers, but Jews and Gentiles alike, discovered at once this new form of the novel and the new subject (so ignored in the thirties) of anti-Semitism. Arthur Miller's first novel, *Focus,* Laura Z. Hobson's *Gentleman's Agreement,* Mary Jane Ward's *The Professor's Umbrella*—there is a whole stream of such books mounting to a kind of flood-peak with John Hersey's *The Wall.* They are profoundly sentimental in theme and tone and are written in the slickly finished style proper to a literary no man's land existing somewhere between Hollywood and Madison Avenue and blanketed with old copies of the *Saturday Review of Literature,* the *New Yorker* and the *Princeton Alumni Weekly.*

What is oddest about such fiction, however, is the way in which it is typically hoked-up; the books are never simply studies of anti-Semitism in action, they are studies of anti-Semitism with a gimmick. Miller, for instance, deals with a man who, though a Gentile, *looks* like a Jew when he puts on glasses and is persecuted when his eyes fail. Mrs. Hobson's book is about a reporter who *pretends* he is a Jew and brings down upon himself the discrimination of anti-Semites. It is not only a certain middlebrow ideal of form which demands the gimmick, but a basic uncertainty which is aptly symbolized by such a tricky device. What, after all, *is* a Jew in this world where men are identified as Jews only by mistake, where the very word becomes merely an epithet arbitrarily applied? It is difficult to make a novel about anti-Semitism when one is not sure exactly what, beside being the butt of anti-Semites, makes a man a Jew.

There are, to be sure, occasional portraits of real Jews beside the imaginary ones; but the former are such monsters of humility and gentleness and endurance and piety that it is impossible to believe in them. Such protagonists are no more real than the happy endings which await them: reconciliations in an atmosphere of goodwill even less credible than the atmosphere of exaggerated hostility with which such fables typically begin. The pattern is set once and for all in a story by Irwin Shaw called "Act of Faith," in which a young man, scared by his father's accounts of anti-Semitism at home, decides to keep as insurance a Luger he has picked up on the battlefield. He thinks, however, of his wartime buddies, "of all the drinks they had had together, and the long marches together, and all the girls they had gone out with together" and decides to sell the pistol after all. "Forget it," he says finally, "what could I use it for in America?" What begins as a political problem (touched with hysteria) is solved as a sentimental one (touched with politics).

From a story of anti-Semitism to one of the war is an easy jump; indeed, the liberal war novel is only one more species of the high-minded literature of social reform: a subvariety, in the hands of Jewish writers in particular, of the novel of anti-Semitism. Shaw's *The Young Lions* is the prime example of the genre, anticipations of which we have already noticed in Mailer's *The Naked and the Dead*. In a fundamental sense, there is nothing *new* in such novels; they do not change the protest form of the war-book invented just after World War I; but the method has been perfected: the tone of superficial realism set by unflinching descriptions of death, rape, and the other usual calamities of combat; the rejection of certain more obvious stereotypes of the enemy, and the exploitation of others: the reactionary American General, for instance, but especially the "representative platoon," with the Jewish Sad Sack to help make up its roster.

One raised entirely on such literature and the movies based on their clichés would believe the United States Army to be carefully organized so that each platoon contains a pure, sentimental sample of the "little people" at war: a cocky, slight Italian, a Brooklyn Jew, a raw-boned, blond farm boy, etc. Certainly, no such group would dare set off without its Jew, the kind of understanding victim who, in the recent liberaloid film *Attack,* is portrayed as reciting *Kaddish* for a Catholic thug who dies while trying to reach a gun and kill (naturally!) an evil officer.

Shaw's Jew is Noah Ackerman, a self-educated intellectual, hated at first by his buddies, in part because a copy of *James Joyce* is found in his footlocker, but later much admired after offering to fight the six or eight toughest men in his platoon. In him, we meet the stereotyped antistereotype of the Jew: since the old stereotype makes the Jew a coward, he is brave; since it makes the Jew a war-resister, he is a combat hero; since it makes the Jew an enemy of personal violence, he is (for quite high-minded reasons) dedicated to it. What Hemingway had satirized as overcompensation in Robert Cohn is here glorified.

There are, however, two other major characters in *The Young Lions* beside the Jew as Fighting Sad Sack: the antistereotype stereotyped Nazi and an enlightened, sensitive American who has passed from Broadway to the front and is the eye of the book. The Nazi is permitted to kill the Jew, but Michael Whiteacre, the emissary from the world of Popular Culture, kills the Nazi. This is all quite satisfactory to the readers; for Michael is clearly intended to be their representative in the action: a projection of the mind for which Shaw is writing, the social group for which he speaks.

His work fulfills the ideal proposed to himself by the bureaucratized intellectual dreaming of what he would do if released by Hollywood or the T.V. network. *The Young Lions* is, one remembers, the book which the gigolo-scriptwriter in *Sunset Boulevard* (and presumably the scriptwriter behind him) reads in his spare time.

Budd Schulberg is, of course, another novelist who speaks for the same audience; and his *What Makes Sammy Run?* is as appropriate a representation of the Hollywood novel on the middlebrow level as *The Young Lions* is of the war novel (or, indeed, as Schulberg's own *On the Waterfront* of the liberaloid labor story).

When Schulberg's earlier book appeared, there was much pointless and confusing comment on the presumably anti-Semitic implications of his portrayal of Sammy Glick—as if this were the first portrait of an evil Jew to have appeared in American literature. In the midst of such properly middlebrow polemics, most readers failed to notice the more unforgivable travesties of Jews in Schulberg's noble scriptwriters, who read Silone's *Fontamara* in *their* spare moments and fought the good fight for the Screenwriters' Guild despite blacklisting and redbaiting.

Schulberg's novel, like all sentimental melodramas, splits into opposing symbolic characters what in fact exists in one contradictory soul. Once understood in this light, the book may be read as a portrait of the artist as a Hollywood employee: that is, a writer like Schulberg (and Shaw) is in part the noble Jewish supporter of the Loyalists and trade-unionism, but in part, too, Sammy Glick, the poor boy on the make. They, too, are sons of a first generation of immigrants which had destroyed itself for their sake in a strange world; they, too, are eager to be heard, to be effective, to be successful—and to break out of the trap of a stereotyped Jewishness without money. They are more complicated men, to be sure, than Sammy Glick; but then everyone is: even Herman Wouk.

Wouk's work does, however, possess a certain importance for revealing on a less sophisticated level ambitions analogous to those which inform *What Makes Sammy Run?* and *The Young Lions.* If Shaw and Schulberg can be said to speak for the mass entertainers with yearnings to transcend their world, Wouk can be understood as representing the ad writers and gag writers who are convinced that the same slick techniques by which they earn their livings can do justice to certain modest liberal values, and that those values are compatible with the suburban lives they lead. Turning from Shaw and Schulberg to Wouk, one notices certain differences: less shock, fewer dirty words, less stylistic pretension. His is a world that cries

"Keep it clean!" and the one thing that that world finds dirtier than four-letter words is highbrow art.

A common sentimentality, however, binds them together and a common store of stock "little people." Greenwald, the Jew of Wouk's war novel, *The Caine Mutiny,* is blood brother to the Ackerman of Shaw's *The Young Lions:* both are Jews who face up to Gentile versions of courage and honor which exclude them, not by challenging those codes but by aping them; both attempt to prove, despite the handicaps of a Jewish physique and a long tradition of nonviolence, that they can outdrink and outfight any *goy.* But Greenwald has adapted to the world that surrounds him even more shamelessly than Ackerman, having neither a taste for James Joyce nor a principled distrust of the armed forces. The villainous intellectual who does is called Keefer and is clearly (thank God!) not a Jew.

The reconciliation which Wouk demands goes far beyond the embracing of one's fellow yahoos in battle camaraderie as advocated by Shaw. It requires embracing the whole military, the whole social order in all its smug security, because, as Greenwald reminds especially his Jewish readers, it was Captain Queeg who kept mama out of the Nazis' soap dish. "Captain Queeg, yes, even Queeg and a lot of sharper boys than any of us. Best men I've ever seen. You can't be good in the Army or Navy unless you're goddam good, though maybe not up on Proust and *Finnegans Wake* and all." *The Stars and Stripes Forever* blend with *A Yiddishe Mamme,* as Gold had once blended the latter with the *International*—and the way is clear for Marjorie Morningstar.

Marjorie is, indeed, our new middlebrow muse, translated from Wouk's book to the cover of *Time* to the movies with scarcely a pause for breath: a portrait of accommodation as the young girl. That she is Jewish is the final touch: a tribute to the triumph of liberalism in the suburbs, the truce with anti-Semitism of the American middle class, and the end of surly intransigeance among the Jews. In the form of Noel Airman, Wouk has isolated all that is skeptical, anti-Philistine, and indifferent to bourgeois values in the Jewish-American tradition; and Airman he has made his villain. With him he identifies everything that stands between the Jew and social acceptance, the novelist and popularity; with Marjorie he identifies all that makes the Jew acceptable and the Jewish novelist a best-seller. It is one of the melodramatic fissions like the one we have noticed in Shaw and Schulberg; though this time the author isolates and casts out of himself symbolically not his greed for success but all that stands between him and that success.

What is truly strange is not that Marjorie should seem representative to the bourgeois Jewish community, but that she should also strike the American community at large as a satisfactory image. Yet it is comprehensible in the end that the enlightened American *allrightnik,* Gentile or Jew, should find in the suburban Jewish housewife the proper symbol of interfaith "tolerance," the vision of unity in diversity possible where no one any longer believes in anything but the hundred-per-cent Americanism of just believing.

This is not yet, however, a total picture of the middlebrow novel as written by the Jewish American writer. If Shaw defines the middle of the middle, and Wouk its lower limits, it is J. D. Salinger who indicates its upper reaches. Though Salinger has written always for the circle of middlebrow periodicals that includes *Good Housekeeping* and the *New Yorker,* he has maneuvered constantly (though at first almost secretly) to break through the limits of that circle. He has piously acknowledged in his stories the standard ritual topics of the enlightened bourgeoisie: the War and anti-Semitism; but he has been concerned underneath with only a single obsessive theme: the approach to madness and the deliverance from it, usually by the intervention of a child. His "little people" are often quite literally little, usually small girls; and his favorite protagonists are under twenty, their typical crisis the last pre-adult decision of deciding whether or not to remain in school.

The themes that find full expression in *Catcher in the Rye* are tried early in short magazine fiction. In "A Girl I Know," there first appears the familiar, six-foot-two, blackhaired boy, cast out of school; though in this case he is eighteen, has been expelled from college, and finds his way to Austria where he becomes involved in a brief, utterly innocent love affair with a Jewish girl, who can speak no more English than he can German. The War separates them, and he returns to Europe to find her dead, killed by Nazis. In the much-reprinted "For Esme with Love and Squalor" the other half of the obsessive fable is sketched in: the story of a man redeemed from a combat breakdown by a gift from an orphaned, twelve-year-old, upper-class girl, with whom he has had a brief tea-table conversation in England.

In *Catcher in the Rye,* the blackhaired boy on the lam from school and the man threatened with insanity are joined together; the savior becomes the little sister—and the sentimental-political background is sloughed away in favor of a discreetly hinted-at world of religious implications. One has the sense that Salinger is making a real bid to break out of the trap of middlebrow "understanding" into the realm of the tragic; but the attempt fails. It is impossible to believe in Holden Caulfield finally, for he is too unreal, a creature of tricks of style, set against an utterly unconvincing family background. One knows that he is intended to represent a holy innocent against whom the rest of the world is measured: a kind of prep-school, upper-income-bracket Huckleberry Finn, who cannot quite light out for the Territory but is redeemed by a little girl in a climax essentially sentimental; yet he ends as the prep-school boy's dream of himself, a slickly amusing model imitated by a hundred seventeen-year-olds in a score of secondary-school magazines from coast to coast.

In "Zooey," a recent novella published in the *New Yorker,* Salinger seems to me to have recast his story, so often unsuccessfully attempted, in much more convincing form. If "Zooey" moves us where *Catcher in the Rye* merely amuses, it is because for once the madness of the theme is allowed to break up the slickness of the style; and the family tragedy which is Salinger's essential theme is uncontaminated by required subject matter, erotic or political, essentially alien to him. The only romance to which he really responds is the family romance: Orestes saved from the furies by Electra (though this time he has reversed the roles); and he has brought his myth in all purity *home,* to his own Manhattan and to the Jewishness with which he has had so much trouble coming to terms. His protagonists may find their final peace in a religious revelation compounded of Zen Buddhism and Christian mysticism; but they begin at least in a Jewish milieu (half-Jewish only, he insists) of quiz kids and memories of the Pantages circuit. Salinger seems to me by all odds the most interesting of the middlebrow writers, torn between a professional knowledge of what is permitted the entertainer and a desire to surrender all striving to the attainment of a mystic's peace. The assertion at the end of "Zooey" that the Fat Lady of the middling audience is "Christ Himself. Christ Himself, buddy!" seems to me one of the wackiest and most winning attempts to compromise these contradictory impulses.

The second major direction of recent fiction, what I have called earlier the Jacobin protest, is a last attempt to maintain the snobbism of the highbrow in a world which undercuts his existence. It is associated, in its Jewish manifestations at least, with *Partisan Review* and the publications that flank it: *Commentary, Encounter,* and the *New Leader,* on the one hand; *Kenyon Review, Sewanee Review,* and certain other literary quarterlies, on the other. It is not especially relevant from our point of view that *Partisan* was originally political in nature, pledged to retaining the purity of Marxism at a time when the official Communist movement was in retreat toward Popular Frontism; what *is* important is that it was pledged also to maintain against the bourgeoisie the alliance of high art and radical thinking.

By the 1950's as a matter of fact, Marxism had become a memory, a special condition of their youth, to most of *Partisan Review's* remaining collaborators; respectability crept inexorably in upon it. At various points, indeed, certain super-Jacobins left the magazine's pages in despair. Not the least interesting of these is Paul Goodman, who wanted to maintain an uncompromised allegiance to pure bohemianism and nonaccommodation. He is at present a lay analyst, influenced in his practice by the teachings of Wilhelm Reich; and his concern with depth psychology helps shape his fiction, which is also based in part on the techniques of Kafka and the devices of Yiddish folk humor.

Yet even those who remain and have most blatantly accommodated to the world around them still share something with further dissenters like Goodman, something which separates them clearly from the middlebrow writers we have been discussing. What is it that they share beneath all their differences? I have called it earlier the snobbism of the highbrow; and their enemies are likely to label it "negativism." Perhaps it is best thought of as a sort of vestigial, spiritual Trotskyism: an obligation to the attitudes of dissent which survives the ideological grounds for dissent. It arises in any case from their early conditioning in endless polemics on Marxian theory and their exposure from adolescence on to Freudian concepts; and makes them more closely kin in certain ways to European intellectuals than to more traditional American writers.

Perhaps most important of all is the fact that such writers possess in common a brand of experience which is rich and suggestive. They are urban; they are second-generation Americans; they are men and women whose adolescence and early youth came between the Great Wars, was influenced by the Civil War in Spain, and haunted by the Depression; they remain strangers in the world of prosperity in which they now, quite comfortably, live. They are joined to each other and separated from the rest of their generation by the experience of having accepted and rejected Communism.

They are, finally, typically Jewish: secularized, uncertain Jews in most cases to be sure; but in all cases possessed by the ghosts of their Jewish past; and they continue to wrestle with the lay messianism which was the gift of that past to them. Their peculiar relationship to their Jewishness emphasizes their sense of alienation (it is a favorite word of theirs, very annoying but inescapable), and protects them against the Wouk-Shaw-Schulberg kind of simpleminded, liberal-middlebrow accommodation.

Yet the blessing which has fallen upon Wouk has also been bestowed (even more fantastically) upon *Partisan Review*. For better or for worse, the time has come when each cultural level in America looks to some Jewish-sponsored myth for a justification of its existence and its dreams; for some the Superman of the comics, for some the moralistic robots of Isaac Asimov, for some Marjorie Morningstar, for some images of urban alienation out of the pages of *Partisan Review*. Certainly, that magazine despite the tininess of its actual subscription list exercises at home and abroad a fantastic influence. If the concept of the highbrow has become for most Americans associated with the notion of the urban, Jewish, former Communist, this is in part the work of *Partisan Review*.

Certainly, as far as literature is concerned, it has introduced over the past fifteen years a group of writers rivaled in their variety and the richness of their common themes only by the Southern group which includes Eudora Welty, Carson McCullers, etc. Among them are writers like Delmore Schwartz, who has not yet produced a novel, but who has, in the short stories collected in *The World Is a Wedding,* managed to evoke the tone and texture of second generation life in America better than anyone I know. To render an undramatized sense of gray people in gray cities, speaking to each other in gray voices and gray words, he has evolved a desperately flat style, which, when it does not succeed, can be boring beyond belief; but which, when it works, carries an unparalleled conviction. There are further the *Partisan Review* adaptors of Kafka, in particular Isaac Rosenfeld, who made in his short stories something new and disturbing of Kafkaesque ambiguity and grotesque humor and who pushed forward the possibilities of Kafkaesque form, the symbolic statement neither quite essay nor quite story.

There is, finally, Bernard Malamud, recipient of one of the *Partisan Review* fellowships in fiction, who is presently enduring an astonishingly universal acclaim, the latest manifestation of the hunger among American readers for occasions to identify with Jewish life. Though his shorter work has appeared chiefly in *Partisan and Commentary,* he is much less political than most of his fellow contributors, free of their (in some cases obsessive) concern with the aftermath of the Communist experience. Close to forty-five, he is only now coming into full possession of his talent and his subject matter, and so has avoided the typical *Partisan Review*-ers' experience of being twice-born, once as a Bolshevik, once as a human. Yet he emerges from the same milieu as his more political colleagues, trades like them (though more fantastically) on the vestiges of urban Jewishness, on the kind of American experience closest to the moral life of Europe. His first novel, *The Natural,* dealt improbably enough with a baseball player (last symbol for the city-dweller of the heroic), handling a symbolic story with gusto and tact. His second book, *The Assistant,* more conventionally centered upon the family of a poor Jewish shopkeeper in the thirties, but ended, quite astonishingly for all its matter-of-fact tone, with the circumcision of its Italian protagonist; a desperate Happy Ending! It is all as if Mike Gold had never existed. Malamud did not, however, really arrive until the publication of his collected short stories (in a volume called *The Magic Barrel*), whose discreet flirtation with sentimentality perhaps made their acceptance easier. These stories tell and retell a fable in which a scholarly, timid, or genteel protagonist, secure or on the verge of security, confronts some seedy, living projection of the lostness and terror which his life denies—some more ultimate Jew; and we come away with the conviction that Malamud remains as a writer (thank God!) a good deal blacker, more *demonic* than he is ever prepared to admit—even to himself.

Malamud's meaning seems to me to be still defining itself and his significance to belong to what lies ahead, unlike that of the two major figures of the last decade to whom I now come. The first is Lionel Trilling, who is to me an endlessly fascinating case, though finally, I fear, a disappointing one. Indeed, the clue to his fascination lies in the last-minute failure of what is a complex and subtle sensibility; in the fact that as a fictionist, he doesn't quite work. Yet he was willing to attempt in *The Middle of the Journey* the novel which some writer of his kind must someday achieve: the story of the allure of Communism and of the disillusion with it. Norman Mailer has tried his hand at it, to be sure, but without having quite lived through the experience, and Isaac Rosenfeld has explored it a little obliquely in one short story; while Leslie Fiedler has endlessly circled around it in his shorter fiction. Only Trilling has made the full-scale attempt; and it is perhaps a certain air of schematism in his approach, a sense of his having reached this item on a list of Important Things to be Done, which mars the book.

The events of the novel, at any rate, finally remain unconvincing, both on the symbolic level (despite their relationship to the central experience of a generation) and on the literal one (despite their resemblance to the newspaper story of Hiss and Chambers); because they come to us refracted through the mind of a singularly unconvincing protagonist, a kind of cross between Matthew Arnold and E. M. Forster, caught at the moment of his entry into middle age and at the point of recovery from a wasting disease. He is both genteel and Gentile, this Laskell, through whom the working-class characters of the book become caricatures and its passion merely literary—not Trilling, of course, but a mask Trilling prefers to assume, a mask of the bourgeois academic who is beyond Judaism as he is beyond the clichés of middlebrow liberalism. I do not know whether Trilling lacks vitality because of his failure to tap his own Jewish sources, or whether he fails to tap those sources because of an initial lack of vitality; but somewhere here there is a clue to his failure, a failure whose outward symbol is the lack of Jewish major protagonists in a novel by a Jew about an experience deeply rooted in Jewish life.

He is much more successful in certain short stories, in "Of This Time, of That Place" and "The Other Margaret," where he can concentrate on a narrower world of university-oriented, genteel, New York, middle-class culture, in which Jewishness survives chiefly as what used to be called "ethical culture," a kind of diffuse moral concern. When he enters the larger world of the novel and confronts in particular the absurdity essential to the Communist experience in America, he is defeated by the very talents which make him so much at home in the world of late nineteenth-century British fiction.

Saul Bellow is quite another matter. The Author of *The Dangling Man, The Victim, The Adventures of Augie March* and a recent collection of shorter fiction called *Seize the Day*, he is already an established writer; although in the annoying fashion of American journalism (he is after all younger than Faulkner or Hemingway) he is still referred to as a "young novelist." Looking at the whole body of his work, one has the sense of a creative restlessness, an adventurousness, which distinguishes him quite sharply from such other established fictionists as Trilling, on the one hand, or Irwin Shaw, on the other. Even such younger, dissident middlebrows as Herbert Gold seem beside him to lack technical courage and real commitment.

Bellow can, on occasion, mute his style as he has done in *The Victim* and in the novella which gives his most recent collection its name; but even under wraps, his language has a kind of nervous life, a tough resiliency unequaled by any other American Jewish writer of the moment. Perhaps the fact that Yiddish was his first language has something to do with the matter; but when he unleashes his fancy and permits himself a kind of rich, crazy poetry based on the juxtaposition of high language and low, elegance and slang, I am reminded of *Moby Dick*. The dialogue of his books possesses a special vitality; he can report a passage of conversation about ideas which leaves one feeling that his characters have exchanged more than words, have really touched each other as with a blow or a kiss.

In the body of his work, the ideas of the *Partisan Review* group (it does not matter how far he thinks he has left them behind) come fully alive in literature for the first time; they exist, that is to say, as they existed at their best in the minds of the men who held them; for those men at their best *lived* such ideas and did not merely believe them. Not only does Bellow have a style more vigorous than that of Trilling; but he moves in a world which is larger and richer and more disorderly and delightful—a world which he calls most often Chicago, though it is the externalization of fancy as well as memory. Implicit from his beginnings is the impulse toward the picaresque, which broke free finally in the sprawling, episodic shapelessness of *Augie March*—whose very formless form protests the attempt to impose tight, aesthetic patterns upon a world whose essence is chaos.

Bellow is, not unexpectedly in an age when writers in general have entered the university and Jews in particular have found a home there, a teacher like Trilling. The Jim Tully ideal of the author-bum, still played at by novelists like Nelson Algren, has never had much appeal for the Jewish writer in America; but though Bellow rejects the mask of the hobo bard, he does not assume that of the cultured humanist. His myth of himself is not that of the morally discriminating bourgeois at home over cocktails; but of the lonely city-dweller moving among boarding houses and cheap hotels, shabby restaurants and gray city streets in the heat of midsummer. The typical Bellow protagonist is the man whose wife has left him or has gone off to her mother's, the man returning to a house in disorder.

He is the person who, all amenities stripped away, feels himself stripped to his human essence. And the human essence, the naked fact of a man in a Bellow book is never an answer but always the question: What am I, after all? What, after all, is man? To which the unpromising answer is returned: You are what asks; go on asking. Here is Bellow's true center as well as what makes him central for all of us; he has realized not more clearly, perhaps, but more passionately than anyone what the collapse of the Proletarian Novel really meant: not the disappearance only of a way of writing, never very fruitful in any case, but also the dissolution of the last widely shared definition of man—as victim or beneficiary of the social order.

Because Bellow does not subscribe to the liberal's illusion that the definition of the human in social terms is still viable; because he knows that Man, in the old sense, is dead—he is able to redeem all the typical books of the middlebrow-liberal canon. *The Dangling Man* is his book about the war; *The Victim,* his novel of anti-Semitism; *Augie March,* his examination of the perils of success; *Seize the Day,* his fable of failure in a world of prosperity—his own *Death of a Salesman.* But in each, ambiguity has replaced sentimentality, the tragic or the joyous displaced self-congratulation and self-conscious piety. The Jew and the anti-Semite, the machiavellian and the *shlemiel* come alike to the same revelation.

It is because he manages to exact from the most unpromising material the stubborn vision of lonely man in a world which no longer provides his definition that Saul Bellow is able at last to create the most satisfactory character ever projected by a Jewish writer in America: Augie March. With the book itself, shrill, repetitious, in spots hysterically euphoric, I have certain quarrels; with Augie, none. He is an image of man at once totally Jewish, the descendant of the *schemiels* of Fuchs and Nathaniel West, and absolutely American—the latest avatar of Huckleberry Finn. In him, there are blended in perfect irony those twin, incompatible American beliefs: that the answer is just over the next horizon and that there is no answer at all.

It is, I think, the final commentary on our age and on the place the Jew occupies in its imagination, that Huck Finn, when he returns to our literature not as an item of nostalgia but as an immortal archetype, returns without his overalls, his fishing pole and his freckles, as a Chicago kid making his way among small-time Jewish machiavellians. More was needed, however, than the age; the moment demanded a Jewish hero, perhaps, but hesitated indifferently between Augie March and Marjorie Morningstar. What was demanded was the talent and devotion and conviction which belong particularly to Bellow, and the rich, complicated milieu out of which he has emerged.

*Missoula, Montana*
—1959

# SEVEN

# The Image of Newark
# and the Indignities of Love:
# Notes on Philip Roth*

IN RECENT years, I have more often gone by Newark than into it, though it is the place where I was born and brought up. Still, seeing even from the Pulaski Skyway the Public Service Building lifted above the Meadows, and imagining around it the yellow trolley buses and the crowds at the curbs, frantic and disheveled as refugees—I feel again the ennui and terror and crazy joy of my childhood. It was at once depressing and exciting to live in a place which we came slowly to realize did not exist at all for the imagination. That Newark was nowhere, no one of us could doubt, though it was all most of us knew. What history the city possessed had been played out before our parents or grandparents were a part of it, and we did not even trouble to tell ourselves that we disbelieved it. What could Robert Treat, the founding father, mean to second generation Jewish boys living on a street of two-and-a-half-family houses with stone lions on the stoops? He was an embossed figure on a teaspoon, steeple-hatted and unreal: a souvenir given away at a forgotten centennial and fought over by the kids when the pot roast was taken off the table and the stewed fruit brought on.

And Newark itself, the whole living city, what was it beyond a tangle of roads defining our own neighborhood and enclosing others

---

* Originally a review of *Goodbye, Columbus.*

118

utterly alien? The city on whose streets we walked with school-books or ice cream cones or packages from the store we could not feel for a moment as one of those magical centers whose very names were thrilling to say: Paris, London, even New Orleans or Chicago or New York—the last only ten miles away. Newark was not even a joke like Brooklyn or Oshkosh or Peoria; vaudeville per-formers with canned gags for everywhere on the circuit could scarcely find one able to extort a perfunctory laugh. In those days, to be sure, there were the Bears, a ball club at least, and always the airport; after a while Dutch Schultz was shot in a local tavern, and for a thrilling moment Longie Zwillman, whose mother we could watch walking our sidewalks with the diamonds he bought her, made the Public Enemy list! Public Enemy Number One, we liked to boast; but I have been afraid to try to verify it, uneasily aware that at best he was only third or fourth.

No, even as kids we felt really how undefined, how character-less our native place was—without a legend older than last week's *Star-Eagle*. We did not *know* its characterlessness, perhaps, but we lived it just as we lived its ugliness. Later we would know, when it was time. In the meanwhile, we prepared for the moment of knowl-edge by reading in that Public Library, in which, fittingly, the pro-tagonist of Philip Roth's longest story works to put himself through college. If Newark, our Newark, had any focal point at all it was The Library; but there those of us who took books seriously learned almost first of all that poor Newark had no writer, and hence no myth to outlive its unambitious public buildings, its mean frame houses. When Bamberger's Department Store was at last closed down and the Prudential Insurance Company had crumbled away, how would anyone learn that we had ever existed? Maybe the name would survive at least on some old commutation ticket for the Hudson Tubes, petrified in coal dust.

There was, to be sure, Stephen Crane, memorialized in the classroom, but his fictional world was a small-town Gentile world called Whilomville, not his native Newark at all; and we found it as alien as most of the teachers who told us about it—or as those Newark *goyim* who are all the time passing by the centers of action of Roth's stories without ever quite impinging on them: the *shikses* in white hats, the Sunday churchgoers walking to and from scarcely conceivable services. For Newark, *our* Newark, to exist for the imagination of strangers and of our own children, Newark would have to produce a writer as vulgar, comical, subtle, pathetic, and dirty as itself. He would have to be Jewish, un-genteel, emancipated from all limitations except those of memory and of the remembered city.

But by the mid-fifties, it was clearly too late for such a writer to appear. With prosperity, the city we had known, the city of *cheders* and lox, "Vote Communist" buttons and college boys working in shoestores, despair in gravel schoolyards and epiphanies in the open stacks, had long since disappeared. A prosperity more final than death had translated the very *yentes* from the brick stoops to the Beach Clubs of Livingston and even more unimaginable suburbs; had removed the sons of leatherworkers and the owners of candy stores to Bucknell or Ohio State or (God forbid!) Princeton. Those who had not lusted for the suburbs or college towns had dreamed of New York; and to each the best he could desire was granted. The houses, the lots, the hedges that had defined our Newark passed now into the possession of the Negroes, from whose midst the laureate would have to come that we had apparently not been able to bring to birth. At best, our Newark would be in the long life of the city, multiple and squalid as Troy's, the Newark *before* the Newark that had become a fact of literature; archaeologists would give us the proper number.

In Philip Roth's stories, however (how can he be only twenty-six?), my own remembered and archaic city survives, or more precisely, lives fully for the first time; I live fully for the first time the first twenty years of my life. Maybe he has only dreamed that world, reconstructed it on the basis of scraps of information recollected from conversations with cousins or older brothers or uncles; or maybe a real city only becomes a mythic one when it is already dead. No matter—he has dreamed truly. In his nightmare vision, that is, a Newark very like the one from which I still occasionally wake sweating has been rescued from history, oddly preserved. At the Little Theatre across the Park from the Museum, Hedy Lamar is still playing in *Ecstasy,* as she played for 39 weeks (or was it 79?) when I was sixteen. Through the landscape of "switchman's shacks, lumberyards, Dairy Queens, and used-car lots," Roth's characters still ascend the one hundred and eighty feet toward suburban coolness—the breath of air of which Newarkers vainly dream all summer long. For it is summer, of course, Newark's infernal season, in Mr. Roth's fictional city—and somebody's aunt and uncle are "sharing a Mounds bar in the cindery darkness of their alley, on beach chairs." It is possible to persuade oneself (though Roth does not say so) that with the proper coupon clipped from the Newark Evening News one could still get *three* transparent White Castle Hamburgers for a nickel.

I would not have believed I could feel nostalgia for the meager world Roth so improbably evokes, and I do not really believe it now; but there is a suspicious kind of satisfaction for me in knowing that world is fixed now forever in his gray authentic poetry. I can smell the sweat of my own lost August nights as I read *Goodbye, Columbus,* and am aware that I must be on guard lest, sentimentally and uncharacteristically (God knows!), I go out to meet Philip Roth more than halfway. I realize that because there is more Newark in the title piece of his book—more passionate social anthropology, rich as invention, depressing as fact, witty as the joke the survivors of Newark have had to make of their lives to live so long—it is for me the most moving of Roth's fictions. But I am convinced that my reaction is more than personal and eccentric.

There is more room in his single novella than in any of his shorter stories for nontheoretical life, for the painful wonder of what is given rather than the satisfactory aptness of what is (however skillfully) contrived to substantiate a point. Random and inexhaustible, such life is, after all, more the fictionist's business than any theme, even the rewardingly ironic and surely immortal one of how hard it is to be a Jew—quite differently elaborated in "Defender of the Faith," and "Eli the Fanatic." For the first, Philip Roth has already received the young Jewish writer's initial accolade: the accusation of anti-Semitism; and both stories are effective, convincing—the second even terrible in its reflections on how these days the holiest madness is "understood" and cured. But their terror and irony alike remain a little abstract—fading into illustrations of propositions out of Riesman, or pressed hard toward some not-quite-committed religious position. I should suppose that if Roth is to be as funny and as terrifying as he has the skill and insight to be, he must move out in the religious direction he has so far only indicated; but at the very least he must learn to risk a certain slovenliness, which in his short stories he evades with the nervousness of a compulsive house-cleaner. Other readers, I know, are more capable than I of responding to his pace, vigor and candor without the nagging sense that they are all a little compromised by something uncomfortably close to slickness; but I cannot deny that feeling in myself.

"Goodbye, Columbus" appeals to me, therefore, precisely because it is untidier than the rest, not so soon or so certainly in control. And in its generous margin of inadvertence, there is room enough for a mythical Newark, truth enough for the real one. In the end, "Goodbye, Columbus" does not quite work as a novella. Its plot (satisfactorily outrageous, but a little gimmicky and eked out with echoes of Mary McCarthy) and its themes tend to fall apart. Unlike some of the short stories, it evades rather than submits to these themes, perhaps because the author is afraid to submit to the old-fashioned motif of love across class lines which struggles to become its point. But love, desperate and foredoomed, love as a betrayal which takes itself for pleasure, is the only subject adequate to the city Roth has imagined. This he knows really, and *incidentally* has exploited fully even in "Goodbye, Columbus."

It is in its incidents rather than in its total structure that the novella comes alive. Its details are as vivid as its themes are inert, its properties more alive, perhaps, than its chief protagonists: the furniture which symbolizes status, refrigerators crammed absurdly with mountains of fruit, a jockstrap hung from the faucet of a bathtub, the record that gives the story its name. *Things* writhe, assert themselves, determine lives in a Dickensian frenzy. But some of the people who are possessed by them or subsist in the margins they leave free come alive, too—like Uncle Leo with his memories of the "oral love" which he learned from a girl called Hannah Schreiber at a B'nai Brith dance for servicemen, and which he exacted later from his wife, who was "up to here with Mogen David" after a Seder. "In fact, *twice* after Seders. Aachh! Everything good in my life I can count on my fingers." Here it seems to me is the profoundly atrocious pathos which is Roth's forte, his essential theme. Love in Newark! Beside it, the reminiscences of childhood, the anecdotes of peacetime army life, even the accounts of the disruption of the Jew's suburban truce with respectability come to seem of secondary importance—preludes to a main theme.

Even as the legendary city which Roth creates is one looked back to at its moment of dying, so is the love which is proper to it. In his fables, the young watch with horror and without sympathy the old yearning desperately for an idyll of sex, whose unreality the decay of their own flesh declares; or the old, sleepless, hear from their beds the zip-zip of the young making out on the downstairs couch. The latter is the subject of "Epstein," for me the most successful of the shorter pieces despite a last-minute concession to sentimentality as banal as the required ending of a box-office movie. Urged by spring, the copulation of the young and the imminent failure of his own flesh, Epstein reaches out for romance with, naturally, the lady across the street. But he moves toward love through the drab horror of Newark whose embodiment he is, sagging, frantic, rather dreaming lust than enduring it; and he ends, as he must, convinced that he has syphilis, facing the prospect of a divorce, overtaken by a heart attack in the very act of love. " . . . his eyes were closed, his skin grayer than his hair. . . . His tongue hung over his teeth like a dead snake." And his wife looms over him with the proper advice, "You hear the doctor, Lou. All you got to do is live a normal life." It should be the end, but Roth gives it away—concludes with a promise of recovery and reconciliation. "You can clean it up? 'So it'll never come back,' the doctor said. . . ."

But maybe even this is all right. Maybe it is better because more terrible to imagine Epstein living than dead: he and his Goldie on their beach-chairs, with their Mounds bars, "in the cindery darkness of their alley"—while their nephew speeds toward a failure as complete as Epstein's, though his dream of love has been transformed from the lady across the street to the girl in Briarpath Hills.

Newark! A Florence it will never be in the minds of men, nor a Baghdad nor a Paris; but after Roth, we can hope that perhaps it will survive on library shelves ravaged by ambitious boys as another Yonville or Winesburg, Ohio—another remembered name for the "cindery darkness" which men build around themselves and in whose midst they suffer the indignities of love.

—1959

# Antic Mailer–Portrait of a Middle-Aged Artist

SURELY THE MOST moving, truest, and saddest book to have appeared in the United States during the last year is Norman Mailer's *Advertisements for Myself*. It is a confession in the form of an anthology, an autobiography disguised as a running commentary on a chronologically arranged collection of Mailer's shorter writings over the past 20 years. There is a little of everything: short stories, newspaper columns, editorials, pseudo-poems, dramatic fragments. There are even selections from Mailer's already published novels (which he assumes, correctly, to have remained unread) and from one which he will clearly never finish.

There is the sense everywhere of a writer, baffled and near despair, trying for one last time to break through to the talent he dreamed he had at 17, to the audience he will not yet admit does not exist. Finally, and despite its occasional outbursts of apocalyptic hope, its praise of the Good Orgasm and the Hip Life, *Advertisements for Myself* is the story of the defeat of the writer in America—a work like, say, Griswold's *Life of Poe* or Edmund Wilson's recension of Scott Fitzgerald's *The Crackup*. Mailer, however, is his own Griswold and Wilson, denigrating critic and adulatory surviving friend all in one; and where he cannot himself provide sufficient occasion for self-hatred or self-pity, he draws on unfriendly reviews, nasty letters to the editor and accounts of private snubs.

"The shits are killing us," he tells us is the motto of his book; and there is evidence enough that he at least has been deeply wounded by the shits in whose world American writers now, as in the time of Poe or Fitzgerald, have to fight for survival. It is the failure of others, of the "squares," that Mailer chiefly describes: the timidity of publishers, the venality or condescension of popular and academic reviewers, the vulgar spite of the purveyors of popular culture. But he betrays also the inadequacy of the hip world he considers his own: its ignorance and insularity, its hysterical pursuit of sensation, its small rivalries and paranoid fantasies. Mailer himself appears to believe that a radio interviewer deliberately doctored a tape to make Mailer's voice sound thin and fruity, his own voice rich and assured. What else can he believe, being convinced that he somehow just missed sparking the Coming Sexual Revolution in the columns of a small-circulation newspaper run by a friend, that it is the fear of his hipster's code of marijuana, jazz, and the orgasm which has made the publication of his books so difficult?

Yet the case Mailer makes against our culture is strengthened rather than weakened by the provinciality and paranoia which cue his accusations. That his frantic dedication to honesty and the unmitigated ambition which has driven him all his life should eventuate in a case history rather than in triumph, this is the final terror, a guilt in which we are all involved. What is there to choose, we are compelled to ask, between resisting the values of our society and acceding to them, if one means writing, like Mailer, inchoate and sentimental articles in *Dissent* (e.g., "The White Negro"), and the other means composing dull appeals for cleaner television, like the article by Arthur Schlesinger Jr. in a recent *TV Guide?*

If there *were* a choice, I would, of course, stand with Mailer, whose enemies at least seem more like my own. But I cannot finally believe there is more than an illusion of choice; for I am haunted by a remembered scene, in which Schlesinger and an editor of *Dissent* are lounging at opposite ends of a fashionable Cape Cod beach and one cannot be sure to which party the Negro maid is hurrying with umbrella and baby bottle. Dying we surely are, but in a style to which it is hard to get accustomed!

As a matter of fact, it is precisely at the seaside in Wellfleet— and in the advertising offices among bright young sociologists, sure that they should be spending their time on something loftier than praising Coca-Cola—that a Mailer revival is now going on. "The conscience literature of the new $30,000-a-year men," one more than ordinarily self-conscious $30,000-a-year man recently called Mailer's novels; and it is this new popularity which Mailer has *not* come to terms with in the present book. It is a final irony before which even he flinches that he—who began as a middlebrow best-seller, then lapsed into obscurity—returns to popularity among a minority who find in his simple-minded intransigence on the subject of sex a metapolitics compatible with their own loss of youth and poverty. Such readers turn to Mailer not as a good writer, but as a rebel whose rebellion threatens (alas) nothing.

Indeed, Mailer is not a really first-rate novelist at all—and it is here that the pathos of his exemplary position is compounded. *The Naked and the Dead* is a cliché-ridden rewrite of the standard post-World War I protest novel, its villain-general half *Daily Worker* Fascist and half G.I. faggot. One is not surprised to learn in this volume that the book had been half-conceived by the undergraduate Mailer before he had ever left Harvard to go to the war. *Barbary Shore* is a belated thirties novel dissolved into incoherence by a hysteria irrelevant to its politics. And *The Deer Park,* for all its evident honesty, loses its sexual point amid the stereotypes of two decades of anti-Hollywood attitudinizing. Only now is Mailer beginning to escape from the limitations of the middlebrow protest novel, as he takes up—late as usual—the cause of the hipster and Reichian genitality.

Perhaps the best thing he has ever written is the outrageous and hilarious account (blow by blow and smell by smell) of a fore-doomed sexual encounter between a culturally pretentious coed (in analysis) and a sexual athlete, whose vanity and obtuseness one hopes Mailer perceives. Called in this collection "The Time of Her Time," the story will presumably be part of an immense novel, whose introduction, incredibly vacuous, concludes this book; and its protagonist is that same Sergius O'Shaugnessy who appeared in *The Deer Park.* Sergius was first imagined, we learn in these pages, as a mythically potent hero dreamed by "a small, frustrated man, a minor artist *manqué.*" But he has unfortunately come to seem real to Mailer—not the embodiment of nostalgia for the unimaginable perfect orgasm but that orgasm made flesh. Without his counterfoil outside the dream he is the least credible male in modern fiction.

In *Advertisements,* however, the dreamer excluded from Mailer's fiction returns under the name of Norman Mailer, a real Hero of Our Time, the artist *manqué* unnerved alike by success and failure, reminded by his wife of how continually he goofs, endlessly engaged in persuading himself that he is tough, although he can never forget he had to learn to fight from books. The Harvard Boy as Hipster and ex-Celebrated Author, he is put down by everyone: writers of letters to the papers, homosexual editors, TV interviewers —and not least of all by his amused, agonized, critical self.

Almost tenderly he anthologizes the insults of minor enemies and the rebuffs of those from whom most of all he wanted love— even the two writers whose child he feels himself, Hemingway and Faulkner. Tremulously, he sent *The Deer Park* to Hemingway, with an inscription asking for a reaction and with a proud, foolish warning that "if you do not answer . . . I will never attempt to communicate with you again." The package to which he entrusted book and love letter came back marked: "Address Unknown—Return to Sender."

With Faulkner, it was a little different, though the final result was not dissimilar. Not Mailer but an alert editor sent to the older writer Mailer's comment that "the white man fears the sexual potency of the Negro." Faulkner responded to this not-very-useful cliché that he had often heard the idea expressed "though not before by a man. The others were ladies . . . usually around 40 to 45 years of age." It was a stand-off: Mailer, who had over the air called Eisenhower a "woman," had been answered in kind, but he could not resist a last retort. His embarrassingly jejune answer does not matter: what counts is the fact that in painful candor he reports it with the rest of the interchange—completing to the final pathetic detail the Portrait of the Artist as a Middle-Aged Man, in which a generation can see itself and squirm: the unfulfilled writer, contemptuous of his peers, rebuffed by the mass audience, read by slobs and snubbed by the few elders he admires. Only a fool would confess to recognizing himself in such an image; but Mailer has had the final intelligence—or grace—to play for the world that torments him precisely such a fool—almost, indeed, the Fool.

—1960

# NINE

# Marx and Momma

IT BECOMES clearer and clearer these days that one of the chief functions of the sixties is somehow to rediscover, re-invent, redeem the thirties which, for the two decades before our own, seemed at a maximum distance from us—remote, unavailable. But the thirties were, of course, the period in which Jews were becoming, for the first time, spokesmen for America, or at least for that sentimental radicalism which best reflected the Depression mood of the United States. Michael Gold's *Jews Without Money* embodied that mood in fiction and Clifford Odets' *Waiting for Lefty* and *Awake and Sing* gave it form on the stage, both exploiting the rhythms of Jewish-American speech and the patterns of the Jewish-American family. What a strange marriage we celebrated then, without quite knowing it, between Karl Marx and the Jewish Mother.

But we can begin to know it now—in an age when everyone has read Henry Roth's *Call It Sleep* and Ph.D. candidates begin to write theses on Nathanael West; an age in which we are ready for Alfred Kazin's reminiscences of that decade and the confrontation most characteristic of it, between what he calls the "typical writers of the Twenties . . . rebels from 'good' families—Dos Passos, Hemingway, Fitzgerald, Cummings, Wilson, Cowley" and the "writers of the Thirties . . . from the working class, the lower class, the immigrant class . . . ," often enough, though not exclusively, the encounter of certain WASPS about to be driven from their positions of power and young Jews, like Kazin, about to make it in America on, to be sure, the highest cultural level.

Kazin's *Starting Out in the Thirties* is not entirely satisfactory as a unified work, moving erratically between personal reminis-

128

cence, capsule literary criticism and social history, but it is a fascinating record, a reminder of how radical politics and *avant-garde* book-reviewing became for the first time in the thirties a method of social climbing, especially viable for young Jews; and of how consequently, our own age of professors and pundits was in fact born.

But Kazin's book aspires to be more than a social record, indeed works best when it comes close to passing over into fiction —in the family scenes, for instance, dealing with his Cousin Sophie, which remind us of his more generally successful first book of reminiscences, *A Walk in the City.* I felt all through the book's scant length a tension between the logic of the material, which aspired to become a novel, and the caution of the writer, not finally trusting his own talent, or not able somehow to attain total honesty in regard to certain personal events that contain the book's truest meanings. The prose itself passes from delicacy and passion to a kind of virtuous woodenness every time the author withdraws from what is most dark, difficult and personal and commits himself to mere literary comment.

Nonetheless, if one is looking for a sense of what it was like to be alive and reading, ambitious, and literate in the thirties, Kazin's little book is an admirable guide. But how much pathos there is in the lapsed reputations of writers like Farrell and Saroyan, whose failed fame Kazin memorializes, or the evocation of an era in which it was possible to think Ralph Bates a great writer, and books like Malraux's *Man's Fate* or Silone's *Fontamara* masterpieces. From the vantage point of the sixties, one remembers that while Silone was being celebrated, the first translations of Alberto Moravia were going absolutely unnoticed in the United States, and relishes the dramatic irony of a note in Kazin's account of a meeting with James T. Farrell about a "young man comfortably draped on the couch" in Farrell's apartment who turned out to be Nathanael West.

A book Kazin does not at all mention, though it appeared in English in 1933 under the title of *The Sinner* and had stirred considerable popular response, is I. J. Singer's *Yoshe Kalb,* just now reissued under its original name and with an introduction by Singer's younger brother, Isaac Bashevis Singer, that darling of the sixties. In the few months since its publication, *Yoshe Kalb* appears to have stirred little or no enthusiasm, though it seems to me on re-reading even more moving and honest than I had remembered it—containing among other things one of the most magnificent portraits of an old country Jewish Bovary that I know.

We live, however, at a moment uncongenial to I. J. Singer's icy and uncompromising rationalism, his impatience with the world of *yiddishkeit* (he strove desperately for a while to find another language to write in) and especially with *chasidism,* about which we have learned—via Buber among others—to be sentimental and nostalgic. There is something ironical about the older Singer returning to us under the auspices of the younger, whose belief in demons we find so much more compatible with our own life than his brother's belief in reason. Nonetheless, *Yoshe Kalb* remains a rich and terrifying book, a vision of a world in decadence, ridden by corrupt and semiliterate rabbis, plagued by its own repressed lusts, but somehow redeemed by its longing to mythologize its experience in a way with which I. J. Singer found it harder than we do to sympathize—yet managed to all the same.

But this year sees the attempted revival of another thirties Jewish writer, also absent from the pages of Kazin's book; for just as he scants I. J. Singer in favor, say, of Malraux, so also he ignores Meyer Levin in favor of Edward Dahlberg, Albert Halper, Henry Roth, Daniel Fuchs, not to mention *goyim* like Henry Miller and Nelson Algren. Yet with the publication of *The Stronghold,* an attempt both historical and allegorical to come to terms with the Nazi experience, and Levin's fifteenth published book, his publishers have launched a campaign to get for him the critical acclaim they obviously (and he, too, of course must concur) feel his due. A pamphlet called "Meyer Levin at 60" lays out the history of his career and cites some of the praise he has been accorded from sources as various as Albert Einstein and Nelson Algren.

Moved by all this, I have been rereading him—not, to be sure, all of his books, which is a task beyond the scope of weak mortality, but much here and there; and once again, I rise from his work baffled. His books are not egregiously false; not embarrassingly inept; they deal with important subjects without unduly trivializing them; they are, in fact (after the false start of his first two novels, *Reporter* and *Frankie and Johnnie),* a continuing valiant effort to close with the meanings of being Jewish in an era which begins with the Leopold and Loeb Case and reaches a double climax with the defeat of Hitler and the emergence of the State of Israel. And if honesty and energy were enough, Levin would be—as he is not, alas—a writer of the first rank.

There is perhaps an unseemly hunger for violence in Levin, reflected in his sympathy with the Stern Gang and his obsession with Leopold and Loeb (though the book I admire most of all he has written is the fictional account of those two premature hipsters, *Compulsion); and* certainly there is a desire for establishing a version of heroism most critical readers find a little dismaying in an age when the antihero, the *shlemiel* as invented by Nathanael West and perfected by a host of latter-day imitators, seems more suitable to the meanings of our time. But it is finally a failure of language, an inability to rise above flatness to anything but vehemence and shrillness that keeps his work from kindling the imagination. *The Old Bunch,* published in 1937, remains still his major bid, his most substantial creation, but compared even to Farrell's *Studs Lonigan* trilogy (a book whose evaluation has continued to sag), it seems unforgivably dull, pulled by the banality of the world it imagines and should redeem into a corresponding banality.

## Theater

There is some nostalgia for the thirties in the theater, too. Herbert Blau, for instance, insisting that the kind of moment he would like to recover for his Repertory Theatre at Lincoln Center is the one at the end of the original production of *Waiting for Lefty,* when the whole audience arose and yelled with the players "Strike!" Chiefly, however, the theater seems to clutch desperately at contemporaneity, the issue of the moment: which is, to be sure, race relations, or more specifically, *The Negro and the Jew.* This *chic* topic Howard Da Silva and company have introduced into the stage version of Dan Jacobson's *The Zulu and the Zayda*—Jacobson spelled it "zeide," but the change of spelling is the least among the degrading transformations of his material the vulgar and stupid play of almost the same name has achieved.

I should begin in all fairness by saying that the performance of Menasha Skulnick as the "zayda" or "zeide," as the case may be, is —though occasionally too cute—on the whole absolutely charming; and if the play could have been redeemed, he would have done so. But even his professional magic palls after what seems like hour upon hour of saying the most utterly banal things possible in *yiddish* (the very sound of which appears to break up the nostalgic audience), and then painfully translating them into English for the benefit of the *goyim,* if any, present. Only a mind childish enough to find inexhaustible fun in a large black African speaking our *mammeloshen* should subject himself to the play; though there is, to be sure, much pious material about race relations inserted between jokes, complete with explanatory sermons. The point of the whole self-righteous parable seems to be that all problems of *apartheid* in South Africa could be resolved if only a kindly old grandfather from the *shtetl* could confront a noble-hearted Zulu out of the *kraal,* and the two could trip through the streets of Johannesburg holding hands like young lovers.

Anybody interested in the original story, however, in which the Zulu wears a beard, the grandfather, who is not kindly, pees in bed, and there are no painfully explicit reflections on race relations, can find it in a recent collection called *Modern Jewish Stories* and edited by Gerda Charles. It is an oddly assorted anthology, containing things as bad as the unspeakable Hyman Kaplan stories of Leo Rosten and the hopelessly sentimental parable of Irwin Shaw, "Act of Faith"; but the original Jacobson study of a struggle between father and son that ends in virtual patricide is there, plus the not easily available story "The Hand that Fed Me," by Isaac Rosenfeld, whose fiction we are likely—to our loss—to forget exists.

## Films

Oddly enough, race relations provide the main theme for the recent Israeli film *Sallah,* too. As a matter of fact, all that is most ticklish and difficult in Israeli life is touched on in this marvelously courageous movie, which, however, finks out at the very end with a conventional and unconvincing happy ending: the Israelis' contempt for the American Jews who subsidize them, the frittering away of the ideal of the *kibbutz* in endless ideological wrangling and the hiring of *Schwarzers* (well, black Jews anyhow) to do the hard labor, the permanence of "temporary housing," etc., etc.

I had expected nothing from the film, since the first Israeli movie I had ever seen—an incredible horse opera with the Israeli-cowboys beating out the Arab-Redskins—was so bad that I had decided Jewish moviemakers somehow mysteriously lost their skills in Israel. But *Sallah* turned out to be fast-moving, well-photographed, truly witty and marvelously acted, especially by Haym Topol who plays the title role. This film, too, has its share of jokes based on the use of Yiddish, but how different they are—the leader of a kibbutz for instance, whose Hebrew is ponderous and full of the loftiest abstractions, slipping into the *mammeloshen* when he counts out money. A little cruel to the tradition of *yiddishkeit,* perhaps, but no crueller than to American tourists, Israeli politicians, graft, fixed elections, and rigid bureaucracies in general.

Only Sallah himself emerges as a fully lovable figure, a kind of Oriental Jewish Old Black Joe, shiftless and conniving, noble-hearted and incorrigibly lazy by nature, earning a living by no work other than taking his Ashkenazi neighbor at backgammon day after day; but a criticism in his essence of the striving and progressive world into which the ingathering has plunged him. Of course, the writer of comedy can have it both ways; and so Ephraim Kishon, author of the script, does here, finally accepting the world his irony undercuts, and resolving his own contradictions by marrying off the children of the Black Jew, Sallah, to proper "white" *kibbutzniks*. It is an ending as easy and false in its way as that Howard Da Silva provides for the racial struggle in South Africa; but, after all, it is not the function of popular entertainers to solve the problems of ethnic conflict in Israel or the United States or Africa, only to charm us into believing in the darkness of the theater that we can dream them away. From this deluding dream great fiction and poetry must awaken us—and for this, too, we wait.

—1966

# TEN

# Some Jewish Pop Art Heroes

IT WAS in 1913 that little Mary Phagan was killed, a thirteen-year-old factory girl, her attempted rape fumbled but her head successfully bashed in, and though it seems painfully clear now that her assailant was a Negro, her boss, a young Jew called Leo Frank, was convicted in court of her murder and lynched for it shortly thereafter. That was 1915, the war already begun which was to cut us off forever from that time of relative innocence; and Americans were going in large numbers to see *The Birth of a Nation,* greatest of all American moving pictures and storehouse of all the most vicious anti-Negro stereotypes. But just those Georgia rednecks, who should have contented themselves with an orgy of hating niggers and cheering the Ku Klux Klan under the auspices of D. W. Griffith, were letting the shiftless and violent Negro whose testimony doomed Frank slip through their fingers in order to indulge stereotypes more deeply buried in the depths of their psyches than any fantasies about Black sexuality. Harry Golden tells us that only a couple of decades ago, back-country performers were still singing the ballad he prints as an appendix to his best-selling book on the Frank Case *(A Little Girl Is Dead),* a ballad which justifies the lynching as sacred revenge against the Jews.

> Leo Frank he met her
> With a brutish heart and grin;
> He says to little Mary,
> "You'll never see home again."
> Judge Roan he passed the sentence;
> He passed it very well;

The Christian doers of heaven
Sent Leo Frank to hell . . .

But why, Harry Golden is worrying all these years later, did the crowd malice of the Deep South, egged on by the rhetoric of Tom Watson, a splendid Populist leader gone sour and turned into nigger-baiter *par excellence,* why did it prefer the Jew to the Negro, given a clear choice? True enough, Frank behaved oddly in his first encounters with the police, appeared guilty of something (though God knows what), evasive, shifty; and by all accounts he seems to have been a singularly unappealing young man. Besides, he was clearly identified as a "capitalist," doubly a capitalist, since to the *lumpen* Socialist mind of the American Populist capitalist equals Jew, and the two together add up to demidevil. And in certain regards, the record seems to bear them out; for Frank did hire child labor, did work it disgracefully long hours at pitifully low wages; and if he did not (as popular fancy imagined) exploit his girls sexually, he walked in on their privacy with utter contempt for their dignity. Like most factory managers of his time, he was—metaphorically at least—screwing little girls like Mary Phagan; and in the undermind of the uneducated the line between metaphor and fact is blurred.

Besides, the kind of Georgians who lynched Frank were the inheritors of a folk tradition in which the Jew had been defined through centuries of song and story as the child-murderer. That tradition had been strong enough to influence great poets like Chaucer and Shakespeare and to create a score of ballads still sung in the rural South, so why should it not have moved the jurors, even before Frank's own lawyer had made the mistake of raising the issue of his Jewishness, and erupted finally in the fury of the lynch mob? In European folk art, the Jew is a villain of a special kind, and before World War I the mind of back-country America was still folk and European; but in American Pop Art (which he plays a decisive role in creating) the Jew is a hero, like Golden himself: successful pop artist and pop idol—to the Gentiles, of course, as well as the Jews—at the same time. No wonder Norman Mailer, fighting the hard fight of the serious writer, who bucks rather than embodies the stereotypes of the mass audience, wrote plaintively once:

"If/Harry Golden/is the Gentile's Jew/can I be-/come the Golden/Goy?" This shift of the Jew from archetypal "Baddie" to mythological "Goodie," and its connection with the shift from folk culture to mass culture is immensely important yet almost totally ignored by literary critics like Irving Malin (in *Jews and Americans,* Southern Illinois University Press), who is committed to defining the nature of the Jewish experience in the United States.

Yet Malin does not mention Harry Golden, for instance, much less other Jewish Pop Art Heroes like Lenny Bruce, Sammy Davis, Jr., Jack Ruby, or Superman. Trying to fit Philip Roth and six other writers (Bellow, Malamud, Karl Shapiro, etc.) into his own seven categories (Exile, Time, Irony, Parable, etc.), he does not find an occasion for treating the difficult and essential subject I have been trying to define. Perhaps this is because "vulgarity" is not one of his rubrics, and it is the vivid and perdurable vulgarity of the Jews (so embarrassing to our official apologists) which lies at the heart of Pop Culture. No Jew on his own would have invented —thank God—the notion of a gentleman, but some Jews invented Miami Beach, some the commercial Musical Comedy, and two, Jerome Siegel and Joe Shuster, the Comic Book—or at least, the first Great Comic Book Hero of them all, Superman.

We live now at a point where the generation (they must be somewhere between twenty-five and thirty-five) that grew up on the classic Comic Book is memorializing it; making a smash success out of the revived Bat Man on TV (pop art wryly remembered is Camp, a kind of genteel tribute to vulgarity); and, I hope, buying in vast quantities the annotated anthology of the genre recently put together by Jules Feiffer, himself a veteran vulgarian *(The Great Comic Book Heroes).*

Jules Feiffer loves the comic books a little better than he understands them, missing, I think, the essential point that they are a special kind of "junk" in the history of subart: *urban junk*—their imagined world simply the city, and their heroes city boys or losers in the very world that makes and peddles the comics (Superman is in "real life" an unsuccessful reporter). But the dreamers in the city are, almost inevitably, Jews—and it is their fantasies by which a generation or two lived, their fantasies by which they discovered they could make it in this Gentile world: beginning in school, let's say, by drawing the pictures erotic or heroic, which their inept neighbors needed to see before they were quite sure what they were dreaming.

Not only Will Eisner's seedy *The Spirit* was Jewish, as Feiffer sees; but all of those more WASPish looking Superfellows, though on another level. They are Jewish versions of the Goy, idealized portraits of the Gentile boy who beats up the Jewish one (no wonder so many of their fictional victims had long noses and puttered about laboratories)—quite like, on their level, Bellow's Henderson or Mailer's Sergius O'Shaughnessy. Did we love them or hate them, those dumb sluggers in their lodge regalia? The answer is there in the record as Feiffer sees quite clearly when dealing with their female opposite numbers, who remind us of that other perfect bully out of the nightmares of our childhood: Mama. ". . . Wonder Woman . . . was every Jewish boy's unfantasied picture of the world as it really was. You mean men were not wicked and weak? . . . You mean women didn't have to be *stronger* than men to survive in this world? Not in *my* house?"

Once he has projected his oppressor as his secret self, however, the Jewish writer, on a pop level or any other, is likely to get in trouble; end like Norman Mailer—or Lenny Bruce—forgetting that he is only Jerome Siegel imagining he is Clark Kent dreaming that he can reveal himself as Superman, and coming to believe that there is only himself, i.e., Super-Jew. Lenny Bruce's autobiography *(How to Talk Dirty and Influence People)* does not take us to the point where he recently fell out of a hotel window, after having capered madly about the room and lifted an imaginary cape, screaming, "I'm Super-Jew." But it does take us through some of his earlier disguises as an Oriental mystic, Roman Catholic priest, transvestite sailor, still uncertain of his destiny as victim, persecuted truth-teller, gross and grotesque prophet—his passion called obscenity, and his madness drug addiction. There is a streak of self-dramatizing sentimentality in Lenny Bruce that tempts him to see himself as Jesus Christ; but there is a saving vulgarity, too, which impels him to realize that he is rather a Comic Book Hero who cannot fly. That vulgarity I'm sure he would be pleased to think of as Jewish; for he is (with scarcely any Jewish education or even background, certainly none of the kind generally called "positive") much concerned with sorting out the world into what he thinks of as its primary categories: "Evaporated milk is goyish even if the Jews invented it. Chocolate is Jewish and fudge is goyish. Spam is goyish and rye bread is Jewish. Negroes are all Jews. Italians are all Jews. Irishmen who have rejected their religion are Jews. Mouths are very Jewish. And bosoms. Baton-twirling is very goyish." In his sense at least, it is still hard to be a Jew; and perhaps the chief value of his book (along with the thousand bitter laughs it provides) is to remind us of this fact.

No one would suspect it, on the other hand, reading Sammy Davis, Jr.'s autobiography; for though, like Lenny Bruce, he is an entertainer who has turned himself into a Pop Art Hero, he is one who has made it—in part, he would have us believe, by identifying with the Good Medicine of Judaism. Waking from a difficult and successful operation, he finds "a clear outline of the Star of David" impressed on his palm from a religious medallion he was clutching; he wears a mezuzah, given him by Eddie Cantor, around his neck and charms everyone; he gains the respect of Sam Goldwyn by refusing to work on Yom Kippur; he wins a beautiful *shiksa* for his wife, who then converts to Judaism and their wedding is a B. O. smash! Yet all through it of course, he is a Negro. Under such circumstances, who wouldn't be a Jew!

His book *(Yes I Can),* though professionally written in that insipid ghost style which robs truth of conviction and fact of reality, is not without interest. For somehow the picture of a vain, driven, essentially unlovable man, at odds with his own Negro community (and what disheartening glimpses we have of their columnists, reporters, and millionaires) and himself, emerges, a gifted entertainer who betrays almost everything and everybody but is blessed with success; and who—in this age of strange conversions—imagines that to begin to become "all right," one must become a Jew. I saw, for my sins, the production of *Golden Boy* just now closing in New York, an utterly incredible revision of Odets' soupy play about Jews updated to get the box office that only Negro drama gets these days; and in the midst of it all Sammy Davis, trying to live the part he acted, a Negro turned Jew being the John Garfield of the sixties. And remembering, of course, Marilyn Monroe and Elizabeth Taylor, I found myself slipping away into a daydream in which Frank Sinatra (second only unto Jehovah in Sammy Davis' pantheon) would end up playing Frankie Alpine in the movie made of Bernard Malamud's *The Assistant,* and insisting upon being really circumcized in the last scene where that character becomes a Jew. And then there would be no goyim left at all in the world of pop culture, not a single one. . . .

But walking down the street afterward, I saw the lines queued up before *Thunderball* and realized that James Bond at least was left, the last of the WASP heroes, as goyish as fudge or twirler girls: something for us to imagine ourselves when we grew weary of the mythic burden of our Jewishness. My relief did not last long, however; for just as there is (in the local drugstore, supermarket, airport newsstand) a Fanny Hillman of our own these days for every one of *their* Fanny Hills, I discovered there is also an Israel Bond, OY-OY-7, the sort-of hero of *Loxfinger,* which surely must rank with the worst books ever written. I will not let chauvinism drive me to calling it unequivocally *the* worst; but if you have wondered where all the weary Semitic jokes went since Hitler scared them out of the goyim they are here (along with Hitler himself), in such a context of Borsht Belt good humor that one must take them as innocently proffered. Next to Sol Weinstein, author of *Loxfinger,* Henny Youngman seems like Oscar Wilde; and it takes a considerable effort to remember the immemorial principle that, despite everything, a Jew has a right to make a living.

Vulgarity passes over into grossness not by excess but by cold-blooded commercial manipulation. What could be more vulgar, for instance, yet still pathetic at least, perhaps even tragic, than Jack Ruby who wanted, like any kid reading *Superman,* to be a hero, too; and even got the chance to do it on television. John Kaplan and Jon R. Waltz have written their recent study of the case *(The Trial of Jack Ruby)* to analyze courtroom strategies, not the vagaries of mass culture; but it is the latter that impressed and disheartened me as I made my way through their book: NBC offering to pick up the tab if Ruby would hire the real-life original of TV's *Sam Benedict;* Judge Brown's public denial of the manuscript about the case by which he hoped to make his fortune; Ruby's lawyers bootlegging pictures of him to sell to *Life,* etc., etc.

In his own deepest consciousness, however, Ruby wanted to sell nothing, only to show the world (on television if possible) that "Jews do have guts," that under his own improbable guise Super-

Jew really lived and would avenge the President that had been kind
to his people. Once convicted and, he felt, vilified, however, it was
quite other fantasies that possessed Ruby's poor paranoid head:
fantasies that "all the Jews in America were being slaughtered,"
"twenty-five million innocent people," and that even his brother
Sam was being "tortured, horribly mutilated, castrated and burned
in the street outside the jail"—that the Jew had, in fact, become
Leo Frank again because he had failed to be Superman.

But Ruby is, of course, wrong. No crowds are gathering for his
lynching or his brother's; and if any ballads are being made now,
they concern not his guilt but his plight, are sung not by rednecks
from the hills but urban folk singers, Jews like Bobby Dylan, the
inventors of "folk-rock," who surely celebrate him something like
this:

> I didn't raise my chubby, sweet,
>     brown-eyed balding boy
> To go out and overdo the doin's
>     of some goy.
> He murdered a man on TV
> They say he has shot another.
> Won't you give some thought to
>     poor Jack Ruby's mother.

—1966

# ELEVEN

# This Year We Are Slaves—
# Next Year We Shall Be Free

To say who the Jews are, to speculate about what the Jews will become (or, alternatively, what will become of the Jews), to remember what the Jews were—surely these have always been the obsessive tasks of those who by that very token we have continued to call
Jews. But when these preoccupations become the center of a novelist's concern, he is driven to attempt that most difficult of forms of
fiction, the historical novel; and it is precisely four historical novels,
four *Jewish* historical novels (plus a pair of Jewish historical films)
about which I have been pondering over the past couple of weeks.

The longest and most ambitious (and by all odds the worst) of
the lot is by a non-Jew, who, despite his detached position, seems to
have been as deeply troubled in his genteel, liberal soul as any genteel, liberal Jew by the two recent events which trouble all the writers with whom I am dealing—the atrocious fact of Hitler's rise and
fall on the one hand, and the ambiguous triumph of Israel on the
other. It is with Israel that James Michener is primarily concerned;
and in *The Source* he uses the device of an archeological dig to
take us back via a series of historical flashbacks some 100,000
years into the past of what used to be called the Holy Land. Even
as popular archeology, this book seems to me dull and thin—the
thickest thin book I have read. Mr. Michener sees the toughness
and courage of the Israelis all right, just as he sees their most difficult problems (discrimination against "Black Jews," tyranny of an
Orthodox rabbinate, etc., etc.), but somehow none of this hurts him

141

enough, ultimately concerned as he is with the pale, Protestant question: how can Judaism remain a valid religion after the appearance of the Christian Church.

Even Stephen Longstreet's *Pedlock and Sons,* for all its commitment to the weariest middlebrow banalities about the meaning of American life and all its obvious popular appeal (lots of outward action, old-fashioned heavy-handed plotting and explicit sex), says a little more about what it feels like to be conscious of one's self as a Jew than Mr. Michener's blandly righteous book. It is about the American scene, of course, that Mr. Longstreet writes, of how the Jews made it in America, and what they did when they got there. But even in his more modest attempt, he has trouble assimilating his gobbets of historical information. For me, the journal entries were an invitation to skipping I could not resist.

Dan Jacobson's attempt in *The Beginners* to do an analogous family saga of the Jews in South Africa is much more sober and serious, the work of a much more gifted writer, though I suspect his gifts qualify him for humor and gentle pathos rather than for the ambitious solemnities of this novel which is profoundly unexciting, technically unadventurous, unforgivably well behaved. Surely the emigration of Jews from the Pale to the New World of South Africa, from South Africa to England and Israel, much less their spiritual wanderings from Orthodoxy to Marxism and Zionism and back to Orthodoxy again cannot be that dull.

Mr. Bassani's *The Garden of the Finzi-Continis* is the slimmest and tightest of the books I have been reading—the most deceptively modest, and finally the most successful. A description of the last days of a Jewish community in a provincial Italian city, Bassani's book stays in the mind with a peculiar persistence. It creates not real Jews, perhaps, but the ghosts of real Jews—as unheroic, tentative and ridden by vanity as any of us, but no more deserving surely of being dead.

To resist the impulse toward the heroic in recalling the recent Jewish past requires a kind of quiet heroism which Bassani, in fact, possesses. Not so the authors (script writer, producer, director) of *Cast a Giant Shadow,* which attempts to memorialize the creation of the State of Israel in what moviemakers like to call "epic" terms

—and which has drafted for its purposes such prototypes of heroism on the screen as John Wayne and Kirk Douglas (the latter casting off at last his *goyish* camouflage and playing the Jewish "jock" he really is). In the end, what was hard enough to believe to begin with is made even more incredible. But perhaps it is the function of the "big movie" to make the truth seem false enough to bear.

How much better the antiheroic tact of *The Shop on Main Street* which plays out the immediate events of the destruction of Mid-European Jewry as if seen through the wrong end of a telescope, reduced in size but increased in intensity of focus. This extraordinary Czech film has just been awarded an Oscar, which seems to me even more extraordinary, since I, at least, expect the Academy Awards to go unerringly where they belong, to standard mediocrity of high technical excellence. But perhaps even in Hollywood there are ceremonial occasions when vice pays tribute to virtue.

Each of these works involves dreaming as well as remembering, evoking, side by side with its political memories, erotic dreams. In *The Source,* the contemporary plot is actually a parable in which a beautiful Israeli archeologist hesitates long over which of three contenders she shall marry: a fellow Israeli, a Catholic American or (a dark horse who enters at the last moment) a rich American Jew. And when this improbable Hebrew Astarte casts her lot with the last, leaves Israel for Chicago, and the pioneer life for suburbia, she expresses surely Michener's own final uneasiness with Israel and the female sexuality he deems appropriate to it.

*Pedlock and Sons* is sexier by far, possessed not by the author's dreams of a Gentile for whom the Jewish girl represents the forbidden sexual object, but the bolder fantasies of a Jew for whom the *shiksa* plays an analogous mythological role; and there are *shiksas* aplenty in its pages—red-haired secretaries, luscious Armenian spies, etc., etc. The best and most auspicious sex in the novel, however, turns out to involve two nice Jewish kids, leading them on to marriage (the girl protests loudly at one point that she is *not* Marjorie Morningstar, but she fools no one).

Dan Jacobson has a harder time being fashionably frank about sex; for despite the assurance of the book jacket that its world is one "of sexual explicitness and racial conflicts," it is really resolutely old-fashioned and muted by archaic reticences.

Perhaps the essential virtue of Bassani's book is that it allows its love story, its dream of love, to make its point without burying it beneath a ponderous superstructure of sociological or political observations.

As everyone knows, however, the real dream girl of the Jewish boy—whether he writes books or not—is his mother; and we are not surprised to find that in both Longstreet's and Jacobson's novels the Beloved who binds the fiction together in feeling and form is the Matriarch. In *Pedlock and Sons* she is, to be sure, more Wife of Bath than standard Jewish Mother; but in *The Beginners* she returns in her conventional form, one whose erotic longing, baffled in her husband, is invested ambiguously in her sons. And Jacobson, aware of her mythological dimensions, even calls her Sarah.

One of the two chief characters of *The Shop on Main Street* is a Jewish-Mother-without-a-son gone senile, who blindly takes in as her substitute son a poor goy, who in turn thinks of himself as exploiting her under cover of the anti-Semitic regulations of the Czech Nazi puppet government. He is, however, not very good at exploiting, this simple-minded peasant, though under pressure he turned out to be (like all of us) adequate enough at betrayal—thus acting out not only the role of the Bad Gentile Neighbor at the time of the Holocaust, but of the Bad Jewish Son at any time.

Indeed, I suspect that part of the enormous appeal of the movie may depend precisely on its stirring the guilt feelings planted in all of us by *our* mothers—along with its portrait of evil personified in the too-sexual wife of the protagonist, its appeal to the audience to cheer or at least grimly approve when at long last he beats the hell out of her. What could be more American, or Jewish for that matter, more Jewish-American, more universal at the moment, than simultaneously to hate the wife, love mama, and deplore the death of Europe's Jews. Maybe, after all, only an Academy Award can signify how terrifyingly near to all of our ugly hearts this beautifully rendered fable comes.

—1966

# TWELVE

# Myths of the Jews on Stage and Screen

IT IS NOT easy to lie about what happened at Auschwitz now that the facts are known, but Peter Weiss in *The Investigation* has managed to do so—and for this he must be given, I suppose, some kind of credit though his method is simple and not original with him. He has merely removed from the story—the Jews. His carefully edited text, drawn from the records of a trial of Nazi war criminals held in Frankfurt between January 1964 and August 1965, omits the word "Jew" as if somehow it were irrelevant or, worse, misleading; as if the bulk of the four million victims destroyed there were Jews only by accident or mistake. I do not believe, as do some more charitable reviewers of his play, that he desires to universalize the terrible events which reached their climax in the gas chambers and ovens. Far from it; the Soviet Union is mentioned quite specifically over and over along with the names of certain large industrial concerns, so that finally we are left with the impression that what really happened to the six million under Hitler was only an incident in the class struggle, or more precisely the clash between German Big Business and the Communist Party. But rendered in light of this simple-minded Marxist interpretation of Nazism, what happened at Auschwitz seems trivialized, desecrated, profaned.

We need a myth of Hitlerism, all right, some large archetypal view in which all that is merely bureaucratic or narrowly political or simply sadistic in the appalling record will be raised to a level above journalism and pornography; but Party-line propaganda will

145

not do. To be sure, one member of the small audience present on the night I attended the play was moved to rise in the balcony and scream: "The United States is doing exactly the same thing, using gas and killing children in Vietnam!" I presume, however, he had brought his politics with him and was merely taking advantage of the occasion to force those foolish enough to be present to endure yet one more small indignity. Never mind the feeble-minded politics, in any case, the obtuseness which made me almost ashamed for the moment of my own opposition to the War in Vietnam; what mattered much more was the gratuitous second destruction of German Jewry, the erasing from history of those history had already killed. And for this, Communist politics (with its own bad conscience about the Jews) is only partly to blame, since Peter Weiss is apparently the victim of a personal hang-up in this regard. I heard him last year, for instance, speaking at Princeton under the auspices of the *Gruppe '47,* deliver a long conversion speech, explaining how he had come to see the light about what was going on in Germany—in which also he did not ever use the word Jew; and I understood for the first time (began to understand, at least) why he pretended that his earlier play about Marx and Freud, which is to say, about a pair of ex-Jews, was actually a dialogue between two unexceptionable *goyim,* Marat and the Marquis de Sade. Peter Brook's splendid version of that first drama, the extraordinary passion and color of the production, had concealed from me Weiss's real limitations: his deficient sense of drama, his banality on the level of ideas, his sick fascination with horror, and his crippling fear of his own Jewishness. The latter two are surely part of the heritage of Hitlerism, telling an implicit truth about Weiss and his world, that on an explicit level he does not know how to confess. And though it perhaps does him more honor than he deserves, we must be willing to identify him as yet one more victim of the ultimate horror, the last flowering of European anti-Semitism which includes in its toll countless thousands of living Jews along with the six million dead.

Hitler is, as I recall, as absent from Weiss's pseudodrama as are the Jews themselves; for the archetypal destroyer baffles the mean secular mind of the journalist-propagandist as utterly as the victims themselves: those we must understand—whatever their personal inadequacies and failures in self-consciousness—to have been bearing witness, "Sanctifying," as some Jews are still able mythologically to say, "the Name." How much more moving, deeply terrifying, *true* is the appearance which Hitler makes in Leonard Cohen's recent novel, *Beautiful Losers* (it is a book which does not fade from my mind, which I find myself driven to recall and mention on all possible occasions), an obscene spirit evoked in the midst of a passage which presents itself as mere fiction, frank pornography—rather than at the heart of a lubricious lie which purports to be a "document." Two of his characters have yielded themselves up to an infinitely versatile exciter of the flesh, an omnipurpose sex machine called a "Danish Vibrator," which has made each of them "nothing but a buffet of juice, flesh, excrement, muscle to serve its appetite." And then:

> There was a professional knock on the blond door.—It must be him, I said.—Should we put our clothes on?—Why bother. We did not even have to open the door. The waiter had a passkey. He was wearing the old raincoat and moustache, but underneath he was perfectly nude. We turned toward him. — Do you like Argentine? I asked for the sake of civil conversation.

And mysteriously, there is evoked not merely a shudder, but a sense of the obscenity of it all, the odd sexual repulsion-allure essential to the tale of the Camps. Though this time around not suffered in self-deception by author and audience, rather caught, exposed, brought out into the open. And I therefore felt reading it *clean,* as I do not coming on articles about the destruction of Jewry in the popular press, or hearing from Weiss's players the whole terrible bit about the nakedness of the victims in the gas chambers, the hardening cement introduced into the vaginas of Jewish women, etc., etc. The sheer *dirtiness* of the experience on the most literal level, the pornographic horror of the Camps is not, I know, incidental but essential—but this is hard to confront, much less to understand. Some light is cast on it, of course, by Weiss's favorite *bête noire,* the Marquis de Sade, but even more by the New Testament; for ultimately it is from that insidious compendium of myth that the whole notion of the "dirty Jew"—on which the anti-Semite's necessary sense of defilement depends—arises. Stripped to the

buff and sent to "the showers": this is how Jews died at Auschwitz
—those obdurate people who would not be washed clean in the
Blood of the Lamb. "Let those who are filthy remain filthy," says
one of the Gospels; and who are in this sense filthier than the killers
of Christ?

We have long been the victims of an obscene myth of ourselves
as the obscene enemies of man and God; and we must make the experience that revealed to victim and victimizer alike the depth of its
obscenity a myth of equal stature and terror—lest its meanings be
frittered away in the "historical record." But where are our mythol-
ogizers? Not Weiss certainly, who will not even grant that we exist
mythologically. And if not even a German Jew steeped in the intimate horror of it all can make myth of the experience, what can we
expect of remoter Americans?

Not very long ago I went finally, though a little reluctantly, to
see Pasolini's extraordinarily deft and beautiful filming of that
deep source of anti-Semitic mythology, *The Gospel According to
Saint Matthew.* How beautiful the faces in it were, and the Italian
countryside, and the costumes right out of Piero della Francesca;
and how terrifying the fable, how satisfactorily villainous the High
Priests and the fickle mob of Jews! For me as a Jew in attendance,
it was an experience much like that of, say, an Indian kid on a res-
ervation watching a cowboy and Indian film and barely resisting
the impulse to cheer for the wrong side. "Remember you're an Indian, for Christ's sake," I found myself telling myself at one point;
and I wanted to scream the same sentence aloud up into the screen,
when I recognized there the talented Italian-Jewish novelist, Natalia
Ginzburg, playing, of all things, the part of Martha: *Remember,
you're an Indian, too.*

There is a fascinating little book which bears on this subject.
Written by a priest called Edward H. Flannery and entitled *The
Anguish of the Jews: Twenty-three Centuries of Anti-Semitism,* it
is currently available in paperback, published by Macmillan, and is
causing at the moment widespread controversy in the liberal Catholic press. Father Flannery tries, God knows, to break the long silence of the Church on this subject, but he cannot resist qualifying,
justifying and apologizing when specifically Christian anti-Semitism
(as opposed to anti-Semitism practiced by Christians despite their

own religion) becomes the issue; finally falling back on earlier authority when the question of the anti-Semitism of the Gospels themselves is posed: "We conclude with Father Baum: There is no foundation for the accusation that a seed of contempt and hatred for the Jews can be found in the New Testament. . . ." But this most Jews find difficult to accept, subscribing—despite occasional temptations to claim Jesus as "one of our boys"—to the belief recently formulated once more by Hugh J. Schonfield in a book called *The Passover Plot:* "The calumny that the Jewish people were responsible for the death of Jesus has all along been an anti-Semitic fraud perpetuated by the Church. . . ." It is hard to take with full seriousness a man who insists on calling himself "Dr." on the jacket and title page of his book; and there is little in Schonfield's book (including the theory that Jesus was drugged and prepared for a fake resurrection, or that his enemies were the "aristocrats" among the Jews opposed to the "common people") which is new or startling. But there is one sentence for which it may be remembered beyond its merits (for which I, at any rate, will recall it with some pleasure), in which the author says of Jesus: "He had what is called in Jewish jargon a *yiddishe hertz,* a Jewish warmth of benevolent affection." Which is, one likes to think, an unacknowledged quotation from that Jewish mother whom misguided Christians insist on thinking of as the Blessed Virgin.

But, of course, Christians have long carried with them, not only the mythology of the New Testament so hostile to us, but our own self-justifying mythology as preserved in what they call The Old Testament—equally a part of their revered "Bible." And John Huston's recent *The Bible* turns out to be, for once, that first half of the Scriptures only, concluding with Abraham's deliverance from the obligation of human sacrifice, in short, *"our* Bible." But John Huston's film is finally, alas, a contribution neither to the well-being of the Jews nor to the art of cinema. It is fine in its first moments, which is to say, until humans and animals appear—spectacularly handsome in its evocation of the creation of the physical universe, of boiling seas and ragged rocks. But from then on it is a shambles: in casting (imagining a naked Eve, Huston naturally imagines a Swedish actress; and conceiving of the first Jews, perversely insists that Sarah our Mother is Ava Gardner and Father Abraham,

George C. Scott); in language (arranged and edited with supplementary revelation by Christopher Fry, the very words of Scripture become banal and flat); but especially in discretion and tact.

The scenes in the Garden of Eden are a kind of coy striptease, in which our naked first ancestors dodge from one conveniently masking bush or tree limb to another, concealing from all the fact that they have nipples or genitals—and revealing themselves at full length only from behind; so that finally we have the sense that the first man and first woman were two pairs of buttocks with nothing on the other side. The Noah's Ark sequence, on the other hand, is for the whole family—a Walt Disney movie in which kindly old Noah moves among animals so impossibly cute that a cynical viewer finds himself wishing they had not made it into the ark. John Huston has always been queer for elephants, but never so flagrantly sentimental about it all. Even so, he is less intolerable as Disney than as Cecil B. DeMille, into whose manner he is tempted by the Tower of Babel and the corruption of Sodom and Gomorrah. But nowhere does he seem fresh or vivid or true. What we are given is a reading of Genesis not as terrifying and primitive myth allegorized into something like wisdom, but as a child's or a fundamentalist backwood preacher's notion of history, passed via classic comic books or illustrated Sunday school texts to the screen. From time to time, Huston pretties up the traditional account to make God look good—perhaps because, like all makers of Biblical Epic Movies, he begins before he is through to think he is God. Perhaps it is too much to expect a sophisticated version of the legends upon which our deepest self-consciousness as Jews largely depends; this is not after all what we go to the movies to get. But at least a man of Huston's immense zest might have given us something as richly vulgar and riotous as, say, the Mystery Plays of the Middle Ages, in which Noah, far from being a benevolent patter of elephants' trunks, was a hoary old drunk harried by a loud-mouthed shrew. Ah well, even from so great a moviemaker as Huston, I suppose, we can expect triumphs of vulgarity only by mistake; and Billy Wilder himself I fear confronted by Scriptures would be overtaken by that solemn piety which has made so many Christians secret haters of their own dearest mythology—and therefore of the Jews who, they dimly surmise, had something to do with the beginnings of it all.

—1967

# THIRTEEN

# Crimes and Punishments

THERE IS AN odd sense these days in the still flourishing community of Jewish-American writers that a certain vein of material is nearing exhaustion, that the mother lode which it once seemed would last forever is at the point of being used up. How long, after all, is it possible to exploit a diminishing tradition of *yiddishkeit,* which becomes finally nothing more than a memory of that diminishing tradition, a tradition of the memory of the tradition, etc., etc., to the point of absolute zero. In the work of such ultimate Jews as Bruce Jay Friedman one has the feeling of a diminuendo in content made all the more terrifying by the mounting laughter it occasions. And the publication of Bellow's *Herzog* seems somehow to have smacked of finality—representing for all its versatility and skill the end of something rather than a beginning. I do not mean to say that *Herzog* may not be a book of first excellence (I do not find it so, but this may arise from some deficiency or weariness in me), merely that its net effect is dispiriting. *Herzog,* in any event, seems to move the middle-aged more than it does the young, and being myself middle-aged, Herzog-aged, to be quite frank, I find this especially dismaying.

It has been quite a while as such things go—in a period where literary generations succeed each other with terrifying rapidity—since there has been a youth best-seller by a Jewish American writer. The last was J. D. Salinger's *Catcher in the Rye,* and even in that case he had to pretend that young Holden was a *goy.* The last two books to have moved large numbers of the young with the sense of speaking from as well as to them have been Christian allegories: William Golding's *Lord of the Flies* and J. R. R. Tolkien's

151

*Lord of the Rings.* But these at least are properly Christian, which is to say, connected in some way with the basic mythology and the great themes of Judaism.

And of all this, at some level or other, Jewish American writers begin to grow aware. I do not think anyone is surprised that the boom in Jewishness has not continued indefinitely; some critics have been predicting for quite a while, I among them, that soon, soon the Negroes would be asserting their right to be spokesmen for America as a whole; and that it was not excluded that the White Anglo-Saxon Protestants might make a sort of posthumous bid for immortality. But no one, I think, had foreseen that the Jewish-American subject matter and diction and style might give out (or worse be institutionalized, become established) before the switch-over came. Who before, in the Western World, had imagined Establishment Jews! But the Negroes have been slow in taking over the spokesman role, and the WASPS somehow do not quite fill the bill; so that we are confronted with a generation of Jewish-American writers, more full of vigor than matter, in search of a new subject.

One at least has made the desperate attempt to renew himself by turning to the past, switching from the evocation of things lived through in his own generation to the re-creation of what happened just beyond the rim of his knowing, in history. Jewish historical novels have been written before, to be sure; but they have tended to come out of a remote, easily romanticized past, not like Bernard Malamud's *The Fixer,* out of a history just over the horizon, as close to us and as related to events that have made our world (consequent anti-Semitism, the Russian revolution) as the Beilis case which provided the documentary evidence of punishment without a crime that Malamud has tried to mythicize and generalize. In the end, however, what appeal his book has for me is not in style or tone, a pastiche of translated Russian and Yiddish books, but in the resonance of the actual case behind it—for which, after all, one might as well read Maurice Samuel's high-level journalistic account, *Blood Accusation.* I do not mean that there is not genuine pathos in Malamud—feeling on the verge but not over the edge of sentimentality is his forte—but that his book resolves nothing of the crisis in the Jewish-American novel in which I feel myself deeply involved. Finally, his book bores me, offends me with the sense that nothing is happening in it except history, old history. What is the point, I find a troubled voice in my head asking, in writing one more nineteenth-century novel past the middle of the twentieth century?

In retrospect, I think more and more that Malamud's best novel was his first one—that mythological study of baseball and the hatred of the Hero called *The Natural*. But he was trying an interesting tack at least in his unsuccessful last one, too, *A New Life*, in which he tried to portray the interior exile of an urban Jew in the American West, the Jew in an improbable, less-exploited locale than New York or Chicago or wherever. His West and his Jew kept coming apart, however, perhaps because of his deficient sense of the former; and so he ended not by writing a Western with a Jewish accent but only one more weary college novel.

David Markson, in a little noticed novel which appeared well over a year ago now, did much better, producing a broad burlesque of Indian and cowboy relations seen with a learned and irreverent eye. His *The Ballad of Dingus Magee* is full of bad jokes and good history, plus some of the best Indian stuff next to the Catherine Tekakwitha story in Leonard Cohen's *The Beautiful Losers* ever to have been produced out of the Jewish-American imagination, specially qualified on this score by detachment and ignorance—two great possible sources for the New Western. Other Jews have tried their hand at the revived Western genre, too—Arthur Miller, for instance, in both the original story and the later screenplay called *The Misfits;* and I myself in my last novel, *Back to China,* as well as the final story in my recent collection of fiction, *The Last Jew in America.*

That story, *The Last Spade in the West,* is, as the title declares, concerned also, in fact primarily, with the Negro; and here, perhaps, is the real chance for the Jewish-American writer bereft of a theme or left with one too long worked over. Not only have Negro writers of real distinction been slow to appear (Baldwin seems at a dead end; Ralph Ellison writes with painful slowness and in the tradition of Kafka; LeRoi Jones finds it hard to make art of an obsession which grows more and more painful until it verges on simple *mishigas),* but there has been developing between Negroes and Jews a kind of relationship which only literature can manage to express in all its involved agony—a relationship of mutual distrust and bafflement which makes all political or sociological wisdom seem inept platitude.

For the first time in modern memory the Jews find themselves not in the traditional position of the exploited, but in the uncomfortable new position of the exploiter—at least in the consciousness of Negroes, yelling to their faces and muttering behind their backs, "Down with Ikey Goldberg." The ironies of this situation no Negro writer has as yet developed on the level of art; but two new novels, *Big Man* by Jay Neugeboren and *Call the Keeper* by Nat Hentoff, developed reflections on the theme from the point of view of the Jewish writer ferociously identifying with the Negro. The Neugeboren book is the less rewarding of the two, content by and large with easy humor and obvious pathos, as it describes the plight of a Negro basketball player, blackballed after the game-fixing scandals in the Garden, and victimized—perhaps with the best of intentions —by a Jewish journalist on the make, who discovers him playing for a B'nai Brith championship in a Brooklyn synagogue. Hentoff, on the other hand, plunges us deep into the world of hipsterism, jazz, and dope, in the midst of which there is improbably re-enacted a new up-to-date version of Dostoevsky's *Crime and Punishment*, but this time American style, with a Negro psychopath in the Raskolnikov role and a Jewish detective as the malign pursuing cop.

And obviously it will not stop here, since the Jewish writer in search of a way out of his self-constructed trap of success will turn inevitably to a subject so rich in possibilities for self-examination and reproach. Already there have been attempts even on the level of slick fiction, Bruce Jay Friedman turning his hand to the theme in the title story of his recent collection of commercial stories, *Black Angels,* which concerns a feckless and abandoned suburbanite (this time Friedman pretends he is an Italian called Stefano, but we recognize him as our old friend, Stern) who falls into the hands of a group of Negroes who come on as incredibly cheap workmen, but in the end reveal themselves as psychiatrists preparing to bleed him to death with exorbitant fees. It is a nightmare vision rendered with all the insouciance of a joke, a blackout gag in the continuing burlesque show of suburban life.

Reading Friedman and Neugeboren and Hentoff, however, we remember the writer who began it all, the Jewish boy out of Harvard who first declared himself a White Negro, Norman Mailer— and suddenly there returns to mind the terrible and triumphant scene out of *An American Dream,* in which Stephen Rojack (himself a half-Jewish Raskolnikov crossed with James, or is it Israel, Bond) beats out the "spade" junkie with a knife for the possession of the blonde Cherry, all-American Wasplet, who stands obviously for that erotic dream of a pale Protestant America waiting to be won, a dream shared by Jew and Negro alike. Maybe we are not so sure of the boast implicit in Mailer that we Jewish boys are still capable of taking the archetypal American *shikse* out of the hands of any "spade," however well armed; but it does us good to dream so in a time of troubles. And if Mailer goes on to tell us, as he does, that the girl finally dies, that we are both, Negroes and Jews alike, left with a ghost only, a disembodied voice on the telephone—this bad news we can stand, too, after the dreamed moment of glory.

—1967

# FOURTEEN

# Some Notes on the Jewish Novel in English or Looking Backward from Exile

"BY THE RIVERS OF Babylon we sat down and wept . . ."; or so at least it is reported in *the* Book: the first—though by no means the last—of those Jewish books which the non-Jewish world has somehow been persuaded is its book, too. Sat down and wept, to be sure, but sang and wrote too, sang of the weeping, wrote of the singing, thus inventing the first Jewish profession, writing in exile—a permanent Jewish profession everywhere. I had thought it in America, only last year. But this year I have looked about me in search of Jewish writers in England, *real* Jewish writers, who write their Jewishness, however vestigial, and their exile, however cozy; and convince non-Jewish readers that in some sense they are Jews, too, and exiles as well, though they had not suspected it before. And I have found none. No Jewish writers in England. How can it be?

The question troubled me from the start, and so I asked those whom destiny (I have been teaching in an English University all year) had put in my power, my poor captive students. How does it happen, I demanded of them, that there is no serious, no considerable Anglo-Jewish Novel? You share with us Americans a common language, the mother-tongue, in fact, of most living Jews, who once wrote in Aramaic or Arabic or Yiddish or German, but now choose English or American or Anglo-American. Way back at the turn of the century you produced Israel Zangwill, one of the first Jewish

156

writers to adopt the new mother tongue. But though in the United States novelists like Bellow and Mailer and Malamud, poets like Allen Ginsberg, speak for all Americans, stand at the center of the scene—almost too established, too successful, so that resentment grows and anti-establishment writers begin to consider them the enemy; nothing remotely similar has happened, is happening here. And why not?

It was a foolish question, perhaps, and so deserved the silence which greeted it, as it greeted most of the misguided American questions I directed at my baffled students in those first weeks. Finally, however, I did get an answer from a girl who, until that point, had always proved more charming than articulate, but was moved at last to say, smiling benignly, "Well—They're All so Rich here, They don't have to write Books, do They?" After which it was my turn to be silent; though I suppose she was really suggesting an answer with her distancing "They" and her offhand evocation of the envious-spiteful stereotype. Maybe it is essentially that mild-as-milk, matter-of-fact anti-Semitism, which I have found everywhere in England, that has prevented Jews here from becoming spokesmen for anything except their own parochial interests, or, alternatively, slightly quaint entertainers like, say, Chaim Bermant.

For better or for worse (so at any rate it seems to me), the Jews in England, quite like the Pakistanis or the Jamaicans, or, for that matter, the Irish, are felt to be English only insofar as they seem to have ceased being Jewish; but this is the absolute opposite of the American case, in which the rule is, has been for a decade or two: the more Jewish, the more American. It is for this reason, then, that the handful of Anglo-Jewish writers of talent actually producing fiction and verse are not felt to add up to anything significant. There are novelists who happen to be Jewish but no Jewish novel.

On the other hand, there is a *female* novel in England, where certain middle-aged women (some of them irrelevantly Jewish) tend to function like certain middle-aged Jews (some of them irrelevantly female) in the United States. I do not read these English ladies often or with much pleasure, but I have enough sense of them to have composed in my head a composite portrait of the typical recent English novelist labeled, for convenience, Muriel Murdoch.

And in moments of perversity, I have tried to imagine mating her with her American opposite number, called, of course, Bernard Bellow. They are not utterly unlike, since M.M. shares with B.B. certain memories of the thirties and World War II, as well as an interest in the language of Existentialism. But her stock-in-trade is her battered sexuality rather than her disappearing ethnic identity; and even if her affairs turn out to be, like his ghetto origins, just another image for alienation, I am afraid I could never get my imaginary couple past the first strains of introduction. Perhaps the true opposite of the Jew is not (as, I seem to recall, Maurice Samuel once suggested) the Gentleman, but the Lady, or, to be quite up-to-date, the ex-Lady; and these opposites do *not* attract.

America has, at any rate, ever since the end of the War against Hitler chosen to identify itself with the Jew—quite disregarding a warning against this rapprochement issued some fifty years ago by D. H. Lawrence, who, however resolutely *not* a gentleman, was as anti-Semitic as any Englishman. Meanwhile, England has chosen to see itself as the aging lady, which means, I suppose, no match—though a transatlantic offspring is possible all the same; since in the realm of the imagination, even the refusal to mate is not a guaranteed contraceptive. But where could he go, this unwanted child of M.M. and B.B., equally unwelcome at both poles of the English-speaking world, except, perhaps, to the no man's land, the Demilitarized Zone of Canada. But if he were, in fact, there, he would be invisible from South of the Border as well as from the Other Side of the Atlantic—since, despite occasional valiant efforts to *find* Canadian literature (Edmund Wilson provides one notable recent example), it remains stubbornly unavailable to English and American readers alike.

Still, I myself have been reading Canadian books for a long time and have been variously amused, dismayed, interested and bored—but not really moved (even enough to want to register my reactions in print) except by the work of two authors, both self-exiled English-speaking Jews from Montreal, one of whom I have known for a long time now, the other of whom I have come across only quite recently: Mordecai Richler and Leonard Cohen. That they both be Jews is fair enough, proving once more that, culturally speaking, Canada is part of the American rather than the British

Commonwealth; and that they have both chosen to exile themselves from their place of birth is appropriate, too, proving once more that the America Canada is really like is always the America of three decades before.

Among us in the United States, exile, particularly to England, seems scarcely a typical strategy these days (imagine Saul Bellow or John Barth or Allen Ginsberg permanently planted in the English countryside); but for Richler it apparently provides the possibility of participating in American culture—contributing to *Commentary,* starring in the first issue of the *New American Review* —without the defensive self-consciousness he would have felt following a similar course at home. From England, at any rate, he seems to able to join, however belatedly, the extended Norman Podhoretz "family" not as a poor relation from the North, but as a distinguished foster-brother from overseas. And England, in addition, has provided him with a new subject, the subject of exile, latterday or post-romantic exile itself, rescuing him from the need to recapitulate earlier American models. *The Apprenticeship of Duddy Kravitz,* for instance, seemed to me when I first encountered it, hopelessly retrospective for all the talent that went into its making —the sort of fictional study of making it out of the ghetto appropriate for Americans only to the thirties. *Having* made it was our new subject—and Richler's, too, though he did not seem to know it at the start. Still, there was apparent in him a lust for surreal exaggeration and the grotesque, and an affinity for the atrocious—the dirty joke turned somehow horrific, the scene of terror altered somehow into absurdity—which made him, before he himself knew it, a member of the group later to be labeled Black Humorists.

Satire was his special affinity—not, to be sure, polished and urbane satire, but shrill and joyously vulgar travesty—directed, all the same, against pop culture, on the one hand, and advanced or experimental art on the other: middlebrow satire, in fact, however deliciously gross, an antigenteel defense of the genteel tradition. It is this which makes Richler so difficult a writer for *me* to come to terms with, and—by the same token—so easy a one for the guardians of official morality to accept. His most recent novel, *Cocksure,* for instance, was simultaneously published in permissive America and in restrictive England; and though it contains one episode in which it is revealed that a prim and aging schoolmarm has been blowing the top boys in her class, there has been no protest from an irate British public, and no action from the British courts which recently condemned and banned *Last Exit to Brooklyn*. Part of the explanation for this must be surely that, never mind *how*, the schoolmarm in question is re-establishing discipline and hard work in a formerly progressive school; and no true-blue Englishman wants to deny what Richler suggests: better *fellatio* than children's productions of plays by the Marquis de Sade. Besides which, in tone and language and indefinable stance Richler himself belongs to the world of mass culture (in which he has labored long, continues to support himself), so that he seems ultimately—*seems*, I think, rather than *is*—as harmless as *The Black and White Minstrel Show*.

It is quite another aspect of his work which makes Richler more dangerous than he seems perhaps even to himself: his concern with exile, his compulsion to define all predicaments in terms of that hopelessly Jewish concept, and his implicit suggestion that, after all, we are—every one of us—Jews. In an oddly uncharacteristic, but to me impressive, book called *A Choice of Enemies* (the structure of which reminds me disconcertingly of Graham Greene), Richler turned his cold satirical eye on certain Hollywood exiles in England, victims of the anti-Communist heresy hunts of the fifties, who, stripped of power and wealth, continue to play the old Machiavellian games which earlier they had carried on behind their mouthing of Communist pieties. And in *The Incomparable Atuk*, he deals with the fate of a Far North Eskimo in the world of Toronto pop culture, moving closer and closer to a level of farce and fantasy whose connections with reality are more like those of a Mack Sennet comedy than a novel of the late nineteenth or early twentieth century.

*The Incomparable Atuk* is not quite a successful book (I notice it is not even included among the earlier Richler books listed opposite the title page of *Cocksure*); but in it Richler seems to have discovered at last where the demands of his real gifts were taking him —toward ultimate, absolute burlesque, i.e., burlesque that includes finally the book itself and its author, the sort of nihilism implicit unawares in all pop art, and consciously exploited in "Pop Art," of which *Cocksure* is an example. But ultimate burlesque requires a sense of the ultimate outsider, the real victim, the true Jew, who— in the realm of Anglo-Saxondom at least—turns out to be the Anglo-Saxon: Richler's poor Mortimer Griffin, a Canadian in the world of Anglo-American T.V. and films, convinced that the Jews are thicker, the Negroes longer than he, who is cuckolded, sacked, and due to be murdered as the book closes. He has discovered before that conclusion that certain powerful Jewish entrepreneurs—in particular a bisexual monster-producer, kept alive with multiple transplants—actually manufacture out of plastic the WASP robots who are the screen idols of the world; and is—naturally enough— taken for mad by those whose peace of mind demands that they believe plastic the ultimate reality. It is a book which seems always on the verge of becoming truly obscene but stops short, alas, at the merely funny. Yet it is so close, so close—the sort of near miss that leaves permanent damage behind.

Perhaps it is close enough, then. Certainly Richler has come as near to saying how it is with us now, when the ultimate exile has proved to be success, as anyone can out of the generation which dreamed that success, at a point when being poor and excluded seemed the only real indignity. Or perhaps it is even possible to say that he has come as near as satire can under any circumstances, since satire is the weapon of one—his deepest self made by a failed father, a deprived childhood—who secretly believes himself weak. The weapon of the strong is joy, of the half-strong pathos and sentimentality; and Leonard Cohen calls on the latter, while he woos the former in hope.

He begins with certain social advantages, aside from all questions of gifts, since he was born in another generation (ten years makes all the difference), another Montreal (not the old ghetto, but suburbia which reveals its dreams as delusions); and he has sought another exile (Greece, the Island of Hydra, which is to say the remotest and most sunlit of all American Bohemias). And being of another generation, his relationship to pop culture is utterly different—not the condescension and self-inclusive scorn of one forced to earn his living in its terms and thinking of it as a kind of prostitution, against which the appropriate revenge is "art"; but the admiration of one to whom it was forbidden by finicky parents when he was a child, and who therefore cannot help believing it a source of power, a guide for redeeming "art" turned genteel. In any case, the pop art which most moves Cohen and provides not the subject so much as the mythology which informs his work is not films and television, but comic books and pop music. Superman and Ray Charles inhabit his imagination as the Hollywood Producer and the M.C. of the Panel Show inhabit Richler's. And he is quite properly, therefore, a successful writer of pop songs (his latest album recently released in England as well as America), in addition to being a poet and novelist. As a matter of fact, I find his song lyrics (in "Suzanne," for instance, and especially "The Sisters of Mercy") more valid than his book-poetry, because the former have found contemporary occasions which justify their pathos and sentimentality, whereas the latter seem moved merely by nostalgia for certain lapsed Romantic styles. He works, at any rate, not in the middlebrow arena of Richler, in which pop and *avant-garde* are felt as complementary threats, but the new post-Modernist world in which the old distinctions between low and high art, mass culture and *belles-lettres* have lapsed completely—and it is therefore, blessedly impossible to be either alienated or outrageous. Vision replaces satire in that world, which aims at transforming consciousness rather than reforming manners.

Nonetheless, Cohen has found no publisher yet in England willing to risk bringing out his extraordinary second novel, *Beautiful Losers,* since in England (particularly after the court decision against *Last Exit to Brooklyn* seemed to give official sanction to it), the art of being outraged by what is not outrageous has been highly developed. I suppose the point is that Cohen does not make dirty jokes at all, certainly not dirty jokes at the expense of what is advanced or experimental, but tries instead to blur the boundaries between the clean and the dirty, even as he has those between serious art and popular entertainment. Or, perhaps, the former is only a particular case of the latter since it is the end of "porn" as an underground, secretly relished genre which books like *Beautiful Losers* threaten. For it is to a place before or beyond the realm of the dirty book that we are taken by scenes like the terrible-lyrical one in which Cohen's two male lovers jerk each other off as they speed in an automobile toward what seems a wall of solid stone; or the terrible apocalyptic one, in which a heterosexual pair, exhausted of passion and drained of all their liquids after a bout with an erotic device called the "Danish Vibrator," rouse to find themselves confronted by Hitler naked beneath a military raincoat. Certainly, Cohen has found to render such scenes a language not gross and elegant by turns, but gross and elegant at once, a poetry of obscenity which makes condescension to him or his subjects impossible. And perhaps it is the possibility of condescension for which the English are fighting in the courts, having lost the battle everywhere else.

I should hate really to deprive anyone who really wants it of that last vestigial pleasure of class consciousness; but it seems even more unfair to rob young readers especially of the pleasures of Cohen's novel with its special blend of scholarship and paranoia, poetry and vulgarity, its intertwined stories (on one level, it recounts the death by self-torture of a seventeenth-century Indian girl converted to Christianity and pledged to chastity for Christ's sake; on the other, it tells of a polymorphous perverse triangle in twentieth-century Montreal moving through joy toward madness and death), and its final vision of redemption, through the emergence of the New Jew—a saving remnant who, Cohen assures us, does not necessarily have to be Jewish at all, but probably does have to be American. It is a possibility in which I find myself believing, in part, of course because I want to (which is always more than half the battle), but in part because the evidence is *there,* in the text and texture of *Beautiful Losers* itself; so that it is not merely prophecy or an idle boast when Cohen writes toward the book's close: "Hey, cried a New Jew, laboring on the lever of the Broken Strength Test. Hey. Somebody's making it!"

—1968

# FIFTEEN

# Negro and Jew

THIS IS A MOMENT for questions, new questions or old ones newly posed, a moment when answers seem impertinent—which is, perhaps, why fiction (a method of posing questions without troublesome question marks) seems the most promising method of attacking the problem of Negro-Jewish hostility. I am thinking of such books as Norman Mailer's *An American Dream,* Nat Hentoff's *Call the Keeper,* and Jay Neugeboren's *Big Man,* as well as (hopefully) my own *The Last Jew in America.* In a strange way it has now become incumbent on the Jewish writer to re-imagine the Negro in terms which will escape the old WASP clichés, sentimental and vicious, and the recent even more soupy and hysterical Spade ones. Eventually, of course, the Negro writer himself will have to invent the New Negro as Harriet Beecher Stowe, Mark Twain, D. W. Griffith and Faulkner have invented the Old Negro. But Jews will apparently have to deal with him in the moment of transition, since the current crop of Negro novelists is fumbling the job: Ellison remaining stubbornly old-fashioned on this score, Baldwin caught between the exigencies of his poetic talent and his political commitment, LeRoi Jones the victim of his own anguish and *mishigas.* But the Jewish writer's assumption of this task can prove in the end only one more possible source of misunderstanding and tension between the two groups.

Some relevant questions then—and all which follows is a series of questions even when passion or strategy leads me to omit the question marks. Would not the proper title for an article on this subject be "Thou shalt not honor the poor man in his cause"—to remind the present-day enlightened Jew of certain therapeutic anti-liberal elements in his own tradition: a priestly admonition that might have protected him in the thirties from illusions about the working class and its parties (but did not); and might now serve as an antidote against delusive hopes about Negroes and their organizations (but probably will not). Or maybe it would be better—in light of my own continuing concerns—to use the title *An End to (Another) Innocence;* since the liberal tradition in America—to which the Jewish intellectual has attached himself, which, indeed, he has all but pre-empted—insists on stumbling from one innocence to another with appropriate bouts of self-recrimination between. It is not mere "white backlash" (the very term is a buttress of naïveté on the defensive) but simple wisdom (what used to be called "good sense") to notice that, like all such movements, the Civil Rights Movement is becoming, had to become with the beginnings of success, self-seeking, self-deceiving, self-defeating—devoted not to a search for justice but to the pursuit of power. But the liberals (the *Jewish* liberals, as Negro critics like to say) will be the last to admit this; since the liberal is a man who can drown in the same river twice—which is, let me be clear, his glory as well as his folly, the function of an incredible generosity of spirit which fades imperceptibly into willful stupidity: a combination, mythologically speaking, of *yiddishe hertz* and *goyishe kop.*

Why not continue to speak mythologically then; for mythology seems the basic way into the problem of Jewish-Negro hostility—which turns out not to exist sociologically at all, i.e., not *consciously* (using the methods of the behavioral sciences, investigators keep discovering to their own satisfaction and the confusion of the rest of us, that Negroes really love, respect, and honor Jews) but only preconsciously, on the level of legend and nightmare.

What, in fact, are the mythologies at work, first in the minds of Negroes concerning Jews and then in the minds of Jews concerning Negroes? "Sub-minds" would be a more precise way of naming the locus of myths: and is it not well to remind ourselves in this regard of the differing weights of mind and submind, conscious and preconscious factors in the case of Negro and Jew? It is no secret, surely, that in America the Jewish Community has largely committed itself to a life of logos, a cultivation of the ego and the whole Gutenburg bit whose demise Marshall McLuhan has been quite un-Jewishly predicting; while the Negro community in large part continues to live (even to make its living) in the world of subliteracy, unrationalized impulse, and free fantasy.

Do not Negroes, in any event, tend to begin with the WASP racist mythology (endorsing it in self-hatred, or inverting it in impotent rebellion) which divides the world into two ethnic-mythic segments only: White and Colored; and which further assumes that the distinction is hierarchal, corresponding roughly to higher and lower. The deep Jewish ethnic-mythic division, on the other hand, is threefold, as the legend of the three sons of Noah reminds us. As descendants of Shem, we were once taught, we have *two* hostile and inferior brothers, Ham and Japheth. The Negro, committed to his simpler mythology, tends to regard the Jew either as a Colored Man who is deviously passing as White; or a goddamned White Man pretending, for reasons hard to fathom, to the fate of the excluded Colored Man. The Jew, meanwhile, is struggling with the vestigial sense of being a third thing, neither-either, however one says it; and he therefore thinks of himself (his kind of awareness driving him compulsively from feeling to thinking) as being free to "pass" in either direction, in a world which oddly insists that he identify himself with one group of strangers or another, Hamitic or Japhetic. And he knows that historically segments of his people have done both (some first pretending to be White, then becoming prisoners of their pretense; some following the opposite strategy): that in Israel, for instance, it is possible to observe these two groups, "Black Jews" and "White Jews," in open conflict. He is, therefore, baffled as well as resentful when he discovers himself denominated "White" without choice and made the victim in a Black-White race riot; just as he was once baffled as well as resentful to discover himself linked without choice to Negroes in being excluded from White clubs and hotels and restaurants. And he is doubly baffled and resentful when the Negro switches from hating him as White to despising him in a mode imitated from those earlier-arrived North European Americans who thought themselves so much Whiter than he.

How can the Jew help seeing Negro anti-Semitism as a kind of culture-climbing, an illegitimate attempt to emulate WASP style —and, inevitably, a belated and misguided attempt; since the

WASPs are abandoning the racist attitudes to which the Negro aspires at the very moment he is assimilating them. Even Hitler, certain more ignorant or frantic Negroes tend to think of as just another White Man—rather more efficient than most, though not quite efficient enough in eliminating his Jew-enemies—and thus they have not felt shamed out of their anti-Semitism by the rise and fall of Nazism, as their WASP opposite numbers (who cannot help feeling Hitler in some sense one of them) have tended to be. It is especially unassimilated, unassimilable Jews, Jews who do not even seem to want to look like all other Americans, who stir the fury of Negro hoods—say, Hasidim with their beards, *peyes* and gabardines.

At the deepest mythological level, is it not the Jewish religion, finally, as well as the Jewish ethnic inheritance which bugs the Negroes? Certainly this would be understandable enough; for insofar as they are Christians, fundamentalist, evangelical Protestants, do they not inherit the simple-minded anti-Jewish mythology of the Gospels (which Catholics long had the good grace to keep out of the hands of subliterates) with its simple-minded melodrama of "our" Christ killed by "the Jews"? And do not Negroes in particular possess the additional sentimental myth of Simon the Cyrenean —kindly Negro by the wayside—who helped Jesus bear his cross as the Jews hooted and howled for his blood? And insofar as they are becoming Muslim (Why could not the first attempt of the ill-fated founder of that movement to establish a Black Judaism have succeeded?), are they not obsessed by the legendary notion of the "Evil Jacob," Israel the Usurper—as well as the myth of Isaac before him doing poor Ishmael out of his heritage? And as Muslims, do not they (along with the members of other non-Mohammedan Afro organizations) identify themselves with an Arab-African anti-Jewish political mythology, which leads them to consider Jews, in America as well as Israel, even wickeder than the rest of the depraved "hoojis"? Are not both Christianity and Islam, finally, being offshoots of a more primitive Judaism, subject to spasms of a kind of collective sibling rivalry, which passes over on occasion into fratricidal strife? And is not the *shul*-goer or temple-attending Jew caught once more in the old bind between the Christian Negro for whom he is not (spiritually) White enough—not sufficiently washed in the Blood of the Lamb—and the Muslim Negro for whom he is not (mythologically) Black enough—not far enough removed from the White Man's God?

It is not, however, only the worshipers of Christ or the followers of Mohammed among the Negroes who are possessed by anti-Jewish mythologies. The hippiest and most advanced Negroes, secular as they may seem to themselves, are committed to a myth system—the Beat Religion, let's call it for the purposes of quick identification, most recent form of an old Romantic anti-Church. And does that Church not necessarily, in view of its archetypal antecedents, see the Negro as the embodiment of (admired) impulse and irrationality, the Jew as the incarnation of (despised) sublimation and rationality? About these matters I have written at some length before; and have thought about them long enough not to be surprised at recent efforts at expelling Allen Ginsberg from the True Church (a kind of apostle to the Beat Gentiles, or maybe better, a Trotsky of the Hip revolution—his position is more than a little anomalous). No one, at any rate, need pretend astonishment when he hears the cry from a Negro at the back of a room in which Robert Creeley is reading aloud, "This is a poem for Allen Ginsberg" —"Hey, man, when you going to stop talking about those Jew poets?" Is it not a rule of the mythological literary life in America that when the Negro is up, the Jew is down? What was true in the twenties is true once again as the Jewish thirties, forties, and early fifties recede from us. Who can serve two masters, after all? One must choose between Saul Bellow and LeRoi Jones, Jerusalem (well, the Northwest side of Chicago at any rate) and Harlem (well, let's make it Newark's Third Ward). Mythological as well as historical factors, that is to say, have determined the fact that certain Hippies at the present moment find themselves protesting a Jewish Literary Establishment ("Norman Podhoretz's floating ghetto," one in-group joke calls it) in the name of a movement whose reigning figures are archetypal *goyim* like Charles Olson, Norman O. Brown and Marshall McLuhan. Jewish writers, from Mailer to Nat Hentoff, may try to escape the mythological hang-up by redefining themselves as imaginary or "White Negroes" (the very term was, of course, invented by a Jew)—just as their more political brethren have tried to assimilate to a world which mythologically rejects them by linking arms with Negroes in protests and demonstrations. But though young Jews have an affinity not only for protest but for folksongs, jazz, and marijuana (how much more readily they assimilate to pot than to the Paleface medicine of whiskey), the whole syndrome, they have trouble making it across the legendary line—remain always in danger of being told that they cannot *really* commit themselves to the Movement, cannot *really* make authentic jazz, cannot *really* sing the blues. The point is that other mythological demands are being made on them—to play the false liberal, or "Mr. Goldberg" or, ultimately, the super-ego in one or another currently unfashionable form.

So much—for the moment—about the Negro or Negroizing mythologies of the Jew; though I suppose a word at least demands to be said about the "Black Socialism" (the term antedates its adoption by actual Blacks), that presumably revolutionary anti-Semitism which poor Negroes have inherited from White workers, *lumpen* proletarians, peasants and "red-necks." This view (to which Leo Frank was once a victim) sees the Jew as rich, powerful, devious, behind the scenes if not at the centers of power—a Boss, in short. But this view tends to become less and less influential as the leading elements of the Negro Movement become prosperous or mobile and educated enough to afford overt anti-Semitism. It is real enough, to be sure, but is it not finally a vestige, as old-fashioned, which is to say, as peripheral in the current situation as the remnants among the aging Jewish bourgeoisie of the simpleminded anti-Negroism appropriate to our social-climbing days: the contempt of the still insecure Jewish housewife for the *schwarze* who cleaned for her, or the Jewish marginal small businessman for his Negro janitor, or the underpaid Jewish salesman for his Negro instalment customer? Do we not enjoy rehashing such elementary prejudices, long after we have made it in a way which renders them irrelevant, precisely because they are no longer urgent; and leaving them, we would have to confront relationships much more difficult to analyze or confess?

Almost as familiar, and therefore quite as ritually satisfying to discuss yet one more time, are certain good old Freudian notions— long since lapsed into semi-popular mythology—about the Negro: the projection onto the Negro male, for instance, of the sadist nightmares about his own women dreamed by the white male, etc.,

etc. These have always been rather confused as far as Jews in America are concerned, by the fact that Jews themselves have played similar mythological-sexual roles in WASP erotic fantasies; and in Norman Mailer's last novel one can see enacted in the form of comic melodrama a kind of contest between his (half) Jewish hero and a particularly potent Spade to see which one will possess the blond all-American *shikse*—which, mythologically speaking, amounts, I suppose, to an argument about which one of us she is dreaming these days. More interesting, and more dangerous to broach, are questions about the role of homosexual rather than heterosexual fantasies in the earlier stages of the Civil Rights Movement. I am not referring to the fact that there has been a strange confluence of the Homosexual Rebellion (the emergence of queer America from underground to the daylight world) and the Negro Movement; but rather to the influence on that Movement of the old antifemale dream of a pure love between males, colored and white, so crucial to our classic literature in the United States. I myself can report having heard several times in various forms from young civil rights workers the cry, so authentically American it was hard at first to believe: "Oh, Christ, things were great when just us buddies Black and White were fighting it out together; but these White chicks are just down here to get laid."

It seems to me, however, that none of these sexual concerns, deep as they may go, are as important at the moment as certain political mythologies. What chiefly exacerbates relations between Negroes and Jews, as far as Jews are concerned, is the persistence among them of the mythology of Liberal Humanism. This troublesome myth system, derived in part from Old Testament sources, most highly developed in modern Anglo-Saxondom, and picked up again in that world by emancipated Jewish intellectuals, includes the following articles of faith: that all men desire freedom and full human status and deny that freedom and status to others only when it has been refused to them; that equality of opportunity leads to maximum self-fulfillment and social well-being; that the oppressed and the injured have been so ennobled by their oppression and injury that they are morally superior to their masters; that all men desire literacy and suffrage—and can exercise those privileges equally well when granted them; that all the foregoing are not the parochial belief of a tiny minority of mankind over a minute span of time, but what all men have always believed, or would have believed given the opportunity. Intertwined with this credo—though not as often avowed as that credo itself—is the Whig Myth of History which sees freedom slowly broadening down from precedent to precedent, country to country and ethnic group to ethnic group. The Jews have always (since their exit from the ghetto and entry into the West, at least) considered themselves more qualified than anyone, less compromised than anyone because of their historical situation certainly, to preach this doctrine. They have felt especially righteous in respect to the application of these principles to the Negroes in the United States, since they were not as a group involved in the enslavement of the Negro, and they know themselves to have long been involved in Civil Rights Movements in numbers all out of proportion to the percentage of the total population which they represent. No Negro ever died for a Jewish cause, Jews tell themselves; but some of our boys have died for Negro rights.

How utterly unprepared they have been, therefore, to find a growing number of Negroes rejecting not only their credo but them in particular as its messengers—spurning in short the whole body of "Jewish Liberalism." "Hear our message and be saved," they cry only a little condescendingly and are dismayed to hear in return: "All we want from you white mothers (or alternatively, Jew mothers) is to get off our backs and out of our road!" Yet worse, much worse, is the fact that the Negroes, whatever their avowed credo, challenge by their very existence a basic article of the Liberal Faith: equality of opportunity will not grant very many of them, brutalized by long brainwashing and bred by a kind of unnatural selection, a decent life or the possibility of prosperity. What they demand, not so much by what they say as by how they are, how they test, how they perform, is *special privilege* rather than equality if they are to make it at all in the very world in which the Jews have so preeminently flourished. And what a shame and embarrassment that some men (i.e., most Jews) have done so well under conditions in which certain fellow-humans seem bound to do ill. What can survive of liberal mythology in the face of this? Is "liberalism," then, only a camouflage for a special sort of privilege, a code by which the peoples who alone have long lived with the alphabet can triumph over all others?

Marxism, especially in its more brutal Bolshevik versions, has long offered an alternative mythology to that of liberalism; but so many intellectual Jews now sufficiently advanced into middle age to have become its spokesmen have been there before. Some, indeed, are alive and articulate at the moment who have lived through the loss of three religions: first Orthodoxy itself, then Stalinism or Trotskyism, finally enlightened liberalism; and for them, what lies ahead but despair? But for the young, and the politically obtuse who remember nothing and have learned nothing, it seems possible, even imperative—in order to justify or explain black violence, black know-nothingism, black racism—to fall back once more on the mythology of an already once-discredited anti-liberal Bolshevik "Humanism." Certainly, there is superficial reassurance at least in the simple-minded theory that the whole vexed problem is "economic"—and that the last vestiges of Black Racism will disappear (like anti-Semitism in the Soviet Union? a nagging voice demands) only after the major means of production have been appropriated by the People's State. But how can a thinking man live by the mythology of a God who died in the declining thirties? And how especially can a Jew come to terms with the fate of his own people by applying a Marxist mythology which denies the Jewishness of the Jews—as is, after all, appropriate to a secular religion invented in large part by recusant Jews. To be sure, any and all "Jewish problems" immediately disappear when the real reference of the adjective is denied; but this is a semantic solution which cannot conceal the fact that actual Jews are being harried and threatened. And if proof is needed that this semantic strategy is not only a lie but an offense, one need only see Peter Weiss' current play, *The Investigation,* that obscene parody of what happened at Auschwitz, from which "the Jews" have been expunged, even as a name to be spoken aloud.

No, more attractive to me than yesterday's defunct mythology —more valid for all the self-pity easily attached to it—is the more ancient mythology which insists that the ultimate villains of history define themselves finally and essentially by their attitude toward the

Jews; and that all enemies of the Jews (with whatever pious slogans and whatever history of suffering they begin) are enemies to the good of mankind, whether they be black, brown, yellow, or white —Haman or Hitler or the CORE leader rising to scream that Hitler should have done a better job of getting rid of us. "Not in one generation alone, but in every generation they have risen up to destroy us," the ritual phrase in the Passover Haggadah runs; and it continues on to reassure us that God has always delivered us out of the hands of our enemies. But what about the hands of our presumed, even our real, allies? And what can we expect anyhow in these dark days when God is dead and only the devil survives: the devil still identified by Ku Kluxers with Negroes, and by some Negroes with the Jews? What does the devil's devil do in a world without God, or even gods?

Despair? Make jokes? Pray to the void? Confess that nothing can be done? That by a joke of history the amends that *must* be made to the Negroes (for indignities for which the Jews bear little or no guilt) must, alas, necessarily do harm to the Jews? That it is our turn again, or really on this continent at long last? Sometimes I feel this way and am tempted toward desolation; until, looking out into the streets, the schoolyards, the coffeehouses, I find my heart leaping up at the sight of young couples linked arm in arm. And I think our daughters will save us, love (not big theoretical, but small sexual love) will save us. I remember a year or two ago riding a plane to Jerusalem and being told by the man seated beside me, who worked for a Jewish adoption agency, that the number of illegitimate Negro babies being produced by Jewish girls was mounting spectacularly. And were there also, I asked, legitimate ones, *even* legitimate ones? But I did not listen for the answer, knowing it was yes, and not quite sure why I needed confirmation. What sunders us may not be first of all but is last of all a sexual taboo; and that taboo is every day being broken, with or without benefit of clergy, Christian or Jewish; and its breaking is the beginning (though *only* the beginning) of the end.

So naturally a new mythology is being invented, appropriate to that new solution; though like all new myths this one, too, contains within it one very old, indeed, the myth of the Jewish Daughter, Hadassah (renamed Esther, which is to say, Ashtoreth) dancing naked for our salvation before the Gentile King. I sat the other day eavesdropping on the conversation of a group of very young white girls—most of them pretty, blonde daughters of Jews with black boyfriends, discussing what they would do when the first race riots broke out in Buffalo. And one of them suggested that they march between the two opposed packs, Black and White, carrying signs which read: MAKE LOVE NOT WAR. It was elegant and vain as the loveliest dream; and I am old and cynical enough, after all, to know it; as I know how much there is dark and desperate even in their young love, and as I realize how much in marriage itself (for some few of them *will* marry their Negro boyfriends, I am sure) is a problem rather than a solution. To make matters worse, I had just been reading in the *East Village Other* a statement by a Negro poet, who not so long before had been able to write that he had "married a Jewish Lady to escape Bohemia," that Jewish girls only married Negroes in order to emasculate them. And I was aware that it was his paranoid and sinister mythology which operated in the tensions that made headlines day after day; but I knew that the counter-mythology of those young girls had power to move men, too. I, at least, prefer to live in its hope rather than the Negro poet's despair, convinced of its superiority to all the weary mythologies of mere politics. The disillusionment it will inevitably breed at least still lies ahead, and (if I am lucky) I may not live so long.

—1966

# SIXTEEN

# Master of Dreams:
# The Jew in a Gentile World

*If there were dreams to sell,*
*Merry and sad to tell,*
*And the crier rung the bell,*
*What would you buy?*

T. L. BEDDOES

"AND JOSEPH DREAMED a dream," the Book of the Jews tells us, "and he told it his brethren: and they hated him yet the more." It is the beginning of a myth whose ending we all know, the opening of a larger dream which a whole community has dreamed waking and aloud for nearly three thousand years. But it is unique among communal dreams, this myth of Joseph and his descent into Egypt; for it is the dream of the dreamer, a myth of myth itself. More specifically (or maybe I only mean more Jewishly), it is the dreamer's own dream of how, dreaming, he makes it in the waking world; the myth of myth making it in the realm of the nonmythic; an archetypal account of the successful poet and the respected shrink, the Jewish artist and the Jewish doctor—hailed in the Gentile world, first by the Gentiles themselves, and as a consequence by their hostile brethren, their fellow-Jews.

I might have hit upon the meaning of the Joseph story in any number of ways, reflecting on the Biblical text itself, or reading Thomas Mann's true but tedious retelling of the tale in *Joseph and His Brethren;* but I did not. And only after I had begun my own

175

ruminations did I come on Isaac Bashevis Singer's exegesis, in a little story called "The Strong Ones," in which he remembers the strange resentment of his childhood friends after he had first revealed to them his secret desire to become a writer: "And even though I asked how I had offended them, they behaved like Joseph's brothers and could not answer amicably. . . . What was it they envied? My dreams. . . ." But the archetypal beginning implies the archetypal ending; and just as mysteriously as they had rejected him, Singer's comrades end by asking his forgiveness: "It reminded me of Joseph and his brothers. *They* had come to Joseph to buy grain, but why had my friends come to me? Since I had not become Egypt's ruler, they were not required to bow down to the earth. I had nothing to sell but new dreams."

Actually it was a chance phrase in a most *goyish* poet which provided me with a clue to the meanings I am pursuing here, a verse in the Sixth Satire of Juvenal, where—describing the endless varieties of goods on sale in Rome, wares especially tempting, he tells us, to women—he remarks that "for a few pennies" one can buy any dream his heart desires "from the Jews." *From the Jews!* It was those few words which fired my imagination with their offhand assumption that dream-pedlary is a Jewish business, that my own people have traditionally sold to the world that commodity so easy to scorn and so difficult to do without: the stuff of dreams. And I found myself reflecting in wonder on the strange wares that have been in the course of Western History Jewish monopolies, real or presumed: preserved mummy, love philtres, liquid capital, cut diamonds, old clothes—Hollywood movies; which brought me almost up to date.

Moving backward in time, however, in reversion from such uncomfortable contemporaneity, I found myself in *Mizraim,* face to face with the archetypal ancestor of all Jewish dreamers, with that Joseph whom his brothers hailed mockingly, saying, "Behold, here comes the Master of Dreams," and whom they cast into the pit, crying out, "And then we shall see what will become of his dreams." But we *know* what, in fact, did become of those self-flattering dreams of that papa's spoiled darling. And how hard it is to believe that there was ever a *first* time when the envious brothers did not know in their deepest hearts what the event would be: how

Joseph, after he had ceased to dream himself, would discover that his own dreams of glory had prepared him to interpret the dreams of others, and how, interpreting them, he would achieve the wish revealed in his own.

Not, however, until he had gone down into Egypt, becoming in that absolutely alien world an absolute orphan, a Lost Son. When the Jew dreams himself in the Gentile world, it is as the preferred offspring of Jacob, which is to say, of Israel—betrayed by his brethren, but loving them still, forgiving all. When the Gentile dreams the Jew in his midst, on the other hand, he dreams him as the vengeful and villainous Father: Shylock or Fagin, the Bearded Terror threatening some poor full-grown *goy* with a knife, or inducting some guileless Gentile kid into a life of crime. But Shylock and Fagin are shadows cast upon the Christian world by that First Jewish Father, Abraham, who is to them circumcizer and sacrificer rolled into one—castrator, in short.

In the deep Jewish imagination, however, Abraham is seen always not at the moment of intended sacrifice, but the moment after —releasing his (only ritually) threatened Son to become himself a Father, and the Father of a Father, to beget Jacob who will beget Joseph. Abraham *and* Isaac *and* Jacob: these constitute that paternal triad which possesses the mythic memory of the Jews. And beyond them there is for us no further Father, only Our Boy, Joseph, who never becomes (mythically speaking) a Father at all—only makes good, i.e., provides salvation for the Gentiles and *nachas* for his own progenitor.

The Gentiles cannot afford the luxury of *our* Joseph, however, having an archetypal Son of their own, who denies his actual Jewish father ("Let the dead bury their dead"), called—appropriately enough—Joseph, too. How like and unlike the figure of the first Joseph is to that Gentiles' Son of the Father, the mythicized Jesus Christ, whose very Jewishness is finally sloughed off in the exportable archetype he becomes. Not for *our* Beloved Son a crucifixion and a translation to glory only after death. Our Dreamer, too, may begin by leaving his father's house on a mission to the Gentiles; but the temptations he must resist are the temptations of this world not the next. Specifically, he must elude not the clutch of Satan but the grasping fingers of the Gentile woman who lusts for him; and survive the slander with which she punishes his rejection of her alien charms. And his reward for virtue is to become a success in this world, the unredeemed here and now (not some New Heaven and New Earth, where he will sit at the right hand of Power), ruled over only by the powers-that-be: those fickle Pharaohs whose favor depends on his providing for them the good dreams they cannot dream for themselves, and therapeutically explaining away the bad dreams they cannot keep from dreaming.

And this means that the archetypal Jewish Son, in whatever *Mizraim* he finds himself, performs not only the function of the artist but also of the Doctor. My Son the Artist, my Son the Doctor —it is the latter which the tradition especially celebrates, the bad jokes recall in mockery; but in the tradition, the two—artist and doctor—are finally essentially one. In life, however, they may be, for all their affinities, split into separate persons, distinct and even hostile: in our own era, for instance, Sigmund Freud, on the one hand, and Franz Kafka, on the other, which is to say, the Healer and the Patient he could not have healed, since he is another, an alternative version of himself. The voice which cries, "Physician, heal thyself!" speaks always in irony rather than hope. Yet both Healer and Patient are, in some sense, or at least aspire to become, Joseph.

How eminently appropriate, then, that Kafka (first notable Jewish Dreamer of a cultural period in which the Jews of the Western World were to thrive like Joseph in Egypt, but also to be subject to such terror as the descendants of Joseph later suffered at the hands of a Pharaoh who knew him not) should have called his fictional surrogate, his most memorable protagonist, by the mythological name of Joseph. This time around, however, Joseph is specified a little, becoming—with the addition of the author's own final initial—Joseph K., a new Joseph sufficient unto his day. This Joseph, at any rate, along with the fable through which he moves, embodied for two or three generations of writers to follow (real Jews and imaginary ones, Americans and Europeans, White men and Black) not only a relevant dream-vision of terror, but also the techniques for rendering that dream in the form that Freud had meanwhile taught us was most truly dreamlike: with a nighttime illogic, at once pellucid and dark, and a brand of wit capable of revealing our most arcane desires.

Yet despite the borrowed name of his surrogate-hero, Kafka could no longer imagine a Happy Ending for either that character or himself, since he no longer dreamed himself the Beloved of his father, but an outcast, unworthy and rejected. In what has become perhaps the best known, since it is, surely, the most available, of his stories, *Metamorphosis,* his Joseph protagonist becomes a vermin in his father's eyes. And we are left with the question: how did the lovely boy in his coat-of-many-colors turn into a loathsome insect, the advisor at the royal ear into a baffled quester, an outsider barred forever from the Courts of the Mighty? But the answer to this question Kafka's own works, whatever difficult pleasure or stimulating example they may provide, do not themselves render up —not even the private and agonized "Letter to My Father," nor that final story, in which Joseph is altered in sex, demoted to Josephine, the Songstress. And the relation of the mouse-artist to the Mice-Nation (i.e., the Jews) is treated with uncustomary explicitness: "But the people, quietly, without showing any disappointment . . . can absolutely only make gifts, never receive them, not even from Josephine. . . . She is a tiny episode in the eternal history of our people, and our people will get over the loss."

No, if we would really discover what went wrong with Kafka's relationship to his own father, which is to say, to Israel itself (he who never mentioned the word "Jew" in his published work) which that father represented, or more generally to his inherited past—to history and myth—we must turn back to another Master of Dreams: the Doctor who preceded and survived the Artist: a latter-day *Baal-ha-chalamoth* (in the sense this time of interpreter rather than dreamer), Sigmund Freud, or better, Dr. Freud. Only at this moment, as we pass into a regime of rulers who know not Joseph, have we begun to outgrow our own dependence on that Healer, to learn to see him stripped of his clinical pretenses and assimilated to the ancient myth.

And mythologically speaking, he is, of course, an *alter ego* of Franz Kafka—or more precisely, of Joseph K.—one who, like the Biblical Joseph and his namesake, descended into the abyss of ridicule and shame for the sake of his vision; then was lifted up and acclaimed a culture-hero: a Saviour of the non-Jewish world which had begun by maligning and rejecting him. Certainly, it is as a solver of dreams that Freud first attracted public notice, with that book born just as the twentieth century was being born, *The Interpretation of Dreams*. Like an artist, he himself tells us—though the comparison did not occur to him—he was granted in that book an unearned illumination, on which he was to draw for the rest of his days. "Insights such as this," he wrote much later, toward the end of his life, "fall to one's lot but once in a lifetime."

And publishing the first fruits of that illumination, he prefaced it with a quotation reflecting his sense of how monumental and monstrous a task he was beginning to undertake: *"Flectere si nequeo Superos, Acheronta movebo."* If I cannot influence the Gods above, I will set the world below in motion—set Hell in motion, he means really, but he chooses to call it "Acheron," to draw on Classical rather than Hebrew mythology, perhaps because he realizes how Faustian, Satanic, blasphemous his boast finally is. And he further clarifies what he means by quoting, in the Foreword which immediately follows, Aristotle's dictum (once more the source is our other, non-Jewish antiquity) that "the dream is not God-sent but of demonic origin." But precisely in his turning from the supernal to the infernal interpretation of dreams, Freud declares himself a true modern, which is to say, quite another sort of Joseph; though the first Joseph, to be sure, began his journey toward success with a descent into the pit.

Unlike the original Joseph, however (for whom there could be no Happy Ending unless his father survived to relish his triumph), Freud could not begin his Acherontic descent until after the death of his father—called Jacob, too, by one of those significant "accidents" which Freud himself would have been the first to point out in the case of another, but on which he never commented in his own. He could not even make the preliminary trip down, much less the eventual trip up, until his darkest wish-dream had been, in guilt and relief, achieved: not to do his rival siblings down in the eyes of his father, but to be delivered of that father—his last tie to the Jewish past—and thus be freed to become an Apostle to the Gentiles, a counselor at the Court of his own doomed Emperor. Yet, before releasing his published book to the Gentile world, or even lecturing on its substance at the Gentile University of Vienna, Freud rehearsed it in one lecture at the Jewish Academic Reading Hall, and two (however incredible it may seem) before that most bourgeois of Jewish Fraternal Organizations, the B'nai Brith—tried out his vision, that is to say, before the assembled representatives of the community to which his dead father had belonged.

Yet, despite the pieties with which he hedged his blasphemy about, Freud's Acherontic "insight" failed at first to impress either the world out of which he was trying to escape, or the one to which he aspired. The handful of reviews his book got responded to it condescendingly, lumping it with old-fashioned "Dream Books" for the ignorant and the superstitious; and it sold, during the first two years after publication, some 350 copies, scarcely any in the next five. But this is hardly to be wondered at since, to Jew and Gentile alike, Freud was proposing a radically new myth of the relation of sons to fathers, of the present to the past: a myth whose inversion of the Joseph legend never occurred to him in those terms at all. What is involved is not merely the flight from Hebrew mythology in general, which we noticed in regard to the epigraph and Foreword to *The Interpretation of Dreams,* but something much more particular.

After all, one figure out of the Old Testament did come eventually to possess the imagination of Freud and to occupy him on the level of full consciousness: the figure of Moses, whose very name —as Freud carefully points out—means in Egyptian "Son," with the patronymic suppressed and whose own fleshly father, Amram, plays no part in his myth, is not even named at the center of the tale. Surely Freud loved Moses because he would brook no father at all, Hebrew or Egyptian or Midianite, killing the surrogate for the Egyptian King who had fostered him, running off from Jethro, the father of the *shikse* he had married, and—most reluctant of Jews—refusing to have his own son circumcised until the Angel of the Lord (so runs the apocryphal extension of the story) had swallowed him from his head down to his testicles. Joseph, however, Freud does not ever mention; though as an old, old man, he wrote once—to his own son naturally—"I sometimes compare myself to the old Jacob whom in his old age his children brought to Egypt. . . ." (And not even this time did he pause to note that in becoming "Jacob," he was becoming his own father.)

In his great pioneering work, however, it is neither Jacob nor Joseph nor Moses himself whom Freud evokes, but a mythological *goy,* two mythological *goyim* out of the dreams of the Gentiles. How casually, how almost inadvertently he calls up King Oedipus and Prince Hamlet side by side in what purports to be a casual three-page digression. Compelling the deep nightmare of fathers and sons dreamed by the Western World from the fifth century before Christ to the seventeenth after his death to give up its secret: "It may be that we were all destined to direct our first sexual impulses toward our mothers and our first impulses of hatred and violence toward our fathers; our dreams convince us that we were. . . ." How calm and objective he keeps his tone, as if the "we" were more impersonal than confessional. Yet everyone knows these days that *The Interpretation of Dreams* was not the product of a sudden revelation alone, but also of a painful self-analysis, into which the death of his father had impelled Freud to plunge and from which he liked to think of himself as having emerged healed.

Unlike Kafka's *Letter to My Father,* Freud's great antipaternal work is a solution, not an exacerbation, or so at least he claimed. In him (it is his proudest boast, and we believe it), obsession is turned into vision, guilt into knowledge, *trauma* into *logos;* while in Kafka, the end is paralysis, a kind of lifelong castration, memorialized by the incomplete and bloody stumps of his most ambitious works. Freud's major works are finished—their completion as much a part of their final meaning as the incompletion of Kafka's was of his. Nonetheless, between them, Kafka and Freud, the crippled poet and the triumphant savant (for, finally, not even a measure of the worldly success of Joseph was denied to the father of psychoanalysis), have helped to determine the shape of Jewish-American writing in the first half of the twentieth century—the shape of the tradition from within which (at the moment of its imminent demise) I write of them both.

From the two, our writers have learned their proper function: to read in the dreams of the present the past which never dies and the future which is always to come; and they have, therefore, registered their vision in a form which wavers between the parable and the discursive essay, art and science. For though the means of the Jewish-American writers from Nathanael West to Norman Mailer are poetic and fictional, their ends are therapeutic and prophetic. Their outer ear may attend to the speech of their contemporaries, in the realist's hope of catching out life as it passes; but their inner ear hears still the cry of Freud: "I am proposing to show that dreams are capable of interpretation." And their characteristic tone is born of the tension between the Kafka-esque wail of *"Oi veh!"* and the Freudian shout of *"Eureka!"*

That tone is established once and for all in the work of Nathanael West, in whom begins (however little the critics may have suspected it in his own time) the great take-over by Jewish-American writers of the American imagination—our inheritance from certain Gentile predecessors, urban Anglo-Saxons and midwestern provincials of North European origin—of the task of dreaming aloud the dreams of the whole American people. How fitting, then, that West's first book—published in 1931, at the point when the first truly Jewish decade in the history of our cultural life was beginning —be called *The Dream Life of Balso Snell* and that it turn out to be, in fact, a fractured and dissolving parable of the very process by which the emancipated Jew enters into the world of Western Culture.

Balso himself gets in by penetrating through the asshole that symbol of tradition and treacherous conquest, "the famous wooden horse of the Greeks." West makes his point with some care, perhaps a little too insistently for subtlety's sake: not only is it the Trojan horse that alone gets us into the beleaguered city; but for us Jews, just to make it into the horse in the first place is a real problem—since, after all, it was built for Greeks. We do not need Balso to tell us that there are only three possible openings, three entryways into any horse, even the most fabulous of beasts; but which way is for us we do not know in advance, and this he is prepared to explain, reporting of his hero, our thirties representative: "The mouth was beyond his reach, the navel provided a cul-de-sac, and so, forgetting his dignity, he approached the last. O Anus Mirabilis!" It is a lovely, an inevitable pun—and not only in 1931, since in any age, the Jewish Dream Peddler must, like Balso, "forget his dignity" to get inside. Not for him, the High Road to Culture *via* the "horse's mouth," nor the mystical way of "contemplating the navel"; only the "Acherontic" Freudian back entrance: the anal-sexual approach. "Tradesmen enter by the rear."

For West's Balso, at any rate, the strategy works; in a moment, he is transformed from outsider to insider, but he does not like it after all. God knows what he had imagined would be waiting for him in the belly of the horse; what he discovers in fact is that it is "inhabited solely by writers in search of an audience," all Josephs and no Pharaohs. And the approval of other approval-seekers is exactly what he neither needs nor wants, though for a while he pursues one of their number, "a slim young girl" called Mary Mc-Geeney, who has written a novel "in the manner of Richardson," the Great WASP Father of the *genre*. It is not as an author, however, that Balso lusts for Mary, but as the archetypally desirable *shikse,* who—at the very moment his tongue is in her mouth—disconcertingly becomes "a middle-aged woman, dressed in a mannish suit and wearing horn-rimmed glasses," which is to say, Potiphar's wife turned schoolmarm. Once revealed, however, Miss McGeeney proves even less of a problem to Balso than her earliest prototype to Joseph: "He hit Miss McGeeney a terrific blow in the gut and hove her into the fountain." After which, she stays inside the limits of his fantasy, returning "warmly moist" to make possible the sexual climax with which the book ends, turning a dry dream wet.

More troublesome to Balso than his Gentile foster mother (to whom he can play Joseph or Oedipus, turn and turn about, with no real strain) is a kind of archetypal Jewish father, who disconcertingly appears in the very bowels of the horse, a self-appointed *kibbitzer* in the uniform of an official guide, from whom Balso has finally to wrench himself "with a violent twist," as the paternal busybody howls in his ear: "Sirrah . . . I am a Jew! and whenever anything Jewish is mentioned, I find it necessary to say that I am a Jew. I'm a Jew! A Jew!" It is the last such explicit declaration of Jewishness anywhere in West's work, on the lips of a character or in the words of the author himself; for after the exorcism of *Balso Snell,* his dreamers dream on presumably free forever of their aggressively Jewish censor. But the dreams that they dream—of Sodom burning, of the destruction of ever purer Josephs by ever grosser Potiphar's wives—we must call Jewish dreams.

Even the madness which cues them, we must call (more in sorrow than chauvinistic pride) Jewish madness; for just such madness, cuing just such dreams, we discover in that other great novel of the thirties, this time frankly Jewish in language and theme, Henry Roth's *Call It Sleep.* How aptly the ending of that book manages to catch, more in the rhythm, maybe, than in their manifest content, the phrasing of the words, that ambiguous moment at a day's end when it is uncertain whether the spirit is falling toward sleep and a dreaming from which it will wake with the morning or toward a total nightmare from which there is no waking ever. The cadences of that close and their hushed terror stay in my head, more than thirty years after Roth first conceived them, a valedictory both to his child protagonist in bed and to his own career as a writer: "He might as well call it sleep. It was only toward sleep that every wink of the eyelids could strike a spark into the cloudy tinder of the dark, kindle out of the shadowy corners of the bedoom such myriad and such vivid jets of images. . . ."

We know, having come so far in the novel, what those images "toward sleep" were, and are, obviously doomed to be until death for Roth and his protagonist: the adoring mother, exposed in her nakedness before jeering kids; the terrible rage of an actual Jewish father and the guilty dream of a *goyish* spiritual one; the Jewish girl betrayed in abject love to a mocking Gentile; the spark out of the bowels of the earth, up from the third electrified rail of the streetcar, bright enough to redeem all from darkness and pain; and, weaving in and out of the rest, the cry of the Prophet: "I am a man of unclean lips in the midst of a people of unclean lips. . . ."

Joseph—the solver of dreams—has become confused with Isaiah in the terrible thirties, learning to talk dirty instead of speaking fair; and he moves, therefore, not toward recognition and acclaim in his own lifetime and his father's, but like West or Roth, toward premature death or madness and silence. If, at long last, posthumous success has overtaken Nathanael West, and almost-posthumous acclaim Henry Roth—this is because the forties and fifties learned once more to believe in the Happy Ending, which the writers of Genesis postulated for the Joseph myth, but which the thirties could imagine no more than Kafka himself. The lowering into the pit, the descent into Egypt or Hell was all of the legend which seemed to them viable; and trapped in the darkness, they looked not to Pharaoh for deliverance, but to the psychoanalysts, the heirs of that Jewish Doctor who had boasted that he could set very Hell in motion.

In our time, however, with benefit of analysis or without, Joseph has once more been haled into Pharaoh's court, once more lifted up in the sight of his enemies and brothers; once more recognized as a true Master of Dreams, under his new names of J. D. Salinger and Bernard Malamud and Philip Roth and Saul Bellow. But this is the achievement of an era just now coming to a close, a decade or more of responsibility and accommodation, in which those erstwhile outsiders, Freud and Kafka, became assigned classroom reading, respectable topics for the popular press: an age which, rediscovering West and Roth, celebrated its own sons who had grown up reading them, the age of the Jew as winner. But how hard it is to love a winner—to love Bellow, let's say, after the National Book Award and best-sellerdom—in this land of ours, where nothing succeeds like failure, and all the world loves a loser.

How much more comfortable we feel with those exceptional figures of the forties-fifties who did not quite make it, dying too soon and still relatively unknown, like Isaac Rosenfeld, or surviving dimly inside of their wrecked selves until they could disappear unnoticed, like Delmore Schwartz. I, at least, find myself thinking often these days of Rosenfeld, who might well (it once seemed) have become our own Franz Kafka and who perhaps *was* (in a handful of stories like "The Pyramids" and "The Party," dreams of parables or parables of dreams) all the Kafka we shall ever have. And even more often my thoughts turn, ever since his pitiful death anyhow—in the same black year for the Jews which also saw Lenny Bruce go—to Delmore Schwartz, with whom the forties began two years before the official opening of the decade.

It was only 1938, even before the start of World War II, when there appeared a volume of his short fiction and verse called, appropriately enough, *In Dreams Begin Responsibilities*—"responsibilities" for the age to come, "dreams" for the long tradition on which he drew. In the title story, at any rate, a young man on the eve of his twenty-first birthday, is portrayed dreaming a dream that becomes a movie (not in technicolor, or even in black and white, but in gray on gray, those authentic Schwartzian colors), the movie of a dream. Asleep, but already on the verge of waking, he watches his parents, sundered by rage and mutual incomprehension before his birth or conception. " . . . and I keep shouting," he tells us, "What are they doing? Don't they know what they're doing? Why doesn't my mother go after my father?' . . . But the Usher has seized my arm and is dragging me away. . . ."

It is a nightmare uncannily apt for the Age of the Cold War and Going-to-the-Movies—an era whose chief discovery was disillusion: this bad dream of the past as irrevocably given and of the impotence of the young in the face of enormities which they inherit (and even understand) but cannot control. Born in reaction, it is a counterdream to the Marxian vision of apocalypse and social change which moved the thirties and of the hysterical despair which underlay it, the paranoia which its myth of the Class Struggle at once nurtured and concealed. But for the antipolitical politics of the forties-fifties, too, there is an appropriate psychosis, as there is for all brands of politics: the conviction of impotence freezing into catatonia—the total paralysis of the will of those with no place to go except *up* into the Counselor's seat at the right hand of the leaders of utterly corrupt states. Both the thirties and the forties-fifties, however, merely *suffered* varying forms of madness bred by Freud's Oedipal dream and the failure of Marxian politics.

It was left to the sixties (which got off to an even earlier start than most decades somewhere around 1955) to *celebrate* psychosis; and to attempt, for the first time, not to pretend that schizophrenia was politics, but to make a politics of schizophrenia recognized for what it is: a total and irrevocable protest against Things-as-They-Are in a world called real. And behind this movement, too, there is a Jewish dreamer, yet one more Joseph sufficient unto his day. I mean, of course, Allen Ginsberg who has escaped the hang-up of finding or not finding the ear of Pharaoh, by becoming a mock-Pharaoh, a Pharaoh of Misrule, as it were. Think of his actual presence at the head of parades or his image looking down at us from subway hoardings—crowned with the striped hat of Uncle Sam.

Ginsberg, however, unlike the Joseph before him, is no father's darling at all, not even such a baffled aspirant for paternal favor as was Kafka. He is a terminal son, to be sure, like the others—but a mama's boy this time, unable to imagine himself assuming papa's role ever ("Beep, emit a burst of babe and begone/ perhaps that's the answer, wouldn't know till you had a kid/ I dunno, never had a kid never will at the rate I'm going"), or saying *kaddish,* that traditional Jewish mourner's prayer which becomes an endearing synonym for "son"—except for his mother, called Naomi, and identified in his mythological imagination with her Biblical namesake, and with Ruth and Rebecca as well, though *not* with Rachel, that favored second wife of Jacob. She was a life-long Communist, that mother who haunts Ginsberg, who died—lobotomized and terror-stricken—in the nuthouse: "Back! You! Naomi! Skull on you! Gaunt immortality and revolution come—small broken woman— the ashen indoor eyes of hospitals, ward grayness on skin."

But her post-Marxian madness, the very paranoia which per-suaded her that she had been shut away at the instigation of "Hit-ler, Grandma, Hearst, the Capitalists, Franco, Daily News, the 20's, Mussolini, the living dead," becomes in her son vision and a program fostered by that vision: "vow to illuminate man-kind . . . (sanity a trick of agreement)." And when his own insanity fails to sustain him, he turns to drugs, singing—on mari-juana and mescalin, Lysergic Acid and laughing gas and "Aya-husca, an Amazonian spiritual potion"—a New Song, appropriate to a new sort of Master of Dreams, the pusher's pusher, as it were. He does not sell the chemical stuff of dreams directly, of course (was this, then what the Jews *did* peddle in the market place of Ju-venal's Rome?), but sells the notion of selling them—crying out in protest: "Marijuana is a benevolent narcotic but J. Edgar Hoover prefers his deathly scotch/And the heroin of Lao-Tze and the Sixth Patriarch is punished by the electric chair/but the poor sick junkies have nowhere to lay their heads. . . ." or insisting in hope: "The message is: Widen the area of consciousness."

The psychedelic revolution, however, whatever its affinities with the traditional Jewish trade of dream-pedlary and its appeal to the sons of Jewish merchants engaged in handling much harder goods, belongs to a world essentially *goyish:* the world of William Bur-roughs and Timothy Leary and (however little he might relish the thought) J.R.R. Tolkien. For a contemporary Master of Dreams more explicitly Joseph-ian, which is to say, Jewish, we must turn to a writer who in his own fantasies is never more than half-Jewish, to Norman Mailer. Those who have read the successive versions of his *The Deer Park* (or have seen it on the stage), and who know his most successful and impressive short stories, "The Man Who Stud-ied Yoga" and "The Time of Her Time," as well as the notes on these in that mad compendium of self-pity and self-adulation, *Ad-vertisements for Myself,* are aware that Mailer once planned a Great American Dream Novel in eight volumes.

Each volume, he tells us, was to have represented one of the "eight stages" in the dream of a defeated Jewish writer (Mailer makes him only one-quarter Jewish, which is to say, minimally though essentially so) called Sam Slavoda, who, in his nighttime fantasy sees himself as a kind of Super-Goy called Sergius O'Shaughnessy. In the dream of Slavoda, O'Shaughnessy, his heroic *alter ego,* is portrayed as eternally strugging with a Jewish father figure (in the recent dramatic version, we learn that he is "half-Jewish—on both sides"), named Eitel, for the possession of a Gentile girl, daughter or mistress or wife (essentially, I suppose, somebody else's wife, i.e., Potiphar's Wife), called Elena. It is all —thanks, alas, to Freud—distressingly explicit; and I for one was not, am not, sorry that the project ended in shipwreck and a ten years' silence; since out of that silence Mailer emerged to write a book less like Kafka and more like Pop Art—more indebted, that is, to the immediate Jewish past (those post-World War II Masters of Dreams, Shuster and Siegal, who inventing Superman for the comics, invented a possible future for the dying novel) than to a remoter one no longer viable.

That book is, of course, *An American Dream,* in which dreamer and dream-actor have become one, Sam Slavoda plus Sergius O'Shaughnessy turning into Stephen Rojack—who is half-Jewish, since in the world of myth a quarter Jew plus a full Gentile equals a half-Jew. But he is precisely the half-Jew, the half of Joseph, that neither Kafka nor the great writers of the thirties could envision: Joseph *after* his recognition, the very archetype of the Man Who Has Made it. No protagonist has entered our recent fiction with so impressive a list of distinctions, for he is a Congressman, a decorated War Hero, the friend of a future President of the United States, the M.C. of a successful T.V. program; as well as a tireless cocksman, who can get away with murdering his own wife, then walk the parapet of a penthouse under the eye of his evil Fascist father-in-law, turn down that Bad Father's homosexual advances, and triumph finally over a Total Conspiracy—in which all of his Bad Brothers (transformed fashionably into members of the Mafia and the C.I.A.) have joined with that Father to destroy him.

Mailer's latest book is, indeed, in its very banality and vulgarity just such an American Dream as its title advertises it to be; but it is also a Jewish Dream: if not Joseph's own dream, at least our dream of Joseph, as well as a Jewish interpretation of the dreams of Pharaoh's (read "John F. Kennedy's") servants. Try as he will, therefore, Mailer cannot basically alter the shape of the myth he has inherited. How desperately he yearns to permit his Joseph (unlike the earlier Josephs from whom he descends) to have all that glory and Potiphar's Wife, too—in fact, all three of the Gentile women into whom Mailer has split the single figure of the original legend. But, in the end, Rojack has to reject them like the Josephs before him, so that his soul may live. Deborah Coughlin Mangravede Kelly he marries and kills, though—or maybe because—she is Pharaoh's Wife rather than Potiphar's. Mailer nowhere says outright, of course, that she is intended to be a portrait of Jacqueline Kennedy; but she reminds us of the mythological Jackie at least. And Rojack, introducing her, explains, "Forgive me, I thought the road to President might begin at the entrance to her Irish heart."

And the mistress once dead, he must destroy the maid who is her extension, too: penetrating all three of her entrances, one by one, but reaching his climax—and cheating her of her own—in the *Anus Mirabilis* (we are back to Balso Snell once more, and this time the identification is explicitly made between asshole and Acheron: "I had come to the Devil a fraction too late, and nothing had been there to receive me. . . ."). Buggery is the essential aspect of a sexual connection whose aim is annihilation not fulfillment; and buggery extorts from the red-headed German Ruta, the confession that she had been a Nazi: " '*Ja.*' She shook her head. 'No, no,' she went on. '*Ja*, don't stop, *ja*.' " After which Rojack is able to declare, "There was a high private pleasure in plugging a Nazi, there was something clean despite all. . . ."

But another third of Potiphar's wife remains to be dealt with; after the Irish aristocrat and the Kraut servant, the ultimately blonde, all-American Wasplet: the Happy Ending Girl, whose name, Cherry, declares, I suppose, that whatever befalls her flesh, mythologically she remains eternally virgin. Cherry, Rojack truly loves, but her, too, he leads to her death—involuntarily, but inevitably all the same; not, however, until he has won her in an archetypal battle with a *really* Bad Brother—a Negro junkie who comes at him with a knife. It is as if Mailer were trying to declare, or his fable in his despite: "Things haven't changed all that much, my colored brothers; a Jewish boy in good condition can still beat out you spade hipsters in the struggle for that archetypal blonde *shikse* who embodies the American psyche." Yet in the end, the spades who cannot keep her in life do her in; the friends of the hipster whom Rojack has earlier defeated, humiliated, in effect, *killed,* destroy our poor Cherry. And Rojack, guiltless of that murder, is released from the burden of actual love—releasing his author at the same moment from all obligations to realism: liberating him into the world if not of pure myth, at least of Pop Art fantasy.

As the book closes, Mailer asks us to believe, Rojack has stopped at a disconnected phone booth in the middle of the Great American Desert; and when he dials (sleeping or waking, we are not sure) the voice of his dead beloved answers—and why not, after all. "Why, hello hon, I thought you'd never call. . . . Marilyn says to say hello." At this point, Mailer's personal fantasy becomes once more our common fantasy, his dream girl ours, as Cherry blends into our own late, perhaps too much lamented, Marilyn Monroe; and somehow we are supposed to be, somehow we *are* at peace. It is a long way from the beginning of Mailer's book to the end: from his evocation of the dead Dream Boy of us all (the novel opens, "I met Jack Kennedy in November, 1946. We were both war heroes and had been elected to Congress"), whose death one crazy Jew, himself now dead, thought he was avenging—to the Dead Dream Girl of us all, of whose death another saner Jew has written a play to prove himself guiltless. But it is a way which leads from madness to sanity, from falling asleep to waking up; from the lunatic wish to be President and screw all the women in the world, to the modest hope of finding someone to love and the resolve to take time out for thinking things over.

"But in the morning," Stephen Rojack ends by saying, "I was something like sane again, and packed the car and started on the long trip to Guatemala and Yucatan." Maybe this, too, is only one more fantasy, the last madness of believing oneself sane; or maybe Joseph *is* sane again, at least as Mailer has re-imagined, re-embodied him; maybe, in exorcising himself of the American Dream, the American version of the flight from Potiphar's wife, Mailer has healed himself—demonstrating that artist and doctor can inhabit the same head. Didn't Freud himself assert (apropos of his own attempt along the same lines, the very book with which we began) that successful self-analysis is possible to one who is "a prolific enough dreamer"?

But even granting all this, we are left with the final question: what does this mean to *us*? What do Joseph's personal healing and his consequent success (after all, *An American Dream* did prove a best-seller, and more, a way back into writing again for its author) mean to those who have helped make that success, critics or readers or nonreading buyers of books? And the answer to that question I have been pursuing throughout—reflecting on how the Jewish Dreamer in Exile, thinking only of making his own dreams come true, ends by deciphering the alien dreams of that world as well; thus determining the future of all those who can only know what lies before them dimly and in their sleep. It is the essence of the myth I have been exploring that Joseph, the Master of Dreams, cannot lie; for dreams tell only the truth, and the Dreamer is also a Dream. But the final word on the subject has been said by Freud himself, in his peroration to *The Interpretation of Dreams:*

> The ancient belief that dreams reveal the future is not entirely devoid of truth. By representing a wish as fulfilled the dream certainly leads us into the future; but this future, which the dreamer accepts as his present, has been shaped in the likeness of the past by an indestructible wish.

*Buffalo, N. Y.*
—1967

# UNFINISHED BUSINESS

# Introduction

IN THIS SECTION, the reader will discover all I shall probably ever get down of two books I have dreamed through most of my life as a writer. It seems clear to me now that I will never produce either the full length study of the thirties which I have been promising myself for so long, or that inclusive and conclusive book on the university with which I have been teasing myself for a somewhat shorter time. My essays on Henry Roth and John Peale Bishop, as well as a more general one called "The Two Memories," will have to make do for the first; while a little piece on freshman composition, plus the longer essays called "Academic Irresponsibility" and "The New Mutants" will have to substitute for the second.

I cannot write a full scale work on the thirties, I discover, not now anyhow, because I am still too deeply involved with memories and feelings still out of my control; while a full and formal treatment of the university seems inevitably to end in banalities, which I cannot bear to sign with my name and send forth into a world weary almost to the point of death of precisely such banalities. Perhaps, all the same, I may someday grow detached enough to do the first and inspired enough to do the second, who knows.

Just six months or a year ago, I would have included among these scraps from unfinished books an essay or two on Shakespeare, but suddenly I am in the process of writing that presumably unfinishable book. Still I could not forbear including in this section an essay called "Caliban or Hamlet," in which Shakespeare is treated not so much as a literary subject as a source for metaphors capable of redeeming politics from the clichés which usually dog it.

195

I have also occasionally proposed to myself a surely unwritable book on the "non-Ethnic" American writers of the twentieth century to whom I have responded passionately, but who have tended to fall out of the categories around which my longer work is usually organized. I have therefore included essays on two such writers, John Hawkes and John Barth, leaving out with regret (because I do not feel that what I have written on them so far is substantial or amusing enough to be preserved) essays on two other "non-Ethnics" whom I equally admire, Wright Morris and Kurt Vonnegut.

Finally, I must mention what I have included in this section, the two brief postscripts to my early essay "Montana, or the End of Jean-Jacques Rousseau" and the article I wrote on Hemingway after a tragic confrontation with him at the moment just before his death. Hemingway and Montana are inextricably intertwined in my own mind, and the conjunction of these two essays may serve to illuminate the mingled piety and horror, love and rejection with which I regard both. These have been hard essays for readers with a taste for simplicity and the single vision to understand, and I sympathize with their confusion, though their failure to make due allowance for my own has led to their difficulties in the first place.

Equally ambivalent and confusing is my attitude toward the Rosenbergs, whose case is treated at length in an essay reprinted in Volume I, and which I take up again here in an article that is really a prescript rather than a postscript, having been written some half-year before the former. That prescript, which I wrote from Italy as a kind of message home as well as a preparation for returning, seemed to me at the moment of its composition too personal and passionate and somehow naked to be printed then. But I discover that I have preserved it over seventeen or eighteen years, and I print it now for the first time, at a moment when the Rosenbergs have become the heroes of a play on Broadway and my own earlier comments are being quoted widely in the press by conservative commentators quite sure I have not changed my mind. Radical students, on the other hand, keep asking me hopefully, "You don't *still* believe that stuff about the Rosenbergs, do you?" The answer to which is, "Yes, I do." But I suspect that neither the conservative journalists nor the radical students quite understand what I said about the Rosenbergs to begin with, and I, therefore, have decided to publish my two Rosenberg pieces side by side in order to make clear just how divided was the mind out of which both came. Let me add only one word from the present, a commentary on the little dialogue reprinted here. Though the character I call "C" has the final word in that dialogue, "A" and "B" also represent the author, which is to say, me. In this piece, therefore, as in so many others which I have written before and since, my attitude finally is as simple as A-B-C, which is, of course, not very simple at all.

# ONE

# The Rosenbergs: A Dialogue

(The scene is the house of A., where A. himself and B., C's two oldest friends, are waiting eagerly to pick up again their twenty year long political wrangle, interrupted by C.'s two years abroad.)

A: Welcome home! (holding out a drink)

B: Home! Home! I hope you're not such a victim of clichés that you take this word too seriously. Just because you go away from a place and come back, that doesn't make it home. What man who respects himself could feel at home in the U.S. in 1953!

C (He takes the drink, and motioning in salute to his two friends swallows it down.) American whiskey! *I* feel at home—and it's not only the bourbon. You have no idea what a pleasure it is to come back to the same arguments, the old familiar language of disagreement and misunderstanding. I haven't felt so much at home for two years—except in my dreams.

B: Some dreams! Nightmares is more like it. The tidal oil lands turned over to private industry, Stevenson beaten, the campaign against the "eggheads" in full swing, snoopers in every college and university, McCarthy—the Rosenbergs—

C: The Rosenbergs! You make me feel as if I were back in Europe again. This is the Europeans' America—the legendary land of horror they *have* to believe in so they can continue to

199

despise us while they sustain what freedom they have left with our money. Rosenberg! I haven't heard that name mentioned since I got back; but in Europe there are posters on every wall, announcements of mass meetings, and every communist cab driver or clerk asking you, "What about the Rosenbergs?" As if you were killing them personally, as if their sentencing were an answer to all the charges against Russia, two people to balance against the millions in the concentration camps!

B: Well?

C: Well, what?

B: In a sense you *are* personally responsible for their deaths—you and all the rest of those who think communism is the main enemy, who don't have the time to protest against McCarthy!

C: I'm bored with the whole business. It's all too obvious, the same arguments over and over.

A: They have to be repeated over and over. Take me. I approve of the death sentence, and I don't hesitate to admit it. If that means personal responsibility, I accept it. These are traitors who acted in the interests of a foreign country and who are too cowardly or too stupidly sly to admit it. They delivered information that may bring destruction to thousands, to millions of their own countrymen, to those very kids of theirs that are being publicly wept over by the professional commie sob sisters. They're guilty as hell—and they should die! Why not?

B: Don't change the subject. For years now all you ex-communists and ex-liberals have been howling for blood. Now you have it. How do you like it?

A: Fine! I like it just fine. Thank God, I've faced up long ago to the part of me that's guilty in the same sense the Rosenbergs are. Fortunately, I never had the chance to do what they did, though once I would have given a lot to have had it. So I don't have to pay publicly for a crime, only internally for an intention.

B: Fine, fine—they should die like scapegoats for your moral benefit, two real human beings, not literary examples, *real* people, with mothers, friends, children—so you can feel clean and smug.

A: That's not the point at all. The real question is: do you think they're *guilty?*

B: Guilty! What does the word mean?

A: I don't mean anything metaphysical. Just the legal fact. Did they pass certain information through Greenglass that—

C: In a sense, I *know* they're guilty, but—

B: You know, you know—did you read the whole transcript?

B: To tell you the truth, I hardly even read the newspaper accounts, but the pattern is so obvious, once you know the types involved, it's clear that it *must* be true, that Greenglass can't be lying. It's the old pattern, classic by now. All one has to do is remember himself of ten or fifteen years before, and the verdict is—

C: Guilty, I know. *You're* guilty, but you're not on trial. It's easy enough to try yourself in a figure of speech—you won't burn. Listen, aside from this look-at-yourself business, it's just one man's word against two others; the word of a man who contradicted himself, a man who hated his relatives, who's trying to save his own skin—

A: The whole point is that it's not just one word against another. As B. says, there's a pattern, a context, a whole framework of possibilities which we can't pretend we don't know, we three, who have in common our experience in the movement, whatever our later differences—

B: Is that proof in court? Why are so many distinguished people convinced that they're innocent? I won't even mention the Pope, but take Urey—Urey isn't satisfied, and he read the whole transcript. Is it proved, *proved!*—not just probable?

C: Jesus, B., you know why most of the protesters are protesting. It has nothing to do with the Rosenbergs. They only want to save *themselves* in their own eyes, to acquit their own youth: pretend to themselves that *they* really wouldn't have done it —or that their communist friends whom they sponsored and protected in the Popular Front days, wouldn't have done it, couldn't have done it, *didn't* do it. Talk about trying yourself!

A: Those are the same people, or at least the same kind of people who protested for Hiss, for Judith Coplon, for all the latest Communist Tens and Twelves and Elevens, and always for the same irrelevant reasons: to clear themselves, to refuse to admit that what they were once so proud of, what they thought of as their "highest principles," should lead only to lying and betrayal and piddling evil.

B Stop ganging up on me, you two. "Evil"! this is the new fashionable word. Once it was "the class struggle"—now it's Good and Evil—and I suppose you've got Original Sin up your sleeve. Put all your cards on the table!

A: Talk about red herrings!

B: All right, let's talk about this "evil," then. Suppose for a minute the Rosenbergs did it, that they passed on the information, whatever it was worth. The question is what they did it *for,* Is this an irrelevant point? Were they paid? Hirelings, sadists, bullies or what? They—

C: You can never be sure about motives. What do you think *we* were in the movement for? For the pure, disinterested reasons we would have given once, or—

B: Listen, hells bells, let's not go too deep. Maybe all virtue is vice disguised, I can't discuss such crap anymore—this is for the college dormitory. But speaking in an ordinary, human, unclinical way, these were people who acted for the *best* motives: for Internationalism, for Peace, for Humanity. Don't you think this should be taken into consideration?

A: There you go. Just what I've been waiting for you to say, part two of the standard justifier's gambit: one, they didn't do it at all—they were framed like Tom Mooney, Sacco and Vanzetti, Guy Fawkes, God knows who; and two, they had a *right* to do it, because—

B: I didn't say they had a right. If they betrayed their country, betrayed us, *me*—they were wrong. This much I know. I'm only saying that they *may* have done it not because they were worse, but because they were better than their neighbors, those fake patriots and black marketeers, who will probably watch the Rosenbergs' execution on television!

A: If you don't say it, the Rosenbergs do. They at least want it both ways: they're innocent spotless lambs, and they're heroes of the struggle against American imperialism. Like Hiss and Remington and all the rest—and because they want it both ways, they're nothing in the end, *liars!*

B: But still you can't deny they began with a desire for peace, a love of humanity—

A: They were always what they are now, stooges, who gave up their minds to the party bureaucrats, stupid and proud, victims of pride, like we were once, like you still are, B.

C: I can't agree. In this respect, B. is right for once. They acted stupidly, certainly, but for motives which I would hate to deny, for ends that may have been practically unattainable, but which I'm glad, *proud* (I'm not scared of the word) I yearned for when I was young and foolish—for Humanity! Is that just a dirty word for us now?

A: We couldn't tell the difference between Humanity and the Soviet Union. We kept saying Humanity—but what we really dreamed of was an eruption of force, getting even, wiping out in blood the world we felt despised us. There was a lot of hate—

C: It's no use. I just feel guilty. I want to cry when I think of their dying—really cry, because *I*'m not dying, because they're paying alone the bill for the rest of us. To hell with their foolish or hypocritical defenders, and with their hypocritical or foolish opponents. I know what they mean!

A: I don't understand it, C. Europe seems to have softened you up. Why all this sentimentality? You certainly didn't talk like this about Hiss.

C: Hiss! But he wasn't sentenced to death. What did he get, after all? A measly couple of years; and the whole respectable world, everybody blessed enough to have gone to Harvard, secretly convinced he couldn't have done it, because he was one of them!

A: What difference does the sentence make? The principles are the same; the sides line up the same way—

C: No, damn it all, the Rosenbergs are the precise *opposite* of Hiss. Take the same twelve people who would have believed at first sight and despite all evidence that Hiss was innocent (so clean-cut!)—and they would swear at the same first sight and on a stack of Bibles that the Rosenbergs are guilty! That they *look* like communists—the dirty kind, not the polite ones you can meet at the Harvard Club.

B: Why don't you say it right out, C. The Rosenbergs are *Jews;* they look like Jews—ugly, drab people with their comical Jello boxes and Bronx background. Why don't you say the word anti-Semitism, my friend?

C: Because it's not anti-Semitism. They were given a fair trial— presided over by a Jewish judge, the case against them conducted by a Jewish lawyer—

B: There were also Jews who helped round up the Nazis' victims in the Warsaw Ghetto!

A: Please, spare us the quotations from the *Daily Worker!*

C: Yet, somehow, no one can deny that the fact of their being Jews had *something* to do with their deaths. That they should be the only ones to pay in this way with their lives, two Jews, it can't be entirely an accident.

A: I'm ashamed of you, C. You're really a racist at heart. That's why you talk so differently about the Rosenbergs than you did about Hiss. Because they're Jews, fellow Jews—that's the only difference. You're just like the Harvard lawyers in their attitude toward *their* boy. You identify completely with these people, who—

C: Who I'd hate if they were in this room, whom I couldn't say three words to without losing my temper, who haven't thought one thought of their own in years. But so harmless, so middling, so unattractive, so much out of a world I know, so *made* to be victims! Why the hell should they pay for being born in the wrong situation, for having just the right combination of guts and stupidity to be caught out for something the Browders and Fosters ought to be paying for. Who's *really* responsible?

A: But don't you see where this leads you? Why stop with Foster? Why not Molotov or Malenkov, the Central Committee of the Russian Party, who really make the policy all their American stooges act out. Or why not Roosevelt himself (okey, he's dead, but just for example) because during the war years, when the crime was committed, he led the propaganda to convince us that Russia was our simon-pure friend—

B: It's true, after all, that Russia *was* our ally in those days. And that shouldn't be forgotten either. The Rosenbergs gave the information, *if* they gave it, to an ally.

A: Let's take one thing at a time. For every crime, society and its leaders are responsible in some sense. But also the individual! Isn't this the whole point, C.? That for all our good intentions, for all our being misled, we were each responsible for what well-meaning evil we did? You wouldn't plead (or would you?) that no one should be executed for anything, since all guilt is spread thin over all of us?

C: Your question is too general. This is a *special* case. It's not just a matter of the diffused overall responsibility of all of us for each other but of a deliberately sponsored political policy whose purpose was to lead such dull individuals to crime— and of an almost equally criminal stupidity, which—

B: Admit it! They're dying because they're Jews; and you're feeling a twinge because their death is a threat against you, C., and you, too, A., if you'd only face facts. If, at least, they hadn't had a Jewish judge, who had to lean over backward, to prove that all Jews weren't accomplices and Bolsheviks! A gentile judge—and we would be having another discussion. Let's even admit that they should have been found guilty, but such a sentence! It's lynch spirit—lynch law—

C: It's true that the sentence is excessive, a scandal! Why should they die, when someone like Fuchs, much more directly, more terribly guilty, is already free? When a Hiss, a real power in our political life for years, is almost ready to leave jail—

B: Naturally, these were not Jews!

C: That's not the point—

A: It really is the point, C. B. gives away your whole racist game.

C: No, no—such perilous matters aside, the sentence is absurd. Why does it shock the whole world?

A: Communist propaganda—subtle enough even to influence you.

C: And the Pope? No, no. There's obvious injustice. First of all, Russia *was* our ally at the time of the crime. And then, nobody can be *sure* that the piddling information Greenglass dug up for the Rosenbergs really helped the communists—Urey says no. And most important, no real harm has been done yet. It's all speculative. A sentence for possible murder—if the victim doesn't commit suicide first.

A: Why do you bring up the issue of murder? Treason is enough. They spied in wartime; they gave information to another country. And let's not kid ourselves. Sooner or later, Russia will find an excuse to attack us—and you can be sure they won't hesitate about using against us the atomic weapon they have in their hands thanks to Ethel and Julius Rosenberg. You don't have any illusions about that? Maybe you think that Russia's having the bomb is an aid to world peace?

C: You know I have no such illusions. It just seems *wrong,* that's all. I can't find the arguments against what you say—it's just irrelevant. The whole thing has a disgusting feel to it, the feel of fear and vindictiveness. It makes me ashamed of my country; and I don't like to be. Naturally, I give answers to the communists—when they bring it up, but—

B: And now the latest move—did you read about it? How they promised immunity to the Rosenbergs, if they would confess. Confess! Exactly like the Russian trials—

A: It isn't exactly like anything. In the first place, they didn't ask for a confession, but for identification of accomplices; and in the second place, it wasn't a promise of immunity, but of conversion of the death sentence, and—

C: Don't let B. bait you with these party line arguments; he knows as well as we do that turning State's evidence is an old democratic procedure—and yet—

A: And yet, what? How can you even consider for a moment comparing this isolated case with the thousands of farcical trials, judicial executions is better, of the communists. Not to mention—

C: You don't have to convince me of the hypocrisy of the communists; even B. knows that!

B: Even! Thank you.

C: I don't give a crap for what the communists say—or how loud their stooges and made-to-order meetings howl and scream in forty countries. Whatever the United States does, good or bad, they'll twist into something good enough to use as propaganda against us—good enough to convince those who are convinced in advance of anything they read in the *Daily Worker* or *Unità* or *Humanité*. I don't even care about the noble statements of the Catholic hierarchy; after all, they're professionals, mercy is their business! But for our own sake as Americans, because it's against our traditions to kill for political dissent—

A: Political dissent! Treason is what you should say.

C: You know what I mean. Politically, practically, a million absolutely unjust executions are infinitely worse than one half-unjust one—but morally each single instance has the same weight. And against this one, against our injustice or excess or mistake, America's act and *mine,* what can I do? What can I feel but guilt! They shouldn't die, that's all!

B: It's hysteria, McCarthyism, the beginning of the end. Naturally, we're nowhere near as bad as Russia now, but one thing leads to another. You start with Red-baiting (even if the communists are wrong, even if they're vicious—they're such small potatoes in the U.S.) and you go on to Jew-baiting and worse!

C: This is not what I feel. It's only that—well, after all, a piece of all three of us will be dying with these Rosenbergs; we should at least have the decency to say out loud that it hurts.

A: Sometimes I just don't understand you, C. I'll bet anything that if the Rosenbergs had been acquitted, or were given some nominal sentence, you'd be howling against the stupidity of the courts, the sentimentality of the American people, our moral immaturity—

B: What do you mean—an old Red-baiter like him (he puts a friendly arm around C.), he'd be yelling for their blood.

C: You're both right—but—I only wish I were! I only wish I were!

Rome, Italy
—1952

# Voting and Voting Studies

IT IS A terrible thing to be a lion in a Daniel's den; but a humanist fallen among social scientists can scarcely help seeing himself in that absurd role. I have been interested for a long time in voting: in the meaning of the act itself and of the choices which that act involves. My interest has been especially poignant because so Platonic; I have, that is to say, actually voted only once in my life—and regretted it immediately afterward. There are, I tell myself, good superficial reasons for my failure to go to the polls: changes of residence and a consequent lack of knowledge of local candidates and issues, an early Marxist indoctrination against the whole notion of parliamentarianism. But I am not really sure why I have so strong a reluctance to vote; and I have sought to answer my questions about myself by speculating on my neighbors. Do they really believe that they are acting meaningfully when they put a cross before one of two names on a printed ballot? Do they vote to make a choice or make a choice in order to be able to vote; that is, is voting an act of social conformity, a symbolic gesture of belonging rather than a way of influencing government? Why do societies succeed in getting more and more people to vote as they become more and more totalitarian? Has the act of voting in its modern mechanical form (I see the voting machine as the visible and outward form of an invisible and inward process of dehumanizing choice) anything to do with traditional democracy at all?

I was disconcerted in turning to the three recent studies of voting I have been looking through (*Straight Fight*, *Voting*, and *The Voter Decides*) not so much by their failure to ask some of the

210

questions that strike me as fundamental, as by their method. Different men must ask different questions, I know; for a study, whatever its pretenses at objectivity, is an attempt to define oneself as well as a social problem. But the dispassionate, scientific air of these approaches left me feeling inadequate, overwhelmed by their modesty and impersonality, and dazzled by the charts and diagrams, the clinical vocabulary (no one "thinks" or "guesses," but "conceptualizes"), the sophistication in the matter of statistics, and the precision of the sampling methods. I am almost ashamed to admit that the very notion of the "panel" interview was unknown to me; and that I had vaguely assumed all my life that a "random sample" was one made at random.

In the face of such professionalism and abstract concern, my own interest seems not merely amateur but almost animal, that is, passionate and instinctive; and so I have been indulging in the sentimental image of myself as a member of a lower species trapped in the lair of the prophets of science. Yet when I have turned to their prophecies, that is, to the results of their investigations, I have been disconcerted once more in quite an opposite direction. *Straight Fight,* for instance, informs us that, in one English urban constituency at least, a greater portion of the old, of women, and of the upper classes vote for the Conservative Party, though, indeed, all three factors may be reducible to the single one of social class. To which the only adequate response is, "Uh-huh," or in more literary terms: we need no prophet come back from the grave (or panel interview) to tell us this! And when the same study goes gravely on to observe that "the behaviour of electors may perhaps be classified in terms of long-term trends and short-term fluctuations," the modest "perhaps" with which this platitude is proffered seems the final insult to one trained to wince at belaboring the obvious. I am similarly offended when it is ponderously established in *Voting* that Catholics tend to vote Democratic, or noted, with the air of having discovered some arcane truth, that "opinions are really formed through the day-to-day exchange of observations and comments which goes on among people." This even the naïvest of poets has observed, as he has also observed, merely by living, what *The Voter Decides* includes in its summary: "the results of both studies may be said to conform to the basic psychological principle that when strong and opposing forces act on an individual the resultant behavior will demonstrate the characteristics of conflict." This assertion, stripped of its technical vocabulary, does not even make the grade of a platitude but remains a simple redundancy: where there is conflict, there is conflict! And such a pleonasm is scarcely redeemed by applying it to the political situation and producing the further conclusion that a voter with contradictory convictions is less likely to vote and more likely to vacillate in his choice than one without them.

I do not wish to appear Philistine on this score; and I want to go on record as believing that sociology will yet survive such self-evident "discoveries," as it will survive parallel ones in other sub-fields, i.e., that rumors are less accurate as they spread out from a center, that people who talk about moving move more often than those who don't, and the like. I feel, however, that such banalities are the price American social science is paying for its current anti-intellectualism, its flight from theory; and I cannot help making some observations on the sociology of such sociology from the point of view of a not wholly unsympathetic outsider. I feel obliged to preface those observations with a note on the sociology of my own sociology of sociology; this is a process which opens up possibilities of endless regression, but here I promise I shall stop!

The humanist's image (or as we prefer to say, "myth") of the contemporary sociologist is that of a heavily subsidized, much-touted and honored scholar, torn at each moment between offers from industry and government—scarcely knowing, indeed, whether to take the rewards offered by the Coca-Cola Company or the Air Force—for his latest documentation of some weary cliché about man, long since a commonplace of literature. The humanist, made especially aware of the spiritual dullness and lack of intellectual curiosity in contemporary society by its indifference to great art, cannot help thinking of the sociologist's statistical wisdom as an ersatz for real insight into the social being of man; and he is likely to be caught muttering bitterly: "Sufficient unto the day is the social science thereof." Perhaps the wittiest expression of this rather unfair, but thoroughly understandable, reaction is found in two lines of Auden, a new commandment for modern life:

Thou shalt not sit with statisticians
Or commit a social science.

The humanist's case must, then, be discounted a little for the professional pique of the excluded which lies behind it; yet it is not without merit. The sort of statistical sociology (or political science) represented by these texts seems to him the result of two phenomena, both peculiar, in their strongest forms at least, to contemporary America: an almost neurotic impulse to self-examination and an almost religious regard for "scientific method." The spiritual hypochondria, the eternal feeling of his own pulse by the contemporary American is a standing joke among Europeans; and this eternal self-examination (rivaled only, if we can believe Dostoevski and Chekov, by nineteenth-century Russians) is not merely a matter of maudlin self-exposure at cocktail parties, but of endless polls, interviews, exposures, and candid statements to the press, ranging from the crassest journalism to the most cautious and methodical research.

These, the average American is not only delighted to participate in, but is pleased to spend his leisure time reading. From Kinsey's improbable best-seller to the latest Gallup or Roper report in the daily newspaper, the American is at once creating and consuming a never-ending "Song of Myself": a monument to obsessive self-concern beside which Whitman's poem seems a masterpiece of selflessness. His voting habits are of especial concern to him since the act of balloting tends to become his only even remotely political activity; and he wants to be told first how he is going to vote, then how he is voting (at two in the morning, he is still up beside his radio; and the great electronic gadgets of which he is so proud are adding him to all the other nameless units awake beside their sets), at last how he has voted. And he is not even averse to being told why, though the simple, gigantic figures are what interest him most. Like the sociologist on his more sophisticated level, the man by the T.V. believes that only quantitative truth is real.

Once given official sanction (and large budgets), such organized curiosity is insatiable; from the polls, to the altar, to the sickbed, to the grave—the experts we have hired to tell us all pursue us doggedly, notebooks in hand. I presume that the only reason we did not drop sociologists and psychologists into Hiroshima with the Bomb was a technical one; and I sometimes have a nightmare of our world after its final war, in which the sole man and woman left alive turn out to be a pair of sociologists, who after questioning each other scientifically, instead of getting down to reproduction, separate to write rival studies of "The Single Survivor." Yet the interest in self which lies behind such phenomena is not, however untrammeled, in itself really reprehensible. As a nation, we come by it honestly enough, out of the tradition of soul-searching so unexpectedly handed down by the Puritans to the emancipated, contemporary American of whatever origin. There is something really satisfactory and amusing in the notion of the social scientists as our Last Puritans.

It is only what the "self" becomes in the electronic calculating machines that gives me pause; for what the IBM cards can record or newspapers report is a statistical datum, abstract and unreal. I cannot finally convince myself that in our desire to know first especially and then exclusively the existence we share with others, experience that is *statistically* meaningful, there is a retreat from inwardness and the person as defined in literature and art. There is a kind of comfort, I am aware, a delightful sense of actuarial helplessness in learning that we are Democrats because of certain probabilities inherent in our generation and ethnic group—or adulterous because of our level of education. The panel method, for all its avowed desire to come to grips with individuals rather than with rows of figures, cannot handle those individuals except as instances of, say, the male sex, the forty-year age group, the Protestant religion. The sort of peace with himself that man used to seek in the conviction that we are all sons of God, he seems now to find in the conviction that we are all specks on a bar graph between the covers of a scholarly book.

I do not believe, of course, that the studies I have been reading are the work of conscious or deliberate enemies of inwardness. They are written by men doing a job as conscientiously as they can in a society organized on the lines of a rigid division of labor. They are, in short, "specialists" rather than men at the moment that they write, and in that sense, the victims of a general panic in our culture, a flight from the person. A first symptom of this is their resolve to attest to their objectivity by drawing their metaphors for the individual from science rather than the humanities. The "sciences of man" (as they are sometimes called in the phrase that already gives away the game) hesitate between the natural sciences and literature and philosophy; but the poles do not stand still. And how can one blame the sociologist for abandoning traditional notions of man, when critics and philosophers, too, are abandoning insight to statistics, poetry to methodology—and even the professor of literature likes to boast that he is producing "research."

The embarrassment of the scientizing political philosopher and literary man alike is that he deals with a field in which there is (in a sense analogous to that of the physical sciences) nothing new to discover; though, indeed, certain older wisdom has to be taught again and again in new languages. I think at this point of Freud's plaint about having to tell men as if it were a revelation what every nursemaid knows. Both poet and social scientist are, therefore, necessarily engaged in redeeming platitudes; but the method of the poet is to specify and complicate the cliché, while the method of the sociologist is to quantify and simplify. A poet's pondering on the problems of filial ingratitude produces *King Lear*. A sociologist might by a series of panel interviews decide that ("perhaps" and "at least in one rather typical small court of pre-Christian England, selected because of etc., etc.") there is more of a tendency among grown daughters of kings showing signs of senility to evidence open hostility, if such kings give over their property completely to such daughters. A really canny investigator might even be able to show, within the normal statistical margin of error, of course, the percentage of such cases in which the father would finally be shoved out into a storm. To put it mildly, such information is irrelevant to any central human concern; though, to be sure, more than one Department of Welfare might be persuaded to put up funds for a continuing study along the same lines.

Yet the notion that knowledge about the relations of men to each other is not useful—not even really *true*—until it can be quantitatively expressed has taken over not only in the social sciences. The accidental (from any philosophical point of view) predominance of physical science in our culture and the confusion of that science in the popular mind with technology have lent prestige to all graphs, mathematical formulations, and equations, however meaningless. The social sciences, precisely because they have come late into the field to which they aspire, and because they are suspected of continuing fraternization with such outmoded elite disciplines as religion, philosophy, and literature, feel obliged to ape especially sedulously the outward appearance of the more prestigeful methods of investigation. In the way a schoolgirl imitates the hair style of the reigning movie actress, so the social scientist imitates the mathematical statement and laboratory attitudes of the physicist. His world, too, can be reduced to numbers! *Wie m' goyisht sich, azoi m' yiddisht sich* (As the gentile is a gentile, so the Jew is a Jew)—the folk saying puts it.

Of course, there are rationalizations. "True," the sociologist retorts, "everyone always knew that things fell when one dropped them; but until such knowledge was quantitatively expressed as $S = \frac{1}{2}gt^2$, that knowledge was not practically of any consequence, and in the same way. . . ." But it is, alas, never the same way; at least, I have never seen any "sociological law" of the order of the law of gravity emerge from the most statistical analysis of a platitude. Indeed, one could scarcely look for such an event until the vagaries of the individual man become as indifferent to us as the wanderings of individual atoms. At this happily scientific stage, I trust we shall never arrive; and, indeed, it is because I feel an impulse in such a direction in statistical sociology and political science that I am a little wary of those disciplines.

One does not have to move to such large objections, however, because of the lack of smaller ones. The "quantitative method" as exemplified in these three studies leads to an insidious sort of half-conscious falsification, disturbing, I am sure, even to advocates of the method. For instance, in *The Voter Decides,* there is a striking instance of the tendency to hypostatize imaginary psychological categories, which can then be statistically manipulated in their interrelationships. In this case, the "manageable number of variables" turns out to add up to the fairy-tale number of three: issue orientation, party orientation, and candidate orientation; and though the writers begin by speaking of these as names, convenient labels, they end by the logic of their method in treating them as *things*.

More disturbing to me and more inevitable, I fear, is the way in which all three books are driven, for the sake of merely getting on with the problem, to treat all Republican or Democratic votes as equivalent to each other. I suppose that if one is to make any generalizations at all on this level about voting behavior, one must assume that all voters are making a choice between two relatively constant and distinguishable alternatives. Yet such are the complications of our party system to begin with, and of human motivation in the second place, that two people who are "black radicals," opposed passionately and ignorantly to the educated and rich, may vote one Democratic ("for the party of the people") and the other Republican ("for the party of the investigators who showed up those Harvard boys in the State Department"). Each of these may be paired off with a quite genuine conservative, one of whom takes the Whiggery of Eisenhower to represent his ideal, the other of whom finds the same ideal better personified in the genteel New Deal nostalgia of Stevenson. In such cases, is it not more bewildering than informative to treat arbitrary labels as indications of a real choice? The same impulse to make quantitative lists rather than qualitative discriminations leads to a lumping together of all nonvoters, though certain refusals to vote may be real political acts, just as certain resolves to go to the polls may be abject surrenders to conformism, the rejection of politics. Such distinctions are perhaps impossible to make inside such an approach as we are examining; and I suspect that many of the investigators would find them as pointless and finicky as a qualitative distinction between orgasm and orgasm would seem to a Kinsey.

My final and chief objection to the statistical method in the social sciences in general is that it represents the triumph of an antitheoretical drift, which seems to me one of the most regressive aspects of American scholarship. It strikes me, to put it as bluntly as possible, as yet another facet of a widespread, academic anti-intellectualism—part of the (real American!) quest to find a democratic substitute for something so aristocratic as ideas, some bureaucratic ersatz for the insight of the individual thinker. Sociological investigation becomes not merely quantitative in method but bureaucratic in its organization, not the child of pure science it would like to claim itself but a hybrid offshoot of mass production and industrial engineering, with techniques as impersonal and ultimately mindless as the production methods of a movie or a news magazine. One imagines the director of research with three phones on his desk, dreaming of the day of complete automation.

"Specialization" first and now "bureaucratization," these have been in the American university, in the schools of a country notorious for its resistance to general ideas, the respectable methods of substituting technology for theory. Such a retreat from speculation to "fact" begins with a healthy desire to escape the "ivory tower," to bring political science, say, down to the level of practical politics —to be immediately useful to ordinary men in their everyday concerns. This is not on the face of it an ignoble ideal; but it turns out to be merely the noblest disguise of the heresy of practicality which has turned our colleges into trade schools. To be sure, the investigation of opinion formation is *useful,* and it is no accident that it blurs into big business on the one side and journalism on the other; but such a usefulness is not the usefulness of science or of pure mathematics. It is the hallmark of the technological: and technology is the slave of the system it serves; it cannot challenge or teach, only blindly implement.

I suppose that below such theoretical levels, the development of mass faculties in mass universities has created an economic pressure for the invention of cooperative disciplines to replace individual talent. Only in an academy of the elite, can one expect Platos and Aristotles; we must find, and are finding, ways in which the mediocre can at once maintain their self-respect and be useful to their society. This is a necessity in a day in which the university is becoming more and more overwhelmingly a refuge for men of indifferent talent in search of status and security. In the beginning, the fact-compilers and the statistics-gatherers were humble and spoke as temple servants. They were mere collectors bringing in a fresh harvest of data against the day when some great, synthesizing mind would make of their harvest a new theory. But let anyone now dare to try to synthesize with the proper rashness and brilliance, and hear the vituperation heaped on him as a popularizer and robber of other men's ideas. The fact-snufflers, the truffle-hounds of science, have come to think of themselves as their own masters; the temple servants have set themselves up in the inner sanctum as priests.

And who is there to challenge them in a society that more and more thinks of "facts" as more honorable than theories, of impersonality as more acceptable than personality, of graphs as more worthy than poems?

Of the three books I am discussing, *Straight Fight* is by all odds the worst offender in this regard: no idea contaminates the purity of its research. *Voting* is, in many respects, an honorable exception. Certainly, in its last two chapters, especially in the latter on "Democratic Practice and Democratic Theory," it moves out freely and interestingly into the realm of speculation; but, truly, I must confess that I find it hard to see how the detailed documentation that precedes those chapters is necessary to the posing of a question of which most of us are surely aware: How is it possible to maintain a belief in classic democracy now that we are conscious (and weren't the formulators of that doctrine conscious of the same thing, after all?) that the individual voter does not come up to the ideal qualifications they dreamed for him? The book does, however, resist the temptation to stay safely ensconced behind its figures and easy clichés, asking finally some of the questions at least which properly follow such an investigation.

It seems to me, however (speaking with all the irresponsibility of one whose primary commitments are elsewhere), that some theoretical speculations must be engaged in before *an investigation*. No one can begin, of course, without prior ideas and expectations; if he is not conscious of those ideas and expectations, he is likely to begin with ill-perceived general assumptions that will betray the finest sampling methods and questioning techniques. There are two areas especially where the lack of insight and theory seems to me evident in the studies with which I am concerned. First, the matter of class. In England, conventional notions of class status, resting on the traditional socio-economic basis, seem to yield viable results; at least, there appears to be a real correlation between "class" in this sense and the way a voter makes his limited party choice. But in America, ordinary (which is to say, European-oriented) conceptions of class are confusing rather than helpful when applied to voting habits.

Let me deal here quite briefly only with the criterion of "education" which is used in *Voting* as one of the three main measures of

SES. To ask only the quantitative question, "How many years of education?" is to establish a standard so gross that all really interesting distinctions escape it. I have a hunch that in America at the present moment a university education is in the process of becoming so general a cultural possession that it can scarcely be considered a cutting line between classes. The important questions now tend to be: night school or daytime classes? city college or college away from home? agricultural school or arts college? general curriculum or school of education? Ivy League or Big Ten? A real distinction in status now could be established not so much from where a person happens to get his education as from where he is able to imagine getting it. If one insists on turning these things into questionnaires anyone can administer, perhaps the key question should be: Where do you look forward to sending your children to college? It seems to me, at least, that the limitation of ambition, even of imagination in such regards, is the clue to actual class status in the United States, not so much the matter of legally or even economically limited possibilities as of the limitation of aspiration and desire.

It is not, for instance, how much money a man has that fixes him in a certain class (for our classes, as they most effectively function, seem to me clearly "cultural" rather than economic), but what kind of ties, say, he would buy if he had money enough to make a free choice. What kind of clothing, what sort of house, which magazines, what books (if any) would he own? Would he drink beer or Martinis? Would he go to wrestling matches or polo matches? These are the matters that count. Indeed, a distinction closer to that we make in ordinary conversation between "highbrow" and "lowbrow" (in which years of education and income are secondary considerations) would be more to the point than inherited notions of socio-economic class, or even the self-ranking of people who do not really share in this regard the assumptions of the questioner.

At least, if one began with such a standard, he would not produce the really useless and confusing conclusion arrived at by most of this research, namely, that the more educated group votes more Republican. This baffles my own firsthand knowledge, for instance, that university faculties (who are, after all, more educated than anyone) tend to be Democratic—or the special fact that in three English departments with which I have had intimate connections less than 5 per cent of the members voted Republican. What are the operative factors here? I certainly find no hint of them in any of the studies. In what groups does one lose caste by voting Republican? In what groups does he gain status by such a vote? What makes a vote either way *what one does?* The authors of *Voting* make the point quite clearly in one place that the voting decision is parallel in its formation to the formation of taste. I should guess that it is, often at least, precisely like other manifestations of taste, a way of asserting one's belongingness to a particular group, and that it should be studied in respect to the whole syndrome of taste. How many readers of comic books vote for Stevenson? How many people who do not know what an artichoke is prefer the Republicans? What is the connection between wearing hand-painted ties and party choice?

Finally, it seems to me (and here I return to where I began) that there is not in any of these studies sufficient prior speculation on the social meaning of the act of voting as such, opposed to the act of choosing one or another candidate; yet I do not see how one can begin to study the latter until he has distinguished from it and clearly understood the former. In recent years and in direct proportion, I would venture to guess, to the decrease in a really passionate concern with the outcome of elections, there has grown up an increasing public concern with having people *just vote,* no matter whom they vote for. Institutional propaganda in the press and over the radio insists more and more (even at the cost of time for publicity for the competing parties) on everyone's getting out to the polls; so that in the consciousness of the American citizen there is slowly established (of all people, he has been in his freedom of movement and choice relatively immune to this) the notion that not the considered act of deciding on candidates and issues but the mere mechanical act of voting is in itself his essential patriotic duty. To "go to church" (but what church?), to vote (but for whom?), to send his children to college (but what *sort* of college?)—these are the demands on anyone who asks respect from the community.

The whole mythology of voting has been transformed; the vote comes to be regarded as a public act of allegiance to an abstract "democracy" rather than a private decision as to what is good and what bad for the state. The "secrecy of the ballot" becomes an outmoded slogan; what matters is that the act of entering the polling place be *not* secret, known to everyone. That this is merely one symptom of a general drive for *participation* as a good in itself—regardless of its end—should be obvious. It links up closely with the parallel propaganda that nags at us from radio and television: Go to church this Sunday. Not to one church or other, just any church —not to assert your difference but your sameness: everyone the same in different places. It is notorious that we are in the midst of the strangest of all religious revivals, a renewed commitment to the abstract idea of religion rather than to any particular manifestation —in a nation where "man" is any man, "the church" is any church.

On every level of cultural life, this hunger for total participation replaces the older ideal of personal preference and threatens especially the freedom simply to withdraw or hang back. Even school children become subject to such pressures; the coming of Valentine's Day, for instance, no longer means that a boy brings, shyly or boldly, to some girl he has mooned over all year a lacy heart and a declaration of love; but that every kid under pressure brings for every other kid in his entire class some machine-produced greeting remembered the day before at the Five-and-Ten. One does not choose a special Valentine, but celebrates Valentine's Day. I have a hunch that our situation is already far gone in this respect when it comes to voting; but I should be interested in having the problem investigated (as long as the machinery is in motion) by someone with the means and techniques for such research. We seem to be at a critical point; for the abandonment of choice is one of the essential symptoms of a drift toward a totalitarianism of spirit and attitude which can presumably grow even inside a technically open society.

It is well known that in the full-fledged, total state, voting (once sentimentally regarded as the sufficient guarantee of democracy), far from being discouraged, reaches new heights of enthusiasm and participation. It is pointless merely to speak of a perversion of the practice; something in the act of voting itself has apparently all along contained the seeds of its present uses. To be sure, in a totalitarian culture, the element of choice, already narrowed for us unredeemably, it seems, to two parties, is further minimized or eliminated altogether; and the whole process becomes purely what it was before only in part, a mass ritual of acceptance and conformity. In what sense and to what degree voting has already become for some of our people such a symbolic gesture of the surrender of personality is a question whose significance cannot be exaggerated. This question, so vital to us at the present moment, I would hope that some future researcher would have the intellectual temerity to ask.

—1954

# THREE

# The Antiwar Novel
# and the Good Soldier Schweik

## I.

WRITTEN IN Prague in the twenties about the events of 1914 and 1915, *The Good Soldier: Schweik* first reached America with the Depression, and returns now, after another war and another peace, strangely involved in history: not only the history of the times it describes, but the history of the times through which it has come down to us. What shifts of taste and allegiance it has survived! What collapsed hopes and betrayed dreams!

Perhaps the kind of pacifism it embodies is the sole product of World War I to have lasted into our era. Certainly the official aims in whose names that war was fought, and which were theoretically assured by the Treaty of Versailles, have not come to very much. The dissolution of the League of Nations, the successes of Stalin and Hitler, and the outbreak of World War II made clear that the outward forms of democracy, national self-determination, and international cooperation, imposed by fiat or invoked in piety, had little to do with the inward meaning of the world after 1919. Not peace and order but terror and instability were the heritage of the postwar years: an institutionalized terror and a stabilized instability, in whose honor two minutes of silence were observed for the score of November elevenths between the first Great Armistice and the second great eruption of violence.

But pacifism, too, was a victim of World War II, which saw thousands of young men, who earlier had risen in schools and colleges to swear that they would never bear arms, march off to battle —as often as not with copies of antiwar books in their packs. Those books were real enough, like the passion that prompted them and the zeal with which they were read; only the promises were illusory. The unofficial war-resisters, who for twenty years had pored over evocations of battlefield atrocities to immunize themselves against the appeals of patriotism, found their own slogans finally as irrelevant as the catch phrases they pretended to despise. To be sure, the end of still another war has seen the upsurge of still another pacifism; but this seems by now part of a familiar pattern, the zig which implies a zag before and after.

Perhaps then, one must content himself with saying more moderately that the chief lasting accomplishment of World War I was the invention of the antiwar novel: a fictional record of the mood out of which the pacifism of between-the-wars was born and of the hopes and fears which sustained it through all the horrors of peace. It is certainly true that before the 1920's that genre did not exist, though it had been prophesied in the first two-thirds of Stephen Crane's *The Red Badge of Courage,* and that since the 1920's, it has become a standard form: both a standard way of responding to combat experience and a standard way of starting a literary career.

In the United States, the examples of Hemingway and Faulkner have ensured the continuing popularity of the genre; the latter struggling as early as *Soldier's Pay* and as late as *A Fable* to give shape to his sense of World War I, and the former providing a classic prototype once and for all in *A Farewell to Arms.* No wonder similar books from abroad have always moved us, from Henri Barbusse's *Le Feu* to *All Quiet on the Western Front,* and notably, of course, *The Good Soldier: Schweik.* And no wonder, too, that the generation of Americans who had broken their pacifist oaths in World War II sought to make amends by keeping faith with the sort of novel that had made war real to them before life itself had gotten around to doing it.

Certainly the flood of antiwar novels that generation has been producing since the forties owes more to certain books that their authors had grown up reading than to the actual fighting that many of them did. A typical case in point is Norman Mailer's *The Naked and the Dead,* begun at Harvard before Mailer had lived through any battles but fictional ones; and quite properly so, since for those of his age *the meanings of their wars had already been established by men twenty and thirty years their senior,* by Hemingway and Faulkner and Jaroslav Hašek, among others.

As a matter of fact, the meaning of their wars has been for most generations established before the fact—in our culture, largely by works of art. The writers of Europe and America who were young enough to fight in World War I were, in this light, unique, endowed with a peculiar freedom their successors have vainly tried to emulate by imitating the forms in which it was expressed. Only the former, however, actually lived in the interval between two conventional ways of understanding war, serving as the gravediggers to one and the midwives to the other.

For a thousand years or so, roughly from the time of Charlemagne to 1914, the wars of Christendom, whether fought against external enemies or strictly within the family, had been felt and celebrated in terms of a single continuous tradition. And those who lived within that tradition assumed without question that some battles at least were not only justifiable but holy, just as they assumed that to die in such battles was not merely a tolerable fate but the most glorious of events. Doubts they may have had, but these could scarcely be confessed to themselves, much less publicly flaunted.

Full of internal contradictions (what, after all, had any military code to do with the teachings of Christ?) and pieced together out of the rag bag of history (tales of Old Testament berserkers like Samson, scholarly recollections of Roman *vertu* and Greek *arete,* popular vestiges of the Germanic combat-religion), nonetheless the Christian heroic tradition proved viable for ten centuries, as viable in the high verse of Dante and Shakespeare and Chaucer as in folk ballads and the sermons of country priests. Yet all the while it lived, of course, it was dying, too, dying with the civilization that had nurtured it, already mourned for by the time of Sir Walter Scott. So slowly did it die, however, that only under the impact of total war were those who fought shocked into admitting that perhaps they no longer believed in what they fought for.

Last to learn that the old tradition had in fact died were the heads of state, kings and emperors, prime ministers and presidents. In their mouths, the shabby slogans For God and Country, For

Christ and King, *Dulce et decorum est pro patria morire*—rang ever less convincingly. But they were not the simple hypocrites their earliest critics took them for; they were merely dupes of history, in whom self-interest conveniently cooperated with confusion. Even more absurd than they, however, seemed the prelates of churches, on whose lips the more bloody battle cries, always a little ironical, appeared suddenly nothing but ironical. Yet it was not the believers who felt the absurdity, only those for whom God was presumably dead.

Small wonder, then, that priest and potentate alike remained unaware that history had rendered them comic, since no one told them except those whose opinions they discounted in advance. Indeed, some to this very day have not realized that the words they speak in all solemnity have been to others for over forty years household jokes. One function of totalitarianism in its manifold forms is precisely to forestall the moment of awakening, imposing by decree the heroic concepts which once flourished by consent. The totalitarian chief counterfeits ever more grotesque versions of the Hero, and in cell and torture chamber attempts to exact from those who dare laugh at him "confessions" that nothing is funny at all. The earliest record of such an attempt, as well as of its gloriously comic failure, is to be found in *The Good Soldier: Schweik*.

Not only in totalitarian societies, however, is the antiheroic spirit assailed by the guardians of the pseudoheroic. In more democratic nations, mass culture is entrusted with the job assigned elsewhere to the secret police; and where those who snicker at pretension are not hauled off to prison, they find it difficult to make themselves heard above the immensely serious clatter of the press and the ponderous voices of official spokesmen, magnified to thunder by P.A. systems. Yet certain writers, like Hašek before them, continue to feel obliged to carry to the world the comic-pathetic news it is reluctant to hear: the Hero is dead. First to know, such writers are the last to forget that ever since World War I they have been called on to celebrate, with due hilarity, the death of the myth of the heroic, even as their predecessors were called on solemnly to celebrate its life.

In the battle front against war, however, there is these days no more possibility of a final victory or defeat than on the battle fronts of war itself. In the former as in the latter, the end is stalemate; for the antiheroic satirists who have carried the day in the libraries and the literary magazines elsewhere seem to have made little impression. The notion of the Christian Hero is no longer viable for the creative imagination, having been destroyed once and for all by the literature of disenchantment that followed World War I; so that no modern Shakespeare could conceive of presenting warriors and kings in the light shed on them by the chronicle plays, nor can we imagine a contemporary Vergil suggesting that death for the fatherland is sweet. Yet we fight wars still, ever vaster and more efficient wars, while senators and commissars alike speak, and are applauded for speaking, in all seriousness the very lines given caricatured senators and commissars in satirical antiwar novels.

Worse still, the antiheroic revolt has itself become in two or three generations a new convention, the source of a new set of fashionably ridiculous clichés. Shameless politicians are as likely to use the slogans of between-the-wars pacifism to launch new wars as they are to refurbish more ancient platitudes. The wild freedom with which the authors of *The Enormous Room* and *Le Feu, The Good Soldier: Schweik* and *A Farewell to Arms,* challenged millennial orthodoxies has been sadly tamed; its fate is symbolized by Picasso's domesticated dove hovering obediently over the rattling spears of the Soviet war camp. Nevertheless, such books still tell us certain truths about the world in which we live, reveal to us certain ways in which men's consciousness of themselves in peace and war was radically altered some four decades ago.

The antiwar novel did not end war, but it memorializes the end of something almost as deeply rooted in the culture of the West: the concept of Honor. It comes into existence at the moment when in the West men, still nominally Christian, come to believe *that the worst thing of all is to die*—more exactly, perhaps, the moment when for the first time in a thousand years it is possible to *admit* that no cause is worth dying for. There are various mitigated forms of this new article of faith: that no cause is worth the death of all humanity, or of a whole nation, or simply of millions of lives; but inevitably it approaches the formulation: no cause is worth the death of a man, no cause is worth the death of *me!*

There are in the traditional literatures of Europe, to be sure, characters who have believed that death was the worst event and honor a figment; but such characters have always belonged to "low comedy," i.e., they have been comic butts set against representatives of quite other ideals, Sancho Panzas who serve Don Quixotes, Falstaffs who tremble before Prince Hals, Leporellos who cower as the Don Giovannis tempt fate. They have been permitted to blaspheme against the courtly codes precisely because those codes have been so secure. And, in any event, their cowardice has always spoken in prose or dialect, worn the garb of a servant or vassal, bowed the knee before an unchallenged master. They represented not a satirical challenge but precisely a "comic relief" from the strain of upholding—against the promptings of our animal nature, the demands of indolence, and greed, and fear—those high values that were once thought to make men fully human. *Non fate fosti viver come bruti, ma perseguir virtute e conoscenza.*

What happens, however, when the Leporellos, the Falstaffs, and the Sancho Panzas begin to inherit the earth? When the remaining masters are in fact more egregious Falstaffs and Leporellos and Sancho Panzas, and all that Don Quixote and Prince Hal and Don Giovanni once stood for is discredited or dead? What happens in a time of democracy, mass culture, and mechanization, a time when war itself is transformed by the industrial revolution? *The Good Soldier: Schweik* addresses itself to answering, precisely and hilariously, this question. And the answer is: what happens is what has been happening to us all ever since 1914, what happens is *us.*

We inhabit for the first time a world in which men begin wars knowing their avowed ends will not be accomplished, a world in which it is more and more difficult to believe that the conflicts we cannot avert are in any sense justified. And in such a world, the draft dodger, the malingerer, the gold brick, the crap-out, all who make what Hemingway was the first to call "a separate peace," all who somehow *survive* the bombardment of shells and cant, become a new kind of antiheroic hero. Of such men, Schweik is the real ancestor. "A great epoch calls for great men," Hašek tell us in a prefatory note. "Today, in the streets of Prague, you can come across a man who himself does not realize what his significance is in the history of the great new epoch. . . . If you were to ask him his name, he would answer . . . 'I am Schweik.' . . . He did not set fire to the temple of the goddess at Ephesus, like that fool of a Herostrate, merely in order to get his name into the . . . school reading books. And that, in itself, is enough."

## II.

Not all of Hašek's book, unfortunately, is devoted to portraying a Falstaff in a world without Hotspurs or Prince Hals. Much of it is spent in editorializing rather obviously about the horrors of war and the ironies of being a chaplain, the shortcomings of the Emperor Franz Joseph and the limitations of the military mind; and toward the end it becomes rather too literary in a heavy-handed way, especially after the introduction of Volunteer Officer Marek, a figure obviously intended to speak directly for the author. From time to time, we feel it as dated, say, as *What Price Glory* or *All Quiet on the Western Front,* for we have grown by now as weary of the phrasemongering and self-pity of conventional pacifism as of the attitudinizing and pharisaism of conventional patriotism.

It is not Hasek's anticlericalism or anti-Semitism, not his distrust of Magyars or of the long-defunct Austrian Empire, not his Czech nationalism or his defense of the Czech tongue against German linguistic imperialism that moves us today. The dream of expropriation, too ("After this war, they say, there ain't going to be any more emperors and they'll help themselves to the big royal estates"), rings hollow for us now, who know how it turned into the nightmare from which Jan Masaryk leaped to his death two wars later.

It is only when Hašek turns Schweik loose among scoundrels quite like himself, the police spy Bretschneider or the atheist Jewish chaplain, Otto Katz, and permits him to speak his own language— only, that is to say, when the anarchist intellectual permits himself to be possessed by his *lumpen* antihero—that the book becomes at once wonderfully funny and wonderfully true. Schweik is fortunately one of those mythical creations who escape the prejudices of their creators even as they elude our definitions; and he refuses to speak with the voice of the 1920 revolutionary, even as he refuses to speak with the voice of councilors and kings.

He will not be exploited by his author any more than he will by the con men and bullies who inhabit his fictional universe; moving through a society of victimizers, he refuses to become a victim. Though Hašek would persuade us that he is surrounded by Pilates ("The glorious history of the Roman domination of Jerusalem was being enacted all over again"), Schweik certainly does not consider himself a Christ. He is neither innocent nor a claimant to innocence. Charged with political crimes by an absurd police spy, he pleads guilty; and to a fellow prisoner who cries, "I'm innocent, I'm innocent," he remarks blandly, "So was Jesus Christ but they crucified Him for all that. Nobody anywhere at any time has ever cared a damn whether a man's innocent or not."

To Schweik malice is simply one of the facts of life, the inexhaustible evil of man a datum from which all speculation about survival must begin. He neither looks back to a Golden Age nor forward to redemption, secular or heavenly, but knows that if he is to survive it must be in a world quite like the one he has always known. A communicant of no church and a member of no party, he considers that neither intelligence nor charity is likely to ameliorate man's condition. "Anybody can make a mistake," he says at one point, "and the more he thinks about a thing, the more mistakes he's bound to make." And at another, he remarks with a straight-faced nihilism before which we can seek refuge only in laughter, "If all people wanted to do all the others a good turn, they'd be walloping each other in a brace of shakes."

Return evil for evil is Schweik's anti-Golden Rule, though often he assumes the guise of nonresistance, along with the semblance of idiocy, to do it. He is, however, neither a pharisee nor a hypocrite, only a simple conniver—in civil life, a peddler of dogs with forged pedigrees; in war, a soldier who will not fight. His resistance to war is based on no higher principles than his business; both are rooted in the conviction that a man must somehow *live* and, if possible, thrive on the very disasters which surround him. In the end, he is a kind of success, as success goes in a society intent on committing suicide; he eats well, drinks well, sleeps with the mistress of one of his masters, and pummels another mercilessly. But above all, he does not die. What more can a man ask?

He is even promoted from a lowly batman to company orderly, though, of course, the one place he will not go to is the Front. No matter how hard history nudges him, no matter what his orders read, nothing will force him into battle. He marches resolutely backward or in circles, but never forward into the sound of shooting; and by the novel's end, he has managed blessedly to be taken prisoner by his own side. Refusing to recognize the reality of disaster, he turns each apparent defeat into a victory, proving himself in the end no more a *schlemiel* than a Victim, or one of those Little Men so beloved in sentimental protest literature. Yet he seems sometimes all three, for it pleases his native slyness to assume such roles, fooling us as readers, even as he fools his superiors in the fiction they share, and as we suspect he fools the author himself. Indeed, he is fond of speaking of himself as "unlucky," but when he explains what this epithet means, it turns out he is unlucky only to others, especially those unwise enough to entrust him with important commissions.

Schweik's affiliation runs back through all the liars of literature to the father of lies himself, back through Falstaff to the sly parasites of Roman comedy and the Vices, those demidevils of medieval literature. He is, in fact, the spirit that denies, as well as the spirit that deceives: but he plays his part without melodrama, among the clowns, his little finger on the seam of his trousers, and his chin tucked in. So plumb, affable, snub-nosed, and idiotically eager to please does he seem, that we are more inclined to pat his head than to cry, "Get thee behind me!"

Yet on his lips the noblest slogans become mockeries. Let him merely cry, "God save the Emperor" and all who listen are betrayed to laughter; for he speaks in the name of the dark margin of ambivalence in us all—that five or ten per cent of distrust and ridicule that lurks in our hearts in regard even to the cause to which we are most passionately committed. And in the world in which Hašek imagines him, there is none to gainsay him, since the spokesmen for the ninety or ninety-five per cent of ordinary affirmation are corrupted or drunken or dumb.

We cannot help knowing, moreover, that not only the slogans of a distant war and a fallen empire, but those most dear to us now—the battle cries of democracy or socialism—would become in that same mouth equally hilarious; our pledges of allegiance intolerable jokes even to us who affirm them. Surely Schweik is not yet dead, but survives in concentration camps and army barracks, in prison cells and before investigating committees, assuring his interrogators of his feeble-mindedness and his good will as their pretenses to virtue and prudence crumble before his garrulous irrelevancies. "Beg to report, sir," he says, looking us right in the eye, "I'm an idiot, sir." And the idiocy of our definitions of sanity becomes immediately apparent.

It seems appropriate that Jaroslav Hašek and Franz Kafka lived at the same moment in the same city; for, though their politics differed as did the very language in which they chose to write, though one was mildly anti-Semitic and the other a Jew, their visions of the world's absurdity were much the same. Perhaps there was no better place from which to watch the decay of Europe and the values which had nurtured it than Prague; no better place to see how *comic* that catastrophe was.

Jewish legend tells us that precisely in Prague, in the attic of that city's ancient synagogue, the *Golem* waits to be reborn: the sleeping man-made Avenger who will awake only when some terror beyond all the Jews have known threatens the world. And maybe, after all, Schweik is no devil, but only that *Golem* in the uniform of a doomed empire, more comic in his second coming than anyone could have foreseen. "Terribly funny," we say putting down the book, and not taking the adverb seriously enough.

Kafka, we remember, thought himself a humorist, yet we shudder reading him. Hašek, it would appear, believed he wrote a tale of terror and was greeted by laughter. Let us leave the final word to Schweik, who reports, getting the names a little wrong, of course, but making his point all the same, "I once knew a Czech author personally, a chap named Ladislav Hajek. . . . He was a cheerful gentleman, he was, and a good sort, too. He once went to a pub and read a lot of his stories there. They were very sad stories and they made everybody laugh, and then he started crying and stood us drinks all around and—"

The account remains unfinished, like the book in which it appears, for the tale of the Good Soldier Schweik can never really be done; and, in any event, Hašek, who roused him from his long sleep in Prague, died at forty of the T.B. he had contracted in the prison camps of World War I.

*Fano, Italy*
*—1962*

# FOUR

# The Two Memories:
# Reflections on Writers and
# Writing in the Thirties

To THINK ABOUT the thirties in the second half of the sixties seems
not a luxury but a necessity: not one of those acts of reminiscence
and nostalgia which are optional, the self-indulgence of a baffled
critic, looking, perhaps, for his own lapsed youth (though surely
there is something of that in me), but the kind of return to roots
and sources so often required for cultural renewal; the re-examina-
tion of a past never quite understood—out of an awareness that unless we understand it now we will not understand the present or our
own surviving selves. We have barely left behind a decade or so
spent in re-evoking and re-evaluating the twenties, reaching back to
the years just after World War I in search of a clue to our identity
in the post-World War II years; and our own times have been altered as well as illuminated by that search. We have exhumed the
Charleston, as well as certain dress styles and hairdos; we have redeemed the fading figure of F. Scott Fitzgerald and revived for a
little while memories of Leopold and Loeb; we have even created a
magnificent pastiche of the period (its legendary slayings and weary
old jokes) in *Some Like It Hot*. And it is the myth of that period, if
not the actual fact, which helped make possible a New Jazz Age, a
revival of Bohemian Life, complete with Pop Art and what we have
agreed recently to call Camp, plus a new sort of Romanticism, ut-

terly without side or solemnity, despite its celebration of feeling over form, and pleasure over piety.

But our hunger for the twenties seems satiated for the moment, as the old-fashioned Beat become the newfangled Hip, and our fantasies demand to be fed with myths of quite another past, for which we ransack the thirties—surrendering nothing, let it be said quickly, of what we have redeemed from the twenties, only seeking to add something other, something more. The way in has been primarily literary so far: a series of studies and reminiscences to begin with —ranging from academic examinations of the past as something dead and therefore fair game for Ph.D dissertations (Walter Rideout's *The Radical Novel,* for instance, and Daniel Aaron's *Writers on the Left,* as well as Allen Guttmann's *The Wound in the Heart)* to more journalistic accounts like Murray Kempton's *Part of Our Time,* or personal memoirs like those of Mary McCarthy and Dwight MacDonald and, most recently, Alfred Kazin's account of "making it" in those bleak years. When the New Establishment remembers its origins (and to become established has always meant to feel obliged to remember) it recalls the thirties.

Even more striking have been the revivals and reprintings of the books which those Establishment figures enjoyed as underground literature in their youth—*not,* be it noticed, those writers whom the official taste of the period itself preferred, Dos Passos, say, or James T. Farrell or even John Steinbeck, despite his almost posthumous Nobel Prize. We tend to agree with the twenties in their adulation of Fitzgerald—grant, in effect, that they understood themselves, or at least chose to celebrate in themselves what we can share; but we correct the thirties even as we revive them—instruct them retrospectively about their own meaning. And we are embarrassed to find European opinion, as expressed by the Nobel Prize Committee, trapped still in the established taste of that much-confused era.

No, it is certain relatively neglected writers of the Depression decade who appeal to us, constitute our mythical thirties—judging at least by what the critics of our age have bullied the paperback publishers into making available once more: Henry Roth's belated best-seller, *Call It Sleep;* the three comic novels of Daniel Fuchs, *Summer in Williamsburg, Homage to Blenholt,* and *Low Company;*

James Agee's *Let Us Now Praise Famous Men;* and especially, of course, the almost lost novels of Nathanael West, *Miss Lonelyhearts* and *Day of the Locust,* in particular, but even his first half-botched piece of Surrealism, *The Dream Life of Balso Snell*—and, *especially* for the cognoscenti, those real hungerers for the thirties, *A Cool Million: or the Dismantling of Lemuel Pitkin.* Latterly, even such indifferent efforts as Tess Slesinger's *The Unpossessed* have been put back into print, and even such egregiously though typically bad prose of the period as Mike Gold's *Jews Without Money* or such correspondingly atrocious poetry as Eli Siegel's "Hot Afternoons Have Been in Montana." Surely there is a certain amount of campy condescension involved in the final two revivals, as well as a certain amount of canniness on the part of publishers to whom it has come through at last: the thirties are in! But there is a kind of vague sense, too, like that which drives the sick dog to consume whatever weeds are nearest by, that the literature of the thirties is good for what ails us.

All the books I have mentioned so far have been American books by urban Jewish Leftists and their fellow travelers, radicals at least of one or another persuasion; but even the works of Southern Agrarians begin to make it onto the supermarket and airport shelves (John Peale Bishop's *Act of Darkness* is about to be republished); and the books of certain European novelists who moved the Depression generation begin to appear again in the hands of the young. Not so long ago, a second edition (revised as thirties books tend to be revised when they are reborn) of Silone's *Fontamara* was issued, and though it has, I fear, won few hearts it had not already won twenty-five years before, the retranslation of Céline's *Death on the Installment Plan* which followed it seems to be moving our younger readers, as the original has already moved a new generation of readers in France.

Besides these revivals on the level of High Style, there have been humbler, more popular rediscoveries, too: sometimes in the form of adaptation, like Clifford Odets' *Golden Boy*—in blackface, with Sammy Davis, Jr. in the title role, straddling the political pieties of two ages; sometimes in the form of remakes, like the long-promised new movie version of *Winterset;* but most often in the form simply of reruns, those twin bills (the very notion of the

Double Feature itself a nostalgic revival) which bring back to the local theater, say, Clark Gable and Greta Garbo, or W. C. Fields and Mae West; after which the real addicts can stagger on home to the Late, Late Show and watch *Grapes of Wrath* or *I Was a Fugitive from a Chain Gang*. One movie face in particular, however, has emerged from the scores called up out of the past, coming to represent the very essence of the period as we redream it: not, oddly enough, Paul Muni or John Garfield who belong to the age completely, but Humphrey Bogart who survived it into the forties and fifties, to the verge of our own era—keeping alive (we are now able to realize) the unshaven cheek and the stiff upper lip of the Depression face through a time when we thought we had forgotten it forever. But there it was all the while, awaiting the moment when we would be able really to see it again, whether worn by Sam Spade in Dashiell Hammett's *The Maltese Falcon,* or the last surviving prospector in *The Treasure of the Sierra Madre,* or Harry Morgan in Hemingway's sole true thirties novel, *To Have and Have Not*— in which, for once, the quite unthirties face of Gary Cooper simply would not do for a Hemingway hero.

And with what astonishment we have lived to discover that face, grown magically young, to be sure, sported again in the sixties by Jean-Paul Belmondo; with what delight learned that we, through Bogey, had been there first. But so, too, were we there first politically; and it is with similar astonishment and delight that we observe the young, on campuses and off, forging once more a Radical Youth Movement, which may be only an analogue of what went on in the thirties rather than a belated offshoot. It hardly matters, however, since, whatever its roots, such a Movement makes possible the kind of dialogue with the past unavailable to those under twenty-five in the forties and fifties. To be sure, there are fundamental differences between their Movement and ours, but precisely this gives us something to talk about, since we are both aware of what divides us as well as of what we have in common—though they, perhaps, tend to be more conscious of the former, and we of the latter.

The Radicalism of the sixties, like that of the thirties, is influenced by the Bohemia which preceded it, and with which it remains uncomfortably entangled; and it differs from its earlier counterpart precisely as the one Bohemia differs from the other. The young radicals of the thirties came out of a world of bootleg and bathtub gin and the tail end of the first Freudian-Laurentian sexual revolution; the young radicals of the Sixties have emerged from the post-1955 world of "pot" and other hallucinogens and that homosexual revolution so inextricably intertwined with the struggle for Civil Rights as well as the quest for "cool." Even in moments of violence, in those demonstrations so satisfactory to the young in any age (and not the young alone), those climaxes of mass action in which the students of the sixties seem to be trying once more—though without full consciousness of the past—to achieve the delusory power felt by the half-million protesters against war on the campuses of the mid-thirties, a new note of almost feminine passivity has entered. Everywhere the desire to *suffer* violence rather than to inflict it seems to possess a generation untouched by the dream of "hard Bolshevism" proper to a world that had not yet learned to detest Stalin and endure Khrushchev—the aspiration to remain innocent even in conflict by playing the role of the raped rather than the rapist, the Jew as opposed to the Cossack.

And more than this, the New Leftist seems oddly, perhaps cripplingly, to *know* that he is indulging in a limited and privileged kind of activity, like joining a fraternity or playing on a team; that after four years or five, or six, he will accommodate to the life around him, run for office, or get a job, in any case, become more like his father than he can really bear quite to acknowledge—unless he leaves politics for drugs, abandons the SDS for LSD; but the real politico cannot abide this way either. But whence, we are driven to ask at this point, the odd passivity and the strange (not cynical but ironic) self-knowledge? And part of the answer lies surely in the thirties and what they have come to mean right now: in the particular way in which the thirties have survived for the activist young, which is to say, in their vicarious memory of that period.

The young have a longer memory than their elders—or even they themselves—are prepared to grant, a memory as long as the imagined lives lived in the books they read; not histories and memoirs and analyses by political scientists, for these seem only dead records of the dead, but fiction and poetry. And the books which have made the mind of this generation turn out to be in large part the sort of thirties book I referred to earlier, the underground literature loved in their youth by that intermediate generation of Saul Bellow, Norman Mailer, and James Baldwin, who have also influenced them, since the time of growing up which that intermediate generation remembers is indistinguishable from the nightmare visions of Nathanael West. West is finally the key figure, at work still as a living influence in the fiction of writers as young as Jeremy Larner, whose Dell Prize novel, *Drive, He Said,* may have a title derived from the poetry of Robert Creeley, but whose vision comes from *Miss Lonelyhearts* and *Day of the Locust.* But the world of West, we must never forget for a moment, that "peculiar half-world," as he called it himself, escaped all the clichés of politics, even of the left-wing orthodoxy to which he himself subscribed. Apocalyptics was his special province; and for the sake of a vision of the End of Things, he was willing to sacrifice what his Communist mentors had taught him was a true picture of society. Once out of his books, he felt obliged to apologize for his vision (writing to Jack Conroy, for instance, "If I put into *The Day of the Locust* any of the sincere, honest people who work here and are making such a great, progressive fight . . . [he is talking about Hollywood] the whole fabric of the peculiar half-world which I attempted to create would be badly torn by them"); but once inside them, he remained utterly faithful to that vision, however alien it might be to the Stalinist's theoretical America.

No wonder it is even more alien to the version of the thirties preserved in official histories, or tenderly recollected by the majority of those now over forty whose proudest boast is that they voted for Franklin Delano Roosevelt three times, or argued over with endless recriminations and counterrecriminations by the survivors of the New Deal. There are, mythologically speaking (and we are in the realm of myth whenever we talk about what survives not in the archives but in the heads of the young), *two* thirties at least— two memories of that legendary era, not merely different but competing. And those who walk about possessed by one such set of memories find it difficult, almost impossible to communicate with those haunted by the other, or committed, for official reasons, to evoking and preserving it. I listened recently—at a ceremonial occasion presided over by political scientists—to the movie actor Edward G. Robinson (himself a survivor of the thirties) not this time playing a gangster role, but reading the documents of *his* thirties: F. D. R.'s First Inaugural Address, topical comments by Will Rogers, etc., etc. And what, I kept asking myself—feeling quite like Saint Augustine crying out, "What has Athens to do with Jerusalem!"—had any of this to do with *my* thirties?

Yet Mr. Robinson's documents illustrated admirably a view of the Depression decade officially sponsored in the golden time of John F. Kennedy, by such court historians as Arthur Schlesinger, Jr.: a view which sees the thirties as a period in which we moved from defeat to triumph—conquering fear and poverty as well as preparing for a victory over the Nazis and Japanese—a time during which Labor came into its own, and the first decisive steps were taken toward the truly Good Society, i.e., the Welfare State. F. D. R. is the hero of this euphoric vision of our not-so-remote past, the true "Happy Warrior," crippled and charismatic, not FDR flanked, perhaps, by Eleanor Roosevelt or Henry Wallace, or some favorite ghost writer, brain truster, trust buster, or whatever. But this vision is embodied in no distinguished work in prose or verse—only in the feeblest sort of pious-commercial plays, the sound tracks of propaganda films prepared by the Department of Agriculture, and the final panels of those wartime comic books showing Roosevelt grasping by the hand Captain America or Superman. Even the elegiac verse occasioned by his death has mercifully faded from the mind.

No, the truly distinguished literature of the time of F. D. R., the books of the period that are preserved in libraries, taught in classes, or—best of all—still passed from hand to hand, scarcely confesses the existence of the New Deal at all; and the figure of Roosevelt, when untypically evoked, signifies irrelevance or impotence, the meaningless world of somewhere else. We can find, if we look hard, an ironical reference or two to his ineffectual legislation in some of the proletarian novels so admired during the period itself: in Clara Weatherwax's *Marching! Marching!*, for instance, first and last winner of the *New Masses* prize for fiction, or in the sort of satirical verse published in that same magazine. Though occasionally, and especially during the early years of his first administration, the Left managed to whip up some public indignation toward Roosevelt, he did not even exist for them as he did for the contemporary extreme Right—as the mythological object of rabid hatred and fear —but only as a subject for condescension and offhand contempt.

Characteristically, *Americana* (an independent left-wing review with which Nathanael West was briefly associated) could manage to say in 1932 only: "As for Mr. Roosevelt personally, we consider him a weak and vacillating politician who will be an apt tool in the hands of his powerful backers." Years later, to be sure, Whittaker Chambers, a literary witness of the era (at least, the period itself had considered him "literary," since certain leading Soviet critics had said kind things about his three published stories; and his play *Can You Hear Their Voices?* produced and directed at Vassar by Hallie Flanagan, had shaken the whole Ivy League) had attributed a somewhat more virulent attitude to his *alter ego* Alger Hiss, reporting of the latter that "the same strange savagery cropped out in a conversation about Franklin Roosevelt." This comment he hastened to explain at some length, in terms oddly reminiscent of D. H. Lawrence's *Lady Chatterley's Lover:* "Hiss's contempt for Franklin Roosevelt as a dabbler in revolution who understood neither revolution or history was profound. It was the common view of Roosevelt among the Communists, which I shared with the rest. But Alger expressed it not only in political terms. He startled me, and deeply shocked my wife, by the obvious pleasure he took in the most simple and brutal references to the President's physical condition as a symbol of the middle-class breakdown." The implicit metaphor is clear enough: F.D.R. as Lady Chatterley's impotent husband the C. P. as her prepotent lover, and the American working class as Constance herself.

Whether this was, in fact, Hiss's opinion scarcely matters (it is a question for the courts and the kind of journalist who loves correcting the courts, not for literary or social critics); it was, beyond doubt, a prevailing one in the thirties among the Communists and those writers influenced by them. But this means among *most* writers of first-rate talent then functioning in the United States, including certain survivors of the twenties, as well as young men just then rising to prominence, and even younger ones who would have to wait for the forties and fifties for recognition. The only considerable group of gifted artists who then operated completely outside the Communist sphere of influence were the Southern Agrarians—who numbered in their ranks poets like John Crowe Ransom and Allen Tate, novelists like Robert Penn Warren, and who had issued at the very beginning of the thirties their own manifesto, *I'll Take My Stand,* in which they had attempted to define a mythologically resonant and intellectually respectable politics of the Right. But F.D.R. in his anti-mythological Middle seemed as alien to them as to the writers of the Left: an irrelevant, faintly distasteful representative of the hated and feared urban Northeast, who, after T.V.A., was revealed as the Enemy.

I have spoken of the poetic invisibility of Roosevelt so far as if it were merely a historical datum to be researched and recorded; but his mythological irrelevance, in fact, belongs to a literary past with which our present is continuous, to which we still respond. The two most influential literary journals of the forties and fifties, the training ground of the writers who most move us now, or have, at least, until only yesterday (all the way from Saul Bellow to Marshall McLuhan, Karl Shapiro to John Berryman), were *The Kenyon Review,* heir to *The Southern Review,* and *The Partisan Review.* But *The Southern Review* came into existence under the doubtful auspices of Huey Long, redneck rabble rouser and fascist; while *The Partisan Review* was the by-product of the Communist-sponsored John Reed Club in New York, and the imported notions of *agitprop* it had presumably been formed to espouse. To be sure, by the time *The Kenyon Review* itself was being published, the disillusion of the respectable Southern Right with their peasant allies (fictionally recorded in Robert Penn Warren's *All the King's Men)* had already occurred; and *The Partisan Review* moved quickly from Stalinist orthodoxy to Trotskyism and Cold War Liberalism. Eventually, in fact, the two movements coalesced in academic amity, uniting to form the School of Letters, in which another generation of writers and intellectuals were trained. But in their most effective years, both journals reflected the traditions of radical dissent, Right and Left, out of which they had been born.

There has been much idle discussion, pro and con, of late about how "Red" the "Red Decade" really was; but as far as serious writers are concerned, there seems little doubt. In 1932, at any rate, more than fifty writers, among them the best known and most respected of their time, issued a statement called *Culture in Crisis,* in which they expressed their joint despair over the prospects of our society surviving its economic collapse, and pledged their support for the Communist presidential and vice-presidential candidates, Foster and Ford. Among the signers were Edmund Wilson, Sherwood Anderson, Lincoln Steffens, Langston Hughes, Erskine Caldwell, and John Dos Passos, who were later joined—in the American Writers' Congress, an organization which institutionalized the attitudes and positions of that first manifesto—by Edward Dahlberg, Katherine Anne Porter, Kenneth Burke, James T. Farrell, Dashiell Hammett, Richard Wright, Theodore Dreiser, and Ernest Hemingway. If we add to their number Henry Roth and Nathanael West, who were deep in the Movement from the start and needed no large public appeal to recruit them, it seems hard to think of anyone (with the exception always of the unreconstructed Southerners) not on the list whom one would expect to find included in a current college course on the literature of the Thirties. And we remember, finally, that a poll of a sample selected from the American Writers' Congress membership in 1936 showed still 36 voting for Earl Browder, six for Norman Thomas, only two for Franklin Roosevelt. How oddly skewed a result as compared with the voting behavior of the total electorate!

But what had moved the writers on the Left to make a commitment which cut them off from the mainstream of American life in so spectacular a way, pledging them at one and the same time to social action and disaffection from the strategies and techniques of action chosen by the overwhelming majority of their fellow citizens? If we look at the 1932 manifesto itself, we will find two quite distinct, though linked, motivations, both operative from the very beginning. The first is a particular brand of self-righteousness, an almost pharisaical smugness in being among the excluded, which seems an inevitable concomitant of all American radicalism and the isolation such radicalism implies in the United States: "Very well, we strike hands with our true comrades. We claim our own and we reject the disorder, the lunacy spawned by the grabbers."

The second is a vision of disaster and a pleasuring in it—a masochistic wish-fear that welcomes the End of Days, the Pangs of the Messiah, the long-awaited Signs of Doom precisely because they herald terror and annihilation. The writers of *Culture in Crisis* see the world around them as "a house rotting away; the roof leaks, the sills and rafters are crumbling"; but they thrill not to a promise of renovation and renewal, rather to the hope of pulling it down around them, of themselves disappearing under the rubble. How ironically the Rooseveltian phrase about having nothing to fear but fear itself rings in this context, where fear seems the last passion; and how oddly the appeal for hope built into F. D. R.'s speeches by anti-apocalyptic ghost writers contrasts with the cherishing of despair dear to the hearts of the doomsters. For the American writer who signs his own name, terror has been the staple of prose and verse ever since (if, indeed, it was ever anything else, in this land where dissent has always meant the rejection of all official optimisms), and the one thing to fear above all else the failure of fear itself.

And what is present in the manifesto only by implication and nuance is spelled out, fleshed out in the explicit images and fables of a hundred books that followed. Straight autobiographical accounts of what it was like to be alive and responding in this way to the America of the thirties are to be found in works like Malcolm Cowley's *Exile's Return* and Edmund Wilson's *American Jitters*— out of which not the outmoded rhetoric, but a single realized image stays in my mind, Wilson's picture of the just-opened Empire State Building in 1931, the tallest American house of them all, and one born rotting away,

> the pile of stone, brick, nickel and steel, the shell of offices, shafts, windows and steps, that outmultiplies and outstacks them all— that, most purposeless and superfluous of all, is being advertised as a triumph in the hour when the planless competitive society, the dehumanized urban community, of which it represents the culmination, is bankrupt. The big loft is absolutely empty, there is nothing to look at in it—with the exception of one decoration: . . . A large male figure is seen standing upright and fornicating, *Venere aversa*, with a stooping female figure, who has no arms but pendulous breasts. The man is exclaiming, "O, man!" Further along is a gigantic vagina with its name in four large letters under it.

And these books are still in print; *again* in print says it more precisely; yet the reader must be careful, for he will find them disconcertingly altered, bowdlerized, as it were, in Wilson's *American Earthquake* or Cowley's revised edition of *Exile's Return*. The author who survives an apocalypse that never comes, can scarcely believe he waited so breathlessly, so hopefully for the End—and tries to keep us from believing it three decades later.

Another kind of record is to be found in the so-called proletarian novels of the period, with their obsessive accounts of strike after strike defeated, defeated, *defeated* (it was Walter Rideout who first observed their distaste for victory in his acute study, *The Radical Novel in America)*. If the events at Gastonia provide the plot for at least six novels of the era, beginning with Sherwood Anderson's *Beyond Desire* and culminating in poor Miss Weatherwax's *Marching! Marching!,* it is surely because their outcome was satisfactorily disastrous for labor—though the imagination of the time could tailor fact to suit its own needs, as in the case of the strike at Aberdeen, Washington, which actually ended in a triumph for the unions, but in each fictional case was revised into a defeat. It is one more instance of the discrepancies of the Two Memories: the history books assuring us that the thirties were a period of immense gains for organized labor, the era of the Wagner Act and the creation of the C.I.O.; and the more poetic accounts seeing only bloody struggle inevitably debouching in defeat, failure, destruction, utter annihilation—this time in contempt of fact, though perhaps not of deeper truth.

Still, the manifestly proletarian books of the Depression era are its least satisfactory achievements, perhaps in part because of our nagging sense that this is not *really* how things went, our realization that the trade unions succeeded, after all, and that (for us still who are children of that age, as well as for the age itself) nothing fails like success. Certainly, the great causes which moved the thirties were *lost* causes: local miscarriages of justice, small or large, beginning with Sacco and Vanzetti and going on and on to a kind of climax in the Scottsboro boys. And what a shabby history of the exploitation of quite genuine misery for specious political ends it all seems from the vantage point of the present—compounded by our recent knowledge that the victims further victimized by their protectors may not even have been innocent to begin with—not even Sacco, not even Vanzetti. But mere facts matter little in such symbolic cases, tending finally to obscure their mythic significance.

So, too, with the war in Spain, that deep "wound in the heart" (the phrase is Camus', borrowed by Allen Guttmann for the title of a book about the literature created to express the pain born of the Loyalists' defeat): the war, which to those with memories like my own, made World War II seem when it came second-best, too-late, hopelessly impure. It was a war in which the New Deal, the pious Middle, refused—despite much soul searching—to become officially involved; the war in which Roosevelt forbade shipments of supplies to the forces fighting Hitler and Mussolini, but to which thousands of Americans (mostly Communists, largely Jews) went anyhow as volunteers, disowning both reality and their own country as they crossed the borders. But it was especially a war which captured the imagination of writers everywhere, a war which prompted even Hemingway to write four stories (chiefly bad), a play (utterly awful), and an ambitious novel (not quite good enough); and to make what must be the only public speech of his entire career.

Even more incredibly, it brought William Faulkner's signature to a petition, and—working at the deep level of his imagination where his old characters were being continually recast and furnished with new adventures, persuaded him to ship Linda Snopes off to drive an ambulance for the Loyalists. Yet what was for our best writers the chief event of the age—confirming their prescience of Doom—a cause incredibly pure (at least as mythicized) overwhelmed by the Fascists from without, and compromised hopelessly, even before the military defeat, by the maneuverings of the Soviet Union from within: this last, best, lost cause scarcely existed in the world of F.D.R. In James MacGregor Burns' thick and fascinating study of his character, *The Lion and the Fox,* for instance, the whole matter is given apologetic short shrift in three or four pages out of over five hundred: "Roosevelt from the start had favored the Loyalist cause. . . . Publicly, however, the President was adamantly neutral. . . . As the months passed Roosevelt felt increasingly distressed. . . . There were arguments and forces on the other side. . . . But nothing happened. . . . To raise the embargo would mean the loss of every Catholic vote in the coming fall election, Roosevelt said." And anyhow he had other fish to fry, other causes closer to his heart. It was left to the poets to celebrate disaster, and if they sputtered away into sentimentalities over bombed children, who then had the *chutzpah* to criticize, or the insight to point out that such images of desolation and impotence were precisely what the age demanded? Instead, they listened as Harold Rosenberg sang

> . . . *All he knew of life was laughing and growing*
> *Till the iron dropped on him out of the sky.*
> *O gaunt horses of Hades*
> *He has not even one weapon*
> *With which to defend himself.*

and Muriel Rukeyser answered antiphonally,

> *Bomb-day's child will always be dumb,*
> *Cannon-day's child can never quite come,*
> *but the child that's born on Battle-day*
> *is blithe and bonny and rotted away.*

And though they wept publicly, they thrilled a little, in private, too, at the notion of the rotting child. They did not know it was a Marquis de Sade they were all the time demanding, though they had one of their very own close at hand—since every revolution, failing inevitably at all of its ends but terror, produces a laureate of terror: the original Divine Marquis in 1789, Nathanael West in 1935.

West, too, is an expert in the indignities of children. Think, for instance, of the letter from "Desperate" to "Miss Lonelyhearts": "When I was a little girl it was not so bad because I got used to the kids on the block making fun of me, but now I would like to have boy friends like the other girls . . . but no boy will take me out because I was born without a nose—although I am a good dancer and have a nice shape . . . I have a big hole in the middle of my face that scares people even myself so I can't blame the boys." But West is not content with pathos, even when sanctified by a political cause; it is ultimate horror he is after, a kind of final terror which he attains not only in such full-fledged evocations of apocalypse as the often quoted ending of *Day of the Locust,* but more modestly and slyly, as in the "dismantling" scene of *A Cool Million,* rendered in cool idiot English imitating the style of Horatio Alger:

> At this both actors turned on Lem and beat him violently over the head and body with their rolled-up newspapers. Their object was to knock off his toupee or to knock out his teeth and eye. When they had accomplished one or all of these goals, they stopped clubbing him. Then Lem, whose part it was not to move while he was being hit, bent over and with sober dignity took from the box at his feet . . . whatever he needed to replace the things that had been knocked off or out.
> . . . For a final curtain, they brought out an enormous wooden mallet labeled "The Works" and with it completely demolished our hero. His toupee flew off, his eye and teeth popped out, and his wooden leg was knocked into the audience.
> At the sight of the wooden leg, the presence of which they had not even suspected, the spectators were convulsed with joy. They laughed heartily until the curtain came down and for some time afterwards.

But West is a virtuoso of the macabre, after all, from whom we come to expect such effects as his stock-in-trade. What truly astonishes us is to find a sober-minded apologist for sweet reason and the status quo betrayed by the mood of the time into precisely such grotesque evocations of terror. Certainly, nobody on the Left in the thirties thought of James Gould Cozzens as an ally, and surely no one now associates him (after a series of books pledged to redeeming himself from his temporary lapse) with deep despair, that ultimate *Angst* before the failed possibilities of our civilization—for which Communism once seemed to provide a handy set of formulations, if not a solution. Yet he wrote in the midst of the Depression a little book called *Castaway,* which caught perhaps better than any other single work (being untroubled by ideology) the mood of the times.

Cozzens' book is a modern Gothic novel set in a department store in a large American city, New York perhaps though we cannot be certain. Mr. Lecky, who is the sole character, remains as unsure as we throughout whether he is in Macy's or Gimbels or the May Company or Hell. It is functionally an island, at any rate, the place on which he wakes to find himself cast away, and he becomes, therefore, a new Robinson Crusoe—even discovering at one point the print of a bare foot in an aisle between two display counters. But Mr. Lecky is a Crusoe at the end rather than the beginning of the era of bourgeois free enterprise, a survivor rather than a founder of the Age of Individualism—a Crusoe lost and starving not in an unexplored desert, but in the very midst of a world of Things which he can no longer manipulate or control in his own interest. And when he finally finds (and kills!) the Man Friday, whose footprint has temporarily lifted up his heart, and whom he has pursued as much in fear as in hope, it turns out to be only himself, his own terrifying reflection in the glass.

> Mr. Lecky beheld its familiar strangeness—not like a stranger's face, and yet it was no friend's face, nor the face of anyone he had ever met. What this could mean held him, he bent closer, questioning in the gloom; and suddenly his hand let go the watch, for Mr. Lecky knew why he had never seen a man with this face. He knew who had been pursued and cruelly killed, who was now dead and would never climb more stairs. He knew why Mr. Lecky could never have for his own the stock of this great store.

But Mr. Lecky—which is to say those of us who came to consciousness in the Thirties—lived on, saved, perhaps, by that very same Roosevelt in whom we never succeeded in believing. Preserving capitalism, the New Deal also preserved us who had been predicting its death and our own. And the doom which befell us, quite as dark in its own way as our blackest vision, turned out to be the opposite of what we had foreseen. We have moved into the Affluent, the Great Society (so we are told, and so—in some sense—we cannot deny); and are assured daily that, Cozzens and the other melancholy writers of the thirties notwithstanding, we can indeed have for our own "the stock of this great store." And though we may protest that, alas, we still do not know how to manipulate or control the things we inherit, we have been taught at least how to want and waste them; which means, in effect, that the End for which so many of us so passionately waited has not come, either with a bang or a whimper.

Perhaps this is why some of the writers most profoundly possessed by the mood of the period stuttered to silence when new possibilities demanded new responses for which they were not prepared. Henry Roth is the most striking example—the victim surely
of personal problems we cannot pretend to know, but in part too, a
casualty of the failed apocalypse. The rediscovery of the Thirties
has apparently convinced him that he as well as his masterpiece
might be reborn; and newspapers stories tell us that he has emerged
from hiding and is off in Spain contemplating a second novel,
about the fifteenth-century persecution of the Jews and Indians.
And maybe he will find a new voice for the new age; though the examples of Dos Passos and Farrell, ghosts haunting their own bodies
and their own later books, should give him pause.

Younger men than he, writers whose first efforts never quite
appeared in the thirties, have managed to be reborn—like Saul Bellow, for instance, with an abortive thirties-type manuscript stored
away for his biographers, or destroyed; and even Nelson Algren,
who apparently rewrote his in the form of *A Walk on the Wild
Side*. Others, like them approaching their fiftieth year or just leaving it behind, have more disconcertingly produced in the late forties
and fifties crypto-thirties works of art, of varying degrees of merit,
Bernard Malamud's *The Assistant*, for example, and Arthur Miller's *Death of a Salesman*—in which a kind of secret nostalgia for
the Depression underlies all more overt meanings.

Yet with what assurance and authority they move among us,
these twice-born younger sons of the thirties: successful authors
now welcomed to the pages of *The New Yorker* or *Esquire* or *Playboy*, though at home still in the *Partisan Review*, where they began,
and which has become quite as established as they; or, alternatively, successful professors of sociology or political science or
American literature, their commitment to poetry and fiction abandoned with other childish things. And what would our universities,
much less our magazines, be without them, these astonishing over-
achievers, blessed with an extra quantum of energy, a demon-on-
call left unemployed for a while after the collapse of the politics of
the thirties?

But we at least among the twice-born who are writers still—or
critics or teachers of writing—though we thrive in post-Depression

America, and, in a certain sense, love our success, cannot love it wholeheartedly. We are still too deeply involved with the persistent memories and defeated expectations I have been trying thus far to define; and like first-century Christians after the failure of the Second Coming, are at our deepest core dead to this world—or convinced anyhow that it is dead to us. It is a hoax, *must* be a hoax (we tell ourselves just before falling asleep, or just after waking up), this depressingly ongoing world with its depressingly immense Gross National Product—all, all illusion. And even at broad noon, we feel ourselves in a kind of interior exile—a comfortable, invisible, but quite real sequestration in the midst of our fellows: profoundly disaffected from everything which our contemporaries with the Other Memory (it scarcely matters whether they be Republicans or Democrats, whether they bless F.D.R. or curse him) consider politics and social action.

For a little while, a vain faith in that eternal loser, Adlai Stevenson, seemed to take us back into the common political arena; and then John F. Kennedy (another loser from the start, though we did not know at first that we knew it) won the allegiance of many of us who had resisted the blandishments of the New Deal—perhaps largely because he created the illusion that if not he, at least his wife, or his wife's sister, read fiction and verse, *our* fiction and verse. But his death produced poetry quite as bad as that which mourned the Happy Warrior before him. And the exacerbation of the situation in Vietnam has completed the process which the intervention in Cuba began (I shall never forget the hippie pickets on that occasion carrying signs which read: *JACQUELINE, VOUS AVEZ PERDU VOS ARTISTES).* The Kennedy *détente* is over; and with what relief we artists and intellectuals—not only veterans of the thirties but our successors as well—have relearned detachment from the great consensus, with what satisfaction settled down to hating L. B. J.

No one as yet has written a great anti-Vietnam poem (as no one, we recall sadly, ever wrote a great anti-Franco one), but those we have are considerably better at least than elegies to middle-of-the-road Presidents—for they draw on *our* memory of the thirties, on a reserve of terror and hopeless protest transmitted via certain poems and books into the creative self-consciousness of the youngest poets and rebels amongst us. There have been a whole series of transitional figures who have tried to straddle the gap between the thirties and the sixties—Norman Mailer, for instance, whose belated flirtation with Trotskyism is recorded in his fascinating if unsuccessful novel, *Barbary Shore.*

Allen Ginsberg, however, is the figure who preeminently represents the link between right now and back then; and in a single remarkable poem called, of course, "America," becomes the living memory of our dying memory of the mythological thirties. He included the poem in his first slim collection, *Howl,* a little book which raised a lot of hell, out of which there emerged finally a new life-style and a new metapolitics that has remained at the center of the cultural scene ever since. There is much that is quite new in "America," testimonies to drugs and fraternal greetings to Jack Kerouac, William Burroughs, and Neal Cassady, names just then beginning to be heard—but there are other names that need footnotes now, which one is tempted to weep composing: Scott Nearing (still alive and very old, an organic food nut these days, somewhere in New England), Israel Amter (does the *Freiheit* still go on, are there survivors still who read *Yiddish* and long for those pristine days?), Mother Bloor (dead, long dead—that wrinkled WASP who used to tie red bandanas around the necks of little Jewish Young Pioneers).

Almost from the start of the poem, we are aware that we are back with our unforgotten past, as the cry, "America when will you be angelic" becomes "When will you be worthy of your million Trotskyites?"; and suddenly the identification is made between "pot" now and Marx then,

> America I feel sentimental about the Wobblies.
> America I used to be a communist when I was a kid I'm not
> sorry.
> I smoke marijuana every chance I get.
> I sit in my house for days on end and stare at the roses in the
> closet.
> When I go to Chinatown I get drunk and never get laid.
> My mind is made up there is going to be trouble.
> You should have seen me reading Marx. . . .

But we are not quite prepared, however, when the old ghosts of those endless protests and defeats begin to arise, the wraith of Ginsberg's mother at the very center of them all,

> America free Tom Mooney
> America save the Spanish Loyalists
> Americo Sacco & Vanzetti must not die
> America I am the Scottsboro boys.
> America when I was seven momma took me to Communist Cell
>     meetings they sold us garbanzos a handful per ticket
>     a ticket costs a nickel and the speeches were free
>     everybody was angelic and sentimental about the workers
>     it was all so sincere you have no idea what a good thing
>     the party was in 1835 Scott Nearing was a grand old man
>     a real mensch Mother Bloor made me cry I once saw
>     Israel Amter plain. Everybody must have been a spy.

Irony, of course, plays everywhere in the passage—irony directed not only outward at the smug vilifiers of the Movement, but inward at its own pretensions (the last lovely touch being that almost inadvertent "1835"); but there is pathos, too.

And the source of that pathos is more fully revealed in the title of Ginsberg's next volume, *Kaddish,* which is to say, the Mourner's Prayer of the Jews: the prayer of a surviving queer son for his dead mother and all she represented to him, Newark, Paterson, lost strikes, Communism, madness—that paranoia which is only the apocalyptic vision, the prescience of defeat lived in the darkness of a lonely head, rather than evoked on a printed page. But here is his litany:

> O mother
> farewell
> with a long black shoe
> farewell
> with Communist Party and a broken stocking
>     *
> with your sagging belly
> with your fear of Hitler
>     *
> with your belly of strikes and smokestacks

with your chin of Trotsky and the Spanish War
with your voice singing for the decaying overbroken workers
with your nose of bad lay with your nose of the smell
                                        of the pickles of Newark
with your eyes
with your eyes of Russia

What, after all, could the (after all) good Jews who stood at the center of things in the thirties have asked better than being thus remembered by their children, with pity and fear equal to their own, being thus turned into poems? To be sure, we had thought of ourselves in our blither moments as the fathers of a new society, in our darker ones as the last sons of the world. That we are remembered as Somebody's Mother is a final irony, but somehow a not unattractive one.

# FIVE

# John Peale Bishop and the Other Thirties

THE REVIVAL OF the literature of the thirties through which we have recently been living—the republication of novels long out of print, the redemption of reputations long lapsed, the compilation of anthologies long overdue—has been oddly one-sided, a revival of one half only of the literary record of that dark decade: the urban, Marxist, predominantly Jewish half, whose leading journal was the *New Masses* and whose monster-in-chief was Joseph Stalin. And this skewed emphasis, though somewhat misleading, is comprehensible enough; for we live at a moment when a large reading public, educated by a second generation of urban Jewish writers (ex-Marxists, this time around), begins by identifying with certain contemporary literary heroes, like Moses Herzog, whose minds were made by this thirties tradition, and ends by wanting to read the books they read: the fiction of Nathanael West and Daniel Fuchs and Henry Roth, even Mike Gold's *Jews Without Money*.

Some writers, however, who move us just now at least as strongly as Saul Bellow, writers ranging all the way from neo-Gothic journalists like Truman Capote to latterday prophets like Marshall MacLuhan, were nurtured on another, rival tradition which also flourished in the thirties: a provincial, Agrarian, primarily WASP tradition, whose chief journal was the *Southern Review* and whose monster-in-chief was Huey Long. We are less likely to know the basic manifesto of that tradition, a compilation of paeans to the old South called *I'll Take My Stand* by "Twelve Southerners," than such Marxist equivalents as Malcolm Cowley's *Exile's Return* or Edmund Wilson's *American Jitters.*

Yet the former is no more dated, no more alien in its aspirations than the two latter, which, indeed, have been drastically rewritten in later editions, as their authors have changed with the times. All three books are exemplary, useful both for illuminating their own age and tempering our enthusiasm for the unguarded goals and hopes of our own. Just as we find it therapeutic to recall that Cowley and Wilson once looked to the Soviet Union for salvation, we may find it equally so to remember that Robert Penn Warren could once write of the Southern Negro that he "is likely to find in agricultural and domestic pursuits the happiness that his good nature and easy ways incline him to as an ordinary function of his being."

And it is well, too, to come to terms with the hopes for literature which the Southern Conservatives, like the Eastern Radicals, attached to their social and political programs in order to savor the full irony of the fact that both movements did, indeed, produce literary revivals, though, in each case, the most moving books arose out of tension and disillusion rather than allegiance and simple faith. The great writer of the South was already on the scene when the thirties began, but he remained as invisible to the doctrinaire advocates of Southern Agrarianism as Nathanael West and Henry Roth were to be to the doctrinaire Marxist critic. Not until 1939 did George Marion O'Donnell give full recognition to Faulkner in the *Kenyon Review*. In 1930, when *I'll Take My Stand* appeared, Donald Davidson, who was entrusted with commenting on the arts, did not even mention him—concentrating instead on Ellen Glasgow and James Branch Cabell, the latter his leading contender for the laureateship of the South. Yet some of Faulkner's very best work had already been published though, indeed, so embattled and bleak a novel as *The Sound and the Fury* provides little of that "repose" and "continuity" which Davidson hoped for from the Old Dominion—part of his problem being, of course, that it was Virginia and not Mississippi which he had in mind when he spoke generally about the South. Madness, stylistic improvisation, and a radical dislocation of the tradition is what Faulkner was then prepared to offer; and that, Davidson thought, was already being supplied in sufficient quantities by certain despised writers from New York and Chicago.

From our present vantage point, it is easy to see that Glasgow and Cabell, addressing the past as they did in hushed and genteel voices (for all Cabell's vaunted pornography), could evoke from it no promise of a renaissance of letters and that Faulkner alone was capable of providing models for the literature to come that was to celebrate the terrible and elegant death of the South. Not, let us recall, the Faulkner of post-Nobel Prize banalities about dignity and endurance, but the shrill and despairing Faulkner, who mocked the world of the mid-thirties with *Sanctuary,* and was able still to write as late as 1944 (in the course of asserting that his real subject matter had never been the South at all): " . . . life is a phenomenon but not a novelty, the same frantic steeplechase toward nothing everywhere and man stinks the same stink no matter where in time."

Before any other Southern writer of distinction, John Peale Bishop seems to have sensed the value and significance of what *this* Faulkner was doing—not merely going on record in praise of his double vision, his capacity to appreciate simultaneously the myth of the Sartorises and the fact of the Snopeses, but imitating his techniques as well, in, for instance, a story called "Toadstools Are Poison," which he published in 1932 in emulation of Faulkner's "That Evening Sun." We are more likely to be aware of such later heirs of the dark Faulkner as Robert Penn Warren and Eudora Welty, Carson McCullers and Truman Capote, even so belated a continuer of the line as Flannery O'Connor. Yet Bishop was there first in picking up the cues for a fiction Gothic, as the fiction of the South has always been since the days of Edgar Poe, but fully aware at last of what before had only been hinted: that the blackness of darkness which haunts it is not merely embodied in the Negro, but quite simply *is* the Negro—that nightmare creature born of the contempt for manual labor and the fear of the sexuality of their own women which had so paradoxically made the White masters of the South heroes but not quite men.

Such a fiction is by definition even further from the possibility of "repose" than that of the industrial North and East; for if the latter is torn between the terrible fact of the present and the dream of a barely possible pure future, the latter is pulled apart between an equally dismal actuality and the dream of a manifestly unreal pure past. Nonetheless, the manifestos of the Agrarians tell the kind of lie which illuminates the truth of the fiction of Faulkner and Warren and Bishop, even as the Marxist manifestos tell the kind of lie which illuminates the truth of the novels of Nathanael West and Henry Roth. If we would recapture the past of three decades ago, we need to relive both the elation of the beautiful lies which nurtured it, and the discomfiture of the grim truths spoken from the heart of those lies. It would, therefore, be a special shame if Bishop's single completed novel, *Act of Darkness,* remained unavailable a moment longer, since in it one committed by birth and temperament to the myth of the South both rehearses it and—passionately as well as tenderly—gives it the lie.

We must, then, if we are to understand Bishop and his age, learn to think of him as perhaps the most important Southern novelist of the thirties* despite the slimness of his production. Yet if we bring him to mind at all these days, we are likely to associate him with a different genre, a different decade, even a different region. Certainly we tend to remember him first as a poet, second as a critic—and only last, if at all, as a writer of fiction. And though this emphasis is, on the one hand, a function of the way in which his influential friends (Scott Fitzgerald, Edmund Wilson, Allen Tate, among others) have chosen to mythicize and preserve him; on the other, it is a result of the way in which his writing career actually developed.

True enough, Bishop may have first captured the imagination of a large audience as the semi-fictional highbrow poet, Tom d'Invilliers, who moves through the pages of Fitzgerald's *This Side of Paradise;* but his verse had already appeared in print under his own name even before the publication of that novel in 1920—in fact, three years before the start of World War I, which is to say, a year before the initiation of Harriet Monroe's *Poetry* and the official beginnings of modernism in American verse. And he continued to

---

* Carson McCullers is his chief rival; but though her first and best book, *The Heart Is A Lonely Hunter,* which appeared in 1936, is a true thirties book, adapting the terror of the Depression to a world of freaks reflected in a child's eye, her reputation belongs to the forties into which she lived, and to which she provided a bridge.

write poems until his death in 1944, publishing four volumes in his lifetime and leaving enough uncollected poetry to justify Tate's putting together a *Collected Poems* in 1948, as well as a special selection for English readers in 1960.

In his preface to the latter volume, Tate celebrated Bishop's achievement as a poet, paid a passing compliment to his fiction, then went on to give the highest praise to his criticism—recording a belief that his dead friend had been "one of the best literary critics of the twenties and thirties." And in this opinion, Edmund Wilson (perhaps even better qualified to judge) had seemed to concur, when he had earlier gathered Bishop's scattered criticism into book form for the first time. But Bishop's critical writing, collected in a single volume, disconcertingly adds up to less than one would have expected from the impressions created by individual pieces; just as his verse, however elegant and accomplished, seems in retrospect too much a fading echo of styles already obsolescent before he had perfected his skills.

No, it is only in Bishop's fiction that I, at any rate, hear an authentic and original voice, only in his one successful novel and a handful of short stories, that I come on rhythms and phrases, images and myths that live on in my head. But he does not seem at first glance a *thirties* writer even in this area of his greatest achievement; for he began to write fiction, too, long before the collapse of post-World War I prosperity had made the thirties possible—publishing his very first stories when the twenties had barely started: one of them, characteristically elegant and unconnected with things to come, in *The Undertaker's Garland,* a volume on which he had collaborated with Edmund Wilson.

Wilson and Fitzgerald, Fitzgerald and Wilson: how inextricably Bishop's life as a writer is involved with theirs, and how inevitably we are tempted to see him through what we know more securely about them. But the clues they seem to offer are likely to lead us astray, suggesting that Bishop's spiritual home was Princeton (where he had met his two friends); that not *The Sound and the Fury* but *The Great Gatsby* provided him with a model for his fiction; and, finally, that he is a twenties writer in his deepest heart. Wilson, to be sure, who began as a true child of that earlier decade, was reborn as a leading spokesman for the radical thirties and survived to become a kind of elder statesman for the generation of the forties and fifties; but Fitzgerald we think of as having belonged so utterly to the era which learned in large part its very life-style from him, that he could not survive its disappearance. And Bishop seems, after all, much more like the latter than the former.

Why not, then, regard him simply as a twenties writer, who, living too long without accommodating to a new era, found himself quite out of fashion. Certain of his allegiances, surely, like a great deal of his rhetoric, he shared with those older writers, who—having barely found their voices before World War I—were bereft by that War of subjects appropriate to those voices; and insisted forever after on regarding its horrors as a personal affront rather than a universal catastrophe. Like many of his contemporaries, too, Bishop subscribed with equal fervor to the cult of self-pity and the religion of art, which seemed for a while—until the coming of more fashionable political faiths—to fill quite satisfactorily the vacuum left by the vanishing of older pieties. And like most of them, he espoused a righteous contempt for the vulgarities of American culture and a yearning for old world charm which, combined with a favorable exchange rate, led to expatriation in the Holy City of Paris.

It was the War which took him to France for the first time; and returning briefly to America, he did not cease to remember it, writing at the close of an essay on his alma mater, which he published in 1921: "If I had a son who was an ordinarily healthy, not too intelligent youth I should certainly send him to Princeton. But if ever I find myself the father of an extraordinary youth I shall not send him to college at all. I shall lock him up in a library until he is old enough to go to Paris." Shortly thereafter he made his first post-War removal to Europe, then a second much longer one, which lasted until 1933, and during which three sons were born to him on the continent to which he had dreamed of sending them if they proved themselves "extraordinary" enough.

And what does all this shuttling between Princeton and New York and Paris have to do with the thirties, which turned from New York and Princeton, as well as Detroit or Sauk City or Newark, New Jersey, toward the Holy City of Moscow (to which only a few were foolish enough to venture in fact)—or alternatively, to the Holy Anti-City of Jefferson's Monticello (to which none, however foolish, could manage to return)? Little enough in fact; indeed, so little that we are not surprised when Bishop, in quest of a setting for his one finished novel, moves backward in time, out of the mid-thirties which saw the publication of the book to the pre-World War I years of his own childhood. And in that relatively remote era, he rehearses—or rather lets his boy hero with whom he shares the almost anonymous name of John rehearse—a familiar tale, not less indebted to certain prevailing modes of the twenties for being so palpably autobiographical. The commonplace which reminds us that life often imitates art, does not make sufficiently clear that it is inevitably yesterday's art, outmoded art, i.e., a cliché, which today's life is likely to repeat.

In *Act of Darkness,* at any rate, we find Bishop, though apparently convinced he is recreating his own early experience, recreating instead fictional patterns already well established by his predecessors and contemporaries at home and abroad. On the one hand, we encounter such standard American plots as the belated flight from mama; or the boy vicariously inducted into maturity by witnessing the fall to woman of an older man on whom he has a homosexual crush. On the other, we are confronted by such fashionable European imports as the direct initiation into manhood at the hands of a whore (fumbled the first time, achieved the second); and especially the fable of conversion popularized by Joyce's *Portrait of the Artist as a Young Man,* in which a baffled youngster—realizing after many wrong turnings that only Art gives meaning to Life—goes forth to write his first novel.

All this familiar stuff is transformed in *Act of Darkness,* however, not only by the subtlety of language and delicacy of cadence which Bishop somehow redeemed from mere elegance by transferring it from verse to prose; but also by the typical thirties tone and voice in which he renders it. It is not finally a social message which gives to the fiction of the Depression years its special character, though the critics of that age once liked to think so. Horace Gregory, who was willing to hail Bishop's book when it first appeared as "one of the few memorable novels of the decade . . .", hastened to add, almost apologetically, that it had "no pretensions of being a 'social document.' " No matter; since the hallmark of the thirties is rather a certain panic shrillness, a sense of apocalypse, yearning to become religious but held by the mode to secular metaphors.

This we find everywhere in the period: in those atypical novels produced then by writers out of another decade—in Faulkner's *Sanctuary*, for instance, or Hemingway's *To Have and Have Not* or James Gould Cozzens' *Castaway;* as well as in the most characteristic work of writers who belong entirely to that dark decade—in Nathanael West's *Miss Lonelyhearts*, say, or Henry Roth's *Call It Sleep*. They are *mad* books all of them, even more disturbingly than they are crypto-religious ones: sometimes actual projections of madness, sometimes accounts of long flirtations with insanity, ending in not quite credible escapes back into reason and peace—as if the political debates which occupied the age were finally mere analogues, leftover nineteenth-century metaphors called on to express a crisis of consciousness for which the times had not yet found a new language.

And of all the books of the period, *Act of Darkness* (along with *Call It Sleep*) comes closest to revealing that not-quite secret. How different its panic mood is from the more theatrical despair typical of the twenties (think of Fitzgerald's *All the Sad Young Men),* which, after all, was never incompatible with euphoria. A comparison of the two types of book reveals how—though the Great War may have been felt chiefly as a personal affront, the Great Depression seemed Armageddon itself, a kind of end of the world. It is odd and maybe even a little degrading to realize how we Americans (not only our writers, finally, but all of us) were driven to ultimate despair not by contemplating the destruction of fabled cities abroad or even the prospect of our own deaths in foreign lands, but by a confrontation at home with the Crash, the end of prosperity and fun and games. The colloquial phrase says it exactly: the Depression struck *home* to us as the War had not; and the image of the desolated American city seemed an image also of our own devastated souls, whereas that of the ravaged European capital had signified only the death of that Culture with which we had never been quite at ease.

Most Depression novels, therefore, played out their fables against the background of the ruined American city, making the native urban landscape for the first time the chief symbolic setting for our kind of Gothic. Not so in Bishop's case, however, despite his commitment after his college years to the Princeton-New York-Paris circuit, despite his father's northern city origins, despite his own final retreat to New England to die. Faulkner himself may have been driven in the Depression years from Jefferson to Memphis, out of whose backalleys Popeye emerges to stalk the pages of *Sanctuary*, that other inverted parable of rape and the Southern Lady. But Bishop turns back, in the midst of the general panic that was possessing the land, to where his own personal panic had begun, to precisely the sort of small Southern community in a farm setting which the Agrarians celebrated; but which for him (despite the kind things he had to say of the South in his more abstract commentary) is the place of horror from which, at the end of his book, he is escaping, even as he escapes the "soft torture" of his mother's love and the temptation to madness.

His poems, on the other hand, do have a kind of urban setting; since in them he imagined himself and his friends (Edmund Wilson, for example, turned not so improbably into an antique Senator) moving through an imaginary city clearly intended to remind us of Rome. But his is *not* the Rome—however much Allen Tate would like us to believe it—created in the fantasy of Southern neo-Classicists like George Washington Custis, delivering his annual Fourth of July oration dressed in a toga, or Thomas Jefferson dreaming the University of Virginia. Bishop's is rather a doomed and decadent city—much like the "unreal City" of T. S. Eliot's *The Waste Land*, or even more like Cavafy's Alexandria: an imperial capital whose great Caesars are all dead, and which is assailed from without by barbarians and Christians, from within by doubt; a city whose inhabitants are waiting—as so many so variously but so nearly unanimously waited in the thirties—for the End:

> We did not know the end was coming: nor why
> It came; only that long before the end
> Were many wanted to die . . .

So, too, his first and unfinished novel, *The Huntsmen Are Up in America*, is set in legendary dying cities—this time called Venice and New York. But that novel stutters away before its intended close in the most legendary part of New York (doubly strange and wonderful for the Southerner), which is to say, in Harlem, where Bishop tries to bring to the surface the underground theme that obsessed him: the idyll which turns nightmare of a sacred union of White and Negro, the pale virgin and black stud. The idyllic names for the partners in that union are Venetian, of course, Desdemona and Othello; but to do justice to its nightmare aspects, Bishop had to take it back to where, in his troubled mind, it really belongs: back to his own birthplace of Charles Town, West Virginia, called in his fiction "Mordington"; though its actual name is distributed to the two leading characters of his completed novel, to the Charlie and Virginia who were for him the prototypes of Othello and Desdemona.

"Mordington" is, at any rate, the background not only for *Act of Darkness,* which he published in 1935, but also for the collection of stories called *Many Thousands Gone,* which had appeared four years earlier. It was apparently Bishop's aim in the five stories which make up the book, as well as in the novel, to create a mythical equivalent of the small town he knew best: his own Yoknapatawpha County, which is to say, a microcosm of the South, true both to its sociological facts and its legendary meanings. Sociologically, Bishop is not nearly so successful as Faulkner; for despite his patent determination to write the sort of "realistic" book his age had convinced itself it admired, his data keeps incandescing (at best) into poetry, or dissolving (at worst) into self-conscious symbolism. Yet in the course of his failed attempt at recording history, he does succeed in releasing from himself and what of the past lives on in his memory their essential myth.

In an extraordinary little story called "If Only," a pair of genteel Southern spinsters known as "the Sabine Sisters," who have survived the Civil War only to confront indigence, find themselves one day possessed of a Negro servant called "Bones." The allegorical import of the names is not less important for being self-evident: the evocation of Rome and rape in the first, of death and the Minstrel Show in the second. Bones, at any rate, almost miraculously restores the decayed household of the sisters to an elegance which they perhaps only dreamed of having had before; but simultane-

ously begins to appear before them in darkly sinister, though incon-
clusively sexual manifestations—winking out at them in naked in-
solence from their bathtub, asleep on one of their beds, "terrible
and tall . . . and very black." Dismayed and horrified, the two
women find themselves incapable of telling whether their ambiguous servant is a madman, or a figment of their own madness: and
they cannot, in any event, disengage themselves from their "nigger," since "with him they lived in terror, but in the tradition."

*Act of Darkness,* which is concerned with the escape from both
the terror and the tradition, is less perfectly achieved; but by the
same token, it seems richer, less a bare parable. And we are finally
more deeply moved and illuminated by it, for all its obtrusive
faults: its two halves which fall apart in tone and tempo, its point
of view which shifts without clear motivation or redeeming grace,
etc. etc. Any teacher of composition could tick off its flaws; yet the
tale it tells survives its technical ineptitude: the story of a boy early
bereft of his father, almost swallowed up by his mother's love and
dogged through his lonely house by a Negro homosexual of his own
age, who at last finds a kind of salvation by attaching himself,
purely and passionately, to his young Uncle Charlie. Uncle Charlie,
however, first seduces a young farm girl whom the boy is prepared
to love though not possess; then takes him to a whorehouse in an
unsuccessful attempt at inducting him into guilt and manhood; finally rapes a not-so-young Southern lady, a friend of and surrogate
for the boy's mother, called by the twice symbolic name of Virginia.

The climax of the book's action and the heart of its meaning is
contained in a long courtroom scene, during which Charlie is, at the
lady's instigation, tried for having assaulted her; and ends by claiming that not he—dandy and bully and restless seducer—but the
woman herself—intellectual and freethinker and virgin—had been
the effective rapist: that "he shamelessly allowed her to complete
his animal rapture," maintaining the whole time "only a passive
prowess." And young John is undone by the confession, pushed
over the brink of a breakdown by what seems to him the ultimate
affront to his own dubious masculinity: "What I could not forgive
was his denying his domination over what had been done in the
darkness of the woods. . . ." But John is not alone in his dismay at
this comic-tragic denouement; for the reader finds himself shaken

as he is shaken only when some inadequate but long-lived archetypal version of the way things are is inverted and extended, an ulterior, and uncomfortable, significance made clear.

I should suppose that the Southern reader especially would be discomfited; for though rape is the subject *par excellence* of Southern literature in the nineteenth and twentieth centuries—a concern as obsessive as that with seduction in eighteenth-century England —it is typically the rape of a white woman by a black man, real or fancied, which lies at the center of the plot. Bishop's novel, however, tells no nightmare tale of a black man grossly offending or falsely accused; though there is an attenuated and dislocated echo of the standard fable in the subplot of the black fairy with whom the white boy narrator flirts in horrified attraction, and who is finally killed off-scene by being pushed out of a window by somebody else. In the main action, a white man, a gentleman—in fact, just such a gentleman farmer as the Agrarians were then making the focus of their hopes for social reform—is responsible, at least passively, for the act of darkness which the color of his skin seems to belie.

But *why*, the book insists that we ask, why such a total inversion of the archetype? Surely not just because it happens to have happened so in some series of actual events from which Bishop may have made his fiction. So easy an answer the novel itself will not let us accept, evoking as a clue toward its close the pair of ill-fated Shakespearian lovers who had already begun to haunt Bishop, as we have seen. Desdemona and Othello appear again and again during the thirties in all of Bishop's work, whether in verse or prose, the first explicit reference, as we might expect, in the book whose protagonist is called "Brakespeare," *The Huntsmen Are Up in America.* Describing the city of Venice, Bishop writes, as if by the way, "it was only there, I am sure, that the ceremony could have been found that would have wed Desdemona to her black Moor." And a gloss on the metaphor is to be found in one of his best poems, a kind of epigraph to the body of his work, which he called "Speaking of Poetry":

> The ceremony must be found
> that will wed Desdemona to the huge Moor.

>              It is not enough—
> to win the approval of the Senator . . .
>                   For then,
> though she may pant again in his black arms
> (his weight resilient as a Barbary stallion's)
> She will be found
> when the ambassadors of the Venetian state arrive
> again smothered . . .
>                    (Tupping is still tupping
> though that particular word is obsolete . . .)

The allegorical meanings are clear enough: elegance must be married to force, art to magic, the mind to the body—*married,* not merely yielded up to the kind of unceremonious possession which turns inevitably into destruction. It is ritual, "ceremony" which makes of passionate attachment a true marriage, as it makes of passionate perception a true poem: which is to say, the marriage of Desdemona and Othello becomes a metaphor for the poetic act. Equally clear is the nature of the appeal of that metaphor to the race-obsessed, sexually queasy Southern mind: the image of black "tupping" white, a miscegenation, which—lacking appropriate ceremonials—is no more than a rape.

Fair enough, then, that after Charlie's trial and conviction, his unnerved nephew—who had earlier found satisfaction in simpler boys' books, idyllic like Audubon or sinister like *Oliver Twist*—should have turned to Bishop's favorite play to learn for himself how the poet can confer order and beauty and significance on what otherwise must remain heartbreakingly chaotic and sordid and meaningless. "Had the actual murderer of Desdemona . . . " Bishop reports him as thinking, "been brought into a Venetian court, his trial would have made no more sense than Charlie's had done in the Mordington courthouse."

But there is no "huge Moor" in the Mordington affair, we want to cry out at this point, no black man at all, only Uncle Charlie. To which Bishop responds through his narrator, evoking for the first time relevant Shakespearian criticism as well as the text: *neither was Othello a "huge Moor" really—only a Venetian nobleman, neither blacker nor whiter than the farmer from West Virginia.*

"The Venetian gentleman," Bishop's John explains to us, "who wore mulberries on his shield, since his name was Il Moro, had, in the repetition of the story of the murder of his wife, been mistaken for a Moor. In time, passing to the North, he had become a black-skinned barbarian, Othello."

The blackness of Othello is, then, *Act of Darkness* insists, a misconception, a mistake; or more precisely, the rapist of white women is black only as the dream of revenge against their emasculating Ladies is black inside the darkness of the white heads of Southern males. The Prosecuting Attorney, pressing for Charlie's conviction, underlines this when he so oddly repeats in his own language the burden of the scholarship on *Othello:* " . . . once more the cry of rape is heard in the land and . . . this heinous and horrible crime, has been committed, not by a man of the colored race . . . but is imputed to one whose former education, training and fair tradition should have predisposed him to a career of honor and worthy actions."

There is another turn of the screw beyond this, however, as we already know; a second and even more terrifying inversion implicit in Charlie's plea that it was he who had been raped, that the true Othello is Desdemona: the pale virgin dreaming her own dark violation, and projecting that dream outward upon the white male who resents her—at the cost of his manhood and honor, and at the risk of his life. But the end of the illusion which concealed this truth from a defeated nation, which survived only by imagining itself the last home of chivalry, means the beginning of the end of that nation's myth and its very existence. Intuiting this, *Act of Darkness* becomes a work of prophecy, a parable of that death of the South which all of us are living through in agony right now.

Its protagonist, at any rate, having been deprived of that illusion by his uncle and Shakespeare, is preparing at the book's end to leave not only the small lies of his mother, but the larger lies of the sweet land which seemed for a while to sustain them, to go North. First, however, he has to return to the whorehouse to which his uncle had earlier taken him in vain, where, this time, he musters up enough "passive power" to accomplish his own deflowering. "It was when her hands were on me," he tells us, "that I knew what was again being accomplished was the act in the woods, that all its gestures must be repeated and forever repeated, the rape of the mind by the body."

But at this point, we are no longer sure (and how did we ever deceive ourselves that we were, even in deepest Dixie?) about which is mind, which body, which White, which Black, who Desdemona, who Othello, who the virgin and who the whore. The mythical marriage which Bishop imagined in his verse has, in fact, been accomplished, the archetypal opposites united in a confusion that begins in madness and ends in poetry.

*Buffalo, New York*
—1966

# Henry Roth's Neglected Masterpiece

IT WOULD NOT BE quite true to say that Henry Roth's *Call It Sleep* went unnoticed when it appeared in 1935. One contemporary reviewer at least was willing to call it "a great novel" and to hope that it might win the Pulitzer Prize, "which," that reviewer added mournfully, "it never will." It never did, the prize going instead to H. L. Davis's *Honey in the Horn,* which was also the Harper Prize Novel of the year and was even touted by Robert Penn Warren in the *Southern Review*—then still being subsidized by Huey Long. Not only the Southern Agrarians were looking elsewhere, however, when Roth's single book was published; almost everyone seemed to have his eye on his own preferred horizon, on which he was pretending to find his own preferred rising star.

The official "proletarian" party was busy hailing Clara Weatherwax for a desolately enthusiastic tract disguised as fiction and called *Marching! Marching! "Marching! Marching!"*—runs the jacket blurb—"is the winner of *The New Masses* contest for a novel on an American Proletarian theme, conducted jointly by *The New Masses* and the John Day Company—the first contest of the kind ever held." It was also the last such contest, partly, one hopes, because of the flagrant badness of the winner (the climax of Miss Weatherwax's book runs as follows: ". . . some of us thinking *Jeez! Bayonets! Machine Guns! They got gas masks on those bags around their necks on their chests—gas!* and others *For God's sake, you guys, don't shoot us! Come over to our side. Why should you kill us? We are your brothers")*—but chiefly, one suspects, because a basic change in the political line of the Comintern instituted

271

in 1936 led to the substitution of the Popular Front novel for the Proletarian one.

John Steinbeck, the most sensitive recorder of that shift, was to publish his resolutely proletarian *In Dubious Battle* in 1936, but this reflects a lag demanded by the exigencies of publishing. *The Grapes of Wrath*, which represents the full-scale political-sentimental novel of the last half of the thirties, did not reach print until 1939. Meanwhile, Dos Passos and Farrell, the most ambitious talents of the first part of the decade, were closing out their accounts by putting between the covers of single volumes those fat trilogies *(Studs Lonigan* actually appeared in 1935; *U.S.A.* was that year in its last stages) which seemed for a while to the literary historians the great achievements of the period. And at the same time, Hemingway was preparing for his own brief fling at being a "proletarian" author, improbably publishing a section of *To Have and Have Not* in *Cosmopolitan* magazine during 1934.

To the more dogged proletarian critics, Henry Roth seemed beside Weatherwax or Dos Passos, Farrell or even Hemingway woefully "poetic" and uncommitted. "He pleads [prefers?] diffuse poetry to the social light . . ." the reviewer for the *New Republic* complained, adding rather obscurely but surely unfavorably that Roth "pinkly through the flesh sees the angry sunset." Actually, there was some point in chiding Roth for not writing a "socially conscious" book, since his dedication to Eda Lou Walton (his teacher, sponsor, and friend, who had identified herself clearly enough with the proletarian cause) indicated a declaration if not of allegiance at least of general sympathy. Certainly Roth did not take his stand outside of the world bounded by the *New Masses,* the *Nation,* and the *New Republic,* as, say, did John Peale Bishop, whose *Act of Darkness* was also published in 1935, or Thomas Wolfe, whose *Of Time and the River* was just then thrilling the adolescent audience for whom he had rediscovered *Weltschmerz* in *Look Homeward, Angel.* Nor was Roth willing to launch the sort of satirical attack on social commitment undertaken only a year later by another young Jewish writer, Daniel Fuchs, in *Homage to Blenholt.*

He was ideologically in much the same position as Nathanael West, whose *A Cool Million* appeared in the same year with *Call It*

*Sleep,* and whose technique, different as it was, also baffled the official "proletarians." Both had reached intellectual maturity inside a world of beliefs which they felt no impulse to deny but which they did not find viable in their art. West died inside that world and Roth apparently still inhabits it insofar as he retains any connection with literary life at all. At any rate, looking back from 1960 and the poultry farm in Maine to which he has finally withdrawn, that is the world he remembers. "Is Yaddo still functioning?" he recently asked an interviewer. "Whatever happened to Horace Gregory and Ben Belitt?" There is a half-comic pathos in the questions and the continuing faith from which they spring that a literary movement to which Roth never quite belonged must still somehow be going on.

But in Roth's novel itself there is little enough manifest social consciousness. Though his scene is Brownsville and the East Side of New York just after the turn of the century and his protagonists are a working-class Jewish immigrant family, there is small sense of an economic struggle. Jobs are gotten and lost because of psychological quirks and dark inner compulsions; money does not corrupt nor does poverty redeem; no one wants to rise like David Levinsky or fears to fall like the harried protagonists of Theodore Dreiser. If there is a class struggle and a revolutionary movement, these are revealed only in an overheard scrap of soapbox oratory at the climax of the novel, where they seem singularly irrelevant to the passion and suffering of Roth's child hero who is living through that climax.

"In 1789, in 1848, in 1871, in 1905, he who has anything to save will enslave us anew! Or if not enslave will desert us when the red cock crows! Only the laboring poor, only the masses embittered, bewildered, betrayed, in the day the red cock crows, can free us!"

But even this prophecy uttered out of a "pale, gilt-spectacled, fanatic face," is turned into a brutal sexual jest, recast in light of the obsession which rides the book, its protagonist, and its author. "How many times'll your red cock crow, Pete, befaw y'gives up? T'ree?" asks a mocking Irish voice from the sidelines.

Perhaps it is this obsessive transformation of all experience into equivocations based on a hated and feared sexuality which put off the kind of reader who might have been expected to hail the kind of book Roth actually wrote. That the *New Masses* critics deplored him and the Southern Agrarians scarcely registered his existence is, after all, to be expected; nor is it proper to feel dismay over the yellowing lists of best-sellers in old newspapers, carefully documented testimony to what the largest audience was reading in 1935 *instead* of Roth. For some the whimsy, Anglophile or pseudo-Oriental, of James Hilton (both *Goodbye, Mr. Chips* and *Lost Horizon* topped the lists) seemed the specific demanded by the pangs of the Great Depression, while others found tranquillity in the religiosity of *The Forty Days of Musa Dagh* or in Mary Pickford's *Why Not Try God?* For those less serious or more chic, there was the eunuchoid malice and sentimentality of Alexander Woollcott's *While Rome Burns;* and the most nearly invisible audience of all (furtive high school boys standing at the circulating library racks in candy stores and their older sisters behind the closed doors of their bedrooms) were reading Donald Henderson Clarke's *Millie* and *Louis Beretti* —the demi-pornography which no library would think of stocking twenty-five years later.

But what of those specifically interested in Jewish literature in the United States, those who, picking up a first novel by a twenty-seven-year-old New Yorker, thought of Mary Antin's *The Promised Land* or remembered Abraham Cahan's breakthrough to the rich disorderly material of Jewish-American life? There is surely no more Jewish book among American novels. Though its young hero, David Schearl, for instance, goes to public school, that Gentile area of experience is left shadowy, unrealized. Only his home and the *cheder* and the streets between become real places, as only Yiddish and Hebrew and the poor dialects of those to whom English is an alien tongue are rendered as real languages. And yet those presumably looking for the flowering of a rich and satisfactory Jewish-American literature were not moved to applaud.

Some of them, on the contrary, protested against the unloveliness of Roth's ghetto images, the vulgarity and poverty of the speech he recorded—as if he had invented them maliciously. "Doggedly smeared with verbal filthiness," one such critic wrote.

*"Call It Sleep* is by far the foulest picture of the East Side that has yet appeared." It is, of course, the typical, the expected response to the serious writer by the official spokesmen of the community out of which he comes. Yet there was in Roth a special kind of offensiveness, capable of stirring a more than conventional reaction; for the real foulness of his book is rendered not directly but through the consciousness of an extraordinarily acute and sensitive boy of seven or eight. Its vulgarity, that is to say, is presented as *felt* vulgarity, grossness assailing a sensibility with no defenses against it.

The technique of *Call It Sleep* is contrived to make manifest at every moment that its real subject is not so much abomination in the streets as that abomination in the mind. Aside from a prelude, in which the arrival of David and his mother in America is objectively narrated, and a section toward the book's end which blends into a Joycean rhapsody the sounds of a score of city voices as overheard by some omniscient Listener—the whole substance of the novel is presented as what happens inside the small haunted head of David. It is only through him that we know the dark cellar swarming with rats whose door he must pass on his way in or out of the warm sanctuary of his home; the rage and guilt of his paranoid father or that father's impotence and fantasies of being cuckolded; his mother's melancholy, and her soft, unfulfilled sexuality; the promise of her body and the way in which it is ogled by others; the fact of sex in general as pollution, the very opposite of love. For David, the act by which he was generated is an unmitigated horror (in a dark closet, reeking of mothballs, he is initiated by a crippled girl, her braces creaking as she embraces him, "Between the legs. Who puts id in is de poppa. De poppa's god de petzel. You de poppa"); and he longs for a purity he cannot find in his world, a fire, a flame to purify him from his iniquity as he has learned in *cheder* Isaiah was once purified.

No book insists more on the distance between the foulness man lives and the purity he dreams; but none makes more clear how deeply rooted that dream is in the existence which seems to contradict it. It is, perhaps, this double insight which gives to Roth's book a Jewish character, quite independent of the subject matter with which he happens to deal. Certainly, it reveals his kinship to Nathanael West, also a novelist of the thirties, whose relationship to his own Jewishness is much more equivocal than Roth's, but who quotes in his earliest book an observation of Doughty's about the nature of Semites in general which illuminates his own work as well as Roth's: the Semite stands in dung up to his eyes, but his brow touches the heavens. Indeed, in Jewish American fiction from Abraham Cahan to Philip Roth, that polarity and tension are present everywhere, the Jew mediating between dung and God, as if his eternal function were to prove that man is most himself not when he turns first to one then to the other—but when he touches both at once. And who can project the awareness of this more intensely and dramatically than the child, the Jewish child?

It is possible to imagine many reasons for Roth's retreating to childhood from adult experience; for retreat it does seem in the light of his second withdrawal, after the publication of a single book, into the silence in which he has persisted until now. To have written such a book and no other is to betray some deep trouble not only in finding words but in loving the life one has lived enough to *want* to find words for it. A retreat from all that 1935 meant to Roth: from the exigencies of adult sexuality and political commitment alike—this is what *Call It Sleep* seems to the retrospective insight of 1960. The book begins in 1907, and though it jumps quickly some five years, never quite reaches the year of the Russian Revolution (the roster of splendid betrayals listed by the street-corner speaker stops at 1905) and the vagaries of Leninism-Stalinism; just as in coming to a close in a boy's eighth year it stops safely short of the point where "playing bad" becomes an act that can end in deflowering or pregnancy. In its world before the falls of puberty and the October Revolution, one can remember 1905 and Mama —play out the dream of the apocalypse and the Oedipal triangle in all naïveté.

Cued by whatever fears, Roth's turning to childhood enables him to render his story as dream and nightmare, fantasy and myth—to escape the limits of that realism which makes of other accounts of ghetto childhood documents rather than poetry. In its own time *Call It Sleep* was occasionally compared to Farrell's *Young Lonigan,* but one cannot conceive of such a foreword to Roth's book as that written for Farrell's by "Frederic M. Thrasher, Associate Professor of Education, New York University, Author of *The Gang.*" Roth's book aspires not to sociology but to theology; it is finally and astonishingly a religious book, though this fact even its latest admiring critics tend to ignore or underplay. Only in the account of a child's experience could a protégé of Eda Lou Walton (it would have been another matter if he had been sponsored by Mary Pickford) have gotten away with a religious resolution to a serious novel about ghetto life; and it was to a child's experience that he was canny enough to turn. An evasion of responsibility? A strategic device of great subtlety? It is not necessary to decide.

David Schearl, at any rate, is portrayed not only as a small boy and a Jew but also as a "mystic," a naïve adept visited by visions he scarcely understands until a phrase from the sixth chapter of Isaiah illuminates for him his own improbable prophetic initiation. Having just burned the leaven of the year in preparation for the Passover ("All burned black. See God, I was good? Now only white Matzohs are left"), David sits watching the play of light on the river and is transported ("His spirit yielded, melted into light. . . . Brighter than day . . . Brighter"). But he is awakened from his ecstasy by the tooting of a barge ("Funny little lights all gone. Like when you squeeze too hard on a toilet . . ."), thrust back into darkness until two Gentile hoodlums persuade him to drop a strip of zinc down into the third rail of a trolley line and he feels that in the dark bowels of the earth he has discovered the source of all light ("And light, unleashed, terrific light bellowed out of iron lips"). This light he identifies with the burning coal that cleansed the unclean lips of Isaiah, though his rabbi mocks him ("Fool! Go beat your head on a wall! God's light is not between car-tracks")—and in his joy he wets his pants.

For better or worse, the prophetic poetry reduced to an exercise learned by rote and beaten into unwilling boys has come alive in David, delivered him from fear so that he can climb the darkest stairway untroubled. ("Gee! Look! Look! Is a light . . . Ain't really there. Inside my head. Better is inside. . . .") Released a little from the warm bondage that binds him to his mother, he can climb now even to the roof of his house, where he meets for the first time the Gentile boy, Leo, a twelve-year-old seducer and eater of forbidden foods, beside whose absolute freedom David's limited release seems slavery still. And in Leo's house he finds new images for the inner light, the purifying flame, in a portrait of Jesus with the Burning Heart and a box bearing the symbolic fish, the name GOD. For the rosary that box contains, he agrees to introduce Leo to his sluttish cousin Esther, whose grimy favors Leo finally wins in the cellar beneath her mother's candy store.

As Leo and Esther squeal and pant in the darkness of one cellar shed, David crouches in another trying to exact light from the holy beads for which he has betrayed his family, his Jewishness, his very desire for cleanliness.

> Past drifting bubbles of grey and icy needles of grey, below a mousetrap, a cogwheel, below a step and a dwarf with a sack upon his back . . . sank the beads, gold figure on a cross swinging slowly . . . . At the floor of the vast pit of silence glimmered the round light, pulsed and glimmered like a coin. —Touch it! Touch it! Drop!

But the light eludes his efforts; and the other two, who have performed the act of darkness at the very moment he sought the light, emerge blaming each other as they are discovered by Esther's sister. "Tell 'er wut I wuz doin', kid," Leo blusters. "Yuh jew hewhs! We wuz hidin' de balonee—Yaa! Sheenee!"

AFTER such a denouement, nothing is possible for David but a plunge into hysteria, a hysteria which overcomes him as he is rereading the passage about the calling of Isaiah, betrays him into telling to his *rebbe* a story compounded half of his father's delusions, dimly perceived, and half of certain reminiscences of his mother, ill understood: his mother is not his *real* mother, he is a bastard, son of a goyish organist in an old country church, etc., etc. This fantasy the *rebbe* hastens to carry to David's home, arriving a moment before the horrified parents of Esther appear with their own scandal. And David, overwhelmed by guilt and fear, offers to his father a whip, grovels at his feet, the rosary falling from his pocket as if to testify to the truth of his illegitimacy, his contaminated blood. At this point, he must run for his life, his father's long rage at last fulfilled, presumably justified; and he runs where he must, toward God in the dark cleft, to the third rail, the coal of fire that can take away iniquity.

He snatches a ladle from beside a milk pail and flees to an obbligato of city voices, which from the girders of a half-finished building, a warehouse, a bar, a poker table speak with unclean lips of lust and greed, hatred and vengefulness. Only David dreams of a consummation that will transcend and redeem the flesh, finally thrusts the metal he bears between the black lips of the tracks and the awful lightning is released, his body shaken by ineffable power, and his consciousness all but obliterated. Yet his intended sacrifice redeems no one, merely adds a new range of ambiguity to the chorus in which one voice blasphemes against the faith of another and all against love. Himself dazzled, the reader hears again certain phrases he has before only half understood, listens again, for instance, to the barroom voice that mocked the street-corner orator, "How many times'll your red cock crow, Pete, befaw y'gives up? T'ree?"—notices the "three," the name "Pete," and remembers the other Peter who, three times before the cock crow, denied his Rabbi.

In the interplay of ironies and evasions the final meaning of the failed sacrifice, the private apocalypse (the boy does not die; the world is not made clean; only his parents are rejoined more in weariness than affection over his bed) is never made quite clear, only the transcendence of that meaning, its more than natural character. Turning the final pages of Roth's book, one realizes suddenly how in the time of the Great Depression all the more serious fictionists yearned in secret to touch a religious note, toying with the messianic and the apocalyptic but refusing to call them by names not honored in the left-wing journals of the time. The final honesty of Roth's book lies in its refusal to call by any fashionable honorific name its child hero's bafflement as he learns the special beauty of a world which remains stubbornly unredeemed: "Not pain, not terror, but strangest triumph, strangest acquiescence. One might as well call it sleep."

—1960

# SEVEN

# Our Country and Our Culture

THE END OF the American artist's pilgrimage to Europe is the discovery of America. That this discovery is unintended hardly matters; ever since Columbus it has been traditional to discover America by mistake. Even in the days when it was still fashionable to talk about "expatriation," the American writer was rediscovering the Michigan woods in the Pyrenees, or coming upon St. Paul in Antibes. How much more so now when the departing intellectual does not take flight under cover of a barrage of manifestos, but is sent abroad on a Fulbright grant or is sustained by the G.I. Bill. The new American abroad finds a Europe racked by self-pity and nostalgia (except where sustained by the manufactured enthusiasms of Stalinism), and as alienated from its own traditions as Sauk City; he finds a Europe reading in its ruins *Moby Dick,* a Europe haunted by the idea of America.

The American writer soon learns that for the European intellectual, as for him, there are two Americas. The first is the America of ECA and NATO, a political lesser evil, hated with a kind of helpless fury by those who cannot afford to reject its aid; the second is the America invented by European Romanticism—the last humanistic religion of the West, a faith become strangely confused with a political fact. To the European, the literature of America is inevitably purer, *realer* than America itself. Finding it impossible to reject the reality of death, and difficult to believe in anything else, the European is perpetually astonished at the actual existence of a land where only death is denied and everything else considered possible. Overwhelmed by a conviction of human impotence, he regards with horrified admiration a people who, because they are too naïve to understand theory, achieve what he can demonstrate to be theoretically impossible.

From Europe it is easy to understand the religious nature of the American belief in innocence and achievement; to see how even the most vulgar products of "mass culture," movies, comic books, subliterary novels are the scriptures of this post-Christian faith—a faith that has already built up in Western Europe a sizable underground sect which worships in the catacombs of the movie theaters and bows before the images of its saints on the newsstands. A hundred years after the *Manifesto,* the specter that is haunting Europe is— Gary Cooper! Vulgar, gross, sentimental, impoverished in style— our popular subart presents a dream of human possibilities to starved imaginations everywhere. It is a wry joke that what for us are the most embarrassing by-products of a democratic culture are, in countries like Italy, the only democracy there is.

It seems to me that it has become absurd to ask whether a democratic society is worthwhile if it entails a vulgarization and leveling of taste. Such a leveling the whole world is bound to endure, with or without political guarantees of freedom; and the serious writer must envision his own work in such a context, realize that his own final meanings will arise out of a dialectical interplay between what he makes and a given world of "mass culture." Even the Stalinists, though they thunder against American jazz and cowboy suits for children, can in the end only kidnap our vulgar mythology for their own purposes. The sense of an immortality here and now, so important to American culture and parodied in Forest Lawn Cemetery, finds its Soviet counterpart in the mummification of Lenin or the touting of Bogomolets; while our faith in progress and achievement finds an ersatz in the Five Year Plans and the statistics doctored to assist belief. In its Russian form, what is possible in America has become compulsory, an unofficial rite has been made an orthodoxy. And even in our own country there have been occasional attempts to impose optimism (and eventually, one can only suppose, youth and naïveté) by law.

Yet for us, hope has never become just official, a mere camouflage for actual exploitation, though indeed two generations of writers just before us believed so; and it was their sense of having alone penetrated our hoax of prosperity and happiness that nourished their feelings of alienation. The error of such writers was double (such errors, naturally, do not preclude good writing; being *right* is, thank God, optional for the writer). Not only was the American *mythos* real and effective, the very opposite of the hypocritical and barren materialism is seemed; but also everywhere, down to the last layer of babbitry, there existed beside this belief its complement: an unspoken realization of the guilt and terror involved in the American experience. In his sense of lonely horror, the writer was most one with everyone else.

Precisely the uncompromising optimism of Americans makes every inevitable failure to accomplish what can only be dreamed an unredeemable torment. Among us, nothing is winked at or shrugged away; we are being eternally horrified at dope addiction or bribery or war, at things accepted in older civilizations as the facts of life, scarcely worth a tired joke. Even tax evasion dismays us! We are forever feeling our own pulses, collecting statistics to demonstrate the plight of the Negro, the prevalence of divorce, the failure of the female orgasm, the decline of family Bible reading, because we feel, we *know* that a little while ago it was in our power, new men in a new world (and even yet there is hope), to make all perfect. How absurd of our writers to have believed that only they were pained at the failure of love and justice in the United States! What did they think our pulp literature of violence and drunkenness and flight was trying symbolically to declare? Why did they suppose that the most widely read fiction in America asks endlessly, "Whodunnit? Where is the guilt?"

I think we are in the position now to understand that the concept of the "alienated artist" itself was as much a creation of the popular mind as of the artist. It is no accident that Edgar Allen Poe is both the prototype of the American Poet as Despised Dandy, and the inventor of the most popular genres of "mass culture." The image of the drunken, dope-ridden, sexually impotent, poverty-oppressed Poe is as native to the American mind as the image of the worker driving his new Ford into the garage beside the Cape Cod cottage; together they are the American's image of himself. Poe, Crane, Fitzgerald—each generation provides itself with its own lost artist—and their biographies are inevitable best-sellers.

I do not mean to imply that the role of scapegoat is not actually painful for the artist; his exclusion and scourging is the psycho-drama of us all, but it is played out in earnest. Poe was in a certain sense a poseur, but he died of his pose; and the end of Fitzgerald was real terror. I want only to insist that the melancholy and rebellious artist has always been a collaborator in American culture—that it is only when he accepts the political or sentimental half-truths of democracy, when he says *yes* too soon, that he betrays his role and his countrymen—and that the popular mind at its deepest level is well aware of this.

Of all peoples of the world, we hunger most deeply for tragedy; and perhaps in America alone the emergence of a tragic literature is still possible. The masterpieces of our nineteenth-century literature have captured the imagination of readers everywhere, precisely because their tragic sense of life renews vicariously the exhausted spirit. In Western Europe, the tragic tension no longer exists; it is too easy to despair and to fall in love with one's despair. Melodrama, *comédie larmoyante,* learned irony and serious parody—these are the forms proper to the contemporary European mind. In the orbit of Stalinism, on the other hand, despair has been legislated away; justice triumphs and the wicked suffer—there is no evil except in the other. Some lies are the very stuff of literature, but this is not among them; it breeds police forces rather than poetry.

Only where there is a real and advancing prosperity, a constant effort to push beyond all accidental, curable ills, all easy cynicism and premature despair toward the irreducible residuum of human weakness, sloth, self-love, and fear; only where the sense of the inevitability of man's failure does not cancel out the realization of the splendor of his vision, nor the splendor of his vision conceal the reality and beauty of his failure, can tragedy be touched. It is toward this tragic margin that the American artist is impelled by the neglect and love of his public. If he can resist the vulgar temptation to turn a quick profit by making yet one more best-selling parody of hope, and the snobbish temptation to burnish chic versions of elegant despair, the American writer will find that he has, after all, a real function.

Indeed, he is needed in a naked and terrible way, perhaps unprecedented in the history of Western culture—not as an entertainer, or the sustainer of a "tradition," or a recruit to a distinguished guild, but as the recorder of the encounter of the dream of innocence and the fact of guilt, in the only part of the world where the reality of that conflict can still be recognized. If it is a use he is after and not a reward, there is no better place for the artist than America.

—1952

# EIGHT

# Caliban or Hamlet:
# A Study in Literary Anthropology

THERE IS A peculiar paradox—the Caliban-Hamlet Paradox, I have chosen to call it—which resides at the heart of American Literature, and which is so intricately bound up with a basic ambiguity at the heart of European-American cultural relations, our endlessly baffled attempt to understand each other, that to study one means inevitably to deal with the other. Yet the first problem seems clearly an aesthetic one, amenable to formalistic or, at any rate, conventional literary approaches; while the other belongs just as clearly to the realm of sociology or social anthropology, which (as any college catalogue will testify) is a realm utterly alien to that of the arts. How, then, to deal with one world without betraying the other, or with both without falsifying both?

I should like tentatively, though not too much so (since I have been working along these lines for a couple of decades now), to attempt here an approach, perhaps best called literary-anthropological, that seems to me to satisfy the difficult conditions I have just defined. To one practising this approach, it scarcely matters whether he begins with the sociological aspect of the problem or the literary one. Indeed, it seemed to me at first best to introduce the subject I have chosen to confront with a consideration of the assassination of President Kennedy—or more specifically, with a pair of quotations extracted from a review that appeared in *Encounter* for June 1964 of Thomas G. Buchanan's odd and unconvincing study, *Who Killed Kennedy?*

"What Mr. Buchanan is trying to establish," the reviewer writes, "is that . . . this pattern [of Kennedy's assassination] does not accord with the popular [American] belief that the murder of a President is necessarily the irrational act of a lonely and isolated individual who is diseased or deranged in mind." But precisely this belief is what the official Warren Commission report has ended by endorsing, drawing for us the portrait of an utterly alienated mama's boy prompted to a revenge whose motives he never quite understood by all the forces of heaven and hell that possessed him. That portrait, I have tried to indicate with certain deliberate echoes of Shakespearian language, assumes or implies a prototype which presumably failed to come to the reviewer's mind: the image, however vulgarized and degraded, of Hamlet.

What does occur to him is a quite different, though equally authentic Shakespearian prototype, appropriate to the political-plot version of Kennedy's death sponsored by Mr. Buchanan and particularly appealing to Europeans. "Mr. Buchanan uses the murder of the President," the reviewer writes in another place, "to hold up a mirror to America which reflects such a Caliban image of brutishness and corruption that her enemies can only view it with glee. . . ." But why the second rather than the first prototype moves men on the other side of the Atlantic, why they continue to search for a millionaire Caliban behind the scenes, while we are content with a *lumpen* Hamlet front and center, cannot be explained as long as we remain on the political or sociological level. Even to begin, we must answer a prior—and more properly literary —question: what do Caliban and Hamlet, which is to say the myths they embody, represent to the deep imagination of both worlds?

Such an answer is found, however, not in newspapers or the transcripts of police interrogations but in novels and plays and poems, and especially in the deep images that lie at their hearts. Let me, then, make a new start by asking a pair of purely literary questions, which may seem at first quite beside the point, but which will eventually lead us toward the kind of explanation we are seeking. First, why did T. S. Eliot at the moment of his recent death, why does he now seem so irrelevant to young readers and writers of poetry? And second, why does Walt Whitman, so long deceased, seem so living a model at the moment—living as he has not been for some three or four decades?

Simply to ask these questions, to recognize that they can, even must be asked, is to suggest that American writers, old as well as young, are turning away after nearly half a century from sophisticated literary cosmopolitanism; and that they are returning—with extraordinary ferocity and what can only be called a willing suspension of intelligence—to the crassest kind of nationalism, nativism, and primitivism: back to Caliban, in short. We hear once more these days (as we have not heard since the triumph of Whitman) of the necessity for exploiting American themes, using the native American language, and inventing—or restoring—native American meters. In this Calibanistic program, the school of poetry once centered at Black Mountain College joins with that once centered in San Francisco—bohemian academies joining extra-academic bohemians to rescue poetry from the Anglophile universities and recreate it in the Anglophobe cafes.

We have lived, consequently, to see not only Walt Whitman himself, but more recent Whitmanizers like Henry Miller, William Carlos Williams and Louis Zukofsky move from the periphery to the center of literary interest; while poets of the generation of Allen Ginsberg do variations on themes from *Leaves of Grass,* and the old Poundian cry, "Break the iambic!" (i.e., the European heritage, the tradition, the accent of *Hamlet)* is echoed and re-echoed, as if from the barricades. "But what does it mean?" one asks further, "What is really at stake?" And the immediate answer at least is that the cultural situation responds to, even perhaps prophetically anticipates, a political and social one: that we have been preparing for an era in which it will become possible for Negro writers (relatively unsophisticated, and culturally—as we like to say—deprived) to act as the principal spokesmen for the American people; and for the life they share to seem the archetypal life of us all, the language in which they communicate our archetypal tongue. The relationship of Whitman to this revolution Garcia Lorca intuitively grasped long ago, writing in *The Poet in New York:* "Sleep, Walt, and let a black boy announce to the golden Whites the arrival of the reign of an ear of corn." But it is desirable, perhaps, to come to terms with that relationship less metaphorically.

As is well known, we Americans are forever re-inventing our-selves in terms of the experience and values, the attitudes and idi-oms of one or another ethnic and cultural group out of the many which constitute our community. When the elected archetypal group is of one kind (genteel, university-educated, Atlantic Sea-board Anglo-Saxons, for example, as in the second half of the nine-teenth century; or New York and Chicago Jews, with vestigial Marxist and Freudian vocabularies, as just before and after World War II), we are likely to think of ourselves as participating in a common cultural enterprise with Europe or the whole Western world. When, however, small-town boys from the Midwest or South —their various inherited cultures, chiefly North European, boiled away in the melting pot—emerge at the center of our culture, as they did just before and after World War I, they tend to think of their art as made against the total European-Mediterranean tradi-tion, in despite or contempt of their cultural heritage. Walt Whit-man composed their manifesto long before they were born:

> Come Muse migrate from Greece and Ionia,
> Cross out please those immensely overpaid accounts,
> That matter of Troy and Achilles' wrath, and Aeneas',
>     Odysseus' wanderings,
> Place "Removed" and "To Let" on the rocks of your snowy
>     Parnassus . . .

How much more the Negroes (and following their example, the Negro-izers, Beat and Hip) tend in the sixties to create for us—and reflect from us—a desire to re-establish our culture on a denial of that Western cosmopolitanism whose political face is White Imperi-alism. Once we have granted that the nationalist-nativist-primitivist strain in our life and art is our most authentic expression, we are compelled to see the Negro as the ultimate, the absolute American —rivaled only by the Indian, to whose image he is assimilated in our classic books. Certainly, he is no transplanted European, but no more is he a displaced African after three hundred years on our soil; he is a new man, made in the U.S.A., a pure product of the New World.

Another way to say this is that the Negro is totally what all other Americans are only in part: the living embodiment of that absolute Other dreamed by Europeans—sometimes sympathetically, more often in fascinated horror—before they had ever dragged an actual Black from Africa to slavery in America. To be sure, that dream was prompted by self-hatred and a reversion from culture, and nurtured by a despair of reason and a yearning for the natural past, which existed only in myth; but it has, nonetheless, vexed Europe ever since the eighteenth century or earlier, eventuating in poems on the one hand, and emigration on the other. And here, of course, is the source of the paradox to which I began by alluding: the reason why the native American when he glories in his naïveté, and thinks he is most anticosmopolitan—is in fact most abjectly submitting to Old World tradition.

In this sense, Walt Whitman and Mark Twain are the most European of our writers, assuming masks and poses with which the reader abroad can be at ease, as we never can be at home; for such writers strive to seem what the European eternally demands we make ourselves for his sake: the mythological anti-European he has defined in his literary tradition. In that tradition, Mediterranean and German and Englishman, rationalist and Romantic and pragmatist find themselves oddly at one. And it is, perhaps, possible to say that Europeans can be aware of their own world as a single cultural unit only against a clearly identified cultural other: Islam once, American more recently. But this is another paradox, for another day and another sort of writer—one looking from rather than toward that Old World, in which the New was invented.

Let me return to my main concern by asking instead: when, then, are American artists most deeply and truly selves of their own contriving, as opposed to the selves Europeans so eagerly foist on them? And let me suggest by way of an answer: when they are permitted, permit themselves rather, freely to ransack their whole cultural heritage (Hebraic-Hellenistic-Renaissance-Romantic, all that they share with Europe); and when they end choosing, not what was already chosen for them before they existed as a people, but at first hand whatever they will. Or, to insist once more on the paradox, our writers are most themselves when they are able to see themselves precisely in borrowed images, images long used for their own purposes by our European forebears.

What images our writers do in fact choose to portray their sense of themselves and of us are fascinatingly various. I shall, however, pass over here all but one: omitting, for instance, the American artist's vision of himself and his people in the guise of Christ—as the Suffering Servant by whose stripes the European Gentiles are healed. Yet this image is of critical importance both in Hemingway and Faulkner and recurs on the edge of unconscious parody in Arthur Miller's *After the Fall,* from which I once heard a baffled lady spectator emerge muttering to herself, "Why, that son-of-a-bitch thinks he's Jesus Christ." Nor shall I deal with the Ulysses image in its peculiarly American form: that non-Homeric, romanticized figure out of Dante by way of Tennyson which so spectacularly haunts the imagination of Ezra Pound.

I prefer instead to concentrate on Hamlet, once more as revised by the Romantic imagination: the peculiarly American Hamlet seen backward through Goethe's young Werther. I choose this figure not only because it makes such a neatly illustrative Shakespearian pair with Caliban, but also because the Hamlet image seems to me the one that has most obsessively concerned our writers, all the way from *The Power of Sympathy,* whose appearance coincided with our birth as a nation, to *The Hamlet of A. MacLeish* or even Hyam Plutzik's Horatio poems. The central document in the history of American Hamletism is surely Melville's *Pierre,* a novel unparalleled until Mailer's *An American Dream* for the unguarded way in which it projects deep fantasies shared by the author and his culture; and the *locus classicus* is the passage in which Pierre stands before his bookshelf:

> His mind was wandering and vague; his arm wandered and was vague. Some moments passed, and he found the open *Hamlet* in his hand, and his eyes met the following lines: 'The time is out of joint, Oh cursed spite,/ That ever I was born to set it right.' He dropped the true volume from his hand; his petrifying heart dropped hollowly within him. . . .

But though it is Pierre who finds the key lines for Americans in *Hamlet,* he is no more Werther-Hamlet-like, after all, than, say,

Poe's Roderick Usher, or any of the Dimmesdale-Coverdale melancholics of Hawthorne, or Faulkner's Quentin Compson, or Saul Bellow's Herzog, for that matter; or, to leave literature for life and remember the place from which we began, than Lee Harvey Oswald. We must understand, at any rate, the long background of convention and expectation against which Prufrock cries out, "No! I am not Prince Hamlet, nor was meant to be," the sense in which simply rejecting that tragic role in favor of the comic Polonius one is in our land a revolutionary gesture, a break with tradition.

What, then, is the special appeal of *Hamlet* to the American imagination; of the plot, on the one hand, with the obligation to revenge fumbled and fumbled, then suicidally achieved; and of the character, on the other, with an anguish and melancholy disproportionate (as Eliot once more has insisted) to the events? Surely, that very anguish and melancholy to begin with; for we inhabit a country where the required optimism of the ruling majority breeds a compulsory *angst* in the writing minority, the drunken revelry of fathers a withdrawn brooding on the part of their sons. And the notion of suicide itself titillates even more, suggesting the possibility of an irrepressible, an unanswerable revolt against inherited obligations. Also, I think, American writers have tended to take the Prince of Denmark at his word when he speaks of his coward-making conscience; for we are experts on the inhibitory nature of conscience, as even Eliot, for all his theoretical anti-Hamletism, testifies:

> Between the conception
> And the creation
> Between the emotion
> And the response
> Falls the Shadow

Finally, however, I am tempted to believe that on some level of consciousness many American intellectuals have found (as I have found certainly) in the Romantics' favorite Shakespearian play, Melville's "form book," an oddly apt parable of our relationship to Europe. While Europeans tend to think of us mythologically as rebellious slaves, which is to say, politically and in the context of society, we need to regard ourselves as wronged sons, which is to say, psychologically and in the context of the family. Both the Christ image and the Hamlet one cater to this inner necessity; for archetypally speaking, Hamlet is Christ after the death of God, a Son of the Father whose progenitor survives only as a dubious ghost and whose single surviving prayer is: *My God, my God* (or, *Father, Father) why hast thou forsaken me?* The Hamlet image is, however, more unequivocally Oedipal and therefore more congenial to us: the figure of a son, who is a university graduate and intellectual as well as a Prince, loving still the soiled mother who has (perhaps) bereft him of his real, i.e., his good, father and put him at the mercy of his bad one: a drunken murderer and usurper whom that son should overthrow, and, indeed, might, were he not robbed of all power except that over words by the monstrous love that ties him more to his whored mama than to any paternal ghost.

The troubled cry of Hamlet when he first realizes his mission and his disability is, at any rate, a peculiarly American one, which we need no Pierre to discover for us:

> The time is out of joint; O cursed spite,
> That ever I was born to set it right.

Here in a couplet is summed up the attitude toward the Old World and all in the New which comes to resemble it (resplendent pomp and established power and presumed injustice) that motivates not only such private vengeances as Oswald's, but also such public ventures as our current campaign in Vietnam, or the often-proposed, often-delayed plan to "liberate Eastern Europe." But while the American, in Saigon or Dallas or Budapest, is imagining himself as Hamlet, the European may well be seeing him as Caliban.

Indeed, Shakespeare, who was not at all thinking about America, of course, when he wrote *Hamlet,* was precisely concerned with the New World when he was conceiving *The Tempest* and inventing Caliban. Despite his perfunctory effort to suggest a non-American setting for *The Tempest,* it is reasonably clear that Shakespeare had been reading accounts of an expedition to the Bermudas, as well as Montaigne's essay on cannibals, while the fable of the play (one of the very few for which no model has been found) was forming in his mind. And it is highly probable that "Caliban" is a deliberate anagram of "cannibal," itself in all likelihood a corruption of "Carib," which is to say, a native of the Caribbean or a Red Indian.

At any rate, we can profitably think of Caliban as one of the earlier European portraits of the indigenous American, *l'homme sauvage* of an already existing mythology transplanted to the New World: part-Indian, part-Negro, all subhuman—indeed, as Shakespeare fancies him (remembering doubtlessly the medieval notion of the Western hemisphere as a watery world), part-fish. Caliban is, however, not only a sketch of the dark-skinned peoples in whose presence white Europeans have attempted to work out their destinies on our continent; he is also the model according to which such transplanted white Europeans have sometimes tried to remake themselves. D. H. Lawrence, as a matter of fact, believed that willy-nilly Americans of European origin do become assimilated to Indians and Negroes, being appropriately "fugitive slaves" to begin with; and he quotes, in the introductory chapter to *Studies in Classic American Literature,* a tag from *The Tempest* as appropriate to all inhabitants of the United States, whatever their origin.

'Ban, 'Ban, Ca— Caliban,
Has a new master— Get a new man.

But what finally does this Calibanistic view of America mean, this vision of the archetypal American not as the son of a usurping false-father and a sullied mother, but as a deformed slave, rebelling against legitimate authority at the instigation of certain European turncoats (more fools even than knaves) who have plied him with liquor? What follows when we have identified the mythological American with the drunken offspring of a witch and the Devil, bent on raping female innocence and overthrowing a mastery imposed in utter reason and benevolence? What can follow except condescension and contempt? Yet there is a qualifying note already present in Shakespeare, in the lines he gives Prospero reflecting Europe's sense of responsibility for America, for the institution of slavery, which was its first gift to us, and for the blackness of darkness embodied in slavery. "This thing of darkness I," Prospero says (and the personal pronoun hangs at the end of the line, confessing Caliban to be the responsibility not of that arrant evil he had presumably left behind in the Old World, but of the best he had been able to bring to the New), "Acknowledge mine."

It is a fascinating dialogue which the Shakespearian analogues suggest to us: the voice that Americans have claimed as their own crying, "O cursed spite. . ."; and the voice which Europeans have preferred answering, with a dying fall, ". . . Acknowledge mine." It does not even matter that certain Europeans later switch sides, i.e., support Caliban against the Master of Arts whose creature he is—hail Whitman, praise John Steinbeck, make a cult of Dashiell Hammett or of those ultimate imaginary Americans, those Calibans thrice removed, the Beatles. Occasions for misunderstanding still arise, opportunities for pathos and comedy—not only in literature but in life, in the councils of the U.N. or on the established routes of tourism—as the American, who is sure that he is Hamlet, confronts the European, who is convinced that he is Caliban.

Even funnier and more pathetic, however, is the confusion of certain American Hamlets attempting to persuade themselves, as the fashion changes at home, that they are in fact Calibans, have been secret sea monsters all along. Karl Shapiro is a case in point, for instance, with his boasted shift from the Eliotic style of his earlier poems to the Whitmanian stance of "The Bourgeois Poet"; and Norman Mailer another, self-transformed into what he calls a White Negro, i.e., Caliban, from the Harvard boy dreaming of combat on the banks of the Charles.

> . . . Rightly to be great
> Is not to stir without great argument,
> But greatly to find quarrel in a straw . . .

Most moving and most significant at the moment, however, is the case of James Baldwin, who, beginning with the delicate and scrupulous examination of conscience in *Go Tell it On the Mountain, Notes of a Native Son* and *Giovanni's Room,* has been impelled to move on toward the brutal histrionics of *Another Country* and *Blues for Mr. Charlie.*

> . . . Examples gross as earth exhort me.

I would suppose that to a Negro (or an Indian) the notion of playing Caliban has a special attraction, since not only most Europeans
but many of their white brethren (eager to keep the number of
Hamlets down) have thrust the role of rapist-rebel-slave upon
them; and it must seem, at any rate, preferable to the alternative
role of Uncle Tom. Even this is more farcical than tragic, however,
deserving not the Hamlet cry I find trembling on my lips ("O
cursed spite. . ." once more) but almost any Calibanistic vaunt:
perhaps best of all those astonishingly chic verses Shakespeare put
into Caliban's mouth, a Beat American poem before its time:

Freedom, high-day! high-day, freedom! freedom!
high-day, freedom!

*Buffalo, New York*
—1965

# NINE

# Toward a Centennial:
# Notes on *Innocents Abroad*

IT IS NOW nearly a hundred years since Mark Twain embarked on "the first organized pleasure party ever assembled for a transatlantic voyage," and began making the notes which were to become that occasionally mad, often tedious, but somehow eminently satisfactory travel book, *The Innocents Abroad or the New Pilgrim's Progress: Being Some Account of the Steamship QUAKER CITY's Pleasure Excursion to Europe and the Holy Land.* A century later, we find it perfectly natural that Twain should have been present as a kind of laureate-*ex-officio* at the initiation of mass tourism in the United States—his way, to the tune of $1,250, paid by a California newspaper; for we know now that with the publication of his "New Pilgrim's Progress," he was launching a literary career marked by an almost obsessive concern with Europe and the quest for American identity.

No one, however, had any sense of this on June 8, 1867, when the *Quaker City* sailed, since—though Twain had already done some newspaper pieces about a voyage to Hawaii—his sole published volume, *The Celebrated Jumping Frog and Other Sketches,* suggested an exclusive concern with quite other, much more parochial material. Yet, over and over, he was to return to the themes of *The Innocents Abroad:* not only in other self-declared travel books like *A Tramp Abroad* or *Following the Equator,* but in such fictions as *The Prince and the Pauper, A Connecticut Yankee in King Arthur's Court, Personal Recollections of Joan of Arc, Tom Sawyer Abroad, The Mysterious Stranger.* Even in his greatest work, *Huckleberry Finn,* the encounter with Europe is represented, despite the exclusively American scene, in the ill-fated meeting between Jim and Huck, on the one hand, and the Duke and the Dauphin, on the other. To be sure, those two self-styled Europeans are arrant frauds; but precisely insofar as they are fraudulent, they embody what Twain took to be the essential nature of Old World aristocracy.

At any rate, Twain's participation in the excursion seems to have been more suffered than welcomed, the representatives of the Plymouth Church (apparently the moving spirit behind the whole enterprise) preferring to advertise such better known prospective passengers as Henry Ward Beecher and General Sherman, neither of whom finally went along. Mark Twain, however, was there on schedule, along with "three ministers of the gospel, eight doctors, sixteen or eighteen ladies, several military and naval chieftains," and other similarly undistinguished but pious fellow-adventurers. "The whole affair," Bret Harte was acute enough to point out in 1870, "was a huge practical joke, of which not the least amusing feature was the fact that 'Mark Twain' had embarked on it." Yet this joke eventuated in a classic work which, without ceasing to be amusing, marks a critical point in the development of our literature, and especially in our attempt through literature to find out who we Americans are.

We have always been aware that ours is a country which has had to be invented as well as discovered: invented even before its discovery (as Atlantis, Ultima Thule, a western world beyond the waves) and re-invented again and again both by the European imagination—from, say, Chateaubriand to D. H. Lawrence or Graham Greene—and by the deep fantasy of its own people, once these existed in fact. Europeans, however, begin always with their own world, the Old World, as *given* and define the New World in contrast to it, as nature versus culture, the naïve versus the sophisticated, the primitive versus the artificial. We Americans, on the other hand, are plagued by the need to invent a mythological version of Europe first, something against which we can then define ourselves, since for us neither the Old nor the New World seems ever given and we tend to see ourselves not directly but reflexively: as the Other's Other. Only when the two worlds become one, as they seem now on the verge of doing, will Europeans and Americans alike be delivered from the obligation of writing "travel books" about each other, i.e., books whose chief point is to define our archetypal differences and prepare for our historical assimilation.

In the past, certainly, most American writers have, either in avowed fictions or presumed factual accounts, created myths of the two worlds and their relationship; from Washington Irving and James Fenimore Cooper, through Poe and Hawthorne and Melville to James and Hemingway, Eliot and Pound, scarcely any of our major authors have failed to face up to this task. Those few who have rejected it—Thoreau and Whitman come first to mind—have felt their refusal in itself as somehow heroic and if not quite a sufficient *raison d'être,* at least a satisfactory *raison d'écrire.* For a long time, however, the general American obligation to accommodate to each other the myths of Europeans and ex-Europeans was oddly parochialized by being entrusted to the small group of highly educated White Anglo-Saxon Protestants from a few Atlantic seaboard cities, who remained for decades the sole public spokesmen of the United States.

It was that group, in any case, who first undertook the archetypal voyage to Europe (Dr. Franklin, in his disguise as a good, gray Quaker, being the mythological forerunner of them all), defining it in letters, articles and books as simultaneously a Descent into Hell and an Ascent to Olympus. The inferno into which the earlier travelers thought of themselves as descending was the Hell of surviving Medievalism, which is to say, of oppression, class distinction, "immorality" (belated vestiges of Courtly Love), and, especially, Roman Catholicism; while the Olympian heights they fancied themselves as scaling were represented by the preserved monuments of antiquity, the reconstructed cathedrals of the Middle Ages and the artistic achievements of the Renaissance as displayed in museums. Unfortunately for their peace of mind, the works of art which such WASP travelers admired to the point almost of worship were hopelessly involved with the values, religious and political, which such travelers most despised. The benign culture-religion into which the faith of their mothers was, by slow and imperceptible degrees, lapsing came into inescapable conflict with the violent anti-Catholicism to which the fiercer faith of their fathers had, just as gradually, shrunk. And though they did not often confess the disease bred by that conflict, they were surely troubled by it.

A little later, their direct descendants, Henry James and Henry Adams, were to suggest a solution, fully achieved only later still by their remoter heirs, T. S. Eliot and Ezra Pound (in whom anti-Semitism tended anyhow to replace anti-Catholicism): the total abandonment of the negative vestiges of Protestantism in favor of the culture-religion and whatever fashionable cults were best adapted to it. But so drastic an accommodation was achieved only at the risk of expatriation and apostasy, which is to say, the surrender of essential "Americanism," as defined in the WASP tradition. How different the Old World was to look to such recusant Puritans only the twentieth century was able to reveal; yet that century revealed, too, how like one half of the older view, at least, their revision of it remained.

One need only contrast their point of view with the versions of Europe and Americans in Europe produced by the quite different kinds of writers to whom the task of re-inventing the two worlds was transferred in the new century: with those birthright Roman Catholics, for instance, like F. Scott Fitzgerald in *Tender Is the Night;* or with those post-Jamesian urban Jews, like H. J. Kaplan in *The Plenipotentiaries* or Bernard Malamud in his Italian stories. The ultimate contrast, however, is with myths of Americans abroad imagined by those absolutely non-European Americans, the Negroes, best represented, perhaps, by James Baldwin in his novel *Giovanni's Room* or his pioneering essay "A Stranger in the Village." We have had to travel far, indeed, on a journey for which the only maps are precisely the books we have been discussing, to get from the Old World of Irving or Longfellow or Hawthorne or Melville, even of James or Eliot, to stand in the Europe Baldwin experiences and overhear his musing, as he watches a group of Swiss villagers: "The most illiterate among them is related in a way I am not to Dante, Shakespeare, Michelangelo . . . the Cathedral of Chartres says to them what it cannot say to me. . . ."

But this is also true of the most illiterate among the Western Americans of the mid-nineteenth century, in whose name Mark Twain pretended to speak; for Twain represents merely the other side of the old WASP ambivalence, its secular Puritanism—that fear of High Art and High Church worship which the followers of Henry Adams had rejected in favor of the religion of Art. Twain may refuse the Virgin and choose the Dynamo, but he remains immeasurably closer to the first American travelers in Europe than any latterday American Catholic or Negro or Jew. Whatever sense of alienation he may feel from Dante, Shakespeare, and Michelangelo, to Shakespeare at least he is bound by a kinship of blood and tradition he can never quite disavow. To be sure, his relationship to Michelangelo is more than a little ambivalent, for Michelangelo was a Mediterranean and a lackey of Cardinals and Popes. "I used to worship the great genius of Michael Angelo," he tells us, " . . . but I do not want Michael Angelo for breakfast—for luncheon—for dinner—for tea. . . . I never felt so fervently thankful, so soothed, so tranquil, so filled with a blessed peace, as I did yesterday when I learned that Michael Angelo was dead."

Yet even here, Twain's is no more the utterly alienated view of a James Baldwin than it is, say, the tormentedly involved response of a second-generation Italo-American, the son of an illiterate peasant from the Abruzzi who has grown rich and returns to confront the world his father had fled. Twain stands on precisely the Protestant Anglo-Saxon middle ground, from which Mediterranean Europe was being surveyed in his time by such more genteel exploiters of experience abroad as William Dean Howells and Bayard Taylor. As a matter of fact, by the time Twain was beginning to write, Taylor himself had decided that Europe was pretty well used up as a literary subject; and in *By-Ways of Europe* (a book about spots off the main lines of travel, published in the same year as *The Innocents Abroad),* had vowed that he would produce no more such essays. Twain, however, being the spokesman for the lowbrow tourism which succeeded the upper middlebrow variety in whose name Taylor had written, follows the old routes with no sense that they have suffered from literary overexposure, or that, indeed, there are any others.

He was, to be sure, the prisoner of a tour plan laid out by organizers for whom the world worth seeing had been defined once and for all by the genteel essayists of the generations before and the writers of guidebooks, who were their degenerate heirs; but he, who protested so much else, does not protest the limits thus imposed on him. Bret Harte, in his otherwise extremely laudatory review, complains of precisely this, "Yet, with all his independence, 'Mark Twain' seems to have followed his guide and guidebooks with a simple, unconscious fidelity. He was quite content to see only that which everybody else sees, even if he was not content to see it with the same eyes. . . ." In one sense, the case can be made even stronger; for more often than anyone seems ever quite to remember, Twain saw those "same sights" with exactly the "same eyes" as those who had gone the same route before him.

He shares especially the bad taste of his generation and its immediate predecessors: admiring extravagantly, for instance, the mediocre Cathedral of Milan ("a poem in marble"), the gross funeral statuary in the cemetery of Genoa, the inferior sculptures exhumed at Pompeii, and even—despite his general contempt for "old paintings"—the Guido Reni "Saint Michael Conquering the Dragon," which the pale heroine of Hawthorne's *The Marble Faun* had also overesteemed. But he shares also their sentimental, hypocritical politics and morality: combining a theoretical hatred of royalty, for instance, with an actual willingness to submit to the charms of emperors, if they are efficient (like Louis Napoleon) or kind to their pretty young daughters (like the Czar of all the Russias); and complementing a theoretical abhorrence for European frankness about sex with an actual eagerness for seeking out occasions to put that abhorrence to work.

Like many of the contemporaries he affected to despise, he wants to have it both ways—to attend unashamedly a performance of the can-can ("I placed my hands before my face for very shame. But I looked through my fingers"), but to be morally offended at the presence beside him of "staid, respectable, aged people." ("There were a good many such people present. I suppose French morality is not of that strait-laced description which is shocked at trifles.") As long as it is understood that sex is for the consumption of men only, and especially of young bachelors, Twain is not morally troubled. He even manages to admire certain pictures "which no pen could have the hardihood to describe," drawn on the walls of what he calls delicately "the only building in Pompeii which no woman is allowed to enter," and barely manages to work up in a dutiful climax, a vision of the wrath of Heaven being visited upon its long-dead clients.

Only when sex threatens the purity of women, or, more precisely, I suppose, of ladies, is his Puritan indignation genuinely stirred; and that indignation is doubled, of course, when a Churchman is involved in the dubious proceedings. Surely, one of the most extraordinary passages in *The Innocents Abroad* (the feeling invoked absurdly out of proportion with the declared occasion) is the long digression on the seduction of Eloise by Abelard and the consequent decline of Abelard's fortunes. With what prurient relish Twain recounts the disasters which overwhelmed "the dastardly Abelard," summing up his downfall finally with that Protestant, bourgeois, American phrase of utter contempt: "He died a nobody. . . ."

But on the way to that climax, he lingers with especial pleasure over Abelard's castration, which he does not name, falling back on a quotation from an anonymous "historian" to hint at it: " 'Ruffians, hired by Fulbert, fell upon Abelard by night, and inflicted upon him a terrible nameless mutilation.' " To which Twain adds: "I am seeking the last resting place of those 'ruffians.' When I find it I shall shed some tears on it . . . and cart away from it some gravel whereby to remember that howsoever besotted by crime their lives may have been, those ruffians did one just deed. . . ."

The notion of an adulterous passion committed and generous enough to be redemptive seems to Twain only "nauseous sentimentality"; for he is as immune to the continental tradition of Courtly Love as any Anglo-American lady novelist. Even in its most attenuated and spiritualized form, as celebrated for instance in the poems of Petrarch to Laura, the Medieval love code finds no sympathetic response in Twain, who only cries by way of protest, "Who glorifies poor Mr. Laura?" Not that he ever blames the young ladies involved, considering them, by definition, innocent victims. "I have not a word to say against the misused, faithful girl," he comments of Eloise herself, taking her side as instinctively as Harriet

Beecher Stowe had taken that of Mrs. Byron, in an article printed in the very issue of *The Atlantic Monthly* in which Howells had reviewed Twain's travel book; for, like Mrs. Stowe, Mark Twain believed that a "reverence for pure womanhood is . . . a national characteristic of the American. . . ."

Certainly, it was a characteristic of those genteel vestigial Puritans to whose company Twain aspired; and whenever he found a living example of that "pure womanhood" ready to hand—as he did in Mary Mason Fairbanks aboard the *Quaker City*—he submitted to her censorship in an act of guilt-ridden hypocrisy, which he apparently took for virtue. "I was never what she thought me," he wrote on the occasion of 'Mother' Fairbanks' death in 1899, "but I was glad to seem to her to be it." Such submission to conscience as embodied in a surrogate mamma of genteel taste and sentimental Christian principles appeared to Twain, at any rate, a way into the cultured WASP world; and this conviction seemed to him justified when the book which had taken final shape under Mrs. Fairbanks's supervision was hailed by William Dean Howells, spokesman-in-chief for that world.

His spontaneous expression of pleasure at that review is, however, a giveaway, not only in its unguarded vulgarity, but in the implications of its metaphor. He had felt reading it, Twain said, like the woman whose baby had come white; and, indeed, with the acceptance of *The Innocents Abroad,* he had been accepted as fully "white," in the sense that the Anglo-Saxon first settlers of America had given that mythological adjective.

But he was not, finally, quite one of them, as was to become embarrassingly evident to his genteel defenders at the infamous Whittier Birthday Dinner, a decade or so after his voyage on the *Quaker City.* Confronting what Stuart P. Sherman would still be able to call as late as 1910, "the leading geniuses of New England," i.e., the most proper literary Bostonians, Twain told into the "black frost" of their disapproval an utterly irreverent, pseudo-Western yarn involving "Mr. Longfellow, Mr. Emerson, Mr. Oliver Wendell Holmes—confound the lot. . . ." Twain was never able really to understand why his homely anecdote had failed to tickle his auditors; but Mr. Sherman, last apologist for the values he had unwittingly challenged, is in no doubt. "I know very well," he asserts, "that Congreve or Addison or George Meredith would have agreed . . . that Mark Twain's reminiscence was a piece of crude, heavy intellectual horseplay—an impudent affront offered to Puritan aristocracy by a rough-handed plebeian jester from Missouri."

But why, Twain must have wondered, was his Whittier's birthday speech rejected by the sort of men who had accepted his European travel book, much of which was precisely the same sort of "crude, heavy, intellectual horseplay," presented through exactly the same sort of *persona,* "a rough-handed plebeian jester from Missouri." Stuart Sherman himself, as a matter of fact, is quite as ready to condemn the book as the speech, and on similar grounds: "The Mississippi pilot, homely, naïve, arrogantly conceited . . . turns the Old World into a laughing stock by shearing it of its humanity —simply because there is nothing in him to respond to the glory that was Greece, to the grandeur that was Rome—simply because nothing is holier to him than a joke." William Dean Howells, however, had not been nearly so severe in his review of the book by the man he kept referring to as "Mr. Clements"—only a little condescending, perhaps: "It is no business of ours to fix his rank among the humorists California has given us, but we think he is, in an entirely different way from all the others, quite worthy of the company of the best."

Finally, however, Howells is willing to exempt the "California humorist" from charges of *lèse-majesté* in the realm of culture: " . . . it is always good-humored humor, too, that he lavishes on his reader, and even its impudence is charming; we do not remember where . . . it is insolent, with all its sauciness and irreverence." Even here the descriptive phrases remain condescending, though they are apt enough, after all, in defining a writer who composed his book to shock (a little) and mollify (a lot) the woman whom he had appointed his shipboard "mother." Charming . . . impudence," "insolent," "sauciness"—these are terms suitable not so much to a man as to a boy, one of those naughty boys who are not in the final analysis downright "bad." And, indeed, Twain himself uses the word "boys" constantly to describe his closest associates among the Pilgrims, the lively few who, with him, constantly sought to flee the more aged and grim members of what he likes to call the "synagogue." Already at the very beginning of his career, he is beginning to trade on that "boyishness" which he never willingly surrendered, in order to get away with what would have been counted sacrilege in a full-fledged man. And a sufficiently perspicuous critic might well have predicted at that point, that the hero in whom Twain was to embody his most mature definition of the American character would necessarily be a juvenile, just one more boy in a cast of boys.

But the "Mark Twain" of *The Innocents Abroad* is a bigger boy than Huck Finn: a boy full-grown enough to regret that his fellow voyagers scanted whist and dancing and love-making in favor of prayers and the singing of hymns, and to wander the streets of Europe in search of good cigars, a decent shave, and an authentic pool table—yet one not too mature to steal bunches of grapes on his way down from the Acropolis, and to torment his guides with childish horseplay. The "Mark Twain" of 1867 was, in short, the kind of boy-man we think of referring to as a "Westerner," one in whom the power of adulthood and the irresponsibility of childhood ideally combine. Twain, however, did not consider himself quite such a "Westerner" as he was later to describe in *Roughing It*, "stalwart, muscular, dauntless, young braves . . . erect, bright-eyed, quick-moving, strong-handed young giants. . . ."; for these exist only as legend, i.e., as someone else.

The character called "Mark Twain" in *The Innocents Abroad* is a comic version of these heroic types, a *schlemiel*—or clown-Westerner—a wandering jester who has learned among the "young braves" (to whom, of course, he had always been a butt) to hate cant, despise sentimentality, distrust sophistication, and who has picked up from them a new vocabulary—a native American diction —in which that hatred, despite and distrust can become a kind of humor acceptable to the New England Brahmins themselves: a way of discharging in laughter the nagging doubts about high art and European civilization that troubled their social inferiors if not them. Moreover, "Mark Twain" had lived in a landscape so terrifyingly beautiful in its aloofness from man's small necessities, so awe-

somely magnificent in its antihuman scale, that beside it the scenery of the Old World was bound to seem pallid, domesticated,
dwarfed.

"Como? Pshaw! See Lake Tahoe," one of his chapter headlines
reads; and in a footnote to another, this time concerned with the
Sea of Galilee, Twain notes: "I measure all lakes by Tahoe, partly
because I am far more familiar with it than with any other, and
partly because I have such a high admiration for it. . . ." Yet each
time he begins by evoking the peaceful splendor of that Western
lake, he ends in rage—rage at the rest of the world, which he considers somehow betrays its mythical splendor. On the shores of the
Sea of Galilee, for instance, he remembers dreamily how on Tahoe
"the tranquil interest that was born with the morning deepens and
deepens, by sure degrees, until it culminates at last in resistless fascination!" But an instant later he is near hysteria, scolding the Pal-
estinian landscape, as it were, for failing him and his memories:
"these unpeopled deserts, these rusty mounds of barrenness . . .
that melancholy ruin of Capernaum; this stupid village of Tiberias
. . . yonder desolate declivity where the swine of the miracle ran
down into the sea, and doubtless thought it was better to swallow a
devil or two and get drowned into the bargain than to have to live
longer in such a place. . . ."

Earlier, taking off from a comparison with Lake Como, he had
been even more extravagant in his praise of Tahoe: "a sea whose
every aspect is impressive, whose belongings are all beautiful,
whose lovely majesty types the Deity!" But he subsides quickly
from the high level banality of such schoolroom English prose, into
pure barroom American—and once more into the rage, which
seems as appropriate to the latter, as platitudes to the former style.
This time, however, his rage is directed, quite unexpectedly, against
the American Indians.

> Tahoe means grasshoppers. It means grasshopper soup. It is
> Indian, and suggestive of Indians . . . . People say that Tahoe
> means "Silver Lake"—"Limpid Water"—"Falling Leaf." Bosh!
> It means grasshopper soup, the favorite dish of the Digger
> tribe . . . . It isn't worthwhile in these practical times, for
> people to talk about Indian poetry—there never was any in

them—except in the Fenimore Cooper Indians. But *they* are an extinct tribe that never existed. I know the Noble Red Man. I have camped with the Indians; I have been on the war-path with them, taken part in the chase with them—for grasshoppers; helped them steal cattle; I have roamed with them, scalped them, had them for breakfast. I would gladly eat the whole race if I had a chance.

It is an astonishing performance, which begins by puzzling us, ends by sending us back to a novel published more than a decade before —to Melville's *The Confidence Man,* a book which Mark Twain doubtless never read, but one whose twenty-sixth chapter, "Containing the metaphysics of Indian-Hating, according to the views of one evidently not so prepossessed as Rousseau in Favor of Savages," serves as a gloss to his meditations beside Como.

Attempting to answer, via a series of shadowy spokesman characters, the question: "Why the backwoodsman still regards the red man in much the same spirit that a jury does a murderer, or a trapper a wild cat," Melville finds himself impelled to define the essential nature of the "backwoodsman," which is to say, precisely the kind of man through whose mask Twain has chosen to comment on Europe in *The Innocents Abroad.* "Though held as a sort of barbarian," Melville tells us, "the backwoodsman would seem to Americans what Alexander was to Asia—captain in the vanguard of a conquering civilization. . . . The tide of emigration, let it roll as it will, never overwhelms the backwoodsman into itself; he rides upon the advance, as the Polynesian upon the comb of the surf. Thus though he keep moving on through life, he maintains with respect to nature much the same unaltered relation throughout; with her creatures, too, including panthers and Indians." And more generally, Melville observes, "the backwoodsman is a lonely man. . . . Impulsive, he is what some might call unprincipled. At any rate, he is self-willed; being one who less harkens to what others may say about things, than looks for himself, to see what are things themselves."

But what does the backwoodsman see, when he "looks for himself, to see what are things themselves" in respect to culture rather than nature, Europe rather than the wilderness, when he becomes an "innocent abroad"? The Westerner's bleak vision of the Old World was recorded much later by Ezra Pound, who was born properly enough in Hailey, Idaho—rendered in verse at the moment of America's entry into World War I, itself, in a sense, the continuation of tourism by other means.

> There died a myriad,
> And of the best, among them,
> For an old bitch gone in the teeth,
> For a botched civilization,
>
> Charm, smiling at the good mouth,
> Quick eyes gone under the earth's lid,
>
> For two gross of broken statues,
> For a few thousand battered books.

Two major American talents had begun to wrestle with the problem, however, long before the nineteenth century was over: the two writers of their generation by whom Europe was most obsessively felt as an enigma to be endlessly attacked, precisely because it could never be entirely solved—Samuel Clemens and Henry James. Both, at any rate, were the authors of novels in which a Western American, defined as pristine Protestant and incorruptible democrat, tries to come to terms with a Europe seen as essentially aristocratic and Roman Catholic.

James's *The American* was not published until 1877, eight years after the appearance of Twain's *The Innocents Abroad,* but in terms of fictional time, their protagonists missed meeting each other in the museums of France by less than a year; for it was, James tells us, "On a brilliant day in May, in the year 1868," that *his* gentleman from San Francisco—called with obvious symbolic intent Christopher Newman—was lounging in the Louvre. Like that other San Franciscan, "Mark Twain," Newman, we learn, was suffering from an "aesthetic headache" in the presence of all those masterpieces; and like his improbable opposite number, he was convinced from the start that the fresh copies of the Old Masters being made by various young ladies right before his eyes were superior to the dim and dusty originals.

It is easy enough to surmise what Newman is supposed to represent, but a certain Mrs. Tristram (who most nearly speaks for James in the book) makes Newman's meaning explicit, by explaining to him, " 'You are the great Western Barbarian stepping forth in his innocence and might, gazing a while at this poor effete Old World, and then swooping down on it.' " At that point, however, the "great Western Barbarian"—whom James never quite understood, in fact—demurs, crying out, "I am a highly civilized man"; and spends the rest of the novel trying to prove it, at considerable cost not only to himself but to his author, who loses thereafter the comic tone on which he has opened in melancholy and melodrama. But if one chronicler of the New Barbarian in the Old World failed because of his distance from the character he was attempting to portray, the other continually risks disaster because of his uncomfortable closeness to the *persona* he has assumed.

Neither the reader nor the author of *The Innocents Abroad* is ever quite sure where Samuel Clemens stops and "Mark Twain" begins, how far Clemens is in fact what Stuart Sherman described as "the kind of traveling companion that makes you wonder why you went abroad" (in more contemporary terms, the kind of American consumer for whom Europe is just one more item on the menu of Mass Culture), and how far he is the satirist of that kind of traveler. There is no doubt, in any case, that his book is primarily about such travelers rather than about the Old World itself; that it is consequently not a "travel book" at all in the traditional sense, but a chronicle of tourism at the precise point when the Puritan aristocrat abroad is giving way to the Puritan plebeian on tour.

What the plebeian—that unforeseen new man—finds wrong with the Old World, the Old Masters, the land of the Old Testament is precisely that they are all *old*, i.e., worn out, shabby, dirty, decaying, down at the heels. This abject prejudice against seediness, however ennobled by time, both Clemens and "Twain" share with their fellow travelers. To be sure, there is ambivalence aplenty in *The Innocents Abroad,* most spectacularly exemplified in the chapters on Venice, where the wary Westerner, the man resolved at all costs not to be had, begins by asserting point-blank, "This famed gondola and this gorgeous gondolier!—the one an inky, rusty old canoe with a sable hearse-body clapped onto the middle of it, and the other a mangy, bare-footed guttersnipe with a portion of his raiment on exhibition which should have been sacred from public scrutiny." But a few pages later, he has apparently changed his mind, observing in conventional panegyric tones, "The Venetian gondola is as free and graceful, in its gliding movement, as a serpent. . . . The Gondolier *is* a picturesque rascal for all he wears no satin harness, no plumed bonnet, no silken tights."

This doubleness of vision, however, this alternation between daytime debunking and nighttime subscription to a dream ("In the glare of day, there is little poetry about Venice, but under the charitable moon her stained palaces are white again. . . .") does not arise out of the dialogue between Clemens the artist and "Twain" the comic innocent; it has lain deep in the heart of every run-of-the-mill tourist ever since that memorable year of 1867, when, for the first time on record at least, "Everybody was going to Europe. . . ." Occasionally, of course, Twain moves from echoing the Americans abroad to mocking them, but never for their vulgarity, their grossness of perception, their smug contempt for culture. What stirs his satirical impulse is rather their pretentiousness, their pitiful attempts at culture climbing: their signing hotel registers in French, or claiming loudly never to have eaten a meal without the proper wine—or, especially, their mouthing of high-flown phrases out of guidebooks in the presence of works of art they do not really understand.

When he is recounting the playful desecration of revered cultural sites, his tone is bafflingly equivocal—as in the episode in the crater of Mount Vesuvius which so infuriated Stuart Sherman. "Some of the boys thrust lone slips of paper down into holes and set them on fire, and so achieved the glory of lighting their cigars by the flames of Vesuvius, and others cooked their eggs over fissures in the rocks and were happy." Surely, there is a note of friendly mockery here, but none of that cold fury with which Twain reports, say, the credulity of Europeans in the face of holy "relics" and "miracles," or the gushing response of some of his fellow Americans to such utterly ruined pictures as da Vinci's *Last Supper*. ("Maybe the originals were handsome when they were new, but they are not now.")

Only at the climax of the book, when the author-protagonist stands face to face with the oldest monument he has encountered, with, that is to say, an ultimate incarnation of the persistence of the past, toward which he has been as ambivalent as any other ignorant American, are his last scruples overcome, his final equivocation resolved. It is the Sphinx that conquers him: "After years of waiting, it was before me at last. . . . There was a dignity not of earth in its mien. . . . It was gazing out over the ocean of Time—. . . . It was MEMORY—RETROSPECTION—wrought into visible, tangible form. . . . And there is that in the overshadowing majesty of this eternal figure of stone . . . which reveals to one something of what he shall feel when he shall stand at last in the awful presence of God." But at this point, when he has been converted, however temporarily, to the religion of culture, Twain looks up and sees on the jaw of the Sphinx "a wart, or an excrescence of some kind," which turns out to be, of course, a fellow American, a companion on the tour—in search of a souvenir.

"We heard," Twain tell us, abandoning himself finally to total rage against just such an "innocent" as he had all along pretended to be, "the familiar clink of a hammer, and understood the case at once. One of our well-meaning reptiles—I mean relic-hunters—had crawled up there and was trying to break a 'specimen' from the face of this, the most majestic creation the hand of man has wrought." Confronted with such absolute sacrilege, however, all Twain can conceive of doing is to call a cop, i.e., a sheik, whom he urges to warn the intruder that his offense is "punishable with imprisonment or the bastinado." A hundred years later, it has become clear just how ineffectual such sanctions are against the American tourist's irrepressible need to chip away piece by piece the Old World he does not quite dare confess borcs him; but what else was there then for Twain to do in response—except, of course, to write a book.

TEN

# The Shape of *Moby Dick*

THAT *Moby Dick* is something more or less than a well-made novel
no critic has ever doubted. Had Henry James taken the trouble to
classify it, he would surely have put it in the category of "loose and
baggy monsters," which, considering its overt themes and secret obsessions is fair enough. But not quite good enough for me, I fear.
*"How* loose, and *why* baggy?"—these are the questions which have
concerned me for some years now, and to which I have not yet
found quite satisfactory answers; for which reason, I worry them
again this evening, beginning with what is most obvious and moving
on—hopefully—to what is most obscure.

But surely the most obvious thing about *Moby Dick* is the fact
that it describes a voyage, *is*—in its mythological essence—a Voyage, or, as we would put it these days, a Trip: a venture There and
Back, temporarily out of this world, away from terra firma into
worlds more fantastic, or to use Melville's preferred metaphor,
more watery. He typically dissolves or dives into vision, rather than
taking off or flipping out as we children of a Space Age would have
it. Nonetheless, he moves on out of here and now, which is to say
out of civilization and sanity, as classic American writers—through
their books, at least, and their imagined surrogates—tend almost
universally to do.

Not only Americans, however, have imagined the Voyage or
the Trip as the essential poetic experience. From the time of the
*Odyssey* on, heroes have been set in motion, often through or into
worlds quite as watery as Melville's, since until the mythologizing
of Outer Space the Sea was the reigning image for Otherwhere. Yet
there is something singular about American versions of the Voyage,

312

which are typically for us, aberrantly for the Western tradition in general, neither quests nor homecomings. Our heroes do not fare forth in search of the Golden Fleece or the Golden Girl who goes with it, nor do they end in the connubial bed of home, rooted like a tree into deepest earth. No, the protagonists we admire and who set in motion our classic books flee *from* home; they are escapees, refugees, men in flight, whose direction is not toward but away: like Ishmael himself or Natty Bumppo before him or Huck Finn to come.

Yet the prototype of them all is Odysseus, though Homer did not know it, Odysseus beyond the point to which the Greek imagination could take him, Dante's Odysseus—or as he, beneficiary of Roman rather than Hellenic sources, prefers to call him: Ulysses. It is in the twenty-sixth canto of the *Inferno* that America is invented for the European mind, as well as the myth of the West and the Western, which is to say, the westering Hero. When Dante makes his Ulysses cry to his "brothers," the shipmates "who through a hundred thousand dangers have reached the West" an appeal to attempt an even more ultimate West, the forbidden watery world, he puts in his mouth words eminently American: "Do not reject the experience—following the course of the sun—of the unpeopled world." After which, of course, only disaster can follow; for when land is sighted in the Western Hemisphere, the God of Europe, who has declared it taboo, sucks Ulysses and his crew down into the bottom of the ocean, whirling them about three times, and then a fourth "until the sea closed over us again."

That Dantesque cadence and image recur again and again in our literature, as our latterday refugees from home, from what Dante had called "the sweetness of having a son, the obligation to an aging father and the legitimate love that should have made Penelope rejoice," head for similar fates at the ends of utterly alien worlds: Gordon Pym, for instance (in the final paragraphs of Edgar Allen Poe's *The Narrative of A. Gordon Pym*) on the verge of his whirlpool, remarking, "And now we rushed into the embraces of the cataract, where a chasm threw itself open to receive us." Thus Melville, speaking in the voice of Ishmael and responding to some recent reading surely of both Dante and Poe, recreates almost exactly the feel of the close of Ulysses' speech: "And now, concentric circles seized the lone boat itself, and all its crew, and. . .spinning, animate and inanimate, all round and round in one vortex, carried the smallest chip of the *Pequod* out of sight. . .then all collapsed, and the great shroud of the sea rolled on as it rolled five thousand years ago."

But it is the relationship between myth and form, archetype and structure that I am interested in this evening. For it seems to me that the structure of our classic books is fugal—of *Moby Dick* preeminently, but also, say, of *Huckleberry Finn*—repeated themes pursuing each other and themselves, overlapping, echoing, inverting —not so much telling a tale as recording the reverberations of the taleteller's voice; and that the reason for this is, quite simply, that form follows myth—an archetypal account of a flight from reason and control and civilization demanding a mode of narration that eschews the rationality of plot, the return home of a well-made fiction. Formally as well as thematically, our authors are always suggesting to us the shape of the wilderness and a longing to light out for the unexplored territory ahead, the next *mondo senza gente,* which is to say, Dante's "unpeopled world."

If all this sounds like "the fallacy of imitative form," it is meant to, since almost all American writers of distinction have subscribed to this fallacy, this peculiarly American literary heresy. In light of all this, it is interesting to reflect that the single great book of our nineteenth century which achieves an orderly structure, a form almost classical in its grace and stability, is Hawthorne's *The Scarlet Letter,* which is the sole classic American book about the rejection of flight, Dimmesdale's refusal in the forest of Hester's suggestion that he flee the established community either to seek (in the image of Fenimore Cooper) a more ultimate Western wilderness, or (in anticipation of Henry James) the once-abandoned corruption of Europe. Correspondingly, the most flagrant of our nineteenth-century nonnovels or antinovels is *Moby Dick,* which begins with Ishmael already in flight and already aware that his taking to sea means an abandonment of ordered reality as well as the homeland: "By reason of these things, then," Melville has him confide in us, "the whaling voyage was welcome; the great floodgates of the wonder-world swung open. . . ."

Nonetheless, even if Ishmael knew himself from the first to be embarked on a dream-fugue, Melville seems to have thought for a while that he was about to write, in some conventional sense, a novel; and in its first chapters, there survive fragments of a failed novel in the realistic mode, "a continuous narrative." At least this was how Melville spoke of the book to others (perhaps thought of it himself) in the early stages, insisting "I mean to give the truth" —as opposed, apparently to the free fantasy of *Mardi*—with perhaps "a little fancy to cook the thing up." But the "continuous narrative"—the account, it can be presumed, of a struggle between a monomaniac Captain and a virtuous sailor, an irresistible demonic force and an immovable angelic obstacle (just such a story as Melville finally got down in *Billy Budd)*—was never written, or rather barely begun. Bulkington, the Handsome Sailor, obviously intended to play protagonist to Captain Ahab's antagonist, is introduced, forgotten, suddenly remembered at the start of Chapter XXIII ("Some chapters back," he writes, "one Bulkington was spoken of, a tall, new-landed mariner. . .") and as quickly hurried out of sight ("Let me only say," he concludes, "that it fared with him as with the storm-tossed ship. . . this six-inch chapter is the stoneless grave of Bulkington. . .").

Something obviously had happened in Melville's mind between Chapter III and Chapter XXXIII, some deep change in purpose and direction overtaken him; and much of the writing about *Moby Dick* in our own time has concerned itself with a quest for the causes of this change—in Melville's rereading of Shakespeare, for instance, and his encounter with Hawthorne, whom he was to love so ill-fatedly forever after. And doubtless, both of these external events helped to make Melville aware of what the internal logic (more properly, illogic, I suppose) of his fugal tale had been all the time demanding: to bury Bulkington, for instance, rather than praise him, to leave only Ahab and Ishmael finally, which is to say, two parts of his duplicitous self, to confront each other in the howling watery wilderness, which is to say, the region of nightmare common to both.

Melville did not, could not, resist the voice of his demon, writing finally the book he had to, rather than the one he thought it wise to do. But the need for money and the pressure of time were on him when he saw his way clear at last; and he attempted to remake his novel without destroying any of the pages already written. To have altered the ironic tone of the opening to accord with the tragic climax to which he felt driven would have taken too long; to have eliminated Bulkington completely would have required tiresome revisions (and besides he was extraordinarily fond of him); to have cut down the sheer bulk of the Queequeg-Ishmael story would have demanded starting all over again. And so, as ever, Melville settled for what he thought of as a "botch." "All my books are botches," he once wrote, and explained, "Dollars damn me." Damned by dollars, saved by his demon; it is the story of his writing life.

But it is not the whole story; for if an account of the Voyage into the World of Myth and Wonder defies, finally destroys, the novel form, invented precisely (as Samuel Richardson himself once boasted) to drive the "marvelous" and "wonderful" from the realm of prose fiction—such Voyage literature suits admirably the older and more honorable form of the Epic. And, indeed, it is toward the Epic that Melville aspired all his life long, an Epic Poem in Prose which he finally wrote in *Moby Dick*. Whitman, with similar ambitions driving him, was to equivocate between prose and verse in *Leaves of Grass;* but Melville seems never to have doubted that a Democratic Epic, the Epic of uncommon common men, must be cast in the humbler and homelier form. Perhaps, after all, it was the chief value of his deceiving himself into thinking that he was writing a novel, that this confusion kept him from the temptation to verse. Consider what grief he came to later on when he did turn to verse in *Clarel*, an epic attempt which fails as notably as *Moby Dick* succeeds.

*Moby Dick* is, however, not merely a Democratic Epic but also a Romantic or Erotic one; and in this sense, too, it owes a debt to the tradition of the novel, which in so many other ways it betrayed. The proper subject of the Epic is War and the Return from War; while the subject *par excellence* of the Novel is love. To be sure, we modern readers, conditioned by two centuries of the post-Richardsonian novel, eagerly seek out in the *Iliad* the story of Briseis and Chryseis, which is to say, the erotic; just as we choose to recall out of all the grim events of the *Aeneid* the sentimental episode of

Dido. But this is a matter of our eccentric taste and should not deceive us. The God of the Epic Poets is Ares not Aphrodite; and in writing of a love which triumphs over death Melville is of the tribe of Richardson rather than of Homer—or, indeed, even of Shakespeare who is so much on Melville's mind as he writes *Moby Dick*.

What misleads us a little at first in *Moby Dick* is the fact that its great love story involves two men, one white and one colored, rather than a man and a woman; but this, after all, is the traditional American way, the deepest of all our native myths of love. When Ishmael arises out of the sea at the book's close (in the epilogue which manages to get past the catastrophic ending that was for Dante a final word), he is clinging to a coffin which has been marked with the patterns originally tattooed on the body of his dearly beloved Queequeg, clinging, in fact (in the metaphor which is poetic fact), to all that is immortal in his dead friend.

It is a strange unheroic Happy Ending for an Epic Hero; but, then, Ishmael is a strange unheroic hero to begin with—one who does nothing after his original feat of running away, except to watch (as one watches in a dream the exploits of all he most fears and adores in his deepest self) the self-destruction of Ahab, the fatal encounter of the Killer and the Beast from the Depths, the mad Yankee Captain and Moby Dick who has castrated him. It is, of course, Ahab rather than Ishmael who seems like the traditional heroic figure of ancient legend: the man with a mission, who raises his lance against the most formidable monsters and conquers them; except that for Melville the ancients' unequivocal Hero is himself a monster who must be destroyed, and who therefore lifts his lance in vain. And why not, after all, since Moby Dick, unlike those pests destroyed by Theseus and Perseus and all the classic rest, is somehow divine: not God himself, perhaps, since there is no God; but a symbol at least of the vacuous mystery which resides at the center of the universe once thought to be filled with the plenitude of God.

Ahab cannot be, then, the real hero of Melville's tale—only the hero-villain of a tale within his tale, or, more precisely, a *play* within his tale (complete with stage-directions and asides), since for Melville all nightmare aspires to Shakespearian form. And this hero-villain, this maimed half-hero is watched by Melville's other half-hero, Ishmael, a character who tends (like Hamlet himself at the moment of *his* play within a play) to fall out of the plot into the audience.

But exactly here is the final clue to the complex form of *Moby Dick,* which embodies at once envelope and enveloped, the dreamer and the dreamed: a Democratic Romantic Epic, pretending to be a novel, which encloses a nightmare pretending to be a lost play by Shakespeare. But it is, however, the pseudonovel, the secret epic which contains the pseudodrama; even as the drama's half-hero, the Warrior turned monomaniac killer, is contained in the epic's half-hero, the runaway who in his flight from reality and death represents the author in his flight from form.

—1967

# ELEVEN

# The Pleasures of John Hawkes

EVERYONE KNOWS THAT in our literature an age of experimentalism is over and an age of recapitulation has begun; and few of us, I suspect, really regret it. How comfortable it is to be interested in literature in a time of standard acceptance and standard dissent—when the only thing more conventionalized than convention is revolt. How reassuring to pick up the latest book of the latest young novelist and to discover there familiar themes, familiar techniques—accompanied often by the order of skill available to the beginner when he is able (sometimes even with passionate conviction) to embrace received ideas, exploit established forms. Not only is the writing of really new books a perilous pursuit, but even the reading of such books is beset with dangers; and it is for this reason, I suppose, that readers are secretly grateful to authors content to rewrite the dangerous books of the past. A sense of *déjà vu* takes the curse off the whole ticklish enterprise in which the writer engages, mitigates the terror and truth which we seek in his art at the same time we cravenly hope that it is not there.

John Hawkes neither rewrites nor recapitulates, and, therefore, spares us neither terror nor truth. It is, indeed, in the interests of the latter that he endures seeming in 1960 that unfashionable and suspect stereotype, the "experimental writer." Hawkes' "experimentalism" is, however, his own rather than that of yesterday's *avant-garde* rehashed; he is no more an echoer of other men's revolts than he is a subscriber to the recent drift toward neo-middlebrow sentimentality. He is a lonely eccentric, a genuine unique—a not uncommon American case, or at least one that used to be not un-

319

common; though now, I fear, loneliness has become as difficult to maintain among us as failure. Yet John Hawkes has managed both, is perhaps (after the publication of three books and on the verge of that of the fourth) the least read novelist of substantial merit in the United States. I recall a year or so ago coming across an ad in the *Partisan Review* in which Mr. Hawkes' publisher was decrying one of those exclusions which have typically plagued him. "Is *Partisan*," that publisher asked, "doing right by its readers when it consistently excludes from its pages the work of such writers as Edward Dahlberg, Kenneth Patchen, Henry Miller, John Hawkes and Kenneth Rexroth?"

But God knows that of all that list only Hawkes really *needs* the help of the *Partisan Review*. Miller has come to seem grandpa to a large part of a generation; while the two Kenneths are surely not without appropriate honors and even Dahlberg has his impassioned exponents. Who, however, reads John Hawkes? Only a few of us, I fear, tempted to pride by our fewness, and ready in that pride to believe that the recalcitrant rest of the world doesn't deserve Hawkes, that we would do well to keep his pleasures our little secret. To tout him too widely would be the equivalent of an article in *Holiday*, a note in the travel section of the *Sunday Times*, might turn a private delight into an attraction for everybody. Hordes of the idly curious might descend on him and us, gaping, pointing— and bringing with them the Coca-Cola sign, the hot-dog stand. They've got Ischia now and Majorca and Walden Pond. Let them leave us Hawkes! But, of course, the tourists would never really come; and who would be foolish enough in any case to deny to anyone daylight access to those waste places of the mind from which no one can be barred at night, which the least subtle visit in darkness and unknowing. Hawkes may be an unpopular writer, but he is not an esoteric one; for the places he defines are the places in which we all live between sleeping and waking, and the pleasures he affords are the pleasures of returning to those places between waking and sleeping.

He is, in short, a Gothic novelist; but this means one who makes terror rather than love the center of his work, knowing all the while, of course, that there can be no terror without the hope for love and love's defeat. In *The Cannibal, The Beetle Leg,* and *The Goose on the Grave* he has pursued through certain lunar landscapes (called variously Germany or the American West or Italy) his vision of horror and baffled passion; nor has his failure to reach a wide audience shaken his faith in his themes. In *The Lime Twig* he takes up the Gothic pursuit once more, though this time his lunar landscape is called England; and the nightmare through which his terrified protagonists flee reaches its climax at a race meeting, where gangsters and cops and a stolen horse bring to Michael Banks and his wife the spectacular doom which others of us dream and wake from, relieved, but which they, improbably, live.

It is all, on one level, a little like a thriller, a story, say, by Graham Greene; and, indeed, there is a tension in *The Lime Twig* absent from Hawkes' earlier work: a pull between the aspiration toward popular narrative (vulgar, humorous, suspenseful) and the dedication to the austerities of highbrow horror. Yet Hawkes' new novel finally avoids the treacherous lucidity of the ordinary shocker, the kind of clarity intended to assure a reader that the violence he relives destroys only certain characters in a book, not the fabric of the world he inhabits. In a culture where even terror has been so vulgarized by mass entertainers that we can scarcely believe in it any longer, we hunger to be persuaded that, after all, it really counts. For unless the horror we live is real, there is no point to our lives; and it is to writers like Hawkes that we turn from the wholesale slaughter on T.V. to be convinced of the reality of what we most fear. If *The Lime Twig* reminds us of *Brighton Rock,* which in turn reminds us of a movie by Hitchcock, it is of *Brighton Rock* recalled in a delirium or by a drowning man—*Brighton Rock* rewritten by Djuna Barnes. Hawkes, however, shares the effeteness of Djuna Barnes's vision of evil no more than he does the piety of Greene's vision of sin. His view avoids the aesthetic and the theological alike, since it deals with the mysteries neither of the world of art nor of the spirit—but only with the immitigable mystery of the world of common experience. It is not so much the fact that love succumbs to terror which obsesses Hawkes as the fact that love breeding terror is itself the final terror. This he neither denies nor conceals, being incapable of the evasions of sentimentality: the writer's capitulation before his audience's desire to be deceived, his own to be approved. Hawkes' novel makes painfully clear how William Hencher's love for his mother, dead in the fire-bombings of London, brings him back years later to the lodgings they once shared—a fat man with elastic sleeves on his thighs, in whom the encysted small boy cannot leave off remembering and suffering. But in those lodgings he discovers Banks and his wife Margaret, yearns toward them with a second love verging on madness, serves them tea in bed and prowls their apartment during their occasional absences, searching for some way to bind them, his memories, and his self together. "I found," he reports of one such occasion, "her small tube of cosmetic for the lips and, in the lavatory, drew a red circle with it round each of my eyes. I had their bed to myself while they were gone." It is, however, Hencher's absurd and fetishistic passion which draws Michael Banks out of the safe routine of his life into crime, helps, that is, to turn a lifetime of erotic daydreaming about horses into the act of stealing a real race horse called Rock Castle.

And the end of it all is sheer terror: Hencher kicked to a pulp in a stable; Margaret Banks naked beneath the shreds of a hospital gown and lovingly beaten to death; Michael, screwed silly by all his nympholeptic dreams become flesh, throwing himself under the hooves of a field of horses bunched for the final turn and the stretch! What each of Hawkes' doomed lovers has proposed to himself in fantasy—atrocious pleasure or half-desired indignity—he endures in fact. But each lover, under cover of whatever images, has ultimately yearned for his own death and consequently dies; while the antilovers, the killers, whose fall guys and victims the lovers become, having wished only for the death of others, survive: Syb, the come-on girl, tart and teaser; Little Dora, huge and aseptically cruel behind her aging schoolmarm's face; and Larry, gangster-in-chief and cock-of-the-house, who stands stripped toward the novel's end, indestructible in the midst of the destruction he has willed, a phallic god in brass knuckles and bulletproof vest.

> They cheered, slapping the oxen arms, slapping the flesh, and cheered when the metal vest was returned to him—steel and skin—and the holster was settled again but in an armpit naked now and smelling of scented freshener.
>
> Larry turned slowly round so they could see, and there was the gun's blue butt, the dazzling links of steel, the hairless and swarthy torso. . . .

"For twenty years," shouted Dora again through the smoke opaque as ice, "for twenty years I've admired that! Does anybody blame me." Banks listened and . . . for a moment met the eyes of Sybilline, his Syb, eyes in a lovely face pressed hard against the smoothest portion of Larry's arm, which—her face with auburn hair was just below his shoulder—could take the punches . . .

And even these are bound together in something like love.

Of all the book's protagonists, only Sidney Slyter is without love; half dopester of the races, half amateur detective, Sidney is at once a spokesman for the novelist and a parody of the novelist's role, providing a choral commentary on the action, which his own curiosity spurs toward its end. Each section of the novel opens with a quotation from his newspaper column, *Sidney Slyter says,* in which the jargon of the sports page merges into a kind of surrealistic poetry, the matter of fact threatens continually to become hallucination. But precisely here is the clue to the final achievement of Hawkes' art, his detachment from that long literary tradition which assumes that consciousness is continuous, that experience reaches us in a series of framed and unified scenes, and that—in life as well as books—we are aware simultaneously of details and the context in which we confront them.

Such a set of assumptions seems scarcely tenable in a post-Freudian, post-Einsteinian world; and we cling to it more, perhaps, out of piety toward the literature of the past than out of respect for life in the present. In the world of Hawkes' fiction, however, we are forced to abandon such traditional presumptions and the security we find in hanging on to them. His characters move not from scene to scene but in and out of focus; for they float in a space whose essence is indistinctness, endure in a time which refuses either to begin or end. To be sure, certain details are rendered with a more than normal, an almost painful, clarity (quite suddenly a white horse dangles in mid-air before us, vividly defined, or we are gazing, close up, at a pair of speckled buttocks), but the contexts which give them meaning and location are blurred by fog or alcohol, by darkness or weariness or the failure of attention. It is all, in short, quite like the consciousness we live by but do not record in books —untidy, half-focused, disarrayed.

The order which retrospectively we *impose* on our awareness of events (by an effort of the will and imagination so unflagging that we are no more conscious of it than of our breathing) Hawkes decomposes. For the sake of art and the truth, he dissolves the rational universe which we are driven, for the sake of sanity and peace, to manufacture out of the chaos of memory, impression, reflex and fantasy that threatens eternally to engulf us. Yet he does not abandon all form in his quest for the illusion of formlessness; in the random conjunction of reason and madness, blur and focus, he finds occasions for wit and grace. Counterfeits of insanity (automatic writing, the scrawls of the drunk and doped) are finally boring; while the compositions of the actually insane are in the end merely documents, terrible and depressing. Hawkes gives us neither of these surrenders to unreason but rather reason's last desperate attempt to know what unreason is; and in such knowledge there are possibilities not only for poetry and power but for pleasure as well.

*Goshen, Vermont*
—1960

# John Barth: An Eccentric Genius

NINETEEN-SIXTY WAS a year in which two American eccentrics of great integrity and power produced ambitious books which (once more!) have received neither the acclaim nor, I suspect, the kind of reading they deserve. The first is Wright Morris, whose *Ceremony in Lone Tree* was received generally with the stony respect it has become customary to accord his work. His latest book is the thirteenth he has published, and at this point the response to him has become ritualized: the small sales, the impassioned pitches of a few critics, the baffled sense that now, *now* he must surely be on the verge of popularity (he has finally one book in paperback, *Love Among the Cannibals).* Certainly, he has become the best-known little-known author in the civilized world—a "case" we would all be loath to surrender; but even this indignity Wright Morris will doubtless endure as he has endured all the others visited on him in his exemplary career.

To be, like Morris, a really American writer these days— doggedly provincial and incorruptibly lonely—requires a special sort of obtuseness, with which Morris is lucky enough to be blessed; and John Barth, who is my second eccentric, shares this obtuseness. In his case, however, I feel somehow that it is an obtuseness chosen rather than given; for Barth is not only a younger man than Morris, but is also, unlike Morris, an academic—with proper degrees and a job in a university. All of which means, it seems reasonable to assume, that Barth approaches each of his inevitable publishing failures with an awareness of their inevitability; while Morris, one surmises, launches each new book with an embittered but unbroken hope. I see the first of these American types as a

325

character played by W. C. Fields and the second as one played by Buster Keaton: comics both of them; though reflecting on the one hand the absurdity of great expectations eternally frustrated, and on the other that of foregone defeat accepted with a kind of deadpan pleasure.

John Barth's *The Sot-Weed Factor*—the title is early American for a tobacco merchant—is his third novel, set like his first two in Maryland, or more precisely in the single country of Maryland which he knows best—his America. (Only such a European-oriented writer as Whitmen at his worst believes that to portray America one must encompass its imaginary vastness, its blurred continental totality.) Barth works his corner of our land, reconstructs it with all the intensity of Morris re-imagining Nebraska, Hemingway Upper Michigan, Faulkner Northern Mississippi, or Whitman (in his less cosmic moments) Brooklyn; though Barth is surely aware that the territory he explores has less ready-made mythic import for other Americans than almost any region to which he might have been born. It does not represent the moral miasma we identify with the Deep South, nor the well-armed innocence of the East, nor the frigid isolation of New England, nor the niggling Know-Nothingism of the small-town Midwest, nor the urban horrors of the industrialized East.

Maryland, in fact, is not yet invented for our imaginations; and the invention of the place he knows is the continuing task Barth has set himself, the continuing interest that binds together his three books. His is not, of course, the interest of the pious antiquary or local colorist; what he discovers is scandal and terror and disreputable joy—which is to say, the human condition, the disconcerting sameness of human particularity. Yet John Barth is, on one level, a historical scholar; and his books, even when they deal with contemporary or nearly contemporary events (like *The Floating Opera* or *End of the Road)* give the odd effect of being worked up from documents, carefully consulted and irreverently interpreted. He finds in history not merely the truth, not really the truth at all—for each of his novels exploits the ambiguities of facts and motives— but absurdity. He is first of all a philosopher, and knows not only what Marx knew (that if history does, indeed, repeat itself, the second time is always comic) but also what Heraclitus knew (that there is only a second time). He is, in short, an existentialist comedian suffering history, not just because it happens to be *à la mode* to be comic and existentialist, but because, born in Maryland in his generation and reborn in graduate school, he can scarcely afford to be anything else. He has, moreover, talent enough to be what he has to be, against all the odds, *unfashionably*.

Granted all this, it was predictable enough that Barth would eventually try what looks like a full-scale historical novel and is in fact a travesty of the form. And the probabilities were all along that when he attempted such a book he would produce one not slim (like the *tour de force* of Lampedusa's "The Leopard") but traditionally, depressingly fat. This is in fact so.

*The Sot-Weed Factor* is a volume of over eight hundred pages, dealing with the adventures of a rather unprepossessing male virgin called Ebenezer Cooke, who in the declining years of the seventeenth century came to America—equipped with a doubtful patent as "Poet and Laureate of Maryland" which somehow involved him not only in the cultural life of his time but also in political and religious struggles, Indian warfare and the miseries of love. That the book is too long is obvious—*i.e.*, it is too long for most reviewers to read through so that, though they are respectful, they are also cautiously brief and non-committal. For fifty pages at a time it can even be boring or confusing or both; but what are fifty pages in so immense a text, and what do a little boredom and confusion matter in the midst of so dazzling a demonstration of virtuosity, ambition and sheer courage?

To have settled for less than eight hundred pages would have been to accept timidly the unwritten edict that in our time only bad books can be long, only the best-seller can risk dullness. Why should the antihistorical novel not be equal as well as opposite to the standard received historical romance in fullest bloat? Why should it not also contain *everything*, though everything hilariously transformed? Though Barth's antihistory does not end as mere parody, it begins as such: the reconstruction of a Good Old Time in which Sir Isaac Newton, with buggery in his heart, pursues his students across the quad; and the portrait of Lord Baltimore, a disguised master spy, who is not even really the spy he claims to be but a more devious counteragent impersonating the impersonator.

Similarly, Barth's antinovelistic form distorts the recognitions and reversals of popular literature, first in the direction of travesty and then of nightmare: brother and sister recognize each other on the verge of rape; Indian and white man find they possess a common father when they confess a common genital inadequacy; the tomahawked and drowned corpses in one chapter revive in the next. Yet somehow the parody remains utterly serious, the farce and melodrama evoke terror and pity, and the flagrant mockery of a happy ending constricts the heart. And all the while one *laughs,* at a pitch somewhere between hysteria and sheer delight.

The book is a joke book, an endless series of gags. But the biggest joke of all is that Barth seems finally to have written something closer to the "Great American Novel" than any other book of the last decade. In *The Sot-Weed Factor* he recapitulates (not by way of imitation but out of a sensitivity to the dark forces that have always compelled such concerns in our fiction) all the obsessive themes common to our classic novels: the comradeship of males, white and colored, always teetering perilously close to, but never quite falling over into, blatant homosexuality; sentimentalized brother-sister incest or quasi-incest; the antiheroic dreams of evasion and innocence; the fear of the failed erection.

And the madness of the scene he calls up strikes us as a familiar madness, no recent surrealist import but that old disjunction of sense and order expected in American books, the homely insanity we scarcely notice in the work of Brockden Brown, Edgar Poe or John Neal. Indeed, in a way delightfully unforeseen, Barth's novel more closely resembles the horrendous farrago of John Neal's *Logan* (first published in 1822) than any more recent fiction, middlebrow or beat; though for the influence of *Werther* and Ossian, Barth has substituted that of Rabelais, Sterne, Sir Thomas Browne, and the Marquis de Sade. No real American book, after all, can be born without some recognizable European ancestors.

The very styles of Barth's novel are based on Baroque and Mannerist models, and one of the charms of *The Sot-Weed Factor* is the insouciance with which it moves in and out of its counterfeits of seventeenth century diction. It is, however, no mere pastiche, but a piece of ingenious linguistic play, a joyous series of raids on half-forgotten resources of the language, largely obscene. If anyone has forgotten how many kennings there are in English for copulation, Barth's book will refresh his memory as it runs the gamut of unions, routine and recherché, between man and woman, man and man, man and beast. One important element of *The Sot-Weed Factor* is pornography, comic and serious; and in the book within a book (a secret diary of Captain John Smith which is discovered piece by piece throughout the action) Barth has succeeded in writing the kind of subversive erotic tale with historic trimmings which Mark Twain tried and failed at in *1601*. The point is that Barth—here parting company with his American predecessors—sees the world he renders primarily in terms of sex, and manages somehow to believe that even in America passion is central to the human enterprise.

He is, in the fullest and most satisfactory sense, a "dirty" writer; and this is one reason for his earlier books having dismayed critics, who want their sex programmatic (as in Lawrence, Miller, Durrell, Mailer, etc.), and the public, which wants it sniggering and sentimental (as in almost all best-sellers). Barth gives us sex straight, gay or vicious but never moralized, the literary equivalent of the painfully hand-copied erotica passed from cell to cell in the men's block of prisons; and since American literature has long lived in a jail labeled "For Men Only," he could not have found a more appropriate model.

*The Sot-Weed Factor* is, finally, not only a book about sex and society, but also one about art, a long commentary on the plight of the artist in the United States by a writer already initiated into contempt and misunderstanding, but preferring still irony to self-pity. After noticing in great detail the difficult relations of the poet with church, state and the opposite sex, the illusions of recognition and the reality of neglect, Barth entrusts his last word to a verse epigraph, presumably composed for his own gravestone by his antiheroic poet, and, of course, left off by his heirs in the interests of piety:

> *Labour not for Earthly Glory:*
> Fame's *a fickly Slut and whory.*
> *From the* Fancy's *chast Couch drive her:*
> *He's a Fool who'll strive to swive her!*

And Barth adds, alluding wryly to the place he himself was born, that his warning must have got about, for the marches of Dorchester in Maryland "have spawned no other poet since Ebenezer Cooke, Gentleman, Poet and Laureate of the Province."

—1961

# Montana: P. S.

ONE BECOMES A Montanan in strange ways. I made my own peculiar kind of peace with this state by writing the article reprinted
below. Not that I knew I was sealing a permanent relationship
when I wrote it—far from it; or that a good many of my readers
accepted it in that sense—even farther from it! Much resentment
and hostility boiled up immediately, not only in the breasts of local
readers (after all, how many people in Montana read the *Partisan
Review,* where the piece originally appeared?), but also of those
who had heard about it from the readers, or even those who had
heard about it from those who had heard about it from the readers.
People who never, I am sure, read *anything,* have approached me
imbued with honest indignation and only the vaguest notion of what
my infamous article on "The Montana Face" was about. It was not
merely that I was biting (they thought) the fine, generous Western
hand that was feeding me; but that I had not even been born in the
state I chose to criticize. Montanans have a special distrust of those
who come here by free choice rather than by the accident of birth.
In my more bitter moments, I suspect that the native Montanan
cannot really understand why anyone from outside would choose to
settle in such a place of his own free will—without some dark and
dirty secret purpose.

I will not say that I have ever actually suffered for what I have
written—or even for having chosen rather than endured becoming
a Montanan. One is protected in Montana (can I make this point
now that I am the father of three children born in the state?) by a
vast intellectual indolence, an indifference to ideas, which Montan-

331

ans sometimes confuse with tolerance or courtesy. I am sure that no one will ever be lynched in this state again, not so much because we have become more law-abiding or less brutal, as because it would take too damned much effort! Nevertheless, I have been annoyed in little ways: once blackballed as a speaker at a religious conference for being "too controversial" a person, though at the last minute I made it, thanks to the burst appendix of a more orthodox participant; and more than once, rather inefficiently slandered. The slander in itself is interesting. I remember one University Freshman, who had been forced to read my essay (not by me, let me add quickly!), telling his teacher that he knew all about the author of this lying "story," an Easterner who considered himself too good to talk to anyone and who made his children call him "sir"! This, for the record, is what one Montanan at least considered the final depths to which a man might sink.

Even more embarrassing to me are the responses of some of those who like the essay: both those, usually disaffected Westerners, who consider me a fellow "debunker," and pluck me by the sleeve to tell me in whispers how many men Calamity Jane slept with and what she charged—or just how sordidly some Great Montanan came to his drunken end—and those, usually self-satisfied Easterners, who are shocked to discover that I still live in Montana, and look at me with pity and admiration for daring to live among the surly natives I have offended. It is only an unworthy desire to stay in character as a hero that keeps me from crying out that I did not write my article to prove Montana blacker than any place else, but only to describe its particular shade of black. This, I know, upsets those who feel their prosperity depends upon pretending that it is white and delights those who take its blackness as a proof of the whiteness of Peoria or Santa Barbara or Hoboken. But such are the risks of telling even the smallest part of the truth one sees.

Reading over my own article now after seven or eight years, I find in it a note of passionate engagement that indicates a *family* quarrel, perhaps the peculiar bitterness of an adopted son. A man has, if not a special right, at least a special obligation to reveal with brutal candor the failures of his own household; and it is beside the point to protest, "But things are as bad everywhere else!" What matters is what is bad about one's own affairs. Maybe I have fallen into local pride and am well on the way to becoming a booster, but it seems to me that in certain areas at least we can assert without boasting that we are even worse than everyone else! At any rate, my criticisms of Montana strike me now not as those of a snide outsider, but as the perplexed reactions of one accepting a fate and a home. A writer, whether native or adopted, is a dangerous citizen at best, since he is a citizen, first of all, of the Republic of Letters, and he tends to seem (before he is safely dead and schools have been named after him) to give aid and comfort to the enemy.

I have heard Montanans sometimes idly wishing, at the appropriate conferences on the arts, that a "great writer" might emerge from their midst—forgetting as they dream the bitter image of Florence left behind by Dante or the terrible portrait of Dublin preserved in the works of Joyce. I would recommend to those who consider their state most justly represented in the literature of Chamber of Commerce bulletins or Northern Pacific ads, to pray nightly that Montana *never* produce a first-rate writer. There is no use being sentimental about such matters. I remember the after-dinner comment of an eminent novelist from the South who was visiting in Missoula. To the young lady who asked him whether he didn't think So-and-So might someday write the Great Montana Novel, since "he loved the state so much!" The Southerner answered: "To write about a place well, you must *hate* it!" And after a pause, he added, "The way a man hates his wife."

There is nothing I would want to change in my original piece, and, barring some stylistic revision, I reprint it as I wrote it. I do not mean that I still see everything the same way, but that I still find truth in that fresher, naïver reaction. Though I have since learned more things about the state and its people that I resent and want to change, I have also become more inured to them. I know them rather than feel them passionately. The prevailing contempt for intellectual achievement and the adulation of mediocrity (the school principals who ask for "C" students as teachers, because "they'll fit in better"); the paralyzing ancestor-worship that wants to fake history rather than investigate it; the brutal drunkenness and W. C. T. U. gentility with only a railroad track to separate them; the self-righteous reproaches against the South for "prejudice," in a state where until recently there was a law against miscegenation and where a Negro can still scarcely find a place to get his hair cut; the uneasy, hypocritical relationship with the Indian; the "cultural" organizations whose yearly elections are bloody battles for social prestige; the mummery and dressing up to attract tourists (with hired Indians wearily parodying their tribal dances)—and the privately expressed contempt for those tourists for being taken in; the smug assumption that the God-given glories of our landscape somehow redeem the gross inefficiency of men who can't keep their streets in good repair or support a decent newspaper—all these have become as familiar to me as the scenery itself.

I sometimes pass weeks without being aware of them, as I sometimes go for weeks without seeing "The Montana Face," my description of which has brought me so much abuse. I am now willing to admit that native Montanans do not see that face, the visible sign of an inner inarticulateness which some of them at least are quite prepared to grant. At first, when they shouted their unawareness at me, fire in every eye, I thought they were lying, engaged in a vast conspiracy of deceit. They see the "Eastern Face," "The New York Face," all right, dark, nervous, over-expressive to their eyes; but their own is to them (and why not?) the face *par excellence,* the face in the Garden that was made in God's image. I did not intend to offend anyone's physical pride, even though I had not yet clearly realized how body-centered pride is in a land where ball teams are subsidized before museums are built or orchestras founded; and I think that now I should try to find a new strategy for saying what I mean that would not send people hurt and puzzled to the mirror. Perhaps, I might call it the "Gary Cooper Face," which would say what I was after, and leave everyone feeling flattered! Having raised this ticklish issue, however, I feel obliged to finish it by confessing that more and more rarely (but not less strongly) my old vision returns to me—and suddenly I see before me faces that have not only been starved of richness and subtlety of experience, but are proud of it! For their deprivation one feels pity, but for the smugness, rage!

"And is there, then, Mr. Critic, nothing good to be said for us?" "And do you really feel, Mr. Holier-than-thou, as superior to everyone else as you sometimes seem to imply?" God forbid! It is only that too many people are only too willing to advertise the good aspects of Montana in bad prose; and that I have (put it down to bad toilet-training or unfortunate prenatal influences) the irreverent desire to tell the other side of the whole truth. I have never felt holier than anyone else—only a little louder, a little less inhibited!

It is vexing to have to say it, but I might as well make clear some place that it is only because I like Montana, after all, that I consider it worth raising my voice over its more flagrant weaknesses. Indeed, it is for and not in spite of those weaknesses that I like it—because there is so much to gripe about, and it is so hard to get anyone to listen; because in the beauty of its natural setting, man, when he is vile (and when is he not?), seems viler than elsewhere. Montana seems to me the hardest place in the world to be a hypocrite, though, indeed, I have neighbors who succeed quite well at that difficult task. For myself I can say that at least I do not try.

When I feel the enervating effect of the mountains overcoming me, and I have no desire to revile my fellow-men for their weaknesses, but want only to lie on a riverbank and hear with closed eyes the noise of the water that tells me: *nothing matters— nothing matters—nothing matters—this is the real Montana,* I leap to my feet and drive, past the rusty beer cans and the white roadside crosses, back to town. To restore myself to my senses it is enough to go to the Monday night meeting of the P.T.A. where some local candidate for the legislature is lying in semi-literate periods about what he intends to do for the underpaid schoolteachers, or to the Thursday night wrestling matches, where the girl in fringed buckskin is screaming, "Break his lousy arm! Break it off! Kill him!" Or best of all, if it is Saturday, I go back to that saloon I wrote about in my original article, with its once-new neon lights beginning to flicker and its linoleum a little scarred. Nothing has changed much, though. The whores have gone for good from the rooms upstairs, but there are the bargirls, fat and seedy enough for anyone; and the poker game on the green table is still going, the same dealer looking gravely through his rimless glasses under the ten-gallon hat. There is a "Western Combo," complete with tenor, the guitars electrified and stepped up so that "Sixteen Tons" sounds like an artillery barrage and no one is tempted to waste good drinking time by attempting conversation. The boss, a little more battered around the ears, is still grinning from behind the bar under the same old fly-specked sign reading, "Yes, we serve crabs. Sit down."

But the boss has a new lieutenant, a younger version of himself, with a beat-up pug's head, too, though less punchy looking; and the two of them take turns setting up drinks on the house. "Haven't seen *you* for a hell of a long time." The lieutenant is wearing new cowboy boots, though he is only two years away from the Near North Side of Chicago; he has just dropped out of the journalism school at the University. "Worth thirty-five bucks," he says proudly, indicating the boots. "I got 'em from a wine-o just off the freights for half a gallon of muscatel. Christ, he needed it bad. Walked next door to drink it *(we* don't let 'em drink from bottles at the tables here, but next door they don't give a damn). Walked out barefoot—*barefoot*—and it was snowing, too. 'Take it or leave it,' I told him, 'half a gallon for the boots.' They were red with yellow threads but I had them dyed black. Look pretty good, don't they? Thirty-five bucks." The band begins to play "You are my Sunshine," good and loud and I can't hear any more, but I get it. I'm home. Montana or the end of you know who.

*Missoula, Montana*
—1956

# FOURTEEN

# Montana: P. P. S.

I RETURNED TO Montana in 1969 after an absence of five years—not to live there for another little while, as I had after trips elsewhere before, but just to visit, like one more tourist from the East. I was disconcerted to discover, however, that I didn't feel like a tourist at all, only oddly, disturbingly at home; so that I found myself growing annoyed, for instance, when a trio of obvious first-time Easterners sitting across the aisle from me in the plane kept nudging each other as we circled down into Hellgate Canyon, crying out, "Are those really the Rocky Mountains? Hey, those are *really* the Rockies." "Those are actually the Bitterroots," I wanted to say, though of course I didn't, except in the silence of my own head, "and in their icy shadow I used to walk, shivering, on winter mornings from my home to my office. Those are *my* Bitterroots."

And yet for nearly thirty years before that moment, I had believed, needed to believe that my relationship to those mountains, to the whole place and its people depended on my feeling myself an eternal stranger in an eternally strange land. I should have known, of course (I had actually come close to saying it, though not, it would seem, really imagining it), that precisely the sense of being alienated from the landscape and all the others who moved through it was what had made me, and would keep me forever—present or absent, waking or sleeping—a true Montanan, which is to say, just such an Eternal Stranger in a land that will, must, remain eternally strange to all white ex-Europeans, no matter what games they play at the Rodeo or on pack trips into the remoter "Primitive Areas."

But it was the surface familiarity of it all that struck me first—not the habitual feeling of alienation, but the sense of having returned to, perhaps of having never really left that accustomed scene. There were the same wooden faces under the broad-brimmed Stetsons and the bright colored headscarves bulging over half-concealed curlers; and I found myself wondering if my face had not through the years come imperceptibly to look more like theirs than those of the dudes who came to buy two weeks of wilderness, frozen into that noncommital mask which had seemed to me at first so hopelessly, almost terrifyingly foreign. In a short time, at any rate, I was no longer looking at the Face but at faces, in search of old friends and enemies who have never ceased, and never will, I suppose, to occupy my dreams.

How odd to be back among those who, by accident as it were, mere chance, know as much of your own private life as anyone outside your skin ever can, and with whose own private lives you are equally familiar; so that you and they are forever joined together, or intimately separated, by something whose name is neither hatred nor love, though it contains elements of both. I am trying to say, I guess, that back in Montana I felt *at home:* as uncomfortable as any returned prodigal sitting down at the family table and listening once more to the old jokes tinged with hostility or tenderness, whose original occasion no one quite remembers.

What else to do under such circumstances except to note (with a kind of desperate if undefined hope) the few small things which had actually changed: a new bridge replacing an old one from which a friend once nearly jumped to her death; a new highway scarring the side of a hill where my two oldest boys at five or six or seven used to play among poisonous ticks for which we would search the hairline at the back of their necks just before bedtime; a new First National Bank, astonishingly elegant, and thus, as it were, a kind of inadvertent reproach to the rest of the crummy storefronts along the main drag; and, finally, the stench of pollution from the pump mill—and the cloud from its chimneys, multicolored and ugly-beautiful as a bruise, hanging trapped between the flanks of Mount Sentinel and Mount Jumbo.

But none of this made any real difference, as we discovered (at this point my wife had joined me) lunching in the Florence Hotel, where without looking up, we could identify the voices at the surrounding tables, and guess the precise note of concern and malice with which they would ask about our current difficulties with the Law, after the initial, "Well, I never—" It was not, however, the smallness of Missoula I had come to find, but the hugeness of Montana—especially the flanks of the surrounding valleys, rock and pine and scrub to their rim of endless sky, places where we had walked and built fires and swum and napped in the sun, though never—despite the importunities of sportsman friends—killed anything larger than an ant or a fly. I think what I would have liked best, given as they say there "my druthers," would have been a trip to the Buffalo Preserve at Moiese and a last encounter with the old albino bull, into whose unreadable blear eyes I used to look through the wire fence, feeling myself each time I returned a little more like that totem beast—a little shaggier, a little heavier, a little whiter.

But he had died in our absence, and so we had to content ourselves (the weather was very hot, very still, very dry, and the heat lightning at night threatened forest fires) with wading across or riding the current of those rivers, still icy though at low, low water, whose names I would sometimes say to myself like a litany or a spell, falling asleep in Buffalo on the shores of a dying lake: the Rattlesnake, the Bitterroot, the Blackfoot, the Clark Fork. A river, however, is for people like me only a place to play in; as, indeed, is the whole high, wide, and handsome expanse of Montana, except for little, tight Missoula, where even the trains come less and less frequently to disturb the real estate agents selling each other property and the lawyers waiting in the wings to sue. Like those agents and lawyers (who at least fished and hunted on weekends), I neither planted nor raised stock, neither cut down trees nor dug into the earth for minerals—only, in the West as in the East, read and talked, wrote and listened, taught and learned.

And so, sandy and bruised but exhilarated somehow, I went back to Missoula, to stand on the edge of the University campus, looking up at the "M" made of white-washed stones on the side of Mount Sentinel, and wondering who had won the five dollar prize this year for suggesting "the best new tradition." But I did not walk into the heart of the Oval, its grass already burned brown by summer, turning instead in the direction of the house in which we had lived for two decades. It had become, I knew, having made the sale after some hesitation, the Meeting House of the Unitarian Fellowship, who, I was pleased to discover, kept faithfully painted on its board fence the four-toed foot which is our family emblem, and which used to bug our neighbors nearly out of their minds. But I could not enter here either, or stay long, for I had remembered what else I did in Missoula, which is to say, drink.

And so I went finally where I had to: to the street which represented for me always the true mythic center of Missoula—not the businessmen's center, nor the lawyers', nor the shopping ladies', but the drinkers', which, when I first arrived in 1941, had seemed to my sentimental Easterner's eye the last remnant of the Old West, the West of the movies I had sat through during all those lost Saturday afternoons of my childhood in Newark, New Jersey. I went to Woody Street, where once the bars and whorehouses had provided a meeting place, a common ground for young instructors escaped from their books, students still trying to leave home, and winos just off of the freights.

But Woody Street was gone. The signs on the corners still said its name, and the same old cracked asphalt street still ran up from the N.P. train station in the same old way; but in place of the open doors and brightly lit windows of saloons were boarded-up fronts and gaps full of dusty rubble. Dorazi's was gone, where the Indians had felt free to come even when they were still being hasseled in other bars; and where we would sit, four or five of us, after the last Friday classes to hear Joe Kramer (now eighty-five!) remind us in his comedian's Yiddish accent of the wisdom we had, it would become clear to us as he shouted us down, travestied or denied all week long. And the Sunshine was closed, too, where—with a couple of electrified guitars and a mike—one indistinguishable cowboy group or other had so filled the place with sound that walking in cold sober felt like walking into a well.

But who in the Sunshine had ever been cold sober? I remember staggering out of its doors one night, as blind drunk and happy as I have ever been in my life, my wife sagging on my arm, equally happy I hope (it was, I recall, a wedding anniversary); and there were a pair of cops waiting to greet us—and, in that lovely time before the fall of us all—to drive us home in jovial solicitude. "Now take it easy, Doc, you're gonna be all right in the morning." But everything changed, as God knows it had to; and before disappearing completely, the Sunshine (or maybe it was that bar next door whose name I could never remember, no matter) was taken over for a while by some university kids from the East, interested in listening, over cups of coffee—along with, I suppose, an occasional joint—to what they called "folk music," i.e., the kind of music the drunks in the Sunshine had always danced to or sung, scarcely knowing there was any other.

It was, however, the Maverick I really wanted to walk into just one more time, having long dreamed of coming back to find Spider still behind the bar: his flattened pug's face turning slowly from side to side as he kept an eye out for trouble; and his back to the pasted-up clipping on the mirror behind him, the article in which I had mentioned his saloon. He would recognize me for sure (I told myself), call me by name or just "Hey, Professor"; and buy me a drink—a bourbon and ditch, what else—which I would nurse for a long time in a back booth between the bandstand, on which that same schoolmarmish-looking lady with the specs would be doing a chorus of "Cold Clear Water" to her own piano accompaniment, and the poker table, at which the same five old men, three shills and a couple of suckers, would be playing poker close to their vests. But the Maverick was dark and empty, too, and I could see nothing between the boards nailed over its broken front window—only imagine I heard a rat skittering through the rubbish inside.

Well, it seemed necessary to drink to Spider dead—to buy myself a drink, since he would not be setting them up again; and raising my glass to the image of myself in some bar-mirror make whatever toast came to mind. But where to buy a drink, *where?* I could not go back to the Florence Hotel or the polite "cocktail bars" on Front Street, and all the other places I knew seemed to be gone. So, I walked down Higgins Avenue toward the Station, until finally there were lights, and a sign saying "Bill's" or "Ed's" or "Jim's," some name I knew even then I would not remember. It was a new place, opened up only a year or two before; but the bartender, it turned out, was an old student of mine, the one in fact who had taken the mad picture of me reproduced on the jacket of *Love and*

*Death in the American Novel;* and the walls of the saloon were decorated with his more recent photographs—huge blowups of assorted old-timers: cowboys, drifters, Indians, and just plain drunks.

Stupidly, I kept walking up and down before them, looking for my own face, and pursued the whole time by a very large Indian lady who kept loudly admiring the curls on the back of my neck— as if I were in fact already developed, fixed, printed, and hung on the wall: one more old-timer from a Montana that no longer existed outside the world of art, if, indeed, it ever had. I was cold sober, had forgotten even to order a drink; but I rushed into the street and shouted up toward the dark mountains, "God damn it, *hier oder nirgends ist Amerika,* here or nowhere is America," to which echo answered (or maybe I just imagine the whole scene, dreaming over a desk in Paris), *"Nirgends ist Amerika."* And only now, writing this, do I know that this means not, as I first thought, "America is nowhere" but rather, "Nowhere is America." "Nowhere" which in Greek is "Utopia."

*Nowhere*
Friday the Thirteenth
1984   minus 14

# FIFTEEN

# An Almost Imaginary Interview: Hemingway in Ketchum

But what a book they both agreed, would be
the real story of Hemingway, not those he
writes but the confessions of the real
Ernest Hemingway . . .

*The Autobiography of Alice B. Toklas*

I AM WRITING NOW the article which I have known for months I must someday write, not merely because he is dead but because there sits on the desk before me a telegram from a disturbed lady whom I can not quite remember or despise. "Your confiding reminiscences of Papa Hemingway," it reads, "reminiscent of Louella (Hearst)." The clichés of "Papa" and "Hearst" date but do not identify the sender; and the fact that she has wired her malice from Seattle only confuses me. Why Seattle? Surely the few cagey remarks I have made to a reporter about my experiences in Ketchum, Idaho do not constitute "confiding reminiscences"—dictated as they were as much by a desire to conceal as to reveal, and concerned as they were with my own dismay rather than the details of Hemingway's life. How did they get to Seattle? And in what form?

I am aware, of course, of having told over the past six months in at least as many states the story of my inconclusive encounter with Hemingway last November. I have never been able to tell it until after the third drink or the fourth, and then always to those who, I was convinced, would understand that I was talking about a

343

kind of terror which rather joined me to than separated me from a stranger whose voice I have known all my adult life—a stranger obviously flirting with despair, a stranger whose destruction I could not help feeling my own calamity, too. After all, I was only talking the way everyone talks all the time about American letters, the plight of the American writer. What could be more banal or harmless?

But I can tell from the poor conventional ironies of the telegram before me what I have come to suspect already from my need to say over and over precisely how it was in Ketchum: that what is at stake is an image by which we have all lived—surviving haters of Hearst, middlebrow adulators of *For Whom the Bell Tolls,* Jews who have managed somehow to feel closer to Jake Barnes than to Robert Cohn—the lady from Seattle, and I. That image I must do my best to shatter, though on one level I cannot help wishing that it will survive my onslaught.

I do not want ever to see the newspaper article that cued the wire. I am willing to accept responsibility for whatever the press in its inaccuracy and confusion made of my own inaccuracy and confusion; but I want to accept it without having read it. If amends are to be made for pieties offended, they must be made by setting down the best version of what I am able to remember, by my writing this piece which perhaps already is being misunderstood by those who have managed to get so far.

I went to see Hemingway just after Hallowe'en last year along with Seymour Betsky, a colleague from Montana State University, the university attended briefly by one of Hemingway's sons; and, much more importantly, the one from which Robert Jordan took off for the War in Spain in *For Whom the Bell Tolls.* From a place as much myth as fact, from Hemingway's mythical home (I am told that during his last trip to Spain he signed tourist autographs, "E. Hemingway, Red Lodge, Montana"), I set out across the three hundred miles to his last actual home near Sun Valley, a winter resort out of season. We were charged with persuading Hemingway to give a public lecture at our school, to make the kind of appearance he had resolutely refused to make, to permit—like a good American —a larger audience to look at him than would ever read him, even in *Life.* Actually, we felt ourselves, though we did not confess it aloud, neither professors nor promoters, but pilgrims—seeking the shrine of a God in whom we were not quite sure we believed.

I had long since put on record my only slightly begrudged acknowledgment of Hemingway's achievement: his invention of a major prose style viable in the whole Western world, his contrivance of the kind of short story young writers are not yet done imitating, his evocation in *The Sun Also Rises* of a peculiar terror and a special way of coming to terms with it that must seem to the future the very hallmark of our age. But I had also registered my sense of his mindlessness, his sentimentality, his failure to develop or grow. And I could not help recalling as I hurtled half-asleep beside the driver through the lucid air of not-yet winter, up and down the slopes of such mountains as haunted Hemingway, a symposium in Naples just ten years before. I had been arguing in a tongue not my own against what I took to be the uncritical Italian veneration of Hemingway; and I was shouting my protest to one of those young writers from Rome or Palermo or Milan who write in translated Hemingwayese about hunting and *grappa* and getting laid—but who have no sense of the nighttime religious anguish which makes Hemingway a more Catholic writer than most modern Italians. "Yes," I remembered saying, "yes—sometimes he puts down the closest thing to silence attainable in words, but often what he considers reticence is only the garrulousness of the inarticulate." This I hoped at least I was managing to say.

What really stirred in me on that long blue ride into dusk and the snowless valley (there was near dismay in the shops and cafés since the season was at hand and no snow had fallen) was an old resentment at those, chiefly but not exclusively Europeans, unable to understand that Hemingway was to be hated and loved not merely as a special American case, but more particularly as a Western writer, even as an imaginary Montanan. It seemed only fair that revolutions and illness and time bring him to Sun Valley to die, to the western slopes of America, rather than to Spain or Africa or Cuba; and it was scarcely ironical that his funeral be held in a tourists' haven, a place where the West sells itself to all comers.

Hemingway never wrote a book set in the Mountain West, but he wrote none in which innocence and nobility, heroism and cowardice, devotion and passion (not love but *aficion)* are not defined as they are in the T.V. Westerns which beguile a nation. The West he exploited is the West not of geography but of our dearest and most vulnerable dreams, not a locale but a fantasy, whose meanings do not change when it is called Spain or Africa or Cuba. As long as the hunting and fishing is good. And the women can be left behind. In Gary Cooper, all at which Hemingway merely hinted was made explicit; for Cooper was what Hemingway only longed to be, the West made flesh—his face, in its inarticulate blankness, a living equivalent of Hemingway's prose style.

It is not at all odd to find a dramatist and a favorite actor collaborating in the creation of character and image; what Tennessee Williams imagines, for instance, Marlon Brando is—or has obligingly become. But a similar collaboration between novelist and actor seems to me unparalleled in literary history— a little strange, though in this case inevitable. How aptly the paired deaths of Cooper and Hemingway, each greeted as a national calamity, climaxed and illuminated their relationship, their joint role in sustaining on upper cultural levels an image of our character and fate common enough in pulps, comic books and T.V. That they did not manage to see each other before Cooper died seemed to the press (and to me) a more than minor disaster, mitigated perhaps by the fact that the one did not long survive the other. And like everyone else, I was moved by Hemingway's telegram offering Cooper odds of two to one that he would "beat him to the barn."

Death had presided over their association from the start, since their strongest link was Robert Jordan, invented by one, played by the other: the Westerner as fighter for Loyalist Spain, the anti-Fascist cowboy, the Montana innocent in a West turned oddly political and complex, a land ravaged not by the conflict of outlaw and sheriff but by the struggle between Communist and Nazi. In such a West, what can the Western Hero do but—despite the example of his immortal prototypes—die? Unlike the War for the American West, the War in Spain was lost by Our Side; and finally only its dead seemed true heroes. Hemingway's vision in *For Whom the Bell Tolls* is something less than tragic; but his self-pity is perhaps more adequate than tragedy itself to an age unsure of who its heroes are or what it would like to do with them.

Only a comic view could have been truer to our times, and this Hemingway notoriously lacks. He never knew how funny the Westerner had come to seem in our world, whether played by Roy Rogers or Cooper or Hemingway himself—only how sad. Of all his male leads, Jake Barnes comes closest to being redeemed from self-pity by humor—the humor implicit in his comic wound. And consequently Jake could no more have been played by Cooper than could the Nick Adams of the earliest stories, or the old men of the last books. Never quite young, Cooper was not permitted to grow really old—only to betray his age and suffering through the noncommital Montana mask. He represents ideally the protagonists of Hemingway's middle novels, Lieutenant Henry and, of course, Jordan; but he will not do for anything in *To Have and Have Not,* a Depression book and, therefore, an ill-conceived sport sufficient unto Humphrey Bogart. The roles on either side of middle age, Hemingway was able to play himself, off the screen yet in the public eye: the beautiful young man of up to twenty-three with his two hundred and thirty-seven wounds, the old stud with his splendid beard and his guns chased in silver. We cannot even remember the face of his middle years (except as represented by Cooper), only the old-fashioned photographs of the youth who became the "Papa" of cover-stories in *Look* and *Life:* his own doomed father, his own remotest ancestor as well as ours.

At any rate, it was a pilgrimage we contemplated, my colleague and I, leaving Missoula some twenty-five years after the fictional departure of Robert Jordan. But it was also—hopefully—a raid: an expedition intended to bring Hemingway home to Montana, where he might perhaps succeed in saying what he had never been able to say to outlanders, speak the meanings of the place in which we had been born or had improbably chosen to live. It was, I suppose, *my* Western I hoped Hemingway would play out (becoming for me what Cooper had been for him); and there would have been something appropriately comic, after all, in casting the boy from Oak Park, Illinois in a script composed by the boy from Newark, New Jersey, both of them on location in the Great West. But, of course, the first words we exchanged with Hemingway made it clear that if he had ever been able to speak in public, he was unable to do so now; that if he did, indeed, possess a secret, he was not about to reveal it from the platform. And how insolent, how absurd the quest seems in retrospect—excused only by a retrospective sense that what impelled us was a need to identify with an image we thought we despised. If it was not an act of love we intended, it was a more typical American effort magically to establish something worthy of love. *Here or Nowhere is America.* Surely the phrase rang someplace in the back of my head as we approached Ketchum; but Here turned out to be Nowhere and Hemingway in the middle of it.

At first, however, we were elated, for we were able to reach quickly the young doctor we had been told was Hemingway's friend and hunting companion; and we were as much delighted as embarrassed (everything seemed to be composing itself more like a poem than a mere event) by the fact that he was called, symbolically, Dr. Saviers. They hunted together during the afternoons, Dr. Saviers told us, though Hemingway could no longer crouch in a blind, only walk in search of birds, his last game. Hemingway worked mornings, but perhaps he would adjust his routine, find some time for us the next day before noon . . . after all, we had driven three hundred miles . . . and even though he never made public appearances, still . . . .

We sat that night in a half-deserted bar, where the tourists had not yet come and the help waited on each other, making little ingroup jokes. No one noticed us nursing over our drinks the elation about which we scarcely dared speak. God knows what unworthy elements fed our joy: a desire for scraps of gossip or occasions for articles, a secret yearning to be disappointed, to find the world figure fatuous or comic or—No, surely there were motives less ignoble at its root: a genuine hope that emanating from greatness (the word came unbidden to our minds) there would be a *mana* we could share, a need somehow to verify the myth. We entered Hemingway's house through a back porch in character with the legend —limp ducks hanging from the rafters, a gun against the wall—the home of the hunter; but to step into the kitchen was to step out of the mythic world. There were the neatly wrapped trick-or-treat packages left over from the week before, loot unclaimed by kids; *The Readers Digest, The T.V. Guide* open on tables; and beyond, the nondescript furniture of a furnished house, a random selection of meaningless books on the half-empty shelves.

And the Hemingway who greeted us, framed by the huge blank television screen that dominated the living room, was an old man with spectacles slipping down his nose. An old man at sixty-one.

For an instant, I found myself thinking absurdly that this must be not the Hemingway we sought but his father, the ghost of that long-dead father—materialized at the age he would have been had he survived. Hemingway's handclasp I could scarcely feel; and I stood there baffled, a little ashamed of how I had braced myself involuntarily for a bone-crushing grip, how I must have yearned for some wordless preliminary test of strength. I had not known, I realized standing dumb before one even dumber, how completely I had been victimized by the legend Hemingway had worn himself out imagining, writing, living.

Why should he not, after all, inhabit a bourgeois house, sit before T.V. with a drink in his hand, while his wife passed out Hallowe'en packages to children? Why the hell not? But he dwindled so abruptly, so touchingly from the great red and white head to his spindly legs, accentuated by tapered pants, legs that seemed scarcely able to hold him up. Fragile, I found myself thinking, breakable and broken—one time too often broken, broken beyond repair. And I remembered the wicked sentence reported by Gertrude Stein, "Ernest is very fragile, whenever he does anything sporting something breaks, his arm, his leg, or his head." The scar of one more recent break was particularly evident on his forehead as he stood before us, inarticulately courteous: a scar just above the eyes that were the wrong color—not blue or grey as they should have been, not a hunter's eyes at all, but the eyes of a poet who dreamed of hunters, brown, soft, scared. . . .

These, at least, I knew could not have changed. Whatever had recently travestied him, whatever illness had ravaged his flesh, relaxed his handclasp, could not have changed his eyes. These must have been the same always, must always have tried to confess the secret he had perhaps more hoped than feared would be guessed. "But Jake Barnes is in some sense then a self-portrait," I almost said aloud. "And that's why *The Sun Also Rises* seems your truest book, the book of fear and fact, not bravado and bullshit." I did not speak the words, of course, and anyhow he was saying in a hesitant voice, after having listened politely to our names, "Fiedler? Leslie Fiedler. Do you still believe that st— st— stuff about Huck Finn?"

He did not stammer precisely but hesitated over the first sounds of certain words as if unsure he could handle them, or perhaps only a little doubtful that they were the ones he really wanted. And when I had confessed that yes, I did, did still think that most American writers, not only Twain but Hemingway, too (naturally, we did not either of us mention his name in this context), could imagine an ennobling or redemptive love only between males in flight from women and civilization, Hemingway tried to respond with an appropriate quotation. "I don't believe what you say," he tried to repeat, "but I will defend to the death your right to say it." He could not quite negotiate this platitude, however, breaking down somewhere in the neighborhood of "defend." Then—silence.

I knew the motives of my own silence though I could only speculate about his. I had been cast, I could see, in the role of The Critic, hopelessly typed; and I would be obliged to play out for the rest of our conversation not the Western I had imagined, but quite another fantasy: the tragicomic encounter of the writer and the mistrusted professional reader upon whom his reputation and his survival depend. That Hemingway was aware at all of what I had written about him somehow disconcerted me. He was, I wanted to protest, a character in my *Love and Death in the American Novel;* and how could a character have read the book in which he lived? One does not imagine Hamlet reading the play that bears his name. But I was also, I soon gathered, a semifictional character—generically, to be sure, rather than particularly—a Hemingway character, an actor in his imaginary world. So that finding me before him made flesh, he felt obliged to play out with me a private drama, for which he would, alas, never be able to frame quite appropriate sentences, an allegorical quarrel with posterity. At least, for an hour he could get the dialogue out of his haunted head.

He had read or glanced at, I could soon see, not only my essays but practically everything anyone had written on the modern novel in the United States. I fancied him flipping the pages, checking the indexes (or maybe he got it all out of book reviews in *Time),* searching out the most obscure references to himself, trying to find the final word that would allay his fears about how he stood; and discovering instead, imbedded in the praise that could never quite appease his anguish, qualifications, slights, downright condemnations. "T-tell Norman Mailer," he said at one point, "I never got his book. The mails in Cuba are— are— terrible." But who would have guessed that Hemingway had noticed the complaint in *Advertisements for Myself* about his never having acknowledged a presentation copy of *The Naked and the Dead*. And yet the comment was not out of character; for at another point he had said, really troubled, "These d-damn students. Call me up in the middle of the night to get something they can h-hang me with. So they can get a Ph.D." And most plaintively of all, "Sometimes when a man's in—when he can stand it least, they write just the things that—"

Between such observations, we would regard each other in the silence which seemed less painful than talk until Seymour Betsky would rescue us. I did not really want to be rescued, it seems to me now, finding silence the best, the only way of indicating that I knew what was racking the man I faced, knew his doubt and torment, his fear that he had done nothing of lasting worth, his conviction that he must die without adequate reassurance. It was not for Hemingway that I felt pity; I was not capable of such condescension. It was for myself, for all American writers. Who, *who,* I kept thinking, would ever know in these poor United States whether or not he had made it, if Hemingway did not. I may even have grown a little angry at his obtuseness and uncertainty.

"A whole lifetime of achievement," I wanted to shout at him, "a whole lifetime of praise, a whole lifetime of reveling in both. What do you want?" But I said nothing aloud, of course, only went on to myself. "Okay, so you've written those absurd and trivial pieces on Spain and published them in *Life*. Okay, you've turned into the original old dog returning to his vomit. But your weaknesses have never been a secret either from us, or, we've hoped at least, from you. We've had to come to terms with those weaknesses as well as with your even more disconcerting strengths—to know where we are and who, where we go from here and who we'll be when we get there. Don't we have the right to expect the same from you? Don't we have the right to—" But all the while he kept watching me warily, a little accusingly, like some youngster waiting for the reviews of his first book and trying desperately not to talk about it to one he suspects may be a reviewer.

And what could I have told him, I ask myself now, that might have helped, and what right did I really have anyhow, brought there by whim and chance? What could anyone have said to him that had not already been repeated endlessly and without avail by other critics or by sodden adulators at bars. The uncertainty that Hemingway betrayed was a function surely of the depression that was about to destroy him; but, in a deeper sense, that depression must have been the product of the uncertainty—of a lifetime of uncertainty behind the bluster and the posturing, a lifetime of terror indissoluble in alcohol and action, a lifetime of fearing the leap out of the dark, never allayed no matter how many beasts he brought down in bush or boondocks.

It was only 9:30 A.M. but, after a longer than customary lapse in our talk, Hemingway broke out a bottle of wine to help ease us all. "Tavel—a fine little wine from the Pyrenees," he said, without, apparently, any defensive irony or even any sense of the comic overtones of the cliché. Silence and platitude. Platitude and silence. This was the pattern of what never became a conversation. And I felt, not for the first time, how close Hemingway's prose style at its best was to both; how it lived in the meager area of speech between inarticulateness and banality: a triumph wrung from the slenderest literary means ever employed to contrive a great style—that great decadent style in which a debased American speech somehow survives itself.

"It's hard enough for me to wr-write much less—talk," he said twice I think, obviously quoting a favorite platitude of his own invention; and, only once, but with equal satisfaction, "I don't want to talk about literature or politics. Once I talked about literature and I got—sick." One could hear in his tone how often he must, in similar circumstances, have used both; but he meant the first of them at least. The word "articulate" became in his mouth an insult, an epithet. Of Norman Mailer, for instance, he said between pauses, quietly, "He's s-so— articu— late—" and there was only a little envy to mitigate the contempt. But he wanted to talk about literature really, or, more precisely, wanted to talk about authors, his colleagues and rivals. Yet his comments on them boiled down to two only: the first for writers over fifty, "Great guy, you should've known him!"; the second for those under that critical age, "That boy has talent!" Vance Bourjaily, I recall, seemed to him the "boy" with the most "talent." The one author he did not mention ever was himself, and I abided by the taboo he tacitly imposed, though, like him I fear, more out of cowardice than delicacy.

When I noticed in a particularly hard moment the *T.V. Guide* beside me open to the Saturday Night Fights, I welcomed the cue, tried to abandon Bourjaily in favor of Tiger Jones, though I really admire the style of the one not much more than that of the other. "Terrible what they make those boys do on television," Hemingway responded, like the joker next to you at the bar who baffles your last attempt at communication. And it didn't help a bit when Mrs. Hemingway entered to apologize in an attractive cracked voice for the state of the house. "If I had only known that someone was coming. . . ." But why was everyone apologizing and to whom?

It was the *politeness* of the whole affair which seemed somehow the final affront to the legend. Hemingway was like a well-behaved small boy, a little unsure about the rules, but resolved to be courteous all the same. His very act of asking us to come and talk during his usual working hours and at a moment of evident distress was a gesture of genuine courtesy. And he fussed over the wine as if set on redeeming our difficult encounter with a show of formality. At one point, he started to pour some Tavel into my glass before his own, then stopped himself, put a little into his glass, apologized for having troubled to remember protocol, apologized for apologizing—finally insisted on drinking to my next book, when I lifted my glass to his.

But what were we doing talking of next books when I could not stop the screaming inside of my head, "How will anyone ever know? How will I ever know unless the critics, foolish, biased, bored, tell me, tell us?" I could foresee the pain of reading the reviews of my first novel, just as I could feel Hemingway's pain reading the reviews of his later work. And I wanted to protest in the name of the pain itself that not separated but joined us: The critic is obliged only to the truth though he knows that truth is never completely in his grasp. Certainly he cannot afford to reckon with private anguish and despair in which he is forbidden to believe, like the novelist, inventing out of his friends and his own shame Lady Brett or Robert Cohn.

And I looked up into Hemingway's smile—the teeth yellowish and widely spaced, but bared in all the ceremonious innocence of a boy's grin. He was suddenly, beautifully, twelve years old. A tough, cocky, gentle boy still, but also a fragile, too-often-repaired old man, about (how could I help knowing it?) to die. It puzzled me a little to discover him, who had never been able to invent a tragic protagonist, so much a tragic figure himself—with meanings for all of us, meanings utterly different from those of his myth, meanings I would have to figure out later. . . . Yet he seemed, too, as we had always suspected, one who had been *only* a boy and an old man, never what the rest of us for too wearily long must endure being— all that lies between. I could not help recalling the passage where Gertrude Stein tells of Hemingway at twenty-three crying out that he was too young to be a father. And I could hear him now in my inner ear crying out that he was too young to be an old man. Too young to be an ancestor.

But he was not too young to be my ancestor, not too young for me to resent as one resents what is terribly there when he is born. I would not be able to say the expected kind things about him ever, I knew, not even after he was dead. And who would understand or believe me when I was ready to say what I could: that I loved him for his weakness without ceasing to despise him for his strength.

We had left Seymour Betsky's car in town, and as the four of us looked at each other now, more than ready to be done with our meeting, Hemingway and his wife offered to drive us back in to pick it up. He had to do some small chores, chiefly go to the bank. But it was a Saturday, as we had all forgotten; and Betsky and I stood for a moment after we had been dropped off watching Hemingway bang at the closed glass doors, rather feebly perhaps but with a rage he was obviously tickled to be able to feel. "Shit," he said finally to the dark interior and the empty street; and we headed for our car fast, fast, hoping to close the scene on the first authentic Hemingway line of the morning. But we did not move quite fast enough, had to hear over the slamming of our car door the voice of Mrs. Hemingway calling to her husband (he had started off in one direction, she in another), "Don't forget your vitamin tablets, Daddy."

—1962

# SIXTEEN

# On Remembering Freshman Comp

I TOOK, as they say, Freshman Composition at New York University Heights in 1938 and 1939, sitting with some twenty-five or thirty others before a teacher whom I can only imagine now as scared and baffled, though glad surely to have a job—however ill-paid—in those Depression days. The indignities he endured in graduate school (I am not certain he ever made it to a Ph.D.) he visited upon us in kind: a minor Terror never quite equivalent to the major Terror he lived with beyond our ken and on his own time. We scarcely suspected this, having no way of knowing that the dictator who threatened us with failure for a single comma fault or run-on sentence might cringe before his thesis director or wake at nights to worry about his prelims. Not realizing the nature of his suffering, I could not know a chief reason for the existence of a freshman course in composition—as therapy for graduate students and recent Ph.D.'s. Just as the aggrieved workingman was once permitted to beat his wife and children on Saturday nights, so the doctoral candidate was once allowed to bully a classful of freshmen. But social progress has changed all of that. The workingman is no longer aggrieved—and the graduate student, then customarily celibate, is now almost required to have a wife and children, on whom surely he vents a good deal of his legitimate spite. And what use to him, therefore, is a class of freshmen? No wonder there is talk of eliminating the comp course altogether.

What assaults of wit we quivered under! What ironical sallies bowed our heads! Sometimes—not sure we understood the nuances of his rancor—our instructor would explain to us how we had just been insulted, translating down for our benefit and his own. It was

355

only then that he confessed we did not speak a common language
—though he never gave up the pretense that we *should* speak one,
persisted in maintaining the hoax that there was one to speak. He
seemed to believe that such a language was actually to be found in
the back pages of *Harper's Magazine,* to which he aspired—or in
which he had been published once, or was about to be published—
we were never sure. At that moment, I was myself seeking a language of my own in magazines like *transition,* which is to say, I was
working hard to learn a not-quite-up-to-date international art jargon—which appealed to my seventeen-year-old desire to use writing more for the purposes of concealment than revelation. As if one
could ever be understood too easily or too soon! As for the rest of
the class, they strove dumbly to protect the living language which
was their heritage: a language which moved at the pace of city life,
which was grayed to the tones of city light, which erupted into the
dull horror of city violence—but which kept also the rhythms of an
almost forgotten Yiddish.

But we were forbidden Yiddishisms as we were forbidden slang;
and though we had our censors outnumbered, our ignorance and
shame kept us powerless. We were, some eighty-five or ninety or
ninety-five per cent of us, urban Jews; our instructor and his colleagues were one hundred per cent Western or Midwestern or
back-country *goyim,* who had (not so long before) abandoned their
Midwestern or Western or back-country dialects for a nonfunc-
tional, unreal Academese, acceptable on its more formal levels in
the pages of *PMLA*—and on its more relaxed levels in *Harpers* or
*Atlantic Monthly* or *The Saturday Review of Literature.* It all
seemed to us a familiar way of choosing up sides for an old unfair
game. We had played by similar not quite kosher rules in grade
school and in high school, becoming in self-defense bilingual—
though already our first language, our native schoolyard tongue had
begun to slip away from us. But we were not yet fully at home with
the lifeless classroom language whose shape was determined by an-
tiquated rules of etiquette (usually called "grammar") rather than
by aesthetic principles or organic needs.

Nobody had ever told us that the American language was still
to be invented—was always to be invented—as it has been invented
and reinvented by urban Jews of approximately my own genera-

tion, Saul Bellow, for instance, and Bernard Malamud, Delmore Schwartz and Grace Paley; and as it had been invented earlier out of their own dialects by Hemingway and Faulkner, Melville and Whitman and Henry James. Our world extended from Beowulf to Thomas Hardy, and the language we studied was called misleadingly "English." How could we discover what was living in our own tongue reading *The Mayor of Casterbridge* (which we did not really like) or *Martin Chuzzlewit* (which we renamed *Martin Chuzzleberg* and managed to love), or learning the scholarly way to crib from Sir Sidney Lee in "research papers" on Shakespeare's *Sonnets*. It was once, I suppose now, the function of freshman comp classes precisely to convince all Americans, farm boys and city dwellers, Slavs and Swedes, Italians and Jews, that they had a common literary language which was quite (or almost) the same as that used by "our British Ancestors." It was simply a matter of straightening out that difficulty about "different than." But the British were not by a long shot *our* ancestors, and we resented the melting pot brainwashing that culminated for us in the first year of college. Here or nowhere our (approximately) Anglo-Saxon mentors had decided, we would be convinced we spoke a common tongue with them: a language capable of uttering only the most correctly tepid Protestant banalities no matter what stirred in our alien innards.

All this I was scarcely aware of then—thinking rather of my private war against gentility and "good taste." In that war, the Enemy included my fellow students, too: those would-be doctors and lawyers eager to be accepted by a world of other doctors and lawyers, a world more polite and less passionate than that of their parents and grandparents. But it was the teachers who represented especially the standards of an established alien taste, represented it as my fellow students could not, partly by virtue of their degree— but chiefly by virtue of certain inflections and idioms as foreign to us as their neckties. Writing my weekly themes on the subway, jostled by elbows and haunted by haggard faces I would stop sometimes to sketch in the little pad I carried with me like a charm—I would know what I wrote against as well as for: against their taste as well as for our own. I can remember now only two of the themes I wrote on "forbidden subjects," risking an F if I did not make an

A. In our classroom, women and love were taboo like the teacher and the course—too sacred to touch without the threat of flunking; but I was seventeen and even on the Lexington Avenue Express it was somehow spring in April and May. Both my remembered efforts were stories, for exposition irked me and I longed to be delivered from the Description of a Process ("How I Tie My Shoes").

The first of my stories described the strange life and death of a woman who had an orgasm every time she passed through a subway turnstile—and who in her last moments attained the ultimate ecstasy, imagining the crucifix above her hospital bed whirling madly against her as she passed into Heaven. The other concerned a man who married a seal but was unable to find a way to consummate their union and perished (along with his bride) of sheer frustration. But the latter was a translation only and lacked the real point of an original version which I had composed in uncertain French—after I had discovered that the French word for seal was *phoque*. On each paper in indignant red pencil my instructor wrote "Good taste!" It seems a naïve enough time from the vantage point of an age in which similar stories would evoke psychoanaltyic interpretations by instructors with subscriptions to the *Partisan Review*. "Good taste!" It was from fellow students I learned about Freud, as it was a fellow student (shortly thereafter dropped from the School of Engineering) who told me on the library steps about a writer called Kafka—and set me to limping through *The Castle* in German. And this is the way it should be, I cannot help believing still: the world of Them, of the Others, of the Past defined in the classroom; the world of Us, of the Young, sought and fought for outside. But having gained certain things we desired (there are now Jewish Chairmen of English Departments, and conservative girls from old-fashioned schools are bullied into saying "It's me" instead of "It is I."), we have lost others we cannot so easily spare. Now in what is called Freshman Composition, students may be asked to read casebooks on Ezra Pound or even the Beats—and are certainly urged in one way or another to pursue the up-to-date, hand in hand with teachers eager to prove that their youth, though longer used, is quite as vigorous as that of the dewiest of their students.

So another traditional function of the classical freshman composition course is abandoned: the attempt to impose yesterday's taste and yesterday's usage on tomorrow's writers, thus defining a world against which the future can define itself. But we have lived long enough to create a world in which everyone inhabits the future and the past belongs to the past—a world in which there is scarcely a freshman teacher who would have nerve or sense enough to flunk the Scott Fitzgerald of this generation. And what is the function of the comp course whose ends are *not* Initiation through Terror, Melting Pot, Brainwashing, and the Induction into Gentility? How we flounder these days in search of a *raison d'être:* functional linguistics, semantics, "close reading," the battle against Mass Culture; how appallingly often new texts with guaranteed new approaches appear. I was in on the birth of one of the first at the University of Wisconsin. Only six years after I was myself a freshman, I found myself teaching a comp course, but one utterly different from what I had endured. Our text (still mimeographed then) was S. I. Hayakawa's adaptation of Korzybski to classroom uses, and we called the course not Composition at all but "Language in Action." "$Cow_1$ is not $Cow_2$ . . ." we taught our students to repeat and somewhere in the background floated a dream of world understanding and no war.

If I permit myself a certain nostalgia for 1938, it is not because I forget the grimmer aspect of the comp course in a school whose unconfessed aim was the final liquidation of the ghetto in favor of the suburb, the conversion of the children of greenhorns into subscribers to *Time* and *Newsweek*. It is only because I appreciate—belatedly—the lovely innocence of those terrible times. We were in some ways, I will not deny, like a class in an occupied country, a group of Alsatians or Czechs, say, under a German master. And we felt ourselves captives, prisoners in the classroom, in a way which it is hard to remember; because outside there was simply nothing—no jobs, no openings, a world without possibility and therefore a world of violence. In the classroom, too, violence seemed always barely tamped down, just ready to explode; but when it came, it came from an unexpected quarter. I think all of us believed that a certain large Italian boy, who slept quietly in the first row (he drove a truck all night) except when browbeaten awake by the lash of our instructor's wit, would someday spectacularly erupt. But oddly enough it was in the biology class that he took his stand, declaring one day in the midst of a lecture that he could not abide being taught natural science by a virgin (we saw his point) and walking out. No, in comp class it was a fifteen-year-old stammerer who blew up for us all, hurling himself at some kid behind him who snickered when he stuck in the middle of explaining, perhaps, the difference between "it's" and "its."

Outside of class, he could usually make it through a sentence at the cost of a little wheezing here and there; but on his feet before a teacher, he would be overwhelmed by all the pressures that had driven him to skip three years of the long way toward a B.A. and certified membership in genteel America. His mouth opened grotesquely and his breath terrifyingly audible, he would seem someone who tried to scream rather than speak, someone who tried to wake from a nightmare—and the clowns around him who did not know that there was a nightmare from which to wake would mock him. When he jumped that day halfway across the room and his mocker went down under him, we all leaped, too, our *Martin Chuzzlebergs* flying; and whether we wanted to make peace or compound the violence we could not have said. Only the teacher stood outside the melee, frozen into silence, alone. . . . It is this scene which possesses me whenever I try to call up the faces and voices of those days, and I like to think that it is somehow a parable. But I should hate to be called on to explain its meanings.

*Athens, Greece*
—1962

# SEVENTEEN

# Academic Irresponsibility

To ARGUE in favor of freedom for the teacher seems at first the most pointless sort of preaching to the converted, since everybody —as everybody hastens to assure you—is already convinced. Difficult enough under the best of conditions, everybody explains, teaching would be virtually impossible without a large degree of liberty. But everybody then adds, at the point where piety ends and candor begins, that the teacher obviously must be "responsible" as well as free; the clear implication is that freedom is *limited* by responsibility—to which everybody else assents, with the sole exception, it sometimes seems, of me.

In my objections to responsibility, I find myself not only lonelier and lonelier but more and more distant from those I had long thought my natural allies. From my earliest reading years, I had understood that Babbitt was the enemy of freedom, and responsibility his hypocritical watchword. Of this I had been assured not only by Sinclair Lewis, who baptized him, but by John Dos Passos in *U.S.A.*, by James Thurber in *The Male Animal,* by the whole consort of writers who had sentimentalized and mythicized the early academic victims of Rotarians, chambers of commerce and boards of trustees—from Thorstein Veblen to Scott Nearing and innumerable other half-forgotten half heroes fired from university posts for defending Tom Mooney and Sacco and Vanzetti or for criticizing monopoly capitalism and the war.

The campaign of vilification and harassment directed against certain leftish academics in the time of Joe McCarthy seemed the climax and confirmation of the whole thing. After the total discred-

361

iting of McCarthy, when political liberty for professors was pretty generally won and Babbitts everywhere had gone into retreat, an occasional rear-guard action on their part seemed more comic and pathetic than sinister or threatening. Picking up, for instance, a Kiwanis Club pamphlet labeled "Freedom," I am tickled rather than dismayed to discover no reference to anything that I mean by freedom, only an appeal to teachers to transmit to the young "an understanding of responsible citizenship, principles of free enterprise and values of our spiritual heritage. . . ." "Free" as in enterprise, but "responsible" in everything; it is quite what the literature I grew up on taught me to expect—something comfortably unchanged in our disconcertingly changeable world.

There is, however, one area at least where the Babbitts, even in retreat, continue to pose a real threat to freedom—a threat because the academic community is on their side. When social behavior rather than politics is involved—especially in matters of sex or the use of banned drugs (associated inevitably with sex in the fantasies of the repressors) and especially when faculty members seem to advocate, or condone, or encourage or simply permit unconventional student practices in these matters—then the faculties of universities tend to speak the same language as the Kiwanis Club. And here I am eternally shocked and disheartened.

For almost a decade now, there has been instance after instance, from the notorious firing of Timothy Leary at Harvard, through the dismissal of certain young "homosexual" instructors at Smith, to the recent failure to rehire the poet Robert Mezey at Fresno State College. Often the real issues are camouflaged, as in Leary's case; the charge pressed was not that Leary had become a published advocate of LSD but that he failed to meet his classes regularly. Or they tend to be blurred, as in Mezey's case; the fact that he opposed the war in Vietnam and defended black power might suggest the recurrence of simple old-fashioned McCarthyism, were it not that thousands of academic opponents of the most unjust of American wars continue to be reappointed or promoted so long as they do not also happen to advocate changes in the existing marijuana laws.

Sometimes the underlying issues are totally hushed up, out of ostensible regard for the reputation of the victims, who, accepting dismissal in order to avoid scandal, provide their colleagues with the possibility of copping out; so that no advocate of academic freedom is called upon to take a principled stand on freedom for potheads or queers; no libertarian is forced to confront the limits of his own tolerance. I am aware of only a single case of this kind fought hard enough and far enough to compel the American Association of University Professors to rethink its own position, defining—from a teacher's presumable point of view—the competing claims of freedom and responsibility: the now nearly forgotten Koch case.

On March 18, 1960, Leo Koch, an assistant professor of biology at the University of Illinois, wrote a letter to the campus paper in which, after some reflections—more banal and less witty than he obviously thought them—on "a Christian code of ethics already decrepit in the days of Queen Victoria," he concluded:

> With modern contraceptives and medical advice readily available at the nearest drugstore, or at least a family physician, there is no valid reason why sexual intercourse should not be condoned among those sufficiently mature to engage in it without social consequences and without violating their own codes of morality and ethics.
> A mutually satisfactory sexual experience would eliminate the need for many hours of frustrating petting and lead to much happier and longer-lasting marriages among our younger men and women.

Whether the course of action that Professor Koch advocated would, indeed, have led to the happiness and marital stability he promised remains yet to be proved, since he inspired no general movement to lead openly the sort of sexual life that many students, whether "sufficiently mature" or not, have been leading covertly, anyhow. If Koch was espousing anything new in his manifesto, it was presumably the abandonment of concealment and that unconfessed pact by which students make it possible for their teachers to pretend they do not know what their students pretend they do not know those teachers know.

Yet his letter had results, all the same, for it brought about a chain of events that ended in his being fired. And his firing, in turn, produced a series of statements and counterstatements about morality and freedom from the president of the university, its board of trustees, the faculty senate and many individual members of the teaching staff. This intramural debate was followed by a prolonged investigation under the auspices of the American Association of University Professors of what had become by that time "the Koch case," an investigation not finally reported on in full until three years later. The report, which appeared in the *A.A.U.P. Bulletin* of March 1963, reveals a division of opinion among college professors themselves, symptomatic of a confusion on the issues involved, that not only divides one academic colleague from another but splits the individual minds of many Americans inside the universities and out.

More interesting to me, however, and more dismaying than any of the disagreements, was a substantial area of agreement between the president and the board of trustees of the University of Illinois (who thought Koch should be fired), the faculty senate of that institution (who thought he should only be reprimanded) and Committee A of the A.A.U.P., the professed guardians of academic freedom (who thought the whole case should have been thrown out of court because of lack of due process). All four agreed that Koch was guilty of a "breach of academic responsibility" and that, regardless of his guilt or innocence, his academic freedom, like everyone else's, was and should have been limited by the academic responsibility that he was accused of having flouted. What academic responsibility means was nowhere very clearly defined in the dispute but was apparently understood by everyone involved to signify an obligation on the part of any professor to keep his mouth shut or only moderately open in cases where there is a clear danger of offending accepted morality, i.e., public opinion.

But how odd it was to find in the conservative and anti-intellectual camp a committee specifically charged with the protection of professors' rights—rights which the committee has often unyieldingly defended. What, then, moved it this time to grant that ". . . we can hardly expect academic freedom to endure unless it is matched by academic responsibility"? Surely, the topic of Koch's letter had something to do with it, and not merely the fact that his thoughts were neither well reasoned nor cogently expressed. If all cases of academic freedom involved the justification of documents as dignified and compelling as, say, Milton's *Areopagitica,* to defend liberty would be as easy as to attack it; but this, as the A.A.U.P. must have learned in its long career, is far from the truth. No, it was the subject of Koch's expostulation that made the difference; for when sex and students are simultaneously evoked, even the hardiest campus civil libertarian seems willing to cry "responsibility" with all the rest.

And the larger community has sensed this, moving in to attack —even when political motives play a considerable role—only when sex and drugs are involved. The young instructors at Michigan State University who helped edit a radical magazine called *Zeitgeist* may have offended their colleagues and administrators in many ways; but when their contracts were not renewed, a year or so ago, it was only the dirty words they had printed that were marshaled as evidence against them. And when, some years before that, Mulford Sibley, a well-known pacifist and political dissident, was brought under attack at the University of Minnesota, what was quoted against him was a speech in which he suggested that the university might be healthier if it could boast "a student Communist club, a chapter of the American Association for the Advancement of Atheism, a Society for the Promotion of Free Love . . . and perhaps a nudist club."

Predictably enough, communism and atheism tended to be soft-pedaled in the accusations brought against him, which lingered most lovingly over the fact that he was "agitating for nudist clubs" and added, apparently as the final proof of his perfidy, that "Dr. Sibley assigned books to his students resembling 'Lady Chatterley and Her Love Affairs.' " I know how disabling such a charge can be in academic circles, since, in an early encounter of my own with a really concerted effort to silence me in the classroom (the only time I ever really ran into trouble before the recent attempt to manufacture a case against me on the grounds of "maintaining a premise where marijuana is used"), I was accused not only of contempt for my then-fellow Montanans but also of having written a "dirty" poem called *Dumb Dick* and a "dirty" story called *Nude Croquet,* which was "subsequently banned in Knoxville, Tennessee." Alas, some of my former colleagues, willing enough to stand with me on political grounds, were shaken by being informed that I was a "dirty writer."

Pornography and nudity, along with trafficking in drugs and indulging in homosexuality, as well as refusing to condemn any or all of these to students, are the stock charges in latterday assaults against the freedom of the teacher by elements in the business community sophisticated enough to know that in our time, old-fashioned accusations of being Red or "soft on Reds" are likely to be laughed out of the court of public opinion and have no status at all in courts of law. But there are statutes that can be invoked against offenses of the former sort, as in the recent police harassment of Leonard Wolf, a member of the English department of San Francisco State College, charged with "contributing to the delinquency of minors."

Wolf is the founder of Happening House, an institution set up to maintain a dialogue between the kind of kids who inhabit the Haight-Ashbury district of San Francisco and the local academic community. During a conference on the problem of runaways, some of those kids, members of a performing dance group, took off all their clothes onstage. Wolf, who was the most convenient adult on the premises, was arrested. He was subsequently tried and acquitted because the prosecution could not prove him responsible for the students' disrobing, but from the start, the intent of the police seems to have been quite clearly to impugn Wolf both as the founder of Happening House and as a teacher. Why else charge him with acting in a way that "causes, tends to cause or encourages unknown juveniles to lead immoral or idle lives"? Whatever college officials thought of his classroom performance or his outside activities, a court conviction would make him a criminal in their eyes—and, as such, his position in the college, as well as his status in the community, would be endangered. And just as clearly, it wasn't only Wolf who was being put on trial, but all teachers who, insofar as they are true to their profession, seek to release their students from parochialism and fear, thus laying themselves open to charges of "corrupting the young" or "contributing to the delinquency of minors." A printed statement from the Leonard Wolf defense recognizes this fact—though it states the dilemma ineptly and misleadingly by insisting that in his case, "The limits of any teacher's responsibility are at stake" and that "If the attack on Professor Wolf proves successful . . . the limits of responsibility will have been unfairly extended in the service of repressive interests."

One cannot effectively fight an opponent whose language, along with its assumptions, has been uncritically accepted. And to grant —even implicitly—that there are just and proper limits somewhere, sometimes, to the teacher's freedom is to give the game away to those ready and eager to seize any show of weakness on the teacher's part. This is especially dangerous these days, when we are threatened on two sides, not just on one, as we have long been accustomed. On the one hand, there are the traditional "repressive interests," plus the courts and cops whom they largely control, to whom a free faculty seems always on the verge of going over to the enemy, i.e., the young, whom they think of as swinging back and forth between an unwholesome flight from reality and untidy demonstrations in the streets. And, on the other hand, there are the young themselves, or at least the revolutionaries among them, to whom the much-vaunted "academic freedom" of their teachers seems only a subterfuge, a cover-up for their subservience to the *real* enemy, i.e., the old, who, if they do not actually wage imperialist war and exploit labor, apologize for both.

I sit at the moment looking mournfully at an "Open Letter" directed to the faculty at the University of Sussex, an English university in which I spent last year as a visiting professor. The document is signed by "The February 21 Committee," a group whose chief political activity was throwing a can of red paint over a speaker from the American Embassy who had attempted to defend United States intervention in Vietnam. An early paragraph reads, in part: "Students say 'free inquiry' or 'free speech' mean that academics must permit their institution to be used for any purpose, this freedom ends logically in irresponsibility. . . ." Syntax and punctuation have broken down a little, but the meaning is clear—and disheartening. Whether Kiwanis Clubber, A.A.U.P. member or Maoist student, one touch of responsibility makes them all kin to one another, and alien to me.

Yet there is a difference, of course, between the Babbitts and the *enragés,* those who boast themselves sane and those who like to think of themselves as mad. Both demand restrictions on political freedom, one from the right and one from the left; but the students, at least, are on the side of erotic and imaginative freedom, in favor of love and dreams—and when such issues are involved or can be evoked, the free professor will find them on his side. In that area, indeed, they are more dependable allies than his own colleagues, since even the most liberal professors have tended to be equivocal on the subject of social, as opposed to intellectual, freedom, for both students and themselves. To the young, more important than the freedom to read what books or take what courses they please is the freedom to make love as they please; and it was therefore quite proper that the recent student revolt in France was touched off at the University of Nanterre by protest over restricted visiting privileges between boys' and girls' dormitories.

This fundamental inconsistency of viewpoint toward social rather than academic freedom has tended to sap the integrity of certain faculty, and sowed a deepening distrust in the minds of students, who, in response, have been on occasion as cavalier about the political rights of their teachers as their teachers have been about their personal liberties. But there is an even more fundamental source of confusion in the definition of responsibility that the academic community—professors first of all, and now the students— has accepted, without sufficient wariness, from the larger community that surrounds and often resents it.

Once the teacher has granted the theory that responsibility equals restriction, restraint, censorship, taboo, he has lost in advance all those "cases" to which he must in due course come. At best, he commits himself to endless wrangles about exactly where freedom (understood as the right to express what he believes without hindrance) yields to responsibility (understood as the obligation to curtail his expression), lest he offend the taste, the conventions or the religious, political, and moral codes of the community that sustains him.

There is no way out of such wrangles and not much point in going on to further debates about who (the teacher, the community, or some impartial referee) is to draw the line between freedom and responsibility, once these have been postulated as opposites. And surely there is even less point in debating after the fact how harshly the "irresponsibles" are to be treated, whether by a lopping of heads or a mere slapping of wrists; i.e., whether they are to be dismissed or reprimanded. I propose, therefore, to define responsibility in quite a different way—as a matter of fact, in two quite different ways—in order to put the problem in a new light and deliver everyone from the frustration and ennui of having endlessly to re-hash the old arguments.

Let me begin with a positive definition of "academic responsi-bility" as the teacher's obligation to *do* something, rather than not to. The teacher—not exclusively, perhaps, but, without doubt, es-pecially—has a single overwhelming responsibility: the responsibil-ity to be *free,* which is to say, to be what most men would call *irre-sponsible.* For him, freedom and responsibility are not obligations that cancel each other out but one and the same thing; and this unity of academic freedom and academic responsibility arises from the teacher's double function in our society: first of all, to extend the boundaries of knowledge by questioning *everything,* including the truths that most men at any given point consider sacred and timeless; and, finally, to free the minds of the young, so that they can continue the same task beyond what he himself can imagine.

I shall not linger over the traditional "research" function of the teacher, since its necessity is granted, with whatever secret reserva-tions, by almost everyone except certain backward students, much given to complaining that their teachers spend more time on re-search than on them—not understanding that there would be noth-ing for those teachers to give them if independent investigation and lonely meditation were ever suspended or drastically curtailed. Thorstein Veblen, prototype of the free teacher, thought it was a mistake to attempt to combine in a single person the schoolmaster and the scholar; but American universities have long since made the decision to try, and it is incumbent on the scholar-schoolmaster to be clear in his own mind, and to make clear to everyone else concerned, the priorities of his commitments. Few of them have been as candid about it as was Robert Frost, himself a schoolmaster for some 50 years, who always insisted from the platform that the teacher's first duty was to himself, his second to his subject matter and only his third to the student. And no one who begins with an understanding of the free teacher's peculiar obligation to the free student could possibly challenge this order.

The problem to begin with is: What can, and what should be, taught? From that start, it was clear to me that teaching was a pas-sion, not a science, and that methods, therefore, are meaningless in the classroom, that lesson plans and pedagogical strategy are vanity and illusion. But it has taken me nearly three decades of teaching to realize that even the subject matter one teaches is quickly—and, in most cases, quite correctly—forgotten, gone, certainly, with the last exam. It should no longer be considered a scandalous secret that the students believe they are hiding from teachers—or vice versa —that course subject matter is at best optional, at worst totally irrelevant.

What is required of the teacher is not that he impart knowledge but that he open up minds, revealing to his students possibilities in themselves that they had perhaps not even suspected, and confirming in them a faith in their own sensibilities and intelligence; not suffering their foolishness or indulging their errors, but all the time revealing to them the double truth that, though the student can often be wrong, he has, like his teacher, the *right* to be wrong; and that, if he is willing to live a life of intellectual risk, he may someday know more, see further and feel more acutely than any of the elders of the community, including his teachers. It is the credo of the free and truly "irresponsible" teacher that no truth except this (not even the ones he most dearly believes in) is final, since the advance of human thought is potentially unlimited.

Such a teacher addresses his students, confronts them, engages with them, in the hope that they will someday go beyond the limitations of vision built into him by the limitations of his training and his time; and that they will even escape the trap of believing that their new vision is a final one, to be imposed forever after on the generations who succeed them. My ideal teacher must teach his students, in short, to be free—which is something quite different from persuading them to write in their notebooks, "Be free!," since freedom cannot be acquired by rote any more than it can be established by law. Freedom cannot be taught by preaching it—as, by writing this, I have betrayed myself into doing—but by acting it out, living it in full view. Once we have realized that the teacher is not just a guide, much less a substitute parent or a charming entertainer (though he can be all of these things, too, if he is so moved), but a model; and that what is learned in the classroom is *him,* the teacher, we will understand that the teacher must become a model of the free man.

And yet how many of our own teachers do we remember as having been even in aspiration, much less in fact, anything like free? How many do we recall with love for having freed us from those fears and doubts about ourselves and our world that we brought with us into school, inextricably intertwined with our ignorance and bravado? There have been only a handful among the scores I encountered in my own school career: one or two in high school, none at all in college, and one in graduate school, whom I cannot forbear naming. Author of once-admired but now-forgotten poems and a splendid book about the shape of his own life, *The Locomotive God,* William Ellery Leonard once gave me, by his splendid example, certain illusions about what teaching and teachers were like that brought me into the university in the first place; and then left me, with even more splendid tact, to find out the truth for myself.

But why have so many, so large a majority not merely of my teachers but of everybody's teachers, failed in their obligation to choose to be free? It is tempting, but finally unsatisfactory to say, in easy cynicism: Well, everyone fails at everything, so why not they? Certainly there are pressures on them from all sides to be of "service" to the community as a whole, or to the past, to the present, to God, to the Revolution, etc. Wherever the free teacher turns, he confronts men, sometimes his own colleagues, convinced that the function of the university is not to free the mind but to inculcate a set of values, to indoctrinate or—as we say when somebody else's values are concerned—to brainwash the student.

But the wielders of such pressures are, in a sense, not hard to resist, especially when they speak from the conservative tradition; since there are habits of response built into most professors from earliest youth that stir a reflex of resistance against movements to ban books by, say, Allen Ginsberg and William Burroughs on the one hand, or by Ché Guevara and Mao Tse-tung on the other, or to fire those who ask students to read them. Whatever our disagreements with the lovers of such literature, we tend to feel them on our side. No, the most conspicuous failure of professors in this regard has been their refusal to protect the dissident right-wingers among them under attack from antilibertarians on our side. Surely one of the most scandalous events of recent academic history has been the quiet dismissal of a distinguished rightist teacher of political science from an equally distinguished Ivy League college, whose own silence was bought by buying up his contract and whose colleagues' silence apparently did not have to be bought at all.

Obviously, those who advocate reticence or "responsibility" from our side are more insidious—and sometimes, it would appear, impossible to resist. For it is our loyalty, rather than our timidity, on which such academic enemies of "irresponsibility" insist: asking us to limit ourselves (lest we give aid and comfort to a common opponent) in the free investigation, say, of the interconnections between the homosexual revolution and the first stages of the civil rights movement, or the importance of anti-Semitism and racism in the later black-power movement. Similarly, they urge us not to take away from the progressive forces certain symbolic heroes of the historical left—not, for instance, to follow up the evidence that at least Sacco, and possibly Vanzetti as well, was guilty as charged in the famous case that mobilized most decent men on their side; and that many of the organizers of the protests against their condemnation already knew the fact and strategically concealed it.

And when the voices that plead with us to lie a little about the importance of Negroes in our history, or to mitigate a little the harsh truth about the last country to betray some revolution in which we once thought we believed, are the voices of our own students, the voices of the young—how even harder it is to resist. We know that their cause, too, will be betrayed, as all causes are ultimately betrayed, but it seems churlish and unstrategic to tell them so; their strength and weakness is precisely not to know this, as our strength and weakness is to know it. And these strengths and weaknesses are complementary, make social life and intercourse between the generations not merely possible but necessary. Why, then, should we not lie to them a little when they come to us, as they do between periods of absolute rejection?

In a way, we are better off, safer, from our own point of view and theirs, when they turn their backs on us, muttering, "Old men, all we want you to do for us is *die!*" But a moment later, they return (being in need of uncles and grandfathers if not fathers: Marcuses and McLuhans and Norman O. Browns), crying, "Underwrite, sanction our revolt, tell us we are righter than you!" Indeed, how could they fail to be righter than we are still, wrong as we were at their age? But it is not our function as free teachers to tell them only how they are right; it is also imperative that we say (at the risk of being loved less, even of finally losing their ear altogether) how they are wrong—what in their movement, for instance, threatens the very freedom that makes it possible, and what threatens to freeze into self-righteousness.

Spokesmen for the "future" forget, even as they fight for it, that the "future" quickly becomes the present, then the past; and that soon they are only fighting for yesterday against the proponents of the day before yesterday. This is why the teacher dedicated to freedom must tell them *right now* the same thing he tells the Kiwanians when they howl down or propose to ban some speaker, some uncongenial idea: If any kind of truth or pursuit of truth—however misguided, however wrong—seems threatening to a cause we espouse, it is time to re-examine that cause, no matter how impressive its credentials. It is also to ourselves, of course, that we're speaking, since without constantly reminding ourselves of this simple principle we will yield to some pressure group, right, left or center. But even taken together, such groups are not our deepest and most dangerous enemy.

What gets us, as teachers, into final trouble is the enemy of our freedom that ordinarily we do not perceive at all: inhibiting forces that are as impersonal and omnipresent and invisible as our total environment or our very selves. Indeed, they are a large and growing part of that total environment, especially in the United States, where more and more education for more and more people remains an avowed goal of society. There are, however, inhibitory and restrictive tendencies built into the very school system to which almost everyone born in America is condemned by the fact of his birth—condemned beyond the possibility of appeal, since what he may feel as a prison was dreamed for him by his forebears as utopia.

For better or worse, in any event, young Americans these days find themselves sentenced by law to a term lasting from their fourth or fifth birthday to their sixteenth—and, by custom and social pressure, to a good deal more: time added, as it were, for good behavior. But though students in large numbers are dimly aware of all this, they have tended to resist it as outlaws rather than as revolutionaries, i.e., to drop out rather than to raise as a slogan, an immediate demand, the right not to go to school. Students have been primarily—and quite properly, as far as it goes—concerned with failures of the school system to provide them with the kinds of freedom to which that system itself is theoretically pledged: the right to demonstrate or petition, to participate and advise, to control in part, at least, their own destinies *in* the schools; but the existence of those schools, and even their traditional function, they have largely taken for granted.

To me, however, the root problem, the essential restriction of freedom, seems compulsory education itself—on both the primary and the secondary levels, where it is enforced by statute and truant officers; and on the higher levels, where it is, more and more broadly, customary and enforced by the peer group plus parents and teachers. Everything begins with the assumption by the community (or some auxiliary private enterprise) of the role traditionally played in the lives of the young by their families, aided and abetted by medicine men, prophets or kindly passing strangers; and is confirmed beyond hope of reform when that community sets up ever more rigid and bureaucratized institutions to do that job for it.

From this initial requirement follows most of what is dangerously restrictive throughout the school system: the regulation of every moment of a student's day (especially in high schools) and a good part of a student's nights (especially for female students, all the way to the university level). This involves, first of all, required attendance, tardiness reports, classes artificially divided into periods and rung off and on by a centrally controlled bell system, proctored examinations and blackmail by grades. And it implies, in the second place, a host of "disciplinary regulations" beginning with the banning of cigarettes on school grounds, or alcohol at school dances, or pot and the pill in dormitories, and ending with petty decrees—totally unconnected to the laws of the larger community—about the length of skirts and pants and hair. Hair, especially, seems the concern of school authorities, whether on the head or on the face—as if somewhere in the collective mind of those authorities, the image persisted of youth as a sort of Samson who to be enslaved must be shorn.

Students have, of course, protested against this; and a good deal of what moves them, plus more that might or should move them, has been beautifully formulated by Edgar Z. Friedenberg, beginning with a book titled *The Vanishing Adolescent*. But their cry of "No more *loco parentis*" is undercut by their clearly contradictory wishes on this score. In general, they seem to want the schools to maintain a certain parental role in warding off police prosecution, yet to surrender that role in maintaining internal discipline. In any case, the protesters do not begin far enough back; for the American school system is essentially—by definition and tradition—*in loco parentis*. And nothing fundamental is solved by persuading it to become a permissive rather than an authoritarian parent—that is, to make itself more like students' actual parents and less like their actual grandparents.

It is, alas, precisely those "permissive" parents who have made the whole school system, from kindergarten to university, what it is, insisting that it act out for them the dark side of their own ambivalence toward their children—be the bad parent they feel guilty for not being—and for wanting to be. If our schools are, in fact, totalitarian under their liberal disguises, more like what the sociologists call "total institutions" (jails, mental hospitals, detention camps) than small democratic communities or enlarged families, this is because the parents of the students in them *want* them to be what they are. Certainly any parent, any full adult in our society, is at least dimly aware of the tendency in himself and his neighbors to project upon children and adolescents sexual and anarchic impulses denied in himself. These impulses he asks his children both to act out and to be blamed for, relieving him of his own double guilt—and providing in its place the double pleasure of vicarious self-indulgence and the condemnation of sin.

In addition, there is the sexual jealousy that inevitably troubles those home-tied by jobs or children, or oppressed by the menopause and the imminence of death when they confront others just emerging into puberty, as well as the desperation of those unable to persuade their children of the value of moral codes in which they only theoretically believe—a desperation that ends in calling out the law to enforce what love could not achieve. And, finally, there is the strange uncertainty of our society about just when a child becomes an adult (whatever that elusive term may mean)—at puberty, at 16, 18, 21; when he votes, drinks legally, goes into the Army or simply becomes capable of reproducing himself. Out of this uncertainty emerge those absurd social regulations that turn the girls' dormitory into a police state, the rules whose goal is to keep those we claim we have to regulate (because they are still "children") from getting pregnant, i.e., from proving to us that biologically, at least, they are fully mature.

Small wonder, then, that our schools and universities have become, like our jails and hospitals and asylums, institutions whose structure works against their own avowed ends—leading not to the free development of free men but to the depersonalization of the student, to his conversion into a code number and an IBM card punched full of data, a fact that he may forget in the midst of the small pleasures that punctuate his boredom but of which he is reminded once, twice, even three times a year by the degrading rituals of examination and registration. The damage done the student by this system we have all begun to notice, as the resentment of his indignity has driven him to construct barricades and hurl fire bombs; but the similar damage done to his teachers we tend to ignore, since they typically respond with silence or statements read only to one another at annual meetings.

It is not merely that the teacher, too, is regulated, right down to such trivial matters as wearing a tie or smoking in class, but that also—and, finally, more critically—he, like the prison guard or the asylum attendant, becomes the prisoner of the closed world he presumably guards, a world in which he begins talking at the ping of one bell and stops at the clang of another, meanwhile checking attendance, making sure no one cheats or lights a cigarette under a NO SMOKING sign or consumes hard liquor or drugs, or, God forbid, takes off his clothes in public. All of this, however, makes him a jailer or a cop, who notoriously resemble their charges; and insofar as he resists, turns him into a hypocrite, acknowledging only the infractions that someone else—the press, a planted police spy, an indignant parent—has noticed first.

How can the teacher who accepts such a system talk freedom to the students before him? Or how can he demand it for himself—academically, politically, personally—at the very moment he is denying it—socially, erotically—to those he asks to emulate his model? The historical struggle of teachers for what has been called "academic freedom"—that is, their own freedom—has been impugned throughout by their hypocrisy. No community, not even a school, can exist one-tenth absolutely free and nine-tenths half slave. It is an unendurable fraud, of which most of us manage to remain absurdly unaware, until some notorious "case"—the Leary case, the Koch case, the Mezey case—forces us to confront it, to confront the contradiction in ourselves. By then, however, it is too late.

Inevitably, at that point we tend to compromise or totally betray for one of us the principles we have already learned to compromise and betray for the students to whom we are, after ourselves, chiefly responsible. And here we have come, at long last, to responsibility. To avoid the word at this juncture would be as abject as having taken refuge in it earlier, since to be responsible means, in the new context, not to be restricted, which is to say, less free—but to be *answerable*, which is to say, more free.

Until a man has learned to be truly free, he cannot begin to be responsible in this deep etymological sense of the word, since the only thing for which a teacher is properly answerable is his own freedom, his necessary prior *ir*responsibility. A slave or a man under restraint, an indoctrinated indoctrinator, a civil servant brainwashed to brainwash others, is answerable for nothing. No matter what charges are brought against him, he can plead innocent; for he is the agent of another, a despicable tool, just another Eichmann, dignified beyond his worth by being brought to the dock.

The free teacher, on the other hand, must not merely suffer but welcome, even invite, criticism of what he espouses and teaches, for his job is to change the minds of the young—which those in established positions seem to view as a kind of "corruption." For him, freedom does not mean freedom from consequences; he takes, as the old Spanish proverb has it, what he wants but he pays his dues. Wanting nothing free of charge, he denies to no one the right to disagree with what he says, to criticize, to try to rebut, even to threaten sanctions. He must always be willing to argue against all comers the basic case for his freedom, which is never, and can never be, won finally and forever. But he must also be prepared to defend—one by one and each on its own merits—all of the tenets, views, opinions and analyses he finds himself free to offer.

Above all, when his ideas are proved wrong, to his own satisfaction, in the debate with those who challenge him, he must feel free to confess his error without in any way diminishing his right to have held those ideas; for he has never had any real freedom at all unless he has been free from the start to be wrong and unless he remains free to the end to change his mind. If, in the debate he has occasioned, however, he continues to believe in his position, he must—with all the assurance that comes of knowing his fallibility as well as that of his opponents—continue to maintain that position. It does not matter at all if a majority is against him, or even everybody; for even everybody has, on occasion, turned out to be wrong, and he is, in any case, not answerable to a popular vote.

He dares not betray the facts as he has learned from his teachers and his colleagues to determine them, but he must always be aware that those "facts" exist finally in his own head. And he is equally answerable to posterity—which means, for a teacher, his students—not those before him at any moment but those yet to come; best of all, those not yet born; and these, too, he must remember live only inside his skull. It is to the unborn, then, that the free man, the true teacher, is finally answerable; but it is the living students, their parents and the community that he inhabits rather than the one he dreams, that judge him and can make him suffer. If that community—parents or students or both—desires to visit sanctions on him, he must not pretend surprise or feel dismay.

Yet they are not hard to please, really, the spokesmen of the past or those of the present; all they ask is a show of subservience either to long-established conventions or to the very latest life style. Only an allegiance to the ever-receding future dismays both; for, driven to imagine a time to come, the responsibles, both old and young, feel their authority slipping from them as they realize that someday they will be dead. But it is precisely this realization that exhilarates some men, making them feel free enough to be irresponsible, irresponsible enough to be free.

—1968

# EIGHTEEN

# The New Mutants

A REALIZATION that the legitimate functions of literature are bewilderingly, almost inexhaustibly various has always exhilarated poets and dismayed critics. And critics, therefore, have sought age after age to legislate limits to literature—legitimizing certain of its functions and disavowing others—in hope of insuring to themselves the exhilaration of which they have felt unjustly deprived, and providing for poets the dismay which the critics at least have thought good for them.

Such shifting and exclusive emphasis is not, however, purely the product of critical malice, or even of critical principle. Somehow every period is, to begin with, especially aware of certain functions of literature and especially oblivious to others: endowed with a special sensitivity and a complementary obtuseness, which, indeed, give to that period its characteristic flavor and feel. So, for instance, the Augustan Era is marked by sensitivity in regard to the uses of diction, obtuseness in regard to those of imagery.

What the peculiar obtuseness of the present age may be I find it difficult to say (being its victim as well as its recorder), perhaps toward the didactic or certain modes of the sentimental. I am reasonably sure, however, that our period is acutely aware of the sense in which literature if not invents, at least collaborates in the invention of time. The beginnings of that awareness go back certainly to the beginnings of the Renaissance, to Humanism as a self-conscious movement; though a critical development occurred toward the end of the eighteenth century with the dawning of the Age of Revolution. And we may have reached a second critical point right now.

At any rate, we have long been aware (in the last decades uncomfortably aware) that a chief function of literature is to express and in part to create not only theories of time but also attitudes toward time. Such attitudes constitute, however, a politics as well as an esthetics; or, more properly perhaps, a necessary mythological substratum of politics—as, in fact, the conventional terms reactionary, conservative, revolutionary indicate: all involving stances toward the past.

It is with the past, then, that we must start, since the invention of the past seems to have preceded that of the present and the future; and since we are gathered in a university at whose heart stands a library[1]—the latter, like the former, a visible monument to the theory that a chief responsibility of literature is to preserve and perpetuate the past. Few universities are explicitly (and none with any real degree of confidence) dedicated to this venerable goal any longer. The Great Books idea (which once transformed the University of Chicago and lives on now in provincial study groups) was perhaps its last desperate expression. Yet the shaky continuing existence of the universities and the building of new college libraries (with matching Federal funds) remind us not only of that tradition but of the literature created in its name: the neo-epic, for instance, all the way from Dante to Milton; and even the frantically nostalgic Historical Romance, out of the counting house by Sir Walter Scott.

Obviously, however, literature has a contemporary as well as a traditional function. That is to say, it may be dedicated to illuminating the present and the meaning of the present, which is, after all, no more given than the past. Certainly the modern or bourgeois novel was thus contemporary in the hands of its great inventors, Richardson, Fielding, Smollett and Sterne; and it became contemporary again—with, as it were, a sigh of relief—when Flaubert, having plunged deep into the Historical Romance, emerged once more into the present of Emma Bovary. But the second function of the novel tends to transform itself into a third: a revolutionary or

---

[1] "The New Mutants" is a written version of a talk given at the Conference on the Idea of The Future held at Rutgers, in June, 1965. The conference was sponsored by *Partisan Review* and the Congress for Cultural Freedom, with the cooperation of Rutgers, The State University.

prophetic or futurist function; and it is with the latter that I am here concerned.

Especially important for our own time is the sense in which literature first conceived the possibility of the future (rather than an End of Time or an Eternal Return, an Apocalypse or Second Coming); and then furnished that future in joyous or terrified anticipation, thus preparing all of us to inhabit it. Men have dreamed and even written down utopias from ancient times; but such utopias were at first typically allegories rather than projections: nonexistent models against which to measure the real world, exploitations of the impossible (as the traditional name declares) rather than explorations or anticipations or programs of the possible. And, in any event, only recently have such works occupied a position anywhere near the center of literature.

Indeed, the movement of futurist literature from the periphery to the center of culture provides a clue to certain essential meanings of our times and of the art which best reflects it. If we make a brief excursion from the lofty reaches of High Art to the humbler levels of Pop Culture—where radical transformations in literature are reflected in simplified form—the extent and nature of the futurist revolution will become immediately evident. Certainly, we have seen in recent years the purveyors of Pop Culture transfer their energies from the Western and the Dracula-type thriller (last heirs of the Romantic and Gothic concern with the past) to the Detective Story especially in its hard-boiled form (final vulgarization of the realists' dedication to the present) to Science Fiction (a new genre based on hints in Poe and committed to "extrapolating" the future). This development is based in part on the tendency to rapid exhaustion inherent in popular forms; but in part reflects a growing sense of the irrelevance of the past and even of the present to 1965. Surely, there has never been a moment in which the most naïve as well as the most sophisticated have been so acutely aware of how the past threatens momentarily to disappear from the present, which itself seems on the verge of disappearing into the future.

And this awareness functions, therefore, on the level of art as well as entertainment, persuading quite serious writers to emulate the modes of Science Fiction. The novel is most amenable to this sort of adaptation, whose traces we can find in writers as various as

William Golding and Anthony Burgess, William Burroughs and Kurt Vonnegut, Jr., Harry Matthews and John Barth—to all of whom young readers tend to respond with a sympathy they do not feel even toward such forerunners of the mode (still more allegorical than prophetic) as Aldous Huxley, H. G. Wells and George Orwell. But the influence of Science Fiction can be discerned in poetry as well, and even in the polemical essays of such polymath prophets as Wilhelm Reich, Buckminster Fuller, Marshall McLuhan, perhaps also Norman O. Brown. Indeed, in Fuller the prophetic-Science-Fiction view of man is always at the point of fragmenting into verse:

> *men are known as being six feet tall*
> *because that is their tactile limit;*
> *they are not known by how far we can hear them,*
> *e.g., as a one-half mile man*
> *and only to dogs are men known*
> *by their gigantic olfactoral dimensions. . . .*

I am not now interested in analyzing, however, the diction and imagery which have passed from Science Fiction into post-Modernist literature, but rather in coming to terms with the prophetic content common to both: with the myth rather than the modes of Science Fiction. But that myth is quite simply the myth of the end of man, of the transcendence or transformation of the human—a vision quite different from that of the extinction of our species by the Bomb, which seems stereotype rather than archetype and consequently the source of editorials rather than poems. More fruitful artistically is the prospect of the radical transformation (under the impact of advanced technology and the transfer of traditional human functions to machines) of *homo sapiens* into something else: the emergence—to use the language of Science Fiction itself —of "mutants" among us.

A simpleminded prevision of this event is to be found in Arthur C. Clarke's *Childhood's End,* at the conclusion of which the mutated offspring of parents much like us are about to take off under their own power into outer space. Mr. Clarke believes that he is talking about a time still to come because he takes metaphor for fact;

though simply translating "outer space" into "inner space" reveals to us that what he is up to is less prediction than description; since the post-human future is now, and if not we, at least our children, are what it would be comfortable to pretend we still only foresee. But what, in fact, are they: these mutants who are likely to sit before us in class, or across from us at the dinner table, or who stare at us with hostility from street corners as we pass?

Beatniks or hipsters, layabouts and drop-outs we are likely to call them with corresponding hostility—or more elegantly, but still without sympathy, passive onlookers, abstentionists, spiritual catatonics. There resides in all of these terms an element of truth, at least about the relationship of the young to what we have defined as the tradition, the world we have made for them; and if we turn to the books in which they see their own destiny best represented *(The Clockwork Orange,* say, or *On the Road* or *Temple of Gold),* we will find nothing to contradict that truth. Nor will we find anything to expand it, since the young and their laureates avoid on principle the kind of definition (even of themselves) for which we necessarily seek.

Let us begin then with the negative definition our own hostility suggests, since this is all that is available to us, and say that the "mutants" in our midst are nonparticipants in the past (though our wisdom assures us this is impossible), dropouts from history. The withdrawal from school, so typical of their generation and so inscrutable to ours, is best understood as a lived symbol of their rejection of the notion of cultural continuity and progress, which our graded educational system represents in institutional form. It is not merely a matter of their rejecting what happens to have happened just before them, as the young do, after all, in every age; but of their attempting to disavow the very idea of the past, of their seeking to avoid recapitulating it step by step—up to the point of graduation into the present.

Specifically, the tradition from which they strive to disengage is the tradition of the human, as the West (understanding the West to extend from the United States to Russia) has defined it, Humanism itself, both in its bourgeois and Marxist forms; and more especially, the cult of reason—that dream of Socrates, redreamed by the Renaissance and surviving all travesties down to only yesterday. To be sure, there have long been antirational forces at work in the West, including primitive Christianity itself; but the very notion of literary culture is a product of Humanism, as the early Christians knew (setting fire to libraries), so that the Church in order to sponsor poets had first to come to terms with reason itself by way of Aquinas and Aristotle.

Only with Dada was the notion of an antirational antiliterature born; and Dada became Surrealism, i.e., submitted to the influence of those last neo-Humanists, those desperate Socratic Cabalists, Freud and Marx—dedicated respectively to contriving a rationale of violence and a rationale of impulse. The new irrationalists, however, deny all the apostles of reason, Freud as well as Socrates; and if they seem to exempt Marx, this is because they know less about him, have heard him evoked less often by the teachers they are driven to deny. Not only do they reject the Socratic adage that the unexamined life is not worth living, since for them precisely the unexamined life is the only one worth enduring at all. But they also abjure the Freudian one: "Where id was, ego shall be," since for them the true rallying cry is, "Let id prevail over ego, impulse over order," or—in negative terms—"Freud is a fink!"

The first time I heard this irreverent charge from the mouth of a student some five or six years ago (I who had grown up thinking of Freud as a revolutionary, a pioneer), I knew that I was already in the future; though I did not yet suspect that there would be no room in that future for the university system to which I had devoted my life. Kerouac might have told me so, or Ginsberg, or even so polite and genteel a spokesman for youth as J. D. Salinger, but I was too aware of what was wrong with such writers (their faults more readily apparent to my taste than their virtues) to be sensitive to the truths they told. It took, therefore, certain public events to illuminate (for me) the literature which might have illuminated them.

I am thinking, of course, of the recent demonstrations at Berkeley and elsewhere, whose ostensible causes were civil rights or freedom of speech or Vietnam, but whose not so secret slogan was all the time: *The Professor is a Fink!* And what an array of bad antiacademic novels, I cannot help reminding myself, written by disgruntled professors, created the mythology out of which that slogan grew. Each generation of students is invented by the generation of teachers just before them; but how different they are in dream and fact—as different as self-hatred and its reflection in another. How different the professors in Jeremy Larner's *Drive, He Said* from those even in Randall Jarrell's *Pictures from an Institution* or Mary McCarthy's *Groves of Academe*.

To be sure, many motives operated to set the students in action, some of them imagined in no book, however good or bad. Many of the thousands who resisted or shouted on campuses did so in the name of naïve or disingenuous or even nostalgic politics (be careful what you wish for in your middle age, or your children will parody it forthwith!); and sheer ennui doubtless played a role along with a justified rage against the hypocrisies of academic life. Universities have long rivaled the churches in their devotion to institutionalizing hypocrisy; and more recently they have outstripped television itself (which most professors affect to despise even more than they despise organized religion) in the institutionalization of boredom.

But what the students were protesting in large part, I have come to believe, was the very notion of man which the universities sought to impose upon them: that bourgeois-Protestant version of Humanism, with its view of man as justified by rationality, work, duty, vocation, maturity, success; and its concomitant understanding of childhood and adolescence as a temporarily privileged time of preparation for assuming those burdens. The new irrationalists, however, are prepared to advocate prolonging adolescence to the grave, and are ready to dispense with school as an outlived excuse for leisure. To them work is as obsolete as reason, a vestige (already dispensable for large numbers) of an economically marginal, pre-automated world; and the obsolescence of the two adds up to the obsolescence of everything our society understands by maturity.

Nor is it in the name of an older more valid Humanistic view of man that the new irrationalists would reject the WASP version; Rabelais is as alien to them as Benjamin Franklin. Disinterested scholarship, reflection, the life of reason, a respect for tradition stir (however dimly and confusedly) chiefly their contempt; and the Abbey of Theleme would seem as sterile to them as Robinson Crusoe's Island. To the classroom, the library, the laboratory, the office conference and the meeting of scholars, they prefer the demonstration, the sit-in, the riot: the mindless unity of an impassioned crowd (with guitars beating out the rhythm in the background), whose immediate cause is felt rather than thought out, whose ultimate cause is itself. In light of this, the Teach-in, often ill understood because of an emphasis on its declared political ends, can be seen as implicitly a parody and mockery of the real classroom: related to the actual business of the university, to real teaching, only as the Demonstration Trial (of Dimitrov, of the Soviet Doctors, of Eichmann) to real justice or Demonstration Voting (for one party or a token two) to real suffrage.

At least, since Berkeley (or perhaps since Martin Luther King provided students with new paradigms for action) the choice has been extended beyond what the earlier laureates of the new youth could imagine in the novel: the nervous breakdown at home rather than the return to "sanity" and school, which was the best Salinger could invent for Franny and Holden; or Kerouac's way out for his "saintly" vagrants, that "road" from nowhere to noplace with homemade gurus at the way stations. The structures of those fictional vaudevilles between hard covers that currently please the young *(Catch 22, V., A Mother's Kisses),* suggest in their brutality and discontinuity, their politics of mockery, something of the spirit of the student demonstrations; but only Jeremy Larner, as far as I know, has dealt explicitly with the abandonment of the classroom in favor of the Dionysiac pack, the turning from *polis* to *thiasos,* from forms of social organization traditionally thought of as male to the sort of passionate community attributed by the ancients to females out of control.

Conventional slogans in favor of "Good Works" (pious emendations of existing social structures, or extensions of accepted "rights" to excluded groups) though they provide the motive power of such protests are irrelevant to their form and their final significance. They become their essential selves, i.e., genuine new forms of rebellion, when the demonstrators hoist (as they did in the final stages of the Berkeley protests) the sort of slogan which embarrasses not only fellow travelers but even the bureaucrats who direct the initial stages of the revolt: at the University of California, the single four-letter word no family newspaper would reprint, though no member of a family who could read was likely not to know it.

It is possible to argue on the basis of the political facts themselves that the word "fuck" entered the whole scene accidentally (there were only four students behind the "Dirty Speech Movement," only fifteen hundred kids could be persuaded to demonstrate for it, etc., etc.). But the prophetic literature which anticipates the movement indicates otherwise, suggesting that the logic of their illogical course eventually sets the young against language itself, against the very counters of logical discourse. They seek an antilanguage of protest as inevitably as they seek antipoems and antinovels, end with the ultimate antiword, which the demonstrators at Berkeley disingenuously claimed stood for FREEDOM UNDER CLARK KERR.

Esthetics, however, had already anticipated politics in this regard; porno-poetry preceding and preparing the way for what Lewis Feuer has aptly called porno-politics. Already in 1963, in an essay entitled *"Phi Upsilon Kappa,"* the young poet Michael McClure was writing: "Gregory Corso has asked me to join with him in a project to free the word FUCK from its chains and strictures. I leap to make some new freedom. . . ." And McClure's own "Fuck Ode" is a product of this collaboration, as the very name of Ed Sanders' journal, *Fuck You,* is the creation of an analogous impulse. The aging critics of the young who have dealt with the Berkeley demonstrations in such journals as *Commentary* and the *New Leader* do not, however, read either Sanders' porno-pacifist magazine or *Kulchur,* in which McClure's manifesto was first printed —the age barrier separating readership in the United States more effectively than class, political affiliation, or anything else.

Their sense of porno-esthetics is likely to come from deserters from their own camp, chiefly Norman Mailer, and especially his recent *An American Dream,* which represents the entry of antilanguage (extending the tentative explorations of "The Time of Her Time") into the world of the middle-aged, both on the level of mass culture and that of yesterday's ex-Marxist, post-Freudian *avant-garde.* Characteristically enough, Mailer's book has occasioned in the latter quarters reviews as irrelevant, incoherent, misleading and fundamentally scared as the most philistine responses to the Berkeley demonstrations, Philip Rahv and Stanley Edgar Hyman providing two egregious examples. Yet elsewhere (in sectors held by those more at ease with their own conservatism, i.e., without defunct radicalisms to uphold) the most obscene forays of the young are being met with a disheartening kind of tolerance and even an attempt to adapt them to the conditions of commodity art.

But precisely here, of course, a disconcerting irony is involved; for after a while, there will be no Rahvs and Hymans left to shock —antilanguage becoming mere language with repeated use and in the face of acceptance; so that all sense of exhilaration will be lost along with the possibility of offense. What to do then except to choose silence, since raising the ante of violence is ultimately self-defeating; and the way of obscenity in any case leads as naturally to silence as to further excess? Moreover, to the talkative heirs of Socrates, silence is the one offense that never wears out, the radicalism that can never become fashionable; which is why, after the obscene slogan has been hauled down, a blank placard is raised in its place.

There are difficulties, to be sure, when one attempts to move from the politics of silence to an analogous sort of poetry. The opposite number to the silent picketer would be the silent poet, which is a contradiction in terms; yet there are these days nonsingers of (perhaps) great talent who shrug off the temptation to song with the muttered comment, "Creativity is out." Some, however, make literature of a kind precisely at the point of maximum tension between the tug toward silence and the pull toward publication. Music is a better language really for saying what one would prefer not to say at all—and all the way from certain sorts of sufficiently cool jazz to Rock and Roll (with its minimal lyrics that defy understanding on a first hearing), music is the preferred art of the irrationalists.

But some varieties of skinny poetry seem apt, too (as practised, say, by Robert Creeley after the example of W. C. Williams), since their lines are three parts silence to one part speech:

*My lady*
*fair with*
*soft*
*arms, what*
*can I say to*
*you—words, words . .*

And, of course, fiction aspiring to become Pop Art, say, *An American Dream* (with the experiments of Hemingway and Nathanael West behind it), works approximately as well, since clichés are almost as inaudible as silence itself. The point is not to shout, not to insist, but to hang cool, to baffle all mothers, cultural and spiritual as well as actual.

When the Town Council in Venice, California was about to close down a particularly notorious beatnik cafe, a lady asked to testify before them, presumably to clinch the case against the offenders. What she reported, however, was that each day as she walked by the cafe and looked in its windows, she saw the unsavory types who inhabited it "just standing there, looking—nonchalant." And, in a way, her improbable adjective does describe a crime against her world; for nonchaleur ("cool," the futurists themselves would prefer to call it) is the essence of their life style as well as of the literary styles to which they respond: the offensive style of those who are not so much *for* anything in particular, as "with it" in general.

But such an attitude is as remote from traditional "alienation," with its profound longing to end disconnection, as it is from ordinary forms of allegiance, with their desperate resolve not to admit disconnection. The new young celebrate disconnection—accept it as one of the necessary consequences of the industrial system which has delivered them from work and duty, of that welfare state which makes disengagement the last possible virtue, whether it call itself Capitalist, Socialist or Communist. "Detachment" is the traditional name for the stance the futurists assume; but "detachment" carries with it irrelevant religious, even specifically Christian overtones. The post-modernists are surely in some sense "mystics," religious at least in a way they do not ordinarily know how to confess, but they are not Christians.

Indeed, they regard Christianity, quite as the Black Muslims (with whom they have certain affinities) do, as a white ideology: merely one more method—along with Humanism, technology, Marxism—of imposing "White" or Western values on the colored rest of the world. To the new barbarian, however, that would-be post-Humanist (who is in most cases the white offspring of Christian forebears), his whiteness is likely to seem if not a stigma and symbol of shame, at least the outward sign of his exclusion from all that his Christian Humanist ancestors rejected in themselves and projected mythologically upon the colored man. For such reasons, his religion, when it becomes explicit, claims to be derived from Tibet or Japan or the ceremonies of the Plains Indians, or is composed out of the non-Christian submythology that has grown up among Negro jazz musicians and in the civil rights movement. When the new barbarian speaks of "soul," for instance, he means not "soul" as in Heaven, but as in "soul music" or even "soul food."

It is all part of the attempt of the generation under twenty-five, not exclusively in its most sensitive members but especially in them, to become Negro, even as they attempt to become poor or prerational. About this particular form of psychic assimilation I have written sufficiently in the past (summing up what I had been long saying in chapters seven and eight of *Waiting for the End*), neglecting only the sense in which what starts as a specifically American movement becomes an international one, spreading to the *yé-yé* girls of France or the working-class entertainers of Liverpool with astonishing swiftness and ease.

What interests me more particularly right now is a parallel assimilationist attempt, which may, indeed, be more parochial and is certainly most marked at the moment in the Anglo-Saxon world, i.e., in those cultural communities most totally committed to bourgeois-Protestant values and surest that they are unequivocally "white." I am thinking of the effort of young men in England and the United States to assimilate into themselves (or even to assimilate themselves into) that otherness, that sum total of rejected psychic elements which the middle-class heirs of the Renaissance have identified with "woman." To become new men, these children of the future seem to feel, they must' not only become more Black than White but more female than male. And it is natural that the need to make such an adjustment be felt with especial acuteness in post-Protestant highly industrialized societies, where the functions regarded as specifically male for some three hundred years tend most rapidly to become obsolete.

Surely, in America, machines already perform better than humans a large number of those aggressive-productive activities which our ancestors considered man's special province, even his *raison d'être*. Not only has the male's prerogative of making things and money (which is to say, of working) been preempted, but also his time-honored privilege of dealing out death by hand, which until quite recently was regarded as a supreme mark of masculine valor. While it seems theoretically possible, even in the heart of Anglo-Saxondom, to imagine a leisurely, pacific male, in fact the losses in secondary functions sustained by men appear to have shaken their faith in their primary masculine function as well, in their ability to achieve the conquest (as the traditional metaphor has it) of women. Earlier, advances in technology had detached the wooing and winning of women from the begetting of children; and though the invention of the condom had at least left the decision to inhibit fatherhood in the power of males, its replacement by the "loop" and the "pill" has placed paternity at the mercy of the whims of women.

Writers of fiction and verse registered the technological obsolescence of masculinity long before it was felt even by the representative minority who give to the present younger generation its character and significance. And literary critics have talked a good deal during the past couple of decades about the conversion of the literary hero into the nonhero or the antihero; but they have in general failed to notice his simultaneous conversion into the non- or antimale. Yet ever since Hemingway at least, certain male protagonists of American literature have not only fled rather than sought out combat but have also fled rather than sought out women. From Jake Barnes to Holden Caulfield they have continued to run from the threat of female sexuality; and, indeed, there are models for such evasion in our classic books, where heroes still eager for the fight (Natty Bumppo comes to mind) are already shy of wives and sweethearts and mothers.

It is not absolutely required that the antimale antihero be impotent or homosexual or both (though this helps, as we remember remembering Walt Whitman), merely that he be more seduced than seducing, more passive than active. Consider, for instance, the oddly "womanish" Herzog of Bellow's current best seller, that Jewish Emma Bovary with a Ph.D., whose chief flaw is physical vanity and a taste for fancy clothes. Bellow, however, is more interested in summing up the past than in evoking the future; and *Herzog* therefore seems an end rather than a beginning, the product of nostalgia (remember when there were real Jews once, and the "Jewish Novel" had not yet been discovered!) rather than prophecy. No, the post-humanist, post-male, post-white, post-heroic world is a post-Jewish world by the same token, anti-Semitism as inextricably woven into it as into the movement for Negro rights; and its scriptural books are necessarily *goyish,* not least of all William Burroughs' *The Naked Lunch.*

Burroughs is the chief prophet of the post-male post-heroic world; and it is his emulators who move into the center of the relevant literary scene, for *The Naked Lunch* (the later novels are less successful, less exciting but relevant still) is more than it seems: no mere essay in heroin-hallucinated homosexual pornography—but a nightmare anticipation (in Science Fiction form) of post-Humanist sexuality. Here, as in Alexander Trocchi, John Rechy, Harry Matthews (even an occasional Jew like Allen Ginsberg, who has begun by inscribing properly anti-Jewish obscenities on the walls of the world), are clues to the new attitudes toward sex that will continue to inform our improbable novels of passion and our even more improbable love songs.

The young to whom I have been referring, the mythologically representative minority (who, by a process that infuriates the mythologically inert majority out of which they come, "stand for" their times), live in a community in which what used to be called the "Sexual Revolution," the Freudian-Laurentian revolt of their grandparents and parents, has triumphed as imperfectly and unsatisfactorily as all revolutions always triumph. They confront, therefore, the necessity of determining not only what meanings "love" can have in their new world, but—even more disturbingly—what significance, if any, "male" and "female" now possess. For a while, they (or at least their literary spokesmen recruited from the generation just before them) seemed content to celebrate a kind of *reductio* or *exaltatio ad absurdum* of their parents' once revolutionary sexual goals: The Reichian-inspired Cult of the Orgasm.

Young men and women eager to be delivered of traditional ideologies of love find especially congenial the belief that not union or relationship (much less offspring) but physical release is the end of the sexual act; and that, therefore, it is a matter of indifference with whom or by what method ones pursues the therapeutic climax, so long as that climax is total and repeated frequently. And Wilhelm Reich happily detaches this belief from the vestiges of Freudian rationalism, setting it instead in a context of Science Fiction and witchcraft; but his emphasis upon "full genitality," upon growing up and away from infantile pleasures, strikes the young as a disguised plea for the "maturity" they have learned to despise. In a time when the duties associated with adulthood promise to become irrelevant, there seems little reason for denying oneself the joys of babyhood—even if these are associated with such regressive fantasies as escaping it all in the arms of little sister (in the Gospel according to J. D. Salinger) or flirting with the possibility of getting into bed with papa (in the Gospel according to Norman Mailer).

Only Norman O. Brown in *Life Against Death* has come to terms on the level of theory with the aspiration to take the final evolutionary leap and cast off adulthood completely, at least in the area of sex. His post-Freudian program for pansexual, nonorgasmic love rejects "full genitality" in favor of a species of indiscriminate bundling, a dream of unlimited subcoital intimacy which Brown calls (in his vocabulary the term is an honorific) "polymorphous perverse." And here finally is an essential clue to the nature of the second sexual revolution, the post-sexual revolution, first evoked in literature by Brother Antoninus more than a decade ago, in a verse prayer addressed somewhat improbably to the Christian God:

> *Annul in me my manhood, Lord, and make*
> *Me woman sexed and weak . . .*
> > *Make me then*
> *Girl-hearted, virgin-souled, woman-docile, maiden-meek . . .*

Despite the accents of this invocation, however, what is at work is not essentially a homosexual revolt or even a rebellion against women, though its advocates seek to wrest from women their ancient privileges of receiving the Holy Ghost and pleasuring men; and though the attitudes of the movement can be adapted to the antifemale bias of, say, Edward Albee. If in *Who's Afraid of Virginia Woolf* Albee can portray the relationship of two homosexuals (one in drag) as the model of contemporary marriage, this must be because contemporary marriage has in fact turned into something much like that parody. And it is true that what survives of bourgeois marriage and the bourgeois family is a target which the new barbarians join the old homosexuals in reviling, seeking to replace Mom, Pop and the kids with a neo-Whitmanian gaggle of giggling *camerados*. Such groups are, in fact, whether gathered in coffee houses, university cafeterias or around the literature tables on campuses, the peacetime equivalents, as it were, to the demonstrating crowd. But even their program of displacing Dick-Jane-Spot-Baby, etc., the WASP family of grade school primers, is not the fundamental motive of the post-sexual revolution.

What is at stake from Burroughs to Bellow, Ginsberg to Albee, Salinger to Gregory Corso is a more personal transformation: a radical metamorphosis of the Western male—utterly unforeseen in the decades before us, but visible now in every high school and college classroom, as well as on the paperback racks in airports and supermarkets. All around us, young males are beginning to retrieve for themselves the cavalier role once piously and class-consciously surrendered to women: *that of being beautiful and being loved.* Here once more the example of the Negro—the feckless and adorned Negro male with the blood of Cavaliers in his veins—has served as a model. And what else is left to young men, in any case, after the devaluation of the grim duties they had arrogated to themselves in place of the pursuit of loveliness?

All of us who are middle-aged and were Marxists, which is to say, who once numbered ourselves among the last assured Puritans, have surely noticed in ourselves a vestigial roundhead rage at the new hair styles of the advanced or—if you please—delinquent young. Watching young men titivate their locks (the comb, the pocket mirror and the bobby pin having replaced the jackknife, catcher's mitt and brass knuckles), we feel the same baffled resentment that stirs in us when we realize that they have rejected work. A job and unequivocal maleness—these are two sides of the same Calvinist coin, which in the future buys nothing.

Few of us, however, have really understood how the Beatle hair-do is part of a syndrome, of which high heels, jeans tight over the buttocks, etc., are other aspects, symptomatic of a larger retreat from masculine aggressiveness to female allure—in literature and the arts to the style called "camp." And fewer still have realized how that style, though the invention of homosexuals, is now the possession of basically heterosexual males as well, a strategy in their campaign to establish a new relationship not only with women but with their own masculinity. In the course of that campaign, they have embraced certain kinds of gesture and garb, certain accents and tones traditionally associated with females or female impersonators; which is why we have been observing recently (in life as well as fiction and verse) young boys, quite unequivocally male, playing all the traditional roles of women: the vamp, the coquette, the whore, the icy tease, the pure young virgin.

Not only oldsters, who had envisioned and despaired of quite another future, are bewildered by this turn of events, but young girls, too, seem scarcely to know what is happening—looking on with that new, schizoid stare which itself has become a hallmark of our times. And the crop-headed jocks, those crew-cut athletes who represent an obsolescent masculine style based on quite other values, have tended to strike back blindly; beating the hell out of some poor kid whose hair is too long or whose pants are too tight—quite as they once beat up young communists for revealing that their politics had become obsolete. Even heterosexual writers, however, have been slow to catch up, the revolution in sensibility running ahead of that in expression; and they have perforce permitted homosexuals to speak for them (Burroughs and Genet and Baldwin and Ginsberg and Albee and a score of others), even to invent the forms in which the future will have to speak.

The revolt against masculinity is not limited, however, to simple matters of coiffure and costume, visible even to athletes; or to the adaptation of certain campy styles and modes to new uses. There is also a sense in which two large social movements that have set the young in motion and furnished images of action for their books— movements as important in their own right as porno-politics and the pursuit of the polymorphous perverse—are connected analogically to the abdication from traditional maleness. The first of these is nonviolent or passive resistance, so oddly come back to the land of its inventor, that icy Thoreau who dreamed a love which ". . . has not much human blood in it, but consists with a certain disregard for men and their erections. . . ."

The civil rights movement, however, in which nonviolence has found a home, has been hospitable not only to the sort of post-humanist I have been describing; so that at a demonstration (Selma, Alabama will do as an example) the true hippie will be found side by side with backwoods Baptists, nuns on a spiritual spree, boy bureaucrats practicing to take power, resurrected socialists, Unitarians in search of a God, and just plain tourists, gathered, as once at the Battle of Bull Run, to see the fun. For each of these, nonviolence will have a different sort of fundamental meaning—as a tactic, a camouflage, a passing fad, a pious gesture—but for each in part, and for the post-humanist especially, it will signify the possibility of heroism without aggression, effective action without guilt.

There have always been two contradictory American ideals: to be the occasion of maximum violence, and to remain absolutely innocent. Once, however, these were thought hopelessly incompatible for males (except, perhaps, as embodied in works of art), reserved strictly for women: the spouse of the wife beater, for instance, or the victim of rape. But males have now assumed these classic roles; and just as a particularly beleaguered wife occasionally slipped over the dividing line into violence, so do the new passive protesters— leaving us to confront (or resign to the courts) such homey female questions as: *Did Mario Savio really bite that cop in the leg as he sagged limply toward the ground?*

The second social movement is the drug cult, more widespread among youth, from its squarest limits to its most beat, than anyone seems prepared to admit in public; and at its beat limit at least inextricably involved with the civil rights movement, as the recent arrests of Peter DeLissovoy and Susan Ryerson revealed even to the ordinary newspaper reader. "Police said that most of the recipients [of marijuana] were college students," the U.P. story runs. "They quoted Miss Ryerson and DeLissovoy as saying that many of the letter packets were sent to civil rights workers." Only fiction and verse, however, has dealt with the conjunction of homosexuality, drugs and civil rights, eschewing the general piety of the press which has been unwilling to compromise "good works" on behalf of the Negro by associating them with the deep radicalism of a way of life based on the ritual consumption of "pot."

The widespread use of such hallucinogens as peyote, marijuana, the "Mexican mushroom," LSD, etc., as well as pep pills, goof balls, airplane glue, certain kinds of cough syrups and even, though in many fewer cases, heroin, is not merely a matter of a changing taste in stimulants but of the programmatic espousal of an antipuritanical mode of existence—hedonistic and detached—one more strategy in the war on time and work. But it is also (to pursue my analogy once more) an attempt to arrogate to the male certain traditional privileges of the female. What could be more womanly, as Elémire Zolla was already pointing out some years ago, than permitting the penetration of the body by a foreign object which not only stirs delight but even (possibly) creates new life?

In any case, with drugs we have come to the crux of the futurist revolt, the hinge of everything else, as the young tell us over and over in their writing. When the movement was first finding a voice, Allen Ginsberg set this aspect of it in proper context in an immensely comic, utterly serious poem called "America," in which "pot" is associated with earlier forms of rebellion, a commitment to catatonia, and a rejection of conventional male potency:

> *America I used to be a communist when I was a kid I'm not sorry.*
> *I smoke marijuana every chance I get.*
> *I sit in my house for days on end and stare at the roses in the closet.*
> *When I go to Chinatown I . . . never get laid . . .*

Similarly, Michael McClure reveals in his essay, *"Phi Upsilon Kappa,"* that before penetrating the "cavern of Anglo-Saxon," whence he emerged with the slogan of the ultimate Berkeley demonstrators, he had been on mescalin. "I have emerged from a dark night of the soul; I entered it by Peyote." And by now, drug-taking has become as standard a feature of the literature of the young as oral-genital love-making. I flip open the first issue of yet another ephemeral San Francisco little magazine quite at random and read: "I tie up and the main pipe [the ante-cobital vein, for the clinically inclined] swells like a prideful beggar beneath the skin. Just before

I get on it is always the worst." Worse than the experience, however, is its literary rendering; and the badness of such confessional fiction, flawed by the sentimentality of those who desire to live "like a cunning vegetable," is a badness we older readers find it only too easy to perceive, as our sons and daughters find it only too easy to overlook. Yet precisely here the age and the mode define themselves; for not in the master but in the hacks new forms are established, new lines drawn.

Here, at any rate, is where the young lose us in literature as well as life, since here they pass over into real revolt, i.e., what we really cannot abide, hard as we try. The mother who has sent her son to private schools and on to Harvard to keep him out of classrooms overcrowded with poor Negroes, rejoices when he sets out for Mississippi with his comrades in SNCC, but shudders when he turns on with LSD; just as the ex-Marxist father, who has earlier proved radicalism impossible, rejoices to see his son stand up, piously and pompously, for CORE or SDS, but trembles to hear him quote Alpert and Leary or praise Burroughs. Just as certainly as liberalism is the LSD of the aging, LSD is the radicalism of the young.

If whiskey long served as an appropriate symbolic excess for those who chafed against Puritan restraint without finally challenging it—temporarily releasing them to socially harmful aggression and (hopefully) sexual self-indulgence, the new popular drugs provide an excess quite as satisfactorily symbolic to the post-Puritans —releasing them from sanity to madness by destroying in them the inner restrictive order which has somehow survived the dissolution of the outer. It is finally insanity, then, that the futurists learn to admire and emulate, quite as they learn to pursue vision instead of learning, hallucination rather than logic. The schizophrenic replaces the sage as their ideal, their new culture hero, figured forth as a giant schizoid Indian (his madness modeled in part on the author's own experiences with LSD) in Ken Kesey's *One Flew Over the Cuckoo's Nest.*

The hippier young are not alone, however, in their taste for the insane; we live in a time when readers in general respond sympathetically to madness in literature wherever it is found, in established writers as well as in those trying to establish new modes. Surely it is not the lucidity and logic of Robert Lowell or Theodore Roethke or John Berryman which we admire, but their flirtation with incoherence and disorder. And certainly it is Mailer at his most nearly psychotic, Mailer the creature rather than the master of his fantasies who moves us to admiration; while in the case of Saul Bellow, we endure the theoretical optimism and acceptance for the sake of the delightful melancholia, the fertile paranoia which he cannot disavow any more than the talent at whose root they lie. Even essayists and analysts recommend themselves to us these days by a certain redemptive nuttiness; at any rate, we do not love, say, Marshall McLuhan less because he continually risks sounding like the body-fluids man in *Dr. Strangelove*.

We have, moreover, recently been witnessing the development of a new form of social psychiatry[2] (a psychiatry of the future already anticipated by the literature of the future) which considers some varieties of "schizophrenia" not diseases to be cured but forays into an unknown psychic world: random penetrations by bewildered internal cosmonauts of a realm that it will be the task of the next generations to explore. And if the accounts which the returning schizophrenics give (the argument of the apologists runs) of the "places" they have been are fantastic and garbled, surely they are no more so than, for example, Columbus' reports of the world he had claimed for Spain, a world bounded—according to his newly drawn maps—by Cathay on the north and Paradise on the south.

In any case, poets and junkies have been suggesting to us that the new world appropriate to the new men of the latter twentieth century is to be discovered only by the conquest of inner space: by an adventure of the spirit, an extension of psychic possibility, of which the flights into outer space—moonshots and expeditions to Mars—are precisely such unwitting metaphors and analogues as the voyages of exploration were of the earlier breakthrough into the Renaissance, from whose consequences the young seek now so des-

---

[2] Described in an article in the *New Left Review* of November-December, 1964, by R. D. Laing who advocates "ex-patients helping future patients go mad."

perately to escape. The laureate of that new conquest is William Burroughs; and it is fitting that the final word be his:

"This war will be won in the air. In the Silent Air with Image Rays. You were a pilot remember? Tracer bullets cutting the right wing you were free in space a few seconds before in blue space between eyes. Go back to Silence. Keep Silence. Keep Silence. K.S. K.S. . . . From Silence re-write the message that is you. You are the message I send to The Enemy. My Silent Message."

The Naked Astronauts were free in space. . . .

—1965

# CROSS THE BORDER—CLOSE THE GAP

# Introduction

AS THE TWENTIETH CENTURY enters its eighth decade and I myself
move on into my sixth, it becomes ever more apparent that I, like
all other literary survivors of "Modernism," whether poets, drama-
tists, novelists, or critics, must come to terms with the death of that
movement. Still seemingly immortal during my own youth, it survived neither that youth nor the second Great War which climaxed
it; but its metaphorical demise passed unnoticed at first among the
real deaths of millions of real men and women. Since 1955, however, no one has been able to doubt that the movement represented
in its declining years by Pound and Eliot and Valéry, as well as by
Proust and Mann and Joyce, is dead and gone—leaving to its heirs
(who can never be sure they are not also its murderers) an obligation to graveside oratory. Some mourn aloud; some pretend to indifference; others frankly and openly rejoice as at a deliverance. But
I am moved to do none of them, willing ever to let the dead bury
the dead and glad only that I am not among them. Instead I have,
as the following essays bear witness, felt obligated rather to proph-
esy what will come next—attempting in a score of ways, all tentative and profoundly ambivalent, to surmise the character and
probable destiny of the movement for which there is still no better
name than Post-Modernism.

To deal with that new movement, quite obviously it will be necessary to develop a really new criticism, free of all vestiges of the
elitism and the Culture Religion which still obsessed our immediate
predecessors. I have, therefore, become more and more interested
in the kinds of books with which such elitist approaches have had
the most difficulty in dealing—turning from the Modernist canon of

403

subtle and difficult works whose readers could scarcely help feeling themselves chosen as well as few to the kind of books which no one has ever congratulated himself on being able to read: books which join together all possible audiences, children and adults, women and men, the sophisticated and the naïve. And in pursuit of such works, I have been willing to cross the border which once separated High Art from Pop.

I am convinced that criticism at the moment can no longer condescend to popular literature as, in fact, my own earlier criticism did; that it must resist all impulses to create hierarchies, even those implicit in what seem harmless distinctions of genre or medium. For this reason, the reader will discover jumbled together in this section reflections on movies, comic books, on pop songs and Japanese woodblock prints, as well as more traditional analyses of novels and poems—which is to say, will perceive that I do my best not to reject those works of art whose muse is a machine and whose fate seems more closely linked to the history of Technology than that of the Spirit. He will further perceive that I have concentrated on the mythic element in all of these, which is to say, on an element which is indifferent to medium, rather than on those formal elements which distinguish one medium from another.

I am quite aware that there is a kind of politics implicit in the critical position I take in these essays, a populist, even anarchist stance based on an impatience with all distinctions of kind created on the analogy of a class-structured society. I feel myself more and more pressed these days toward the position so outrageously expressed by Tolstoi in his essay *What is Art?* I am still resisting the temptation, however, finally to embrace the point of view which urges that the only art worth preserving and praising is the art which joins all men together at their deepest and simplest level of response. In fairness to my own past and my own work as a novelist and poet, I feel it necessary to retain still a respect for traditional high art. Nonetheless, I grow more and more uncomfortably aware that the cult based on the appreciation of works available only to a few has proved not only repressive in a political sense, but even more damaging in a psychological one.

If I live long enough, perhaps I shall finally grow young enough to disavow all vestiges of the humanistic tradition that persist in my thinking—turning my back on the past, recent and remote, quite as if, like some fifteen-year-old, I, too, inhabit a world I never made. The truth is that I feel myself in such an alien world, having been reborn for the second time in my life some five or six years ago and being therefore very young, indeed. Like many in my generation, I have been *thrice* born—first into radical dissent, then into radical disillusion and the fear of innocence, finally into whatever it is that lies beyond both commitment and disaffection. This means that for me the model of Dionysus no longer works, since he was only twice born: once of the Mother, the next time of the Father. What remains, I suppose, is to dare—without mythological precedent—to be born of one's own children.

In any case, the reader should be aware that this second volume of my essays is the product of my third birth, as the first volume is of my second; my original innocence is recorded in print nowhere at all, since I have never published anything I wrote before the age of thirty. My first book (retrospectively called *An End to Innocence*) appeared, in fact, as I was approaching the close of the fourth decade of my life, so that I have felt free with the passage of years to invent and live into a youth which belongs not to history but to myth, not to fact, but to my dreams. Somewhere in his letters Mark Twain casually observes that he had never dreamed himself anything but a young man, and I suspect this is true of all of us. But this is a way of saying, is it not, that however far we may have progressed past innocence in our waking lives, once asleep we revert to that pristine state of innocence which apparently did not, cannot end once and for all. That innocence we are continually beginning to end.

# Some Notes on Ukiyoe:
# A Word on the History of Taste and
# Three Dissenting Opinions

I AM GRATEFUL to Mr. Michener's book* for two reasons: first, because it is high time that there be a popular book by an American on an art which is both popular and (in a real though secondary sense) American; and second, because I have been long waiting for an occasion to say something about an art form that has moved and shaped me in a way to which I find it hard to do justice. From about the time of the Restoration of the Stuarts to the beginning of our own Civil War, a group of middle-class Japanese painters, who did not consider themselves artists in any serious sense of the word, produced for mass distribution what they called *ukiyoe* or floating world pictures, which possess, accidentally, as it were, the merits of high art. These pictures have in common a technique and a subject matter; they are printed from wood blocks in several colors and portray (more than three-quarters of them at any rate) popular actors and well-known prostitutes—or, as the Japanese prefer to say, *bijin*, "beautiful persons." They are, in a word, pin-ups.

It is difficult for such pictures, which are neither singular examples of technique nor portrayals of traditional subjects, to find honor inside of their own culture. Especially in Japan, where one by one the arts, the skills, the sports—the very looking at a maple leaf or drinking a cup of tea—have been subsumed under the contempla-

---

* James A. Michener, *The Floating World.*

tive ideals of Zen Buddhism, where everything to be thought worthy had to be rethought in terms of eternity, it is nearly impossible to take seriously so resolutely secular an art. Only sex in Japan has remained a matter of fact; for in that culture, the attempt so basic to our own to religify sex and sexualize religion has not, so far as I know, ever been made; and *ukiyoe* are, as we shall see, fundamentally sexual.

Even yet, most qualified Japanese will not grant *ukiyoe* to be an art at all. As an *art,* it was invented from certain examples which happened to survive—twice over: once by the French "decadents" of the end of the nineteenth century; and once by rich Americans intent on making us truly the heirs of all the ages. To the "decadents" (I use the Continental name rather than our more honorific word "symbolists" to help make the point), there was in these prints a whiff of something at once delicate and corrupt, nonrealistic and sexual, which they confused with the newly rehabilitated pre-Raphaelites, certain contemporary tendencies in painting, etc. Those epicene, barely adolescent little dishes of Harunobu, for instance, they blended in their own minds with the Virgins of Fra Angelico, making that hash of titillation and religiosity which tickled them.

As for the American millionaires, they were apparently delighted to find a style at once so exotic and congenial. *Ukiyoe* is, of course, bourgeois and open—the most undifficult and human of the Oriental arts. One has to think only of the way in which the human figure is annihilated by symbolic nature and space in a Zen painting and compare it with the way the face of a pretty girl possesses the whole area of a *ukiyoe* print to get the point. In addition, the prints were relatively cheap; and the sense of getting a bargain, of buying at the lowest rate what its owners do not know to be a treasure, attracts the businessman even out of hours. The Japanese soon caught on, to be sure, upping the prices and producing the excellent counterfeits of which our museums are full; but meanwhile the decisive moment was past. The handbills and souvenirs of the red-light district of eighteenth-century Tokyo were well on the way to becoming an art of the American museum.

The moment at which *ukiyoe* as a living form disappears is the moment of the opening of Japan by the American fleet. This art, which must have seemed another country to the Japanese officially closed off during its life to all other countries, is ready to hand when America begins the attempt to assimilate culturally what it has inherited politically. Along with the garishness of Chinese Manchu art, it is the Orientalism easiest to come to terms with at a time when Orientalism was becoming the keynote of American acquisitive interior decorating. From the interiors of Beacon Street, *ukiyoe* found its way into the museums of Boston and westward from there along the main lines of Chautauqua culture. At any rate, for better or worse (and astonishingly, it is for better), America possesses at the moment the largest collections of Japanese prints anywhere.

Sufficient unto these collections is Mr. Michener's book. For my taste it is in spots a little offhand and breezy, sometimes popularizing rather than popular; but it is informative and enthusiastic —a labor of love, its scholarship, as far as I can tell, scrupulous. My sole large objection, and it is a very large one, is to the quality of the reproductions, which are abominable in every regard. The colors are so poor that reference from textual comment to reproduction often leaves one utterly confused, the famous sensitive line blurred and broken.

I do not, of course, agree with all of Mr. Michener's judgments and explanations; and I should like to register three special dissents, based on a taste and a method of interpretation quite different from his own. "Therefore *ukiyoe*. . .," Mr. Michener says at one point, "was a religious word carrying strong Buddhist overtones; the sad, floating, evanescent, grief-stricken world. . . . A less appropriate title for the kinds of pictures we shall meet in this book would be difficult to devise." This is hard even to understand, much less agree with. Mr. Michener could scarcely deny that the world of *ukiyoe*—the world of entertainers paring their toenails, rouging their lips, hurriedly suckling babies between customers, or watching in mirrors the comb passing through the curtain of hair before their hidden face—is a world of vanity. Perhaps he only intends to say that it is hardly a "grief-stricken" world, that its proper tone is a joy which does not even imagine, much less contemplate fearfully, a tomorrow. But the painters in the backrooms of brothels knew the half-world in which they lived: the cages outside of the houses in which the girls were displayed, the guards at the gates of the district to keep them from escaping the realm of "pleasure." There is a melancholy, a nuance of sickly sweet disgust behind their bright flat patterns, the sparkle of their mica backgrounds. One cannot scrupulously follow the month to month shift of fashionable hair-dos (so that experts date the prints from the changing coiffures), or shift subject as popular preference shifts from beauty to beauty, without acquiring some awareness of the treachery of sense and time.

But there is more than this. The two great compulsive themes of *ukiyoe* are the prostitute and the actor, the paid simulator of pleasure and the paid performer of rage and grief; and these archetypes, these living reminders of the difference between "seems" and "is" give the Japanese print a metaphysical dimension. The actor prints especially present simulation *in depth,* being counterfeits in ink and paper of an actor imitating a puppet imitating a human being (for such is *kabuki,* the dramatic art the printmakers exploited). To this subject matter the manner of *ukiyoe* perfectly corresponds.

It is, at first glance, all manner, a mannerist art. Mr. Michener quite properly protests against the older moralizing histories of *ukiyoe* which presented this fact as a condemnation of *ukiyoe,* a revelation of its "decadence." But though his individual judgment of merit differs from those of the moralists, his understanding of what mannerism in general is remains the same as theirs; and he fails to get their essential point or to see them in terms of the non-Japanese art they most resemble. *Ukiyoe* not declines into but begins with distortion and device: the trifling with point of view, the search for effect. And the neck of an impossible Utomaro woman is extended in the same way and for the same reasons as that of the infamous "Virgin of the Long Neck" of Parmagianino.

But we know now the metaphysics to which such distortion aspires, and we do not despise an Utomaro any more than a Tintoretto or an El Greco. The mannerism of the Japanese is not like ours learned or mystical; but the printmakers who learn to show in a single print a woman's face through her hair, behind a fan or a screen and in a mirror; who illuminate one scene from three different sources of light; who study the human body and its distortion at the point where, say, a foot passes from air into water; soon discover that, whatever their intent, they have invented a language for discoursing on appearance and reality.

The key symbol of *ukiyoe* is the mirror: the maiden bent to her glass to discover the illusion which is her face—or the wild girl peering through the tangle of her hair into the pool caught in the hollow of a rock. "Vanity, vanity!" is the text; and we do not need the scallops of cloud that Harunobu and others use for the upper frames of their pictures to tell us conventionally that all this, too, shall pass away.

"One is struck by certain similarities between the fate of *ukiyoe* in Japan and the state of poetry in America. Each was once a popular art. . . . Each became sterile and died for the lack of vital new ideas. Belatedly . . . the reborn art had to be content with an esoteric existence." Wrong again—wrong on all counts. Poetry was, of course, never a popular art, in any meaning of that word; and insofar as it died at all, died precisely because it sought to become one. The comparison proper to *ukiyoe* is not with a formal and traditional art of any kind, but with the movies, with the comics, with television, and jazz.

"Popular" is too ambiguous a word to trust; for two of its commonest meanings are middlebrow and folk. But *ukiyoe* is lowbrow and urban—a mass-produced art of the city. Like all other mass arts, its rise is coincident with the development of a new mechanical device which makes possible mass production. The cases of the movies and television are obvious; and even jazz could not become generally accepted before the perfection of cheap phonograph recordings. The invention which made *ukiyoe* possible was *kento,* a reliable system of guides to insure perfect superimposition of several color blocks.

The Japanese print, it must be pointed out, is not a wood-block engraving in our usual understanding of the term; it is a strange enough thing in all conscience: the mechanical reproduction of a drawing that never existed outside of a shorthand indication. Like all the mass arts, it is not only antigenteel and antisentimental, but also without any consciousness of itself as art—and therefore quite content to be produced on the assembly line. And yet somehow the original conception of the artist manages to survive the engraver, the printer and the publisher; for the wood block on which the latter collaborate is not a medium but a means of distribution.

It is hard to see even any change in the conventions of drawing brought about by the transition from painting to printings. The single exception may be the matter of line, which began as the thick, modulated stroke of the writing brush and was thinned in time into a penlike sensitivity. The trend is from abstraction to representation, from (in the case of the *bijin)* calligraphy to pornography. In the beginning, the outlines of the female figure are almost Chinese characters for woman; in the end, they respond sensitively to the current conventions of sexual attractiveness.

Most important of all, the mass art begins not as ritual, but as "entertainment," which is to say, as titillation wrapped as a commodity in a secularized world. If it becomes high art, it must do so secretly, behind the backs of its consumers and even sometimes of its creators. Its mere popularity is not hopelessly inimical to seriousness, but it is discouraging; and certainly it stands in the way of the critics who find it hard to consider such work seriously. It requires a peculiar sort of sophistication to go in search of excellence in Krazy Kat or Charlie Chaplin or Louis Armstrong; and the Japanese did not themselves develop such a sophistication. It required the intervention of American appreciators to make the leap, in a way not unlike that in which French musicologists had to lead the way to serious analysis of our own jazz.

It is the hopeful lesson of *ukiyoe* that even the most mechanical and debased demand for "entertainment" can stir into life a true art and that such an art can manage to get by in a society which fundamentally despises it. But it is also the lesson of *ukiyoe* that such an art quite quickly exhausts its meager resources, and, being forbidden real experimentation, cannot renew itself. The modern attempts of a few Japanese to redeem this lapsed mass art on an "esoteric" level suggest to me not Eliot or Pound, whom Mr. Michener's comparison seems intended to evoke, but the not quite convincing, middlebrow efforts of a Gershwin or a Brubeck.

"Anyone familiar with western art who studies the prints reproduced in this book must conclude that one of the striking characteristics of *ukiyoe* is its freedom from erotic content. *Ukiyoe* avoids nakedness and foregoes slick suggestiveness." Of the four *ukiyoe* prints I myself own, one is a triple print by Utamaro showing a group of abalone fisherwomen in varying degrees of nakedness; the second a study of a nude stepping into her bath by Harunobu; the third, also by Utamaro, the head and upper torso of a girl from "one of the six best houses," fully clothed to be sure; and the fourth an anonymous piece of hopeful pornography showing an ancient gentleman with a grotesquely oversized phallus addressing himself rather dreamily to a *bijin,* whose face is all calm and submission. Both the old gentleman and the girl are fully dressed except for adjustments necessary to their sport. It is only in this latter sense that *ukiyoe* "avoids nakedness."

Even excluding the simple pornography of which my last item is an example, one could assemble an interesting and worthy collection of nudes and quasi-nudes from the masters of *ukiyoe.* It is a subject which intrigued not only Utamaro and Harunobu but even the more "classical" Koryusai. In an art which so desperately sought to render texture without shading, one would expect a concern with the contrast of silk and flesh, the bare breast falling out of the kimono, etc. The Japanese printmaker is almost always averse to showing mere nakedness, to be sure; even in my Harunobu print, where the girl is quite nude, her kimono hangs on a screen behind her. The point is the opposite of what it may seem. For the Japanese, the folds of the kimono itself, the constriction of the obi, the formalization of the female which denies the mere natural curves of the body is more erotic that the blatant display of nakedness.

It is easy enough to say that the nudes in the triple Utamaro are merely working girls, stripped for their trade—but why this concern with their trade? I remember quite well the Japanese who sold it to me asserting with a sly grin that this was a "spring picture," a term that I did not then understand, but which I have learned since means simply pornography. Of course, it was all in part salesmanship—this appeal to the barbarian; but there was, too, a conviction that nudeness portrayed under any pretext was aimed at provocation. The distinction between the "dirty book," which Mr. Michener tells us took almost half the time of the greatest talents of *ukiyoe,* and their other work is not nearly so great as he assumes.

From the lower left-hand corner of my Harunobu, a little green frog looks directly upward into the unseen shadow of the raised leg of the bather about to get into the tub. He is the symbol of the springtime in a hundred poems, of the Buddhist awakening to a new life; and the leap he signifies in this secular study is a gentle and melancholy parody of spiritual rebirth. But my clothed Utamaro beauty is the most voluptuous of all, though all her hidden body must be declared by her face; the slit eyes, the willow eyebrows, but especially the outrageously cruel and tiny mouth with the stiff curled prong of its protruding tongue.

Even the actors who constitute the second great theme of *ukiyoe* are essentially erotic objects, whether the frail players of female parts with their epicene charm or the great, virile lady-killers of legend—their front hair shaved off according to the law that sought to protect the virtue of their beholders; but the purple scarf that conceals their mutilated manly beauty itself a flaunting provocation.

It is the subtlety which I am afraid fools Mr. Michener, the nuance where we expect the blatancy of calendar art or Rubens. *Shibui* is the adjective that represents the life style toward which Japanese ethos aspires; and *shibui* means something between astringent and austere. To the true Zen devoté, the *shibui hito* with his cracked brown teapot and the single character by an ancient calligrapher on his wall, the impact of the *bijin* is like Marilyn Monroe. To our earlier critics, those girls of Harunobu, as supple and evasive as an erotic dream, looked like the angels of a fourteenth-century Italian fresco; and even to Mr. Michener their promise of the subtlest of frictions seems "aloof, solemn and proper." Alas!

*Missoula, Montana*
—1954

# The Middle Against Both Ends

I AM surely one of the few people pretending to intellectual respectability who can boast that he has read more comic books than attacks on comic books. I do not mean that I have consulted or studied the comics—I have read them, often with some pleasure. Nephews and nieces, my own children, and the children of neighbors have brought them to me to share their enjoyment. An old lady on a ferry boat in Puget Sound once dropped two in my lap in wordless sympathy: I was wearing, at the time, a sailor's uniform.

I have somewhat more difficulty in getting through the books that attack them. I am put off, to begin with, by inaccuracies of fact. When Mr. Geoffrey Wagner in his *Parade of Pleasure* calls Superboy "Superman's brother" (he is, of course, Superman himself as a child), I am made suspicious. Actually, Mr. Wagner's book is one of the least painful on the subject; confused, to be sure, but quite lively and not in the least smug; though it propounds the preposterous theory that the whole of "popular literature" is a conspiracy on the part of the "plutos" to corrupt an innocent American people. Such easy melodrama can only satisfy someone prepared to believe, as Mr. Wagner apparently does, that the young girls of Harlem are being led astray by the *double-entendres* of blues records!

Mr. Wagner's notions are at least more varied and subtle than Mr. Gershon Legman's, who cries out in his *Love and Death* that it is simply our sexual frustrations which breed a popular literature dedicated to violence. But Mr. Legman's theory explains too much: not only comic books but Hemingway, war, Luce, Faulkner, the

415

status of women—and, I should suppose, Mr. Legman's own shrill hyperboles. At that, Mr. Legman seems more to the point in his search for some deeply underlying cause than Frederic Wertham, in *Seduction of the Innocent,* with his contention that the pulps and comics in themselves are schools for murder. That the undefined aggressiveness of disturbed children can be given a shape by comic books, I do not doubt; and one could make a good case for the contention that such literature standardizes crime woefully or inhibits imagination in violence, but I find it hard to consider so obvious a symptom a prime cause of anything. Perhaps I am a little sensitive on this score, having heard the charge this week that the recent suicide of one of our college freshmen was caused by his having read (in a course of which I am in charge) Goethe, Dostoevski, and *Death of a Salesman.* Damn it, he *had* read them, and he *did* kill himself!

In none of the books on comics* I have looked into, and in none of the reports of ladies' clubs, protests of legislators, or statements of moral indignation by pastors, have I come on any real attempt to understand comic books: to define the form, midway between icon and story; to distinguish the subtypes: animal, adolescent, crime, Western, etc.; or even to separate out, from the deadpan varieties, tongue-in-cheek sports like *Pogo,* frank satire like *Mad,* or semisurrealist variations like *Plastic Man.* It would not take someone with the talents of an Aristotle, but merely with his method, to ask the rewarding questions about this kind of literature that he asked once about an equally popular and bloody genre: what are its causes and its natural form?

A cursory examination would show that the superhero comic *(Superman, Captain Marvel, Wonder Woman,* etc.) is the final form; it is statistically the most popular with the most avid readers, and it provides the only new legendary material invented along with the form rather than adapted to it.

Next, one would have to abstract the most general pattern of the myth of the superhero and deduce its significance: the urban

---

* Oddly enough, in the few years since 1955, this became a historic essay. The comic book is dead, killed, perhaps, by the tit-magazines, *Playboy,* etc.— or by T.V., on which violence has retreated to the myth from which it began, the Western.

setting, the threatened universal catastrophe, the hero who never uses arms, who returns to weakness and obscurity, who must keep his identity secret, who is impotent, etc. Not until then could one ask with any hope of an answer: what end do the comics serve? Why have they gained an immense body of readers precisely in the past fifteen or twenty years? Why must they be disguised as children's literature though read by men and women of all ages? And having answered these, one could pose the most dangerous question of all: why the constant, virulent attacks on the comics, and, indeed, on the whole of popular culture of which they are especially flagrant examples?

Strategically, if not logically, the last question should be asked first. Why the attacks? Such assaults by scientists and laymen are as characteristic of our age as puritanical diatribes against the stage of the Elizabethan Era, and pious protests against novel reading in the later eighteenth century. I suspect that a study of such conventional reactions reveals at least as much about the nature of a period as an examination of the forms to which they respond. The most fascinating and suspicious aspect of the opposition to popular narrative is its unanimity; everyone from the members of the Montana State Legislature to the ladies of the Parent Teachers Association of Boston, Massachusetts, from British M.P.'s to the wilder post-Freudians of two continents agree on this, though they may agree on nothing else. What they have in common is, I am afraid, the sense that they are all, according to their lights, righteous. And their protests represent only one more example (though an unlikely one) of the notorious failure of righteousness in matters involving art.

Just what is it with which vulgar literature is charged by various guardians of morality or sanity? With everything: encouraging crime, destroying literacy, expressing sexual frustration, unleashing sadism, spreading antidemocratic ideas, and, of course, corrupting youth. To understand the grounds of such charges, their justification and their bias, we must understand something of the nature of the subart with which we are dealing.

Perhaps it is most illuminating to begin by saying that it is a peculiarly American phenomenon, an unexpected by-product of an attempt, not only to extend literacy universally, but to delegate taste to majority suffrage. I do not mean, of course, that it is found only in the United States, but that wherever it is found, it comes first from us, and is still to be discovered in fully developed form only among us. Our experience along these lines is, in this sense, a preview for the rest of the world of what must follow the inevitable dissolution of the older aristocratic cultures.

One has only to examine certain Continental imitations of picture magazines like *Look* or *Life* or Disney-inspired cartoon books to be aware at once of the debt to American examples and of the failure of the imitations. For a true "popular literature" demands a more than ordinary slickness, the sort of high finish possible only to a machine-produced commodity in an economy of maximum prosperity. Contemporary popular culture, which is a function of an industrialized society, is distinguished from older folk art by its refusal to be shabby or second-rate in appearance, by a refusal to know its place. It is a product of the same impulse which has made available the sort of ready-made clothing which aims at destroying the possibility of knowing a lady by her dress.

Yet the articles of popular culture are made, not to be treasured, but to be thrown away; a paperback book is like a disposable diaper or a paper milk container. For all its competent finish, it cannot be preserved on dusty shelves like the calf-bound volumes of another day; indeed, its very mode of existence challenges the concept of a library, private or public. The sort of conspicuous waste once reserved for an elite is now available to anyone; and this is inconceivable without an absurdly high standard of living, just as it is unimaginable without a degree of mechanical efficiency that permits industry to replace nature, and invents—among other disposable synthetics—one for literature.

Just as the production of popular narrative demands industrial conditions most favorably developed in the United States, its distribution requires the peculiar conditions of our market places: the mass or democratized market. Subbooks and subarts are not distributed primarily through the traditional institutions: museums, libraries, and schools, which remain firmly in the hands of those who deplore mass culture. It is in drugstores and supermarkets and airline terminals that this kind of literature mingles without condescension with chocolate bars and soap flakes. We have reached the end of a long process, begun, let us say, with Samuel Richardson, in which the work of art has approached closer and closer to the status of a commodity. Even the comic book is a last descendant of *Pamela,* the final consequence of letting the tastes (or more precisely, the buying power) of a class unpledged to maintaining the traditional genres determine literary success or failure.

Those who cry out now that the work of a Mickey Spillane or *The Adventures of Superman* travesty the novel forget that the novel was long accused of travestying literature. What seems to offend us most is not the further downgrading of literary standards so much as the fact that the medium, the very notion and shape of a book, is being parodied by the comics. Jazz or the movies, which are also popular urban arts, depending for their distribution and acceptance on developments in technology (for jazz the gramophone), really upset us much less.

It is the final, though camouflaged, rejection of literacy implicit in these new forms which is the most legitimate source of distress; but all arts so universally consumed have been for illiterates, even stained glass windows and the plays of Shakespeare. What is new in our present situation, and hence especially upsetting, is that this is the first art for *post*-literates, i.e., for those who have refused the benefit for which they were presumed to have sighed in their long exclusion. Besides, modern popular narrative is disconcertingly not oral; it will not surrender the benefits of the printing press as a machine, however indifferent it may be to that press as the perpetrator of techniques devised first for pen or quill. Everything that the press can provide—except matter to be really read—is demanded: picture, typography, even in many cases the illusion of reading along with the relaxed pleasure of illiteracy. Yet the new popular forms remain somehow prose narrative or pictographic substitutes for the novel; even the cognate form of the movies is notoriously more like a novel than a play in its handling of time, space and narrative progression.

From the folk literature of the past, which ever since the triumph of the machine we have been trying sentimentally to recapture, popular literature differs in its rejection of the picturesque. Rooted in prose rather than in verse, secular rather than religious in origin, defining itself against the city rather than the world of outdoor nature, a by-product of the factory rather than agriculture, present-day popular literature defeats romantic expectations of peasants in their embroidered blouses chanting or plucking balalaikas for the approval of their betters. The haters of our own popular art love to condescend to the folk; and on records or in fashionable night clubs in recent years, we have had entertainers who have earned enviable livings producing commercial imitations of folk songs. But contemporary vulgar culture is brutal and disturbing: the quasi-spontaneous expression of the uprooted and culturally dispossessed inhabitants of anonymous cities, contriving mythologies which reduce to manageable form the threat of science, the horror of unlimited war, the general spread of corruption in a world where the social bases of old loyalties and heroisms have long been destroyed. That such an art is exploited for profit in a commercial society, mass-produced by nameless collaborators, standardized and debased, is of secondary importance. It is the patented nightmare of us all, a packaged way of coming to terms with one's environment sold for a dime to all those who have rejected the unasked-for gift of literacy.

Thought of in this light, the comic books with their legends of the eternally threatened metropolis eternally protected by immaculate and modest heroes (who shrink back after each exploit into the image of the crippled newsboy, the impotent and cowardly reporter) are seen as inheritors, for all their superficial differences, of the *inner* impulses of traditional folk art. Their gross drawing, their poverty of language, cannot disguise their heritage of aboriginal violence, their exploitation of the ancient conflict of black magic and white. Beneath their journalistic commentary on A-bomb and communism, they touch archetypal material: those shared figures of our lower minds more like the patterns of dream than fact. In a world where men threaten to dissolve into their most superficial and mechanical techniques, to become their borrowed newspaper platitudes, they remain close to the impulsive, subliminal life. They are our not quite machine-subdued Grimm, though the Black Forest has become, as it must, the City; the Wizard, the Scientist; and Simple Hans, Captain Marvel. In a society which thinks of itself as "scientific"—and of the Marvelous as childish—such a literature must seem primarily children's literature, though, of course, it is read by people of all ages.

We are now in a position to begin to answer the question: what do the righteous really have against comic books? In some parts of the world, simply the fact that they are American is sufficient, and certain homegrown self-contemners follow this line even in the United States. But it is really a minor argument, lent a certain temporary importance by passing political exigencies. To declare oneself against "the Americanization of culture" is meaningless unless one is set resolutely against industrialization and mass education.

More to the point is the attack on mass culture for its betrayal of literacy itself. In a very few cases, this charge is made seriously and with full realization of its import; but most often it amounts to nothing but an accusation of "bad grammar" or "slang" on the part of some schoolmarm to whom the spread of "different than" seems to threaten the future of civilized discourse. What should set us on guard in this case is that it is not the fully literate, the intellectuals and serious writers, who lead the attack, but the insecure semiliterate. In America, there is something a little absurd about the indignant delegation from the Parent Teachers Association (themselves clutching the latest issue of *Life*) crying out in defense of literature. Asked for suggestions, such critics are likely to propose *The Reader's Digest* as required reading in high school or to urge more comic book versions of the "classics": emasculated Melville, expurgated Hawthorne, or a child's version of something "uplifting" like "The Fall of the House of Usher." In other countries, corresponding counterparts are not hard to find.

As a matter of fact, this charge is scarcely ever urged with much conviction. It is really the portrayal of crime and horror (and less usually sex) that the enlightened censors deplore. It has been charged against vulgar art that it is sadistic, fetishistic, brutal, full of terror; that it pictures women with exaggeratedly full breasts and rumps, portrays death on the printed page, is often covertly homosexual, etc., etc. About these charges, there are two obvious things to say. First, by and large, they are true. Second, they are also true about much of the most serious art of our time, especially that produced in America.

There is no count of sadism and brutality which could not be equally proved against Hemingway or Faulkner or Paul Bowles—or, for that matter, Edgar Allan Poe. There are certain more literate critics who are victims of their own confusion in this regard; and who will condemn a Class B movie for its images of flagellation or bloodshed only to praise in the next breath such an orgy of high-minded sadism as *Le Salaire de la Peur*. The politics of the French picture may be preferable, or its photography; but this cannot redeem the scene in which a mud-and-oil-soaked truck driver crawls from a pit of sludge to reveal the protruding white bones of the multiple fracture of the thigh. This is as much horror-pornography as *Scarface* or *Little Caesar*. You cannot condemn *Superman* for the exploitation of violence, and praise the existentialist-homosexual-sadist shockers of Paul Bowles. It is possible to murmur by way of explanation something vague about art or catharsis; but no one is ready to advocate the suppression of anything merely because it is aesthetically bad. In this age of conflicting standards, we would all soon suppress each other.

An occasional Savonarola is, of course, ready to make the total rejection; and secretly or openly, the run-of-the-mill condemner of mass culture does condemn, on precisely the same grounds, most contemporary literature of distinction. Historically, one can make quite a convincing case to prove that our highest and lowest arts come from a common antibourgeois source. Edgar Allan Poe, who lived the image of the Dandy that has been haunting high art ever since, also, one remembers, invented the popular detective story; and there is a direct line from Hemingway to O'Hara to Dashiell Hammett to Raymond Chandler to Mickey Spillane to Richard S. Prather.

Of both lines of descent from Poe, one can say that they tell a black and distressing truth (we are creatures of dark impulse in a threatened and guilty world), and that they challenge the more genteel versions of "good taste." Behind the opposition to vulgar literature, there is at work the same fear of the archetypal and the unconscious itself that motivated similar attacks on Elizabethan drama and on the eighteenth-century novel. We always judge Gosson a fool in terms of Shakespeare; but this is not the point—he was just as wrong in his attack on the worst written, the most outrageously bloody and bawdy plays of his time. I should hate my argument to be understood as a defense of what is banal and mechanical and dull (there is, of course, a great deal!) in mass culture; it is merely a counterattack against those who are aiming through that banality and dullness at what moves all literature of worth. Anyone at all sensitive to the life of the imagination would surely prefer his kids to read the coarsest fables of Black and White contending for the City of Man, rather than have them spell out, "Oh, see, Jane. Funny, funny Jane," or read to themselves hygienic accounts of the operation of supermarkets or manureless farms. Yet most school-board members are on the side of mental hygiene; and it is they who lead the charge against mass culture.

Anyone old enough to have seen, say, *Rain* is on guard against those who in the guise of wanting to destroy savagery and ignorance wage war on spontaneity and richness. But we are likely to think of such possibilities purely in sexual terms; the new righteous themselves have been touched lightly by Freud and are firm believers in frankness and "sex education." But in the midst of their self-congratulation at their emancipation, they have become victims of a new and ferocious prudery. One who would be ashamed to lecture his masturbating son on the dangers of insanity, is quite prepared (especially if he has been reading Wertham) to predict the electric chair for the young manundrel with a bootlegged comic. Superman is our Sadie Thompson. We live in an age when the child who is exposed to the "facts of life" is protected from "the facts of death." In the United States, for instance, a certain Doctor Spock has produced an enlightened guide to child care for modern mothers—a paperback book which sold, I would guess, millions of copies. Tell the child all about sex, the good doctor advises, but on the subject of death—hush!

By more "advanced" consultants, the taboo is advanced further toward absurdity: no blood-soaked Grimm, no terrifying Andersen, no childhood verses about cradles that fall—for fear breeds insecurity; insecurity, aggression; aggression, war. There is even a "happy," that is to say, expurgated, Mother Goose in which the three blind mice have become "kind mice"—and the farmer's wife no longer hacks off their tails, but "cuts them some cheese with a carving knife." Everywhere the fear of fear is endemic, the fear of the very names of fear; those who have most ardently desired to end warfare and personal cruelty in the world around them, and are therefore most frustrated by their persistence, conspire to stamp out violence on the nursery bookshelf. This much they can do anyhow. If they can't hold up the weather, at least they can break the bloody glass.

This same fear of the instinctual and the dark, this denial of death and guilt by the enlightened genteel, motivates their distrust of serious literature, too. Faulkner is snubbed and the comic books are banned, not in the interests of the classics or even of Robert Louis Stevenson, as the attackers claim, but in the name of a literature of the middle ground which finds its fictitious vision of a kindly and congenial world attacked from above and below. I speak now not of the few intellectual converts to the cause of censorship, but of the main body of genteel book-banners, whose idol is Lloyd Douglas or even A. J. Cronin. When a critic like Mr. Wagner is led to applaud what he sees as a "trend" toward making doctors, lawyers, etc. the heroes of certain magazine stories, he has fallen into the trap of regarding middling fiction as a transmission belt from the vulgar to the high. There is no question, however, of a slow climb from the level of literature which celebrates newspaper reporters, newsboys, radio commentators (who are also superheroes in tight-fitting uniforms with insignia), through one which centers around prosperous professionals, to the heights of serious literature, whose protagonists are suicides full of incestuous longings, lady lushes with clipped hair, bootleggers, gangsters, and broken-down pugs. To try to state the progression is to reveal its absurdity.

The conception of such a "trend" is nothing more than the standard attitude of a standard kind of literature, the literature of slick-paper ladies' magazines, which prefers the stereotype to the archetype, loves poetic justice, sentimentality, and gentility, and is peopled by characters who bathe frequently, live in the suburbs, and are professionals. Such literature circles mindlessly inside the trap of its two themes: unconsummated adultery and the consummated pure romance. There can be little doubt about which kind of persons and which sort of fables best typify our plight, which tell the truth—or better: a truth in the language of those to whom they speak.

In the last phrase, there is a rub. The notion that there is more than one language of art, or rather, that there is something not quite art, which performs art's function for most men in our society, is disquieting enough for anyone, and completely unacceptable to the sentimental egalitarian, who had dreamed of universal literacy leading directly to a universal culture. It is here that we begin to see that there is a politics as well as a pathology involved in the bourgeois hostility to popular culture. I do not refer only to the explicit political ideas embodied in the comics or in the literature of the cultural élite; but certainly each of these arts has a characteristic attitude: populist-authoritarian on the one hand, and aristocratic-authoritarian on the other.

It is notorious how few of the eminent novelists or poets of our time have shared the political ideals we (most readers of this magazine and I) would agree are the most noble available to us. The flirtations of Yeats and Lawrence with fascism, Pound's weird amalgam of Confucianism, Jeffersonianism, and Social Credit, the modified Dixiecrat principles of Faulkner—all make the point with terrible reiteration. Between the best art and poetry of our age and the critical liberal reader there can be no bond of shared belief; at best we have the ironic confrontation of the skeptical mind and the believing imagination. It is this division which has, I suppose, led us to define more and more narrowly the "aesthetic experience," to attempt to isolate a quality of seeing and saying that has a moral value quite independent of *what* is seen or heard.

> Time that with this strange excuse
> Pardoned Kipling and his views,
> And will pardon Paul Claudel,
> Pardons him for writing well.

But the genteel middling mind which turns to art for entertainment and uplift, finds this point of view reprehensible, and cries out in rage against those who give Ezra Pound a prize and who claim that "to permit other considerations than that of poetic achievement to sway the decision world . . . deny the validity of that objective perception of value on which any civilized society must rest." We live in the midst of a strange two-front class war: the readers of the slicks battling the subscribers to the "little reviews" and the consumers of pulps; the sentimental-egalitarian conscience against the ironical-aristocratic sensibility on the one hand and the brutal-populist mentality on the other. The joke, of course, is that it is the "democratic" center which calls here and now for suppression of its rivals; while the elite advocate a condescending tolerance, and the vulgar ask only to be let alone.

It is disconcerting to find cultural repression flourishing at the point where middling culture meets a kindly, if not vigorously thought-out, liberalism. The sort of right-thinking citizen who subsidizes trips to America for Japanese girls scarred by the Hiroshima bombing and deplores McCarthy in the public press also deplores, and would censor, the comics. In one sense, this is fair enough; for beneath the veneer of slogans that "crime doesn't pay" and the superficial praise of law and order, the comics do reflect that dark populist faith which Senator McCarthy has exploited. There is a kind of "black socialism" of the American masses which underlies formal allegiances to one party or another: the sense that there is always a conspiracy at the centers of political and financial power; the notion that the official defenders of the commonwealth are "bought" more often than not; an impatience with moral scruples and a distrust of intelligence, especially in the expert and scientist; a willingness to identify the enemy, the dark projection of everything most feared in the self, with some journalistically-defined political opponent of the moment.

This is not quite the "fascism" it is sometimes called. There is, for instance, no European anti-Semitism involved, despite the conventional hooked nose of the scientist-villain. (The inventors and chief producers of comic books have been, as it happens, Jews.) There is also no adulation of a dictator figure on the model of Hitler or Stalin; though one of the archetypes of the Deliverer in the comics is called Superman, he is quite unlike the Nietzschean figure —it is the image of Cincinnatus which persists in him, an archetype that has possessed the American imagination since the time of Washington: the leader who enlists for the duration and retires unrewarded to obscurity.

It would be absurd to ask the consumer of such art to admire in the place of images that project his own impotence and longing for civil peace some hero of middling culture—say, the good boy of Arthur Miller's *Death of a Salesman,* who, because he has studied hard in school, has become a lawyer who argues cases before the Supreme Court and has friends who own their own tennis courts. As absurd as to ask the general populace to worship Stephen Dedalus or Captain Ahab! But the high-minded petty-bourgeois cannot understand or forgive the rejection of his own dream, which he considers as nothing less than the final dream of humanity. The very existence of a kind of art based on allegiances and values other than his challenges an article of his political faith; and when such an art is "popular," that is, more read, more liked, more bought than his own, he feels his *raison d'être,* his basic life defense, imperiled. The failure of the petty bourgeoisie to achieve cultural hegemony threatens their dream of a truly classless society; for they believe, with some justification, that such a society can afford only a single culture. And they see, in the persistence of a high art and a low art on either side of their average own, symptoms of the re-emergence of classes in a quarter where no one had troubled to stand guard.

The problem posed by popular culture is finally, then, a problem of class distinction in a democratic society. What is at stake is the refusal of cultural equality by a large part of the population. It is misleading to think of popular culture as the product of a conspiracy of profiteers against the rest of us. This venerable notion of an eternally oppressed and deprived but innocent people is precisely what the rise of mass culture challenges. Much of what upper-class egalitarians dreamed for him, the ordinary man does not want—especially literacy. The situation is bewildering and complex, for the people have not rejected completely the notion of cultural equality; rather, they desire its symbol but not its fact. At the very moment when half of the population of the United States reads no *hardcover* book in a year, more than half of all high school graduates are entering universities and colleges; in twenty-five years almost all Americans will at least begin a higher education. It is clear that what is demanded is a B.A. for everyone, with the stipulation that no one be forced to read to get it. And this the colleges, with "objective tests" and "visual aids," are doing their reluctant best to satisfy.

One of the more exasperating aspects of the cultural defeat of the egalitarians is that it followed a seeming victory. For a while (in the Anglo-Saxon world at least) it appeared as if the spread of literacy, the rise of the bourgeoisie, and the emergence of the novel as a reigning form would succeed in destroying both traditional folk art and an aristocratic literature still pledged to epic, ode, and verse tragedy. But the novel itself (in the hands of Lawrence, Proust, Kafka, etc.) soon passed beyond the comprehension of those for whom it was originally contrived; and the retrograde derivations from it—various steps in a retreat toward wordless narrative: digests, pulp fiction, movies, picture magazines—revealed that middling literature was not in fact the legitimate heir of either folk art or high art, much less the successor of both, but a *tertium quid* of uncertain status and value.

The middlebrow reacts with equal fury to an art that baffles his understanding and to one which refuses to aspire to his level. The first reminds him that he has not yet, after all, *arrived* (and, indeed, may never make it); the second suggests to him a condition to which he might easily relapse, one perhaps that might have made him happier with less effort (and here exacerbated puritanism is joined to baffled egalitarianism)—even suggests what his state may appear like to those a notch above. Since he cannot on his own terms explain to himself why anyone should choose any level but the highest (that is, his own), the failure of the vulgar seems to him the product of mere ignorance and laziness—a crime! And the rejection by the advanced artist of his canons strikes him as a finicking excess, a pointless and unforgivable snobbism. Both, that is, suggest the intolerable notion of a hierarchy of taste, a hierarchy of values, the possibility of cultural classes in a democratic state; and before this, puzzled and enraged, he can only call a cop. The fear of the vulgar is the obverse of the fear of excellence, and both are aspects of the fear of difference: symptoms of a drive for conformity on the level of the timid, sentimental, mindless-bodiless genteel.

—1955

# THREE

# What Shining Phantom: Writers and the Movies

In *The Boys in the Back Room,* a little book first published in 1941 (which is to say, at the end of the decade during which serious writers first went in large numbers to Hollywood), Edmund Wilson turns uncustomarily to verse—perhaps because for once he is moved too deeply for prose. *What shining phantom, he asks, folds its wings before us?/ What apparition, smiling yet remote?/ Is this—so portly yet so lightly porous—/ The old friend who went west and never wrote?* And toward the end of that same book, reflecting on the then recent deaths of F. Scott Fitzgerald and Nathanael West, both friends like the anonymous nonwriter in his poem, Wilson turns to prose to make explicit his intent. "Both West and Fitzgerald," he explains, "were writers of a conscience and with natural gifts rare enough in America or anywhere; and their failure to get the best out of their years may certainly be laid partly to Hollywood, with its already appalling record of talent depraved and wasted."

In prose or verse, however, what Mr. Wilson provides us is more poetry than truth, a conventional elegy rather than a series of insights, as might well be expected from a critic whose range of understanding did not extend to the world of pop culture in general, or that of the "pratfall," the "weenie," the "gag," and the "big take" (movie jargon which Mr. Wilson uses with all the unconvincingness of Walt Whitman turning on his French) in particular. What was involved in the flight of writers to Hollywood and their inevitable defeat there was not so much a series of betrayals and appropriate punishments, as the first stage in a revolution—only recently defined by such commentators as Marshall McLuhan—which would make print obsolete and the first panicked attempts of those committed to the old regime of words to come to terms with the future.

Yet once upon a time Mr. Wilson's fable (only lately reprinted without the prefatory verses in *Classics and Commercials)* was taken as literal fact; and it remains, in certain nostalgic quarters—especially where reinforced by vestiges of thirties-type liberalism—a staple of pretentious journalism. Malcolm Cowley, for instance, writing in 1966 about William Faulkner (whose example should have taught him better), submits to the old routine: ". . . Hollywood, which used to have a notorious fashion of embracing and destroying men of letters," he starts in an offhand way; and continues, "After publishing an admired book, or two or three, the writer was offered a contract by a movie studio; then he bought a house with a swimming pool and vanished from print. If he reappeared years later, it was usually with a novel designed to have the deceptive appeal of an uplift brassiere."

Perhaps it was necessary not only to have sold oneself to the movies but also to have bought a swimming pool to make it into Mr. Cowley's category of the damned; for surely the post-Hollywood novels of both Fitzgerald and West, *The Last Tycoon* and *The Day of the Locust,* have an appeal based on something more substantial than foam rubber. More specious than either, to be sure, are the Pat Hobby short stories of Fitzgerald, purely commercial ventures in which Fitzgerald travestied and stereotyped his own situation as an unsuccessful writer of scripts; and among the clichés deployed in these seventeen or more attempts at pandering to popular notions of life in Hollywood is Pat's memory of the magnificent swimming pool he possessed in his time of glory. ". . . When Pat had his pool in those fat days of silent pictures," Fitzgerald tells us in "A Patriotic Short," "it was entirely cement, unless you should count the cracks where the water stubbornly sought its own level through the mud."

West, too, however—in work considerably above the level of potboiling—is obsessed by the banal image (a motion picture image, really, its ironies obvious enough for the obtusest audience), taking time out from the grimmer concerns of *The Day of the Locust* to let us know that Claude Estee—the single successful screen writer in the book—has the required pool with its required significances. But West, of course, redeems this cliché in the same surreal fashion he redeems so many others, by putting a dead horse (a *fake* dead horse, naturally) at the bottom of the pool. Yet even a dead horse does not help for long—disappearing for instance, from the pool in Evelyn Waugh's *The Loved One,* to make possible once more the pristine Wilsonian sentimentality. In the course of describing the house of Sir Francis Hinsley (formerly "the only knight in Hollywood" and "chief script-writer in Megalopolitan Pictures"), Waugh lingers over his now abandoned swimming pool, which, he informs us, "had once flashed like an aquarium with the limbs of long-departed beauties" before it had become "cracked and over-grown with weeds." All of which was quite literally reproduced on the screen—where it belonged to begin with—in the recent film version of Waugh's novel.

Well, swimming pools have ceased, even mythologically, to represent Hollywood, not because any banality ever wears out on its own; but because prosperity has brought that legendary pleasure from dreamland to the backyards of suburbia, and—in what survives of its former legendary glory—to that storehouse of the dreams of the thirties, Hugh Heffner's pleasure palace in Chicago. The suburban swimming pool is memorialized in a story by John Cheever called "The Swimmer," which recounts the dream legend of a commuter who swam all the way home from the station through pool after pool after pool of his neighbors; and even now that story is—of course, of course—in the process of becoming a movie.

Yet the legend survives its trappings; the myth of "the old friend who went west" outlives the Hollywood swimming pool. Some such "old friends" at least are still wincing, perhaps protesting too much: Daniel Fuchs, for instance, who comes closest to having lived the mythological history of Wilson's "shining phantom." Fuchs had written three novels before going off to Hollywood toward the end of the thirties, *Summer in Williamsburg, Homage to Blenholt,* and *Low Company,* none of which were much "admired" (the word is his) when they appeared. "The books didn't sell—400 copies, 400, 1200," Fuchs himself reports. "The reviews were scanty, immaterial." And so, he went to Hollywood, made it there, lived long enough to see his reputation revived, his novels reprinted in the sixties—but remained bugged all the time, it would appear, by the judgment implicit in Wilson's vision. At any rate, he uses the occasion of the re-issue of his fiction in a single volume in 1961 to go on record: "The popular notions about the movies aren't true. It takes a good deal of energy and hard sense to write stories over an extended period of time, and it would be foolish to expect writers not to want to be paid a livelihood for what they do. But we are engaged here on the same problems that perplex writers everywhere. We grapple with the daily mystery. We struggle with form, with Chimera . . . 'Poesy,' my father used to call it, and I know I will keep at it as long as I can, because surely there is nothing else to do."

It would be easier to believe Fuchs if he seemed really to believe himself; but he is as much of a child of his age and Wilson's, of those mythicized and mythicizing thirties, as was James M. Cain, who had already cried out against Wilson twenty years before—and with more apparent cause, being one of the "boys in the backroom" specifically attacked by Wilson. "Edmund Wilson. . . in an article he wrote about me . . .," James M. Cain complained in 1942 in a preface to three of his own novelettes, "attributed these socko twists and surprises to a leaning toward Hollywood, which is not particularly the case." And he goes on to explain that, despite the tutoring of a script writer called Vincent Lawrence, he himself just "couldn't write pictures," which he takes to be some guarantee, we gather, of virtue as well as of ineptitude. But we remember that, though Mr. Cain may have written no successful scripts, he was the author of "Double Indemnity," as well as of *The Postman Always Rings Twice,*" which is to say, of certain not very good books which *became* very good films—the sort of transitional figure between a Gutenberg era and a non-Gutenberg one (the late Hemingway would be another example, and Steinbeck most of the time), whom we have not understood very well until now: the author of embryo movies which only pretend to be books. Cain, indeed, must be given double credit; since he not only provided the cue for several first-rate American screenplays, but the inspiration as well for Visconti's *Ossessione* (born of an encounter between *The Postman Always Rings Twice* and the Italian director's characteristic blend of social protest and High Camp), with which "neorealism" was born.

All this, however, has to do not with being "depraved and wasted" in any conventional sense but with being fulfilled and completed in a quite unforeseen way. No, the notion of being "depraved and wasted," or, alternatively, "embraced and destroyed" belongs to the legendary literature of defunct "modernism"—to what we can readily see now is the realm of myth rather than that of history or sociology. It is a special development, which flourished chiefly in the thirties, of that Cult of Self-Pity which underlies much of the literature of the first half of the twentieth century. The notion of society as a conspiracy against the individual, and of art as a protest against that conspiracy goes back as far as the beginnings of Romanticism at least. Originally, however, the artist himself was not thought of as the sole or exclusive victim of the world, women and children and noble savages, even peasants and workers being quite understandably preferred.

After World War I, however, writers in Anglo-Saxon countries (responding belatedly to cues from the French) began to portray the poet himself as the victim *par excellence* and to shop about for the institutions most inimical to his career. To such basically European writers as James Joyce, for instance, the traditional institutions of Christendom seemed quite satisfactory: the Family, the Church, the State; but these have struck latterday Americans as somehow outdated compared with the newer institutions (the threat of the future rather than the encumbrance of the past) of mass culture, including mass war. But the notion of total war as particularly reprehensible because of the masterpieces it inhibits or destroys (a notion pathetically developed in, say, Dos Passos's *Three Soldiers)* seems finally a little absurd. And, in any case, our writers have chosen to think of themselves as being destroyed—more ironically than pathetically—by advanced technological substitutes for their own discipline: advertising, script writing, publish-or-perish scholarship, television.

Besides, most men, even writers, are *drafted* into wars—raped as it were, whereas, they are *tempted* into other areas of mass culture, seduced or prostituted. In Peter Viertel's *White Hunter, Black*

*Heart,* which appeared late enough (1953) to seem a retrospective catalogue of all the anti-Hollywood clichés, a semifictional character, transparently modeled on John Huston, is permitted to comment at length on this metaphor, crying out, "They mean the whores when they say Hollywood. . . . Now get this, Victor . . . whores have to sell one of the few things that shouldn't be for sale in this world: love. But there are other things that shouldn't be for sale beside love, you know. . . . There are the whores who sell words and ideas and melodies. . . . Now I know what I'm talking about . . . because I've hustled a little in my time, a hell of a lot more than I like to admit I have. . . . Well, anyway, my point is that it's the whores who put up Hollywood as a big target, and very often they shoot at it themselves just to feel clean again. . . ." Once more we find ourselves in that dim area of protest and apologetics in which muddled voices cry, "You're one, too!" or "I may be one, but not full time," or, "not as much as you."

Money and guilt and the denial of guilt: these are, at any rate, key terms in all accounts of Hollywood; though for a long time, as a matter of fact, not "selling oneself" but "selling out" (another one of those slightly alien terms imported by Marxists into American life during the thirties), an image more sociological than erotic, possessed the minds of those who sought to make fiction of an experience already fictional in essence. The anti-Hollywood Novel—that writer's ultimate, even sometimes posthumous revenge on his seducer-employers—is basically a Depression product; for the heyday of the in-and-out writer in Hollywood, the classic period memorialized in the classic books, coincides almost exactly with that somewhat more than a decade we call the thirties.

The thirties as a social-psychological phenomenon begins with the stock-market crash of late 1927 or, perhaps, with the execution of Sacco and Vanzetti earlier in that same year, and ends with the Japanese attack on Pearl Harbor on December 7, 1941; while the legendary era for the writer in Hollywood begins with the perfection of "talking pictures" in 1927—with Al Jolson in *The Jazz Singer,* let's say, making it on the screen by singing the death of two worlds: the Minstrel Show and Orthodox Judaism—and ends with a corresponding double death, the demise within a few days of each other, during December 1940, of Scott Fitzgerald and Nathanael West. The novels which comment on that era reflect inevitably, then, its fashionable class consciousness; but since the experience which produced them had to come first, they do not begin to appear until that class consciousness, at first vulgar and surly and truly embattled, had become attenuated and sentimental and token.

They are a subvariety not of the Proletarian Novel proper, which belongs to pre-1935, the time of Mike Gold and Grace Lumpkin and Jack Conroy, but of the Popular Front Novel, like *Grapes of Wrath,* for instance, which arises out of a world conditioned by the rhetoric of such Hollywood politicos as Donald Ogden Stewart, and which disappears back into the clichés of that world without a struggle. In the declining thirties, as a matter of fact, when writers of real eminence were deserting the ranks of the communist fellow travelers, hack script writers were replacing them in the leadership of movements like the League Against War and Fascism; and the old vision of the high-paid Hollywood professional as necessarily a whore and sellout had to be qualified.

A division began to be made, in popular mythology and fiction alike, between the kind of successful screen writer who joins the Screen Writers Guild and/or tries to smuggle favorable references to Loyalist Spain and the Soviet Union into his scripts, and the kind who refuses to pay dues in the workers' cause and/or give lip service to "Humanity" as defined by the Communist Party. In the encoded cant of the time, the former, being only half whores or not-quite-whores, were referred to as the "decent and progressive forces"; and it came to be believed that "decent and progressive" novelists, desiring to treat justly the environment which bred them, ought to populate their novels with a preponderance of such types. Woe unto those who did not! Even poor Budd Schulberg, who in his best-selling *What Makes Sammy Run* had rewarded his Jewish narrator-hero ("a decent, generous and gifted" screen writer and Guild member) with the hand of an Anglo-Saxon heroine (an even more "decent, generous, and gifted" screen writer and Guild member), was abused for having insisted too much on the villainy and success of the Jewish heel who gives his book its name.

But he made amends by carrying over into his second book about the movies, *The Disenchanted,* a minor "decent, gifted, etc."

character from the first, a certain Julian Blumberg, whom he permits to be kind to a sodden, aging, unsuccessful screen writer, obviously intended to represent Scott Fitzgerald; and appears himself, faintly disguised, to lecture the same failing lush on the virtues of "progressivism." It is all a little disheartening, but fair enough, I suppose, in light of the fact that Fitzgerald had in fact flirted with left-wing politics, perhaps under the influence of Donald Ogden Stewart, with whom he had worked on a script; and had paid his respects to that flirtation in the embarrassingly bad scene in *The Last Tycoon* which describes a fist fight between the brilliant but failing Jewish producer, Monroe Stahr, and a (Jewish?) communist organizer called Brimmer ("a little on the order of Spencer Tracy. . ." poor Fitzgerald describes him). At the close of the scene, the producer lies on the floor, cold-cocked with a single symbolic punch; and to make the allegorical meanings of the encounter clear, Fitzgerald has his girl narrator, partly responsible for the conflict and a witness throughout, comment about Brimmer, ". . . afterward I thought it looked as if he were saying, "Is *this* all? This frail half-sick person holding up the whole thing?"

Only Nathanael West managed to resist the temptation to redeem the Hollywood writer by reminding us that he was tithing himself for Spain or meeting secretly with others of his kind to condemn the system by which he lived; and even West felt obliged to apologize privately, in a letter to the now almost forgotten Proletarian Novelist Jack Conroy: "If I put into *The Day of the Locust* any of the sincere, honest people who work here and are making such a great, progressive fight. . . the whole fabric of the peculiar half-world which I attempted to create would be badly torn by them." In the letter itself, we watch his rhetoric go fashionably soft and realize that only his exclusion of those whom the age (with West assenting) conspired to think virtuous kept his novel as bleak and antisentimental as it had to be for truth's sake.

When the "progressive" self-deception of the Popular Front had given way to the "anticommunist" self-righteousness of the McCarthy era, the "sincere, honest people" who had persuaded themselves that somehow they were *really* boring from within, even as they made it big in Hollywood, were disconcertingly taken at their word by Congressional Investigating Committees; and they had, therefore, to choose between public recantation and informing, on the one hand, or silence and exile, on the other, exile from the industry that had for so long permitted them both swimming pools *and* clean consciences. There have been two major attempts at dealing with those who made the choice, one way or the other: the first by Norman Mailer, who deals with a recanter; and the other by Mordecai Richler, who treats those who stood firm and were exiled; and oddly enough (though perhaps not unexpectedly) the recanters come off a little better than the unreconstructed.

Mailer's *The Deer Park* begins as the outsider's dream (nurtured in part by other earlier books) of Hollywood people disporting themselves at Palm Springs, and ends as a sympathetic study of the vain and gifted director, an almost hero, who gives up his lifelong resistance to the world in which he flourishes, when he learns first to love, then to be defeated and die. Richler, on the other hand, begins completely outside of Hollywood and its environs, portraying in *Choice of Enemies* the life in England (where Richler himself, a Canadian by birth, is a screen writer) of certain left-wing refugees from Hollywood, who still try to play, without power and on immensely diminished funds, the old games of backbiting and ass-kissing and self-congratulation and betrayal. Both Mailer's book and Richler's, however, though obviously the products of talented younger writers, seemed even at the moment of their appearance, imitations or refinements of a mode still viable, perhaps, but no longer mythically potent.

By 1955, surely, when *The Deer Park* was published, we needed no Sergius O'Shaughnessy come back from the grave to tell us the truth about Southern California and the movies; for the truth had been invented before the fact and, whatever its effectiveness once, had long since ceased to move anyone but actors. How much more remote and unconvincing, then, that same world of Mailer's seemed in 1967, when, after long long delays, the play he had been making of his novel all those years finally got onto the stage, where (with true lack of discretion) it is being presented right now, not as a period piece but as something current or, at least, timeless. Such trifling with time is necessary, I suppose, if *The Deer Park* is eventually to be made into a movie, since the men who make movies cannot really confess that they are dead, that all their writers are ghost writers, their players ghost players, and even the producers ghosts like the rest. And *The Deer Park must* be made into a movie so that we can all be quit of a legend we seem to have known forever, without that knowledge having ever done any of us a bit of good. Certainly it did not help Mailer, who—knowing what he must have known, what his book reveals he knew—went anyhow to Hollywood. But why, we ask, *why?* And not only of Mailer; since delusion was built into Hollywood from the start, and no one ever went there without his eyes open. Into wars, writers may have carried for a little while illusions to be lost; and similarly the universities once dangled before them fair promises and enticing hopes, as did even the Revolutionary Movement of the Depression years and the Popular Front Days which followed. But what ever drew writers to Hollywood?

The search for destruction, I am tempted to answer off the cuff, a desire to play Russian roulette, if not to die—to act out in their own particular lives the fate of the literary art to which they have committed themselves, the fate of books in the world of Hollywood, whose normal temperature is Fahrenheit 451 (the temperature at which as everyone now knows—since Ray Bradbury's book of that name has been consumed in a film, too—all paper burns). But perhaps it is much simpler than that—they go just to make money, as Wilson suggested, or to find a subject for a book, as all the rebuttals to him have really answered, whatever they pretended to say. Or maybe after all, it is a mythological journey, in the full sense of the word, as a descent into all that Hell used to be; for surely "Hollywood" is just as polysemous and attractively sinister a word as any of the traditional names for the underworld; though like hell itself, it has become a cliché.

Let us try once more, then, to penetrate the cliché, by turning once more to Peter Viertel's handbook of banality, to *White Hunter, Black Heart* at the place where his producer-director-villain continues to cry out in protest against platitudes: "You see, the way Vic uses the word 'Hollywood' is an insult. Now, don't contradict me. I've heard it before. In the Army, in the theater in New York —hell, everywhere. People say 'Hollywood' when they want to insult you. But it isn't an insult, really. . .Hollywood is a place where they make a product; it's the name of a factory town, just like Detroit, or Birmingham, or Schaffhausen. But because the cheap element in that town has been overadvertised, it is insulting to remind a man that he comes from there. . . but it doesn't bother me so much when they say it, because I know they're talking about the hustlers, and the flesh peddlers, and the pimps who sit in the sun out there, around the swimming pools. . . . They're not talking about the guys who work out there, who try to do something worth-while. They mean the whores. . . ."

But this takes us right back to where we started, indicating that the longest way around is the only way home (or to hell, if you please), that the swimming pools and the whores are not incidental but essential to Hollywood, which, if it is, indeed, "a factory town," is quite unlike others in that it produces not machines but men and women, living meat for use and pleasure, though (by the canny use of machines) it manages to produce them twice over—once in what *they* take for actuality, i.e., life itself, and once on what *we* take for actuality, i.e., the screen. That these men and women, this living meat be "hustlers, flesh peddlers and pimps," is precisely necessary; since Hollywood is, on the first mythological level, Sodom, or—to use Mailer's alternative title—"the Deer Park": "that gorge of innocence and virtue, in which were engulfed so many victims who when they returned to society brought with them depravity, debauchery, and all the vices they naturally acquired from the infamous officials of such a place. . . . Indeed who can reckon the expense of that band of pimps and madames. . . ." Now that the hand-held camera and a kind of ultimate vertical social mobility has placed the journey to hell within the reach of everyone, and we need no Deer Parks, no Sodom, no Hollywood—we can consider with detachment the special sexual function Hollywood once fulfilled.

It was the place (in a world which had lost the secret pleasure palaces of the aristocrats as locuses for fantasy, and which had not yet learned fully to democratize sexual reverie as well as sexual fact) which simultaneously created—and fulfilled by proxy—the wet dreams of everyone. No wonder that there is scarcely a book which uses Hollywood for a setting that does not include scenes in a whorehouse, or encounters with a pimp, or descriptions of private showings of dirty films for the makers of public films (the movies within the movie world—at least according to the anti-Hollywood novelists—were explicitly, banally pornographic, i.e., totally unclothed). But the special fable which haunts the writers of books about the bookless world of Hollywood is the actual pursuit and possession of a female star, one of those standardized erotic objects nightly possessed in fantasy by millions—superwhores, as it were, in possessing whom in fact one joins himself in fantasy with all the other males of his world, potent or demipotent or without even the power to dream unaided.

Sometimes, to be sure, we are presented, in the fictions made of the Hollywood experience, with the caricature of this sexual encounter, as the hero embraces or, better still, fails to embrace not some recognized and celebrated actress but the frantic anonymous slut aspiring to the role of the Love Goddess. In Mailer's *The Deer Park,* however, or in Fitzgerald's short story "Crazy Sunday" (his first attempt to come to terms in print with Irving Thalberg and the alluring image of Norma Shearer who was his wife) we are given fantasy triumphing over frustration: the universally desired women privately (if only momentarily) possessed. This is the place where the fiction about Hollywood aspires to poetry rather than revenge —or rather, perhaps, where the poetry of celebration and the prose of revenge improbably approach each other, two opposed traditions becoming one. Ever since films became a part of our common culture, poets—who, unlike novelists, have gone not to Hollywood with the chosen few, but just to the movies with the unnumbered many—have been singing the charms of the not-quite-unreal ladies who move through those films: from Vachel Lindsay's coyly gallant "Mae Marsh, Motion Picture Actress" ("She is a madonna in an art/ As wild and young as her sweet eyes:/ A cool dew flower from this hot lamp/ That is today's divine surprise") to Joel Oppenheimer's considerably franker "Dear Miss Monroe" (" . . . some nights i think, while/ i/m in bed, of how lovely your/ body must be, and i don/t mean of/ when the king/s hand is sneaking/ under the sheets while you two/ kiss, i mean of when you and i/ would kiss. . ."). Closer to the poems than to Fitzgerald or Mailer's evocations in prose of bitch goddesses without minds are those transformations of Marilyn *(last,* it now becomes clear, of her once apparently inexhaustible line) at the end of Mailer's own later *An*

*American Dream* or the first pages of Leonard Cohen's post-Hollywood novel, *Beautiful Losers*.

And somewhere on the other side of both poems and novels, behind the screen, as it were, where neither form of literature had reached before, is the strange saga of the Writer and the Star that Arthur Miller lived-wrote by first marrying Marilyn Monroe; then casting her as the anonymous aspirant to all she actually was in *The Misfits* (where she insisted all the same on being only what the screen had composed, not what Miller thought he had rewritten, loving a tree, subduing Clark Gable); then when she was dead, playing her story—the story Hollywood and the myth had determined for her—on the stage, even printing it, as if he had made it up out of the whole cloth, and were waiting for the Hollywood that no longer existed to find another starlet to play it, another John Huston to direct it, another Arthur Miller to be given the job of writing the script: as if the whole thing could continue to go round and round, as if the exact point of it all were not that it was finished, done with. *Basta.*

But what fun and games we have had before it was finished; and how our authors large and small have responded, running the whole gamut of the ambivalence proper to our culture: from nauseated horror (as in Faulkner's single, queasy story out of his Hollywood experience, "Golden Land," in which the drunken and eminently successful father of a faggot and a whore wakes to find his daughter's photograph under the headlines, APRIL LALEAR BARES ORGY SECRETS) to the kind of wistful longing, the dumb hope that rises in the heart of Mailer's dumb hero in *The Deer Park,* when a cynical producer, urging him to turn actor, cries, "You think you're going to enjoy goosing waitresses when you've been boffing the best? Brother, I can tell you, once you've been bed-wise with high-class pussy, it makes you ill, it makes you physically ill to take less than the best. . . ."

It is Nathanael West, however, who preserved the flavor and balance of the ambivalence most perfectly—in the yearning of the studio artist Tod Hackett (nearest thing to a self-portrait of West in *The Day of the Locust)* for Faye Greener, the girl who will never be a star but who embodies the erotic allure of the film heroine all the more convincingly: available to anyone with the going price of tail or with the face and body of a movie actor—but unobtainable by that very token to the only one capable of imagining her, that is, to the poor artist. A luscious seventeen-year-old in the dress of a twelve-year-old child, she flashes across the screen, her long legs "like swords" suggesting to Tod destruction and death; while behind her run (in the painting Tod dreams, at least, which only can give meaning to her life) the book's other major grotesques: a lustful dwarf, a parody cowboy, a troupe of Eskimo acrobats; and behind them, a howling crowd of witnesses—caricatures of the passive and resentful audience—enter at last upon the violence which they have too long only dreamed. The title of Tod's picture is "The Burning of Los Angeles," but the destruction of the city is only the public fantasy which masks his private dream-wish: to rape and destroy that green and golden girl (always golder and "greener" on the other side of the invisible, unpassable fence between audience and screen image), or better yet to be destroyed by her: "Her invitation wasn't to pleasure, but to struggle, hard and sharp, closer to murder than to love. If you threw yourself on her, it would be like throwing yourself from the parapet of a skyscraper. You would do it with a scream. You couldn't expect to rise again. Your teeth would be driven into your skull like nails into a pine board and your back would be broken. . . ."

It is such a love in such a setting that the writer has sought in Hollywood, or so at least West would have us believe, so he shrilly insists in the pages of the best book anyone has ever written about that oddest of "factory towns." In his vision, the metaphorical whore, who calls himself an artist ("When the Hollywood job had come along, he had grabbed it despite the arguments of his friends who were certain that he was selling out. . ."), grapples with the actual one, who calls herself an actress (" 'She's a whore!' he heard Homer grunt. . . ."), even as Sodom turns to ash, and the doomed avengers of all they have themselves desired and loved and despised riot in the streets: ". . . a great united front of screwballs and screwboxes to purify the land. No longer bored they sang and danced joyously in the red light of the flames."

But if, on the one hand, the force which took the American writer to Hollywood is a dark and inverted passion that makes him seek destruction in the arms of the blonde child whore, his corrupt and death-dealing sister, on the other hand, he is moved by a more beneficent love that takes him westward in search of an alien and unlikely father—more technician than artist, more businessman than creator—but a dreamer and peddler of dreams all the same, quite like himself. The relationship resembles that of Stephen Dedalus to Leopold Bloom in *Ulysses,* that blind man's word-bound book, which, after more than half a century, someone has been bold or foolish enough to try to make into a film; and as in Joyce's novel, so in our lives the mythical father of the artist in flight from tradition to Nighttown is a Jew.

How oddly the love affair between the Gentile writer and the Jewish producer-director, the young philo-Semite and the aging Jew, emerges in our literature, which, as late as the twenties and on into the thirties, was continuing to portray chiefly anti-Semitic heroes and antipathetic Jewish foils, in the poetry of Pound and Eliot as well as in the prose of Dreiser and Sherwood Anderson and Hemingway and even Fitzgerald himself. But the latter—after the first rude shock of Hollywood, after the experience of confronting the Jews on their own home grounds, as it were, in a world where not they but the Gentile author seemed the intruder—learned to create an image of the Jew vastly different from the threatening bogeyman, Wolfsheim, who haunts the pages of *The Great Gatsby.* Monroe Stahr, the Jewish tragic hero of *The Last Tycoon,* the wary boy gang leader from the Bronx who has made himself top dog in Hollywood and is ready for destruction, represents for Fitzgerald not only a triumph of art but a victory over prejudice.

To *see* him, much less to love him was not easy for Fitzgerald, whose initial reaction, as recorded in "Crazy Sunday," was to find Hollywood's Jews funny, fit subjects only for burlesque. In that story he tells how his protagonist (himself, surely) begins at his first big movie party an intendedly hilarious takeoff "in the intonations of Mr. Silverstein": '—a story of divorce, the younger generators and the Foreign Legion. . . . But we got to build it up, see?. . . —then she says she feels this sex appil for him and he burns out and says, 'Oh, go on destroy yourself—' '' But Fitzgerald's alter ego is greeted with boos and blank stares. "It was the resentment," the author explains, "of the community toward the stranger, the thumbs-down of the clan." And all, of course, played out in the house of that most eminent of doomed Jews, the figure which was to become eventually Monroe Stahr.

The word "Jew" is not mentioned, to be sure, any more than it is in Nathanael West's brief retelling of what may have been the very same incident, or one very like it, introduced as background conversation during a minor episode in *The Day of the Locust;* but this time we hear it in the voice of the "clan." " 'That's right,' said another man. 'Guys like that come out here, make a lot of money, grouse all the time about the place, flop on their assignments, then. . . tell dialect stories about producers they've never met.' " But when Fitzgerald attempts a full scale treatment of Stahr and his wife—the redemptive father-husband, and the dangerous actress-wife who were in real life Irving Thalberg and Norma Shearer— when he turns to them again in his unfinished novel, he is on top of his own Jewish problem, to the extent at least of being able to name names; registering what may have been his own first impressions in a detached and objective way, through the consciousness of a certain Prince Agge, who sitting at lunch with the executives of a great studio, notes: "They were the money men—they were the rulers. . . . Eight out of ten were Jews—. . . . As a turbulent man, serving his time in the Foreign Legion, he thought that Jews were too fond of their own skins. But he was willing to concede that they might be different in America under different circumstances, and certainly he found Stahr was much of a man in every way. . . ."

With Agge's final opinion the two spokesmen characters into whom Fitzgerald has split himself agree, Cecilia Brady, female and Irish and a worshipper of the great, loving Stahr unabashedly for his alien masculinity; and Wylie White, WASP presumably and tyro writer, admiring him for his control of the new narrative skills which make words seem obsolete. But *The Last Tycoon* remained unfinished and Stahr exits—or better, fades away—in a confusion of other loves: one of which Fitzgerald had borrowed for him out of his own life, exploiting his then current affair with Sheila Graham, who was herself, though not until years later, to exploit both his exploitation and the affair itself (not without the help of a ghost writer, of course) in a popular book, which, becoming a movie, brought Fitzgerald (not without the help of an actor, of course) back in triumph to the world of Hollywood from which he had died in despair. "There are no second acts in American lives," he had written in the notes to himself appended to the manuscript of *The Last Tycoon,* and "not one survived the castration." But he had forgotten about what was then still called "the silver screen."

No matter—for better or worse what exists of *The Last Tycoon* had fixed forever (or perhaps merely caught once and for all) a pattern which has been repeated over and over again in books as vastly different from each other as Christopher Isherwood's *Prater Violet,* Norman Mailer's *The Deer Park,* and Robert Penn Warren's *Flood.* Expatriate Englishman, wandering Jew, and transplanted Southern Agrarian, they portray each in his own way the romance of Celt or WASP writer and Jewish moviemaker, a sentimental allegory signifying the capitulation of High Art to Pop Art, not in terror, however, but in pity and affection. Isherwood, perhaps because he is confessedly a homosexual, is able to reveal the meaning of the encounter and the surrender with an uncustomary candor (though he, for reasons of his own, eschews the word "Jew"), permitting the one of his ill-matched pair who bears his own name to comment just before the novel's close: "Mother's Boy, the comic Foreigner with the funny accent. Well, that didn't matter. . . . For, beneath our disguises . . . we knew. Beneath outer consciousness, two other beings. . . had met and recognized each other, and had clasped hands. He was my father. I was his son. And I loved him very much."

But, of course, Isherwood's Herr Bergman, the director in flight from the Nazis and toward Hollywood, *is* a Jew—just as is Mailer's Charles Francis Eitel, in flight from Congressional Investigating Committees toward death, and even Robert Penn Warren's Yasha Jones, camouflaged behind an assumed last name and oddly at loose ends in the American Deep South. Yet each of these authors plays games with the deepest mythological identity of the adopted father, who represents to each the real maker of the movies for which they aspire to be given screen credits at least. Mailer is less coy and cagey about Eitel's origins in the dramatic version of *The Deer Park* than he was in the earlier novel; but even in the later work, Eitel when challenged admits only to being "half Jewish—on both sides" and in a context which makes it clear that he habitually lies about such matters. And though Brad Tolliver, the WASP-writer of

Warren's *Flood* would clearly love his director to be a Jew, the author will not grant him this mythological satisfaction—insisting that Yasha Jones is a "déraciné Georgian—. . . Georgia in Russia"; and when Brad says wistfully, "I thought you were a Jew," his longed-for foreign father answers oddly, "I sometimes think I am. . . . But we Georgians have a noble history, too."

Perhaps the problem arises in large part simply because, in the years since *The Last Tycoon,* the typical American novelist has ceased to be a provincial Gentile and has become himself an urban Jew; while the refugees to Hollywood (Daniel Fuchs, for instance and West himself) were already often Jewish even in Fitzgerald's own time—so that the contract of pre-Gutenberg Gentile and post-Gutenberg Jew was ceasing to be viable at the moment it was being first imagined. Yet how hard that mythological vision is to surrender even for Jews themselves, who, like Mailer, project *goyish* alter egos to represent their own entry into Hollywood; or, like Peter Viertel, invert the legendary romance—pitting a Jewish obsolescent writer against an Old Hollywood Pro turned super-Goy, or more precisely, maybe, super-Hemingway. Hemingway's name is, at any rate, often on the lips of Viertel's John Wilson, who views himself as having followed in the steps of the Master, only to go beyond by rendering the simplicity and silence which Hemingway pursued, in unspeaking images more appropriate than words. But maybe *all* Hollywood Pros tend to think of themselves as Hemingways, even the Jews, in a penultimate irony which demands that the gravediggers of books find a metaphor for their own lives in the career of a writer of books—who himself, in a more ultimate irony, defined his life style in imitation of that movie cowboy, Gary Cooper. Fitzgerald, certainly, whose own attitudes toward Hemingway were more complex than this, thought it all a sad joke, jotting down among his notes for the background of *The Last Tycoon:* "Tragedy of these men was that nothing in their lives had really bitten deep at all. Bald Hemingway characters."

Viertel's Hemingway-character is quite another matter, however, more like the author's flattering image of himself than Fitzgerald's wry vision of his bald imitators, a true communicant in the Church of Raw Experience and Mortal Danger, appropriately portrayed at play in the jungles of Africa. But he is no anti-Semite like the first Hemingway, this second one turned moviemaker; and he is shown choosing to insult the latterday Lady Brett of *White Hunter, Black Heart* rather than join her in vilification of the updated Robert Cohn, who is his companion and surrogate for the book's author. ". . . and suddenly the lady next to me," Wilson tells his own anti-Semitic lady-interlocutor, as his put-down begins, "and she was a beautiful lady, said that the one thing she didn't mind about Hitler was what he'd done to the Jews. Well, dear, I turned to her, and everyone was silent, and I said, 'Madam, I have dined with some ugly, goddamn bitches in my time. I've dined with some of the goddamnedest, ugliest bitches in the world, but you, dear, are the ugliest bitch of them all.' "

This is not just a pious political stand, a final development of Popular Front politics before it fades into general American liberalism, required of all men of good will after Hitler—though it is this in large part. It is also a declaration of allegiance to the movies themselves and the force that made them; since the movies *are* Jewish, after all: a creation of Jewish ingenuity and surplus Jewish capital, a by-product of the Jewish Garment Industry, which began by blurring away class distinctions in dress and ended by blotting out class distinctions in dreams. But the movies are, alas, ceasing to be Jewish, which is to say, they are dying—dying into something else.

These days there is scarcely a film produced which is not in fact an embryo T.V. program; its brief appearance in the neighborhood theater as clearly an intermediate step on the way to a lifelong run on the Late, Late Show—as the appearance in hard covers of a new book by, say, James Michener, has been for a long time an intermediate step to a film at that neighborhood theater. And (peace to Lenny Bruce, who first revealed to me the scope and depth of this distinction) as surely as chocolate is Jewish and fudge *goyish,* so are the movies Jewish and T.V. *goyish.* What the implications of this are beyond the fact that new mythologies of Pop Culture will have to be invented to suit new needs, and that the figure of the Jew is almost sure to be absent from them—I, the spiritual child of those Jewish Sages, Marx and Freud, leave to those sitting even now at the feet of *goyish* Gurus like Marshall McLuhan and Norman O. Brown.

*Buffalo, N.Y.*
—1967

# FOUR

# A Night with Mr. Teas

THE IMMORAL MR. TEAS was approaching the end of a nine-month run at the little movie house in Seattle where I first saw it. Paired with it was *The Mouse that Roared,* a film I had accidentally seen twice before and one for which I have small affection. I am dismayed at its sentimental-liberal clichés espousing Love and deploring the Bomb. Naturally, I arrived too early and had to endure once more the final cuteness of "The Mouse," its technicolor reassurance that our world would survive—and that its survival would be an unmitigated Happy Ending. It was technicolor I really hated, I told myself; nothing could be true or good or beautiful in those never quite convincing tones, just as nothing could be high, wide, or handsome on the nonscale of the wide screen. "Justify God's ways to man—in color and VistaVision," I imagined the modern muse telling some new Milton; and foresaw the miserable event: four stars in the *Daily News,* ennui for any sensitive beholder.

*Mr. Teas,* however, turned out to be in technicolor, too—its opening all the vulgar tints of urban Southern California: a sun-dazzled city bus stop and our hero, briefcase in hand, beside a street-corner bench endorsed with an ad for a Jewish funeral home. Los Angeles and the undertakers again. Another cliché, I found myself thinking, the by-now-not-quite-fresh-or-moving metaphor for Hell in Our Time. And I was not reassured by the Monsieur Hulot-type music of the score—tinkle-jangle-tinkle, the submelody of city life, as Mr. Teas switched from bus to bike, changed from mufti to a pair of cerise-terra cotta overalls, and began to pedal along his insipid round of work: delivering false teeth to dentists' offices.

This at least was an apt metaphor, I argued with the self that wanted to get the hell out—a quite unhackneyed figure for a setting and routine as glistening and meaningless as death: the detached smile fixed in a polished vise. But one part of me still kept asking what I was doing there anyhow.

The last erotic picture I had been to see—also after a nine-month run—had been "Ecstasy"; but that had been some twenty-five or thirty years before, in another world. How different a world became clear quite soon, as I found myself laughing at a spectacle so antiromantic that it verged, for me, at least, on the anaphrodisiac. In *Mr. Teas* there was not only no passion, but no contact, no flesh touching flesh, no consummation shown or suggested. I remembered from the earlier film the pearls slipping from Hedy Lamarr's throat, her face blurred in the ecstasy advertised by the title. For pornography the woman's angle of vision is necessary, but here were no women outside of Bill Teas's head; and Bill Teas was nobody's dreamed lover, only a dreamer, with his half-modest, half-comical beard, his sagging pectoral muscles, his little lump of a belly creased by baggy shorts or hidden by overalls.

And Mr. Teas could touch no one—not in lust or love or in the press of movement along a street. Once in the film he lays his hand on flesh, the shoulder of an eight-year-old girl working out with a hula hoop, and she beans him with a rock. Any really nubile, desirable female is doomed to disappear into the ladies' room or the arms of some lover whose face we never see—as unreal, finally, as the girl he embraces. Mr. Teas conducts his odd business and carries his frustrated dreams through a world of noncontact and noncommunication.

In his wanderings from office to office, from home to lunchroom, the violently overalled Mr. Teas finds occasional refreshment in staring down the more than half-revealed bosoms of receptionists, waitresses, and cashiers. In his otherwise quite arid world, all females are singularly and lushly *décolleté,* as if they existed chiefly to titillate his impotent desire, and as the plot unfolds with all the step-by-step deliberateness of a strip tease, Mr. Teas is shown developing a talent for imaginarily stripping ever closer to the buff the girls who torment him on his rounds. An injection in a dentist's chair from an assistant, whose breasts become in fantasy the headrest which supports him, helps Mr. Teas create the first of his visions; but awake and undrugged, he continues to fabricate them, finally comes to regard them as a disease from which he asks a psychiatrist to deliver him.

The visions of Mr. Teas are, however, strange in a way which at first we do not notice, because their strangeness is an accepted part of a world in which we all live. That is to say, the nudity he creates is never *complete* nudity. Sitting, for instance, in a café, gnawing on an obscenely large slab of watermelon, Mr. Teas finds that the waitress who serves him has become quite naked, except for the merest doily of an apron covering the meeting place of thighs and belly. Admiring the nonchalance of Mr. Teas as he gnaws his cool fruit and pretends to ignore the feast beside him, we realize that the joke has adapted to the conditions which make the showing of the film possible: there must be an apron; he must not touch her.

It is not finally just a matter of observing certain rules of the censors, but of making those very rules the subject of the picture, the butt of its jokes. For what we are shown when the rules are observed is not female flesh, but pin-up pictures—moving pictures of moving pin-up pictures, life twice removed; and this is why *Mr. Teas,* funny as it is (and it *is* funny—chiefly because of the discretion of its cameraman, Russ Meyers, and the skill with which Bill Teas projects the impassive, dogged, low-keyed lust of its *schlemiel*-hero), is also a quite serious film. It is not merely like the strip tease, the candy-box cover, the girlie calendar, and the fold-out magazine nude; it is about them.

In one sequence, during which he presumably searches for escape at the beach, Mr. Teas stumbles on a professional photographer who is running through her paces a model or hopeful starlet, first in an ultimate bikini, then stripped of her bra and finally clothed only in the surf. How icily the girl simulates the poses of lewd appeal, wild abandon, and sexual allure, though for the camera only and on cue as the camera clicks. Meanwhile, Mr. Teas, too, has a camera, a miniature Brownie that cannot compete with the equipment of the professional any more than the meager personal dreams of Mr. Teas can compete with those professionally produced. He inhabits a world of prefabricated fantasies, stumbling into one situation after another in which those fantasies are being manufactured for men powerless to evoke for themselves even the intangible shadow of sex.

We are, therefore, constantly being reminded of how we, too, live in a world where, whatever the natural bent of our desires, we are forced by billboards, night clubs, stage entertainments, cartoons, and photographs, by the very ads which assail us for brassieres and Kleenex and Pepsi-Cola, into playing the Peeping Tom; and of how we, too, are not only teased by the ten thousand commercially produced provocations, but become finally our own teasers—stripping but not possessing (not even in the deepest imagination), as we have been taught. There is one unforgettable scene, in which, as Mr. Teas aimlessly walks down a street, a window shade springs up and, plastered almost against the pane, a female body is revealed from just below the shoulders to just above the waist—a noseless face in which the nipples make wide eyes above the pursed, tiny mouth of the navel; a face which seems to stare back at the starer, as if all flesh (not only male flesh, as our convention demands) had become eyes and the only communication in either direction were peeping.

As the picture draws to a close, we follow Mr. Teas on a day's outing to a lake, where he is after the same game as always, though by now he has become terrified by his talent, thinks he flees what he seeks; and he finds it. This time there is not just a single girl, but four at once, who, quite naked, rock themselves on hammocks, dip and splash in the shallow water or swim where it is deeper, row boats, and toss a ball, while Mr. Teas ogles and spies, smiling his half-beatific, half-idiotic smile, and separated from them still, as if by the invisible glass pane of the TV toothpaste commercial.

So stylized, so indistinguishable from mass-produced fantasies in every premeditated, robotic gesture are the girls he watches that it is difficult to tell whether the whole episode is intended to be taken for an actual event or merely the most extended of Mr. Teas's dreams. Certainly what of the audience remained to the end the night I first saw the movie (several more clean-cut pairs of college sweethearts had walked out early in the game) argued about it vehemently from either side. But the point, I suppose, lies really in this ambiguity, this irreality. And just as the girls were, in their gestures, more the fabrications of mass culture than of nature, so they were also in their dimensions and their textures. It is impossible to remember, two days after leaving the theater, what color their hair was.

These girls do not quite seem to be women, adapted as they are to the mythical dimensions of pin-ups and to a more than mythical smoothness of texture. Nowhere is there pimple or blemish or sagging skin or untoward wrinkle or mottled flesh. The loving, patient camera (not really a moviemaker's camera at all, but that of the still photographer) that follows the play of light and shade on haunch and hollow finds no human imperfection, not even goose flesh or beads of sweat. Such girls seem more like fruit than flesh— hothouse fruit, serenely perfect and savorless, not to be touched or eaten. Only looked at. Unreal. Unreal. Unreal. This is the sadness of *Mr. Teas.*

As old restrictions crumble in our society, the naked flesh assumes its proper place among the possible subjects for movies, the place it has always held in the other, less public arts; but meanwhile, in the United States, we have been long corrupted by the pseudo-arts of tease and titillation, conditioned to a version of the flesh more appropriate for peeking than love or lust or admiration or even real disgust. In European films like *Room at the Top* or *Hiroshima, Mon Amour,* we have been offered newer versions of nudity appropriate to serious art, versions of a nudity not so much seen as felt, responded to in tenderness and desire. Whether equivalent versions will prove possible in American films seems to me doubtful; perhaps our way will have to be comic rather than passionate or even sentimental. If this is so, *Mr. Teas,* for all its lapses into the obvious, may someday seem a pioneering effort. Its makers have not attempted to surmount the difficulties which confront the American moviemaker who desires to make nakedness his theme; but they have, with absolute good humor, managed at once to bypass and to illuminate those difficulties. The end result is a kind of imperturbable comedy, with overtones of real pathos.

How especially stupid in light of all this are the cuts demanded by the censors of New York, who, in deleting some twenty minutes, have eliminated not only the nipples and buttocks they were obviously after but also the wit and pathos and point of *Mr. Teas.* To

New York moviegoers I am moved to say: Stay away from what will be called *The Immoral Mr. Teas* in your theaters. It will be a tease in the worst sense of the word, the merest leering hint, the dullest remnant of a once witty film—a joke of its own kind on public standards of decency. Decency! How hard it is to believe that the names of those involved in the production are not anticipatory jokes which this final one fulfills. But DeCenzie is apparently the actual name of the producer of the film, Bill Teas that of the chief actor, and Cantlay the real name of a real California street. It pays to be lucky!

I do not know whether the makers of *Mr. Teas* were merely lucky or really aware of the implications of the movie they were making; and New York viewers will have no way of deciding for themselves without a trip to Atlantic City, where an uncut version is being shown. Perhaps DeCenzie and Russ Meyers, the cameraman, are themselves only two more victims of the process which reduces sex in America to sex in the eye, and are critics of the process only inadvertently. I have been reading press releases about how Russ Meyers, who shot *Mr. Teas* in four days at the cost of only twenty-four thousand dollars and dreams of earning a million on it, has produced another film, another bareback quickie, called *Eve and the Handyman*. Maybe from the start he has just been cashing in on the new freedom which provides new ways of exploiting the mindless audience. I would like to believe that this is not so, that he knew all along not merely how funny but how sad *Mr. Teas* really was. In the end, it doesn't matter. The artist is entitled to whatever can be found in his work. I hope he makes the million.

—1959

# FIVE

# The Death of *Avant-Garde* Literature

THAT WE HAVE been living through the death of *avant-garde* literature over the past couple of decades most of us now know. What we are still trying to find out is how to come to terms with that fact, beyond deploring or applauding it, or, in stoical despair, simply refusing to do either. We would scarcely feel at such a loss if we confronted merely the rejection by certain leading authors of advanced or experimental art, for this has been customary in America. Certainly our greatest writers of the 1920's began their careers precisely by turning their backs on the extremes of modernism to woo the mass audience through the mass magazines. Scott Fitzgerald, we remember, was at home in the *Saturday Evening Post* from the start, and that same magazine opened its arms to Faulkner at the very moment he was contemplating *Absalom, Absalom!;* while Hemingway, after a brief flirtation with the little magazines and a vicious parody of their modes in *Torrents of Spring*, headed via *Esquire* toward the maximum audience provided by *Life*. Fair enough. Such adjustments are in the American grain; even Henry Miller has become at last a garrulous, platitudinous old man, and a tourist attraction to boot.

But our major novelists have customarily placed themselves *against* an *avant-garde* tradition which flourishes elsewhere, in Europe or in certain peripheral writers of our own—Djuna Barnes, for example, or Gertrude Stein. They have consciously chosen another direction. Now, alas, there is no choice. The European gravediggers of the *avant-garde*, whether talented survivors of the times of *tran-*

454

*sition,* like Samuel Beckett, or slick young counterfeiters of the experimental, like Robbe-Grillet, do not constitute a counterforce sufficient to make newer ambitious middlebrows like, say, Harvey Swados or John Cheever seem either desperately inept or rewardingly reactionary.

But neither does membership in the academy contrived of yesterday's *avant-gardism,* the nostalgic imitation of techniques revolutionary and exciting in the heyday of James Joyce, produce a literature advanced for us. The very youngest among us may think so briefly, of course, since they are disposed to regard kindly the pioneers of modernism without really knowing them; and it is to such readers that academically "advanced" journals like the *Evergreen Review* are likely to seem less intolerably dull than they in fact are. Such readers, too (and they can be of all ages), have helped, surely, in giving to the warmed-over Proustianism of Durrell's Alexandrian books the cachet of *avant-garde.* What is fashionable, however, cannot properly claim the rewards appropriate to the antifashionable; no writer can have the rewards of book-club adoption and of alienation at the same time.

With the aid of the mass media, antifashion becomes fashion among us at a rate that bewilders critics and writers alike; and nobody will find so many staunch friends and supporters as the man who labels himself an outcast or an enemy of society. A pair of public figures like Arthur Miller and Tennessee Williams illustrate the situation with all the grossness that pertains to the commercial theater; but their tragicomedy of accepted alienation is played out monthly, with a little more verve and grace, in the pages of ladies' magazines, like *Vogue* and *Harper's Bazaar,* or in the sophisticated slicks, like *Esquire.*

No techniques can be devised these days, at any rate, for which the literature major (trained in some Ivy League haven by a highbrow, defeated or biding his time) is not appallingly well prepared; or toward which his wife (who, with the years, does more and more of his reading for him) is not dishearteningly well-disposed. But the literature major and his wife, along with the second-generation literature majors who are their children, constitute the new middlebrow audience, whose appearance testifies to the technical exhaustion of the *avant-garde.* Certainly the devices which once characterized such art (the fractured narrative line, stream-of-consciousness, insistent symbolism, ironic allusion) seem today more banal than the well made plot, the set description, the heavy-handed morality that they were invented to displace. The whole meaning of advanced art was never contained, however, in mere technique, which was only one of the many modes of offending the philistine reader.

It is, after all, *offense* on many fronts which distinguishes *avant-garde* from other kinds of writing. Lowbrow or frankly unadventurous art asks of its readers *identification,* trying to persuade them that it speaks their language, the language of all but a handful of snobs, and embodies their values, the values of all but a handful of nuts. Middlebrow or pretentiously vacuous art offers as its hallmark *protest,* trying to persuade its readers that they are joined with the author and an enlightened not-too-few in a gallant struggle against some quite unambiguous evil, sponsored only by members of the Other Side: slavery, McCarthyism, anti-Semitism, cruelty to dogs or children, The Bomb. Its techniques, therefore, are intended to create neither a private language nor a public one, but only the jargon of a party, in power and defending itself, or out and trying to get in.

Highbrow or truly experimental art aims at *insult;* and the intent of its typical language is therefore exclusion. It recruits neither defenders of virtue nor opponents of sin; only shouts in the face of the world the simple slogan, *épater le bourgeois,* or "mock the middle classes," which is to say, mock most, if not quite all, of its readers. Once the highbrow could offend such readers simply by sporting a contempt for syntax and capital letters, like e. e. cummings, or merely by displaying too much anxiety over the intricacies of writing well, like Henry James. But such easy strategies are no longer available to us, in a time when even journalists have learned to sham a concern with style, and even college rhetorics teach toleration of deviant mechanics and grammar.

No, if offense is still to be given, the good burghers still to be bugged, it must be done by ideas and not by techniques, a program of action rather than an aesthetic code. But what ideas remain offensive in a time in which not merely grammars and dictionaries, but guide books for raising children and for living the good life insist that everything is relative and to know all is to forgive all? Once the advocacy of alcohol and sex, drunkenness and adultery was enough to enrage the respectable; but the long fight to drink and make love as one pleases, memorialized in hundreds of books since the first lost generation announced its lostness in *The Sun Also Rises,* has passed by way of the cocktail party and the fifty-minute hour with the psychiatrist into polite society. *The Sun Also Rises* has ceased being a dangerous book to become a required one, a bore assigned in class; and the mass arts complete the degradation mass education begins, making it next an O.K., which is to say, very bad, movie.

With what a sense of daring, however, the hitherto dirty word "impotent" was first spoken aloud in that film. Yet how quickly we have come to accept since more and more formerly forbidden words: "whore" and God knows what, allowing them first, of course, in foreign films, then in ill-lighted, iow-budget domestic ones, i.e., art films (needing some guaranty that old taboos are being broken in the name of something higher than mere entertainment), then, at last, in commercial films themselves. Who a couple of decades ago would have thought the brutal sexual humor of Billy Wilder possible in neighborhood theaters, or the horror-pornography of Tennessee Williams?

It is not that we Americans have given up our hatred and fear of sex, on which indeed our very sense of our selves and our ties with the past depend; it is only that we now expect, even demand, that our traditional distaste be spoken aloud in four-letter words rather than whispered in genteel polysyllables. Think of the success of J. D. Salinger, in whom sex is consistently presented as a temptation or threat to his teen-age saints—of Holden Caulfield fleeing seduction in classrooms and elevators and hotel rooms, and of Franny crying out in effect, "I'd rather have a nervous breakdown than sleep with you, dear!" In any event, we listen these days to both sides, as they say, even on the level of the popular arts; and both sides speak the same language—a language against which only a diminishing minority of ever more comical bigots cries out in protest.

And what, then, is the serious writer to do in his search for occasions for offense now that the rank and file have overrun his old positions? How can he shock those who, when they do not agree with him, tolerate him? He can, of course, raise the ante higher and higher, *i.e.,* advocate more and more sex, polygamy compounded to hypergamy; or strip it of sentimentality, making the orgasm itself rather than anything called love the goal; or describe more and more closely, with attention to more and more senses, and in language less and less clinical or idyllic, the act itself. He can become, that is to say, Norman Mailer or Jack Kerouac, but he cannot keep the new middlebrows from loving him.

Still he pleases rather than offends, sells well rather than being ignored, returns home to find not the cops waiting for him, but the photographers from *Life,* and a delegation of students inviting him to lecture to their class at City College. Mailer produces what has been described as the conscience literature of the present $30,000-a-year ex-radicals; and Kerouac provides fantasies for the future $40,000-a-year ex-Beatniks. Only in night clubs can the grossest language or the sternest contempt for banal morality stir up the police (so that if giving offense be the hallmark of the *avant-garde,* Lenny Bruce is the last *avant-garde* artist in America); between the covers of books, hard or soft, anything goes—at least with that growing public that ransacks the past for banned novels and stops in the supermarket between groceries and cigarettes to pick up *Fanny Hill* or D. H. Lawrence or the *Kama Sutra.* Already the time is in sight when the only forbidden book will be *Little Women.*

Does anything at all then shock the enlightened middlebrow as he stands, Martini in hand, Freud on shelf, and the slogans of yesterday's *avant-garde* turned to platitudes in his mouth? For a little while at least, it seemed as if homosexuality and drug-taking provided for him the *frisson* proper to *avant-garde* art. Did not even the most emancipated of his own teachers shudder when confronted for the first time by a generation of students crying out, "Freud is a fink!"—meaning that they preferred not to make *ego* of *id,* rationality of impulse, but to extend the range of waking consciousness with the aid of the hallucinogens: peyote or marijuana or LSD? Did not his own even more emancipated wife tremble hearing for the first time the sons of her fellow members in the League of Women Voters insist that they wanted not more and freer sex with more and freer girls, but each other?

Certainly, in response to these new possibilities of offense, a new literature arose, best exemplified, perhaps, by the novels of William Burroughs, *Naked Lunch* and *The Soft Machine,* and the poetry of Allen Ginsberg, particularly *Howl;* though a figure of greater mythical potency than either, perhaps, is Jean Genet—"St. Genet," who has been lucky enough to have Jean-Paul Sartre as his St. Paul. These laureates of homosexual love and drug-taking have set themselves the task not merely of offending the most tolerant, but of redeeming for them some sense of the real horror of a world they so peacefully and self-righteously contemplate, programs of reform in hand. The nightmare reality created by Genet and Burroughs out of their own fantasies and obsessions, their flirtation with madness and contempt for the rational, defies tolerance and reform alike. It is tempting to dismiss their work as mere scare literature, play-terror; but they evoke a vision of the end of man as we have conceived him from the time of the Greeks to the age of Freud—surely terror genuine enough for anyone.

But how quickly their breakthrough to new frontiers of offense has been followed up by imitators and vulgarizers. In our time of rapid communication, the first discoverers have scarcely staked out a territory before the tourists have come, then the carpetbaggers, and at last the middlebrow suburbanites—eager to set up housekeeping on prime sites overlooking the first landing places. So Burroughs' lonely island has turned into a suburb—complete with writer's clubs and home courses in creative writing; so his kind of *avant-garde* has become *Kitsch.* In how few years we have lived to see a popular subliterature made on the model of his *Naked Lunch* and Genet's *Our Lady of the Flowers,* the creation of a new genre recounting the adventures of the homosexual prostitute in nighttown, a kind of *Adventures of Freddie Hill*—since it is really Fanny's brother rather than Fanny herself who interests us.

Her trials and triumphs have begun to seem, indeed, a little dull, too normal to titillate or appall any but the dullest middlebrows passing an idle hour in bus stations or airports. Perhaps John Rechy's recent *City of Night* (described on the jacket as "dealing with the little-known world of hidden sex") represents as well as anything the subsidence of a newer sort of pornography into a newer sort of *Kitsch*, the latest rapid transformation of *avant-garde* art to everybody's entertainment. We can interpret, surely, the end to which his hero comes as symbolic for us all, since he returns from "the clandestine world of furtive love" to childhood and mother and Texas, where the weary clichés of magazine fiction for ladies rise up in his mind; and he leaves us (as if it were *Woman's Day* we had been reading) with the plaint of a small boy for his dog: "And the fierce wind is an echo of angry childhood and of a very scared boy looking out the window—remembering my dead dog outside by the wounded house and thinking: It isn't fair! *Why can't dogs go to Heaven?*" But when will the moving picture version be made?

—1964

# SIX

# Cross the Border—Close the Gap

To DESCRIBE the situation of American letters at the end of the sixties is difficult indeed, almost impossible, since the language available to critics at this point is totally inappropriate to the best work of the artists who give the period its special flavor, its essential life. But precisely here is a clue, a way to begin: not with some presumed crisis of poetry or fiction, but with the unconfessed scandal of contemporary literary criticism, which for three or four decades now has vainly attempted to deal in terms invented to explain, defend, and evaluate one kind of book with *another* kind of book—so radically different that it calls the very assumptions underlying those terms into question. Established critics may think that they have been judging recent literature; but, in fact, recent literature has been judging them.

Almost all living readers and writers are aware of a fact which they have no adequate words to express, not in English certainly, nor even in American. We are living, have been living for two decades—and have become acutely conscious of the fact since 1955 —through the death throes of Modernism and the birth pangs of Post-Modernism. The kind of literature which had arrogated to itself the name Modern (with the presumption that it represented the ultimate advance in sensibility and form, that beyond it newness was not possible), and whose moment of triumph lasted from a point just before World War I until one just after World War II, is *dead,* i.e., belongs to history not actuality. In the field of the novel, this means that the age of Proust, Mann, and Joyce is over; just as in verse that of T. S. Eliot, Paul Valéry, Montale and Seferis is done with.

461

Obviously *this* fact has not remained secret: and some critics have, indeed, been attempting to deal with its implications. But they have been trying to do it in a language and with methods which are singularly inappropriate, since both method and language were invented by the defunct Modernists themselves to apologize for their own work and the work of their preferred literary ancestors (John Donne, for instance, or the *symbolistes),* and to educate an audience capable of responding to them. Naturally, this will not do at all; and so the second or third generation New Critics in America, like the spiritual descendants of F. R. Leavis in England (or the neo-neo-Hegelians in Germany, the belated Croceans in Italy), end by proving themselves imbeciles and naïfs when confronted by, say, a poem of Allen Ginsberg, a new novel by John Barth.

Why not, then, invent a New New Criticism, a Post-Modernist criticism appropriate to Post-Modernist fiction and verse? It sounds simple enough—quite as simple as imperative—but it is, in fact, much simpler to say than do; for the question which arises immediately is whether there can be *any* criticism adequate to Post-Modernism. The Age of T. S. Eliot, after all, was the age of a literature essentially self-aware, a literature dedicated, in avowed intent, to analysis, rationality, anti-Romantic dialectic—and consequently aimed at eventual respectability, gentility, even, at last, academicism. Criticism is natural, even essential to such an age; and to no one's surprise (though finally there were some voices crying out in dismay), the period of early twentieth-century Modernism became, as it was doomed to do, an Age of Criticism: an age in which criticism began by invading the novel, verse, drama, and ended by threatening to swallow up all other forms of literature. Certainly, it seems, looking back from this point, as if many of the best books of the period were critical books (by T. S. Eliot and Ezra Pound and I. A. Richards, by John Crowe Ransom and Kenneth Burke and R. P. Blackmur, to mention only a few particularly eminent names); and its second-best, novels and poems eminently suited to critical analysis, particularly in schools and universities: the works of Proust-Mann-and-Joyce, for instance, to evoke a trilogy which seems at the moment more the name of a single college course than a list of three authors.

We have, however, entered quite another time, apocalyptic, antirational, blatantly romantic and sentimental; an age dedicated to joyous misology and prophetic irresponsibility; one, at any rate, distrustful of self-protective irony and too great self-awareness. If criticism is to survive at all, therefore, which is to say, if criticism is to remain or become useful, viable, relevant, it must be radically altered from the models provided by Croce or Leavis or Eliot or Erich Auerbach, or whoever; though not in the direction indicated by Marxist critics, however subtle and refined. The Marxists are last-ditch defenders of rationality and the primacy of political fact, intrinsically hostile to an age of myth and passion, sentimentality and fantasy.

On the other hand, a renewed criticism certainly will no longer be formalist or intrinsic; it will be contextual rather than textual, not primarily concerned with structure or diction or syntax, all of which assume that the work of art "really" exists on the page rather than in a reader's passionate apprehension and response. Not words-on-the-page but words-in-the-world or rather words-in-the-head, which is to say, at the private juncture of a thousand contexts, social, psychological, historical, biographical, geographical, in the consciousness of the lonely reader (delivered for an instant, but an instant only, from all of those contexts by the *ekstasis* of reading): this will be the proper concern of the critics to come. Certain older critics have already begun to provide examples of this sort of criticism by turning their backs on their teachers and even their own earlier practices. Norman O. Brown, for instance, who began with scholarly, somewhat Marxian studies of Classic Literature has moved on to metapsychology in *Life Against Death* and *Love's Body*; while Marshall McLuhan, who made his debut with formalist examinations of texts by Joyce and Gerard Manley Hopkins, has shifted to metasociological analyses of the mass media in *Understanding Media,* and finally to a kind of pictographic shorthand, half put-on and half serious emulation of advertising style in *The Medium is the Massage.*

The voice as well as the approach is important in each case, since neither in Brown nor McLuhan does one hear the cadence and tone proper to "scientific" criticism of culture, normative psychology or sociology attached to literary texts. No, the pitch, the rhythms, the dynamics of both are mantic, magical, more than a little *mad* (it is a word, a concept that one desiring to deal with contemporary literature must learn to regard as more honorific than pejorative). In McLuhan and Brown—as in D. H. Lawrence earlier, Charles Olson when he first wrote on Melville—a not so secret fact recently hushed up in an age of science and positivism is candidly confessed once more: criticism is literature or it is nothing. Not amateur philosophy or objective analysis, it differs from other forms of literary art in that it starts not with the world in general but the world of art itself, in short, that it uses one work of art as an occasion to make another.

There have been, of course, many such meditating works of art in the past, both fairly recent (Nietzsche's *Birth of Tragedy*) and quite remote (Longinus *On The Sublime),* which make it clear that the authority of the critic is based not on his skills in research or his collection of texts but on his ability to find words and rhythms and images appropriate to his ecstatic vision of, say, the plays of Euripides or the opening verses of *Genesis.* To evoke Longinus or even Nietzsche, however, is in a sense misleading, suggesting models too grandiose and solemn. To be sure, the newest criticism must be aesthetic, poetic in form as well as substance; but it must also be, in light of where we are, comical, irreverent, vulgar. Models have appeared everywhere in recent years but tentatively, inadvertently as it were—as in the case of Angus Wilson, who began a review of *City of Night* some years ago (in the pages of an ephemeral little magazine), by writing quite matter-of-factly, "Everyone knows John Rechy is a little shit." And all at once we are out of the Eliotic church, whose dogmas, delivered *ex cathedra,* two generations of students were expected to learn by heart: "Honest criticism and sensitive appreciation are directed not upon the poet but upon the poetry. . . . The mind of the mature poet differs from that of the immature one not precisely on any valuation of personality, not by being necessarily more interesting, or having 'more to say,' but rather by being a more finely perfected medium in which etc., etc."

Unless criticism refuses to take itself quite so seriously or at least to permit its readers not to, it will inevitably continue to reflect the finicky canons of the genteel tradition and the depressing pieties of the Culture Religion of Modernism, from which Eliot thought he had escaped—but which in fact he only succeeded in giving a High Anglican tone: "It is our business as readers of literature, to know what we like. It is our business, as Christians, *as well as* readers of literature, to know what we ought to like." But not to know that such stuff is funny is to be imprisoned in Church, cut off from the liberating privilege of comic sacrilege. It is high time, however, for such sacrilege rather than such piety; as some poets have known really ever since Dada, without knowing how to keep their sacrilege from becoming itself sacred; as the dearest obscenities of Dada were sanctified into the social "art" of Surrealism under the fell influence of Freud and Marx.

The kind of criticism which the age demands is, then, Death-of-Art Criticism, which is most naturally practiced by those who have come of age since the death of the "New Poetry" and the "New Criticism." But it ought to be possible under certain conditions to some of us oldsters as well, even those of us whose own youth was coincident with the freezing of all the madness of *symbolisme*-Dada-*surréalisme* into the rigidities of academic *avant-garde*. In this sense, the problem of the aging contemporary critic is quite like that of the no-longer-young contemporary novelist, which one necessarily begins to define even as he defines the dilemma of the critic.

In any case, it seems evident that writers not blessed enough to be under thirty (or thirty-five, or whatever the critical age is these days) must be reborn in order to seem relevant to the moment, and those who inhabit it most comfortably, i.e., the young. But no one has even the hope of being reborn unless he knows first that he is dead—dead, to be sure, for someone else; but the writer exists as a writer precisely for someone else. More specifically, no novelist can be reborn until he knows that insofar as he remains a novelist in the traditional sense, he is dead; since the traditional novel is dead—not dying, but dead. What was up to only a few years ago a diagnosis, a predication (made, to be sure, almost from the moment of the invention of the novel: first form of pop literature, and therefore conscious that as compared to classic forms like epic or tragedy its life span was necessarily short) is now a fact. As certainly as God, i.e., the Old God, is dead, so the Novel, i.e., the Old Novel, is dead. To be sure, certain writers, still alive and productive (Saul Bellow, for instance, or John Updike, Mary McCarthy or James Baldwin), continue to write Old Novels, and certain readers, often with a sense of being quite up-to-date, continue to read them. But so do preachers continue to preach in the Old Churches, and congregations gather to hear them.

It is *not* a matter of assuming, like Marshall McLuhan, that the printed book is about to disappear, taking with it the novel—first form invented for print; only of realizing that in all of its forms—and most notably, perhaps, the novel—the printed book is being radically, functionally altered. No medium of communication ever disappears merely because a new and more efficient one is invented. One thinks, for instance of the lecture, presumably superannuated by the invention of moveable type, yet flourishing still after more than five centuries of obsolescence. What is demanded by functional obsolescence is learning to be less serious, more frivolous, a form of *entertainment*. Indeed, it could be argued that a medium begins to be felt as entertainment only at the point where it ceases to be a necessary or primary means of communication, as recent developments in radio (the total disappearance, for instance, of all high-minded commentators and pretentious playwrights) sufficiently indicates. Students at any rate are well aware of this truth in regard to the university lecture, and woe to the lecturer (of whom, alas, there are many) who does not know it!

In any event, even as the "serious" lecture was doomed by the technology of the fifteenth century, and the "serious" church service by the philology of the eighteenth and nineteenth—so is the "serious" novel, and "serious" criticism as well, by the technology and philology of the twentieth. Like the lecture and Christian church services, its self-awareness must now include the perception of its own absurdity, even impossibility. Since, however, the serious novel of our time is the Art Novel as practiced by Proust, Mann, and Joyce and imitated by their epigones, it is that odd blend of poetry, psychology, and documentation, whose real though not always avowed end was to make itself canonical, that we must disavow. Matthew Arnold may have been quite correct in foreseeing the emergence of literature as scripture in a world which was forsaking the Old Time Religion: but the life of the New Scriptures and the New Time Religion was briefer than he could have guessed.

Before the Bible of the Christians and Jews ceased to be central to the concerns of men in Western society, it had become merely a "book" among others; and this, indeed, may have misled the Arnoldians, who could not believe that a time might come when not merely *the* Book ceased to move men, but even books in general. Such, however, is the case—certainly as far as all books which consider themselves "art," i.e., scripture once removed, are concerned; and for this reason the reborn novel, the truly new New Novel must be anti-art as well as antiserious. But this means, after all, that it must become more like what it was in the beginning, more what it seemed when Samuel Richardson could not be taken *quite* seriously, and what it remained in England (as opposed to France, for instance) until Henry James had justified himself as an artist against such self-declared "entertainers" as Charles Dickens and Robert Louis Stevenson: popular, not quite reputable, a little dangerous—the one his loved and rejected cultural father, the other his sibling rival in art. The critical interchange on the nature of the novel to which James contributed "The Art of Fiction" and Stevenson "A Humble Remonstrance" memorializes their debate —which in the thirties most readers believed had been won hands down by James's defense of the novel as art; but which in the dawning seventies we are not sure about at all—having reached a time when *Treasure Island* seems somehow more to the point and the heart's delight than, say, *The Princess Casamassima.*

This popular tradition the French may have understood once (in the days when Diderot praised Richardson extravagantly, and the Marquis de Sade emulated him in a dirtier book than the Englishman dared) but they long ago lost sight of it. And certainly the so-called *"nouveau roman"* is in its deadly earnest almost the opposite of anything truly new, which is to say, anti-art. Robbe-Grillet, for example, is still the prisoner of dying notions of the *avantgarde;* and though he is aware of half of what the new novelist must do (destroy the Old, destroy Marcel Proust), he is unaware of what he must create in its place. His kind of antinovel is finally too arty and serious: a kind of neo-neo-classicism, as if to illustrate once more that in the end this is all the French can invent no matter how hard they try. Re-imagined on film by Alain Resnais, *Last Year at Marienbad* speaks to the young; but in print it remains merely *chic,* which is to say, a fashionable and temporary error of taste. Better by far, and by the same token infinitely more pertinent is Samuel Beckett, who having been born Irish rather than French, finds it hard to escape being (what some of his readers choose to ignore) compulsively and hilariously funny.

Best of all, however, and therefore totally isolated on the recent French scene (except for the perceptive comments of that equally ambiguous figure, Raymond Queneau) is Boris Vian, especially in his most successful work of fiction, *L'écume des jours*, recently translated into English as *Mood Indigo*. Indeed, Boris Vian is in many ways a prototype of the New Novelist, though he has been dead for a decade or so and his most characteristic work belongs to the years just after World War II. He was, first of all, an Imaginary American (as even writers born in the United States must be these days), who found himself in total opposition to the politics of America at the very moment he was most completely immersed in its popular culture—actually writing a detective novel called *I Will Spit On Your Grave* under the pen name of Vernon Sullivan, but pretending that he was only its translator into French. In fact, by virtue of this peculiar brand of mythological Americanism he managed to straddle the border, if not quite close the gap between high culture and low, belles-lettres and pop art. On the one hand, he was the writer of pop songs and a jazz trumpeter much influenced by New Orleans style; and on the other, the author of novels in which the thinly disguised figures of such standard French intellectuals as Jean Paul Sartre and Simone de Beauvoir are satirized. But even in his fiction, which seems at first glance quite traditional or, at any rate, conventionally *avant-garde,* the characters move toward their fates through an imaginary city whose main thoroughfare is called Boulevard Louis Armstrong.

Only now, however, has Vian won the audience he all along deserved, finding it first among the young of Paris, who know like their American counterparts that such a closing of the gap between elite and mass culture is precisely the function of the Novel Now— not merely optional as in Vian's day, but necessary. And though most of the younger American authors who follow a similar course follow it without ever having known him, by a shared concern rather than direct emulation, he seems more like them than such eminent American forerunners of theirs as Faulkner or Hemingway (except perhaps in Hemingway's neglected early burlesque, *Torrents of Spring,* and Faulkner's self-styled "pot-boiler," *Sanctuary.)*

Vian, unfortunately, turned to the form of the Pop Novel only for the work of his left hand, to which he was not willing even to sign his own name, writing in *L'écume des jours* what seems superficially a traditional enough love story to disarm the conventional critics; though it is finally undercut by a sentimentality which redeems its irony, and reflects a mythology too Pop and American for neo-neo-Classicists to bear.

The young Americans who have succeeded Vian, on the other hand, have abandoned all concealment, and when they are most themselves, nearest to their central concerns, turn frankly to Pop forms—though not, to be sure, the detective story which has by our time become hopelessly compromised by middlebrow condescension: an affectation of college professors and presidents. The forms of the novel which they prefer are those which seem now what the hard-boiled detective story once seemed to Vian: at the furthest possible remove from art and *avant-garde,* the greatest distance from inwardness, analysis, and pretension; and, therefore, immune to lyricism, on the one hand, or righteous social commentary, on the other. It is not compromise by the market place they fear; on the contrary, they choose the genre most associated with exploitation by the mass media: notably, the Western, Science Fiction, and Pornography.

Most congenial of all is the Western, precisely because it has for many decades now seemed to belong exclusively to pulp magazines, run-of-the mill T.V. series and Class B movies, which is to say, has been experienced almost purely as myth and entertainment rather than as "literature" at all—and its sentimentality has, therefore, come to possess our minds so completely that it can now be mitigated without essential loss by parody, irony—and even critical analysis. In a sense, our mythological innocence has been preserved in the Western, awaiting the day when, no longer believing ourselves innocent in fact, we could decently return to claim it in fantasy. But such a return to the Western represents, of course, a rejection of laureates of the loss of innocence like Henry James and Hawthorne: those particular favorites of the forties, who despite their real virtues turn out to have been too committed to the notion of European high art to survive as major influences in an age of Pop. And it implies as well momentarily turning aside from our beloved Herman Melville (compromised by his New Critical admirers and the countless Ph.D. dissertations they prompted), and even from Mark Twain. To Hemingway, Twain could still seem central to a living tradition, the Father of us all, but being Folk rather than Pop in essence, he has become ever more remote from an urban, industrialized world, for which any evocation of pre-Civil War, rural America seems a kind of pastoralism which complements rather than challenges the Art Religion. Folk Art knows and accepts its place in a class-structured world which Pop blows up, whatever its avowed intentions. What remains are only the possibilities of something closer to travesty than emulation—such a grotesque neo-Huck, for instance, as the foulmouthed D. J. in Norman Mailer's *Why Are We in Vietnam,* who, it is wickedly suggested, may *really* be a Black joker in Harlem pretending to be the White refugee from respectability. And, quite recently, Twain's book itself has been rewritten to please and mock its exegetes in John Seelye's *Huck Finn for The Critics,* which lops off the whole silly-happy ending, the deliverance of Nigger Jim (in which Hemingway, for instance, never believed) and puts back into the tale the cussing and sex presumably excised by the least authentic part of Samuel Clemens' mind—as well as the revelation at long last, that what Huck and Jim were smoking on the raft was not tobacco but "hemp," which is to say, marijuana. Despite all, however, Huck seems for the moment to belong not to the childhood we all continue to live, but to the one we have left behind.

Natty Bumppo, on the other hand, dreamed originally in the suburbs of New York City and in Paris, oddly survives along with his author. Contrary to what we had long believed, it is James Fenimore Cooper who now remains alive, or rather who has been reborn, perhaps not so much as he saw himself as in the form D. H. Lawrence re-imagined him en route to America; for Cooper understood that the dream which does not fade with the building of cities, but assumes in their concrete and steel environment the compelling vividness of a waking hallucination, is the encounter of Old World men and New in the wilderness, the meeting of the transplanted European and the Red Indian. No wonder Lawrence spoke of himself as "Kindled by Fenimore Cooper."

The Return of the Redskin to the center of our art and our deep imagination, as we all of us have retraced Lawrence's trip to the mythical America, is based not merely on the revival of the oldest and most authentic of American Pop forms, but also projects certain meanings of our lives in terms more metapolitical than political, which is to say, meanings valid as myth is valid rather than as history. Writers of Westerns have traditionally taken sides for or against the Indians; and unlike the authors of the movies which set the kids to cheering at the Saturday matinees of the twenties and thirties, the new novelists have taken a clear stand with the Red Man. In this act of mythological renegacy they have not only implicitly declared themselves enemies of the Christian Humanism, but they have also rejected the act of genocide with which our nation began—and whose last reflection, perhaps, is to be found in the War in Vietnam.

It is impossible to write any Western which does not in some sense glorify violence; but the violence celebrated in the anti-White Western is guerrilla violence: the sneak attack on "civilization" as practiced first by Geronimo and Cochise and other Indian warrior chiefs, and more latterly apologized for by Ché Guevara or the spokesman for North Vietnam. Warfare, however, is not the final vision implict in the New Western, which is motivated on a deeper level by a nostalgia for the Tribe: a form of social organization thought of as preferable both to the tight two-generation bourgeois family, from which its authors come, and the soulless out-of-human-scale bureaucratic state, into which they are initiated via schools and universities. In the end, of course, both the dream of violence in the woods and the vision of tribal life, rendered in terms of a genre that has long been the preferred reading of boys, seems juvenile, even infantile. But this is precisely the point; for what recommends the Western to the New Novelist is pre-eminently its association with children and the kind of books superciliously identified with their limited and special needs.

For the German, brought up on Karl May, the situation is quite similar to that in which the American, who grew up with Cooper or his native imitators, finds himself. What has Old Shatterhand to do with Art, asks the one, even as the other asks the same of Chingachgook. And the answer is *nothing*. The legendary Indians have nothing to do with Art in the traditional sense, everything to do with joining boy to man, childhood to adulthood, immaturity to maturity. They preside over the closing of the Gap which aristocratic conceptions of art have opened between what fulfills us at eight or ten or twelve and what satisfies us at forty or fifty or sixty.

In light of all this, it is perhaps time to look again at the much-discussed "immaturity" of American literature, the notorious fact that our classic books are boy's books—our greatest novels at home in the Children's Section of libraries; in short, that they are all in some sense "Westerns": accounts of an idyllic encounter between White man and Non-White in one or another variety of wilderness setting. But suddenly this fact—once read as a "flaw" or "failure" or "lack" (it implies, after all, the absence in our books of heterosexual love and of the elaborate analysis of social relations central to the Continental novel)—seems evidence of a real advantage, a clue to why the Gap we now want to close opened so late and so unconvincingly, as it were, in American letters. Before Henry James, none of our novelists felt himself cut off from the world of magic and wonder; he had only to go to sea or, especially, to cross our own particular Border, the Frontier, to inhabit a region where adults and children, educated and uneducated, shared a common enchantment.

How different the plight of mid-nineteenth-century English writers, like Lewis Carroll or Edward Lear or George Macdonald, who had to pretend that they were writing exclusively for the nursery in order to enter the deep wonderland of their own imaginations. Even in our own time, a writer like J. R. R. Tolkien found it necessary to invent the Hobbits in a book specifically aimed at children, before he could release the fearful scholarship (another device foreign to American mythologies) and presumably adult magic of the Rings Trilogy. It makes a difference, after all, whether one thinks of the World Across The Border as Faerie or Frontier, fantasy or history. It has been so long since Europeans lived their deepest dreams—but only yesterday for us. And this is why even now, when we are at last sundered from those dreams, we can turn rotten-ripe without loss of essential innocence, be (what has become a model for the young of all the world, as Godard's *Weekend* testifies) decadent children playing Indians; which is to say, imaginary Americans, all of us, whether native to this land or not. But to be an American (unlike being English or French or whatever) is precisely to *imagine* a destiny rather than to inherit one; since we have always been, insofar as we are Americans at all, inhabitants of myth rather than history—and have now come to know it.

In any case, our best writers have been able to take up the Western again—playfully and seriously at once, quite like their ancestors who began the Revolution which made us a country by playing Indians in deadly earnest and dumping all that English Tea into the salt sea that sundered them from their King. There are many writers still under forty, among them the most distinguished of their generation, who have written New Westerns which have found the hearts of the young, particularly in paperback form; since to these young readers, for reasons psychological as well as economic, the hardcover book with its aspiration to immortality in libraries begins to look obsolete. John Barth's *The Sotweed Factor* represents the beginning of the wave that has been cresting ever since 1960 and that has carried with it not only Barth's near contemporaries like Thomas Berger (in *Little Big Man)*, Ken Kesey (in both *One Flew Over the Cuckoo's Nest* and *Sometimes a Great Notion)*, and most recently Leonard Cohen (in his extraordinarily gross and elegant *Beautiful Losers)*—but has won over older and more established writers like Norman Mailer whose newest novel, *Why Are We in Vietnam?*, is not as its title seems to promise a book about a War in the East as much as a book about the idea of the West. Even William Burroughs, expert in drug fantasies and homosexual paranoia, keeps promising to turn to the genre, though so far he has contented himself with another popular form, another way of escaping from personal to public or popular myth, of using dreams to close rather than open a gap: Science Fiction.

Science Fiction does not seem at first glance to have as wide and universal appeal as the Western, in book form at least, though perhaps it is too soon to judge, for it is a very young genre, indeed, having found itself (after tentative beginnings in Jules Verne, H. G. Wells etc.), its real meaning and scope, only after World War II. At that point, two things become clear: first, that the Future was upon us, that the pace of technological advance had become so swift that a distinction between Present and Future would get harder and harder to maintain; and second, that the End of Man, by annihilation or mutation, was a real, even an immediate possibility. But these are the two proper subjects of Science Fiction: the Present Future and the End of Man—not time travel or the penetration of outer space, except as the latter somehow symbolize the former.

Perhaps only in quite advanced technologies which also have a tradition of self-examination and analysis, bred by Puritanism or Marxism or whatever, can Science Fiction at its most explicit, which is to say, expressed in words on the page, really flourish. In any case, only in America, England, and the Soviet Union does the Science Fiction Novel or Post-Novel seem to thrive, though Science Fiction cartoon strips and comic books, as well as Science Fiction T.V. programs and especially films (where the basic imagery is blissfully wed to electronic music, and words are kept to a minimum) penetrate everywhere. In England and America, at any rate, the prestige and influence of the genre are sufficient not only to allure Burroughs (in *Nova Express*), but also to provide a model for William Golding (in *Lord of the Flies*), Anthony Burgess (in *The Clockwork Orange*), and John Barth (whose second major book, *Giles Goatboy*, abandoned the Indian in favor of the Future).

Quite unlike the Western, which asserts the difference between England and America, Science Fiction reflects what still makes the two mutually distrustful communities one; as, for instance, a joint effort (an English author, an American director) like the movie *2001: A Space Odyssey* testifies. If there is still a common "Anglo-Saxon" form, it is Science Fiction. Yet even here, the American case is a little different from the English; for only in the United States is there a writer of first rank whose preferred mode has been from the first Science Fiction in its unmitigated Pop form. Kurt Vonnegut, Jr., did not begin by making some sort of traditional bid for literary fame and then shift to Science Fiction, but was so closely identified with that popular, not-quite-respectable form from the first, that the established critics were still ignoring him completely at a time when younger readers, attuned to the new rhythm of events by Marshall McLuhan or Buckminster Fuller, had already made underground favorites of his *The Sirens of Titan* and *Cat's Cradle*. That Vonnegut now, after years of neglect, teaches writing in a famous American university and is hailed in lead reviews in the popular press is a tribute not to the critics' acuity but to the persuasive powers of the young.

The revival of pornography in recent days, its moving from the periphery to the center of the literary scene, is best understood in this context, too; for it, like the Western and Science Fiction, is a form of Pop Art—ever since Victorian times, indeed, the *essential* form of Pop Art, which is to say, the most unredeemable of all kinds of subliterature, understood as a sort of entertainment closer to the pole of Vice than that of Art. Many of the more notable recent works of the genre have tended to conceal this fact, often because the authors themselves did not understand what they were after, and have tried to disguise their work as earnest morality (Herbert Selby's *Last Exit to Brooklyn,* for instance) or parody (Terry Southern's *Candy).* But whatever the author's conscious intent, all those writers who have helped move Porn from the underground to the foreground have in fact been working toward the liquidation of the very conception of pornography; since the end of Art on one side means the end of Porn on the other. And that end is now in sight, in the area of films and Pop songs and poetry, but especially in that of the novel which seemed, initially at least, more congenial than other later Pop Art forms to the sort of private masturbatory reverie which is essential to pornography.

It is instructive in this regard to reflect on the careers of two publishers who have flourished extraordinarily because somehow they sensed early on that a mass society can no longer endure the distinction between low literature and a high, especially in the area of sex; and that the line drawn early in the century between serious, "artistic" exploitation of pornography (e.g., *Lady Chatterley's Lover),* and so-called "hard-core" pornography was bound to be blurred away. Even the classics of the genre straddle the line: *Fanny Hill,* for example, and de Sade's *Justine,* as do more recent works like John Rechy's *City of Night* or Stephen Schneck's *The Night Clerk,* whose sheer dirtiness may be adulterated by sentiment or irony but remains a chief appeal. This, at any rate, Maurice Girodias and Barney Rosset appear to have sensed; and from both sides of the Atlantic they have, through the Olympia Press and Grove Press, supplied the American reading public, chiefly but not exclusively the young, with books (including, let it be noted, Nabo-kov's *Lolita,* the sole work in which the pursuit of Porn enabled that emigré writer to escape the limitations of early twentieth-century *avant-garde)* exploiting, often in contempt of art and serious-ness, not just Good Clean Sex, but sadism, masochism, homosex-uality, coprophilia, necrophilia etc. etc.

The standard forms of heterosexual copulation, standardly or "poetically" recorded, seem oddly old-fashioned, even a little ridic-ulous; it is *fellatio,* buggery, flagellation that we demand in order to be sure that we are not reading Love Stories but Pornography. A special beneficiary of this trend has been Norman Mailer, whose first novel, *The Naked and the Dead,* emulated the dying tradition of the anti-war art novel, with occasional obscenities thrown in, presumably in the interest of verisimilitude. But more and more, Mailer has come to move the obscenity to the center, the social commentary to the periphery, ending in *Why Are We in Vietnam?* with an insistence on foul language and an obsession with scatology which are obviously ends in themselves, too unremitting to be felt as merely an assault on old-fashioned sensibility and taste. And even in his earlier Pop Novel, *An American Dream,* which marked his emergence from ten years in which he produced no major fic-tion, he had committed himself to Porn as a way into the region to which his title alludes: the place where in darkness and filth all men are alike—the Harvard graduate and the reader of the *Daily News,* joined in fantasies of murdering their wives and buggering their maids. To talk of such books in terms of Dostoevski, as cer-tain baffled critics have felt obliged to do, is absurd; James Bond is more to the point. But to confess this would be to confess that the old distinctions are no longer valid, and that critics will have to find another claim to authority more appropriate to our times than the outmoded ability to discriminate between High and Low.

Even more disconcertingly than Mailer, Philip Roth has with *Portnoy's Complaint* raised the question of whether "pornography," even what was called until only yesterday "hard-core pornography" any longer exists. Explicit, vulgar, joyous, gross and pathetic all at once, Roth has established himself not only as the laureate of mas-turbation and oral-genital lovemaking but also as a master of the "thin" novel, the novel with minimum inwardness—ironically presented as a confession to a psychiatrist. Without its sexual interest, therefore, the continual balancing off of titillation and burlesque— his book has no meaning at all, no more than any other dirty joke, to which genre it quite clearly belongs. There is pathos, even terror in great plenty, to be sure, but it is everywhere dependent on, subservient to the dirty jokes about mothers, Jews, shrinks, potency, impotency; and Roth is, consequently, quite correct when he asserts that he is less like such more solemn and pious Jewish-American writers as Saul Bellow and Bernard Malamud, than he is like the half-mad pop singer Tiny Tim (himself actually half-Arab and half-Jew).

"I am a Jew Freak," Roth has insisted, "not a Jewish Sage"— and one is reminded of Lennie Bruce, who was there first, occupying the dangerous DMZ between the world of the stand-up comedian and that of the proper maker of fictions. But Bruce made no claim to being a novelist and therefore neither disturbed the critics nor opened up new possibilities for prose narrative. Indeed, before *Portnoy's Complaint,* the Jewish-American novel had come to seem an especially egregious example of the death of belles-lettres, having become smug, established, repetitive and sterile. But *Portnoy* marks the passage of that genre into the new world of Porn and Pop, as Roth's booming sales (even in hardcover!) perhaps sufficiently attest.

It is, of course, the middle-aged and well-heeled who buy the hardcover editions of the book; yet their children apparently are picking it up, too, for once not even waiting for the paperback edition. They know it is a subversive book, as their parents do not (convinced that a boy who loves his mother can't be all bad), and as Roth himself perhaps was not at first quite aware either. Before its publication, he had been at least equivocal on the subject of frankly disruptive literature; full of distrust, for instance, for Norman Mailer—and appears therefore to have became a Pop rebel despite himself, driven less by principle than by a saving hunger for the great audience, quite like that which moved John Updike recently out of his elitist exile toward best-sellerdom and relevance in *Couples.*

There is, however, no doubt in the minds of most other writers whom the young especially prize at the moment that their essential task is to destroy once and for all—by parody or exaggeration or grotesque emulation of the classic past, as well as by the adaptation and "camping" of Pop forms just such distinctions and discriminations. But to turn High Art into vaudeville and burlesque at the same moment that Mass Art is being irreverently introduced into museums and libraries is to perform an act which has political as well as aesthetic implications: an act which closes a class, as well as a generation gap. The notion of one art for the "cultured," i.e., the favored few in any given society—in our own chiefly the university educated—and another subart for the "uncultured," i.e., an excluded majority as deficient in Gutenberg skills as they are untutored in "taste," in fact represents the last survival in mass industrial societies (capitalist, socialist, communist—it makes no difference in this regard) of an invidious distinction proper only to a class-structured community. Precisely because it carries on, as it has carried on ever since the middle of the eighteenth century, a war against that anachronistic survival, Pop Art is, whatever its overt politics, *subversive:* a threat to all hierarchies insofar as it is hostile to order and ordering in its own realm. What the final intrusion of Pop into the citadels of High Art provides, therefore, for the critic is the exhilarating new possibility of making judgments about the "goodness" and "badness" of art quite separated from distinctions between "high" and "low" with their concealed class bias.

But the new audience has not waited for new critics to guide them in this direction. Reversing the process typical of Modernism —under whose aegis an unwilling, aging elite audience was bullied and cajoled slowly, slowly, into accepting the most vital art of its time—Post-Modernism provides an example of a young, mass audience urging certain aging, reluctant critics onward toward the abandonment of their former elite status in return for a freedom the prospect of which more terrifies than elates them. In fact, Post-Modernism implies the closing of the gap between critic and audience, too, if by critic one understands "leader of taste" and by audience "follower." But most importantly of all, it implies the closing of the gap between artist and audience, or at any rate, between professional and amateur in the realm of art.

The jack of all arts is master of none—professional in none, and therefore no better than any man jack among the rest of us, formerly safely penned off from the practitioners we most admire by our status as "audience." It all follows logically enough. On the one hand, a poet like Ed Sanders, or a novelist like Leonard Cohen grows weary of his confinement in the realm of traditional high art; and the former organizes a musical Pop Group called the Fugs, while the latter makes recordings of his own Pop songs to his own guitar accompaniment. There are precedents for this, after all, not only as in the case of Boris Vian, which we have already noticed, but closer to home: in the career, for instance, of Richard Farina, who died very young, but not before he had written that imperfect, deeply moving novel, *Been Down So Long It Looks Like Up to Me,* and had recorded a song or two for the popular audience.

Meanwhile, even more surprisingly some who had begun, or whom we had begun to think of, as mere "entertainers," Pop performers without loftier pretensions, were crossing the line from their direction. Frank Zappa, for example, has in interviews and in a forthcoming book insisted on being taken seriously as poet and satirist, suggesting that the music of his own group, The Mothers of Invention, has been all along more a deliberate parody of Pop than an extension of it in psychedelic directions; while Bob Dylan, who began by abandoning Folk Music with left-wing protest overtones in favor of electronic Rock and Roll, finally succeeded in creating inside that form a kind of Pop surrealist poetry, passionate, mysterious, and quite complex; complex enough, in fact, to prompt a score of scholarly articles on his "art." Most recently, however, he has returned to "acoustic" instruments and to the most naïve traditions of country music—apparently out of a sense that he had grown too "arty," and had once more to close the gap by backtracking across the border he had earlier lost his first audience by crossing. It is a spectacular case of the new artist as Double Agent.

Even more spectacular, however, is that of John Lennon, who coming into view first as merely one of the Beatles, then still just another rock group from Liverpool, has revealed himself stage by stage as novelist, playwright, movie maker, guru, sculptor, etc., etc. There is a special pathos in his example since, though initially inspired by American models, he has tried to work out his essentially American strategies in English idioms and in growing isolation on the generally dismal English scene. He has refused to become the prisoner of his special talent as a musician, venturing into other realms where he has, initially at least, as little authority as anyone else; and thus provides one more model for the young who, without any special gift or calling, in the name of mere possibility insist on making all up and down America, and, more tentatively perhaps, everywhere else in the world, tens of thousands of records, movies, collections of verse, paintings, junk sculptures, even novels, in complete contempt of professional "standards." Perhaps, though, the novel is the most unpromising form for an amateur age (it is easier to learn the guitar or make a two-minute eight-millimeter film), and it may be doomed to become less and less important, less and less central, no matter how it is altered. But for the moment at least, on the border between the world of Art and that of non-Art, it flourishes with especial vigor in proportion as it realizes its transitional status, and is willing to surrender the kind of "realism" and analysis it once thought its special province in quest of the marvelous and magical it began by disavowing.

Samuel Richardson may have believed that when he wrote *Pamela* and *Clarissa* he was delivering prose fiction from that bondage to the *merveilleux* which characterized the old Romances; but it is clear now that he was merely translating the Marvelous into new terms, specifically, into bourgeois English. It is time, at any rate, to be through with pretenses; for to Close the Gap means also to Cross the Border between the Marvelous and the Probable, the Real and the Mythical, the world of the boudoir and the counting house and the realm of what used to be called Faerie, but has for so long been designated mere madness. Certainly the basic images of Pop forms like the Western, Science Fiction and Pornography suggest mythological as well as political or metapolitical meanings. The passage into Indian Territory, the flight into Outer Space, the ecstatic release into the fantasy world of the orgy: all these are analogues for what has traditionally been described as a Journey or Pilgrimage (recently we have been more likely to say "Trip" without altering the significance) toward a transcendent goal, a moment of Vision.

But the mythologies of Voyage and Vision which the late Middle Ages and the Renaissance inherited from the Classical World and the Judaeo-Christian tradition, and which froze into pedanticism and academicism in the eighteenth and nineteenth century, have not survived their last ironical uses in the earlier part of the twentieth: those burlesque-pathetic evocations in Joyce's *Ulysses,* Eliot's *The Waste Land,* Mann's *Joseph and His Brothers* or the *Cantos* of Ezra Pound. If they are not quite dead, they should be, *need* be for the health of post-Art—as, indeed, Walt Whitman foresaw, anticipating the twenty-first century from the vantage point of his peculiar vision more than a hundred years ago.

> Come Muse migrate from Greece and Ionia,
> Cross out please those immensely overpaid accounts,
> That matter of Troy and Achilles' Wrath, and Aeneas'
>     Odysseus' wanderings,
> Place "Removed" and "To Let" on the rocks of your
>     snowy Parnassus,
> Repeat at Jerusalem . . .

Pop Art, however, can no more abide a mythological vacuum than can High Art: and into the space left vacant by the disappearance of the Matter of Troy and the myths of the ancient Middle East has rushed, first of all, the Matter of Childhood: the stuff of traditional fairy tales out of the Black Forest, which seems to the present generation especially attractive, perhaps, because their "progressive" parents tended to distrust it. But something much more radically new has appeared as well: the Matter of Metropolis and the myths of the Present Future, in which the nonhuman world about us, hostile or benign, is rendered not in the guise of elves or dwarfs or witches or even Gods, but of Machines quite as uncanny as any Elemental or Olympian—and apparently as immortal. Machines and the mythological figures appropriate to the media mass-produced and mass-distributed by machines: the newsboy who, saying SHAZAM in an abandoned subway tunnel, becomes Captain Marvel; the reporter (with glasses), who shucking his civilian garb in a telephone booth is revealed as Superman, immune to all but Kryptonite—these are the appropriate images of power and grace for an urban, industrial world busy manufacturing the Future.

But the Comic Book heroes do not stand alone. Out of the world of Jazz and Rock, of newspaper headlines and political cartoons, of old movies immortalized on T.V. and idiot talk shows carried on car radios, new anti-Gods and anti-Heroes arrive, endless wave after wave of them: "Bluff'd not a bit by drainpipe, gasometer, artificial fertilizers," (the appropriate commentary is Whitman's), "smiling and pleas'd with palpable intent to stay"—in our Imaginary America, of course. In the heads of our new writers, they live a secondary life, begin to realize their immortality: not only Jean Harlow and Marilyn Monroe and Humphrey Bogart, Charlie Parker and Louis Armstrong and Lennie Bruce, Geronimo and Billy the Kid, the Lone Ranger and Fu Manchu and the Bride of Frankenstein, but Hitler and Stalin, John F. Kennedy and Lee Oswald and Jack Ruby as well; for the press mythologizes certain public figures, the actors of Pop History, even before they are dead —making a doomed President one with Superman in the Supermarket of Pop Culture, as Norman Mailer perceived so accurately and reported so movingly in an essay on John F. Kennedy.

But the secret he told was already known to scores of younger writers at least, and recorded in the text and texture of their work. In the deep memory of Leonard Cohen writing *Beautiful Losers,* or Richard Farina composing *Been Down So Long It Looks Like Up to Me,* or Ken Kesey making *Sometimes a Great Notion,* there stir to life not archetypal images out of books read in school or at the urging of parents; but those out of comic books forbidden in schools, or radio and T.V. programs banned or condescendingly endured by parents. From the taboo underground culture of the kids of just after World War II comes the essential mythology which informs the literature of right now. As early as T. S. Eliot, to be sure, jazz rhythms had been evoked, as in "O O O O that Shakesperherian Rag—It's so elegant, So intelligent . . .," but Eliot is mocking a world he resents; and even in Brecht's *Three Penny Opera,* the emulation of Pop music seems still largely "slumming." In the newest writers, however, mockery and condescension alike are absent, since they are not slumming; they are living in the only world in which they feel at home. They are able, therefore, to recapture a certain rude magic in its authentic context, by seizing on myths not as stored in encyclopedias or preserved in certain beloved ancient works—but as apprehended at their moment of making, which is to say, at a moment when they are not yet labeled "myths."

In some ways the present movement not only in its quest for myths, but also in its preference for sentimentality over irony, and especially in its dedication to the Primitive, resembles the beginnings of Romanticism, with its yearning for the Naïve, and its attempt to find authentic sources for poetry in folk forms like the *Märchen* or the ballads. But the Romantics returned exclusively toward the Past in the hope of renewal—to a dream of the Past, which they knew they could only write, not actually live. And, indeed, there persists in the post-Modernists some of that old nostalgia for folk ways and folk-rhythms, curiously tempered by the realization that the "folk songs" of an electronic age are made not in rural loneliness or in sylvan retreats, but in superstudios by boys singing into the sensitive ear of machines—or even by those machines themselves editing, blending, making out of imperfect scraps of human song an artifice of simplicity only possible on tape. What recent writers have learned, and are true enough children of the Present Future to find exhilarating, is not only that the *Naïve* can be machine produced, but that dreams themselves can be manufactured, projected on T.V. or Laser beams with all the vividness of the visions of Saints. In the first wave of Romanticism, pre-electronic Romanticism, it took an act of faith on the part of Novalis to be able to say, "Life is not a dream, but it can be and probably should be made one." And echoing his German producer, in the pages of both *Lilith* and *Phantastes*, George Macdonald, maddest of the Victorian mad visionaries, echoes the tone of desperate hope. But to the young in America, who have learned to read Macdonald once more, along with his English successors, Charles Williams and C. S. Lewis and Tolkien, the declaration of faith has become a matter of fact.

The Dream, the Vision, *ekstasis:* these have again become the avowed goals of literature; for our latest poets realize in this time of Endings, what their remotest ancestors knew in the era of Beginnings, that merely "to instruct and delight" is not enough. Like Longinus, the new novelists and critics believe that great art releases and liberates as well; but unlike him, they are convinced that wonder and fantasy, which deliver the mind from the body, the body from the mind, must be naturalized to a world of machines—subverted perhaps or even transformed, but certainly not destroyed or denied. The ending of Ken Kesey's *One Flew Over the Cuckoo's*

*Nest* expresses fictionally, metaphorically, that conviction, when the Indian who is his second hero breaks out of the Insane Asylum in which "The System" has kept him impotent and trapped—and flees to join his fellows who are building a fishing weir on a giant hydroelectric power dam. The Dam and Weir both are essential to postelectronic Romanticism, which knows that the point is no longer to pursue some uncorrupted West over the next horizon, since there is no incorruption and all our horizons have been reached. It is rather to make a thousand little Wests in the interstices of a machine civilization, and, as it were, on its steel and concrete back; to live the tribal life among and with the support of machines; to shelter new communes under domes constructed according to the technology of Buckminster Fuller; and warm the nakedness of New Primitives with advanced techniques of solar heating.

All this is less a matter of choice than of necessity because, it has turned out, machine civilization tends inevitably to synthesize the primitive, and *ekstasis* is the unforeseen end of advanced technology, mysticism the by-product—no more nor no less accidental in penicillin—of scientific research. In the antiseptic laboratories of Switzerland, the psychedelic drug LSD was first developed, first tried by two white-coated experimenters; and even now Dow Chemical which manufactures napalm also produces the even more powerful psychedelic agent STP. It is, in large part, thanks to machines—the supermachines which, unlike their simpler prototypes, insist on tending us rather than demanding we tend them— that we live in the midst of a great religious revival, scarcely noticed by the official spokesmen of established Christian churches since it speaks quite another language. Yet many among us feel that they are able to live honestly only by what machines cannot do better than they—which is why certain poets and novelists, as well as pop singers and pornographic playwrights, are suggesting in print, on the air, everywhere, that not Work but Vision is the proper activity of men, and that, therefore, the contemplative life may, after all, be preferable to the active one. In such an age, *our* age, it is not surprising that the books which most move the young are essentially religious books, as, indeed, pop art is always religious.

In the immediate past, however, when an absolute distinction was made between High Art and Pop, works of the latter category tended to be the secret scriptures of a kind of shabby, store-front church—a religion as exclusive in its attempt to remain the humble possession of the unambitious and unlettered, as the canonical works of High Art in their claim to be an esoteric Gospel of art itself, available only to a cultivated elite. But in a time of Closing the Gap, literature becomes again prophetic and universal—a continuing revelation appropriate to a permanent religious revolution, whose function is precisely to transform the secular crowd into a sacred community: one with each other, and equally at home in the world of technology and the realm of wonder. Pledged like Isaiah to speaking the language of everyone, the prophets of the new dispensation can afford to be neither finicky nor genteel; and they echo, therefore, the desperate cry of the Hebrew prototype: "I am a man of unclean lips in the midst of a people of unclean lips."

Let those to whom religion means security beware, for it is no New Established Church that is in the process of being founded; and its communicants are, therefore, less like the pillars of the Lutheran Church or Anglican gentlemen than they are like ranters, enthusiasts, Dionysiacs, Anabaptists: holy disturbers of the peace of the devout. Leonard Cohen, in a moment of vision which constitutes the climax of *Beautiful Losers,* aptly calls them "New Jews"; for he sees them as a saved remnant moving across deserts of boredom, out of that exile from our authentic selves which we all share, toward a salvation none of us can quite imagine. Such New Jews, Cohen (himself a Jew as well as a Canadian) adds, do not have to be Jewish but probably do have to be Americans—by which he must surely mean "Imaginary Americans," since, as we have been observing all along, there were never any other kind.

—1970

# SEVEN

# In Quest of George Lippard

GEORGE LIPPARD, the author of *The Quaker City,* or *The Monks of Monk Hall,* is a little-known figure in the history of American literature. For many years, as a matter of fact, his very existence was kept a secret in the official histories of the novel in the United States, as if he represented a shameful episode in a past we were all doing our best to forget. In recent years, however, scholarly candor has triumphed over patriotic shame; and beginning with Alexander Cowie in *The Rise of the American Novel* (1948), historians of our fiction have been making an effort to come to terms with Lippard and his "dirty" book.

It is, after all, impossible to ignore forever a writer who produced one of the all-time best-sellers, a book which he himself boasted "has been more attacked, and more read, than any work of American fiction ever published"; and which, in fact, sold 60,000 copies in 1844, the year of publication, and was still being bought at the rate of 30,000 a year in 1854, the year of Lippard's death. Not only in America, but in England and on the Continent, Lippard was read by those who pretended to be scandalized as well as by those who didn't even realize that they ought to be shocked. In Germany the "most immoral work of the age" seems to have been a special favorite; and, ironically, during the period when *The Quaker City* had disappeared from our own literary histories, it continued to be listed in German ones as the work of Friedrich Gerstäcker under the title *Die Quackerstadt und ihre Geheimnisse.*

Lippard is an immensely attractive figure, a revolutionary dandy who, in the short thirty-two years of his life, managed to

486

dazzle and provoke the Philadelphia society in which he moved, romantically wrapped in a Byronic cape and always armed against paid assassins whom he imagined everywhere. Brought up to be a minister, he found no church liberal enough to suit his beliefs, and became a kind of lay apostle preaching the doctrine of socialism. All forms and conventions of the community in which he lived seemed to him intolerable; and he married his wife, for instance, by the simple process of taking her hand as they stood together on a high rock overlooking his native city.

He was not only an immensely prolific novelist, author of innumerable books, *The Legends of the American Revolution, Blanche of Brandywine, The Mysteries of Florence, The Memoirs of a Preacher, The Empire City, The Bank Director's Son, The Entranced, New York: Its Upper Ten,* etc.; he was a lecturer as well and fancied himself a natural political leader. He founded, in fact, a radical organization called The Brotherhood of Union (later renamed The Brotherhood of America), of which he appointed himself the "Supreme Washington"; and he issued revolutionary manifestos insisting "When Labor has tried all other means in vain— . . . then we advise Labor to go to War . . . War with the Rifle, Sword and Knife!" Moreover, he considered his fiction another weapon to be used in the struggle. "LITERATURE merely considered as an ART is a despicable thing. . . . A literature which does not work practically, for the advancement of social reform . . . is just good for nothing at all." But this, surely, is one clue to Lippard's long eclipse.

Had he been just a "dirty" writer, he might have survived change of fashion and critical neglect, survived as an underground classic; and had he been a properly pious socialist, his memory might well have been preserved by Marxist critics in search of literary ancestors. To be a "dirty" socialist writer, however, is to lose on all counts. Yet Lippard does not stand alone in his allegiance, on the one hand, to sensation and smut, and, on the other, to social reform. Indeed, to come to terms with him we must come to terms with a whole school of fiction which the habit of contempt and the limitations of our own hopelessly elitist views of art have made it difficult for us to understand. Outside the context of that stream of literature, Lippard can only seem an eccentric, a freak, rather than one of the group of literary pioneers who first tried to create a true popular literature.

It is tempting to see Lippard in an American setting, which is to say, one too parochial really to explain him; and, as a matter of fact, he himself encourages us to do so. His most famous novel is dedicated to Charles Brockden Brown, to whom he also wrote a moving tribute in a contemporary magazine; and his name, otherwise excluded from respectable notice, was associated in literary history with Edgar Allen Poe, whom he befriended. What is easier, then, and superficially more satisfactory than to associate him with these two exponents of the American Gothic, both of whom had connections of one kind or another with Lippard's native Philadelphia.

Lippard is, however, very different indeed from either of his two fellow countrymen, not only in his resolve to address a mass audience rather than to woo an elite one, and in the slapdash style and open form he felt suitable for that end—but in theme and setting as well. It is the city which concerns him, the contemporary American city, New York and Philadelphia in particular; and he therefore rejects equally the brand of exoticism that moved Poe to set many of his dream-fugues against a half-imaginary European background, and that which impelled Brockden Brown (as well as Poe in his single novel) to evoke the shadowy terror of the American wilderness.

In order to find writers whom he really resembles, one has to look beyond rather than before him on the American scene—to Jack London, Theodore Dreiser, and Norman Mailer[1], for instance, who, like him, combine a taste for the sentimental and sensational with an ideological commitment to socialism. Dreiser, moreover, shares with him an appalled fascination with the city and its depraved masters, though he rather lacks what Lippard, London, and Mailer possess in an eminent degree—a kind of natural access to the erotic dreams and paranoid fantasies of the male members of the working class.

---

[1] Mailer's *An American Dream* seems, in fact, closer to what Lippard was doing in *The Quaker City* than anything written between, and this is, perhaps, because it was written serially and under pressure for a popular magazine. If only it had been illustrated as well!

Poe, on the other hand, touches the imagination of childhood, appealing to what remains most childlike in us and thus creating fantasies appropriate to the impotence of that state, as opposed to those arising out of the deprivations of the poor. It is perhaps because the child tends to dream of withdrawing from the world which excludes him, triumphing over it in proud loneliness, rather than of making it in that world like the workingman, that Poe—despite having helped invent so basic a pop form as the detective story —has become a founding father of *avant-garde* literature intended for an elite audience. The descendants of Poe are French dandies, not American radicals—Baudelaire and Mallarmé rather than London and Dreiser and Mailer.

It is finally, however, not even Lippard's American successors, much less his predecessors, who provide the essential clue to what he is after, but certain of his contemporaries in England and Europe: in particular, the popular German novelist Friedrich Gerstäcker (1816–1872), the English publisher, journalist, and writer of fiction G. W. M. Reynolds (1814–1879); and, especially, that super best-seller in a time of best-sellers, the French novelist Eugène Sue (1804–1857). All three of these novelists, along with Lippard himself, were responding to the special challenges of their period, as were, in their own way, their more respectable contemporaries like Dickens and Balzac; and like the latter they aimed at commercial success before critical acclaim.

In the case of Gerstäcker, Reynolds, Sue, and Lippard, however, there is a tendency to abandon utterly traditional standards of "art"; while Dickens and Balzac were somehow having it both ways —triumphing in the market place, and yet preparing a place for themselves in the libraries and classrooms of the future. The radical popular writers, however, accommodated to the new possibilities and new audiences of their time in a fashion which won them the disfavor of the squeamish and genteel generations which immediately succeeded them, but which begins to seem to us now, in another antigenteel time, at a second stage of the Pop Revolution, immensely suggestive and admirable.

As in our era, so in the time of Lippard it was new technology which determined the new aesthetics; and, indeed, this is the essential nature of Pop Art. Certain technological advances had, in any event, made possible the printing of books at a price much lower than anybody had hitherto envisaged: the new rotary steam press; a new method of making paper, first introduced into England by John Gamble in 1801, but resisted by the industry until around 1820; the perfection of the stereotype, making possible quick reprintings; and, finally, the commercial development of lithography by the German émigré Rudolph Ackermann, who also persuaded the great caricaturists of the era to become illustrators. Those inventions were intended chiefly to facilitate the publication of popular newspapers, but they served also to bring about a marriage of journalism and fiction, creating that odd hybrid, the newspaper serial. And, indeed, the cheap novel, the "penny dreadful," *is* the newspaper novel: stereotyped on newsprint, copiously illustrated and appearing in weekly or monthly penny installments—the author never more than a chapter or two ahead of his readers.

Technology, however, could only make possible mass production of fiction; mass distribution depending ultimately on the creation of a mass audience, and this was the work not of engineers but missionaries. The spread of literacy in the time of Lippard was carried on chiefly in institutions established by the evangelical churches and various philanthropic organizations dedicated to the "cultural enrichment" of the laborer: Charity Schools, Sunday Schools, Mechanics Institutes. Once readers were present in large numbers and the price of books had been brought within their reach, the ingenuity of the businessman (particularly in England) soon created new ways of getting books into more and more hands.

In the age of Lippard and Reynolds and Sue, this meant the circulating library, as it had since the eighteenth century; and especially the railway-station bookstall, which was new. The stagecoach had proved a notably inappropriate mode of conveyance for reading, combining a maximum of disruptive motion with a minimum of light; but the railway carriage provided lighting conditions which made it quite possible to read, as well as a kind of comfort which bred that traveler's ennui which makes *not* reading almost impossible. The period, therefore, saw the emergence of a new view of reading, still alive in our time, as the form of relaxation or escape most appropriate to the trip into the country, or the start of a holiday, as well as to that happy state between waking and sleeping induced by the motion of trains.

The use of movies and stereo music on transcontinental and transoceanic air flights perhaps marks the beginning of the end of this period, but bookstands remain to this very moment a conspicuous adornment of all depots and airports. And the same sort of people still line up before them, as departure time approaches, grabbing a handful of books which must be cheap enough to be thrown away or left behind, and which must guarantee somehow total irresponsibility. Such readers, to be sure, are now—as they were then—not typically workingmen at all, but middle-class people, even students, slumming as it were: temporarily taking a holiday from the "serious literature" on their library shelves at home. Yet a large part of the readership of Sue and Reynolds and Lippard must have been drawn from this class—out of which, indeed, came those critics who in middle age disavowed what in their youth they had enjoyed, though even then (they were to claim at least) only as an unworthy indulgence, a minor vice.

It was not, however, primarily to or for such readers that Lippard and his colleagues wrote. He may have managed to earn between three and four thousand dollars a year with their help, but his books (like Sue's or Reynolds') do not represent a purely commercial response to opportunities opened up by advances in technology and new developments in bookselling; they are also, in a deeper sense, "popular," which is to say, aimed at educating the working-class elements of their audience to live better lives and even to make for themselves a better world. Lippard lived through difficult times as a youth, but is not himself of working-class origin, any more than were Sue and Reynolds and Gerstäcker; yet he was a convinced socialist, and, like his contemporaries, got into trouble because of his political activism. It must be understood, however, that his revolutionary doctrine was pre-Communist Manifesto socialism: not the "scientific" theory developed, with appropriate statistics and "laws," by Marx and his followers; but the sort of utopian, idealistic, sentimental dream expressed, with appropriate rhetoric and poetry, by Fourier and others, only to be mocked and belittled by Marx.

Yet whatever the lack in precision and sophistication of its social doctrine, the 1840s were a period at least in which for the first time it had become possible to speak of a "working class" rather than of "the lower orders" or "the poor"; and in which, therefore, it was also possible to imagine a kind of literature appropriate to a group thus redefined. Condescension had not disappeared entirely with the invention of a new nomenclature (any more than it disappears entirely among us now that we have learned to say "Black" rather than "darky" or "colored man" or "Negro"), since men like Sue and Reynolds were quite remote from their readers in social origin. Yet, unlike the kind of literature written at "the lower orders" and "the poor," fiction for the "working class" was relatively free of advice to its audience to know their places and accept their lot. Rather it held out to them the possibility of imagining (perhaps someday creating) a world in which they would fare better; or at least one in which the corruption of their masters would be exposed to scorn.

Quite obviously, the "penny dreadful" did not operate to change the visible world, as did, for instance, the revolutionary pamphlets and books of Marx and Engels; and yet it changed hearts and minds, altered both the self-consciousness of the workers and the consciousness of them among the bourgeoisie. Thinking of something like this, George Bernard Shaw, himself a life-long socialist, was once moved to remark that Dickens' *Little Dorrit* was a more revolutionary book than Marx's *Das Kapital*. And surely, even more directly and crudely than Dickens, Sue and Reynolds and Lippard used their kind of fiction to demythologize the upper classes and to mythologize the lower ones, to expose and debunk aristocratic life and to sentimentalize and glorify the life of the humble.

And precisely because it was addressed not to the reason but to the sensibilities of its readers, this fiction could not afford to be merely didactic or tendentious but aimed above all at telling stories of breathless suspense, creating vivid images of horror and lust, thus rousing passion and releasing it, over and over in a series of orgasmic explosions. The development of this sort of fiction is not linear like conventional plotting, but up and down, from peak to valley, tumescence to detumescence and back.

"Excitement" rather than "instruction and delight" is the end sought by the writers of the popular literature of the 1840's; and in quest of it they exploited, with the virtuosity of old pros, two basic human responses: sex and aggression. Theirs was, that is to say, a kind of fiction thoroughly sado-masochistic and at least demipornographic, though always in terms more political than domestic, more public than private. The brothel and the gallows were their preferred scene—areas where commerce and sex, law and violence oddly consorted. And this concern with public issues constitutes a bid for respectability of a sort.

Such pious and sado-masochistic subpornography must, therefore, be seen as occupying an unsuspected middle ground between that pre-empted by the novels intended for the "proper Victorians" and that exploited by those writers whom Stephen Marcus has called the "other Victorians." Unlike the pure Porn provided by the latter, political demiporn contains no crudely explicit language, no forbidden words, no actual descriptions of the sexual encounter, only a constant teasing of the imagination, a constant invitation to finish for one's self scenes which fade out in a swoon and discreet silence. We are often invited into ladies' beds or permitted to peep into their boudoirs, but never permitted to remain to the point of penetration of their lovely flesh.

And though there is some exploitation of female nudity, both in the text and the accompanying illustrations, to feed the erotic fantasies so essential to popular fiction, such nakedness extends only to the navel. There is typically—usually in the course of a lingering description of a disrobing as a prelude to seduction or rape—considerable exposure of what such writers are fond of calling "snowy globes," though of nothing below the waist. And, indeed, there is no more breast-centered concern with the female form anywhere in world art, with the possible exception of the Fountains of Rome and the center fold-out of *Playboy*.

It should be clear that the literature of the 1840's is a specific subgenre of popular literature—not merely produced by men only but intended for an exclusively male audience. It was, therefore, doomed to a temporary eclipse at least, not only by the more ambitious literature contemporary with it, the work of, say, Balzac and Dickens—but also by the pop literature which immediately succeeded it: those genteel best-sellers of the 1870's *(The Lamp-lighter,* parodied by Joyce in the Gertie MacDowell episode of *Ulysses* is an example) which represented an attempt to come to terms with the re-emergence of a bourgeois female audience—first appealed to by Richardson—as the controllers of the literary market-place.

In any case, it is the temporary dissolution of a politically minded male audience with a taste for subpornography, in favor of the domestically oriented female audience with a taste for pure sentimentality which explains the loss of approval suffered by Lippard's kind of fiction. And when that male audience reasserted itself at the very end of the nineteenth century and the beginning of ours, it had grown somehow less political, was willing at any rate to satisfy itself with the exotic adventure story, the detective novel and the Western—each projecting in its way a nostalgic dream of innocence rather than fantasies of exposure and revolution and sex.

The later pop forms for men only tend, in fact, to be tales of men only; but in the 1840's no male best-seller was without its female victims, raped or seduced by the evil rich, rescued and redeemed by the worthy poor—or more usually, by renegade aristocratic champions of the poor. Descriptions of the female form were as essential to the genre as they were to the sentimental literature read by the wives, mothers, and sisters of its fans. Yet how different those descriptions, in direct response to the differences of the fantasies which fed them and were in turn fed by them.

Here, for instance, are two contrasting passages, the first from the *Family Herald* of 1850, the second from Reynolds' *Wagner: the Wehr-Wolf.* They are quoted side by side in a study by Margaret Dalziel called *Popular Fiction 100 Years Ago,* presumably to illustrate Reynolds' superior skill and candor as compared to other contemporary mass entertainers; but they illustrate rather the diversity of the images of woman demanded, on the one hand, by the female popular audience and, on the other, by the male.

> Alice was one of those tall, aristocratic-looking creatures, who notwithstanding a certain slimness, realise, perhaps, the highest ideal of female beauty. Her figure was of the lordly Norman type, and perfect in its proportions; while every movement was grace-

ful, yet dignified. Her face was of that almost divine beauty we see in the Beatrice Cenci of Guido. The same dazzling complexion, the same blue eyes, the same golden hair. . . . Her countenance, always lovely, was now transcendently beautiful, for it glowed with enthusiasm.

She was attired in deep black; her luxuriant raven hair, no longer depending in shining curls, was gathered up in massy bands at the sides, and in a knot behind, whence hung a rich veil that *meandered over her body's splendidly symmetrical length of limb in such a manner as to aid her attire in shaping rather than hiding the contours of that matchless form.* The voluptuous development of her bust was shrouded, not concealed, by the stomacher of black velvet which she wore, and which set off in strong relief the dazzling whiteness of her neck.

And now Lippard in a similar vein:

Her head deep sunken in a downy pillow, a beautiful woman lay wrapt in slumber. By the manner in which the silken folds of the coverlid were disposed, you might see that her form was full, large and voluptuous. Thick masses of jet-black hair fell, glossy and luxuriant, over her round neck and along her uncovered bosom, which swelling with the full ripeness of womanhood, rose gently in the light. . . . And over that full bosom, which rose and fell with the gentle impulse of slumber, over that womanly bosom, which should have been the home of pure thoughts and wifely affections, was laid a small and swarthy hand, whose fingers, heavy with rings, pressed against the ivory skin, all streaked with veins of delicate azure, and clung twiningly among the dark tresses that hung drooping over the breast, as its globes rose heaving into view, like worlds of purity and womanhood.

Even from so scant a sampling it should be clear that the popular male novel of the 1840's is distinguished not only by a common subject matter and a shared stock of imagery, but also by a special style, which, invented in French, manages to survive in German, as well as in both British and American English. That style tends toward the breathless, the ecstatic, the rhapsodic, as is appropriate to a kind of prose in which the cadences of emotion are always threatening to break through the limits of syntax. And in some of the writers of the school, conventional marks of punctuation give way to dashes or dots to indicate the replacement of logic by passion, as in Reynolds, for instance.

> Even while he reflected upon other things—amidst the perils which enveloped his career, and the reminiscences of the dread deeds of which he had been guilty,—amongst the reasons which he had assembled together to convince himself that the hideous countenances at the gate did not exist in reality,—there was one idea—unmixed—definite—standing boldly out from the rest in his imagination,—*that he might be left to die of starvation!*

Sometimes the full stop is replaced not by the dash but by the exclamation point, or even double exclamation points, while paragraphs shrink to the single exclamatory sentence, as in Reynolds once more:

> A week contains a hundred and sixty-eight hours.
> And he worked a hundred and nineteen hours each week!
> And he earned eight shillings!!
> A decimal more than three farthings an hour!!!

The intent is clear, in any case: to write "badly" at all costs, which is to say, to choose an air of slapdash carelessness over any pretense at polish; to prefer clichés to well-turned phrases; and to let grammar take care of itself. Squeamish critics, both then and now, have tended to be put off by this affectation of banality and subliteracy, which is in fact, somehow functional and effective. I myself, writing about Lippard earlier[2], have fallen into that trap—betraying my own genuine fondness for his mad book by condescension, and thus revealing the "double standard" toward High

---

[2] In *Love and Death in the American Novel* (1960), where along with many observations which seem to me valid still, I felt obliged to talk about "a slapdash literary level considerably below that of his predecessor . . .," "shamefully masturbating dreams," etc. But throughout that study, it seems to me now, I tried to justify my quite valid determination to deal with "pop books" as well as "classics" with snide or ironical asides. It is one of the few things I would now change if I could without falsifying my earlier version.

and Pop Art which I find difficult to transcend. And yet reading in other critics such typical ploys as, "One cannot condemn Elvis Presley for not being like Gigli. On the other hand it is not enough . . . ." or "One can study pornography by its own standards, but one has always to make it clear . . . ." I know the limitations of such a double view, shudder to think how strongly and for how long it affected my own criticism.

In both realms of art, if in fact they are two, form follows function as it properly should. The structure of the subpornographic novel, for instance, is as unorthodox as its sentences, since—like many pop genres, e.g., the daytime radio and television serial—it tends to be all middle, with no real beginning or conclusion. The books of Lippard and Sue and Reynolds are, in essence, endless books. *The Quaker City,* though itself a fairly thick volume, is one of the smallest of the lot; seeming, indeed, almost slim for all its five-hundred-odd pages, when compared to Reynold's *Mysteries of the Court,* which ran to some four and a half million words, and Sue's *Mysteries of the People,* which covers two thousand years of history in enough pages to make perhaps fifty modern novels. What is reflected in their bulk is not so much the dream of writing the "total novel," a model of all human experience, like, say, Balzac or Faulkner, but rather the hope of entertaining forever an insomniac public quite as tyrannical as the story-loving Sultan of Scheherazade. The pop novel of Sue and Reynolds and Lippard represents, that is to say, a model not of swarming life but of the mass media themselves—an unremitting stream of words intended to combat a finally unmitigatable ennui.

Styleless and structureless, in any classic sense, the genre is also —and most disturbingly, perhaps—characterless. The multitude of persons who move through its pages are not portrayed in any kind of psychological depth; and certainly they never change, since they are representative rather than individual, *given* once and for all rather than developed in time. When such characters become memorable at all, it is as mythic figures, names of mysterious resonance inextricably associated with certain immutable qualities and postures; not as fictional personages, endowed with souls and lifestyles, pasts and futures. Moreover, as mythic figures they rapidly pass out of their inventor's hands into the public domain, where they are borrowed with no pangs of conscience by other writers, who sense, perhaps, that their presumed creators merely found them in the communal imagination.

The single book of Charles Dickens which belongs wholly to the popular genre is *The Pickwick Papers*[3]*;* and the archetypal character of Pickwick (suggested by an engraver to begin with) was appropriated by painters and potters and playmakers, as well as rival pop writers, in especial G. W. M. Reynolds, who sent him to France in *Pickwick Abroad,* gave him a wife in *Pickwick Married,* and actually turned him into a teetotaler in *Noctes Pickwickianae.* But why *not,* after all? Had not Dickens himself played a similar game, attempting to re-appropriate his own characters (quite as vainly as Shakespeare trying to revive Falstaff in *The Merry Wives of Windsor)* in *Master Humphrey's Clock?* Pop Art, even in the age of individualism, tended to be collective, collaborative—like the slowly accreting epics on one end of the time scale, and corporately produced movies on the other. Perhaps Sue and Lippard, maybe even Reynolds, may have regarded themselves on occasion as lonely artists trying to make a name as well as a fortune by their art. Typically, however, the author of this kind of fiction seems to think of himself as helping, along with his predecessors, contemporaries, and ghost writers, to compose an immense, cooperative, nearly anonymous work: a monstrous super novel, which exists not in the pages of any book with its author's name on the spine but in the heads and hearts of the mass audience.

Difficult as it has been for traditional criticism to come to terms with the antiform of the popular novel, it has been even harder for it to arrive at any final understanding of what its anti-ideas, which is to say, its nonphilosophical themes, really signify. There is, however, an essential clue to this in the word "mystery" or "mysteries," which appears in so many of the titles. As a matter of fact, even Lippard's book smuggles this key word into its second subtitle, "A Romance of Philadelphia Life, Mystery, and Crime"; and his German translator-adapter gave it an even more prominent place, calling his version *The Quaker City and Its Mysteries.*

---

[3] *Oliver Twist* and *Old Curiosity Shop* remain basically pop as well; but all of Dickens' novels after them aspire to become symbolist rather than mythological—tend, that is to say, toward "High Literature."

In recent times, the word has survived only in our habit of calling detective novels "mystery stories," as if the sole mystery in our existence was "Who done it?"; but this represents a reduced and demythicized use of a magic term with a long history. It is well to remember that it goes back, in fact, to the early days of the Gothic Romance, when Anne Radcliffe published *The Mysteries of Udolpho,* a classic example of the genre dedicated to evoking the darkness of medieval times. The mysteries of the 1840's, however, were concerned not with what was inscrutable and sinister in the outlived past, but what remained inscrutable and sinister in the living present; not with the darkness of the dungeons below medieval castles, but with the darkness of the urban underworld: all that lies beneath the glittering surfaces of the Big City.

Insofar as the subpornographic novel for males represents an attempt to redeem the modern city for the imagination, to invent a myth of the City as moving and mysterious as the ancient myths of Sea and Forest, it belongs to the mainstream of early "modernist" art; joining the "lowbrow" Sue and Reynolds not only to the ambiguously "middlebrow" Balzac and Dickens and Dostoevski, but also to such "highbrows" as Baudelaire and Whitman. The obsession with the infernal city suggests, moreover, a link between Lippard and Herman Melville; for the latter attempted at least twice (for London in *Redburn,* for New York in *Pierre*) the evocation of urban horror, calling on his memories of Dante, for whom "The City" had been a favorite metaphor for hell itself.

The concern with the city as landscape and symbol never quite dies out of "modernism" (think, for instance, of the "Unreal City" of Eliot's *The Waste Land);* but from the time of, say, Arnold Bennett to that of James T. Farrell, there was an attempt to demythify the City—to present it as banal, rather than horrific. To Lippard all cities may have seemed like Cities of the Plain ("Woe Unto Sodom!" cries the slogan on the title page of *The Monks of Monk Hall),* but to those who thought of themselves as "realists," such Biblical analogues came to appear merely sensational—and finally irrelevant. In pop culture, however, the image of the City as hidden horror never died, though it was driven underground—to Soho, the Bowery, the Tenderloin, into the aptly named "underworld" of the detective story and the thriller.

Then in our own century, it has begun to re-emerge—all the more terrifying because of its advanced technology—in Science Fiction: first, perhaps, in certain German films, in Fritz Lang's *Metropolis,* for instance; and next in comic books, whose versions of the Big City have fed the imagination of a generation of novelists and poets just now coming of age. Such writers have been especially impressed by the urban wilderness of Superman and Captain Marvel: that crime-ridden megalopolis—so conveniently supplied with phone booths for quick costume changes, and seen always from above—through which Siegel and Shuster's superhero has been pursuing his foes for a quarter of a century now; and that similar one—seen from below, from the abandoned subway tunnel (once more we are underground, which is to say, mythologically at home)—in which the newsboy Billy Batson, by saying the mysterious word "SHAZAM," becomes Captain Marvel.

But the task of mythologizing the threat of the City remains divided up in our world—a function shared by the movies, the comics, the novel. Reynolds and Lippard and Sue were moviemakers and cartoonists (with some aid from their illustrators) and makers of fiction in one, encyclopedic pop artists competing with no one except each other. Besides, the mythological city they evoked was still fully erotic, still *female,* as it were—neither desexed by technology, nor transformed by the skyscraper into an icon of a kind of permanent and sterile male tumescence endlessly repeated against the sky. Women could be had, if only in terror—raped, seduced, even killed in passion—in the mythic city of the 1840's; but in the comic-book metropolis of post-World War II, they could only be eternally fled in a general flight from passion. Sex, the female principle, persists only as the mechanical womb of the telephone booth or the subway, in which human flesh is converted into a kind of superplastic, invulnerable to bullets or love. No wonder that it was necessary to pretend that the pop-horror of the 1950's was intended for kids only![4]

---

[4] Interestingly enough, there has been an attempt in the dying 1960's to introduce sex—even pornography—into the comic books themselves; but this has so far been confined to certain "head" comics, produced for a special audience, the hippie community for whom Mr. Natural seems a more useful symbol than Captain Marvel himself or other more recent inventions for the mass audience like Sub-Mariner or The Hulk.

For the subpornographers of the 1840's, however, the essential image of the mystery under the city was the Gothic whorehouse: a hidden place where, among all the other commodities for sale in the great urban market places, daughters and sisters and wives are being offered to the purchaser rich enough to acquire them. Typically this place is disguised—as a fashionable milliner's shop in Reynolds, for instance—though it may simply be buried away out of sight, as in Lippard. In any event, it must finally be revealed, exposed—in an age where exploitation, social and sexual, is no longer blatant and open as in pre-Revolutionary days, but concealed behind the facade of "business as usual."

The classic Gothic Novel was radical in its politics, but radical in an oddly retrospective way; which is to say, its authors attacked the inherited evils of the past as represented especially by the Inquisition and the remnants of the feudal aristocracy. The writers of popular Gothic, on the other hand, fought against the new masters, not the old, the hidden rather than open exploiters: factory owners, capitalists, merchants, as well as the pimps and thugs who serve them, and the lawyers and clergy who provide them cover and camouflage. The popular novel thinks of itself, then, as exposing, revealing, muckraking; and in this sense, it is closely allied with the illustrated comic newspaper, which appeared just before it, to provide the "inside dope" on those in power—stripping the rich and beautiful naked to provide the impotent poor a kind of vicarious revenge, as well as a sexual *frisson*. Unlike such newspapers, however, the popular novel was aimed not merely at provoking a snigger and grin but a real shudder of horror as well, repulsion tempered with wonder and awe. The popular novel did not utterly reject the comic, but it yearned for the "marvelous," too. And here James Fenimore Cooper provided a more useful model than, say, *Figaro in London* or *Figaro in Sheffield* or *Figaro in Birmingham,* which were already being published in the early 1830's.

Cooper may seem, at first glance, an oddly inappropriate guide for writers about urban life; but there is, as those authors make sufficiently manifest, a sense in which the City can, indeed *must,* come to represent for modern man, as the Sea and Forest had for his ancestors, what remains hidden and uncontrollable in his own psyche, what survives in him of "The Wilderness": the primitive world out of which his waking self has emerged long since, but to which his dreaming self returns. Intending to build a shelter, a refuge against all that was savage and dark around him, man had (he discovered as the mid-nineteenth century approached) constructed in his cities only a new kind of jungle, a jungle of stone and glass, into which he ventured as into a strange land. Civilized man, which is to say, the literate European of the 1840's, felt first dismay at his alienation in the cities he had built, then excitement. If he was not at home in the urban landscape, he could visit there like a traveler, a tourist.

The popular novels of the 1840's are, then, like Cooper's, exotic novels, expressions of a kind of armchair tourism. And their exoticism had been made possible, even necessary, as a wider and wider gap had opened between the ordinary city dweller and, on the one hand, the Very Rich, on the other, the denizens of the urban underworld, who came, finally, to seem as remote and romantic as the savages of the American West: the real Apaches—as, in fact, the inhabitants of the Underworld of Paris actually were called.[5] Eugene Sue was aware of how much he owed to Cooper in his mythologizing of the urban wilderness; and it is instructive to read his own words on the subject:

> Everybody has read the admirable pages in which Cooper, the American Walter Scott, has traced the fierce customs of the savages; the picturesque and poetic language, the thousand ruses with the aid of which they kill or pursue their enemies.
> We are going to try to put before the eyes of our reader some episodes from the life of other barbarians, also outside of civilization, barbarians different from the savage tribes so well depicted by Cooper.
> Only the barbarians of whom we are speaking are in our very midst. We can brush against them if we adventure into the

---

[5] Romantic exoticism seeks to escape the tedium and alienation of bourgeois life by flight in four directions, Back, Out, In, and Down: backward in time like Sir Walter Scott; outward in space like Robert Louis Stevenson; inward toward the murky depths of the unconscious like Rimbaud; or down the social scale like Sue and, after him, the so-called "Naturalists." (It is interesting that Zola wrote one of the last "mysteries," *The Mysteries of Marseille.*) All forms of Romantic exoticism are kinds of vicarious tourism—the downward variety vicarious "slumming."

hideouts in which they live, where they gather to plot murder, theft; to share the spoils of their victims.

These men have customs of their own, women of their own, a language of their own—a mysterious language full of dark images and of bloody and disgusting metaphors.

How much better Sue understood the real meaning of Cooper, and, consequently, of popular literature than did Poe, who associated the appeal and limitations of both that novelist and his mode exclusively with the primitive setting. In a review of *Wyandotté* published in 1843 (when, in fact, Sue's *Mysteries of Paris* had already begun to appear serially, perhaps at the very moment that Sue was setting down his own response to Cooper), Poe wrote:

> . . . we mean to suggest that this theme—life in the Wilderness—is one of intrinsic and universal interest, appealing to the heart of man in all phases; a theme, like that of life upon the ocean, so unfailingly omniprevalent in its power of arresting and absorbing attention, that while success or popularity is, with such a subject, expected as a matter of course, a failure might be properly regarded as conclusive evidence of imbecility on the part of the author . . .

And he then adds, a little ruefully—though he had already tried his hand at both the sea-story and the Western in his single complete novel, *The Narrative of A. Gordon Pym* (1837–38), and the abortive *Journal of Julius Rodman* (1840)—that the themes of life on the ocean and in the wilderness were to be avoided at all costs by the "man of genius . . . more interested in fame than popularity."

It is an elitist declaration of faith, based on the conviction that of the "two great classes of fiction," the class represented by Cooper, "the popular division," is distinguished by the fact that its authors are inevitably "lost or forgotten; or remembered, if at all, with something very nearly akin to contempt." Yet though this may be true of George Lippard, it can hardly be said to be so of Eugène Sue—whose characters may be forgotten (who now remembers Rodolphe or Fleur-de-Marie?), but whose name has become, like Poe's own, almost a common noun; used sometimes, to be sure, with more than a touch of contempt and yet also of something else, something more.

At any rate, from the very beginning Sue thought of himself as of Cooper's party, rather than, like Poe, on the side of "Mr. Brockden Brown, Mr. John Neal, Mr. Simms, Mr. Hawthorne," writers of whom it can be said, still according to Poe, that "even when the works perish, the man survives." Long before he embarked on the *Mysteries of Paris,* he had, in fact, already written sea-stories modeled on Cooper's *The Pilot,* and had even received, at one point, a fan letter from "The American Walter Scott" himself, who was then voyaging in France. But Sue did not discover until he was well into his greatest book the sense in which he had managed to remain faithful still to his old master, still an exoticist and laureate of the primitive, though he had abandoned the ocean for the city.

Quite another model had been proposed to him by the friend who first suggested that Sue take up a brand-new subject matter, in order to reach "the people" and find "the future." Yet what exactly that new model was is hard to tell, though quite clearly it was English rather than American. Sue's latest biographer, Jean-Louis Bory, reports confusingly that "Gosselin brought to Sue an illustrated English publication, whose illustrations and text depicted the 'Mysteries' of London." The word "Mysteries" causes difficulties, setting the reader immediately to thinking of G. M. W. Reynolds; but the chronology is all wrong, backward—since it was Sue who inspired Reynolds, not vice versa. And, in the end, it seems probable that Gosselin's gift to his friend must have been Pierce Egan's *Life in London,* which appeared in 1821 with a dedication to George IV, the infamous "Georgie Porgie" who had kissed the girls and made 'em cry, while still the Prince Regent—with his plump popsie in Brighton and his mad father in London.

What an unlikely source Egan seems for a new literature aimed at what Gosselin described as "the world just ahead, the future, the people. . . ." His book, despite the feeblest pretense at moralizing, was in fact a tongue-in-cheek, satirical picture of young Oxonians lost in the midst of London's "sporty life": a kind of guide to "flash" debauchery. Its tone is indicated clearly enough by a prefixed song, also written by Egan, a kind of ballad to the first "swinging London":

> London Town's a dashing place,
> For everything that's going,

There's gig and fun in every face,
So natty and so knowing. . . .

Take your Daffy, All be Happy;
And then dash on, In the fashion,
Dancing singing full of glee,
O London London town for me. . . .

No "mysteries" here, certainly, or room for revolutionary fervor. And yet the clue must have been there somehow, somewhere, for an imagination trained by Cooper. Sue found it, perhaps, in the engravings by the Cruikshank brothers, those caricatures closer to the grotesque and more attuned to the terrors and wonders of "slumming" than anything in the bland text itself: in the plate, for instance, called "Lowest Life in London"—depicting with something nearer horror than farce "the unsophisticated Sons and Daughters of Nature at 'All Max' "; or in the almost queasy scene in which a spectacled voyeur at the harpsichord peeps over his shoulder at Jerry dancing with "Corinthian Kate," her breasts bared to the nipple. Even for the modern reader, Pierce Egan seems as often as not to be limping after his illustrator, to be, as it were, merely illustrating the illustrations, often lamely enough, when he is not simply writing captions. Certainly he views his own art in metaphors compulsively pictorial, as his chapter headings reveal from the start: "A Camera-Obscura View of the Metropolis, with the Light and Shade attached to 'seeing Life' "; "A Short Sketch of the Author's Talents in taking a Likeness . . . A Pen-and-Ink Drawing of Corinthian Tom."

It is more than mere accident that the popular novel of the 1840's begins with an author at a loss appropriating from sketches intended for someone else's work, someone else's quite different purposes, the images necessary to release his own deepest fantasy. A similar thing had already happened with Dickens, who had come upon Pickwick in an attempt to provide a text for certain sketches of "sporting life" already contracted for and delivered. But the novel only *finally* became pictorial, after having been first epistolary and dramatic. The first truly pop form of the Western world, it was invented over and over in its first two centuries of existence on the basis of models provided by other genres. Created by Samuel Richardson out of the letter book, it was re-created by Fielding on the basis of stage techniques and parody of epic, then recast by Scott on the pattern of Shakespeare become Closet Drama. Only in the forties was the last element added (we do not think of Richardson or Fielding or Scott, as we do, say, of Dickens as necessarily illustrated), opening a real link with the future (Gosselin was right, after all) not provided by the more traditional models of letter or drama. Once words are thought of, however provisionally, as secondary or subsidiary to pictures—or rather, cartoons—we are well on the way to comic books and Walt Disney, and the "silent film" that is to give a shape to the movies forever after.

Eugene Sue, however, seems to have had little or no sense of all this at first. The tone of Egan, as well as his resolutely *un*-mythicized versions of low life, began by merely disgusting him; and his initial response to Gosselin ran (we are dependent here on the professional liar, Alexander Dumas, but why not?): "My dear friend, I don't like what's filthy and smells bad." But his dear friend hastened to remind him that, as a doctor and descendant of doctors, he should surely understand that remedies for sickness are often found precisely by delving into "the stench and rot of corpses." Once into the stinking heart of the "mysteries," in any case, Sue seems to have forgotten his distaste for filth; or rather, discovered that he *liked* delving in it, found it, after all, *amusing*. *"C' est peut-être bête comme un chou. Cela m' a bien amusé à faire, mais cela amusera-t-il les autres à lire? Violà la douteux."* Stupid stuff, maybe, but it tickled me to do it. Will it tickle anyone else to read it, that's the question.

Real or pretended, Sue's final doubts proved as groundless as his initial ones, for his book was an immediate and spectacular success, hailed—despite a certain detached irony, an amused distance from "the people," which he maintained throughout—not only by bourgeois readers, but by "the people" themselves; and even by *La Phalange,* journal of the utopian socialist followers of Fourier. Professional critics, too, were overwhelmed, as were Sue's fellow novelists in Europe and America, delighted to have been given at last a model for democratizing the Gothic, politicalizing a literature of the Marvelous. Sue had finished the *Mysteries* in October of 1843; the dramatic version (which ran for seven hours!) was played to enthusiastic audiences in 1844; and in that very year Sue began his second dazzling success, *The Wandering Jew.*

It was an extraordinary year for the then New Literature, 1844: a year in which Balzac was publishing *Splendeurs et Misères des Courtisanes,* Dumas *The Three Musketeers* and the *Count of Monte Cristo,* and Dickens was finishing (his mind turned round by his first trip to America) *Martin Chuzzlewit.* Meanwhile Cooper himself, driven by the competition from England to sell his books at twenty-five cents a volume, was doing *Afloat and Ashore,* and Walt Whitman, grieving over the failure of his single novel, *Franklin Evans,* was secretly preparing to become a poet. It was, in short, a time of revolutionary beginnings and endings, of the exhaustion of old possibilities and the opening of new.

To the moment itself, however, it seemed chiefly the time of the triumph of Sue; and in a matter of months, the dramatic adaptations and adulatory reviews were followed by the imitations, as if to make clear forever (but how soon the records were to grow dim, the memory to be lost) that Sue had not merely written a bestseller, he had also invented a genre, infinitely adaptable wherever men lived in cities and longed to mythologize them. Paris itself occasioned an astonishing number: *The Mysteries of the Bastille, The True Mysteries of Paris, The Mysteries of Old Paris, The Mysteries of New Paris,* etc.; and the rest of the world hastened to enter the mythic circle: *Mysteries of Berlin, Mysteries of Munich, Mysteries of Brussels, Hungarian Mysteries*—and, of course, several *Mysteries of London,* including one by Paul Féval, who assumed for the purpose of writing it the "Anglo-Saxon" name of Sir Francis Trolopp.

Sue himself was to do a great deal more before his career was over, but nothing else which would stir the creative imagination of his time as his own had been stirred reading Pierce Egan, or rather looking at the caricatures of the Cruikshank brothers through the eyes of Fenimore Cooper. Even *The Wandering Jew,* despite its phenomenal success, represented in some sense a regression to earlier Gothic themes; the key figure of the Jew, for instance, came out of late medieval lore, and the obsessive concern with the threat of the Jesuits seemed something left over from the eighteenth century: *Ecrasez l' infame!* But the mode itself had been established once and for all, the mixture of gore and sex and socialism, sentimentality and sadism, eros and politics: a true literature of the world ahead, the people and the future.

The triumph of the reactionary forces in France sent Sue into exile after 1852, but it only confirmed his radical politics, and, indeed, made his late fiction increasingly didactic and doctrinaire. The incredibly long and pious *Mysteries of the People,* which traces the history of a working-class family from the time of the Druids to the verge of Sue's present, is the culmination of that trend—a homily in fictional form, translated into English appropriately enough by Daniel De Leon, whom Lenin once described as America's greatest socialist.

G. W. M. Reynolds was perhaps the most important writer to be influenced by Sue; but in a perverse way he seems to have followed his predecessor's path backward, beginning with imitations of the kind of neo-Gothic fiction suggested by *The Wandering Jew,* and only later writing books on the model of *The Mysteries of Paris.* One of Reynolds' first novels was called *The Mysteries of the Inquisition,* followed very shortly by *Faust,* and then by his earliest real success, a newspaper serial called *Wagner: The Wehr-Wolf.* That Sue was in Reynolds' head there is no doubt; for he had spent several years in Paris, where he had gone at the age of twenty-one to begin a new life with the twelve thousand pounds left to him at the death of his father. His parents had intended him for a career in the army, actually sending him to Sandhurst, but his commitment was to a life of journalism, and he invested his patrimony in a magazine, actually published in Paris, on which he employed Thackeray among others.

He was, in fact, the publisher-editor-chief-contributor of several magazines during his career, the most famous of which was called *Reynolds' Miscellany of Romance, General Interest, Science and Art.* In some ways his activities as a writer remained always subsidiary to his interests as an editor, or rather as a journalist-reformer intent on rescuing the working class from intellectual torpor as well as economic exploitation; and he therefore had no scruples about writing voluminously without reflection or revision—and even, on occasion, calling on the aid of ghost writers. Yet despite all of this, Reynolds was, in fact, a highly talented writer, unfortunately cast into the shadow by the immense presence of that contemporary genius, Charles Dickens. By a further ironical turn of the screw, however, it turned out to be the example of Dickens which inspired Reynolds, turning him from an initial interest in fantasy based on the past to a concern with the contemporary scene, especially with low life and the language appropriate to it.

Just as Sue had been triggered by reading Pierce Egan through the eyes of James Fenimore Cooper, Reynolds was awakened to his true vocation by reading Pickwick through the eyes of Sue. Reynolds' relationship with Dickens is not, finally, as one-sided as it may seem at first, since Dickens in the latter part of his career apparently learned a great deal from Sue, borrowing certain stereotypical characters and themes, even adapting certain incidents which struck his fancy. And at the very end of his life he was wrestling with a dark and difficult book, called (untypically for Dickens) *The Mystery of Edwin Drood*, which not only in its title pays a kind of homage to the tradition of the "Mysteries" brought to England by Reynolds.

Reynolds, however, is temperamentally altogether different from Dickens; for there is in him a certain element of Puritanism in regard to drink, quite opposite to the attitude which made Dickens almost Dionysiac in tone whenever he described men on the way to drunkenness. In an act of what seems deliberate blasphemy, Reynolds, in his first pseudocontinuation of the Pickwick series, turned Pickwick himself, that god of brandy and water (along with Sam Weller and his father), into a teetotaler; and then in another actually married him off—removing him from that blessed state of bachelorhood, that world exclusively male, in which drinking is a consummation as high and holy as sex in marriage.

Sex constitutes, in fact, the other major area of difference between Reynolds and Dickens; Dickens is notorious for his squeamishness in dealing with female sexuality, his resolve to keep his women, however passionate or theoretically depraved, fully clothed; whereas female nudity is for Reynolds a central image, almost an obsession.

Reynolds is a master of the strip tease, a near-genius at contriving occasions for disrobing his female characters, and for making the reader his accomplice in peeping at them through windows and keyholes and from behind curtains. There is, for instance, an extraordinary scene in his *Mysteries of London,* in which a handsome young preacher receives as a present from a lady parishioner a nude statue which turns out, in fact, to be that lady herself! But what Dickens and Reynolds do share, and what the native English tradition of "Newgate" literature—the celebration in verse and prose of criminals who came to a bad end—encourages in both of them, is an obsession with violence, especially as it is practiced by the law itself in the form of public executions. The sole form of explicit pornography which Dickens permits himself is horror pornography, the pornography of crime and punishment—Bill Sykes strangling Nancy, Fagin in his cell—and in this Reynolds is almost his equal; though Reynolds had some kinks of his own, including a fascination with body-snatching, the rape of the dead.

Reynolds had a long career as an exploiter of death and sex, and is the author of an almost incredible number of books, but the two which established his reputation as a popular entertainer *par excellence* and friend of the people are *The Mysteries of London* and *The Mysteries of the Court.* In a certain sense, *The Mysteries of the Court* represents a regression from his earlier work, a kind of retreat in time to the era of the Prince Regent, who was later to become George IV, and a shift in subject matter from low life to high life: from an attempt to portray the sufferings of the poor to a projection of fantasies about the corrupt pleasures of the rich. And it was this side of Reynolds which seems to have appealed especially to George Lippard, who, beginning his career younger than any of his contemporaries, had a larger store of dreams than of actual experience to draw on for the making of his fictions—dreams he had dreamed himself in loneliness and anguish, plus the dreams dreamed precisely for such alienated boys as himself by Reynolds, and, for that matter, Sue. Indeed, it is impossible to tell in Lippard's case, so single and communal is the tradition, which writer provided a form for his reverie; the Frenchman who had, in fact, appeared in American translation almost immediately, or the Englishman who had become a best-seller in the United States almost as quickly as in his own country.

We do know that in the case of Friedrich Gerstäcker, it was Lippard himself rather than either of his European predecessors who provided the model; though doubtless Gerstäcker's mind had already been prepared to embrace what Lippard was doing by the example of the other two. What Gerstäcker seems really to have wanted, however, and what only Lippard could provide, was the European tradition of the "Mysteries" rendered with an American accent; for Gerstäcker had made his career precisely as the expert on all that was exotic on the American scene. Most of his books, as a matter of fact, dealt with the American West in its wilder and more brutal aspects; and he survives to this day chiefly as a writer of boys' "Westerns," his books being continually republished in large print, with brightly illustrated editions, and garish covers showing sudden death among trappers and Indians.

He actually journeyed in the United States from 1837 to 1843, and his account of his experiences appeared in an English translation rather inaccurately titled *Wild Sports in the Far West.* In this account one finds, interestingly enough, no descriptions whatsoever of the kind of lynch-mob violence and banditry which he was later to describe in his best-selling *The Regulators in Arkansas* (1845) and *The River Pilots of the Mississippi* (1848). As a matter of fact, he seems to have spent his time when he was not hunting or sight-seeing at Niagara Falls, peacefully visiting settlements of fellow Germans, or baiting, like the good German he himself was, such occasional Jewish peddlers as he encountered. There are some literary references in his travel book about America to Cooper and to Dickens, quite as one would expect; but there is no mention at all of George Lippard whose *Quaker City* he doubtless acquired during his journey, and perhaps had already started to translate or adapt on his way back home. What Lippard's novel suggested to him was, quite obviously, an alternative form of New World exoticism, the evocation of the specifically American city—of Philadelphia, in fact, already associated in the European mind with that earlier American exotic, Benjamin Franklin.

But what *is* specifically American about Lippard's fiction? What, in fact, had he added to or subtracted from the already established European tradition in the book which Gerstäcker was to rename *The Mysteries of Philadelphia?* Most of what he provides is the standard fare for which the popular audience had already been prepared by Reynolds and Sue: much violence and much sex, plus

a good deal of socialist piety. Yet it has all been rendered in a setting at least theoretically different from London or Paris or, for
that matter, any European city; though Lippard's "Philadelphia"
seems most often to be located in a mapless universe of nightmares
rather than in the America of real geography.

Still we do hear on occasion voices undoubtedly American,
communicating not in Sue's argot or the "flash" slang of Reynolds'
underworld types—but in accents well on the way to becoming burlesque or vaudeville stereotypes, *American* burlesque or vaudeville stereotypes, "authentic" enough for a European ear like
Gerstäcker's at least. Here, for instance, is the "Devil-Bug," representing general American low life, in a style which seems a clumsy
foreshadowing of Huck's "Pap": "It don't skeer me, I tell ye!
. . . Ain't it an ugly corpse? Hey? A reel nasty Christian, I
tell ye! Jist look at the knees, drawed up to the chin, jist look at the
eyes, hanging out on the cheeks . . ." And here the equally evil
Negro Glow-worm, "the long rows of his teeth, bustling from his
thick lips": "Massa Gusty no want de critter to go out ob dis 'ere
door . . . 'spose de nigger no mash him head, *bad* . . . did you
ebber see dis chile knock an ox down. Hah-hah!" And, finally, for
the first time, perhaps, in American fiction, the Jewish accent of
Gabriel Van Gelt, "Ven te tings vos done, you vos to gif me ten
tousand tollars in goldt. Vot have you done? Left me to rots in dat
hole—viles you valksh on Cheshnut Streets? Got-tam!"

Aside from all this, what sets Lippard's book apart from those
on which he modeled it is a peculiar emphasis, somehow characteristic of America, on the sanctity, in a world otherwise profane, of
brother-sister relationships. Behind Sue's first venture into popular
fiction, there lurks a kind of family myth, too, but his involves a
father's long search for his lost daughter, whom he finally discovers
living as a whore; and whom he delivers—to the apparent satisfaction of European readers—from the brothel to a nunnery, from
utter corruption to total chastity. Lippard's fantasy, on the other
hand, imagines a brother in breathless quest of a sister whose virtue
is momentarily threatened: a brother who arrives too late to save
that sister's honor, but in time enough to kill her seducer, to whom
he is equivocally bound by affection from the start.

It is not merely the seduction of an unprotected poor girl by a privileged gentleman which furnishes Lippard with a key image for social injustice, but the setting of that act in an odd sort of ménage, which seems all siblings and no parents; reinterpreting seduction, as a matter of fact, as a kind of incest—the worst of threats to the integrity of the family. And in both of its aspects this refantasizing of seduction (long since given the status of a myth by Samuel Richardson and his first female imitators) is peculiarly American; since the obsession with brother-sister incest haunts the American novel from its beginnings in William Hill Brown's *Power of Sympathy,* through the early fiction of Hawthorne and Melville's almost incoherent *Pierre,* to that strangely but aptly titled book with which American "realism" begins, Theodore Dreiser's *Sister Carrie*—and finally to Faulkner's *Absalom! Absalom!*

Moreover, the impulse to understand social injustice not as an offense of person against person, or of society against the individual, but rather of the impious against the family, is also basically American. In *Uncle Tom's Cabin,* for instance, which appeared only a decade or so after *The Monks of Monk Hall,* Harriet Beecher Stowe attempted to convince her vast audience that slavery was wrong by portraying it as an offense against the sole institution presumably unquestioned by anyone, which is to say, the family once more. And doing so she helped release a flood of sentimental energy, which—joined to certain political and economic forces—changed a world by changing its mind, or rather its heart. Mrs. Stowe possessed, however, the power of making or evoking myths to a degree unapproached by Lippard; and, for better or worse, with Uncle Tom and Topsy she succeeded in mythicizing the Negro, as Lippard could not do at all with such comic-malign images of the Black Man as Glow-worm or his companion, Musquito. His true Negro, his absolute victim, was the seduced girl, *la traviata,* whom he more sentimentalized than mythicized, thus preparing the way not for a revolution, but only for more Pop Art—in fiction and drama and, especially, in song.

On the other hand, Lippard's book did produce social results in its own small way. The immediate occasion for *The Monks of Monk Hall* was an incident in which a Philadelphian who had killed the seducer of his sister was held for a while in a New Jersey prison, tried in a New Jersey court, and then, to the total satisfaction of his fellow citizens, acquitted by New Jersey justice. The popular acclaim which followed the release of the murderer led to the writing of Lippard's novel, which in turn helped create a wave of public opinion that resulted in the passage of an antiseduction law in the state of New York in 1849; though in the novel itself not the courts but a brother, taking the law into his own hands, revenges the wronged girl.

There is, in fact, something ambiguous, and yet once more peculiarly American, about Lippard's use of the seduction theme to justify the principle of vigilante justice, in the name of which the Ku Klux Klan would later be defended in the fiction of George Dixon and D. W. Griffith's film *The Birth of a Nation;* and as it had already been glorified in Gerstäcker's *Regulators of Arkansas.* "I determined to write a book," Lippard tells us, "founded upon the following idea: *That the seduction of a poor and innocent girl, is a deed altogether as criminal as murder . . . the assassin of chastity and maidenhood is worthy of death by the hands of any man, and in any place.*" If the tone seems shriller than art or even rhetoric demands, this is surely because Lippard is ridden by an almost pathological obsession with the theme of a sexual assault against the sister; so that he is driven to identify at once with the seducer and the avenger—thus granting himself, as well as his reader, the double privilege of violating the incest taboo and inflicting punishment for such a violation.

His style, at any rate, in the passage toward the conclusion of the book in which he plunges into a kind of dithyrambic song of triumph, presumably sung by a murderer-brother over the fallen body of his sister's lover, reveals a passionate celebration of justified violence, inevitable, certainly, in any guilt-ridden mind; but perhaps essential as well to any revolutionary movement, and to the sort of literature which reflects and sustains its spirit. It is tempting to dismiss the writing as simply "bad," since Lippard lacks even the minimum amount of discretion and control which keep Reynolds and Sue just within the bounds of literary respectability. But everything that is "bad," i.e., indiscreet, vulgar, fulsome, about the following passage represents, at their most embarrassing, effects deliberately sought: the authentic music of the popular-erotic-sentimental-revolutionary novel, before "scientific" Marxism had taught socialists a rhetoric which separated them from the people and their preferred literature.

"Ha, ha!" the shout burst from his lips. "Here is blood warm, warm, aye warm and gushing! Is that the murmur of a brook, is that the whisper of a breeze, is that the song of a bird? No, no, but still it is music—that gushing of the Wronger's blood! Deeply wronged, Mary, deeply, darkly wronged! But finally avenged, Mary, aye to the last drop of his blood! Have you no music there, I would dance, yes, yes, I would dance over the corse! Ha, ha, ha! Not the sound of the organ, that is too dark and gloomy! But the drum, the trumpet, the chorus of a full band; fill heaven and earth with joy! For in sight of God and his angels, I would dance over the corse, while a wild song of joy, fills the heavens! A song— huzza—a song! And the chorus, mark ye how it swells! Huzza!

—1970

# EIGHT

# Chutzpah and Pudeur

IF *chutzpah* and *pudeur* seem an ill-assorted pair of words, one of those mixed marriages (or unblessed acts of miscegenation) which everyone thinks should not and cannot last, but everyone knows most often do, this is because they are in fact such a mismatch; which is to say, made not in heaven but in the head of some perverse matchmaker, some misguided *shadchan*—in this case, me. I had never seen them consorting together on a printed page, the delicate French word, appropriate to a tradition of tact and learning, and the vulgar Yiddish one, so suitable to a countertradition in which arrogance and self-deprecating irony reinforce rather than cancel each other out.

Yet why should they not lie side by side in cold print, I found myself thinking, since they already lived side by side not only in my own divided self, but also in the general culture around me—in American literature, surely, ever since Nathanael West, whose first book boldly displayed its affiliations with the most cryptic, i.e., *pudique,* of French schools, surrealism; and whose last shyly confessed its link with Jewish *chutzpah* by introducing an Indian, called only, in a bad Yiddish joke, "Chief Kiss-My-Towkus," meaning kiss my ass.

Not to have made the conjunction public, once it had occurred to me, would have been to betray a lack of gall, nerve, *chutzpah,* to put it precisely; but not to have regretted it a little almost immediately, would have been to reveal so total an absence of decorum that the very notion of boldness would have lost all meaning. In either event, I would have confessed myself half a man, half an artist, as these are defined in our oddly hybrid tradition, whose two poles Matthew Arnold (being an Englishman at home) termed quite catholically Hebraic and Hellenic, and Philip Rahv (being a recently arrived immigrant) renamed rather parochially Redskin and Paleface; but which I feel obliged to call (feeling neither just arrived nor quite at home) *chutzpah* and *pudeur*. It is not merely a matter of speaking in two tongues neither really mine, but also of insisting on a modicum of irony—that highest academic form of *pudeur*—and thus escaping from both the myth of Antiquity and that of the West, though risking, I suppose, a fall into the equally legendary present, into fashion rather than piety.

I am, at any rate, interested in exploring the basic polarity, as well as the basic ambivalence behind it, which this pair of words seems to me to define more suggestively than any other: a basic polarity in our very understanding of what constitutes art and literature. I am not meaning to suggest that the peculiar Western tradition of art is explained wholly or even chiefly by the tension between *chutzpah* and *pudeur*—merely that this tension plays a large part in determining our essential double view of what it is the artist says or does or makes. I have, as a matter of fact, reflected earlier on two other sets of polarities and ambivalences which also underlie our definition of art: Archetype and Signature in 1952, Mythos and Logos in 1958; and there is some continuity of a complementary if not a developmental kind between those earlier explorations, especially the first, and the present one.

This essay is, in intent, however, complete—not a total explanation but a self-sufficient one: the working out of an extended metaphor or conceit which, in theory at least, should provide a "model" for a large body of literature, otherwise difficult even to see wholly, much less to understand. Yet it is with some regret that I enter on this third (and, I promise myself, final) venture into literary theory. It is a literary form which I practice seldom and reluctantly, finding it a disconcertingly attenuated form of poetry, or more specifically, I guess, prose fiction, in which neither horror nor humor—two effects of which I am, perhaps inordinately, fond, seems quite suitable.

All forms of literary criticism I take to be art forms, but general or theoretical criticism is so genteel or super-*pudique* that it is driven to pretending it is science or philosophy—something else and presumably better, truer, more dependable. It is, however, the very shamefastness of literary theory, its love of disguise, which gives the game away; for, after all, the very essence of literature, or what at least we have agreed to call "literature" in the Western World, is a special use of words which sometimes alternately, sometimes simultaneously, reveals and conceals, exposes and hides: a dialectic movement back and forth between what threatens to become arrogant narcissism and what trembles on the verge of bashful dumbness.

This dialectic can be fruitfully discussed either historically or psychologically: either as it is recapitulated in the experience of the child or youth who begins to define his craft and the image of himself within our tradition, at first feeling, living rather than knowing that tradition; or else as it has been reflected in the long, slow evolution of that tradition itself, in terms, that is to say, of that tradition as it has come to be known. I intend, for reasons which I hope will become clear, to be chiefly historical in my approach, setting the problem in the context of what I take to be history, though others more positivist in their approach might prefer to call it myth or mytho-history: a particular version of the past best suited to illuminate what concerns me in the present.

I cannot, however, resist insisting to begin with on what most readers must already know—on the way in which, even at the earliest stages of his career, a nascent writer may well keep a secret journal, complete with lock and key; but which he ("she" is more apropos here, perhaps, since, mythologically speaking, *pudeur* is female) leaves lying about, unlocked, to be discovered by the first passer-by, even that ultimate invader of privacy, the parent. In a recent article on child poets, for instance, which appeared in *The New York Times,* the caption under a shy-proud ten-year-old face reads: "They don't know I write them"—and the reference of the pronouns is clear; the duplicity involved betrayed by the fact that the phrase was presumably spoken to a reporter and into a camera.

But it is not quite as simple even as that; for the young writer of the locked-unlocked, concealed-revealed journal will probably have developed a not-quite-legible hand, or a system of more or less deliberate misspellings to baffle his hoped-for discoverer. And at the next stage, the almost ultimate one (some writers, indeed, get no further ever), the still virginal artist will have invented for himself a special style, opaque, oblique, overgarrulous, underarticulate—somehow *diversionary* in any case—out of a shamefast desire not to be understood, not to be caught out, even if read! Think of those artists fixated on one or another of these deeply ambivalent, regressive styles: the reticence of Emily Dickinson, the endless qualifications of Henry James, the playful assault on syntax and punctuation of e. e. cummings.

But what exactly does the would-be artist play at concealing so transparently, and why? What, after all, did he produce long before he could muster words, which he was taught he must in all decency hide? What was he, in fact, applauded and praised for doing *out of sight?* The answer is obvious, and explains why so often the bashful beginning writer asked to show his work will answer, "Ah, it's all hogwash or crap or shit." The toilet is in our tradition, the prototype of the hideaway workshop, atelier, studio: the single habitually locked room in a house, where one performs in theoretical secrecy what "they" know in actuality he must be doing.

No wonder the most *pudique* and secretive writers are such palpable monsters of anality: Swift with his still secret "little language," and his obsession with excrement; Gerard Manley Hopkins with his poems tucked away, as it were, in his guilty asshole; Mark Twain with his hoard of shameful manuscripts concealed until after his death, and the give-away clue in his piece of privately circulated pornography, which begins with an attempt to conceal the real author of a fart and ends with an old man peeing away an erection. But the example of Twain's *1601* adds a disconcerting new factor, since the place of love is, he reminds us, quite as St. Augustine had earlier, *intra urinas et faeces.* Indeed, our earliest as well as our latest erections may be caused not by lust but by the simple need to urinate. The locked bathroom is, finally, also a spot for masturbation—for fantasies if not actual works of love, as well as for flushing away shameful wastes; and between its antiseptic white walls, two guilts are compounded into one beside the potentially symbolic roll of blank paper.

If anality signifies shame and implies concealment, orality, on the other hand, is a source of praise and a school for showing off.

The child is urged not to hide the first sounds he learns to make through his mouth, but to repeat them for an audience; and though he is quickly taught to excrete in private, his eating is a public performance. The high chair and the grownup's table are the prototypes, therefore, of the spotlight and the platform from which one recites, prototypes of publication.

How tempting in view of all this to make the easy Freudian identification of the artist's two conflicting impulses, *chutzpahdik* and *pudique,* with the mythological orifices on either end of the alimentary canal; to think of them as biologically, physiologically determined and therefore inevitable, universal. Such an identification would, however, profit by being itself exposed to history, examined in time; a process which might remind us that Freud's basic mythology of oral and anal was, as it were, toilet-trained into him: the product of a Middle European, bourgeois, Jewish mother, crying, as her descendants have ever since, "Eat! Eat! Talk! Talk! But, remember, keep clean, do it in the pot!"—with an implicit "for me, for your mama!" after each injunction.

It would be amusing, therefore, perhaps even instructive, to imagine the son of a non-Middle European, nonbourgeois, non-Jewish mother, who taught her child to eat in private lest he bring shame on her, and to do all his talking to himself behind lowered shades; and who further insisted that the best way of proving his love for her was to crap as frequently and copiously as possible—preferably in the presence of guests. "Fast! Fast!," such a mother might say, "but remember, too, bigger bowel movements or you'll break my heart!" A rather contradictory set of instructions, one must grant, but what mother was ever quite consistent or what mythology ever logical. And one can surmise, in any case, what different symbolic values our two alimentary openings would have, as well as how different "poets" and "artists" might be in such a world: professing macrobiotics, no doubt, indulging in milk shakes only in secret, but boasting to their proud mamas (laconically—or in gestures) how profligately they had spent their seed, and before how many bystanders they had produced record-breaking stools.

For me, in any event, psychological explanations tend to end in fantasies like these, once history has, as it must, broken in on their purity; and I propose, therefore, to start with a mytho-historical approach and let psychology break in only when it can no longer be resisted. Let us* begin then at the Beginning, with the more or less mythological assumption that at that primordial moment, before history existed at all, every song was sung and every story told in a single holy language, *lashon-ha-kodesh:* an esoteric tongue belonging to priests and shamans. At that point, there was not, in our sense, any "literature" at all, only "Scriptures," which is to say, "Revelation": something spoken through and, after a while, even written down by those priests and shamans. But writing itself was a further mystery—not a means of communication, but only another sign of the supernatural origin of what was revealed, one more warranty that in fact (i.e., in myth) it had come from the God or Goddess, Jehovah or the Muse: some supernal authority outside and before the human self.

Such a state, mythology tells us, could not long endure; since before history began, in order for history to begin, there was a Fall, the *Second* Fall according to the Hebrew tradition: a Fall which occurs not in the Garden of Nature, where man can only eat what is given him, not eat what is forbidden; but in the City, in the very midst of what men build with their hands, at the very height, in fact, of their presumably unlimited erection. Unlike the Fall in Eden, which is a fall from grace into morality, the Fall at the Tower of Babel is from the Tongue into many tongues, from "Revelation" to "literature."

From this point on, there exist for every would-be writer two languages: the Holy Language, which he may not even know but inevitably knows *about;* and the secular or vulgar language, his own "mother tongue," as we have come to call it. Thus history and "literature" are invented at the same time; since "literature" as opposed to "Scripture" is first spoken, then written (in a kind of unwitting parody of the sacred texts) in the *mammaloshen,* the *lingua materna.* This means that in a world divided rather than united by language, each man comes to speak for himself, and to others who always may not, frequently do not, really understand him. And it further implies that writing itself ceases to be a Revelation of a

---

* The canny reader will note that with this "us," my paper begins to move from the *chutzpahdik* first person to the *pudique* third—thus illustrating in its own form the thesis it is presenting—or rather, *I* am presenting.

single truth to all mankind, and becomes instead Confession-Communication of a personal vision to those few, if any, who will hear and comprehend.

No longer is it possible for the poet to pretend that he is a sort of divine ventriloquist's dummy or holy conduit. The very formulas with which he introduces his message are profoundly altered. Invocations to the Muse, where they persist at all, are felt as mere metaphors; nor does any manipulator of words dare assert, like his prelapsarian ancestors, "Thus sayeth the Lord," or "It is written." Instead, he is likely to stammer, "What I mean is. . . ," which amounts to little more than "What 'I' means is," or "What I mean am, what I am means. . .": a series threatening continually to end in the whimper: "That is not what I mean at all." The game of words, in short, is played now not in the light of eternity, but in the world of mortality, where the winner achieves not salvation but only fame. What is at issue when one claims to speak for God is life and death; while the confession that one speaks only for himself means that nothing but honor and shame are at stake.

Yet occasionally, even after the fall to literature and history, some blessed Bard (self-blessed, to be sure, but that is good enough) will arise, convinced that the Universe is infinitely hospitable, after all—at least to him—and he will cry his message loud and clear, as if Babel had never fallen and his own language were that spoken in Heaven. We know the names of those serenely *chutzpahdik* Bards, Dante and Shakespeare, for instance; and reading them, we are almost convinced that if not in the Empyrean itself, at least in the Earthly Paradise, the guardian angels converse in Italian or English. But most writers since the Fall have imagined themselves inhabitants of a Universe something less than friendly, a universe threatening at every turn to publish the news which they surmised from the start: that they are *rejected*. Think of the bugaboo of the young writer and all that is implied by its metaphorical name, the "rejection slip." No wonder most poets begin on guard, creating protections against being shamed, even as they invent strategies for winning recognition.

It may well be, as William Faulkner observed of Albert Camus in a moving little obituary, that no author since Babel has ever wanted to do anything more (or less) than to write on the fallen walls of the world, "I was here" and to sign his name. Certainly,

Milton suggested much the same thing in his own language, on a similar occasion: "Fame is the spur." But if *chutzpah,* in the seventeenth century or the twentieth, urges that the worst event of all is to die unknown, *pudeur,* at either point in time, answers that "Shame! Shame! Everybody knows your name!" is the most terrible of reproaches. And so the writer tries to have it both ways at once, *can* have it both ways at once, since all that we call literature was invented with this in view. He writes his name on the already scribbled wall, writes it large and dark to compel attention. But he encrypts it, encodes it—thus emulating those wily prototypes of the artist, Ulysses and Huck Finn, who never tell the truth right away: never begin by giving their right name, or telling the real story of where they have come from, whither they are tending.

Yet if poetry is, after all—as Dante himself confessed, for all his show of assurance—a *bella menzogna,* most beautiful of lies, then the true name of the poet is revealed precisely by giving a false one; since his most secret and authentic title is Liar, Deceiver, Man of Many Devices. He will begin with the joke of a pseudonym, inscribing: KILROY WAS HERE. MARK TWAIN WAS HERE. GEORGE ELIOT WAS HERE—meaning SOMEBODY ELSE WAS HERE. NOT ME. Or, as the shoddiest of all jests has it, "Boss, there's nobody in here but us chickens." At the end, however, he is likely to be joking more seriously, kidding on the square, as it were, by insisting in his last extremity (once more like the prototypical Ulysses) that he is really *OU TIS,* NOBODY AT ALL. *Pudeur,* in short, drives the writer first to plot disguises, and next to dream invisibility; so that he may be heard unseen and unscathed.

Not only Nathanael Hawthorne, then—as Poe once commented in an unfriendly review—but *all* writers—as Poe certainly should have understood—write in invisible ink, on occasion at least. And why not; since with one eye they tend to see themselves as spies, secret agents in a world so unremittingly hostile, that even, perhaps especially, at home they are in enemy territory. And so they feel compelled to communicate with their unknown compatriots (how can they ever be sure who they are, or even whether they exist?) in a secret language, in code.

For this reason, therefore, proper literary criticism, which is to say, the analysis of what is really new or forever inexhaustible in the realm of art, must be in large part cryptanalysis. Insofar as the artist is an agent, the critic must be a counteragent, engaged in a special brand of detective work made easy because the criminal he pursues has taken pains to leave clues everywhere. In fact, the artist is precisely the kind of outlaw or traitor who wants his crime to be found out: found finally not to be a crime at all; but only an act of supreme virtue, a true act of love, though committed with all the show of guilt proper to a crime. Sometimes that strange guilt for love is manifested in the sneaking shamefastness of *pudeur,* sometimes in the brazen arrogance of *chutzpah;* but it is all the same, for they represent finally not two impulses but one: a genuine ambivalence rooted in a single basic response.

Of what, then, does the artist perhaps not quite fear himself guilty, but surely fear he may seem guilty to others, so that in their presence, finally even alone, he is driven to cringe or swagger? If a crime at all or a sin, writing is essentially a lonely crime or sin, an offense without victims; and in this respect it oddly resembles masturbation—constituting a kind of reversed or mirror image of it, in fact. Like onanism, the creation of "literature" is an auto-erotic act, accompanied by, or rather creating, maintaining, certain fantasies. But in the realm of "literature" the auto-erotic act itself remains invisible, existing only in metaphor, by analogy; while the fantasies, once they have been committed to writing, are quite visible, palpable, one is tempted to say, real. But this is, of course, quite the opposite of masturbation.

Even if we think of the act of writing as a kind of aggravated masturbation, which is to say, as exhibitionist auto-eroticism, practiced in the hope (and fear) of attracting an audience, which the writer hopes (and fears) will be stimulated to follow his example, the writer has displayed in public no living flesh of his own, only fantasies whose exposure is banned by no law of God or man. And should his act provoke widespread imitation, it would only make him a best-seller rather than a real seducer; since the masturbatory orgy set off by a work of art, however successful, is one in which no one assaults anybody but himself, and even that within the private chambers of his own head. Where then is the offense; and if any can be presumed to exist, who is the offended?

But once more we have been betrayed by analogy and introspection into the trap of fantastic psychologizing, from which only a return to history can deliver us. And, indeed, if the questions to which we have come can be answered at all, the answers must lie hidden in history itself: *real* history this time, which is to say, the actual records of the emergence of vernacular poetry in Provence toward the end of the eleventh century—the second beginning of "literature" in the Western world.

It is the essence of our culture that in it art was twice-born, poetry twice-invented, the first time in the Near East, the second in Southern France; and the living sense of that second time is preserved for us in the eleven surviving poems (one with its musical setting) by William, the ninth Duke of Aquitaine and the seventh Count of Poitou, sometimes known simply as William of Poitou. He was, his early biographer tells us, distinguished by his royal connections ("he had a daughter who was wife to King Henry of England, and mother of the young King . . .") and his skill at seduction ("he went about the world for a long time to deceive women . . ."). History remembers him, however, as one of the unquestioned firsts of literature: first vernacular poet of the modern world.

There is some indication, in fact, that certain traditions had already begun to gel before the time of William, though in poems which have not come down to us. But they could not have been long in existence, since the deep Middle Ages were hostile not only to the making of poems as such, but to any use of the vernacular in writing whose ends were not immediate and practical. Christianity had, as every schoolboy knows, begun by attacking the "literature" of Greco-Roman civilization—in part because it was hopelessly secular from the parochial point of view called in the Middle Ages "Catholic"; in larger part, perhaps, because its canon clearly constituted a kind of "Scriptures" for a rival, pagan faith. But the war of the church against, say, Ovid (who was bootlegged and preserved anyhow) was not so much a war against a poet or poets as one aimed at destroying the very concept of art which had sustained them.

The Saints who cried, "What has Athens to do with Jerusalem?" provided the ammunition for an onslaught against all culture after Babel, an attack on any kind of Confession-Communication opposed to a single Revelation. And the dream they inspired in the leaders of the Roman Church was a dream of a world reunified around a single canonical Book, *The Book,* as the Christian Scriptures were commonly called, translated into a single, universally understood tongue, i.e., a New Holy Language. Oddly enough from a mythological point of view, though understandably from the point of view of history, that language turned out to be neither Hebrew nor Aramaic nor Greek, in which the Old Testament and the New had originally been written, but Latin, through which the Caesars had tried to unify an empire. But to build with hands in history is to recreate Babel, and the Roman Catholic Tower of Babel, though presumably built on Rock rather than sand, fell like the Tower which was its prototype.

This time, however, the Confusion of Tongues occurred not in myth but in history, and its record can be read in letters and memorial inscriptions and casual graffiti. Not instantaneously as in legend, but slowly over the centuries, Latin became Italian and French and Provençal; so that finally even crying assent to the Christian God, the inhabitants of the old Roman realm heard themselves shouting out variously, *"Si"* and *"Oui"* and *"Oc."* Small wonder they chose to address, feeling free for the first time, those lesser divinities, the women they loved, in those same divided tongues. It was, in fact, in the *langue d'oc,* the language of Rome's First Province, that "literature" was reborn; and William, to whom it was not even really native, picks it up, his lines trembling still for the sensitive ear—not only with the shudder of passion released, but with an additional tremor of delight at exploiting precisely what was *not* a Holy Language—the first vulgar tongue in which it had become possible to say again the personal "I," to write again a signed poem.

Over and over, his poems begin with slight variations on the single formula: *I will make a poem, a verse, a little song*—as if he can never exhaust the wonder and newness of his enterprise: the "I" singing, after long silence, its own vision of the world in the *lingua materna.*

> *Companho, faray un vers ... convinen:*
> *Farai un vers de dreyt nien:*
> *Farai un vers, pos mi sonelh ...*
> *Farai chansoneta nueva ...*

Four times he manages the formula in the first line, then once in the second:

*Pos de chantar m'es pres talentz,*
*Farai un vers, don sui dolenz:*

And the repetition conveys finally something more, something other than a sense of joy and release. *Grand seigneur* that he was, William, one suspects, must have been a little scared—aware of what was dangerous, or would be found so by the Church, in his unprecedented venture. Yet how could he have known what lay ahead, what he was releasing in his playful or melancholy comments on his adventures with women?

Perhaps it is only our retrospective knowledge of the terror and beauty which followed him in history—the scores of poets who followed his example and the repression which ensued—that leads us to read an undertone of bravado and terror into his verse. It was not, after all, the poetry of William or any other *jongleur* that cued the Albigensian Crusade, but profound doctrinal differences, a conflict of religions. And yet when the culture of Provence was destroyed by the armies of the Church, not only the alleged Manichaean faith of the *Cathari* went down with it, but also the cult of *Joia,* of sexual pleasure, to which Provençal poetry was dedicated. That kind of poetry moved elsewhere, to be sure—into the languages of *oui* and *si* first of all; but it had died forever in the lovely tongue William once chose as specially suited to his needs. *"Qu'eu non ai soing d'estraing lati,"* he had written long before the blow fell, *"Qu'e m parta de mon Bon Vezi."* "I need no stranger's tongue, no alien Latin, which might separate me from my Good Neighbor."

Even with a shift into *"estraing lati",* which is to say, foreign vernaculars, William's example continued to impose itself; for he had somehow hit upon two poetic modes whose uses and possibilities have not yet been exhausted. Neither an especially subtle thinker, nor a very sensitive lover, nor an extraordinarily gifted technician, he managed somehow to invent, re-invent, find in the *langue d'oc* two forms appropriate to the two poles of the ambivalence about making verses which was to trouble his successors, if it did not already trouble him: the Enigma to express *pudeur* (in the poem beginning *"Farai un vers de dreyt nien"*), the Pornographic Song to register *chutzpah* (in the one opening *"Farai un vers, pos mi sonelh"*).

The Enigma or the Riddle is a genre which we are likely to associate these days solely with the nursery and the child's book, though it is closely related to an adult form much prized in recent decades—the Conceit, which is to say, the extended, farfetched metaphor as practiced pre-eminently by John Donne. If we had not been told, for instance, in the sixth stanza of the perhaps-too-often cited "A Valediction Forbidding Mourning" that the poet is describing "Our two souls . . . which are one"—and reminded again in the third line of the seventh—the pair of stanzas which follow would be a Riddle rather than a Conceit:

> If they be two, they are two so
> As stiff twin compasses are two;
> . . . the fix'd foot, makes no show
> To move, but doth, if th'other do.

> And though it in the centre sit,
> Yet, when the other far doth roam,
> It leans, and hearkens after it,
> And grows erect, as that comes home.

An Enigma is, in fact, nothing but a Conceit which conceals one pole of its similitude in its tail, instead of presenting it forthrightly at its head. Moreover, even as the Conceit tends to become the Enigma, which, in a sense, it was in the beginning; the Enigma aspires to become—teases us with the possibility, even occasionally succeeds in becoming—the meta-Enigma, or Ultimate Riddle, fit symbol of the mystery at the heart of our existence: the Question without an Answer. Surely many children, all children, perhaps, must feel (as I myself once did) that the "answers" to certain well-loved riddles are irrelevant, a delusion and disappointment, a grown-up hoax intended to persuade them of what they instinctively know to be untrue: *that there is an answer to everything* and that it is the function of language to reveal that answer in story and song.

No wonder the wise child loves so desperately, before he realizes quite why, such anti-Riddles as Lewis Carroll's "Why is a
raven like a writing desk?", to which the proper response is silence,
or even better, laughter. Wonderland is, indeed, the school in which
he learns to respond for ever after to the meta-Enigma, whether
proposed jocosely, as in *Finnegans Wake,* in the form of a
dreamed pun, "Why do am I look alike two poss of porter pease?";
or proffered quite seriously, as at the opening of Thoreau's *Walden,*
in the guise of a confession or anticonfession:

> I long ago lost a hound, a bay horse, and a turtledove,
> and am still on their trail. Many are the travelers I have
> spoken to concerning them, describing their tracks and what
> calls they answered to. I have met one or two who have heard
> the hound, and the tramp of the horse, and even seen the dove
> disappear behind a cloud, and they seemed as anxious to recover
> them as if they had lost them themselves.

In Thoreau the question mark by which we are accustomed to
identify the Riddle has been ingested, as it were; and we are confronted not with the puzzle itself but with a narrative about puzzle-
asking ("I have spoken . . . describing their tracks . . .") and
the bafflement of those asked. And we are here very close to what
is generally called—once more with connotations of the nursery—
Nonsense, i.e., the unanswerable Riddle without even a mark of in-
terrogation to tease us into believing that there are answers at the
back of *somebody's* book.

Nonsense always trembles on the verge of the ridiculous,
though sometimes its practitioners seem blessedly unaware of the
fact, as was Edgar Allan Poe, along with his French translators and
imitators, Baudelaire and Mallarmé. A case in point is the following excerpt from *Ulalume:*

> These were days when my heart was volcanic
>   As the scoriac rivers that roll—
>   As the lavas that restlessly roll
> Their sulphurous currents down Yaanek,
>   In the ultimate climes of the Pole—
> That groan as they roll down Mount Yaanek,
>   In the realms of the Boreal Pole.

And for those still unaware of how funny the last two lines are, a reading of the notes in a recent scholarly edition (explaining the "Boreal Pole" is *really* the South Pole; and "Yaanek" a name derived either from "an Arabic execration, . . . probably obscene" or a term "sometimes used by Polish Jews for an unkindly Christian.") will perhaps suffice to illustrate at least the joke of seriously trying to solve Nonsense, or even Non-Sense, no matter how grave its tone. But Edward Lear—whom W. H. Auden has described as Poe's sole real imitator *in English*—guessed the secret long before us, revealing it in poems clearly intended as comic Nonsense (as opposed to mantic Non-Sense), though echoing Poe in cadence and sound pattern and especially in the invention of exotic-ridiculous place names.

> And in twenty years they all came back,
>     In twenty years or more.
> And every one said, 'How tall they've grown!
> For they've been to the Lakes, and the Torrible Zone,
>     And the hills of the Chankly Bore';
> And they drank their health, and gave them a feast
> Of dumplings made of beautiful yeast;
> And everyone said, 'If we only live,
>     We too will go to sea in a Sieve,—
>     To the hills of the Chankly Bore!'

But what a crew they are, after all, these not-quite-askers of insoluble riddles; what guilt-ridden evaders of the public eye, what deviously invisible or masked men: Lewis Carroll and Henry David Thoreau, Edgar Allan Poe and Edward Lear. What artful dodgers into the nursery or the Azure—where fantasies of pederasty or necrophilia or incest, of sexual transgressions dreamed rather than dared are barely glimpsed past the concealing devices suggested by extreme *pudeur*. Not much doubt remains in their cases, that the Enigma is the form to which a writer turns when his awareness of guilt inclines him toward the pole of *pudeur;* when he lays, as it were, his finger to his lips or sticks his thumb in his mouth, thus betraying what he cannot, will not confess: *"I am guilty as hell, but no one knows it or ever will;* for how can they suspect, accuse, convict an Angel in Exile, or a mere child in adult form, of ultimate iniquity.

*I* was a child and *she* was a child,
In this kingdom by the sea;
But we loved with a love that was more than love—
I and my Annabel Lee—

Finally, however, precisely the pretense that the Riddle is a child's game gives away the sexual secret it tries to conceal; verifying what we learn from other sources: that everywhere in mythology, the Enigma is associated with the threat of incest—as Claude Lévi-Strauss reminds us in a remarkable passage of his inaugural address at the Collège de France. "Between the puzzle solution and incest there exists a relation," he writes, "not external and of fact, but internal and of reason. . . . Like the solved puzzle, incest brings together elements doomed to remain separate. . . ." And he then goes on to explain that "the audacious union of masked words or of consanguines unknown to themselves . . . engenders decay and fermentation, the unchaining of natural forces . . ."; and therefore brings on "an eternal summer . . . licentious to the point of corruption," yet often chosen in history and myth over "a winter just as eternal . . . pure to the point of sterility. . . ."

The unsolved and insoluble Enigma, the Non-Sense Riddle, for which William provided the prototype, is quite another matter, however; since it represents averted rather than achieved incest, guilt without consummation. William's model opens, as a matter of fact, with a disavowal of all guilt, a disavowal of everything; but the order of that everything amounts to a backhand confession.

*Farai un vers de dreyt nien:*
*Non er di mi ni d'autra gen,*
*Non er d'amor ni de joven,*
*Ni de ren au . . .*

"I will make a poem of pure nothing," he begins; and we are reminded, a little absurdly, of the adolescent's answer in the old joke: "Where are you going?" "Out." "What are you doing?" "Nothing." But then he starts to specify, "It is not about me or anybody else; it is not about love or youth, or anything else." "*I* will make a poem," the boastful formula asserts; but by the second line the singer has begun to deny his singing self, the "I" released by the vernacular tradition. First the self, and then love and youth; these are the foci of his guilt—and what therefore his poem must aver is *not* his subject, though it cannot help naming them. And who can blame him, in any case, for what floats to the surface of his mind, since he has dreamed it all (he hastens to assure us next) "asleep and on horseback."

> *Qu'enans fo trobatz en durmen*
> *Sobre chevau.*

Why then is he trembling at the point of death a couple of stanzas later, afflicted by a malady of which he knows only "what they tell me"?

> *Malautz suy e tremi murir,*
> *E ren no•n sai mas quan n'aug dir* . .

He may assure us over and over that he couldn't care less about whatever is really at stake behind all his mystification ("I prize it no more than a mouse . . . I esteem it no more than a cock . . ."), but the note of melancholy and terror will not be exorcised; the counterpoint of *timor mortis conturbat me.* And lest we have forgotten, or never quite realized, that it is a Riddle we have been presented, the final line teases us with the hope of a solution, a key, *"la contraclau,"* that can only be provided by another, answering poem. *Fag ai lo vers,* the poet has assured us only five lines earlier, "and now my story is done." But, of course, it is not—since the meta-Enigma, the Riddle Without an Answer, is in essence endless, a tale without a conclusion.

"Every telling has a tailing," James Joyce was to insist more than eight centuries later, "and that's the he and she of it." But the Absolute Riddle has precisely no "tailing" *("Non er d'amor ni de joven"),* no "audacious union of . . . consanguines . . ."; and without consummation there is no conclusion. The unsolved puzzle like the taboo mother is Ever Virgin, never quite possessed. William, however, wrote not only of love as forbidden and therefore repressed, but also of passion as forbidden yet irrepressible—providing a prototype for the poetry of *chutzpah* even as he had for that of *pudeur.*

That other prototype, however, turns out to be quite simply the pornographic poem: the vaunt of potency, the boast of full genitality —delivered not from the crouch of shame with the finger to the lips, but with a sexual swagger, the hips thrust forward and the arms spread wide for an embrace. Whenever poetry, in fact, becomes *chutzpahdik* rather than *pudique,* in Walt Whitman, say, or Allen Ginsberg, it learns again to talk dirty. Before the arrogant poet can be loved he must first be condemned as "the dirtiest beast of the age," then, not cleared of that charge but found through it, loved for it, quite as in the case of Whitman. The shamefast poet, on the other hand, must first be blamed for his *obscurity,* then without being absolved, found through it and loved for it, quite like Gerard Manley Hopkins. Whitman and Hopkins—they seem ideal, almost allegorical opposites; and yet as Hopkins himself was driven to confess (shyly, his finger characteristically to his lips): "I always knew in my heart Walt Whitman's mind to be more like my own than any other man's living. . . ." It is as close to confessing the particular guilt that dogged him, the homosexuality he shared with Whitman, as Hopkins could come; but it is also a reminder of the sense in which *chutzpah* and *pudeur* are originally and finally one, two faces of a single ambivalence.

But William alone could suffice to remind us of this, since his most successful piece of pornography is about a *chutzpahdik* character (called once more quite simply "I") who managed by shamming the discretion of *pudeur* to achieve a kind of total sexual satisfaction: "Eight days or more" in a Provençal Pornotopia, with a pair of uninhibited women, who first feed him up on capons, white bread, good wine and "pepper in abundance," then almost screw him to death.

> *Tan las fotei com auzirets:*
> *Cen e quatre vint et ueit vetz,*
> *Q'a pauc no·i rompei mos corretz*
> *E mos arnes,*
> *E no us puesc dir lo malaveg,*
> *Tan gran m'en pres.*

"So much I fucked them," William sings, "as you shall hear: One hundred and eighty-eight times, so that I almost broke my braces and my straps; and I can't tell you what misery ensued, it was so great."*

In order, however, to attain that good, which, as he tells us in another poem, men desire more then all else in the world *("esta ben . . . D'acho don hom a plus talen"),* but which, as we learn from this one, can end in pain, the poet finds it necessary to simulate precisely the dumbness associated with *pudeur.* He is, in fact, the least faithful of all versifying lovers to the vow of secrecy theoretically essential to Courtly Love. Not only does he boast again and again in his *chutzpahdik* songs of his sexual prowess in general ("I've never had a lady at night who has not eagerly awakened me next morning. . . . I could have earned a living by my skill. . . ."), but he names names: denominating, for instance, the pair he fucked one hundred and eighty-eight times, first by their husbands' names, then by their Christian ones.

In the poem itself, however, he responds to their courteous-erotic greeting—delivered, as he puts it, in the vernacular of one of the ladies *("en son latin")*—in the nontongue of the deaf-mute: not *"but"* or *"bat"* but only *"Babariol, babariol, Babarian);* and says no more, though, to test him, they drag their long-clawed, vicious cat down his naked back. *"Babariol, babariol, Babarian,"* it is a nonsense poem, a riddling song—a way of saying nothing, of guaranteeing that he is constitutionally incapable of exposing what actual *chutzpah* lurks behind their superficial *pudeur.*

Once loose from the prison of their bedroom, however, the poet finds his shameless tongue; singing once more between waking and sleeping, though this time afoot and in the broad daylight, how lustful and wicked and guilty they were, women are—how sly and indefatigable and *innocent* he turned out to be, men always turn out to be. It is the typical stance of the *fabliaux,* not of the love songs of Provence with their pretense of male humility, their vows of discretion and silence; and suggests disconcertingly the sense in which much of that poetry might be, or at least can be, understood as

---

* In the standard scholarly text, *Les Chansons de Guillaume IX,* edited by Alfred Jeanroy, there is a running translation of the text into modern French, but this stanza is coyly represented (in a book revised in 1964!) by a row of dashes; nor does the verb *fotre* appear at all in the appended glossary—which is, I suppose, a case of academic *pudeur* at its most ignominious in vain combat with the artist's *chutzpah.*

*mock*-humble only, a strategy in the game of seduction. It is what comes of singing at the unguarded moment of falling asleep on the broad highway: "I will make a verse, since I am falling asleep, walking and taking the sun."

The poems of *chutzpah,* William's poetry suggests, are written on the verge of sleep, just as those of *pudeur* are composed in its very depths: the one in the reverie that prepares us for the fatal loss of consciousness, the other, at the moment when, disturbed, we must either dream or start awake. And how finally appealing they both are—the dirty story, so appropriate to the eternal adolescent in us, and the riddle, so suitable to the immortal child; the wet dream which we prepare for ourselves before we have quite lost consciousness, and the irrational sequence of the not-quite-nightmare, which our unconscious prepares for us to forestall a little the advent of guilt-ridden awareness; the fantasy of consummation without guilt, and its twinned opposite of guilt without consummation.

Neither, though, not even both together, served to keep William (representative in this respect of the Christian conscience of Europe) quite at peace, waking or sleeping. And he closes his career by inventing or perfecting a third prototype: the poem of recantation, which begins untypically: *"Pos de chantar m' es pres talentz"* —but in which the old formula *"farai un vers"* appears in the second line, this time qualified, however, with the word *dolenz,* sorrowful, mournful, melancholy. Yet even at this point, he cannot forgo a boast in retrospect, confessing—half ruefully, half proudly —even as he assures us that he wishes to surrender all for the sake of God and his own salvation, "I knew joy and pleasure, far and near and in my own domain." Nonetheless the recantation does in theory represent a disavowal of everything which the opening up of a vernacular, secular tradition had seemed to promise: a rejection of songs of joy in favor of songs of sorrow, of the celebration of self in favor of the denial of self, of poetry in favor of piety. But for piety, not the *"latin"* of Agnes, wife of *en* Guari, but that of the Church, which is to say, real rather than mock Latin is appropriate.

The tradition which William helped to inaugurate did not, however, disappear when he lost, or played at losing, his nerve. Men have, as every reader knows, continued to write in the *lingua ma-*

*terna;* and such writers, along with those readers, have tended ever since his time to divide their allegiances between his two prototypes. The majority have always preferred pornography, the poetry of sexual consummation and its celebration—though most often they have bowdlerized it, saying *amar* rather than *fotre,* out of respect for the *pudeur* of their lovers or their audiences or the official censors. But a considerable minority, all the way from the academy to the nursery, have opted for the Riddle—though this, also, has been bowdlerized, by those too proud or scared to confront the Total Enigma, the Question without any Answer at all.

Academics, especially, have proved *chutzpahdik* enough behind their masks of *pudeur* to prefer the quasi-Enigma, the Riddle insoluble to the uninitiated many, yet decipherable by the tiny congregation of the chosen: a symbol not of the opacity of all existence, but of the mystery of election. "Many are called but few are chosen," sing the poets of the quasi-Enigma; to which the quasipornographers answer in chorus, "All the world loves a lover." And the Provencals had invented quite early names for both of these schools; calling the former *trobar clus,* which is to say, hermetic or private poetry, and the latter *trobar leu,* which means light or open verse.

Arnaut Daniel is the master of the *trobar clus,* "the greatest craftsman of *la lingua materna,*" according to Dante, who actually wrote eight verses in Provençal, the first of mother tongues and Daniel's own, to show his love for the earlier poet as well as the skill he thought he owed to his example. Moreover, Dante composed sestinas, too, imitating the difficult form Daniel had presumably invented. Dante's grave and tormented poems, however, have little of the playfulness, the willingness to walk the brink of nonsense, which characterizes the Provençal poet, who set himself the task of ringing changes on the words for "fingernail" and "uncle" (in the *langue d'oc, "ongla"* and *"oncle,"* words which tease us with their closeness of sound, their dissonance of meaning) in his famous sestina; and whose boast was, in love as well as art, that he "yoked the ox and the hare" and "swam against the current."

What Dante did understand is that the poetry of *pudeur,* the true *trobar clus,* is no mere pastiche of rare words and rich rhymes but a kind of verse built to keep out rather than let in—a way of

CHUTZPAH AND PUDEUR 537

using words as if they were opaque: not as windows opening on the soul, but reflecting jewels which redouble whatever light we cast on them, and end by dazzling us, blinding us with their icy splendor. *Trobar clus* is the poetry of winter light and winter cold—celebrating, in fact, precisely that "winter just as eternal . . ." to which Lévi-Strauss alluded, "pure to the point of sterility. . . ." And this, too, Dante comprehended, beginning his own hermetic sestina:

> To small daylight and the great circle of shade
> I've come, alas, and to the blanching of the hills,
> The season when the color leaves the grass. . .

quite on the model of Arnaut Daniel, who opens one of his thorniest, most forbidding poems:

> The bitter air
> Makes branchy boughs
> Quite bare
> That the sweet made thick with leaves. . . .

The poets of the *trobar leu,* on the other hand, of whom Bernart de Ventadorn is the most eminent and best remembered (nearly fifty of his poems have been preserved, as opposed to eighteen by Daniel), set their songs against a landscape not white but green, not chill but warm. Spring is their symbolic season:

> The sweet paschal season
> With its fresh greening
> Brings leaf and flower
> Of diverse color . . .

Their weather is not quite Lévi-Strauss's "eternal summer . . . licentious to the point of corruption," of which, in some ways, William's overheated interiors inhabited by overstuffed lovers—that world of glowing coals and plenteous hot pepper— seems a nearer analogue; and certainly when William does take us outdoors, it is into a sweet springtime appropriate to a poetry of unabashed sensuality: *la dolchor de temps novel,* in which trees burgeon and birds sing, as if an eternal summer lay just ahead. Springtime represents, perhaps, a compromise, a withdrawal to the moment of promised rather than accomplished bliss, on the part of poets more timid than William, but not less committed finally to the cult of *joia*. And even when they seem to celebrate an eternal April without a June, an eternally retreating horizon, at least it is a benign one. Not, in fact, until the time of T. S. Eliot does any poet portray April as more cruel than kind; since only the tradition of "modernism" and the *avant-garde* permits, as it were, the frozen winter of *trobar clus* to creep past the vernal equinox.

Yet the poetry of the Waste Land is not unprecedented in making the impossibility of love its central subject, innocence as a function of impotence its second theme. Nor is it different from the main stream of *pudique* verse in its resolve to be deliberately "difficult" or "obscure," i.e., in determining to encode its secrets in a language comprehensible only to those already in the know. What is new is the particular language it employs—that blend of allusion and demiquotation in a Babel of tongues, which represents at once the climax and dissolution of a linguistic experiment carried on ever since the Renaissance: the attempt to create a "glorified" or "illustrated" vernacular, a proper "poetic diction," different, on the one hand, from the Christian Holy Language, which was Latin, and, on the other, from the simple prattle of women and children. It was certain insecure academics who had learned to be ashamed of not speaking the languages of Classical Antiquity, and therefore speculated on the possibility of creating a kind of half-holy tongue by splitting their own *lingua materna* into two dialects: one thought fit for the refinements of Art and Love, the other considered appropriate only for the gross business of every day. But various early vernacular poets, from William to Dante, had been there first, creating out of *chutzpah* what the scholars would feel obliged to justify in the name of *pudeur*.

That initial *chutzpah,* however, soon ran out, even for the poets that followed; and, in any case, those who wrote in the "glorified" or subholy tongues could no longer pretend to speak—or even to translate, render at a second remove—the Word of God, but only the words of men, which is to say, of themselves. And though with the passage of centuries and the replacement of the Church by the University as the chief instrument of education, certain humanistic texts began to seem more orthodox than heretical, finally canonical, they constituted no real Scriptures; only pseudo-Scriptures sufficient unto that pseudo-Cult, the Art Religion according to Matthew Arnold—or, in its revised American form, the Great Books Religion according to Robert Hutchins or the New Critics.

It is characteristic of aggravated *pudeur* that it tries to disguise even itself, pretending it is piety rather than mere bashfulness and shame and guilt; but the hermetic tradition, as it has passed from Arnold to Eliot to Leavis and Cleanth Brooks, is revealed finally as mere gentility, i.e., *pudeur* utterly bereft of *chutzpah*. To be sure, our early twentieth-century gentility is more highfalutin, perhaps, than the middlebrow gentility practiced in the middle of the last by, say, Longfellow; but it is equally hollow in its pretenses, redeeming neither language nor souls. Without an adequate faith to justify it, any venture at defining a canonical literature, like any attempt to separate a sacred language from a profane is revealed as one more spasm prompted by the castrating shame which has been haunting Western Art ever since the first Western artist set out to sing of sex and the "I." The chill that freezes the marrow of worshippers at the altars of High Art is not just the cold that possesses all empty churches, but the zero weather of the Eternal Winter, which sets a new generation of readers to shivering even in our superheated classrooms and libraries.

What, then, is to be done? To deliver the Waste Land of our Universities from shame-ridden sterility, shall we swing to the opposite pole—woo the Eternal Summer in which the Bacchae can dance in the *Aula Magna,* as well as on the lonely peaks; and all distinctions of high and low, kith and kind will be melted away in ecstasy? There is always conceivable at least, if never quite possible, a third way eloquently described by Lévi-Strauss in the inaugural lecture quoted earlier.

> In the face of the two possibilities which might seduce the imagination—an eternal summer or a winter just as eternal, the former licentious to the point of corruption, the latter pure to the point of sterility—man must resign himself to choosing equilibrium and the periodicity of the seasonal rhythm. In the natural order, the latter fulfils the same function which is fulfilled in society by the exchange of women in marriage and the ex-

change of words in conversation, when these are practiced with the frank intention of communicating, that is to say, without trickery or perversity, and above all, without hidden motives.

"Never quite possible," I have written (and I return in conclusion to the first person, since that is what I must remain in the silence, the blank space that follows my final phrase), thinking of communal life or even the psychic life of the individual; since in the first "perversity" is the rule, and in the second "hidden motives" are inevitable; and "equilibrium," therefore, in either case merely a wish, a fantasy, a dream. Perhaps this has not always been so; but certainly it is so now, when we no longer possess—in a world of air-conditioning and travel so rapid that summer and winter are hours rather than months apart—the inescapable pattern of "periodicity" provided by the "seasonal rhythm" of the natural year.

Only in poems does man create the balance which Lévi-Strauss proposes and himself momentarily achieves on the page: in the use of language we call "literature," and which, keeping faith with both poles of our ambivalence, relies upon "trickery" and is shaped by motives hidden even from ourselves. Only at the moment of becoming a poet can the anthropologist create the ideal community, the perfect marriage which as a citizen, lover, father, even teacher he inevitably betrays; and he does so, ironically enough, by abandoning or transcending "the frank intention of communicating" in favor of the deviousness of the artist.

It therefore matters not at all whether the poet is asserting the possibility or impossibility of "equilibrium" in the world outside his text. His success in the world depends not on his declared allegiance, but on his undeclared ambivalence. And this is equally true if, like Lévi-Strauss, he is projecting the hope of such a solution, or, like Euripides in *The Bacchae,* singing its inevitable failure: the terror of repression, the terror of release not complementing or fulfilling each other, but only destroying turn and turn about those who have committed themselves either way. In either case, the end is irony; since in the former the equilibrium achieved in the lecture hall is lost in the streets, and in the latter the equilibrium achieved in the theater belies the message which is its occasion. Yet the second kind of irony seems more appropriate to a historical moment in which not the long-term goals for which we demonstrate, but the short-lived Demonstration itself seems to provide all the community we shall ever have; and in which, therefore, not marriage—as for Lévi-Strauss—but the Orgy—as for the Bacchae themselves—becomes the key Utopian image.

Small wonder, then, that *The Bacchae* of Euripides is currently on everyone's mind, as it has been continually on mine in these reflections on the seasons of the soul; that it among the surviving plays of the Attic theater occupies for us the central position held for our immediate predecessors by Sophocles' *Oedipus Rex*. At one point, during the past year, there were playing in the major theaters of the Western world, five new adaptations, free, faithful, naked, clothed, of that play; and as I walk the corridors of my own university, I see posted on the wall just outside our graduate student lounge (itself recently decorated in the course of a "mind-fuck" with painted slogans: FEMINISM LIVES. EAT SHIT. FAR FUCKIN' OUT. TOUCH ME FEEL ME HEAL ME) a casting call for the chorus of yet another production of the same play.

Clearly not every director who revives the *Bacchae*, in this time of a major shift from the tyranny of *pudeur* to the reign of *chutzpah*, realizes that Euripides is singing the inevitable failure as well as the inevitable resurgence of the dream of Eternal Summer. But all are aware that we have somehow used up the personal-psychological myth of the son who knows all the answers, yet does not know he has murdered his father and married his mother; and stand in the need of one more communal-political: the archetypal tale of the repressive son who, in the name of the *Polis*, the State, imprisons his mother's God, only to be ripped apart by her hands for the sake of her *Thiasos*, the Pack that worships her God on the hills.

Both myths seem at a glance equally absurd, yet the first has proved amenable to rational analysis from Aristotle to Freud; while the second stubbornly resists rationalization, leading only to nonwisdom, the ironic tag with which Euripides chose to end this last of his plays, as he had earlier at least three others.

> What we look for does not come to pass;
> The God finds a way for what we did not foresee.
> Such was the end of this story

It is less elegant as well as less hopeful than Lévi-Strauss's peroration: an absolute conclusion beyond which nothing can be imagined, an ending which consumes all beginnings, past and to come. But perhaps it is, by that token, closer than any prophecy to the true myth of our history, though whether more *chutzpahdik* or more *pudique* I am at a loss to say.

*Buffalo, New York*
—1969

# INDEX

# Index

545